D1738704

Irish Playwrights, 1880–1995

In general, the profiles in this book consist of the following components, designed to allow the flexibility necessary to accommodate the range of dramatists included while providing a unified structure to allow the reader easiest access to the materials presented:

1. *Biographical Overview*: A thumbnail sketch of significant events in the playwright's life, generally to be considered a basic introduction to the playwright. Whenever possible, at the end of the overview are ''Selected Biographical Sources,'' references available for gathering further biographical information.

2. *Major Plays, Premieres, and Significant Revivals: Theatrical Reception*: A selective list with dates (usually for first production) and runs of significant productions, including important revivals. Summaries of the published critical receptions of these productions (generally from newspaper and magazine reviews) follow.

3. *Additional Plays, Adaptations, and Productions*: Includes theatrical events that were less significant in the playwright's career.

4. *Assessment of the Playwright's Career*: Includes general assessments that incorporate summary references to published evaluations from critics/scholars as published in magazines, journals, dissertations, and books.

5. *Archival Sources*: When known to exist, a listing of locations housing unpublished materials by and/or about the playwright.

6. *Primary Bibliography*: A selective list of the playwright's published plays and of essays and articles by the playwright relevant to the theater and/or his or her playwriting career.

7. *Secondary Bibliography*: A selected list of materials relevant to the playwright's life and career, including materials referenced in the preceding sections. Secondary material referred to within the profile by authors of multiple entries in the Secondary Bibliography is distinguished by [1], [2], and so on.

8. *Bibliographies*: If available, bibliographies concentrating on the playwright are listed for further referral to material not included in the Secondary Bibliography.

Each contributor to this volume has striven to select materials most significant to future scholarship on his or her respective playwright, but few, if any, of the entries should be viewed as comprehensive in their bibliographic references. The selected general bibliography at the end of this volume supplements the material included in the profiles in this book. The work of Robert Hogan either alone or with a series of collaborators deserves special mention for his sustained effort to document the performance history of Irish drama using reviews and other original source material.

Newspapers are difficult to work with because few libraries have comprehensive newspaper collections, even libraries in major centers like New York and Dublin. The Newspaper Library of the British Library (London) is perhaps the finest in the world, but reductions in funding over the years have made the use of these holdings difficult. A further difficulty is that no Irish newspaper is as yet indexed; neither are most American and British newspapers. Nevertheless, there is one annually produced collection of New York reviews, unfortunately available only since 1940 (vol. 1): *The New York Theatre Critics' Reviews* (New York: Critic's Theatre Reviews). Also available is a bibliography of *New York Times* theater reviews: *New York Theater Reviews 1870–1919* (6 vols.) and *1920–1980* (15 vols.) (New York: Random House). London reviews between 1989 and 1991 have been collected in a periodical entitled *London Theatre Record*. Subsequently, an attempt has been made to include provincial productions as well as London performances, and the periodical's name has been changed to *Theatre Record* to indicate its more inclusive nature.

Bernice Schrank
William W. Demastes

Samuel Beckett

(1906–1989)

TJEBBE WESTENDORP

Samuel Barclay Beckett was born on Good Friday, 13 April 1906. His parents were William Frank Beckett, Jr. (1871–1933), a quantity surveyor, and Mary (Molly or May) Roe (1871–1950), originally from Kildare. He had one brother, Frank Edward (1902). They lived in "Cooldrinagh," Foxrock, a not unfashionable suburb of Dublin. The family was well-to-do, middle class, and Church of Ireland.

William is usually remembered as a fairly jovial outdoorsman. He took his son for long Sunday walks. May Beckett was stricter than her husband. Deirdre Bair, still Beckett's only biographer, describes her as "reserved and austere in dress and demeanour" and unpleasant and stern toward her husband, but after his death in 1933 she grieved for him until she died in 1950.

Samuel Beckett was sent to an Irish school, Portora Royal, in Enniskillen, County Fermanagh, Northern Ireland, where Oscar Wilde had been a student. Beckett made a greater impression as a sportsman than as a student. His brother, Frank, captained the school cricket team, and Samuel quickly made the first eleven. He was an enthusiastic sportsman, became cricket and rugby captain, and, in the course of time, took up boxing, golf, chess, and bridge, rode a motorcycle, and kept generally very fit.

At the early age of seventeen he was admitted to Trinity College, Dublin, where he studied modern English literature, French, and Italian (Dante). Not until the end of his third year did he show any exceptional promise, when he wrote a learned essay on Proust and studied Descartes and the seventeenth-century Belgian Arnold Geulincx.

He took up teaching jobs at Portora and taught briefly at Campbell College, Belfast. From 1928 to 1930 he was exchange "lecteur" at the École Normale Supérieur in Paris. In the years 1930–1932 he was assistant lecturer in French at Trinity, but he suddenly resigned after four terms, to the surprise and disappointment of his friends. In the 1930s he made frequent visits to Kassel, Germany, where his mother's sister lived. He showed a great interest in the German language.

After 1932 until he settled in Paris at the beginning of the World War II, he spent time in Germany and in Paris, where he frequently saw Jack B. Yeats, Thomas MacGreevey, James Joyce (whom he assisted in his work sometimes), and other expatriate Irishmen. He apparently met W. B. Yeats just once.

At the beginning of World War II, Beckett was in Paris, where he played a useful part in the ''résistance'' against the German occupation. When his associates were betrayed and nearly captured in 1942, he escaped to the unoccupied southern zone of France.

He returned to Paris in 1946 for a highly active period of writing. From then on, his life was devoted to the writing of his literary oeuvre. His cynical wit and his attempts to confront the existential issues of his time as expressed in novels such as *Murphy* and later in his plays, coupled with his public reticence, made him a cult figure, *malgré lui-même*. In 1961 his long-standing relation with Suzanne Deschevaux-Dumesnil was legalized, but after their legal marriage Suzanne remained in the background as before. In later years they spent more and more time away from each other.

Beckett's biographer Deirdre Bair has detailed accounts of Beckett's relations to young women (Peggy Guggenheim and others) as well as his depressions and physical ailments. Her work sheds little light on how Beckett's innate disposition or the experiences of his early years contributed to his career as one of the century's most significant playwrights. Beckett was awarded the Nobel Prize in literature, in October 1969.

There is some irritation in Beckett circles about inaccuracies on the part of Beckett's biographer Deirdre Bair and about her unwillingness to join debates with the Beckettians about her scholarship. Her preoccupation with the psychological complexity, depressions, and psychosomatic ailments of Beckett has been considered unwarranted. Interesting, though, are Bair's references to Wilfred Bion, the Jungian psychoanalyst who worked at the Tavistock Clinic in London and treated Beckett for a while, and to the Tavistock lectures that the sixty-year-old Carl Jung gave in 1935. Beckett attended some of them. Bair discusses Beckett's interest in Jung's idea that the unconscious projects images and characters who become stage figures in the imagination. She quotes Jung: ''Because complexes have a certain will power, a sort of ego, we find that in a schizophrenic condition they emancipate themselves from conscious control to such an extent that they become visible and audible. They appear as visions, they speak in voices, which are like the voices of definite people. . . . When [a dramatist] creates a character on the stage . . . he thinks it is merely a product of his imagination, but that character in a secret way has made itself'' (Bair, p. 208).

More light will be shed on the life of Beckett by his letters—Martha Fehsenfeld, from Chapel Hill, North Carolina, and Lois Overbeck, Emory University, Atlanta, Georgia, are the editors—and by the authorized biography by James Knowlson, of the University of Reading, England.

Selected Biographical Sources: Bair; Ellmann; Harrington; Kennedy; Ricks.

MAJOR PLAYS, PREMIERES, AND SIGNIFICANT REVIVALS: THEATRICAL RECEPTION

Le Kid. 1931. He wrote and produced this for a Trinity Drama Festival.

It was a parody on Corneille's neoclassicism and on critics who insist on the three unities. The performance was as outrageous as Alfred Jarry's *Ubu Roi* (1896) and was greatly appreciated by the local audience. At the back of the stage a character is turning the hands of a huge clock and, to maintain the fiction of the unity of time, he must increase their speed as the character up front speaks more quickly. No text survives.

Human Wishes. 1937. A play in English.

The title refers to Dr. Johnson's famous affair with the attractive and much younger Mrs. Hester Thrale. The four-act play was abandoned, but one scene survives and has been published.

Éleuthéria. 1947. A play in three acts, with seventeen characters.

Offered to Roger Blin in 1951, together with *Waiting for Godot*, but rejected by him and by others. Not translated into English and never performed. Victor Krapp (cf. *Krapp's Last Tape*) is the protagonist; Olga Skunk is his fiancée. The play anticipates many later themes.

Waiting for Godot. 1953. A play in two acts, called by Beckett a tragicomedy, translated by him from the original *En attendant Godot*. The French play opened in Paris, Théâtre de Babylone, 5 January, directed by Roger Blin. Pierre Latour was Estragon, Lucian Raimbourg was Vladimir, Jean Martin was Pozzo, and Roger Blin was Lucky.

Alain Robbe-Grillet commented, "Everything happens as if the two tramps were on stage *without having a role*" (in Cohn [3], 20). With Jacques Audiberti he set the discussion going, but it took two anxious years of financial and other problems before Peter Hall succeeded in producing the London premiere (3 August 1955) at the private Arts Theatre Club. Paul Daneman was Vladimir, Peter Woodthorpe was Estragon, Timothy Bateson was Lucky, and Peter Bull was Pozzo. From the beginning the play was received unfavorably. The spirit was hostile, and spectators started leaving soon after the beginning. Thanks to the unbiased reviews of two drama critics in the weekend papers, Harold Hobson and Kenneth Tynan, the play was kept going. Alan Simpson's Irish premiere quickly followed at the Pike Theatre, Dublin, and was well received. On 3 January 1956 Alan Schneider directed the American opening at the Coconut Grove Playhouse in Miami, which failed miserably until the play went to New York. In England the first unexpurgated *Waiting for Godot* was directed by

Anthony Page at the Royal Court, London, December 1964, with Alfred Lynch, Nicol Williamson, Paul Curran, and Jack MacGowran. Ten years after the play had been dismissed by many London critics as incomprehensible, it was revived at the Royal Court Theatre and was most respectfully received. *Waiting for Godot* had become a landmark and is frequently revived. Producers take liberties with it that do not always strengthen the performance.

From the start Beckett had objected to symbolist readings of his plays, but precisely such interpretations turned out to be popular with the critics. The repetitious rhythms and the perfect timing of Irish banter and cross talk from the music hall, of Charlie Chaplin's and Buster Keaton's comic acts, and of the dialogues of the Marx Brothers were as close to Beckett's heart as existentialist symbolism. The play is a classic now and has been treated as such: it has had an all-women cast and has been produced in all kinds of settings and in many languages. It has liberated the modern stage from many of its stifling conventions.

All That Fall. 1957. A play for radio (60 to 90 minutes), written in English, commissioned by Martin Esslin. First broadcast by the BBC, 13 January; directed by Donald McWhinnie. Mrs. Maddy Rooney, a Dublin woman in her seventies, was played by Mary O'Farrell; Mr. Slocum by Patrick Magee; Tommy by Jack MacGowran. Dan Treaton directed Bosco Hogan and Aidan Grennell in the Irish version. An American cassette version, with Billie Whitelaw and David Warrilow, was made in 1986 and directed by Everett C. Frost. *All That Fall* was revived at the Beckett Festival in Dublin on 6 October 1991, on RTE I.

The title is derived from the psalm "The Lord upholdeth all that fall." This play, with its eccentric local characters and their wonderful Irish banter, anticipates the more tragic themes of the later writings, such as that of someone who is "never truly born." Beckett's radio plays and readings from his fiction were very well received.

Endgame. 1957. A one-act play, translated by Beckett from the French *Fin de partie*. The latter had its premiere at the Royal Court, London, 3 April, with Jean Martin and Roger Blin. It moved on to the Studio de Théâtre des Champs Élysées in Paris. After 100 performances, in which Blin played Hamm, and Jean Martin was Clov, it closed. It was invited to the Biennale in 1958. Blin made a film of it in 1962. The first English-language production, in Beckett's translation, was 28 January 1958 at the Cherry Lane Theatre in New York, with Alan Schneider as director. In October 1958 the first production in England came to the Royal Court, in which George Devine played Hamm, and Jack MacGowran was Clov. In 1964 Beckett was unofficially the director of the "English Theatre in Paris" revival in the Studio des Champs Élysées. It ran for nine weeks and was highly acclaimed. It then moved to the Aldwych in London, where it ran to packed houses for two seasons, with Patrick Magee as Hamm and Jack MacGowran as Clov. Another revival took place in 1976, at the Royal Court, with Donald McWhinnie as director, at the celebration of Beckett's seventieth birthday, with Patrick Magee as Hamm. In 1980 Beckett directed the San Quentin Drama Workshop in Chicago. There have been frequent revivals in America: at the Manhattan Theater Club, directed by Joseph Chaikin (1980), at the Harold Clurman Theater, staged by Alvin Epstein (1984), at the American Repertory Theater, directed by JoAnne Akalaitis (1985), and a production by the Quentin Drama Workshop, directed by Alan Mandell (1991). The most recent revival in Dublin was at the Beckett Festival (16–21 October 1991), staged by Antoni Libera, with Alan Stanford and Barry McGovern.

In February 1965 both Blin and Jean-Louis Barrault staged revivals of *Fin de partie*. It opened in Germany as *Endspiel* in 1967 at the Schiller-Werkstatt, Berlin, with Beckett as director. A film was made of it with Horst Bollmann and Werner Stock. The Dublin University players staged the Irish premiere, but the reception was critical.

The stage directions indicate a bare interior with two small windows with curtains. Stage builders have made it into a womb, a skull, a prison, or a chicken coop or have stressed the apocalyptic dimension of the play. Hamm is blind and sits in a wheelchair, asleep. Clov is the servant and the master of his small kitchen. Two old ash bins in the room are the dwelling places of his parents, Nagg and Nell. The names of the characters can be associated with hammer and nails (Fr. *clou* and German *Nagel*; English "nail"). Hamm suggests "ham actor," whose theatrical self-lament "Can there be misery more lofty than mine?" reminds us of Pozzo.

The basic tension of the play is between two men who are eager to leave each other but are incapable of doing so. Beyond their unwanted bond there is nothing. Critics have suggested that in chess an endgame suggests a world that is reduced to a few last pieces confronting each other. "Finished, it's finished, nearly finished, it must be nearly finished" are Clov's opening lines. The moves in the play are, in good Beckettian fashion, repetitious and follow certain (geometric) rules. Critics have mostly addressed the existential issues raised by the text.

Act without Words I. 1957. A mime for one player, music by John Beckett (a cousin), translated by Beckett from the French *Acte sans paroles I*. First English performance: 3 April, at the Royal Court Theatre, London, with Deryk Mendel as director and dancer. It has often been revived: in London, at the In-Stage in 1962; in 1963 with Jack MacGowran under the direction of Chloe Gibson and Donald McWhinnie; in New York at the Lincoln Center and at the Beckett Festival in 1970 (November), as well as at the Dublin Beckett Festival in 1991 (October 11 and 12), with *Not I* and *What Where*.

The short mime has baffled spectators but has proved popular. A small tree, scissors, cubes of different sizes, and a carafe are held out to a single actor who resembles Tantalus. He is prodded into action by dazzling flashes of light and sharp whistles. At the end the carafe "dangles and plays about his face. He does not move. The carafe is pulled up and disappears."

Krapp's Last Tape. 1958. A play written for the Northern Irish actor Patrick Magee, who was Krapp in the first performance: 28 October at the Royal Court Theatre, London, direction by Donald McWhinnie. In 1960 it was staged at the Provincetown Playhouse, New York, with Alan Schneider as director. It was quickly acknowledged as a masterpiece. Roger Blin was in charge of the French opening in March 1960 at the Théâtre Récamier. It was played again at the Sarah Bernardt Théâtre in Paris in 1961. A BBC production with Cyril Cusack (1963) was followed in 1972 by another BBC broadcast, both with the original director and actor. The French *La dernière bande* opened at the Théâtre Recamier in 1970 with Jean Martin and was revived in 1975 in the Petite Salle, Théâtre d'Orsay, with Beckett as director. Revivals: 1969 in German, *Das Letzte Band*, at the Schiller-Werkstatt, Berlin, with Beckett as director and Martin Held as Krapp. In 1988 a recording was made with Rick Cluchey as Krapp at the San Quentin Drama Workshop, Walter D. Asmus directing. At the Dublin Beckett Festival Pat Laffan directed David Kelly (4, 5, 9, 10, 20 October 1991) for another revival.

Krapp's Last Tape has been one of the most popular of the plays: the image of this "wearish old man" listening to the tape recordings he made in the past, realizing that he is caught in his past, refusing to give up his memories and dreams of love, is very powerful. The critics have concentrated on the subtleties employed by actors and directors in staging the play rather than on its accessible text.

Act without Words II. 1959. A mime for two players, from the French *Acte sans paroles II*, Beckett's translation. It opened at the Clarendon Press Institute, Oxford, with John McGrath. London premiere: 25 January 1960 at the Institute of Contemporary Arts, London, with director Michael Horovitz. Revived by Charles Marowitz (the In-Stage, London, 15 July 1962) and at the Gate Theatre in Dublin for the Beckett Festival, in 1991 (2, 3, 4, and 18 October) in a bill with *Come and Go* and *Play*.

One character, A, is slow, and awkward, while the other character, B is brisk, rapid, and precise. They are prodded into motion by a goad.

Embers. 1959. A radio play in one act, first transmitted 24 June on BBC Third Programme, with Patrick Magee and Jack MacGowran, directed by Donald McWhinnie.

Embers won the Prix Italia. The listener seems to be inside Henry's head. It has not had the acclaim of *All That Fall*, possibly because too much is left unspecified, and too much is demanded from the audience. It was revived by RTE I as part of the Dublin Beckett Festival, 1 October 1991, produced by William Styles.

The Old Tune. 1960. A conversation piece for radio, adapted from the French text by Robert Pinget. The BBC Third Programme broadcast it on 23 August: Jack MacGowran as Cream, Patrick Magee as Gorman; production by Barbara Bray. The first stage performance was in 1964 at the Traverse Theatre, Edinburgh, with Leonard Maguire as Gorman and Declan Mulholland as Cream, directed by Michael Geliot. Revived for the Dublin Beckett Festival on 9 October 1991 for RTE I.

Critics have suggested that Beckett placed his originally French text deliberately in the Irish tradition of *All That Fall*.

Happy Days. 1961. A play in two acts. Translation of *Oh les beaux jours*, by Beckett. World premiere at the Cherry Lane Theatre, New York, 17 September, with Ruth White as Winnie, directed by Alan Schneider. England: 1961 at the Royal Court Theatre, London; director George Devine. In 1971 Beckett was its director at the Schiller Theater in Berlin. In 1971 at the Théâtre de France, in Paris, Madeleine Renaud as Winnie, and Jean-Louis Barrault as Willie, directed by Roger Blin. In 1975 the Old Vic in London had Peter Hall direct Peggy Ashcroft. In 1979 at the Royal Court in London Beckett directed Billie Whitelaw. There is a television recording by the BBC. In 1979 Anton Serban directed *Happy Days* at the Public Theater in New York. In 1987 Shivuan O'Casey directed the play at the Global Village, New York. At the Dublin Beckett Festival (8–14 October 1991) *Happy Days* was revived with Fionnula Flanagan as Winnie and Bill Golding as Willie, directed by Caroline Fitzgerald.

Winnie's imprisonment in a low mound at center stage and her minimal communication with her husband have been interpreted as a brilliantly dramatized existential and marital situation.

Words and Music. 1962. A piece for radio, with music by John Beckett, first broadcast by BBC Third Programme, 13 November. Directed by Michael Bakewell. With Patrick Magee as Words, Felix Felton as Croak. Revived in the United States in 1987 (Voices International, directed by Everett C. Frost) and for the Dublin Beckett Festival in 1991 for RTE I.

There are three characters: Croak, a poet, and his two servants, Words and Music. They all play their part in the attempted composition of a poem.

Cascando. 1963. A play for radio, originally in French, with three characters, Opener, Music, and Voice. Music by Marcel Mihalovici. First broadcast in French by ORTF, 13 October, with Roger Blin as director, and in English by BBC Third Programme, 6 October 1964, directed by Donald McWhinnie. Magee was Voice, and Felix Felton was Opener. For the UL-AVC David Rainer Clark directed the play in 1984. In America Everett C. Frost directed it for Voices International (1988). It was revived by RTE (with *Rough for Radio II*) as part of the Dublin Beckett Festival, 15 October 1991, produced by William Styles; original music by Gerard Victory.

The play dramatizes the tension of creation in which the self-assurance of

Opener ("I open . . . and I close") is opposed to the creative Voice ("Can't see . . . jammed down").

Play. 1963. A one-act play in English. First performance at the Ulmer Theater 14 June (in Elmar Tophoven's translation) as *Spiel*. Directed by Deryk Mendel. First American performance 4 January 1964 at the Cherry Lane Theatre, New York, directed by Alan Schneider. The first British performance on 7 April 1964 was at the National Theatre by the Old Vic, with Rosemary Harris and Billie Whitelaw as w1 and w2, and with Robert Stephens, under the direction of George Devine. This performance in the National Theatre was widely reviewed, but for some reviewers the meticulous staging was seen as a sign of Beckett's lack of affinity with the recognized dramatic traditions. The first Irish perform- ance was at the Abbey Theatre in Dublin, 1967. It was revived at the Royal Court, London, in 1978 (Donald McWhinnie as director). *Spiel* was revived in 1978 in Berlin with Beckett as director at the Schiller-Werkstatt. It was per- formed in French as *Comédie*, at the Pavillon Marsan (1964), and reconstituted two years later at the Odéon. It was brought back for the Dublin Beckett Festival (2, 3, 4, and 18 October 1991) at the Gate, with *Come and Go* and *Act without Words I.*

In *Play* three figures, half-hidden in identical urns, tell their own version of a melodramatic triangle situation in a monotonous voice. At the end the whole play is repeated. Over the years productions have increasingly suggested a pur- gatorial atmosphere, which has deepened the play's meanings.

Film. 1964. A film scenario of 24 minutes. The film was shot in New York in the summer, by Alan Schneider, with assistance from Beckett, and with Buster Keaton as protagonist. First shown at the New York Film Festival 1965 in the Evergreen Theatre. Remade in 1979 by the British Film Institute, directed by David Rayner Clark, with Max Wall.

The film's point of departure is George Berkeley's "To be is to be per- ceived." The main character is split into two: the one who sees E and the camera and the one who is seen. Until the end of the film, O is seen in an "angle of immunity," an angle of less than 45 degrees. In the third part, O is seen from behind but is suddenly perceived from the front: O and E turn out to be the same person. Beckett was not happy with the result, though he admired Buster Keaton greatly. Keaton kept introducing his old routines into the film.

Come and Go. 1966. A very brief play, or dramaticule, originally *Va et vient.* Opening 14 January at the Schiller-Werkstatt, Berlin, as *Kommen und Gehen* (Elmar Tophoven's translation), directed by Deryk Mendel. French version 1966, at the Odéon Théâtre de France. In English, 28 February 1968 at the Peacock Theatre, Dublin, with Edward Golden as director. First British perform- ance 9 December 1969 at the Royal Festival Hall, London. Revived at the Dublin Beckett Festival, 2, 3, 4, and 18 October 1991 at the Gate, with *Act without Words I* and *Play.*

The delicate movements of the three women, "as alike as possible," are balanced by the suggested viciousness of their comments on each other.

Eh Joe. 1966. A television play in one act. Broadcast 4 July in a BBC television production that Beckett directed with Alan Gibson. Jack MacGowran, the Northern Irish actor, was Joe, and Sian Phillips the Voice. World premiere 13 April 1966, German Süddeutscher Rundfunk Stuttgart, directed by Samuel Beckett. It was revived in German, directed by Beckett and Walter D. Asmus in 1979. Jean-Louis Barrault and Madeleine Renaud took part in the 1968 French production, which was directed by Michel Mitrani. Critics agreed that director Michel Mitrani allowed Barrault to sin against one of Beckett's basic tenets, that an actor should not show emotions, and a voice should not have "color." In a stage version David Warrilow acted in Alan Schneider's production at the Autumn Festival in Paris, 1981, and Rick Cluchey directed *Eh Joe* at the Goodman Theater, Chicago, 1983. It was revived for the Beckett Festival in Dublin on 30 September 1991 on RTE I in the form of a television showing of Alan Gilsenan's film for Yellow Asylum, with Tom Hickey and the voice of Siobhan McKenna. Beckett has called television "a peephole art."

In this play the camera shows Joe, who does not speak but listens to a woman's voice. The camera keeps closing in. Thus the medium manages to suggest the idea or illusion that we are in Joe's head and that he imagines and creates the voice himself. But Beckett has stated: "It is a concrete person for Joe. . . . She really is whispering inside his head. He hears her." It is dramatically too simple to assume that the voice is that of his conscience. Jonathan Kalb calls the play "accessible," and for that reason critics have either praised it highly (Martin Esslin) or called it his worst (Kalb, p. 103).

Breath. 1969. A sketch of 35 seconds. Written for Kenneth Tynan's erotic show *Oh! Calcutta!* First performance 16 June at the Eden Theatre, New York. Director Jacques Levy. First British performance October 1969, Close Theatre Club, Glasgow, 1969. Director Geoffrey Gilham. Revived at the Dublin Beckett Festival (18 and 19 October 1991), a Gate Theatre Production.

When the play opens, it discovers a feebly lit rubbish heap. When the light grows stronger, a cry is heard. It grows weaker, and a cry is heard. Then silence, and the curtain drops. The directions say that the amplified cry is an "instant of recorded vagitus." In *Breath* life is reduced to a period between two screams. The play is like a visualization of Pozzo's words (*Waiting for Godot*): "They give birth astride of a grave, the light gleams an instant, then it's night once more." Beckett was allegedly furious when he heard that on the stage in the background Jacques Levy, the director in New York, had introduced a few naked people among "the miscellaneous rubbish" in the background of the stage.

Not I. 1972. A one-act play in English, of about 17 minutes. Translated into French by Beckett as *Pas moi.* World premiere at the Beckett Festival, New York, 22 November, Lincoln Center, with Jessica Tandy as Mouth and Henderson Forsythe as auditor. Director was Alan Schneider. In England *Not I* opened 16 January 1973, at the Royal Court, London, with Billie Whitelaw as Mouth and Anthony Page as director. Beckett attended rehearsals and found Whitelaw's performance "miraculous" (see interview, Billie Whitelaw). First French production: Théâtre d'Orsay, with Madeleine Renaud, directed by Jean-Marie Serrau, 1976. In 1978 *Pas (Steps)* and *Pas moi (Not I)* were played together here. *Not I* was revived with Adele King, at the Dublin Beckett Festival, 1991 (11 and 12 October), in a program with *What Where* and *Acts without Word I*.

Not I heralds a new era in Beckett's career as dramatist and anticipates in the virtuosity of the staging his later equally intriguing and spellbinding drama. The actress' disembodied Mouth is visible, upstage, at a height of eight feet, through a hole in the black curtain. An actress (Mouth) speaks a monologue at breakneck speed to a figure hovering in the darkness below her, entirely cloaked in a black djellaba and of uncertain gender. The subject of her speech is the story of a "she," which appears to be that of her own life. The play demands a great deal from the actress playing Mouth, and the quality of her performance has decided the level of the public response. The performances of Billie Whitelaw and Jessica Tandy in this revolutionary and fascinating play were considered brilliant. In Paris (Jean-Marie Serreau directing Madeleine Renaud) the audience was not close enough to the stage (1976), and the play flopped. Beckett assisted Anthony Page in 1977 in the direction of the excellent BBC television recording of *Not I*, with Billie Whitelaw. A wider appreciation of *Not I*, unfortunately, is still lacking, mainly for lack of opportunity to see it.

That Time. 1976. A play in one act, written for Patrick Magee, who was Listener in the premiere (2 May), Royal Court Theatre, London, directed by Donald McWhinnie. The American opening was directed by Alan Schneider, at the Arena Stage, Kreeger Theater, Washington, D.C., in 1976. The German opening was in 1976 at the Schiller-Werkstatt, Berlin as *Damals*. David Warrilow played the French version *Cette fois* at the Dublin Beckett Festival in 1991 with *Solo*. Stephen Rea was Listener in the English version (18 and 19 October) in a combination with *Breath* and *A Piece of Monologue*.

Footfalls. 1976. A play in one act, translated into French by Beckett as *Pas*. It was written for Billie Whitelaw, as May, and Rose Hill, as a woman's voice. First performance at the Royal Court Theatre, London, 20 May, directed by Beckett. The German version *Tritte* was played at the Schiller-Werkstatt, Berlin, in 1976. *Footfalls* was revived in a triple bill (with *Rough for Theatre I* and *Rockaby*, 10–14 October 1991) at the Dublin Beckett Festival, with Suzanne Fitzgerald and Maureen Potter as Voice.

A disheveled and ghostlike figure called May—the name of Beckett's mother—has a dialogue with her invisible, bedridden mother while she paces up and down a strip of nine steps. As the play moves on and slows down, the mother's voice is subsumed in May's. Beckett said about *Footfalls*, "We are not trying to do this play realistically or psychologically but musically,'' and Billie Whitelaw said that she felt like a musical instrument playing notes. The precision of Beckett's stage directions creates the ghostlike atmosphere (May's dress, the voices, the decreasing light), which has led critics like Katharine Worth to introduce the term ''purgatorial'' for this and other late plays.

Rough for Theatre I. 1976. A sketch, originally in French, written in the late 1950s, published in 1976 but barely noticed by the critics. Opened in Germany, May 1979 at the Schiller Theater, Hamburg, directed by Walter D. Asmus. Revived 1987 by La Mama, New York. Revived (with *Footfalls* and *Rockaby*) at the Gate Theatre, 10–14 October 1991.

Rough for Theatre II. 1976. A sketch, originally in French but abandoned (1958). English version published in 1976. World premiere at the Schiller Theater, Hamburg, May 1979, with *Rough for Theatre I.* Performed at the Dublin Beckett Festival at the Gate Theatre, with *Ohio Impromptu* and *Catastrophe* (17, 19 October 1991).

Rough for Radio I. 1976. A play for radio, broadcast on BBC Radio 3, for Beckett's seventieth birthday. Richard Rijnvos directed it in 1991 for Dutch television, with Michael Gough, Joan Plowright, and John Cage.

Beckett felt it had been overtaken by *Cascando*.

Rough for Radio II. 1976. A radio play, which Martin Esslin directed for the BBC in 1976, with Patrick Magee as Fox, Billie Whitelaw as Stenographer, Harold Pinter as Animator, and Michael Deacon as the mute Dick. In 1989 Voices International had Everett C. Frost direct it in the United States. It was revived by RTE (in a program with *Cascando*) as part of the Dublin Beckett Festival, 15 October 1991, produced by William Styles, with new music by Gerard Victory.

Ghost Trio. 1977. A television play, 20 minutes, first broadcast 17 April on BBC 2, with Billie Whitelaw as v and Ronald Pickup as f. Direction Donald McWhinnie. Beckett supervised the filming. In 1977 he directed the German version for the German Süddeutscher Rundfunk in Stuttgart, as *Geister Trio*.

This intriguing play demands an unusual amount of close attention and patience from the viewer.

. . . but the clouds. . . . 1977. A play for television. This short play was first broadcast by the BBC on 17 April, directed by Donald McWhinnie and Samuel Beckett. M was Ronald Pickup, and w was Billie Whitelaw. The title is from Yeats' poem ''The Tower.'' Revived for the Beckett Festival in Dublin, 7 October 1991 for RTE I (with *Quad*).

A Piece of Monologue. 1979. A dramatic monologue, written at the request of David Warrilow, who acted in it and produced it (14 December) in La Mama Theatre, New York, with Rocky Greenberg. It was repeated on 19 August 1984, at the Edinburgh Festival, and in Paris in 1985. At the Dublin Beckett Festival, Warrilow played the French version *Solo* (14 October 1991) with *Cette fois* (*That Time*), while Stephen Rea was Speaker in the English version (18 and 19 October), in a combination with *Breath* and *That Time*, all directed by Judy Friel.

Rockaby. 1981. A play in one act, in English, opened at the Center for Theater Research in Buffalo, New York, 8 April, with Billie Whitelaw, directed by Alan Schneider. First British performance: 9 December 1982 at the National Theatre, London. Television production BBC 2, 15 December 1982, with Billie Whitelaw. Revived in the Samuel Beckett Theatre, New York, 16 February 1984, directed by Alan Schneider. Revived, with Maureen Potter, at the Dublin Beckett Festival, 10–14 October 1991, with *Rough for Theatre I* and *Footfalls*.

An old woman (referred to as W; prematurely old, unkempt gray hair, huge eyes in white, expressionless face, the directions say) sits in a rocking chair, the chair and her face weakly lit. She is listening to a voice that reacts to her command "more." The recorded voice and the rocking of the chair are "together." When the curtain drops, the chair stops its rocking. How is this to be interpreted? As Jonathan Kalb has written, "[A]ll possible meanings refer to the idea of death" (p. 23). The play demands near perfection (such as Schneider gave it) to have its full impact.

Ohio Impromptu. 1981. A play, 20 minutes, opened at Ohio State University, 9 May, with David Warrilow as R (reader) and Rand Mitchell as L (listener). Directed by Alan Schneider. The play was transferred to New York, and produced at the Harold Clurman Theatre (1983), where Elvin Epstein took over as R. First British performance: 13 August 1984 at the Edinburgh Festival. It was revived at the Gate Theatre for the Dublin Beckett Festival, with *Rough for Theatre II* and *Catastrophe* (17 and 19 October 1991).

On the stage two old men, dressed identically in black, sit at a table. On the table are a black, wide-brimmed hat and a book from which R, facing the audience, reads. Beckett suggested to Warrilow that he read it as a bedtime story, but the surprising variety of the several performances has given rise to varied interpretations. The play's sculpturesque and mysterious nature has given it a high reputation with Beckett's admirers.

Quad. 1982. A television mime (or ballet?), opened 8 October, German Süddeutscher Rundfunk, directed by Beckett and performed by the Stuttgart Preparatory Ballet School, under the title *Quadrat*. On the BBC it was performed 16 December 1982 for Beckett's seventy-fifth birthday. Revived for the Dublin Beckett Festival in 1991, 7 October RTE I, with *. . . but the clouds. . . .*

Four nearly identical, cloaked figures shuffle across the stage in geometric permutations.

Catastrophe. 1982. A one-act play in French, directed by Stephen Meldbegg at the Avignon Festival, 21 July, as part of "Une nuit pour Václav Havel," a night for the Czech playwright and politician Václav Havel. In Paris (1983) Pierre Chabert directed it with advice from Beckett. The first British performance was at the Edinburgh Festival, 13 August 1984. This production had opened in June 1983 at the Harold Clurman Theatre, New York, with David Warrilow, directed by Alan Schneider. It was revived under Pierre Chabert's direction at the Gate with Stephen Brennan and Helene Montague, for the Dublin Beckett Festival in 1991 (17 and 19 October), as part of a bill with *Ohio Impromptu* and *Rough for Theatre II*.

On the stage we see the director of the play (D) as a political dictator. The protagonist (P) stands midstage on a block like a live statue and is forced into all kinds of attitudes by the female assistant (A), who executes D's orders. At the end there is "a distant storm of applause. P raises his head, fixes the audience. The applause falters, dies." A's unexpected resilience, coupled with the self-reflexive nature of the scene—the stage applause dies down at the precise moment when the actual audience is about to start its applause—creates a highly dramatic climax. The play, with its explicit political implications, has been very well received.

Nacht und Träume. 1983. A television play without words. First broadcast 19 May by the German Süddeutscher Rundfunk, directed by Samuel Beckett.

It is about a dreaming man and a few words ("Lovely dreams, return again") from Schubert's song. Revived for the Dublin Beckett Festival, 14 October 1991, together with *Ghost Trio*.

What Where. 1983. A 10–minute television play without spoken words, for four male figures, "as alike as possible." In French, *Quoi où*. First performance at the Graz Festival. The English version opened at the Harold Clurman Theatre, New York, 15 June 1983, directed by Alan Schneider and with David Warrilow. The first British performance was in Edinburgh and directed by Alan Schneider (1984). It was revived at the Dublin Beckett Festival in 1991 (October 11, 12), with *Not I* and *Act without Words I*.

In *What Where* we see Bem, Bim, and Bom and hear the voice of Bam. Of a fifth character (Bum?) we have no name. Critics have seen a cynical political fable of Stalinist clowns in which the roles of victim and torturer are constantly reversed. Another interpretation is that the often repeated "You gave them the works" refers not to torture but to the manipulation of a writer or stage director or to the great works of philosophy. The play has not created much interest.

ASSESSMENT OF BECKETT'S CAREER

In his Dublin years Beckett was directly and indirectly involved in amateur theater. At Trinity there was a group called the Dramiks. He attended rehearsals of the Dun Laoghaire Theatre Group. His play *Le Kid* was produced by his fellow students. He liked the work of Sean O'Casey and attended first nights of his plays.

After World War II, Samuel Beckett settled in Paris, where he started writing plays in earnest. He is responsible for two major revolutions in the history of the theater: his *Waiting for Godot* was first performed in 1953 and created a great deal of controversy and discussion both in Paris and in London. It was followed by three plays in the same mode, *Endgame* (1957), *Krapp's Last Tape* (1958), and *Happy Days* (1961). By 1965, when *Waiting for Godot* returned to London, the name of Beckett was popularly associated with plays in which nothing happened and in which the actors stood about waiting for somebody who will not turn up. Variations on the phrase "waiting for" have become part of the English language. The two tramps, Pozzo and Lucky, the blind man with dark glasses in his wheelchair, his servant, the old man Krapp, listening to a tape recording of his own voice recorded in the past, the parents in the garbage cans asking for fresh sand, and Winnie with her body half-buried in a low mound have become familiar to the general public. The self-awareness of the actors and the self-reflexivity of the language and the action, which comment on them-selves, are the most characteristic and conspicuous elements of Beckett's early drama.

A completely different but equally revolutionary type of dramatic entertain-ment emerges in *Play* (1962), *Film* (1963), and, in its starkest form, *Not I* (1972). After this, *Footfalls* (1976), *Rockaby* (1981), *Catastrophe* (1981), and *Ohio Im-promptu* (1982), each in its own way, confirmed Beckett's descent into the world of shades and ghosts. In *Play* three heads protrude from gray urns and tell us three different stories about their relationships. *Film* is a self-reflexive work about perception and "perceivedness" (Beckett's term). The late plays are so short that they do not fill an evening. *Not I* is a 17–minute ranting speech by a disembodied Mouth, which both repels and attracts the spectator. In *Rockaby* and *Footfalls* Beckett enters the world of shades and spirits as the elderly and ghostly female protagonists take stock of their lives. The number of characters and the action are further reduced, the stage becomes darker, and it becomes increasingly difficult for the spectator to see and hear what is going on. *Catas-trophe* and *Ohio Impromptu* show the psychological mastery with which Beckett manipulates his audience: the very subject of the drama brings this out. By their ghostlike atmosphere Beckett's late theater and television plays approximate the other arts: music, television, dance and ballet, mime, painting, and sculpture. Beckett was frequently on the scene as a very demanding director, and no detail escaped him, but he allowed many changes to be made during rehearsals, as can be seen in the production notebooks.

Though perhaps too many scholars limit their comments to the written texts, members of a small but dedicated group of Beckettians from the worlds of the theater and the academies convene at festivals. In Dublin, for instance, the Gate Theatre, Trinity College, and RTE organized a three-week festival (October 1991) that combined performances with academic lectures and discussion, as did a ten-day Festival at The Hague on Beckett in the Nineties (April 1992). Beckett's late drama has not yet conquered the larger public, but his influence on twentieth-century drama and in particular on playwrights like Ionesco, Pinter, Stoppard, Fugard, Mamet, and Shepard has been considerable.

ARCHIVAL SOURCES

Two indispensable references are *The Samuel Beckett Manuscripts: A Study*, Richard L. Admussen, G. K. Hall, Boston, 1979; and John Pilling and Mary Bryden, *The Ideal Core of the Onion: Reading the Beckett Archive*, Beckett International Foundation, University of Reading Library, Reading, 1992.

Beckett holdings are to be found in the following libraries: McMaster University, Hamilton, Ontario; John J. Burns Library, Boston College; Sterling Memorial Library, Yale; University of Santa Barbara, Santa Barbara, California; Southern Illinois University, Carbondale; University of Indiana, Bloomington; Boston University; John Olin Library, Washington University, St. Louis; Baker Memorial Library, Dartmouth College, New Hampshire; New York Public Library; Syracuse University, New York (correspondence with Grove Press); Ohio State University, Columbus; Samuel Beckett Archives at the University of Reading, Reading; Trinity College, Dublin; Harry Ransom Humanities Research Center, University of Texas, Austin. Smaller holdings at Harvard, University of Chicago, SUNY at Geneseo, New York; Beckett Audio-Visual Archive, New York University, for filmed and television material.

There are five libraries with major holdings: John Olin Library, Washington University, St. Louis, (mainly 1961–1967: mostly prose, but texts with many variant versions); Baker Memorial Library, Dartmouth College (mainly prose works); Ohio State University, Columbus (especially *Fin de partie, Happy Days*); University of Reading Library, Reading (a rich collection; includes nonmanuscript material and copies of major manuscripts from St. Louis collection); Humanities Research Center, University of Texas, Austin (first thirty years of Beckett's career).

The correspondence of Beckett with Éditions de Minuit is not available.

PRIMARY BIBLIOGRAPHY

Collected Shorter Plays. London: Faber and Faber, 1986.
The Collected Works. 16 vols., New York: Grove Press, 1970.
The Complete Dramatic Works. London: Faber and Faber, 1986.
Ends and Odds. New York: Grove Press, 1976; London: Faber and Faber, 1977.

Plays

Act without Words I. New York: Grove Press, 1958.
Act without Words II. New Departures, I, (summer 1959).
Acte sans paroles II. Paris: Éditions de Minuit, 1957.
All That Fall. New York: Grove Press, 1957; Faber and Faber, 1957.

Breath, Gambit. International Theatre Magazine 4. 16 (1970).

. . . but the clouds . . . In *Ends and Odds.*

Cascando. Evergreen Review (May–June 1963).

Catastrophe. New Yorker (10 January 1983); Faber and Faber, London, 1984.

Come and Go. London: Calder and Boyars, 1967.

Comédie, et *Actes divers.* Trans by the author. Expanded version. Paris: Éditions de Minuit, 1972.

Eh Joe (Act without Words II and *Film).* London: Faber and Faber, 1967 (and other writings).

Embers. In *Evergreen Review* (Nov.–Dec. 1959), with *Krapp's Last Tape.* London: Faber and Faber, 1960; New York: Grove Press, 1960.

En attendant Godot. Paris: Éditions de Minuit, 1956.

Endgame, followed by *Act without Words I.* New York: Grove Press, 1958; London: Faber and Faber, 1958.

Film (complete scenario, with an essay on directing *Film* by Alan Schneider). London: Faber and Faber, 1967.

Film, suivi de *Souffle.* Paris: Éditions de Minuit, 1972.

Film, with *Eh Joe.* London: Faber and Faber, 1967.

Fin de partie, suivi de *Acte sans paroles I.* Paris: Éditions de Minuit, 1957.

Footfalls. New York: Grove Press, 1976; also in *Ends and Odds.*

Ghost Trio. Journal of Beckett Studies (Winter 1976); Also in *Ends and Odds.*

Happy Days. New York: Grove Press, 1961; London: Faber and Faber, 1962.

Happy Days. Ed. James Knowlson. London: Faber and Faber, 1985; New York: Grove Press, 1985 (Samuel Beckett's Production Notebook).

Happy Days / Oh les beaux jours. Ed. James Knowlson. London and Boston: Faber and Faber, 1978.

Human Wishes. Ed. Ruby Cohn. London: John Calder, 1983.

Krapp's Last Tape. In *Evergreen Review* (summer 1958).

Krapp's Last Tape, Embers. London: Faber and Faber, 1959.

Krapp's Last Tape Ed. James Knowlson. London: Brutus Books, 1980; Faber and Faber, 1992 (theatre Notebook I).

Nacht und Träume. In *Collected Shorter Plays.*

Not I. London: Faber and Faber, 1973.

Ohio Impromptu. In *Rockaby and Other Pieces* and in *Three Occasional Pieces.*

Oh les beaux jours. Paris: Éditions de Minuit, 1963.

Pas. Paris: Éditions de Minuit, 1977.

Pas moi. Paris: Éditions de Minuit, 1975.

A Piece of Monologue. Kenyon Review (Summer 1979); and in *Three Occasional Pieces.*

A Piece of Monologue, Rockaby, Ohio Impromptu. London: Faber and Faber, 1982.

Play. Evergreen Review (December 1964).

Play, and *Two Short Pieces for Radio.* London, Faber and Faber: 1964.

Quad. In *Collected Shorter Plays.*

Rockaby. In *Rockaby and Other Short Pieces.* New York: Grove Press, 1981; and in *Three Occasional Pieces.*

Rough for Radio I and *Rough for Radio II* in *Ends and Odds.* New York: Grove Press, 1976; London: Faber and Faber, 1977.

Rough for Theatre I. New York: Grove Press, 1976; and in *Ends and Odds.*

Solo and *Catastrophe*. London: Faber and Faber, 1984.
Solo, suivi de *Catastrophe*. Paris: Éditions de Minuit, 1982.
That Time. New York: Grove Press, 1976.
Tous ceux qui tombent. Paris: Éditions de Minuit, 1957.
Va et vient. Paris: Éditions de Minuit, 1966.
Waiting for Godot. London: Faber and Faber, 1956 (A tragicomedy in two acts).
Waiting for Godot. First unexpurgated and rev. ed. London: Faber and Faber, 1965 (a
    tragicomedy in two acts).
What Where. In *Collected Shorter Plays*.
Wilkinson, Marc. *Voices from the play Waiting for Godot by Samuel Beckett*. Universal
    ed., London, 1960. (score for contralto, flute, E-clarinet, violoncello, with text in
    English and German).
Words and Music. *Evergreen Review* (November–December 1962).

SECONDARY BIBLIOGRAPHY

On Beckett as Director

Asmus, Walter D. [1]. "Beckett Directs Godot." *Theatre Quarterly* 5 (1975): 19–26.
———. [2]. "Practical Aspects of Theatre, Radio and Television: Rehearsal Notes for
    the German Première of Beckett's *That Time* and *Footfalls*, at the Schiller-Theater
    Werkstatt, Berlin, (directed by Beckett)." *Journal of Beckett Studies*, no. 2 (sum-
    mer 1977): 82–95.
Chabert, Pierre. "Samuel Beckett as Director." Ed. James Knowlson. In *Samuel Beckett:
    Krapp's Last Tape.*
Fehsenfeld, Martha, and Dougald McMillan III. *Beckett at Work in the Theatre*. Vol. 1
    from *Waiting for Godot* to *Krapp's Last Tape*. London: John Calder; and New
    York: Riverrun Press, 1988.
Knowlson, James. "*Krapp's Last Tape*: The Evolution of a Play 1958–1975." *Journal
    of Beckett Studies*, no. 1 (winter 1976): 50–65.
MacGowran, Jack. "MacGowran on Beckett: Interview by Richard Toscan." *Theatre
    Quarterly* (July–September 1973).
Schneider, Alan. " 'Anyway You Like Alan': Working with Beckett." *Theatre Quarterly*
    4 (1975): 27–38.
Whitelaw, Billie. "Practical Aspects of Theatre, Radio, and Television." *Journal of
    Beckett Studies*, no. 3 (summer 1978): 85–90 (interview with James Knowlson).

On Beckett's Drama

Journals

The Irish University Review, Beckett Issue 14.1 (Spring 1984).
Journal of Beckett Studies.
Journal of Modern Literature (February 1977) 6.1 (Ed. Enoch Brater).
Modern Drama 9.3 (1966); 19.3 (1976); 25.3 (1982); 28.1 (1985).
Revue d'ésthetique (Hors série). (1986) (Ed. Pierre Chabert); rev. ed., 1990.

Criticism

Admussen, Richard L. *The Samuel Beckett Manuscripts: A Study*. London and Boston: G. K. Hall, 1978.

Alvarez, A. *Beckett*. London: Fontana/Collins, 1973.

Armstrong, Gordon S. *Samuel Beckett, W. B. Yeats, and Jack B. Yeats: Images and Words*. Lewisburg, Pa.: Bucknell University Press, 1990.

Bair, Deirdre. *Samuel Beckett: A Biography*. London: Jonathan Cape, 1978; New York: Harcourt Brace Jovanovich; rev. ed., New York: Vintage, 1990.

Beja, Morris, S. E. Gontarski, and Pierre Astier, eds. *Samuel Beckett: Humanistic Perspectives*. Columbus: Ohio State University Press, 1983.

Ben-Zvi, Linda, ed. *Women in Beckett: Performance and Critical Perspectives*. Urbana: University of Illinois Press, 1990.

Brater, Enoch. [1]. *Beyond Minimalism: Beckett's Late Style in the Theater*. Oxford and New York: Oxford University Press, 1987.

―――, ed. [2]. *Beckett at 80/Beckett in Context*. Oxford and New York: Oxford University Press, 1986.

Bryden, Mary. "Figures of Golgotha: Beckett's Pinioned People." In *The Ideal Core of the Onion: Reading the Beckett Archive*. Ed. John Pilling and Mary Bryden. Reading, Pa.: Beckett International Foundation, University of Reading Library, 1992.

Buning, Marius, Sjef Houppermans, and Danièle de Ruyter, eds. *Beckett Today / Aujourd' hui: Beckett 1970–1989*. Amsterdam and Atlanta, Ga.: Rodopi, 1992.

Butler, Lance St. J., ed. *Critical Essays on Samuel Beckett*. Aldershot: Scolar Press, 1993 (includes many reviews).

Butler, Lance St. J., and Robin J. Davis, eds. [1]. *"Make Sense Who May": Essays on Samuel Beckett Later Works*. Totowa, N.J.: Barnes and Noble, 1988.

―――. [2]. *Re-thinking Beckett: A Collection of Critical Essays*. London: Macmillan, 1990.

Calder, John. ed. *Beckett at Sixty: A Festschrift*. London: Calder and Boyars, 1967.

Chevigny, Bell Gale, ed. *Twentieth-Century Interpretations of Endgame*. Englewood Cliffs, N.J.: Prentice-Hall, 1969.

Cohn, Ruby. [1]. *Back to Beckett*. Princeton, N.J.: Princeton University Press, 1973.

―――. [2]. "Beckett's German Godot." *Journal of Beckett Studies*, no. 1 (winter 1976): 41–49.

―――. [3]. *Casebook on "Waiting for Godot": The Impact of Beckett's Modern Classic: Reviews, Reflections and Interpretations*. New York: Grove Press, 1967.

―――. [4]. *Just Play: Beckett's Theatre*. Princeton, N.J.: Princeton University Press, 1980.

―――. [5]. *Samuel Beckett: A Collection of Beckett Criticism*. New York: McGraw-Hill, 1975.

Duckworth, Colin. *Angels of Darkness: Dramatic Effects in Samuel Beckett with Special Reference to Eugene Ionesco*. London: Allen and Unwin, 1972.

Ellmann, Richard. *Four Dubliners: Wilde, Yeats, Joyce and Beckett*. London: Hamilton, 1987.

Esslin, Martin. *The Theatre of the Absurd*. Rev. ed. Harmondsworth: Penguin Books, 1968.

Gidal, Peter. *Understanding Beckett: A Study of Monologue and Gesture in the Works of Samuel Beckett*. London: Macmillan, 1986.

Gontarski, S. E. [1]. *Happy Days, an Analysis of the Manuscripts*. Athens, Ohio: Ohio State University Press, 1977.

———. [2]. *The Intent of Undoing*. Bloomington: Indiana University Press, 1985.

Gontarski, S. E., Morris Beja, and Pierre Astier, eds. *Samuel Beckett: Humanistic Perspectives*. Columbus: Ohio State University Press, 1986.

Graver, Lawrence. *Samuel Beckett: Waiting for Godot*. Cambridge: Cambridge University Press, 1989.

Graver, Lawrence, and Raymond Federman, eds. *Samuel Beckett: The Critical Heritage*. London and Boston: Routledge and Kegan Paul, 1979.

Harrington, John P. *The Irish Beckett*. Syracuse, N.Y.: Syracuse University Press, 1990.

Hassan, Ihab. *The Literature of Silence: Arthur Miller and Samuel Beckett*. New York: Knopf, 1967.

Hessing, Kees. *Beckett on Tape, Productions of Samuel Beckett's Work on Film, Video, and Audio*. Leiden: Academic Press Leiden, 1992.

Homan, Sidney. *Beckett's Theatres: Interpretations for Performances*. Lewisburg, Pa.: Bucknell University Press, 1984.

Junker, Mary. [1]. *Beckett: The Irish Dimension*. Dublin: Wolfhound Press, 1995.

———. [2]. "Samuel Beckett and the Irish Dimension in Five of His Plays." Ph.D. diss., Münster University 1991.

Kalb, Jonathan. *Beckett in Performance*. New York and Cambridge: Cambridge University Press, 1989.

Kennedy, Andrew K. *Samuel Beckett*. Cambridge: Cambridge University Press, 1989.

Kenner, Hugh. *A Reader's Guide to Samuel Beckett*. London: Thames and Hudson, 1973; repr., 1988.

Knowlson, James. *Samuel Beckett: An Exhibition Held at the University of Reading Library*. London: Turret Books, 1971.

Knowlson, James, and John Pilling. *Frescoes of the Skull: The Later Prose and Drama of Samuel Beckett*. London: John Calder, 1979.

Maxwell, D. E. S. *A Critical History of Modern Irish Drama 1891–1980*. Cambridge: Cambridge University Press, 1984; repr., 1988.

Mays, J. C. C. "Samuel Beckett." In *The Field Day Anthology of Irish Writing*. Vol. 3. Derry: Field Day, 1991.

Mercier, Vivian. *Beckett/Beckett: The Truth of Contradictions*. New York and Oxford: Oxford University Press, 1977.

Morot-Sir, Edouard, Howard Harper, and Dougald McMillan III, eds. *Samuel Beckett: The Art of Rhetoric*. Chapel Hill: University of North Carolina, Department of Romance Languages, 1976.

Morrison, Kirstin. *Canters and Chronicles: The Use of Narrative in the Plays of Samuel Beckett and Harold Pinter*. Chicago and London: University of Chicago Press, 1983.

Reid, Alec. *All I Can Manage, More Than I Could: An Approach to the Plays of Samuel Beckett*. Dublin: Dolmen Press, 1968.

Ricks, Christopher. *Beckett's Dying Words*. Oxford: Clarendon Press, 1993.

Simpson, Alan. *Beckett and Behan*. London: Kegan, 1962.

Westendorp, Tjebbe. "Catharsis in Beckett's Late Drama: A New Model of Transaction?'' In *Beckett Today/Aujourd'hui*. Ed. M. Buning et al. Amsterdam: Rodopi, 1992.

Worth, Katharine, ed. *Beckett the Shape Changer, a Symposium*. London: Routledge, 1975.

Zilliacus, Clas. *Beckett and Broadcasting: A Study of the Works of Samuel Beckett for and in Radio and Television*. Åbo, Finland: Åbo Akademi, 1976.

BIBLIOGRAPHIES

Andonian, Cathleen Culotta. *Samuel Beckett: A Reference Guide*. Boston: G. K. Hall, 1989 (covers material before 1985).

Beckett on File. Comp. Virginia Cooke. London: Methuen, 1985 (repr. in 1986 as *File on Beckett*).

Davis, Robin J. *Samuel Beckett: Checklist and Index of His Published Work, 1967–1976*. Sterling, Scotland: Library, University of Sterling, 1979.

Federman, Raymond, and John Fletcher. *Samuel Beckett, His Works and His Critics: an Essay in Bibliography*. Berkeley and Los Angeles: University of California Press, 1970.

Fletcher, Beryl S., and John Fletcher. *A Student's Guide to the Plays of Samuel Beckett*. London and Boston: Faber and Faber, Rev. ed., 1985.

Brendan Francis Behan
(1923–1964)

MAUREEN S. G. HAWKINS

Brendan Behan's dramatic fame rests on his two best-known plays, *The Quare Fellow* and *The Hostage*, which, with Beckett's *Waiting for Godot* and Osborne's *Look Back in Anger*, inaugurate the contemporary movement in Irish and British drama. Critics are divided about which is the better play (and, for that matter, whether either is a great play) as well as about the extent and effect of directorial intervention on their final texts. However, all agree that Behan's public behavior often focused more attention on him than on his plays and that his diabetes and alcoholism took a severe toll of his artistic control before they took his life.

On 9 February 1923, near the end of the Irish civil war, Brendan Behan was born into a Dublin working-class family with equally strong connections to the socialist wing of the Irish Republican movement and to the Dublin theater. His mother, Kathleen Kearney Behan, married his father, Stephen Behan, a housepainter, union leader, and Irish Republican Army (IRA) member, after the death of her first husband, Rory Furlong, also an IRA member; Stephen Behan is said to have first seen Brendan through the bars of his cell in Kilmainham Prison, where he was incarcerated for IRA activity. One uncle, Peadar Kearney, author of "The Soldier's Song," Ireland's national anthem, had fought in the Easter Rising, the Black and Tan War, and the civil war and had found time in between to work as stage manager for the Abbey Theatre; another uncle, P. J. Bourke, a playwright-actor-manager, ran the Queen's Theatre. Behan's brothers and cousins include two other playwrights, a theater manager, and an organizer for the Socialist Labour League.

Behan began writing patriotic poetry and prose while a member of the Fianna Eireann, the Irish Republican equivalent of the Boy Scouts. In 1937, he graduated from the Fianna to the IRA at the same time that he entered Day Apprentice School to become a housepainter. His mother dissuaded him from joining the International Brigade, but in November 1939, shortly after his step-grandmother Furlong and two of her daughters were arrested in England for making bombs during the IRA bombing campaign, Behan was arrested in Liverpool for possession of explosives and sentenced to three years' detention in Borstal, Britain's enlightened juvenile detention center and the setting of his autobiographical novel *Borstal Boy*, which Frank MacMahon later dramatized. In November 1941, Behan was released early and deported to Ireland, where he was shortly thereafter arrested for firing, with intent to kill, at a detective who was about to arrest three IRA men following an IRA ceremony at Glasnevin Cemetery on 5 April 1942. He was sentenced to fourteen years' penal servitude, of which he served five before being released during a general amnesty in November 1946. Following his release, he was arrested in Manchester in March 1947 for helping an IRA operative escape from prison and was briefly imprisoned; twice after that, he was arrested in England for breaking his deportation order and deported again.

During his imprisonment, Behan wrote his first play, *The Landlady* (ca. 1942–1943) and sold his first short story. He also studied Irish, in which he became fluent enough to write six articles, several highly praised poems, and three plays: *Casadh Súgáin Eile* (The Twisting of Another Rope—a pun on the title of the first play in Irish produced at a professional theater, Douglas Hyde's *Casadh an tSúgáin* [The Twisting of the Rope]), which he later expanded in English into *The Quare Fellow* (1954); *An Giall* (The Hostage) (1958), which formed the basis of his later play in English, *The Hostage* (1958); and *"Lá Breágh San Reilg"* (A Fine Day in the Graveyard), which became the basis of his unfinished play in English, *Richard's Cork Leg* (1972), completed and first produced by Alan Simpson after Behan's death. He also translated *The Landlady* into Irish.

Not all of Behan's time was spent in prison. By his own account, he worked from 1946 to 1951 as a housepainter, as a smuggler, and, in Paris, as a pimp and a pornographer. From 1951 to 1956, he was a freelance journalist as well as a link-writer and ballad singer for Radió Éireann's "The Balladmaker's Saturday Night." He serially published a crime novel, *The Scarperer*, in the *Irish Times* in 1953, and, from 1954 to 1956, he had a weekly column in the *Irish Press*. In 1955, he married Beatrice ffrench-Salkeld, the daughter of Cecil Salkeld, a noted Dublin artist.

Behan's first play, *Gretna Green; or, Ash Wednesday* (1947) was produced for an IRA fund-raising concert, and, in 1952, Radió Éireann commissioned him to write two short radio plays, *Moving Out* and *A Garden Party* (which were later combined and staged as *The New House* [1958]). His first professionally staged play, *The Quare Fellow* (1954), opened at Dublin's tiny (fifty-five seats), adventurous Pike Theatre Club under the direction of Alan Simpson and was later produced in London by Joan Littlewood's Theatre Workshop at the Theatre Royal in Stratford East (1956). Despite good reviews, it was not widely noticed by the public until a week later, when Behan appeared incoherently drunk on

Malcolm Muggeridge's BBC interview show, "Panorama," where he became, in the words of Donal Foley, "the toast of every Cockney pub overnight" (quoted in O'Connor 185) and began his ultimately self-destructive international career as a media figure.

The subsequent success of *The Quare Fellow* led the BBC to commission Behan to write a one-act radio play, *The Big House* (1957), which was later staged at the Pike (1958). It also led Gael Linn, an Irish-language group, to commission *An Giall* (1958), which was produced at Dublin's Damer Hall; translated, adapted, expanded, and workshopped with her company, it was later produced as *The Hostage* by Littlewood's Theatre Workshop (1958).

Due to his increasing problems with alcoholism, *The Hostage* was the last of Behan's plays produced during his lifetime. During the next few years, he made tours of the United States and Canada, tape-recorded three books of impressions and memoirs, which his editor, Rae Jeffs, put in publishable form, and worked on *Lá Breágh San Reilg* (Richard's Cork Leg), into which he incorporated parts of his unfinished novel, *The Catacombs*. However, he was unable to complete the play in actable form in either Irish or English before he died of diabetes and fatty degeneration of the liver on 20 March 1964, only a few months after the birth of his daughter, Blanaid. He had asked for and received an IRA funeral, the illegality of which was ignored by the many Irish government figures who attended it with the international media and a large portion of the Dublin working class, to whom Behan had always remained one of their own.

Selected Biographical Sources: Brendan Behan, *Brendan Behan's New York, Borstal Boy*; Boyle; Gerdes; Kearney [1, 2]; O'Connor; Simpson [1, 3].

MAJOR PLAYS, PREMIERES, AND SIGNIFICANT REVIVALS: THEATRICAL RECEPTION

The Quare Fellow. 1954. Opened on 20 November at the Pike Theatre Club, Dublin, for 28 performances, directed by Alan Simpson. Opened on 25 May 1956 at the Theatre Royal, Stratford East, London, for two months, produced by the Theatre Workshop and directed by Joan Littlewood; moved to the Comedy Theatre, London, West End, on 24 July 1956 for six months. Opened at the Abbey Theatre, Dublin, on 8 October 1956 for over four weeks. Opened at the Circle-in-the-Square, New York, on 27 November 1958 for 118 performances, directed by José Quintero. Opened as *Der Mann Morgen früh* at the Schiller-theater, Berlin, on 16 March 1959 and as *Le Client du Matin* at the Théâtre de L'Oeuvre, Paris, on 17 April 1959. Broadcast by Radió Éireann on 8 December 1956 and by the BBC on 5 November 1958. The film, written and directed by Arthur Dreifus, premiered at Cork Film Festival (Ireland) on 22 September 1962.

Having been rejected by the Abbey and the Gate, *The Quare Fellow* premiered at Alan Simpson's Pike Theatre Club, after some revision by Simpson's wife, Carolyn Swift. Most reviewers, such as Fallon [2] and Leventhal, were very favorable, drawing attention to its liveliness and exuberance and to the efficacy of its anti–capital punishment stance, though they also commented on its technical and/or structural flaws. Fallon [2] compared Behan to O'Casey. J. F. (who complained of overcrowding) and Robinson were less complimentary; the latter is said to have defended his lack of enthusiasm on the grounds that he could not enjoy a play he had turned down for the Abbey (Boyle). Forced to close because the Pike was too small to support such a large production, Simpson sought another Dublin venue, but *The Quare Fellow* was not produced again in Dublin until after its London success, when the Abbey finally produced it to positive reviews, especially from Fallon [3] and Fox [1].

The London reviewers, despite similar criticisms of the play's structure, were also complimentary, considering *The Quare Fellow* lively, artistic, and good propaganda (Findlater, Richardson). Cain [1] and Tynan [2] praised its gallows humor and use of comic relief, development of tension, and treatment of language. When it moved to the West End, Hobson's [1] second review elevated Behan to the ranks of great Irish dramatists from Goldsmith to Beckett.

The New York reviews were mixed, though most of the critics commented on both the play's technical weaknesses and its exuberance. Crist [2], in particular, was unimpressed; she thought it derivative, unfunny, and undramatic. However, Atkinson, Hewes [3], and McLean differed; Atkinson particularly praised its originality and perceptiveness as well as its vitality. On the balance, *The Quare Fellow* was largely well received everywhere save in Berlin, where Friedrich Luft of *Die Welt* found it boring (see King).

An Giall. 1958. (The Hostage in Irish). Opened in Damer Hall, Dublin on 16 June. Produced by An Club Drámaíochta under the auspices of Gael Linn. Directed by Frank Dermody. According to Wall [1], it was produced seven times for about 50 performances between 1958 and 1984, including a television adaptation by Padráig Ó Siochrú for Radió Telefís Éireann broadcast on 17 March 1968 and 30 August 1973. It should be noted that some revivals incorporated material translated into Irish from Behan's later English translation/adaptation, *The Hostage* (1958).

The reviews of the first production were mixed. Most critics thought that the play needed further editing and tightening, and some thought Behan's treatment of the IRA unfair. However, R. S. professed himself moved to tears by it. According to Wall [1], the reviews in Irish, even the most balanced, were often harsher than those in English, which "praise[d] the play's liveliness, satiric wit, realistic dialogue, sharply etched characters and dramatic tension."

Reviewers of revivals frequently compare *An Giall* to *The Hostage*, sometimes to the former's detriment as too simple (see Ó Glaisne's review of the 1979 revival quoted in Wall [1]). Others, however, prefer *An Giall* for its greater simplicity and chastity. (See Kennedy's and Brogan's reviews of the same production quoted in Wall [1].)

The Hostage. 1958. Opened on 14 October at the Theatre Royal, Stratford East, London, for nine months, produced by the Theatre Workshop and directed by Joan Littlewood; moved to the Théâtre des Nations Festival in Paris as Britain's entry on 3 April 1959; moved to Wyndham's Theatre, London, West End, on 11 June 1959, coproduced by the Theatre Workshop and Wolf Mankowitz; moved to the Cort Theatre, New York, on 20 September 1960, produced by Leonard S. Field and Caroline Burke Swann; moved to the Ethel Barrymore Theatre, New York, and then to the Eugene O'Neill Theatre, New York, for a combined New York run of three and one-half months. Revived at the Lyric Opera House, Hammersmith, London, on 13 February 1961 and at One Sheridan Square, New York, on 12 December 1961 for 196 performances. Opened at the Gaiety Theatre, Dublin, 13 July 1964 for two weeks. Revived at the Abbey Theatre, Dublin, 28 April 1970. Theatre Workshop production under Joan Littlewood's direction revived at Theatre Royal, Stratford East, London, June 1972.

Most of the London critics were positive about—if sometimes a bit bewildered by—*The Hostage* in both its Theatre Royal and West End productions. The most common criticism was of its lack of conventional form: Trewin [1] found this inexcusable, but Shulman [3], Jones, Tynan [4], and Hobson [5] thought that its vitality excused its flaws. Tynan [3] conceded the play's transgression of generic boundaries but saw that as a positive quality in keeping with contemporary practice, and Hobson [5] particularly admired Teresa's curtain speech.

Many critics, such as Hobson [5], so enjoyed the play's liveliness and were so delighted by the laughing impartiality of its treatment of Anglo-Irish relations that they failed to delve very deeply into it. However, two critics were more perspicacious. Brien admired its treatment of the force of the political illusions imposed by the ruling class on oppressor and oppressed alike, and Gilliatt praised it for putting politics in the midst of life as well as for its exuberant language.

The Hostage was the hit of the Théâtre des Nations Festival, where it won the prize for the best play of the year. It received ten curtain calls and a three-minute ovation from an audience of twelve hundred, and the reviewers for *Figaro Littéraire* and *L'Express*, who admired its demolition of conventional generic boundaries, found it forceful and provocative (quoted in O'Connor). Translated into French as *Un Ôtage*, it was chosen the best play of the year in Paris in 1962. Again, however, the Germans disliked Behan's work; Ulick O'Connor says that when *The Hostage* had its German premiere in Ulm, the audience hurled smoke bombs to protest their boredom.

As in Paris, *The Hostage* received ten curtain calls at its New York premiere at the Cort and was largely well reviewed by critics such as Aston, Brustein [2], Chapman [2], Taubman, and Watts, who, like their British counterparts, found it uneven, unstructured, even confusing, but great fun. Brustein [2], though denying its seriousness, recognized the constriction of the human world that its violent humor protests. Kerr [1] and Gilbert penetrated more deeply, seeing it as a serious work with, Gilbert said, affinities to a modern morality play. Only McClain was totally negative, criticizing the play for its lack of conventional structure and its off-color humor and language.

The Hostage has been frequently revived. Perhaps spurred by the mounting Troubles in Northern Ireland, it was revived three times in New York and once in London—by Littlewood's Theatre Workshop—in 1972 alone. As Hunt's review of Littlewood's revival indicates, the situation in Northern Ireland colors its reception even as its message of the need to put life and love above the destructive effects of the past—and of the difficulty of doing so—becomes ever more pertinent. It remains, as the *Times Literary Supplement* reviewer ("Death and the Irish") wrote in 1974, timely.

Richard's Cork Leg. 1972. two-act. Opened at the Peacock Theatre (the experimental theater of the Abbey, Dublin, 14 March. Directed by Alan Simpson. Performed by the Abbey Theatre Company with the popular folk group, the Dubliners, in leading roles. Moved to the Opera House, Cork, and then to the Olympia Theatre, Dublin, on 30 May 1972 for ten weeks for a total run of five months. Opened at the Royal Court Theatre, London, 19 September 1972. Directed by Alan Simpson with many of the original cast.

In incomplete, multiple drafts and rejected in its English version by Joan Littlewood and in its Irish version by Gael Linn at the time of Behan's death, *Richard's Cork Leg* was edited, added to, completed, and directed by Alan Simpson [3], as he believed Behan would have wished, in 1972. The Irish reviewers were not impressed; Finegan [1] found it thin and, noting its similarities to *The Hostage* (some of which, such as the manner in which Cronin dies—and is "resurrected"—are Simpson's additions), wondered whether Behan had been trying to repeat the previous play's success. Nonetheless, it was one of the three best draws in Dublin that year, adequately filling the fifteen-hundred-seat Olympia as well as the smaller Abbey for much of its run.

The London reviewers were more charitable, treating it much as they had *The Hostage*. Brustein [1, 3], Hobson [4], and Billington applauded its joyous exuberance, though Billington questioned whether it traveled well. All the critics recognized its still fragmentary nature, but Hobson [4] and Brustein [1, 3] thought that its unifying theme, death, provided adequate structure.

ADDITIONAL PLAYS, ADAPTATIONS, AND PRODUCTIONS

Behan's first play, *The Landlady* (ca. 1942–1943), a three-act play, was neither produced nor published (see De Búrca for an account of it). His second, *Gretna Green; or, Ash Wednesday* (1947), was never published and does not survive; De Búrca says that it was poorly received. Two one-act radio plays, *Moving Out* and *A Garden Party* (1952), were commissioned and broadcast by

Radió Éireann, and *The Big House* (1957), a one-act radio play, was commissioned and broadcast by the BBC Third Programme. Alan Simpson staged it at the Pike in 1958 on a double bill with Sartre's *Men without Shadows*, which ran for a month before Simpson replaced Sartre's play with *The New House*, a staged version of *Moving Out* and *A Garden Party. The Big House* was produced again by the Theatre Workshop at the Theatre Royal in Stratford East in London on 29 July 1963 as part of a Festival of Irish Comedy.

Frank MacMahon's stage adaptation of *Borstal Boy*, directed by Tomás Mac Anna, opened at the Abbey on 10 October 1967 for 146 performances and was sent to Paris as part of the Abbey's contribution to the Théâtre des Nations Festival in 1969. It opened in New York on 31 March 1970 at the Lyceum Theatre for 71+ performances. Produced by Michael McAloney and Burton C. Kaiser in association with the Abbey Theatre, it was directed by Tomás Mac Anna and won the New York Drama Critics' Circle Award and the Antoinette Perry (Tony) Award for the best play of 1969–1970. Alan Simpson [3] later directed it in Galway in an Irish translation by Sean Ó Cara. Besides this adaptation, two one-man shows constructed from Behan's writings have been produced: Ulick O'Connor's *Brendan* (1971) at the Peacock Theatre (the experimental theater of the Abbey, Dublin) and Shay Duffin's *Shay Duffin as Brendan Behan* (1973) at the Abbey Theatre (New York). There is also a Swedish film, *A Jar with Brendan Behan* (1971).

ASSESSMENT OF BEHAN'S CAREER

Both critical estimation and serious analysis of Behan's plays have suffered from the very factors that first brought him and his work to international attention: his larger-than-life public persona and his work with Joan Littlewood's Theatre Workshop. The former factor has drawn attention from his work to his life and personality, and this has led some critics to avoid analyzing his works by (in effect, dismissively) characterizing them as dramatizations of his personality. Both of these tendencies have resulted in more interviews and reminiscences of the man than critical evaluations of the plays.

The latter factor has led to accusations that much of his drama, particularly *The Hostage*, is really the work of others, especially Littlewood (Gascoigne, Grene, Maxwell [1, 2]; Ulick O'Connor; Taylor [1]; Wall [1, 2]). This claim seems supported by Simpson's assertion that Behan was so careless a writer with such a deficient sense of dramatic structure that Simpson's wife, Carolyn Swift, had to rewrite parts of *The Quare Fellow* (Simpson [1, 3]), as well as by the implication that because Littlewood did not believe in the sanctity of the text or the author's intentions, she must have thoroughly rewritten Behan's plays, especially *The Hostage*, with little or no creative or organizing input from Behan, and that she in some way hoodwinked him into accepting her changes (O'Connor; Wall [1, 2]). However, Boyle and Robert Hogan [1] point out that, for very good reasons, attributing Behan's plays to Simpson or Littlewood is, at the very least, an overstatement. Furthermore, Murphy, who acted in both *The Quare Fellow* and *The Hostage*, claims that Littlewood and her company made few changes to the former play and made changes to the latter one with Behan's cooperation, input, and approval, leaving the play, in all essence, Behan's. That Behan approved of suggested kinds of changes and additions—such as the large-scale incorporation of song, dance, and music hall elements—that may have been proposed by Littlewood and her company would seem to be substantiated by his practice when not working with Littlewood of incorporating such elements into his work (though in lesser degree) as seen in both *The Quare Fellow* and *An Giall*, as well as in his extensive use of such elements in the rough drafts of *Richard's Cork Leg*—incorporations that would seem to suggest that Behan wished to use such techniques and found his work with Littlewood liberating in that it put him in touch with theatrical traditions that, unlike the Abbey realism that dominated the legitimate Irish stage, sanctioned and encouraged the use of such techniques for serious drama.

Even more to the point, it seems significant that such charges are not leveled against other, later dramatists, such as Caryl Churchill and Carol Bolt, who have workshopped many of their plays from a far more fundamental point with the companies that produced them or against dramatists, such as Peter Shaffer, who give extensive credit to the directors and stage designers who helped to give their plays final shape; in both cases, the assumption seems to be that the ultimate control was the playwright's and that the play embodies her or his design and intent. One possible reason that Behan is often not granted the credit of this assumption is that his work with Littlewood's company was pioneering; *The Hostage*, in particular, was one of the first workshopped works to gain widespread public attention. But if critical attitudes to this practice have so far changed with the broader use of this technique as to grant full credit to later playwrights who use it, it would surely seem time to retroactively extend those attitudes to Behan's plays.

Another possible reason that Behan is not given the same kind of credit that dramatists such as Bolt, Churchill, and Shaffer are is that these techniques are not integrated into a fully structured text in *Richard's Cork Leg*, his last play and one written without Littlewood's presumably guiding "authorial" presence. However, the unstructured condition of *Richard's Cork Leg* is hardly de facto proof that Behan was unable to write a coherent, organized play and that he was merely imitating these techniques with no dramatic or structural sense of how to use them; an unfinished text in multiple, fragmentary drafts written when a playwright is incapacitated by diabetes and alcoholism and is near death can hardly stand as evidence of his habitual compositional strategies for finished texts when in good health and in control of his work.

Another reason such credit is not often given to Behan may be that some critics, particularly Irish ones, find the accusation that Littlewood is the real author of his works, especially *The Hostage*, useful for devaluing them as "un-Irish" in terms that sometimes echo those used to criticize Sean O'Casey's postexilic work (Kilroy [2]; Wall [1, 2]; and, especially, O'Connor). However, one must agree with Krause [2], who suggests that such reactions may say more about the critic's sense of Irish national pride than about Behan's artistry. It might be well to add that they also say more about how the critic wishes to define the Irish dramatic tradition than about Behan's place within that tradition.

It is important in this context that, from the very beginning, Behan has been compared to O'Casey (Fallon [2]). Some of these comparisons have been relatively superficial and/or undetailed (Gascoigne; Rollins), but a good start has been made on examining Behan's debt to O'Casey and/or to the influences that shaped O'Casey, such as Shakespeare (Edwards; Kleinstück; Krause [2]) and popular drama and music hall at the Queen's Theatre (Armstrong; Farragher; Hawkins [1]; Kosok [2]; Krause [1, 2]). Given that postexilic O'Casey, too, has been placed outside the Irish dramatic tradition, it could be valuable to consider the roles of both dramatists within that tradition, if only to query whether it is a singular, unified tradition or if it is really made up of multiple strands that place it within a broader European and North American framework.

Within such a framework, it would also be useful to examine the frequent assertion that the use of music hall performance elements, such as song, dance, direct addresses to the audience, and metatheatrical self-reflexivity in *The Hostage, Richard's Cork Leg*, and, to a lesser extent, *The Quare Fellow*, is "Brechtian" (Brien; Brustein [2]; Kitchin; Krause [2]; Rusinko; Trewin [1]; Tynan [3])—though one must also examine Kleinstück's reason for denying it, that Behan does not try to change the world through theater. One reason for ascribing Brechtian practice to Behan's plays was their production by Littlewood's company, whose techniques were assumed to be uniformly Brechtian, thus creating the presumption that such performance elements must be incorporated to create Brechtian alienation effects. However, as Esslin [1] points out, exactly what Brecht's theories and practices entail was not really understood by English critics in Behan's period—and one might wonder whether that has totally changed. The majority of reviewers of Behan's plays seem, by their own testimony, to have been caught up, and drawn in, by the songs and dances, not distanced, "alienated," or discouraged from empathizing and/or encouraged to analyze, which suggests that, if the purpose of including these performance elements was Brechtian, it failed. Given, however, that O'Casey often used similar performance elements, drawn from similar popular theatrical sources, to draw his audience in (among other purposes), an examination of Behan's plays within the contexts of both Brechtian and O'Caseyan practice could provide a more fruitful analysis of his drama, Irish dramatic tradition(s), and the influences on the development of contemporary drama.

Certainly, Behan's use of these elements deserves more detailed attention. Even those who approve of their inclusion tend often to speak of them as fitting a Littlewood "formula" that therefore needs no further analysis, and those who disapprove, such as Gascoigne, Taylor [1], and Wall [1, 2], see their use, particularly in *The Hostage*, as self-indulgent and destructive. However, as Taylor [1] points out, it was not Littlewood's usual practice to allow such elements to overwhelm a work or destroy its structure. His conclusion, that deficiencies in Behan's play forced the irrelevant overinclusion of such elements to cover them up, need not be the only one. A large number of critics, even some as recent as Winkler, have made broad generalizations about the functions of such elements in Behan's work, and some, such as Hendrickx, Krause [2], and Maxwell [1, 2], have more specifically examined the nature of Behan's debt to popular music and music hall traditions. However, only a few have examined in any detail how and why those music hall elements are used. Hays, MacInnes, and Maxwell [1, 2] have examined the structural, characterizational, and thematic functions of "The Old Triangle" in *The Quare Fellow*; Wall [1, 2] has ably discussed the thematic and characterizational use of much of the music and dance in *An Giall*; Wickstrom and Hawkins [1, 2] have examined some of the functions of Leslie's resurrection and song at the end of *The Hostage*, and Cardullo [2, 3] has given an interesting account of the functions of "We're Here Because We're Here" and of its singers, Rio Rita, Princess Grace, and Mulleady, in *The Hostage*. However, much more remains to be done in this area.

The use of these elements is frequently associated with another charge made by critics from Aston to Wall [1, 3] against Behan's dramaturgy: that one, some, or all of his plays lack structure, a charge that Simpson [1, 3, 4], in particular, appears to substantiate by his assertions that Behan's inabilities in this area forced him to have parts of *The Quare Fellow* rewritten and that those inabilities are a cause of the fragmentary nature of *Richard's Cork Leg*. It is instructive, in this case, to examine the kinds of changes that Simpson and Swift thought it necessary to make to *The Quare Fellow*. Besides eliminating repetition (see Simpson [1, 3]), they corrected Behan's tendency to allow characters to begin a topic and drop it only to reintroduce it later or to change topics in midspeech (see Simpson [1, 2, 3])—techniques that had been acceptable even in naturalistic drama since Chekhov. A closer examination of many of the critics who consider Behan's plays lacking in structure, form, or organization frequently suggests that they are either repeating received opinions and/or seeking the kind of nineteenth-century naturalistic structure derived from Aristotle via Scribe. Yet Maxwell [1] can call the structure of *The Quare Fellow* "tightly knit and almost classically unified," and other critics, such as Boyle, Gerdes, Hawkins [1], Hendrickx, Kearney [2], Kitchin, Krause [2], and Wickstrom, find evidence of complex and well-organized structures in *The Quare Fellow* and *The Hostage* (though they are not all in agreement on the nature of those structures). Even in the fragmentary, incomplete *Richard's Cork Leg*, the *Times Literary Supplement* reviewer ("Death and the Irish") finds evidence of an inherent organizing principle that leaves him dissatisfied with Simpson's ending on the grounds that Behan has prepared a different, more poignant, and truly comic ending through the earlier action. Part of the key to understanding Behan's structuring principles may lie in Krause's [2] assertion that Behan was in rebellion against nineteenth-century naturalistic form, in Brustein's [2] intuition that Behan's work has affinities with that of Ionesco, and in Boyle's development of Brustein's intuition into an assertion that, structurally, Behan's drama has affinities with the theater of the absurd, for, as Esslin [2] points out, one of the criteria for theater of the absurd is that form must reflect content. Boyle, in particular, has attempted to examine the relationship between form and content in *The Quare Fellow* and *The Hostage*, but much remains to be done in examining Behan's use of structure and deconstruction and hybridizing of generic boundaries, too.

Finally, inadequate attention seems to have been given to Behan's role in ushering in the contemporary movement in English-language drama, a movement that is usually dated from Osborne's introduction of working-class, angry naturalism in *Look Back in Anger* and Beckett's introduction of European antinaturalistic dramaturgy in *Waiting for Godot* to the English stage. However, Behan's two major plays are concurrent with these two landmark plays, and, whatever Littlewood's contributions to their final form, it is indisputable that they, particularly *The Hostage*, first drew broad-based, approving attention to workshopping drama and that, despite the clowning so prominent in Beckett's work and the growing critical interest in Brecht, they most strongly introduced and made acceptable the incorporation of popular and self-reflexive theatrical elements into serious drama, thus opening the way for a host of dramatists such as Churchill and Bolt and companies such as Joint Stock, Monstrous Regiment, and Theatre Passe Muraille. Without *The Quare Fellow* and *The Hostage*, contemporary drama and theater would undoubtedly have a somewhat different form.

Given all this, it should be clear that, despite the efforts of a number of excellent critics, Behan criticism is barely past its infancy. Besides the areas just discussed, little has been done in areas such as gender analysis or Behan's place in postcolonial studies, though Hawkins [1, 2] and Ragheb have touched on them. O'Connor's contended claim that Behan was homosexual (or, more properly speaking, bisexual) as well as his introduction of "queers" into *The Hostage* would seem to invite an investigation of his work from the perspective of gay and lesbian studies, but nothing appears to have been done in this area, either. All told, Behan's work offers avenues of investigation much broader and far-reaching than those that have already been explored.

ARCHIVAL SOURCES

At the time of her death in 1993, Beatrice Behan held two acts in longhand of the unpublished play *The Landlady* and an almost complete typescript of *Richard's Cork Leg* as well as manuscripts and typescripts of some of Behan's nondramatic work. One act, in Irish, of *The Landlady* is held by the Abbey Theatre Archives, and Alan Simpson [3] stated that he possessed a manuscript of *The Quare Fellow*. Other nondramatic manuscripts and typescripts are housed in the Special Collections of Morris Library, Southern Illinois University at

Carbondale, and in the University College Library, Cork, Ireland. Besides those in the possession of their recipients, letters by Behan are housed in the Fales Library, New York University; in the National Library of Ireland; and in the Library and Museum of the Performing Arts, New York. For more details, see Mikhail [3] 104–5.

PRIMARY BIBLIOGRAPHY

Plays

An Giall. Baile Átha Cliath: An Chomhairle Náisiúnta Drámaíochta, n.d. (in Irish, with Behan's name given in its Irish form: Breandán Ó Beacháin).
An Giall and *The Hostage.* Trans. and ed. Richard Wall. Gerrards Cross, Buckinghamshire: Colin Smythe; Washington, D.C.: Catholic University of America Press, 1987.
The Big House. Evergreen Review 5 (Sept.–Oct. 1961): 40–63.
———. In *Brendan Behan's Island: An Irish Sketch-Book.* London: Hutchinson; New York: Bernard Geis, 1962.
Brendan Behan: Poems and a Play [An Giall] *in Irish.* Ed. Prionsias Ní Dhorchaí. Dublin: Gallery Press, 1981.
The Complete Plays. (The Quare Fellow, The Hostage [rev. ed.], *Richard's Cork Leg, Moving Out, A Garden Party, The Big House.*) Ed. Alan Simpson. London: Eyre Methuen; New York: Grove Press, 1978.
The Hostage. London: Methuen, 1958; New York: Grove, 1959; rev. ed., London: Methuen, 1962.
Moving Out and *A Garden Party: Two Plays by Brendan Behan.* Ed. Robert Hogan. Dixon, Calif.: Proscenium Press, 1967. (Also, as *The New House,* in *Best Short Plays of the World Theatre: 1958–67.* Ed. Stanley Richards. New York: Crown, 1968.)
The Quare Fellow. London: Methuen, 1956; New York: Grove; Toronto: Ryerson, 1957; London: Methuen, 1960.
The Quare Fellow and *The Hostage* (1958 ed.). *Two Plays by Brendan Behan.* Rev. ed. New York: Grove, 1964.
Richard's Cork Leg. Ed. with additional material by Alan Simpson. London: Eyre Methuen; New York: Grove Press, 1973.

Major Nondramatic Works

After the Wake. Ed. Peter Fallon. Dublin: O'Brien; Greenwich, Conn.: Devin, 1981 (short story collection).
Borstal Boy. London: Hutchinson, 1958: New York: Alfred A. Knopf, 1959; London: Corgi, 1960; New York: Avon, 1964 (autobiographical novel).
Brendan Behan's New York. London: Hutchinson; New York: Bernard Geis, 1964.
Confessions of an Irish Rebel. London: Hutchinson, 1965; New York: Bernard Geis, 1966.

The Letters of Brendan Behan. Ed. E. H. Mikhail. London: Macmillan; New York: Barnes and Noble, 1992.

The Wit of Brendan Behan. Comp. E. H. Mikhail. London: Vision Press; New York: Leslie Frewin, 1968.

SECONDARY BIBLIOGRAPHY

Alvarez, A. "The Anti-Establishment Drama." *Partisan Review* 26 (Fall 1959): 606–11.

Archer, Kane. "*Richard's Cork Leg* at the Olympia." *Irish Times* (31 Mar. 1972): 10.

Armstrong, William A. *Experimental Drama.* London: G. Bell, 1963.

Aston, Frank. " 'Hostage' Breaks Rules, But It Is Enchanting." *New York World Telegram* (21 Sept. 1960): 23.

Atkinson, Brooks. "Theatre: 'Quare Fellow.' " *New York Times* (28 Nov. 1958): 34.

B., P. F. [1]. "New Behan Play." *Dublin Evening Herald* (17 June 1958): 3.

———. [2]. "*The New House.*" *Dublin Evening Herald* (6 May 1958): 4.

Barber, John. [1]. "A Hangman Calls—A Jail Waits." *London Daily Express* (25 May 1956): 7.

———. [2]. "I'd Just Hate to Tie Down Mr. Behan, But—." *London Daily Express* (15 Oct. 1958): 9.

———. [3]. "Rag-Bag of Behan's Ribald Writings." *London Daily Telegraph* (20 Sept. 1972): 13.

———. [4]. "The Two Dramas of Irishman Behan." *London Daily Express* (25 July 1956): 7.

Barker, Felix [1]. "A Drop of the Irish." *London Evening News* (30 July 1963): 3.

———. [2]. "It's Bedlam with Behan!" *London Evening News* (12 June 1959): 7.

———. [3]. "*Richard's Cork Leg*: Royal Court Theatre." *London Evening News* (20 Sept. 1972): 11.

Barnes, Clive. [1]. " 'Borstal Boy': Abbey Brings Story of Young Brendan Behan." *New York Times* (1 Apr. 1970): 38.

———. [2]. "Theatrical Curiosity of Behan's *The Hostage.*" *New York Times* (11 Oct. 1972): 50.

Behan, Beatrice. With Des Hickey and Gus Smith. *My Life with Brendan Behan.* London: Leslie Frewin, 1973; Los Angeles: Nash, 1974.

Behan, Brian. *With Breast Expanded.* London: MacGibbon and Kee, 1964.

Behan, Dominic. *My Brother Brendan.* London: Leslie Frewin, 1965; New York: Simon and Schuster, 1966.

Billington, Michael. "*Richard's Cork Leg* at the Royal." *The Guardian* (20 Sept. 1972): 8.

Bordinat, Philip. "Tragedy through Comedy in Plays by Brendan Behan." *West Virginia University Philological Papers* 29 (1983): 84–91.

Boyle, Ted. E. *Brendan Behan.* New York: Twayne, 1969.

Boyne, Sean. "Sparkling Show of 'Hostage.' " *Irish Press* (29 Apr. 1970): 3.

"Brendan Behan's Fatted Calf." *Irish Press* (9 Oct. 1956): 6.

"Brendan Behan's Fine Play in Irish." *Irish Times* (17 June 1958): 8.

Brien, Alan. "Political Pantomime." *Spectator* 201 (17 Oct. 1958): 513–14.

Browne, Joseph. "Violent Prophecies: The Writer and Northern Ireland." *Éire-Ireland* 10 (Summer 1975): 109–19.

Brustein, Robert. [1]. "A Behan Celebration." *Observer* (24 Sept. 1972): 36.

———. [2]. "Libido at Large." *New Republic* 143 (3 October 1960: 20–21.

———. [3]. "Two Plays about Ireland: *Richard's Cork Leg* and *The Ballygombeen Bequest.*" *The Culture Watch: Essays on Theatre and Society, 1969–1974.* New York: Alfred A. Knopf, 1975. 53–56.

Buchloh, Paul G. "The Transposition of Politics in Anglo-Irish Drama: Brendan Behan on German Stages." *Literary Interrelations: Ireland, England and the World, I: Reception and Translation.* Ed. Wolfgang Zach and Heinz Kosok. 3 vols. Tübingen: Narr, 1987. 131–39.

Cain, Alex Matheson [1]. "Death's Jest Book." *Tablet* (9 June 1956): 540.

———. [2]. "French without Laughs." *Tablet* (27 June 1959): 573.

Calta, Louis. "Behan's *The Hostage.*" *New York Times* (13 Dec. 1961): 55.

Cardullo, Bert. [1]. "Behan's *The Hostage.*" *Explicator* 43.1 (Fall 1984): 56–57.

———. [2]. "*The Hostage* Reconsidered." *Eire-Ireland* 20.2 (Summer 1985): 139–43.

———. [3]. "Mulleady, Princess Grace, and Rio Rita in *The Hostage.*" *Notes on Contemporary Culture* 18.3 (May 1988): 3–4.

Carthew, Anthony [1]. "Behan Is So Good—and So Bad." *London Daily Herald* (15 Oct. 1958): 3.

———. [2]. "I Say, Old Behan." *London Daily Herald* (25 July 1956): 3.

Chapman, John. [1]. "Behan's *Borstal Boy* in a Shiny Shamrock." *New York Daily News* (1 Apr. 1970): 82.

———. [2]. "In Behan's *The Hostage* There's No Such Thing as a Little Gaelic." *New York Daily News* (21 Sept. 1960): 55.

Clurman, Harold. [1]. [Review of *Borstal Boy.*] *Nation* 210 (20 Apr. 1970): 473.

———. [2]. [Review of *The Hostage.*] *Nation* 191 (8 Oct. 1960): 236.

———. [3]. [Review of *The Hostage.*] *Nation* 215 (30 Oct. 1972): 410–11.

———. [4]. *The Naked Image: Observations on the Modern Theatre.* London: Collier-Macmillan; New York: Macmillan, 1966.

———. [5]. [Review of *The Quare Fellow.*] *Nation* 188 (3 Jan. 1959): 20.

Crist, Judith. [1]. "First Night Report: *The Hostage.*" *New York Herald Tribune* (13 Dec. 1961): 18.

———. [2]. " 'Quare Fellow' Presented at Circle-in-the-Square." *New York Herald Tribune* (28 Nov. 1958): 14.

Darlington, W. A. [1]. "Irish Plays Fail to Inspire." *London Daily Telegraph* (30 July 1963): 12

———. [2]. "An Irish Prison Play." *London Daily Telegraph* (25 May 1956): 11.

———. [3]. "Mr. Behan Charms Away the Grimness." *London Daily Telegraph* (12 June 1959): 14.

"Death and the Irish." *Times Literary Supplement* (26 Apr. 1974): 44.

De Búrca, Séamus. *Brendan Behan: A Memoir.* Newark, Del.: Proscenium Press, 1971.

Edwards, Philip. *Threshold of a Nation.* Cambridge: Cambridge University Press, 1979.

Esslin, Martin. [1]. "Brecht and the English Theatre." *Tulane Drama Review* 11.2 (Winter 1966): 63–70.

———. [2]. *The Theatre of the Absurd.* Rev. ed. Garden City, N.Y.: Doubleday, 1969.

"An Extravaganza with Roaring Vitality." *Times* (12 June 1959): 15.

F., J. "Last Night's New Play: Song instead of Curtain Speech." *Dublin Evening Herald* (20 Nov. 1954): 6.

Fallis, Richard. *The Irish Renaissance.* Syracuse, N.Y.: Syracuse University Press, 1977.

Fallon, Gabriel. [1]. "Behan Play Opens at the Pike." *Dublin Evening Press* (15 Apr. 1958): 4.

———. [2]. "Behan's Play Should Not Be Missed." *Dublin Evening Press* (20 Nov. 1954): 3.

———. [3]. "The Makings of a Masterpiece." *Dublin Evening Press* (9 Oct. 1956): 4.

Farragher, Bernard. "Brendan Behan's Unarranged Realism." *Drama Critique* 4 (February 1961): 38–39.

Findlater, Richard. "Waiting for the Hangman." *London Tribune* (8 June 1956): 8.

F[inegan], J. J. [1]. "Behan Play with Hardly a Leg to Stand On." *Dublin Evening Herald* (15 Mar. 1972): 4.

———. [2]. "*Borstal Boy* at the Abbey: A Triumph—The Epitaph to Brendan." *Dublin Evening Herald* (11 Oct. 1967): 3.

———. [3]. "*The Hostage* Comes Down to Earth." *Dublin Evening Herald* (14 July 1964): 5.

———. [4]. "Original Touches in Abbey 'Hostage.'" *Dublin Evening Herald* (29 Apr. 1970): 5.

———. [5]. "Prison Drama at the Abbey." *Dublin Evening Herald* (9 Oct. 1956): 5.

———. [6]. "Tragedy and Comedy in Pike's Twin Bill." *Dublin Evening Herald* (15 Apr. 1958): 4.

"First Night: Woolly and Wonderful." *Newsweek* 56 (3 Oct. 1960): 57.

F[ox], R. M. [1]. "Best Abbey Play for a Long Time." *Dublin Evening Mail* (9 Oct. 1956): 6.

———. [2]. "Full Marks for Comedy Element." *Dublin Evening Mail* (6 May 1958): 6.

———. [3]. "Gay and Tragic Plays at the Pike." *Dublin Evening Mail* (15 Apr. 1958): 6.

———. [4]. "Prison Strike at Pike." *Dublin Evening Mail* (20 Nov. 1954): 6.

Gascoigne, Bamber. *Twentieth-Century Drama*. London: Hutchinson, 1962.

Gellert, Roger. "O'Booze." *New Statesman* 66 (9 Aug. 1963): 178.

Gerdes, Peter R. *The Major Works of Brendan Behan*. Bern: Herbert Lang, 1973.

Gibbs, Patrick. "Comedy-Drama of a Hanging: *The Quare Fellow*." *London Daily Telegraph* (25 July 1956): 8.

Gilbert, Justin. "Behan's 'Hostage' Earthy, Ludicrous." *New York Mirror* (21 Sept. 1960): 27.

Gill, Brendan. "The Theatre: Glad Tidings." *New Yorker* 46 (11 Apr. 1970): 81–82.

Gilliatt, Penelope. "Brendan Beano." *Encore* 5.4 (Nov. 1958): 35–36.

"Good Talkers All: Mr. Brendan Behan's Extravaganza." *Times* (15 Oct. 1958): 8.

Grahame, Paul. [1]. "In the Shadow of the Rope." *London Daily Worker* (25 May 1956): 2.

———. [2]. "Theatre." *London Daily Worker* (30 July 1956): 2.

Gray, Ken. "Alias *The Hostage*." *Irish Times* (21 Mar. 1968): 12.

Grene, Nicholas. "Distancing Drama: Sean O'Casey to Brian Friel." *Irish Writers and the Theatre*. Ed. Masaru Sekine. Gerrards Cross, Buckinghamshire.: Colin Smythe; Totowa, N.J.: Barnes and Noble, 1986. 47–70.

Gussow, Mel. [1]. "Juilliard Unit Presents Behan's Timely *Hostage*." *New York Times* (12 May 1972): 24.

———. [2]. "Shay Duffin as Brendan Behan." *New York Times* (3 Jan. 1973): 50.

Hawkins, Maureen S. G. [1]. "*An Giall, The Hostage* and *Kongi's Harvest*: Post-Colonial

Irish, Anglo-Irish and Nigerian Variations on a Postmodern Theme.'' *The Internationalism of Irish Drama and Literature*. Ed. Joseph McMinn. Gerrards Cross, Buckinghamshire: Colin Smythe; Totowa, N.J.: Barnes and Noble, 1992. 63–74.

———. [2]. ''Women, 'Queers,' Love, and Politics: *The Crying Game* as a Corrective Adaptation of/Reply to *The Hostage*.'' *Representing Ireland: Gender, Class, Ethnicity*. Ed. Susan Shaw Sailer. Forthcoming.

Hayes, Richard. ''The Irish Presence.'' *Commonweal* 69 (23 Jan. 1959): 438–39.

Hays, H. R. ''Transcending Naturalism.'' *Modern Drama* 5.2 (May 1962): 27–36.

Heiney, Donald, and Lenthiel H. Downs. ''Brendan Behan.'' *Essentials of Contemporary Literature of the Western World*. Vol. 2. Woodbury, N.Y.: Barron's Educational Series, 1974. 140–42.

Hendrickx, Johan. ''The 'Theatre of Fun': In Defence of Brendan Behan's *The Hostage*.'' *Anglo-Irish Studies* 3 (1977): 85–95.

Hewes, Henry. [1]. ''Brendan and His Double.'' *Saturday Review* 53 (18 Apr. 1970): 26.

———. [2]. ''Brendan Behan's Soup.'' *Saturday Review* 43 (8 Oct. 1960): 32.

———. [3]. ''Broadway Postscript: The Quare World of Brendan Behan.'' *Saturday Review* 41 (13 Dec. 1958): 27–28.

Hirschhorn, Clive. ''Theatre.'' *London Sunday Express* (24 Sept. 1972): 23.

Hobson, Harold. [1]. ''The Pity of It.'' *Sunday Times* (29 July 1956): 4.

———. [2]. ''Theatre.'' *Sunday Times* (4 Aug. 1963): 25.

———. [3]. ''Theatre: *The Hostage*.'' *Sunday Times* (14 June 1959): 23.

———. [4]. ''Theatre: Worlds Apart.'' *Sunday Times* (24 Sept. 1972): 37.

———. [5]. ''Triumph at Stratford East.'' *Sunday Times* (19 Oct. 1958): 21.

Hogan, Patrick Colm. ''Class Heroism in *The Quare Fellow*.'' *Etudes Irlandaises* 8 (Dec. 1983): 139–44.

Hogan, Robert [1]. *After the Irish Renaissance: A Critical History of the Irish Drama since The Plough and the Stars*. Minneapolis: University of Minnesota Press, 1967; London: Macmillan, 1968.

———. [2]. ''Since O'Casey.'' *''Since O'Casey'' and Other Essays on Irish Drama*. Gerrards Cross, Buckinghamshire: Colin Smythe; Totowa, N.J.: Barnes and Noble, 1983. 119–54.

Hogan, Robert, Bonnie K. Scott, and Gordon Henderson. ''The Modern Drama.'' *Anglo-Irish Literature: A Review of Research*. Ed. Richard J. Finneran. New York: Modern Language Association, 1976. 518–61.

Hunt, Albert. ''A Game No More.'' *New Society* (8 June 1972): 524.

Jeffs, Rae. *Brendan Behan: Man and Showman*. London: Hutchinson, 1966; New York: World, 1968.

Jones, Mervyn. ''No Boos for Brendan.'' *Observer* (14 June 1959): 25.

Jordan, John. [1]. ''Brendan Behan's *The Hostage*.'' *Hibernia* 24 (Dec. 1960): 25.

———. [2]. ''*The Hostage*.'' *Hibernia* 15 (May 1970): 22.

Kearney, Colbert. [1]. ''Brendan [Francis] Behan.'' *The Macmillan Dictionary of Irish Literature*. Ed. Robert Hogan, Zack Bowen, William J. Feeney, James Kilroy, Mary Rose Callaghan, and Richard Burnham. London: Macmillan, 1980. 102–5.

———. [2]. *The Writings of Brendan Behan*. Dublin: Gill and Macmillan, 1977.

Kelly, Seamus. [1]. ''Abbey: The Living Theatre of Ireland.'' *Irish Times* (11 Oct. 1967): 8.

———. [2]. "Brendan Behan—Dubliners Combination at Peacock." *Irish Times* (15 Mar. 1972): 12.

———. [3]. "Old Age Creeps Up on *The Hostage*." *Irish Times* (29 Apr. 1970): 10.

Kerr, Walter. [1]. "First Night Report: 'The Hostage.' " *New York Herald Tribune* (21 Sept. 1960): 18.

———. [2]. "No Claim on Our Sympathy." *New York Times* (12 Apr. 1970): sec. 2: 9.

———. [3]. *The Theatre in Spite of Itself.* New York: Simon and Schuster, 1963. 108–12.

Kilroy, Thomas. [1]. "*The Hostage*." *Studies: An Irish Quarterly Review* 48.189 (Spring 1959): 111–12.

———. [2]. "Groundwork for an Irish Theatre." *Studies: An Irish Quarterly Review* 48.190 (Summer 1959): 192–98.

Kitchin, Laurence. *Mid-Century Drama.* London: Faber and Faber, 1966.

Kleinstück, Johannes. "Brendan Behan's *The Hostage*." Trans. R. Hausen. *Essays and Studies* 24 (1971): 60–82.

Kosok, Heinz. [1]. "Brendan Behan: *The Hostage*." *Das englische Drama der Gegenwart: Interpretationen.* Ed. Horst Oppel. Berlin: Erich Schmidt, ca. 1976. 30–48.

———. [2]. "Juno and the Playwrights: The Influence of Sean O'Casey on Twentieth-Century Drama." *Irish Writers and the Theatre.* Ed. Masaru Sekine. Gerrards Cross, Buckinghamshire: Colin Smythe; Totowa, N.J.: Barnes and Noble, 1986. 71–86.

Krause, David. [1]. "The Barbarous Sympathies of Antic Irish Comedy." *Malahat Review* 22 (Apr. 1972): 99–117.

———. [2]. *The Profane Book of Irish Comedy.* Ithaca, N.Y.: Cornell University Press, 1982.

Kretzmer, Herbert. "Behan's Last Laugh—*Richard's Cork Leg*." *London Daily Express* (20 Sept. 1972): 17.

Kroll, Jack. "Tough Thrush." *Newsweek* (13 Apr. 1970): 83.

Landstone, Charles. "From John Osborne to Sheila Delaney." *World Theatre* 7.3 (Autumn 1959): 203–16.

Leventhal, A. J. "Dramatic Commentary: *The Quare Fellow* by Brendan Behan. The Pike Theatre Club." *Dublin Magazine* 22.1 (Jan.–Mar. 1955): 47–48.

M., I. [1]. "Pike Theatre Re-opens with Two Premieres." *Irish Independent* (15 Apr. 1958): 10.

———. [2]. "Prison Life Drama." *Irish Independent* (9 Oct. 1956): 8.

MacInnes, Colin. "The Writings of Brendan Behan." *London Magazine* 2 (Aug. 1962): 53–61.

Malcolm, Donald. "Off-Broadway: An Objection Sustained." *New Yorker* 34 (6 Dec. 1958): 123–24.

Marshall, Oliver. "The Peacock: 'Cork Leg' Leads a Merry Dance." *Irish Press* (15 Mar. 1972): 7.

Martin, Augustine. [1]. "Brendan Behan." *Threshold* 18 (1963): 22–28.

———. [2]. "A Superb Tale Superbly Told." *Irish Press* (11 Oct. 1967): 5.

———. [3]. "Old Age Creeps Up on *The Hostage*." *Irish Times* (29 Apr. 1970): 10.

Maxwell, D. E. S. [1]. "Brendan Behan's Theatre." *Irish Writers and the Theatre.* Ed. Masaru Sekine. Gerrards Cross, Buckinghamshire: Colin Smythe; Totowa, N.J.: Barnes and Noble, 1986. 87–102.

————. [2]. *A Critical History of Modern Irish Drama, 1891–1980*. Cambridge: Cambridge University Press, 1984.

McCann, Sean, ed. *The World of Brendan Behan*. London: New English Library, 1965; New York: Twayne, 1966.

McCarten, John. "Gaelic Gyrations." *New Yorker* 36 (1 Oct. 1960): 128.

McClain, John. "Not Even Mr. Behan Rolled in the Aisles." *New York Journal American* (21 Sept. 1960): 21.

McG., P. "Satire and Fun in *An Giall*." *Dublin Evening Herald* (11 Oct. 1968): 4.

McLean, John. "*The Quare Fellow*." *New York Journal American* (28 Nov. 1958): 18.

McMahon, Sean. "The Quare Fellow." *Eire-Ireland* 4.4 (Winter 1969) 143–57.

Mikhail, E. H., ed. [1]. *The Art of Brendan Behan*. London: Vision Press; New York: Barnes and Noble, 1979.

————. [2]. *Brendan Behan: Interviews and Recollections*. 2 vols. London: Macmillan; Dublin: Gill and Macmillan: 1982; New York: Barnes and Noble, 1983.

Murphy, Brian. "Brendan Behan at Theatre Workshop: Storyteller into Playwright." *Prompt* 5 (1964): 4–8.

Nathan, David. [1]. "Brendan Saves the Irish." *London Daily Herald* (30 July 1963): 5

————. [2]. "The Inside Story of the Final Drop." *London Daily Herald* (25 May 1956): 5.

"New Behan Play at the Pike." *Irish Times* (15 Apr. 1958): 9.

O'Connor, Ulick. *Brendan Behan*. London: Hamish Hamilton; Englewood Cliffs, N.J.: Prentice-Hall, 1970.

O'F[arrell], M[aureen]. [1]. "Behan Play Has Little Lustre." *Dublin Evening Press* (14 July 1964): 3.

————. [2]. "Idea Works like a Charm." *Dublin Evening Press* (11 Oct. 1967): 3.

Ó hAodha, Micheál. [1]. *The Abbey—Then and Now*. Dublin: Abbey Theatre, 1969.

————. [2]. Introduction. *Moving Out* and *A Garden Party: Two Plays by Brendan Behan*. Ed. Robert Hogan. Dixon, Calif.: Proscenium Press, 1967. 3–6.

————. [3]. *Theatre in Ireland*. Totowa, N.J.: Rowman and Littlefield, 1974.

O'Kelly, Emer. "Behan's Hostage." *Dublin Sunday Press* (3 May 1970): 25.

Oliver, Edith. "Off-Broadway: Behan's Dubliners." *New Yorker* (21 Oct. 1972): 50.

"Pike: *The New House* by Brendan Behan." *Irish Times* (6 May 1958): 9

Porter, Raymond. *Brendan Behan*. New York: Columbia University Press, 1973.

Power, Richard. "Behan Play an Easy Mixture." *Dublin Evening Press* (11 Oct. 1968): 5.

"*The Quare Fellow* at the Abbey Theatre." *Irish Times* (9 Oct. 1956): 3.

"*The Quare Fellow* at the Pike." *Irish Times* (20 Nov. 1954): 9.

"*The Quare Fellow*: Mr. Brendan Behan's Play at Comedy Theatre." *Times* (25 July 1956): 5.

Ragheb, Aida. "Behan's *The Hostage* and Hammouda's *El Raha'in*." *The Internationalism of Irish Drama and Literature*. Ed. Joseph McMinn. Gerrards Cross, Buckinghamshire: Colin Smythe; Totowa, N.J.: Barnes and Noble, 1992. 120–33.

Richards, Dick. [1]. "B. B. Takes the Mickey Out of the Trouble." *London Daily Mirror* (15 Oct. 1958): 16.

————. [2]. "A Rather Seedy Affair." *London Daily Mirror* (12 June 1959): 16.

Richardson, Maurice. "O'Casey Goes to Jail." *New Statesman* 51 (2 June 1956): 624–26.

R[obinson], L[ennox]. "Acting Was Superb in Behan Play." *Irish Press* (20 Nov. 1954): 9.

Robinson, Robert. "The Square Fella." *New Statesman* (25 Oct. 1958): 560.

Rollins, Ronald G. "O'Casey, Yeats, and Behan: A Prismatic View of the 1916 Easter Rising." *Sean O'Casey Review* 2 (Spring 1976): 196–207.

Rosen, Carol. *Plays of Impasse: Contemporary Drama Set in Confining Situations.* Princeton, N.J.: Princeton University Press, 1983.

Rosenfeld, Ray. "Behan Play as Burlesque in Belfast." *Irish Times* (12 Oct. 1968): 5.

Rushe, Desmond. [1]. "Abbey: Behan Adaptation Outstanding." *Irish Independent* (12 Oct. 1967): 6.

———. [2]. "Dublin: The Flourishing Trend of One-Man Shows." *New York Times* (4 Oct. 1971): 52.

———. [3]. " 'Hostage'—Too Few Grains amid So Much Chaff." *Irish Independent* (29 Apr. 1970): 26.

———. [4]. "A Vastly Better Production of *The Hostage*." *Irish Independent* (14 July 1964): 7.

Rusinko, Susan. *British Drama, 1950 to the Present: A Critical History.* Boston: Twayne, 1989.

S., L. G. "Irish Play Is Nearly Great." *Stage* (16 Oct. 1958): 12.

S., R. "New Irish Play Begins at Damer Hall." *Irish Independent* (17 June 1958): 8.

Shulman, Milton. [1]. "A Drop of Irish, but the Flavour Is Weak." *London Evening Standard* (30 July 1963): 4

———. [2]. "Mr. Behan Has Fun with His IRA Heroes." *London Evening Standard* (12 June 1959): 6.

———. [3]. "Mr. Behan Makes Fun of the IRA." *London Evening Standard* (15 Oct. 1958): 13.

———. [4]. "Mr. Behan Spares No Goulish Detail." *London Evening Standard* (25 July 1956): 6.

———. [5]. "*Richard's Cork Leg*." *London Evening Standard* (20 Sept. 1972): 23.

Simpson, Alan. [1]. *Beckett and Behan and a Theatre in Dublin.* London: Routledge and Kegan Paul, 1962.

———. [2]. "Behan: The Last Laugh." *A Paler Shade of Green.* Ed. Des Hickey and Gus Smith. London: Leslie Frewin, 1972. 209–19.

———. [3]. Introduction. *Brendan Behan: The Complete Plays.* London: Eyre Methuen, 1978. 7–25.

———. [4]. Introduction. *Brendan Behan: Richard's Cork Leg.* London: Eyre Methuen, 1973; New York: Grove Press, 1973. 5–11.

Taubman, Howard. "Behan Buffoonery: *The Hostage* Makes Debut at the Cort." *New York Times* (21 Sept. 1960): 42.

Taylor, John Russell. [1]. *Anger and After: A Guide to the New British Drama.* London: Methuen, 1962.

———. [2]. "*The Big House*." *Plays and Players* 40.1 (Oct. 1963): 42.

Tee, Robert. "It's Quare—But Successful." *London Daily Mirror* (25 July 1956): 15.

"Theatre: Black Irishman's Mood." *Newsweek* (8 Dec. 1958): 66–67.

"Theatre Workshop: *The Quare Fellow*." *Times* (25 May 1956): 3.

Tracy, Robert. "Ireland: The Patriot Game." *The Cry of Home: Cultural Nationalism and the Modern Writer.* Ed. E. Ernest Lewald. Knoxville: University of Tennessee Press, 1972. 39–57.

T[rewin], J. C. [1]. "Go-As-You-Please." *Illustrated London News* (1 Nov. 1958): 764.

———. [2]. "Through Irish Eyes: *The Quare Fellow* (Comedy)." *Illustrated London News* 229 (11 Aug. 1956): 238.

———. [3]. "The World of the Theatre." *Illustrated London News* (10 Aug. 1963): 216.

Trussler, Simon. "Old Tunes before Noisy New Turns." *London Tribune* (29 Sept. 1972): 9.

Tynan, Kenneth. [1]. "Dubliners in the East End." *Observer* (4 Aug. 1963): 17.

———. [2]. "The End of the Noose." *Observer* (25 May 1956): 11.

———. [3]. "New Amalgam." *Observer* (19 Oct. 1958): 19.

———. [4]. *A View of the English Stage: 1944–63.* London: Davis Poynter, 1975.

W., S. J. " 'Hostage' Staged with Gusto." *Irish Press* (14 July 1964): 7.

Walker, Roy. "At the Theatre." *Observer* (29 July 1956): 10.

Wall, Richard. [1]. Introduction. *An Giall and The Hostage.* By Brendan Behan. Trans. and ed. Richard Wall. Gerrards Cross, Buckinghamshire: Colin Smythe; Washington, D.C.: Catholic University of America Press, 1987. 1–21.

———. [2]. "*An Giall* and *The Hostage* Compared." *Modern Drama* 18 (June 1975): 165–72.

———. [3]. "The Stage History and Reception of Brendan Behan's *An Giall.*" *Literary Interrelations: Ireland, England and the World, I: Reception and Translation.* Ed. Wolfgang Zach and Heinz Kosok. 3 vols. Tübingen: Narr, 1987. I: 123–29.

Wardle, Irving. *Richard's Cork Leg.*" *Times* (20 Sept. 1972): 7.

Watts, Richard, Jr. "The Exuberance of Brendan Behan." *New York Post* (21 Sept. 1960): 32.

Wellwarth, G. E. *The Theatre of Protest and Paradox.* New York: New York University Press, 1964.

Wickstrom, Gordon M. "The Heroic Dimension in Brendan Behan's *The Hostage.*" *Educational Theatre Journal* 22 (1970): 406–11.

Winkler, Elizabeth Hale. *The Function of Song in Contemporary British Drama.* Newark: University of Delaware Press; London and Toronto: Associated University Presses, 1990.

Witoscek, Walentyna. "The Funeral Comedy of Brendan Behan." *Etudes Irlandaises* 11 (Dec. 1986): 83–91.

Wraight, Robert. [1]. "A Perishin' Broth of a Frolic." *London Star* (12 June 1959): 17.

———. [2]. "Quare Fellow and 'The Job.' " *London Star* (25 May 1956): 3.

BIBLIOGRAPHIES

King, Kimball. "Brendan Behan." *Ten Modern Irish Playwrights: A Comprehensive Annotated Bibliography.* New York and London: Garland, 1979. 1–33.

Mikhail, E. H., ed. [3]. *Brendan Behan: An Annotated Bibliography of Criticism.* London: Macmillan; New York: Barnes and Noble, 1980.

Paul Vincent Carroll

(1900–1968)

DAWN DUNCAN

Paul Vincent Carroll is considered the best Irish playwright of the 1930s and 1940s. Famous for two consecutive winners of the New York Drama Critics' Circle Award for Best Foreign Play, *Shadow and Substance* (1938) and *The White Steed* (1939), Carroll's critical acclaim diminished during the 1950s, though a number of his works received major productions.

Paul Vincent Carroll was born 10 July 1900 in Blackrock, near Dundalk, County Louth. The son of Kitty Sandys Carroll and Michael, a schoolmaster, Carroll was educated by his father until the age of thirteen, then attended parochial school. While in Dublin from 1916 to 1920 studying at St. Patrick's Training College, Carroll wrote short stories and poetry for *Ireland's Own* and the *Irish Weekly Independent*. After college, Carroll returned to Dundalk but refused to teach under a confining clerical authority, so he moved to Glasgow in 1921. From 1921 until 1937, Carroll taught school in Glasgow and wrote plays, short stories, and book reviews. In 1923 he married Helena Reilly, a dress designer.

During the 1930s Carroll gained fame and enough fortune as a playwright to make writing his full-time profession. In 1930 the Abbey's Peacock Theatre produced *The Watched Pot*. In 1931 Carroll won an Abbey Theatre prize for *Things That Are Caesar's* (originally titled *The Bed of Procrustes*), subsequently produced in 1932. In 1933, along with two friends, Carroll founded a neighborhood theater in Glasgow. The Irish Academy of Letters presented the Casement Award to Carroll in 1936 for *Shadow and Substance*. In 1937 the Abbey produced both *The Coggerers* and *Shadow and Substance*, the latter establishing Carroll on Broadway. Though Carroll submitted *The White Steed* to the Abbey, the theater's board rejected the play as too critical of the Catholic clergy. Some critics shortsightedly argue that this rejection is the beginning of the end for

Carroll (see Fallis). However, *The White Steed*, produced on Broadway and selected by critics as the best foreign play, further established Carroll's importance.

The year 1939 marks a turning point in Carroll's career. Following his rejection by the Abbey, Carroll wrote *Kindred*, a play about the need for a world in which artists rule. Because of its elitism, this play alienated audiences. At the same time Carroll began writing a number of lighter plays published in *Plays for My Children* (1939). Also in 1939, Carroll became resident playwright for the Rutherglen Theatre near Glasgow. In 1940 *The Old Foolishness* was produced on Broadway and in London.

During the war years, Carroll helped as a member of a rescue squad and once again used the world's turmoil to produce drama. In 1942 he helped found the Glasgow Citizens Theatre, for which he wrote *The Strings, My Lord, Are False*, a play based on his war experiences. Playing to packed houses in Glasgow and Dublin, the war drama was not as successful in New York. Following this European success, the Abbey produced Carroll's proletarian drama *The Wise Have Not Spoken* in 1944.

In 1945 Carroll moved to England and became actively involved in the film industry, acting as author or adviser for both movie and television productions. The most notable of his film scripts are *Saints and Sinners* (1949) and *Farewell to Greatness!*, a drama based on Dean Swift, produced by BBC television in 1957.

While working on film scripts, Carroll continued writing plays. In 1948 *Weep for Tomorrow* premiered in Glasgow, followed by *Chuckeyhead Story* in 1950 and *Green Cars Go East* in 1951. The second of these Scottish productions is set in Ireland and has little in common with the other Scottish scripts. Carroll revised this play as *The Devil Came from Dublin*, a farce about law versus Irish liberty, and the production packed a Dublin theater in 1955. Turning increasingly away from the didactic bent of earlier years, Carroll wrote *The Wayward Saint*, produced on Broadway in 1955, a whimsical farce about a charming, though not so innocent, candidate for sainthood. In this final play, Carroll combines his heartfelt Catholicism with his humanistic humor to great effect.

As the result of a heart condition, Paul Vincent Carroll died on 20 October 1968. His plays continue to be revived, with some being published posthumously.

Selected Biographical Sources: Boylan; Castronovo; Doyle; Kinsman and Tennenhouse; Kunitz and Haycraft; Weimer.

MAJOR PLAYS, PREMIERES, AND SIGNIFICANT REVIVALS: THEATRICAL RECEPTION

The Watched Pot. 1930. Opened 17 November at the Peacock Theatre, Dublin, the Abbey's experimental venue, and ran through 24 November. Produced by the Abbey. Directed by Lennox Robinson.

A morality tale about peasants waiting for an elderly grandfather to die so that they can collect his insurance, this first attempt by Carroll caught the attention of W. B. Yeats and Lennox Robinson. Doyle attributes its gloom to the influence of Synge, but Carroll acknowledges in a signed note on the manuscript that the gloom is due to Tolstoy's influence.

Things That Are Caesar's. 1932. Opened 15 August at the Abbey Theatre, Dublin, ran through 10 September; moved 17 October to the Martin Beck Theatre, New York, for 4 performances; reopened 28 August, 1933 at the Abbey for 7 performances. Produced by the Abbey. Directed by Lennox Robinson.

Dramatizing the artistic soul at odds with social expectations, Carroll impressed audiences on both sides of the Atlantic. Byram, while noting some overwriting in the first act, praised Carroll for writing an excellent critique of Irish society. Hayes declared that Carroll's play was the most important theatrical event in Ireland since Sean O'Casey's debut. In London, Morgan faulted Carroll for making Eilish too saintly.

Shadow and Substance. 1937. Opened 25 January at the Abbey Theatre, Dublin, for 6 performances, with additional short runs in August and again in May 1939; moved to Philadelphia January 1938 and on to the John Golden Theatre, New York, 26 January for 274 performances. Produced by the Abbey. Dublin director—Hugh Hunt; New York director—Peter Godfrey. Revivals: Abbey Theatre, Dublin, February–March 1940, November–December 1941, July 1944, November–December 1949, March 1953, April–May 1963; Off Broadway, July 1946 and 1953–1954 season; Temple Theatre, New York, March 1956; Tara Theatre, New York, November 1959.

Carroll's drama speaks with eloquence of the sacrifice of spiritual innocence to intellectualism and cynicism. Atkinson [8] credited the play with evoking Ireland's spirit and going far beyond the usual folk play. Young praised the sensitive character portrayals. Calta [1, 2] declared the play timeless.

Coggerers. 1937. (one act). Opened 22 November at the Abbey Theatre, Dublin, and played through 27 November. Produced by Abbey. Directed by Hugh Hunt. Opened 20 January 1939 at Hudson Theatre, New York, (billed with Niggli's *Red Velvet Goat* and Giraudoux's *Mr. Banks of Birmingham*) for 3 performances. Produced by One-Act Repertory Company. Directed by Emjo Basshe. Revivals: Off Broadway, 1959–1960 season; Theatre de Lys, New York, 22 March 1960. Revised and retitled *The Conspirators*.

Receiving little critical attention and rarely performed, *Coggerers* has earned the praise of a few important critics. Atkinson [7], while panning the other plays presented on the same bill, singled out *Coggerers* for its originality and congratulated both the writer and the actors for a skillful and professional performance. Later critics would return to *Coggerers* and voice their admiration for the unusual combination of tragifantasy and comedy (see Hogan and Krause [2]). This play, in which a cleaning lady talks with the statues of martyred Irish heroes as her son takes part in the Easter 1916 Rebellion, calls for imaginative staging if the complexity of tragedy-comedy-fantasy is to work. Gelb credits director Robert Glenn with a successful revival in 1960 because of his manner of staging the living statues.

The White Steed. 1939. Opened 10 January at the Cort Theatre, New York, for 136 performances. Produced by Eddie Dowling. Directed by Hugh Hunt. Revival: Embassy Theatre, London, March 1947.

Pits the spirited individual against tyrannical social moralists. Sparking controversy from the start, the play divided the critics. Gilder [3] praised Carroll's dialogue for both its poignant commonness and its poetic power. Angoff decried a lack of warmth and wished that Carroll might have a bit more of O'Casey in his touch. Krutch [2] found the play sentimentally satisfying, especially to American audiences, because of the triumph of tolerance over moral snoops. Ferguson concluded that the plot could take place anywhere. However, Wyatt [2] insisted that the play could be performed only by an Irish cast familiar with what he considered a distinctly Irish problem. Without reservation, Nathan [5] termed *The White Steed* the best play of the season, a powerful story with universal appeal.

Kindred. 1939. Opened 25 September at Abbey Theatre, Dublin, for 6 performances. Produced by the Abbey. Directed by Prionnsias MacDiarmada. Reopened 26 December at Maxine Elliott's Theatre, New York, for 16 performances. Produced by Edward Choate and Arthur Shields. Directed by Robert Edmond Jones.

Having read the manuscript before its production, Nathan [2] warned the theatrical world that this play was completely unlike the preceding Carroll contributions. Focusing on the artist's longing for freedom, *Kindred* emphasizes bonds of spirit rather than blood. Smith [2] declared the play a stinging indictment of status quo politics and daily greed, praising the Abbey production for successfully mounting a complex drama that is both philosophical and experimental as it leaps twenty-five years between parts one and two. Gilder [1] thought Carroll confused the audience by showing the artist's faults and the merchant's appeal. Atkinson [2, 3] panned the New York production, faulting Jones' direction but also calling Carroll's plot and philosophy nothing better than elitist hogwash.

The Old Foolishness. 1940. Opened 20 December at the Windsor Theatre, New York, for 3 performances. Produced by John Golden. Directed by Rachel Crothers. Revival: 7 May 1943 at the Arts Theatre, London.

A drama that, on one level, is about the foolishness of men who fall in love too late in life and, on another level, might be an allegory about lusty pagan Ireland and the impotence caused by socialized religion, this play blends symbolism and reality with a deft touch that recalls O'Casey's late plays (see Hogan). However, critics longed for a return to the simple poetry of *Shadow and Substance*. Whipple called the play a disappointment. Gilder [2] and Lockridge agreed that there were flashes of the Carroll poetic power but not much else except a lot of words that amounted to little. Mantle declared that Carroll should turn his attention back to spiritual and social problems and not waste his time on love stories. Watts [2] found the premise less than persuasive, while John Mason Brown [2] could not buy the allegorical possibilities of Maeve as Ireland and the brothers as impotent Irish types.

Green Cars Go East. 1940. Glasgow Citizens' Theatre. Revival: Glasgow Citizens' Theatre, 1951.

Takes place in a Glasgow tenement, portraying the effects of slum life on one family. Mary, a teacher, rescues her family and wins back her fiancé. A realistic drama flawed by a romantic ending.

The Strings, My Lord, Are False. 1942. Opened 16 March at Olympia Theatre, Dublin, for nine weeks. Presented by Shelah Richards. Reopened 10 May, at the Royale Theatre, New York, for 15 performances. Produced by Edward Choate. Directed by Elia Kazan. Adapted for BBC radio by Carroll.

Based on Carroll's wartime experiences as a member of a rescue squad, this timely play pleased European audiences. Smith [1] recognized the power of the play to touch audiences as they watch war strip away all but the most basic goodness left to people—courage and kindness. However, in New York, Nichols agreed with a *Newsweek* review (Review of *The Strings*) that the play, over-burdened with dialogue, unnecessary episodes, and multitudes of characters, confused the audience. Krutch [1] revealed his own American shortsightedness when he wrongly identified Carroll as English and the setting of the play as England while complaining that all English war plays seem the same, and this is only one more melodramatic air raid.

The Wise Have Not Spoken. 1944. Opened 7 February at the Abbey Theatre, Dublin, for 24 performances. Produced by the Abbey. Directed by Frank Dermody. Revivals: King's Theatre, Hammersmith, London, March 1946; Cherry Lane Theatre, New York, February 1954.

A drama with proletarian leanings (see Pallette), the story revolves around force versus faith as pressures mount against a family who cannot hold on to their land or their lives. Stokes observed that the characters were terrific chances for any actor but that the theme became lost in a haze, even if the need for human faith and understanding did come bleeding through. Atkinson [12] allowed himself to be pleasantly lost for a while in the fog of Carroll's symbolism but concluded that once again Carroll had tried to pack too much meaning into a drama that could have benefited from simplification. Later critics (see Doyle and Pallette) recognized the portrait of Francis, the revolutionary, as one of the most striking of its kind ever to be put on stage.

Weep for Tomorrow. 1948. Glasgow Citizens' Theatre. Revised and retitled *Goodbye to the Summer.*

A failure on the Scottish stage, Carroll revised the play, which was published posthumously under its new title (see Doyle).

Set in a dying Scottish town, the play is burdened with too many characters and story lines. The chief character, schoolmaster Angus Skinner, dreams of saving his town but is blocked by a local businessman. Ibsen's influence, especially *Enemy of the People*, is noticeable.

The Wayward Saint. 1955. Opened 17 February at the Cort Theatre, New York, for 21 performances. Produced by Courtney Burr and John Byram. Directed by John Gerstad.

A comic fantasy about a Saint Francis–type of Irish canon who talks to animals and works various miracles, to the consternation of clerical authorities and a suave but sinister satanic henchman. Hatch saw nothing new or notable in the play, and McClain thought the story did not pick up until the third act. However, the general critical reception was overwhelmingly favorable. Atkinson [9, 10] noted that the limited scope of the writing did not matter because the spirit of the play is so delightfully innocent that it cannot fail to charm. Hawkins, Hewes, Kerr, Lewis, and Watts [1] all celebrated the sparkling comedy and sweet character of Canon McCooey, though they bemoaned the casting of Paul Lukas as the Mephistophelian character. The critics and Carroll himself (see Doyle) believed that the production did not do justice to the writing. Nonetheless, the magic of the material came shining through, proving, as Robert Coleman said, that there are still dreamers who delight in the idea of a gentle spirit triumphing over the devil. Zolotow, departing from his colleagues' criticism of Lukas, thoroughly enjoyed the entire production, praising the play as one of the high points of the season. Wyatt [1] declared the play such a wonder that it should remain a part of repertory theater for years to come.

The Devil Came from Dublin. 1955. Opened in May at the Olympia Theatre, Dublin, for four weeks. Produced and directed by Josephine Albericci. Revival: Margo Jones Theatre, Dallas, October 1958. (Originally titled *The Chuckeyhead Story* and given a short run in summer 1951 at the John Drew Memorial Theatre, East Hampton [NY] before revision.)

A comedy about a town of smugglers on the Northern Irish border who outwit an incorruptible judge. Atkinson [1] considered the production and the audience response sophomoric. However, Nathan [4] praised the wit of the writing for never falling too far into farce or burlesque but making the most of both verbal and physical humor. Bcth Nathan [4] and Doyle credit Carroll with writing a realistic comedy about the problems of making a living on the Irish border.

ADDITIONAL PLAYS, ADAPTATIONS, AND PRODUCTIONS

Three play scripts were never produced: two dramas, *We Have Ceased to Live* and *Bitter Harvest*, and the television play *The Darling of Erin*, based on Robert Emmett's life. In 1949 Carroll authored a screenplay version of *The Wayward*

Saint, which Lopert produced with the film title of *Saints and Sinners*. A long-time favorite with German audiences (see Doyle), *The Wayward Saint* has been translated by Elisabeth Freindlich, performed numerous times over the years by the German State Theatre, and adapted as a German light opera in 1968 by Mark Lothar. In 1957 BBC television produced Carroll's *Farewell to Greatness!* with Micheál Mac Liammóir starring as Dean Swift. Carroll also wrote a number of television scripts produced by Douglas Fairbanks, quite a few children's plays that continue to be performed by children's theater companies, and an adaptation of Zola's *Thérèse Raquin*.

ASSESSMENT OF CARROLL'S CAREER

Chiefly a protest playwright who often succeeded at crafting his philosophy into entertainment, Carroll did at times fail to center and clarify his story. In fact, getting a clear picture of Carroll's career is difficult due to the complications of his plays and the conflicting opinions of critics with regard to his form and style.

The protest theme central to all of Carroll's work is that of the spirited individual versus the mechanical mentality of any system (see Conway). Sometimes Carroll targeted the clerical administration, but never the Catholic faith. Sometimes he took aim at politicians and merchants, but not without also revealing the individual humanity of these characters. Sometimes he scorned peasant mentality but praised the simple exercise of faith that combined paganism and Catholicism.

A number of critics take Carroll to task for failing to fully indict the target of his criticism. For instance, Maxwell praises Carroll when Carroll savagely attacks, but Maxwell insists that Carroll too often relinquishes his stronghold. With regard to the clergymen of *Things That Are Caesar's, Shadow and Substance, The White Steed*, and *Farewell to Greatness!*, Hogan, like Maxwell, complains that Carroll treats his characters too fairly, yet argues that the faults Carroll exposes are indicative of the failure of religion. However, Sister Anne Coleman concludes that Carroll is not attacking religion when he attacks narrow-minded conformity and fanatical intolerance. Tolerance is the key to why Carroll can never mount a complete frontal attack against his targets (see Doyle). When Maxwell faults Carroll for avoiding clear judgments in *Shadow and Substance* and refusing to completely displace church in favor of secularized individualism in *The White Steed*, he misses the central characteristic Carroll pleads for in his characters—tolerance. Brigid in *Shadow and Substance* tries to conciliate the intellectual canon and the cynical schoolmaster and to protect them both from the misunderstanding mob. Canon Lavelle in *The White Steed* condones the merging of pagan passion and Christian faith in his vision of a tolerant Catholic Ireland. Canon Courteney provides a haven from the warring factions of the world in *The Strings, My Lord, Are False* and encourages his housekeeper to cease thinking that only her Irish compatriots are her kin. Father Tiffney, the silenced priest in *The Wise Have Not Spoken*, best understands Francis, the militant atheist, and goes to the heart of how he believes humans are to live— by love, not by laws that divide us. John Mason Brown [1] analyzes correctly that Carroll's nature is not merely to rage but rather to cure with human warmth and, at times, laughter. So, though his protest does not have the hard edges that some critics desire, and his message sometimes seems muddied by sentiments that soften the conflict, Carroll remains true to his central theme of protesting the need for tolerance for the sake of the individual spirit.

Constructing a dramatic line of inheritance for Carroll is almost as difficult as clarifying his target of protest. Having often been compared to Ibsen (see Hogan; Maxwell; and Sitzmann) and O'Casey (see Conway; Fallis; Hayes; McHugh; and Harmon) because of his social criticism and celebration of the life spirit, Carroll also laces his dialogue with poetics that hearken to Synge and Yeats (see Conway). With regard to language and peasant characters, Carroll admitted to taking lessons from Synge (see Sitzmann). Yeats' influence with regard to fusing mythic qualities to create allegories of Ireland is also readily recognizable (see Doyle; Sitzmann). However, it is still O'Casey to whom Carroll is most often compared. After his first real success with *Things That Are Caesar's*, critics suggested that Carroll might become O'Casey's successor (Hayes). John Mason Brown [3] declared *Shadow and Substance* the best Irish play since O'Casey's *Juno and the Paycock* and *Plough and the Stars*. Like O'Casey, Carroll attacks the social materialism that kills the individual spirit (Jeffares). Significantly, O'Casey (see Krause [1]) recognized that Carroll's social critique certainly did not imply a communist philosophy, an accurate appraisal considering Carroll's attack on communism in *Weep for Tomorrow*. Pallette argues that, despite the occasional proletarian tone, the changes that Carroll advocates with his dramas are not systematic changes on a social level but individual changes of heart. Comparisons may be helpful in determining influences, but clearly Carroll was evolving his own style to suit his individual concerns.

Scholars and critics have a hard time dealing with Carroll's stylistics. Described as a writer of the well-made play (see Conway), Carroll also takes experimental risks, most notable perhaps in the time leap of *Kindred*. Praised at various times for his symbolism, realism, fantasy, and satirical comedy, Carroll does not fit neatly into any category. Perhaps even as he pleaded for tolerance in human relations, Carroll tried to open up stylistic borders, a possibility not readily recognized by any of his critics. Maxwell argues that Carroll epitomizes the Abbey's obsession with Irish realism. Crediting Carroll with dialogue and characters that are almost documentary, Maxwell's assessment ignores much of what Carroll created.

Symbolism plays its part in virtually all of Carroll's plays. John Mason Brown [3] suggests that the spirit of Cathleen Ni Houlihan is hiding in the allegorical *Shadow and Substance* and that Carroll's early dramas maintained a Celtic tradition of allegory [1]. Certainly *The White Steed*, with its titular allusion to

Niamh and Ossian, insists upon an allegorical reading. Yet, here too, reality reigns in the allegory. Atkinson [11] praised Carroll for leaving behind much of the mysticism of *Shadow and Substance*, bringing his story down to earth, and peopling it with characters whose voices ring with sharp reality. Occasionally, Carroll's allegory overwhelmed the balancing touch of reality, as in *Kindred*, a highly poetic but deeply flawed text. Likewise, *The Old Foolishness* suffers from a bit too much mysticism (Atkinson [5]).

In *Shadow and Substance, The Coggerers*, and *The Wayward Saint*, Carroll weaves the Irish acceptance of the seemingly fantastic into the fabric of his plays. Yet always, there is the ever-present hint of satire (see Sitzmann). Carroll illuminates the worst faults of the Irish (see Mac Liammóir) yet never loses his love for his people anymore than he gives up his faith in his church (see Sitzmann).

Hogan observes that a weakness in Carroll is his inability to settle on a point of view or discernible style, pointing out that Carroll, who criticized drab realism, wrote his best when avoiding experiments and sticking to the realistic drama. However, it is possible that Carroll was ahead of his critics. His world is not in black and white, as Hogan would have it, but full of colorful figures who need one another's acceptance if their world is to survive.

The question of whether or not Carroll's work has any lasting worth must still be answered. Does it have merely a local significance bound by time, or can it have universal appeal? Fitz-Simon, while acknowledging its permanent place among Irish literature, declares that Carroll's work has only local appeal and is without universal meaning. Doyle concludes that Carroll has earned an honored place in modern drama not only by virtue of his greatest plays—*Things That Are Caesar's, Shadow and Substance, The White Steed, The Wise Have Not Spoken, The Devil Came from Dublin*, and *The Wayward Saint*—but because he has created the most realistic Irish clergymen in the history of drama, a significant contribution both historically and dramatically. Coleman concurs with this opinion and points out that a portrait of Irish culture cannot be complete without the priests of Carroll's plays. However, the priestly portraits in no way confine the importance of Carroll's plays to Ireland. Sitzmann calls Carroll the most important twentieth-century satirist of the Catholic Church, a satirist who works from within the system that he is satirizing and carries on an intimate relationship with his target. Given the immense numbers of Catholics across the world, this possibility alone broadens the appeal of Carroll's work. Numerous critics point to universal significance in a number of Carroll's plays. Smith [2] compares Robert Fennet of *Kindred* to Sinclair Lewis' Babbitt, stressing the universality of the greedy merchant. Smith [1] also argues that any people anywhere who experience war will respond to *The Strings, My Lord, Are False*. Pallette affirms the humanist appeal of Carroll, an appeal that leaps past borders of religion or nationality. Conway observes that Carroll's work is bent on touching the positive in people. However, he concludes that Carroll is ultimately an alien in a nihilistic twentieth century accustomed to real despair.

Though some of Carroll's works are seriously flawed by overly positive endings or messy allegories that lose focus, a great many of his plays are capable, perhaps more now than when they were written, of speaking meaningfully to their audiences. Scholars would do well to take another look at the subject matter and style of Carroll's plays. Possibilities for future investigation might include a clarification of Carroll's philosophy through a comparison of his various clergymen and the targets of his protest, an analysis of his stylistic evolution with special attention to links with Yeats and O'Casey, documentation on the significance of his work in children's theater, and reconsideration of his later plays and their production possibilities. A classroom anthology including Carroll is long overdue.

ARCHIVAL SOURCES

Notebooks, reviews, and manuscripts—of both published and unpublished works—are located in the Paul Vincent Carroll Collection and the W. R. Rogers Collection, both housed in the Harry Ransom Humanities Research Center, University of Texas at Austin.

PRIMARY BIBLIOGRAPHY

Plays

Chuckeyhead Story (original version of *The Devil Came from Dublin*). New York: Rialto
      Service Bureau, n.d.
Coggerers (with *The White Steed*). New York: Random House, 1939.
Conspirators (also called *Coggerers*). London: Samuel French, 1947.
Farewell to Greatness! Dixon, Calif.: Proscenium, 1966.
Goodbye to the Summer (rev. version of *Weep for Tomorrow*). Newark, Del.: Proscenium
      Press, 1970.
Green Cars Go East. London: Samuel French, 1947.
Interlude. London: Samuel French, 1947.
The Old Foolishness. London: Samuel French, 1944.
Shadow and Substance. New York: Random House, 1937; London: Macmillan, 1938;
      French, 1944; Dramatists Play Service, 1948.
Things That Are Caesar's. London: Rich and Cowan, 1934.
The Wayward Saint. New York: Dramatists Play Service, 1955.
We Have Ceased to Live. Journal of Irish Literature (1972).
Weep for Tomorrow. London: M. Hemery, 1948.
The White Steed (with *Coggerers*). New York: Random House, 1939.
The Wise Have Not Spoken. London: Samuel French, 1947; New York: Dramatists Play
      Service, 1954.

Anthologies

Irish Stories and Plays (eight short stories; three one-acts: "The Conspirators," "Beauty Is Fled," "Interlude"; full-length play: *The Devil Came from Dublin*). New York: Devin-Adair, 1958.

Plays for My Children. ("The King Who Could Not Laugh," "His Excellency—the Governor," "St. Francis and the Wolf," "Beauty Is Fled," "Death Closes All," "Maker of Roads." Each of these one-acts was published separately—London: Samuel French, 1947.) New York: Julian Messner, 1939.

Three Plays. (*The White Steed, Things That Are Caesar's,* and *The Strings, My Lord, Are False.*) London: Macmillan, 1944.

Two Plays: The Wise Have Not Spoken—Shadow and Substance. London: Macmillan, 1948.

Essays and Articles on Drama and Theater

"Irish Eyes Are Smiling." *New York Times* (17 Apr. 1938): sec. 10: 1–2.
"The Irish Theatre (Post-war)." *International Theatre.* Ed. John Andrews and Ossia Trilling. London: Sampson Low, 1949. 122–28.
"The Rebel Mind." *New York Times* (24 Jan. 1960): sec. 2: 3.
"Reforming a Reformer." *New York Times* (13 Feb. 1935): sec. 2: 1–3.
"The Substance of Paul Vincent Carroll." *New York Times* (30 Jan. 1938): sec. 10: 1.

SECONDARY BIBLIOGRAPHY

Angoff, Charles. [Review of *The White Steed.*] *North American Review* (Summer 1939): 371–72.
Atkinson, Brooks. [1]. [Review of *The Devil Came from Dublin.*] *New York Times* (3 June 1955): 27.
———. [2]. [Review of *Kindred.*] *New York Times* (27 Dec. 1939): 17.
———. [3]. "Kindred of All Nations." *New York Times* (7 Jan. 1940): sec. 9: 1.
———. [4]. "Liam Redmond Plays Role at Cort Theatre." *New York Times* (18 Feb. 1955): 17.
———. [5]. [Review of *The Old Foolishness.*] *New York Times* (24 Dec. 1940): 18.
———. [6]. "Paul Vincent Carroll's 'The Old Foolishness' Is a Story of Love in County Down of Ireland." *New York Times* (21 Dec. 1940).
———. [7]. "Program of Three Dramas." [Review of *The Coggerers.*] *New York Times* (21 Jan. 1939): 18.
———. [8]. [Review of *Shadow and Substance.*] *New York Times* (27 Jan. 1938): 16. (Also 6 Feb. 1938: sec. 10: 1.)
———. [9]. "Theatre: 'Wayward Saint' in Ireland." *New York Times* (18 Feb. 1955).
———. [10]. [Review of *The Wayward Saint.*] *New York Times* (27 Feb. 1955): sec. 11: 1.
———. [11]. [Review of *The White Steed.*] *New York Times* (11 Jan. 1939): 16.
———. [12]. "*The Wise Have Not Spoken*, by Paul Vincent Carroll, at the Cherry Lane." *New York Times* (11 Feb. 1954): 35.
Boylan, Henry. *A Dictionary of Irish Biography.* 2d ed. New York: St. Martin's, 1988.

Brown, Ivor. [Review of *Shadow and Substance*.] *New York Times* (23 Jan. 1938): sec. 9: 1.

Brown, John Mason. [1]. *Broadway in Review*. New York: Norton, 1940.

———. [2]. "Mr. Carroll's 'The Old Foolishness' Presented." *New York Post* (21 Dec. 1940).

———. [3]. *Two on the Aisle: Ten Years of the American Theatre in Performance*. New York: Norton, 1938.

Byram, John. "That Old Irish Mother." *New York Times* (18 Oct. 1932): 23.

Calta, Louis. [1]. "*Shadow and Substance* Presented at Tara." *New York Times* (4 Nov. 1959): 42.

———. [2]. "*Shadow and Substance* Revived Off Broadway." *New York Times* (14 Mar. 1956): 38.

Castronovo, David. "Carroll, Paul Vincent." *Encyclopedia of World Literature in the 20th Century*. Vol. 1: A–D. Rev. Ed. Leonard S. Klein. New York: Ungar, 1981. 417–18.

Coleman, Anne Gertrude. "Paul Vincent Carroll's View of Irish Life." *Catholic World* 192 (Nov. 1960): 87–93.

Coleman, Robert. " 'Wayward Saint,' at Cort, Stimulating, Rewarding." *Daily Mirror* (18 Feb. 1955).

Conway, John D. "Paul Vincent Carroll's Major Dramatic Triumphs." *Connecticut Review* (Apr. 1973): 61–69.

Doyle, Paul A. *Paul Vincent Carroll*. Lewisburg, Pa.: Bucknell University, 1971.

Ellis-Fermor, Una. *The Irish Dramatic Movement*. 1939. London: Methuen, 1971.

Fallis, Richard. *The Irish Renaissance*. Syracuse, N.Y.: Syracuse University Press, 1977.

Ferguson, Otis. "Delectable Mountains." *New Republic* (8 Feb. 1939): 17.

Fitz-Simon, Christopher. *Irish Theatre*. Dublin: Eason and Son, 1979.

Fox, R. M. [Review of *The Strings Are False*.] *Theatre Arts* (Oct. 1942): 659.

Gelb, Arthur. [Review of *The Coggerers*.] *New York Times* (23 Mar. 1960): 33.

Gilder, Rosamond. [1]. "Brain and Brawn." [Review of *Kindred*.] *Theatre Arts* (Mar. 1940): 165–66.

———. [2]. [Review of *The Old Foolishness*.] *Theatre Arts* (Feb. 1941): 97.

———. [3]. [Review of *The White Steed*.] *Theatre Arts Monthly* (Mar. 1939): 172–73.

Hatch, Robert. [Review of *The Wayward Saint*.] *Nation* (12 Mar. 1955): 226–27.

Hawkins, William. "Devil Gets His Due in 'Wayward Saint.' " *New York World Telegram* (18 Feb. 1955).

Hayes, J. J. [Review of *The Things That Are Caesar's*.] *New York Times* (18 Sept. 1932): sec. 9: 1.

Hewes, Henry. "Gods and Little Fishes." *Saturday Review* (5 March 1955): 26.

Hogan, Robert. *After the Irish Renaissance: A Critical History of the Irish Drama since The Plough and the Stars*. Minneapolis: University of Minnesota Press, 1967.

Jeffares, A. Norman. *Anglo-Irish Literature*. New York: Schocken, 1982.

Kerr, Walter F. [Review of *The Wayward Saint*.] *New York Herald Tribune* (18 Feb. 1955).

Kinsman, Clare D., and Mary Ann Tennenhouse, eds. *Contemporary Authors*. Vols. 9–12. first rev. Detroit: Gale, 1974.

Krause, David, ed. [1]. *The Letters of Sean O'Casey, 1910–1941*. Vol. 1. New York: Macmillan, 1975.

————. [2]. *The Profane Book of Irish Comedy.* Ithaca, N.Y.: Cornell University Press, 1982.

Krutch, Joseph Wood. [1]. "The Heart of a Wookey." *Nation* (30 May 1942): 637–38.

————. [2]. [Review of *The White Steed.*] *Nation* (21 Jan. 1939): 100–102.

Kunitz, Stanley J., and Howard Haycraft. *Twentieth Century Authors: A Biographical Dictionary of Modern Literature.* New York: H. W. Wilson, 1942.

Lewis, Theophilus. [Review of *The Wayward Saint.*] *America* (12 Mar. 1955): 629–30.

Lockridge, Richard. "Carroll's 'The Old Foolishness' Opens at the Windsor Theater." *New York Sun* (21 Dec. 1940).

Mac Liammóir, Micheál. "Problem Plays." *The Irish Theatre: Lectures Delivered during the Abbey Theatre Festival Held in Dublin in August 1938.* Ed. Lennox Robinson. 1939. New York: Haskell House, 1971. 199–227.

Mantle, Burns. " 'The Old Foolishness' Goes Back to Love on the Heights." *New York Daily News* (21 Dec. 1940).

Maxwell, D. E. S. *A Critical History of Modern Irish Drama, 1891–1980.* Cambridge: Cambridge University Press, 1984.

McClain, John. "Charm of Fantasy Arrives Bit Late." *New York Journal American* (18 Feb. 1955).

McHugh, Roger, and Maurice Harmon. *Short History of Anglo-Irish Literature: From Its Origins to the Present Day.* Totowa, N.J.: Barnes and Noble, 1982.

Morgan, Charles. [Review of *Things That Are Caesar's.*] *New York Times* (29 Jan. 1933): sec. 9: 1.

Nathan, George Jean. [1]. "Carroll Comes Again." *Newsweek* (29 Aug. 1938): 20.

————. [2]. "Carroll's New One." *Newsweek* (19 June 1939): 34.

————. [3]. Foreword. *Five Great Modern Irish Plays.* New York: Modern Library, 1941.

————. [4]. "Mr. Nathan Goes to the Play." *Theatre Arts* (Nov. 1951): 21, 66–67.

————. [5]. "The Season's Best Play." *Newsweek* (23 January 1939): 24.

Nichols, Lewis. [Review of *The Strings, My Lord, Are False.*] *New York Times* (20 May 1940): 24.

Pallette, Drew B. "Paul Vincent Carroll—since *The White Steed.*" *Modern Drama* 7 (February 1965): 375–81.

Sitzmann, Marion. *Indomitable Irishery: Paul Vincent Carroll: Study and Interview.* Salzburg: IESL, 1975.

Smith, Hugh. [1]. "Dublin Applauds New Carroll Play." *New York Times* (18 Mar. 1942): 3.

————. [2]. [Review of *Kindred.*] *New York Times* (8 Oct. 1939): sec. 9: 3.

Stokes, Sewell. [Review of *The Wise Have Not Spoken.*] *Theatre Arts* (June 1946): 356.

Review of *The Strings, My Lord, Are False. Newsweek* (1 June 1942): 67.

Watts, Richard, Jr. [1]. "A Fantasy about a Modern Saint." *New York Post* (18 Feb. 1955).

————. [2]. "Irish Sadness." *New York Herald Tribune* (21 Dec. 1940).

Weimer, M. J. "Paul Vincent Carroll." *Dictionary of Literary Biography, Vol. 10: Modern British Dramatists, 1900–1945: Part 1: A–L.* Ed. Stanley Weintraub. Detroit: Gale, 1982. 85–94.

Whipple, Sidney B. "Beauty in Carroll's Latest Play." *New York World Telegram* (21 Dec. 1940).

Wyatt, Euphemia Van Rensselaer. [1]. [Review of *The Wayward Saint.*] *Catholic World* (Apr. 1955): 68.

———. [2] [Review of *The White Steed.*] *Catholic World* (Mar. 1939): 727–28.

Young, Stark. "Drama Critics Circle Awards." *New Republic* (4 May 1938): 396.

Zolotow, Maurice. [Review of *The Wayward Saint.*] *Theatre Arts* (May 1955): 87.

BIBLIOGRAPHIES

Carpenter, Charles A. *Modern Drama Scholarship and Criticism 1966–1980: An International Bibliography.* Toronto: University of Toronto Press, 1986.

Conner, Billie M., and Helene G. Mochedlover. *Ottemiller's Index to Plays in Collections: An Author and Title Index to Plays Appearing in Collections Published between 1900 and 1985.* Metuchen, N.J.: Scarecrow, 1988.

Keller, Dean H. *Index to Plays in Periodicals.* Metuchen, N.J.: Scarecrow, 1979.

Palmer, Helen H., and Anne Jane Dyson, comps. *European Drama Criticism.* Hamden, Conn.: Shoestring Press, 1968.

Salem, James M. *A Guide to Critical Reviews: Part III: Foreign Drama, 1909–1977.* 2d ed. Metuchen, N.J.: Scarecrow, 1979.

Austin Clarke
(1896–1974)

DAVID J. SORRELLS

Thomas Kinsella, author of the introduction to *Selected Poems* by Austin Clarke, praised Clarke by saying that his ''is one of the notable modern poetic careers; a view of modern poetry which does not take his work seriously into account is not adequate.'' The same must be said of Clarke's contribution to Irish theater. In the course of fifty years, he wrote eighteen verse plays, three prose romances, over 250 poems, and over 1,400 articles, essays, and reviews. He founded the Dublin Verse-Speaking Society and Lyric Theatre Company, as well as writing and directing many of their productions.

Austin (Augustine Joseph) Clarke was born 9 May 1896 in Dublin in the blossom of the Irish Literary Renaissance. Clarke's father, Augustine, and mother, Eileen Patten (Browne) Clarke, zealous Irish Catholic nationalists, enrolled him at the age of seven in Belvedere College, the rigorous Jesuit school that James Joyce made infamous in *A Portrait of the Artist as Young Man.* In fact, much of Clarke's young life is strikingly similar to Joyce's. He tells anecdotally that three forces most influenced his childhood and adolescence: his ambivalent feeling toward religion, particularly the Catholic Church; his intense interest in nationalism; and his passion for, first, music and, then, literature. Clarke attended University College in Dublin from 1913 to 1917, where he studied Irish literary history under Douglas Hyde and Thomas MacDonagh. He also learned to read Irish mythology in the original Gaelic, and he studied Anglo-Irish poetry. In 1917, Clarke received a B.A. and M.A. with honors in English and assumed the assistant lectureship at University College that had been held by MacDonagh, who had been executed by the British that year for his part in the Easter Rising of 1916.

Clarke's first volume of poetry, *The Vengeance of Fionn,* was published in 1917. It is an epic narrative based on the legend of Diarmuid and Grainne. In

1921, Clarke revisited mythology in two new epic poems: *The Sword of the West*, based on the Cuchullin saga, and *The Fires of Baal*, which recounts Hebrew legends about the events before Moses' death. That year, Clarke lost his teaching position at the University College because the Catholic university administration was displeased by Clarke's short-lived civil marriage to Lia Cummins. As a result, Clarke left for England the next year, where he was to remain for the next fifteen years working as a literary journalist.

The Son of Learning (also called *The Hunger Demon*), Clarke's first verse drama, appeared in *Dublin Magazine* in 1927. The highly nationalistic Ireland, while supporting writers who produced in Gaelic, was suspicious of authors who wrote in English; therefore, in 1929, all of Clarke's writing was banned, which led to his devotion to repealing censorship in his later years. This ban ironically came during the same year of the publication of Clarke's first major collection of poems, *Pilgrimage and Other Poems*. This volume is important for Clarke, for these poems feature experiments with assonance and internal rhyme to better reflect the sounds of Gaelic poetry. Also, Clarke began a thematic shift from a focus on Irish mythology to the Celtic Romanesque.

Clarke's one-act poetic drama *The Flame* was performed at the School of Speech Training in Edinburgh in 1932. That same year, George Bernard Shaw and Yeats invited Clarke to join them by becoming a charter member of the Irish Academy of Letters, of which he would serve as president from 1952 to 1954. He later received the Gregory Medal, the academy's major literary award.

The poetic playwright returned to Ireland in 1937; he settled with his wife, Nora, and their three children at Bridge House, Templeogue, a village near Dublin where he lived until he died in 1974. In 1940, Clarke and Robert Farren founded the Dublin Verse-Speaking Society, which sought to promote the recitation of rhythmic speech. The society broadcast the dramatic poems of Robert Browning, Vachel Lindsay, G. K. Chesterton, and Clarke on Radió Éireann. With the success of the Verse-Speaking Society, which virtually assured the continuation of verse drama in Ireland, Clarke turned in the 1940s to writing mostly drama.

From 1939 to 1942 and 1946 to 1949, Clarke was the president of the Irish P.E.N. During his terms of office, Clarke organized efforts to ban the Irish censorship that he fell victim to earlier in his career. Years later the organization nominated Clarke for a Nobel Prize. The year 1941 saw the debut of a Clarke play at the Abbey Theatre. *Black Fast* opened on 28 December, but Clarke's real successes were at the Peacock Theatre, the Abbey's experimental venue. Along with plays by Gordon Bottomley and Mary Davenport O'Neill, the Verse-Speaking Society produced Clarke's *The Kiss* in May 1942 and *The Plot Is Ready* in October 1943.

In 1944, Clarke teamed with Robert Farren again to form a strictly theatrical unit of the Verse-Speaking Society, the Lyric Theatre Company. Clarke claimed that the company was founded to "save from neglect the tradition of verse drama left to us by Yeats" (Coskren). The Lyric presented plays by Irish authors in the Abbey Theatre until 1951, when fire caused the company to move. Almost all of Clarke's earlier plays were produced by the Lyric Theatre Company; three of Clarke's plays were premiered: *The Viscount of Blarney* (1944), *The Second Kiss* (1946), and *The Plot Succeeds* (1950).

Several factors contributed to the rapid decline in dramatic output by Clarke in the 1950s. Public interest in verse drama declined: in 1952 the Lyric Theatre Company closed, followed by the final broadcast of the Verse-Speaking Society in 1953. In 1955, Clarke published his first book of poetry since 1938, *Ancient Lights*, which revitalized his interest in poetry and began what is his greatest output of creative effort. The last play premiered in Clarke's lifetime was *The Moment Next to Nothing*, first broadcast by the Verse-Speaking Society in 1953 and later produced at Trinity College in 1958.

The Arts Council of Ireland published in limited edition the *Collected Plays* of Austin Clarke in 1963. The publication of this volume, along with the publication of Clarke's *Later Poems* and *Flight to Africa*, brought the playwright/ poet to America and Britain. Clarke died on 19 March, 1974.

Selected Biographical Sources: Coskren; Halpern; Harmon; Ricigliano.

MAJOR PLAYS, PREMIERES, AND SIGNIFICANT REVIVALS: THEATRICAL RECEPTION

The Son of Learning. 1927. Opened 31 October at the Cambridge Festival Theatre, Cambridge. Produced by Herbert M. Prentice. Directed by Terence Gray. Reopened at the Abbey Theatre in June 1945 by the Lyric Theatre Company.

Based on the Irish folk legend *Aislinge Meic Conglinne* (The Vision of Mac Conglinne), Clarke's first attempt at playwriting recounts the wandering adventures of poet Anier Mac Conglinne. Mac Conglinne rids his king of a hunger demon and himself of a death sentence by incredible feats prescribed by over-zealous monks. The play owes its poetic stylings to Yeats, but the comic style is Clarke's own: he satirizes both the behavior by, and the institutions of, religion. Mac Conglinne is often thought to be Clarke's alter ego—he is a poet and scholar who is drawn to the church and its themes, but not always with pious intent (Halpern). Reynolds recognizes *The Son of Learning* as Clarke's greatest achievement in verse, but Bailey contends that it is formless and "leaves us without sufficient light." Batterham suggests that the play would have been more successful in prose. (Also entitled *The Hunger-Demon.*)

The Flame. 1932. First performed orally in June at the School of Speech Training, Edinburgh, by the members of the School of Speech Training and Drama. Reopened at the British Drama League Festival in 1936 by the Questors and again at the Oxford Festival of Spoken Poetry in 1938. First dramatic performance in Ireland by the Dublin Verse-Speaking Society in 1941. Revived by the Lyric Theatre Company at the Abbey Theatre.

Like *Sister Eucharia, The Flame* is set in a convent where the main character breaks the rules but is forgiven in the end. Sister Attracta, the novitiate assigned to watch the flame of St. Brigid, which burned for centuries at Kildare, passionately did not want to cut her hair, a symbol of worldly vanity. Because of this conflict, Sister Attracta cannot pray. She is afraid and does not want to be left alone to attend the sacred fire. The flame of St. Brigid wanes when she leaves it; the nuns wail in distress. Finally, Attracta receives a vision of Absalom, and she prays to St. Brigid to hide her. The flame dies. In the darkness the nuns discover that they forgot to fill the lamp with oil. They quickly claim that the spark was miraculously preserved, and the abbess rebukes the nuns for their weak faith. *The Flame* features what came to be known as one of Clarke's trademark endings: a miracle with a dubious source and enigmatic significance (see Harmon). Buchanan wrote that the action and miraculous ending of *The Flame* were too distant for modern minds to relate to.

Sister Eucharia. 1939. Opened July at the Gate Theatre, Dublin. Presented by the Earl of Longford and produced by Noel Illiff.

Sister Eucharia, like Sister Attracta in *The Flame*, is delivered from shame by the uncertain miraculous intervention that is Clarke's trademark, when her intense mystical visions alienate her from the remainder of her order (see McHugh). Sister Eucharia wants to die so she can go to heaven; her anticipation is heightened by visions of people glad to be in purgatory. However, the nuns and clerics of the order see her passion for death as excessive. The convent bells peal as Sister Eucharia advances toward the chapel; when Sister Eucharia dies in the chapel, the reverend mother interprets her death as a sign that Eucharia has been made a saint. The real theme of this play, according to McHugh, is the difficulty of a modern Irish person to be a saint. McHugh claims that the source of this play is the tale of an ascetic prefect who, on his way to a retreat, stripped and jumped into a bed of thorns. His conviction was undermined, though, when the priest told the monastery that the prefect had had a small accident.

Black Fast. 1941. Opened 28 December at the Abbey Theatre, Dublin. Produced by Michael Clarke.

Black Fast marks the first performance of a Clarke play to be performed at the Abbey Theatre. This one-act play is a humorous treatment of the seventh-century debate between the Ulster and Munster factions over the exact date of Easter (see Halpern). The Ulster home of Connal More is divided, because Connal follows the Ulster calendar, and his wife, Blanaid, follows the Munster calendar. Because they believe Easter falls on different dates, they also believe the Lenten fasting period is different. Connal has observed the Ulster Lent and Easter, but Blanaid insists that he respect the Munster Lent that she observes by removing certain foods from his table. Blanaid invites Romanus and other

Irish Playwrights, 1880–1995

A RESEARCH AND PRODUCTION
SOURCEBOOK

Edited by
BERNICE SCHRANK
and WILLIAM W. DEMASTES

GREENWOOD PRESS
Westport, Connecticut • London

Library of Congress Cataloging-in-Publication Data

Irish playwrights, 1880–1995 : a research and production sourcebook /
    edited by Bernice Schrank and William W. Demastes.
       p. cm.
    Includes bibliographical references and index.
    ISBN 0–313–28805–4 (alk. paper)
    1. English drama—Irish authors—Bio-bibliography—Dictionaries.
  2. English drama—20th century—Bio-bibliography—Dictionaries.
  3. English drama—19th century—Bio-bibliography—Dictionaries.
  4. Dramatists, Irish—Biography—Dictionaries. 5. English drama—
  Irish authors—Dictionaries. 6. Ireland—In literature—
  Dictionaries. 7. Theater—Ireland—Dictionaries. I. Schrank,
  Bernice. II. Demastes, William W.
  PR8789.I67   1997
  822.009'9415—dc20
  [B]   95–48349

British Library Cataloguing in Publication Data is available.

Library of Congress Catalog Card Number: 95–48349
ISBN: 0–313–28805–4

First published in 1997

Greenwood Press, 88 Post Road West, Westport, CT 06881
An imprint of Greenwood Publishing Group, Inc.

Printed in the United States of America

The paper used in this book complies with the
Permanent Paper Standard issued by the National
Information Standards Organization (Z39.48–1984).

10 9 8 7 6 5 4 3 2 1

Contents

Preface

Irish dramatists have been writing plays for hundreds of years. These dramatists include such distinguished theatrical notables as William Congreve, George Farquhar, R. B. Sheridan, and, later, Oscar Wilde and George Bernard Shaw. Irish drama, however, is a phenomenon of this century, rooted in large part in the political and social ferment out of which Ireland as an independent nation emerged. Although the absence of theatrical opportunities made émigrés and exiles of Congreve, Farquhar, Wilde, Shaw, and the others, their rhetorical brilliance separated them from their English contemporaries and betrayed their Irish origins. That rhetorical brilliance would surface in the work of later Irish playwrights and would become one of the hallmarks of an indigenous Irish drama.

The creation of Irish drama is primarily the story of the Abbey from its origins in 1897 as the Irish Literary Theatre, founded by Lady Gregory, Edward Martyn, and William Butler Yeats, to its present status as Ireland's national theater. Its existence and its role have, over the years, been challenged and critiqued. Theaters like the Gate in Dublin rejected the insistent Irishness of the Abbey and sought to introduce Irish audiences to the drama of continental Europe. There was also a lively theatrical tradition in Ulster, although it was, in the main, derivative. Notwithstanding such challenges, the Abbey has never been displaced from its central position in the emergence of a distinct and distinguished Irish drama.

Its history has been variously recounted. When read in sequence, Ernest Boyd's *The Contemporary Drama of Ireland* (1918), Andrew Malone's *The Irish Drama: 1896–1928* (originally published in 1929), Dawson Byrne's *The Story of Ireland's National Theatre* (1929), Peter Kavanagh's *The Story of the Abbey Theatre* (1950), Lennox Robinson's *Ireland's Abbey Theatre: A History 1899–1951* (1951), Gerard Fay's *The Abbey Theatre: Cradle of Genius* (1958),

Micheál Ó hAodha's *The Abbey—Then and Now* (1969), and Hugh Hunt's *The Abbey, Ireland's National Theatre, 1904–1979* (1979) provide a continuous chronicle of the Abbey's development and continuing influence.

The founders of the Abbey (Lady Gregory, Yeats, and, to a lesser degree, Martyn) had an aesthetic agenda. All three hoped to create an indigenous theater in which the reality of Ireland might be presented, and the stereotypical stage Irishman destroyed. Here they succeeded. More than the others, Yeats wanted more from the Abbey. He hoped the Abbey might nurture a poetic drama that would provide a viable alternative to the realistic theater of Ibsen and Shaw that dominated the stage in the early decades of the twentieth century. Una Ellis-Fermor, in *The Irish Dramatic Movement* (1939; revised 1954), and Katharine Worth, in *The Irish Drama of Europe from Yeats to Beckett* (1978), have argued that Yeats' poetic drama successfully established such a poetic tradition. They also argue that Yeats was the most influential dramatist produced by the Abbey. In a more recent study, *Modern Irish Drama 1891–1980* (1984), D. E. S. Maxwell suggests that Yeats' influence was less significant in the evolution of Irish drama than either Ellis-Fermor or Worth indicates. In Maxwell's view, with the exception of Yeats, the dramatists associated with the Abbey, playwrights like Synge and O'Casey, explored and expanded the parameters of stage realism. Their language is particularly interesting because, although it belongs to the prose realist tradition, it is often so heightened and extravagant as to approach poetry in its effects.

Indeed, the ability of dramatists associated with the Abbey (like Synge and O'Casey) to create stage languages that move effortlessly between prose and poetry, verisimilitude and vision, is at the heart of a distinctly Irish drama. In time, Irish drama became less tied to the Abbey. Later Irish dramatists like Brendan Behan, Samuel Beckett, and Brian Friel, who did not have close connections to the Abbey, nevertheless show the same capacity to create, each in a different way, an inflected dialogue that ranges between the absurd and the metaphysical.

The dramatists included in this book were selected not only because of their Irishness but also because of their diversity and the importance of their achievement. A study of the performance history of Irish dramatists provides strong empirical evidence of the degree to which Irish dramatists have transcended the borders of their nationality. Many of the authors included in this volume have distinguished themselves not only in Dublin and Belfast but in London, New York, and elsewhere. Irish drama has become both a national and an international phenomenon. The playwrights chosen include the "canonized" and familiar figures of Irish drama as well as a significant number of lesser-known writers. Although a conscious effort was made to be inclusive, limitations of space circumscribed this attempt. The editors regret all the inevitable omissions, especially because research on Irish performance history is at an early stage. We are confident, however, that these profiles will encourage and facilitate further research in this area.

monks of Munster to fast with her. Connal calls in the Abbot-Bishop Cummian and the monks of Ulster to defend his cause. During the argument, Cummian and his followers walk out. Darkness falls, accompanied by the rumbling of thunder and rattling dishes. When the lights come up, the table is bare. Romanus exclaims that God's will is done. Just as Connal is about to concede, a messenger rushes in and proclaims that he has just seen the dishes of food passing through the air to the monastery of the Ulster monks. The curtain falls on renewed debate. Like many of Clarke's plays, *Black Fast* lampoons the religious superstitions of the church that claim a foothold in the orthodox community (see Coskren). Mercier [1] likens the play to the medieval morality and miracle plays of England.

As the Crow Flies. 1942. First aired 6 February 1942 on Radió Éireann by the Dublin Verse-Speaking Society, under Austin Clarke's direction. Premiered on stage at the Abbey Theatre on 14 November 1948.

This allegorical tale, set in medieval Ireland, is ideally a one-act radio play. It uses the sounds of thunder, wind, oars, and voices to establish the action of the story: an eagle's quest for knowledge is undermined by an evil crow. During a storm three monks are forced to seek shelter in a cave. Above them, an eagle has built her nest, where the evil crow has also found shelter. The eaglets are calmed by their mother's tale of her long existence. When they ask her if this storm is the worst that ever raged, she departs from the nest, leaving her young in the crow's cave. She finds the answer by asking the wise Fintan, the Salmon of Assaroe, but she is distraught when she finds that the crow has sent the eaglets plummeting to their deaths. The mother eagle throws herself against the cliff in agony. The monks observe, shivering, that all beings are afraid of death and that no stronghold or knowledge can prevent the inevitable. McHugh finds this play's poetic force "arresting," and Harmon concurs that the radio techniques are quietly effective. Halpern finds that the tale's terror stems from its "fundamental naive folktale" structure, but the simple story verges on the grotesque. Farren suggests that *Crow* features Clarke's best lyrics, and he compares them to pieces of sunstricken stained glass.

The Kiss. 1942. Opened 12 May at the Peacock Theatre, the Abbey Theatre's experimental venue, by the Dublin Verse-Speaking Society. Produced by Ria Mooney. Opened June 1944 at the Abbey Theatre by the Lyric Theatre Company.

Written in rhymed pentameter couplets, this one-act comedy is the first of three plays that feature the French pantomime stock characters Pierrot and Pierrette. Pierrette is Uirgeal, the legendary hag whose youth and beauty can be restored only by the first kiss of a young and innocent man, Pierrot. Pierrot is torn between his commitment to help Uirgeal and his repulsion by her. Uirgeal, in her ethereal form, identifies with the ideal woman, while Pierrot suggests that they should enjoy the realistic pleasures of physical love. After their kiss, Uirgeal disappears, and Pierrot melodramatically mourns her. Harmon suggests that the theme of the play is ideal love: Uirgeal visualizes the ideal woman, and Pierrot dreams of ideal love. These ideals, proposes Halpern, suggest a utopian Ireland.

The Plot Is Ready. 1943. Opened 26 October at the Peacock Theatre by the Dublin Verse-Speaking Society. Produced by Ria Mooney. The Lyric Theatre Company reopened the play at the Abbey Theatre in December 1944.

A blank-verse play in four scenes, *The Plot Is Ready* returns to the medieval Ireland of which Clarke is so fond for its base tale. Muireadach Mac Erca, the High King, is deathly ill. He is attended by his mistress Osna, who won the king's favor over his wife and children. Because the abbot believes the king will die soon, he has his monks dig a deep burial plot. Crede, Muireadach's wife, has forgiven her husband's indiscretions, and her mercy sways the abbot to allow the king to live. In a hallucinatory dream, Muireadach refuses the abbot's counsel to leave his mistress and reclaim the bonds with his wife. While rushing away, Muireadach falls into the grave the abbot had previously dug. In what Mercier calls the "coup de théâtre," Muireadach's spirit rises in glory to take his mistress along with him to eternity (quoted in Halpern). Critics have hailed *The Plot Is Ready* as Clarke's best and most moving play (Sealy; Halpern). The ancient tale is revivified into a Clarkean satire of conflict between church dogma and individual will, and, as in several other Clarke plays, the resolution of the conflict is supernatural. Mercier [4] calls this play the "coping-stone" of Clarke's plays to date.

The Viscount of Blarney. 1944. Opened 3 December at the Abbey Theatre by the Lyric Theatre Company. Produced by Evelyn MacNeice.

Based on a Wexford folktale by Patrick Kennedy, this dream-vision one-act play is set around the turn of the century, near the Blackstairs Mountains. It features stock folktale characters—an innocent young girl, the Pooka, Jack O'Lantern, and the viscount of Blarney, who is the devil. Cauth Morrisey is subjected to a succession of evil manifestations in brief episodes that are, according to Harmon, "all a part of a psychological drama, each evocative of Cauth's fear, each connected with female sexuality." Ironically, the Viscount, who is the devil incarnate, is a glorified figure who is so perfect that no one could mistake him for the typical parochial Irishman. An anonymous reviewer suggests that the play is as "graceful and vivacious" as it is "fantastic or supernatural." Fallon [2] contends that *Viscount* is "a little better than Clarke's best."

The Second Kiss. 1946. Opened 3 June at the Abbey Theatre by the Lyric Theatre Company. Produced by Cyril Cusack.

This one-act comedy is the second of three plays that feature Pierrot and Pierrette, stock figures from French pantomime. It is written in rhymed pentameter couplets and features a kiss three seconds longer than the "emotional duration'' prescribed by the film censor, since there was no stage censorship at the time (see Halpern). Pierrette, who frequently poses as Columbine, thinks that Pierrot's suggestion to ''misbehave'' is impossible, since they are now married. Pierrot's fascination with extramarital activities is punctuated by his uneasy and perfunctory responses to Pierrette's conversation. Their marriage, according to Halpern, is one of the mechanical marriages of Ireland that Clarke sees around him constantly. An anonymous reviewer (''Articulate Pierrot'') calls *The Second Kiss* a ''welcome fantasy for a world shorn of delusion and too wary for confidence.''

The Plot Succeeds. 1950. Opened 16 February at the Abbey Theatre by the Lyric Theatre Company. Produced by W. O'Gorman and Austin Clarke. Reopened at the Lyric Theatre, London, in November 1950.

This ''poetic pantomime'' features Mannaun Mac Lir, the mythical shape-shifting sea god, as the host of a medieval revel in which two married couples exchange shapes with each other and with two monks. This play, which should be seen rather than read, satirizes a number of Clarke's favorite targets: the sexual dynamics in marriage and the conflict between matrimony and religious orders (see Halpern; McHugh). Coskren points out that the blind nature of love is similar to that in a Shakespearean idyll, with conventional couples, transformations, supernatural forest settings, and the inexplicable force of love on the humans. Coskren also suggests that the easy interchangeableness of marriage partners is ''intentionally subversive of Ireland's divorce laws.'' An anonymous reviewer (''Two Poetic Dramas'') found *The Plot Succeeds* to be swift, kaleidoscopic, and sensuous.

The Moment Next to Nothing. 1953. First aired 8 November on Radió Éireann. Stage debut in January 1958 at the Players' Theatre, Trinity College, Dublin. Produced by Evelyn MacNeice.

This three-act play is based on a medieval Irish tale, *Altram Tige Da Medar* (The Fosterage of the Houses of the Two Mothers), edited by Lilian Duncan in *Eriu XI*. Set in Ireland at the time of St. Patrick, it is the same tale on which Clarke based his prose romance *The Sun Dances at Easter*. Ceasan, a monk who is spending a year of solitude in the woods, falls in love with Eithne, a non-Christian who seems to be a normal young woman. Ceasan tries to convert her to Christianity, but his arguments for his beliefs ring hollow, while Eithne's pagan actions are sincere. Eithne understands Ceasan's ministrations supernaturally: she is beyond the very concepts of original sin and salvation. When Ceasan tries to baptize Eithne, Aongus Og, Eithne's father, takes her from him. Although Coskren suggests that the meaning of the play is elusive, he concludes that Clarke is attempting to regain paradise by transcending Christian and pagan consciousness. McHugh concurs, but he suggests that a dilemma of conscience may be thematically important. Halpern concludes that the ''play is a negation of Christianity—this time because it stifles the creative, the vital.''

ADDITIONAL PLAYS, ADAPTATIONS, AND PRODUCTIONS

In 1965 Clarke began writing his first plays in twelve years. Clarke's adaptations of Cervantes' *Interludes* (1968) are *La Cueva de Salamanca* (The Cave of Salamanca) and *El Viejo Celoso* (The Silent Lover). Typical of Clarke, both playlets subvert the image of authority, especially the church. *The Impuritans* (1963) is a one-act adaptation of Nathaniel Hawthorne's short story "Young Goodman Brown." The original setting is preserved, but Clarke updates the tale by a prediction of life in America in the mid-twentieth century: America's obsession with the Bible is the country's source of evil. *The Visitation* (1974) is a futuristic spoof set in thirteenth-century Ireland. In *The Third Kiss* (1976), Clarke returns to the commedia dell'arte characters Pierrot and Pierrette, this time staging them as actors in the Abbey Theatre in 1913. Harmon calls it a "little masterpiece." *Liberty Lane: A Ballad Play* (1978) is based on F. R. Higgins' 1935 play *Deuce of Jacks*. "St. Patrick's Purgatory" and "The Frenzy of Suibhne" remain only in manuscript.

ASSESSMENT OF CLARKE'S CAREER

Austin Clarke is best known as a poet whose concern for rhythmic speaking and love for the stage spurred him to write eighteen verse dramas over the course of almost fifty years (see Harmon; Halpern; Ricigliano). Clarke's plays are typically set in the Celtic Romanesque, the period from the beginnings of Christianity in Ireland to the Norman invasion, from the sixth to the twelfth centuries. They usually feature characters involved in theological debate (see Maxwell; McHugh). The plays are often biting satirically, frequently whimsical, and always written in verse (Coskren; McHugh; Halpern). Generally, Clarke's plays written with a comic sense of entertainment—*The Son of Learning, The Kiss, Black Fast*—are more successful than those that explore the serious effects of moral choices on individuals (see Coskren; Harmon).

Clarke's most important achievement is his extending the tradition of poetic drama beyond Yeats and into the mid-twentieth century. Clarke studied carefully the "cold, clear ascetic" quality of Yeats' poetry, and he imitated Yeats' bent toward short one-act plays rather than full-length ones. Clarke also examined T. S. Eliot's plays and found them to be self-defeating, because they were neither spontaneous nor intense. Nor did Clarke care for Eliot's meter. He was, according to Halpern, attempting to find a medium between Yeats and Eliot.

In a note to his 1963 *Collected Plays*, Clarke asserts that "stage speech only resembles natural speech and goes more easily, being set to definite patterns." Critics naturally disagree on the effectiveness of verse drama in general and Clarke's verse drama in particular. Mercier [1] asserts that Clarke's plays are both "good drama and good poetry," insisting that the dramatic effect of the action is reinforced by the rhythm. McHugh concurs that, usually, Clarke's verse is strong: he finds that it is dexterous and flexible enough to mold to dialogue and description, although sometimes the focus on legendary themes is too erudite for audiences not versed in medieval Irish history (McHugh). In an article for *Bell* in 1951, Fallon [2] declares that Clarke's lyrics are too elaborate for a staged performance, that "rhythmic writing is enough." An anonymous review of *Collected Plays* describes Clarke's verse as "cramped" and declares that the rhyme is stiff, despite passages of brilliance. Herring, in a 1966 review of *Collected Plays*, suggests that the effect of the verse is "like still born drama." Hogan summarizes those critics who are cautious about verse drama: prose is a more natural medium for stage work than poetry.

Through the efforts of Clarke and Robert Farren and their work with the Dublin Verse-Speaking Society and the Lyric Theatre Company, verse drama was saved from virtual extinction at the Abbey and Gate Theatres (Coskren). For this accomplishment Austin Clarke's name is remembered in Irish theatre history (McHugh).

ARCHIVAL SOURCES

Notebooks, reviews, and manuscripts are located in the Austin Clarke Collection housed in the Harry Ransom Humanities Research Center, University of Texas at Austin.

PRIMARY BIBLIOGRAPHY

Plays

As the Crow Flies, a Lyric Play for the Air. Dublin: Bridge Press, 1943.
Black Fast, a Poetic Farce in One Act. Dublin: Orwell Press, 1941.
The Flame. London: Allen and Unwin, 1930.
The Impuritans. Dublin: Dolmen, 1973.
Liberty Lane. Dublin: Dolmen, 1978.
The Plot Succeeds. Dublin: Bridge, 1950.
The Second Kiss. London: Williams and Norgate, 1947.
Sister Eucharia. London: Williams and Norgate, 1939.
The Son of Learning, a Poetic Comedy in Three Acts. London: Allen and Unwin, 1927.
The Third Kiss. Dublin: Dolmen, 1976.
Two Interludes Adapted from Cervantes: The Student from Salamanca, La Cueva de Salamanca; and The Silent Lover, El Viejo Celosa. Dublin: Dolmen, 1968.

Anthologies

Collected Plays. Dublin: Dolmen, 1963.
The Collected Poems of Austin Clarke. London: Allen and Unwin, 1932. Includes *The Flame* and *The Son of Learning.*
The Viscount of Blarney and Other Plays. Dublin: Bridge Press, 1945. Includes *The Viscount of Blarney, The Kiss, The Plot Is Ready.*

Plays in Periodicals

The Flame. Dublin Magazine 4 (Oct.–Dec. 1929): 15–22; 5 (Jan.–Mar. 1930): 15–25.
The Kiss. Dublin Magazine 17 (July–Sept. 1942): 5–18.
The Second Kiss. Dublin Magazine 21 (Apr.–June 1946): 5–19.
Sister Eucharia. Dublin Magazine 13 (July–Sept. 1938): 1–25.
The Son of Learning. Dublin Magazine 1 (July–Sept. 1926): 33–50.

Essays and Articles on Drama and Theater

Introduction. *The Plays of George Fitzmaurice: Dramatic Fantasies.* Dublin: Dolmen,
     1967. "Love in Irish Poetry and Drama." *Motley* 1,5 (Oct. 1932): 3–4.
"Poetic Drama." *Spectator* 152 (6 June 1934): 934.
"The Problem of Verse Drama Today." *London Mercury* 33 (Nov. 1935): 34–38.
"Verse Speaking." *Bell* 15.3 (Dec. 1947): 52–56.
"Verse-Speaking and Verse Drama." *Dublin Magazine* 12, new series 4 (Oct.–Dec.
     1937): 9–17.
"W. B. Yeats and Verse Drama." *Threshold* 19 (Autumn 1965): 14–29.

SECONDARY BIBLIOGRAPHY

"Articulate Pierrot." *Times Literary Supplement* (25 October 1947): 550.
"Austin Clarke Special Issue." *Irish University Review* 4.1 (Spring 1974).
Bailey, Ruth. "A Verse Play." *London Mercury* 39.24 (Apr. 1939): 659.
Batterham, E. [Review of *The Son of Learning.*] *Times Literary Supplement* (1 Sept.
     1927): 589.
Buchanan, G. "Drama." *Times Literary Supplement* (15 Oct. 1931): 804.
Colum, Padraic. "Two Poets." *Dublin Magazine* 2.4 (Oct.–Dec. 1927): 39–44.
Coskren, Robert. "Austin Clarke." *Dictionary of Literary Biography.* Vol. 10. *Modern
     British Dramatists, 1900–1945.* Ed. Stanley Weintraub. Detroit: Gale, 1982.
Fallon, Padraic. [1]. "Book Reviews." *Dublin Magazine* 20.1 (Jan.–Mar. 1945): 57–58.
———— [2]. "Journal." *Bell* 17.9 (Dec. 1951): 48–54.
Farren, Robert. *The Course of Irish Verse in English.* New York: Sheed and Ward, 1947.
Fiacc, Padraic. "Austin Clarke." *Irish Bookman* 2.3 (Dec. 1947): 28–32.
Gwynn, Stephen. *Irish Literature and Drama in the English Language: A Short History.*
     London: Nelson, 1936.
Halpern, Susan. *Austin Clarke, His Life and Works.* Dublin: Dolmen, 1974.
Harmon, Maurice. *Austin Clarke 1896–1974: A Critical Introduction.* Totowa, N.J.:
     Barnes, 1989.
Herring, Thelma. [Review of *Collected Plays.*] *AULLA: Journal of the Australasian Uni-
     versities Language and Literature Association* 25 (May 1966): 136.
Hogan, Robert. *After the Irish Renaissance: A Critical History of the Irish Drama since*
     The Plough and the Stars. Minneapolis: University of Minnesota Press, 1967.
Loftus, Richard J. *Nationalism in Modern Anglo-Irish Poetry.* Madison: University of
     Wisconsin Press, 1964.
M., W. P. [Review of *The Moment Next to Nothing.*] *Dublin Magazine* 30.2 (Apr.–June
     1954): 42–44.
MacDonald, J. F. "Poetry." *Canadian Forum* 8.87 (Dec. 1927): 476.

MacNamara, Brinsley, ed. *Abbey Plays, 1899–1948*. Dublin: At the Sign of the Three Candles, 1949.

Mahoney, Tina Hunt. "The Dublin Verse-Speaking Society and the Lyric Theatre Company." *Irish University Review* 4.1 (Spring 1974): 65–73.

Maxwell, D. E. S. *A Critical History of Modern Irish Drama, 1891–1980*. Cambridge: Cambridge University Press, 1984.

McHugh, Roger. "The Plays of Austin Clarke." *Irish University Review* 4.1 (Spring 1974): 52–64.

McHugh, Roger, and Maurice Harmon. *Short History of Anglo-Irish Literature, from Its Origins to the Present Day*. Totowa, N.J.: Barnes, 1982.

Mercier, Vivian. [1]. "Austin Clarke: The Poet in the Theatre." *Life and Letters and the London Mercury* 53.116 (Apr. 1947): 7–18.

———. [2]. "The Arts in Ireland." *Commonweal* 46.8 (June 1947): 183–85.

———. [3]. *The Irish Comic Tradition*. Oxford: Clarendon, 1962.

———. [4]. "The Verse Plays of Austin Clarke." *Dublin Magazine* 19.2 (Apr.–June 1944): 39–42.

Miller, Liam. "Eden and After: The Irish Theatre 1945–1966." *Studies* 55.219 (Autumn 1966): 231–35.

Ó hAodha, Micheál. "Austin Clarke's Witty Verse Plays." *Irish Press* (17 August 1963): 12.

Owens, Coilin, and Joan Radner. *Irish Drama 1900–1980*. Washington, D.C.: Catholic University of America Press, 1990.

"Portrait of a Professional Poet before the Mike." *Irish Times Pictorial* (radio supplement) (10, 17 Dec. 1952): 1,4.

Redshaw, Thomas Dillon. "His Works, a Memorial: Austin Clarke (1896–1974)." *Éire-Ireland* 9.2 (1974): 107–15.

Reynolds, Horace. "Ireland in Austin Clarke's Poems." *New York Times Book Review* (23 May 1937): 20–21.

Ricigliano, Lorraine. *Austin Clarke: A Reference Guide*. New York: Hall-Macmillan, 1993.

Robinson, Lennox. *Ireland's Abbey Theatre: A History 1899–1951*. London: Sidgwick and Jackson, 1951; rpt., Port Washington, N.Y.: Kennikat, 1968.

Ryan, Stephen P. "Ireland and Its Writers." *Catholic World* 192.1148 (Nov. 1960): 149–55.

Sealy, Douglas. "Austin Clarke: A Survey of His Work." *Dubliner* 6 (Jan.–Feb. 1963): 28.

Tapping, G. Craig. *Austin Clarke: A Study of His Writings*. Dublin: Academy Press, 1981.

"Theatre." *Times Literary Supplement* (27 Jan. 1945): 47.

"Touch of a Leprechaun." *Times Literary Supplement* (2 Jan. 1964): 10.

"Two Poetic Dramas." *Times Literary Supplement* (18 May 1951): 306.

Ussher, Arland. "Austin Clarke: A Tribute." *Hibernia* 32.14 (29 Nov.–12 Dec. 1968): 7.

BIBLIOGRAPHIES

Conner, Billie M., and Helene G. Mochedlover. *Ottemiller's Index to Plays in Collections: An Author and Title Index to Plays Appearing in Collections Published between 1900 and 1985*. Metuchen, N.J.: Scarecrow, 1988.

Drury, F. W. K. *Drury's Guide to Best Plays.* Washington, D.C.: Scarecrow, 1953.

Keller, Dean H. *Index to Plays in Periodicals.* Metuchen, N.J.: Scarecrow, 1979.

Kierran, Tom. "Cataloguing the Austin Clarke Library." *Poetry Ireland Review* 22, 23 (Summer 1988): 157–58.

Lyne, Gerard. "Austin Clarke—A Bibliography." *Irish University Review* 4.1 (Spring 1974): 137–55.

Mikhail, Edward. *A Research Guide to Modern Irish Dramatists.* Troy, N.Y.: Whitston, 1979.

Salem, James M. *A Guide to Critical Reviews: Part III: Foreign Drama, 1909–1977.* 2d ed. Metuchen, N.J.: Scarecrow, 1979.

Padraic Colum

(1881–1972)

KAY S. DIVINEY

Padraic Colum is known primarily for his contribution to the development of realistic Irish peasant plays, in *Broken Soil* (1903), *The Land* (1905), and *Thomas Muskerry* (1910). Many critics, however, feel that Colum's departure from this genre in later years was unsuccessful and that the promise of these early plays remained unfulfilled.

Padraic Colum was born on 8 December 1881 in the Longford County workhouse. When his father, Patrick Collumb, the workhouse master, lost his job and went to America to seek work, Colum's mother, Susan McCormack Collumb, moved the family to her mother's home in County Cavan. The family was eventually reunited in Sandy Cove, near Dublin, where Colum was able to attend the Glasthule national school. In subsequent visits to the country, Colum confirmed his commitment to the people of the Irish countryside.

Colum began work at the Irish Railway Clearing House, Dublin, at age seventeen, becoming associated with Cumann na nGaedeal, the Fays' National Theatre Society, and the Gaelic League. His early poems attracted the patronage of George Russell (AE) and W. B. Yeats. As a founding member of the Irish National Theatre Society, he submitted himself to a dramatic apprenticeship that bore fruit in the production of *Broken Soil.*

Broken Soil aroused interest because its author was a Roman Catholic rooted in the country who could speak with authority and sympathy (but not necessarily flattery) for the Irish peasant. It was followed by *The Land* and *Thomas Muskerry*, while Colum revised *Broken Soil* as *The Fiddler's House* in 1907. Colum himself by then had broken his association with the Abbey Theatre, joining the 1906 secession when the original communitarian Theatre Society was superseded by an arrangement that left artistic control with Yeats, Synge, and Lady Gregory. Colum helped to organize the Theatre of Ireland, becoming its honorary secretary.

In 1912, Colum married the writer and critic Mary Maguire; in 1914, the couple embarked on what was to be a peripatetic life, in which long-term residence in New York was interspersed with stays in Ireland, France, and Hawaii. Even before his emigration, Colum had begun work on a play with a Persian setting whose eventual production, at the Gate in 1931 as *Mogu of the Desert*, was sparsely attended and poorly received. The fanciful *Balloon*, published in 1929, was not produced until 1946, when it was tried out in the provinces (Ogunquit, Maine) for a Broadway staging that did not materialize.

Although Colum continued to revise his earlier plays over the decades and coauthored an adaptation of a German work, *Grasshopper*, which appeared at the Abbey in 1917, his most important literary work between 1911 and 1960 was not in drama but in poetry, fiction, and children's literature. In later years, Colum conducted classes in comparative literature with his wife at Columbia University.

After Mary's death in 1957, Colum embarked on an extraordinary literary regeneration in poetry, fiction, and drama. Three of his five experimental, Noh-inspired "plays for dancers," *Glendalough, Monasterboice,* and *Cloughoughter*, were produced in Dublin (*The Challengers*, 1964). Although Colum wrote them in his eighties, they combine the multiple perspectives of one who has survived many changes with a dramatic power that critics found absent from the works of his middle years.

At the time of his death at the age of ninety, Colum was still working on plays and poems. He died on 11 January 1972, in Enfield, Connecticut; seven days later he was buried in Ireland.

Selected Biographical Sources: Bowen [1, 2]; Denson [1]; Hogan and Burnham [1]; Miller; Sternlicht.

MAJOR PLAYS, PREMIERES, AND SIGNIFICANT REVIVALS: THEATRICAL RECEPTION

Broken Soil. 1903. Performed 3, 4, and 5 December at Molesworth Hall, Dublin (double-billed with W. B. Yeats' two one-act plays, *The Hour-Glass* and *A Pot of Broth*); produced in London on 6 March 1904 (double-billed with Yeats' *The King's Threshold* and *The Pot of Broth* and Synge's *In the Shadow of the Glen* and *Riders to the Sea*). Produced by the Irish National Theatre Society; directed by W. G. Fay.

Rewritten as *The Fiddler's House*. Opened 21 March 1907 at the Rotunda, Dublin (double-billed with Alice Milligan's *The Last Feast of the Fianna*). Produced by the Theatre of Ireland; directed by Fred Morrow. A New York production directed by Augustin Duncan, ca. 1910. Revival: Abbey Theatre, 19 August 1919 (directed by Lennox Robinson). Abbey Theatre, 22 February 1923.

Broken Soil, one of the first of the Irish National Theatre Society's peasant plays, focuses on the struggle of the aging fiddler Conn Hourican to resist the call of the road and of his art and the effects on his family when he fails to do so. The *Irish Times* ("Irish National Theatre Society") praised the dialogue and construction, noting Colum's youth and great promise. While "Spealadoir" (James H. Cousins) criticized its immaturity and complained that the author had not yet learned to express himself, Gogarty defended its sublimity and skill, setting the tone for future critics by noting not only the extent to which its plot and catastrophe arise "out of temperament, religion, and traditions peculiar to the Irish people" but also the gift for characterization that sets him apart from many of his contemporaries.

In its revision as *The Fiddler's House*, Colum put heavier emphasis on the conflict between the father and daughter and the feminist fear of male possessiveness (see Colum, Preface). *The Fiddler's House* was held to improve upon the original, while still retaining signs of an apprentice's labor (see "The Abbey Theatre"). Later critics tend to view the play *Broken Soil* as a milestone in the development of Irish dramatic realism; Sternlicht, for instance, lauds it as a "fine national drama" that depicts the Irish peasant "with mild comic irony, dignified sadness, and evocative beauty."

The Land. 1905. (A play in three acts). Opened 9 June at the Abbey Theatre, Dublin, for 4 performances. Produced in England, November–December 1905. Produced by the Irish National Theatre Society; directed by W. G. Fay. Produced in Gaelic as An Talamh (trans. "Torna"), 9 August 1906, by the Theatre of Ireland, at the Rotunda.

The Land's depiction of the domestic conflict within two peasant families at the culmination of the land war was favorably received by critics and general public alike. Reviewers were touched and excited by the depiction of character, the obvious closeness of the artist to the life of the soil, and its "luminous relation" to Irish life (see Rev. of *The Land*, *Freeman's Journal*), although one critic alleged immaturity and structural uncertainty ("The Land Hunger"). Holloway [1] found the play to be "seething with matter vital to the moment in Ireland" and admired the naturalness of both dialogue and acting, while the *Irish Times* (Rev. of *The Land*) praised it as the work of "an artist who loves the smell of ploughed earth and the falling rain." Malone thought it a great play, certainly Colum's best, and "equal to the greatest in the Irish Theatre." More recently, Maxwell focuses on Colum's development of a creditable dramatic voice for peasant characters touched by the modern world in *The Land*, noting a "delicacy of manoeuvre" that is "Colum's distinction as a 'realist' playwright."

Thomas Muskerry. 1910. (A play in three acts). Opened 5 May at the Abbey; Irish National Theatre Society, directed by Lennox Robinson. (Produced earlier in London.) Performed in London at the Royal Court Theatre on 11 June 1910. Revival: Abbey, 6 August 1936.

This unflinching depiction of the Lear-like descent of the master of the workhouse from prosperity and petty authority to penury and abject powerlessness provoked strong reactions from those who disliked its grim social realism. "Jacques" focused on a perceived insult to the Irish character and complained of the coarseness of the dialogue, the grossness of the realism, and the "unrelieved dullness" of the whole. Ella Young's praise of *Thomas Muskerry* as "a great play, an achievement" initiated a stormy exchange in *Sinn Fein*, whose reviewer "X" saddled the play with the pejorative coinage "Muskerryism." The *Times* ("Royal Court Theatre") found the London performance moving and effective, with "the vitality and vibration of a work of art." Later critics have seen the work as among Colum's finest. Maxwell admires the assurance of its "stark, suggestive idiom of its predecessors," while Hogan, Burnham, and Poteet judge it "probably [Colum's] lasting contribution to the modern Irish drama." Malone, on the other hand, while recognizing its sociological accuracy, thinks it "in almost every respect inferior to *The Land* and *The Fiddler's House*." Holloway [2], who found the 1936 revival "full of beauty and understanding," quotes Sean O'Faolain's opinion that the play was "the greatest in the Abbey's repertoire."

Grasshopper. 1917. (A play in four acts, with E. Washburn Freund). (Trans. of *Ein Fruhlingsopfer*, Hermann Keyserling, 1903.) First produced in New York, directed by Ben Iden Payne and produced by David Belasco. Opened in Dublin, at the Abbey Theatre on 24 October 1922, directed by Lennox Robinson.

Grasshopper (or *The Grasshopper*) concerns a young girl's compact with the Blessed Virgin to sacrifice herself in return for her foster mother's life. The beauty of the play's "uncanny atmosphere" and the acting of Eileen Crowe in the title role captivated some observers (see M. H. J. B.; "The Grasshopper"; Holloway [3]), but others criticized the play's construction, performance, foreign origins, and audience (for instance, "Jacques" [1] and "New Abbey Play"). Bowen [2] and Sternlicht largely ignore the play, believing the manuscript to have been lost in a fire at the Abbey. Recently, however, Hogan and Burnham [2] have located and reconsidered the play, whose value for them lies in showing the "realistic strengths of Padraic Colum in their last dramatic embodiment."

Mogu of the Desert. 1931. Opened 29 December at the Gate, Dublin, for 2 performances; directed by Micheál Mac Liammóir.

The performances of this play, which details the rise and fall of an abject desert wanderer who becomes for a time a high Persian official, were lavishly designed (see Fitz-Simon), sparsely attended, prone to onstage accidents, and little noted by critics. Holloway [2] thought that the separate scenes of the play did not sufficiently coalesce into a coherent drama, although some of the scenes were very beautiful. Burgess later traced, at length, Colum's revisions of, and ongoing commitment to, the play, whose conception Colum thought had been pirated in Knobloch's enormously popular *Kismet*. Bowen [2] thought it a weak play whose "hybrid form" makes it "an unsuccessful experiment in fairy tale drama."

Balloon. 1964. (A comedy in four acts). Opened 12 August in Ogunquit, Maine, for a two-week extended run. Produced by Mrs. Walter Hartwig's Manhattan Repertoire Company; directed by Michael Myerberg.

An anticipated Broadway run did not materialize, although a review ("Some Novelists") of the 1929 publication of *Balloon* thought that, if staged, it could "prove highly popular." Bowen [2] links the play's concern with success and nostalgia for vanished ways with *The Land* but finds the plot too thin and the echoes of Strindberg and Joyce unconvincing, sentiments that are echoed by Sternlicht.

ADDITIONAL PLAYS, ADAPTATIONS, AND PRODUCTIONS

Colum wrote several early one-act plays that were never produced: *The Children of Lir* (1899), *The Kingdom of the Young* (1902), *Eoghan's Wife* (1902), and *The Foleys* (1902); *Brian Boru*, written ca. 1899, was neither published nor performed. Also unproduced were a one-act reworking of *The Second Shepherds' Play* of the Wakefield Cycle, called *The Shepherd's Play* (1912); and *Swift's Pastoral* (1921).

Several other one-act plays received minor productions. *The Saxon Shillin'*, which W. G. Fay put into rehearsal but then discarded on the basis of weak construction, was produced on 15 May 1903 by the Daughters of Erin, at the Grocers Assistants' (Banba) Hall, Dublin. *The Miracle of the Corn* was rehearsed but not performed by the Irish National Theatre Society in 1904; on 22 May 1908, it received an all-but-inaudible production by the Theatre of Ireland (Fred Morrow; at the Abbey Theatre. See "The Theatre of Ireland.") An amateur cast gave two performances of *The Destruction of the Hostel*, one for St. Enda's School, Dublin (5 February 1910) and one at the Abbey Theatre (9 April 1910). *The Betrayal* was produced by B. Iden Payne's at the Theatre Royal, Manchester (7 April 1913).

Excerpts from *The Bear Keeper's Daughter* (1957; originally, *Theodora*) were performed at the Irish Literary Society in New York (Jennie Egan). Bowen [2] regards Colum's scenario for an animated puppet film of *Hansel and Gretel* (directed by John Paul, 1954) as showing Colum "at his lyrical, imaginative best." Other adaptations include *The Show Booth*, a translation with Vadim Uraneff of a one-act play by Alexander Blok (1921), and *Ulysses in Nighttown* (with Marjorie Barkentin; produced in New York, 1958).

Three of Colum's five poetic Noh plays have been produced. *Glendalough*, *Monasterboice*, and *Cloughoughter*, about Charles Stuart Parnell, James Joyce, and Roger Casement, respectively, played as a trilogy in Dublin under the name *The Challengers* (1964). *Moytura*, which focuses on Sir William Wilde, and *Kilmore*, about the Ulster leader Henry Joy McCracken, remain unproduced. A dramatization of a selection of Colum's poetry, *The Road round Ireland* (Basil Burwell), was staged in Norwalk, Connecticut, in 1967. As *Carricknabauna,* it played for 21 performances in New York (Larry Arrick, opened 30 March 1967).

ASSESSMENT OF COLUM'S CAREER

During his long and varied playwriting career, Padraic Colum experimented frequently with dramatic genres; yet most critics limit their conception of his dramatic art to his realistic depictions of the Irish peasantry alone. Colum's three plays of peasant realism (*Broken Soil*, *The Land*, and *Thomas Muskerry*) indeed make a neat and coherent grouping, whereas the wandering course of Colum's life and career tends to divide his later work by time, place, subject, and genre from the rest. While it is true that Colum achieved his greatest force and made his main contribution to Irish drama in his realistic portrayals of rural sociology, aspiration, and character, of which *Thomas Muskerry* remains the most powerful, Colum's dramatic experiments after his Abbey Theatre and Irish days should not be overlooked.

Colum's drama began as an expression and exploration of Irish nationalism and remained largely so even when his plays were not set or performed in Ireland. From the outset—that is, from the appearance of Colum's first one-act plays when he was in his late teens and early twenties—Colum used various forms and voices to dramatize his keen nationalism. He began not with realism but with Irish myth and historic lore: in *The Children of Lir* and later in *The Destruction of the Hostel*, Colum makes available a revivified Irish heroic model as a source of cultural pride for his contemporaries. On the other hand, several of Colum's one-act plays, such as *The Foleys*, the incendiary *The Saxon Shillin'*, and *The Betrayal*, mine an explicitly political vein. A mythologized religious version of heroic self-sacrifice is grafted onto the political concern of *The Foleys* and informs *The Miracle of the Corn* and *Grasshopper* as well.

Thus, the realistic nationalism of *Broken Soil, The Land,* and *Thomas Muskerry* is only one of several modes of dramatic inquiry that Colum explored during his first decade as a playwright. There can be no doubt, however, that he made his mark in the genre of peasant realism. Colum himself regarded *The Land, The Fiddler's House,* and *Thomas Muskerry* as explorations of three distinct character types, the small farmer, the artist, and the public official. Years after the fact, he suggested that he left this kind of drama—and the Irish theater—when he ran out of types that he wanted to "make articulate" (Preface). Colum's ability to realize character types convincingly as individuals impressed his early critics, like Holloway [1], who observed that "nothing could be more natural" than the dialogue in *The Land*. Furthermore, Colum's depiction of the peasantry had a reassuring credibility for an audience that was trying to come to terms with *In the Shadow of the Glen* and *Playboy of the Western World*. Although in later years it has certainly not been the case, Colum sometimes got the better of Synge in contemporary criticism, especially when critics like O'Donnell wanted to castigate the tawdry bent of Synge's imagination.

The realistic plays share other features, including, as Katz Clarke notes, their presentation of features and problems of rural life ranging from fair days to emigration. Weygandt notes the theme of the hardness and alienation of youth in these plays, as well as in *The Kingdom of the Young* and *The Foleys*. They represent only one of Colum's dramatic voices, however. If Colum abandoned it after *Thomas Muskerry*, it was, in part, to return to other dramatic impulses that had, for a time, remained dormant. The fabulous, mythical, and folkloric elements of Colum's largely overlooked and often scorned (see Sternlicht) plays *Mogu of the Desert* and *Balloon* were, to some extent, developments of the mythical, historical, and supernatural dimensions of some of his earliest plays.

In other ways, plays like *Mogu* and *Balloon* are indeed coherent with Colum's realistic plays. For one, in spite of the exotic settings and fantastical plots, in spite of their dozens of characters (and, as Burgess makes clear, dozens of revisions), the dramatic construction of these plays shows the hand of the author of *Thomas Muskerry*. Furthermore, *Mogu*'s exploration of worldly success and inevitable decline and *Balloon*'s consideration of the meaning of heroism grow naturally from Colum's earliest nationalist concerns. The persistent query of Caspar in *Balloon* ("Is a man born a hero, or does he become one through heroic action?") evidences Colum's continuing revision of nationalistic concepts of heroism, a topic that Loftus has shown to be at the center of much of Colum's work.

Colum's most thoroughgoing dramatic experiment, his five late Noh-influenced plays, is, among other things, a vast synthesis of his many dramatic interests and approaches. In them, Colum returns to Ireland, to Irish heroic materials, and to an intertwining of the mythological, political, and sociological manifestations of his earlier nationalism. While Sternlicht finds the plays' interweaving of many levels of time disconcerting and dramatically questionable, they allow Colum to explore the interactions between different levels of history, in each play centered on a single place and personage. Though multichronous, they are also, in a sense, synchronous, in that by plumbing many temporal strata, they string together those particular moments of the past that create, illumine, and heighten one critical moment, which—as in *The Land* and *The Fiddler's House*—is always a moment of decision. The open form allows Colum to avoid a reductive certainty in his presentation: the resonances between historically separate but thematically parallel situations do not always produce identical outcomes. For example, in *Glendalough*, Saint Kevin and Parnell face similar temptations but make different decisions, each with historically significant consequences. The Noh technique allows Colum to represent in full complexity Ireland's storied, layered, but not always coherent past.

Writing in 1913, Weygandt pronounced prematurely what many have taken to be the last word on Colum's dramatic career: "To be after ten years a dramatist of promise is to be essentially at a standstill." Colum did not achieve dramatic prominence after he left Ireland, the Abbey, and peasant realism, but many of his experiments with the genre bore fruit. While a passionate nationalist and an ardent believer in the power of the dramatic movement to intensify the emerging sense of Irish cultural identity, Colum—unlike many of his critics— clearly did not believe that the only good plays were Irish peasant plays. His achievement in this genre undoubtedly marks the pinnacle of his career, yet the Noh plays are a second, if less spectacular, peak. Their achievement has been obscured by Colum's age, his temporal and geographic remove from the Irish theater, his experimentalism—unexpected and unwelcome to some—and his enduring commitment to ideas of character and nation building that had fallen out of vogue by the time these plays came to be produced.

Maxwell suggests that Yeats was the first and most influential critic to misjudge Colum's art. Yeats' preference for the rhythms of Synge's Aran-like speech and Lady Gregory's Kiltartenese deafened him to the quieter music of Colum's dialogue and influenced many of those around him. Then, too, Colum lost his audience when he left Ireland in 1914. He was not able to recover it for his later Dublin productions, nor did he share with New York or London theatergoers the shared background and purpose of the Dublin audience, however quixotic and demanding, during the Revival. The many faces of Colum's nondramatic career also distract critics from his achievement in the theater. Colum created notable works of poetry and fiction throughout his life, and indeed his dramatic monologues and the storytelling elements of his folklore-based children's works and other fictions all bear the mark of his early immersion in the theater. But Colum himself told Charles Burgess that he was *"primarily* a man of the theatre" (italics added): "If I am not a playwright, I am nothing." His nontheatrical ventures should not obscure the tremendous contribution he made to the development of peasant drama or the value of his later plays. Being realistic rather than visionary (*Cathleen Ni Houlihan*), poetic (*Riders to the Sea*), or comic (*In the Shadow of the Glen, Spreading the News*), Colum's peasant plays deepened the contemporary conception of the nature of rural Irish people and problems and showed the beauty and pathos that existed in even humble and unextraordinary cottage scenes. They were also but one facet of an innovative dramatic talent and taste that produced inventive and appealing plays in several dramatic genres.

ARCHIVAL SOURCES

The Colum Collection of the Library at State University of New York at Binghamton houses an extensive collection of manuscripts, working notebooks, printed materials, letters, and photographs; this library also has a Mary and Padraic Colum Collection. Manuscripts may also be found in the Berg Collection of the New York Public Library and in the National Library of Ireland.

PRIMARY BIBLIOGRAPHY

Plays

Balloon. A Comedy in Four Acts. New York: Macmillan, 1929.
"The Betrayal." *Drama* 11 (Oct. 1920): 3–7.

The Children of Lir: A Poetic Tragedy in One Act. Weekly Independent (Dublin) (1899).
The Desert: A Play in Three Acts. Dublin: Devereux, 1912.
Eoghan's Wife, a Monologue for a Woman. United Irishman (20 Dec., 1902).
The Fiddler's House. Dublin: Maunsel, 1907.
The Foleys, a Play in One Act. United Irishman (10 May, 1902).
James Joyce's Ulysses in Nighttown. Dramatized and transposed by M. Barkentin, under the supervision of Padraic Colum. New York: Modern Library, 1958.
The Kingdom of the Young, a Play in One Act. United Irishman (14 June, 1902).
The Miracle of the Corn. In *Studies.* Tower Press Booklets, Series 2, No. 2. Dublin: Maunsel, 1907.
Mogu the Wanderer; or, The Desert. A Fantastic Comedy in Three Acts. Boston: Little, Brown, 1917.
Moytura: A Play for Dancers. Dublin: Dolmen, 1963.
The Saxon Shillin', a Play in One Act. United Irishman (15 Nov., 1902).
"Swift's Pastoral." *Dramatic Legends and Other Poems.* New York: Macmillan, 1922.

Anthologies

Selected Plays of Padraic Colum. (*The Land, The Betrayal, Glendalough, Monaster-boice.*) Ed. Sanford Sternlicht. Syracuse, N.Y.: Syracuse University Press, 1986.
Three Plays. (*The Fiddler's House, The Land, Thomas Muskerry.*) 1917; rpt., Dublin: Allen Figgis, 1963.

Essays and Articles on Drama and Theater

"Early Days of the Irish Theatre." *Dublin Magazine* 24 (Oct. 1949): 11–17; 25 (Jan. 1950): 18–25. (Rpt. *The Abbey Theatre: Interviews and Recollections.* Ed. E. H. Mikhail. Totowa, N.J.: Barnes and Noble. 59–71.)
"Ibsen and the National Drama." *Sinn Fein* (2 June 1906): 8.
"The Irish Literary Movement." *Forum* 53 (1915): 133–48.
Preface. *Three Plays.* Dublin: Allen Figgis, 1963.
"The Promise of Irish Letters." *Nation* 117 (1923): 396–97.

SECONDARY BIBLIOGRAPHY

"The Abbey Theatre." *Irish Times* (20 Aug. 1919).
Bowen, Zack. [1]. "Ninety Years in Retrospect: Excerpts from Interviews with Padraic Colum." *Journal of Irish Literature* 2.1 (Jan. 1973): 14–34.
———. [2]. *Padraic Colum: A Biographical-Critical Introduction.* Carbondale: Southern Illinois University Press, 1970.
Burgess, Charles. "A Playwright and His Work." *Journal of Irish Literature* 2.1 (Jan. 1973): 40–58.
Fitz-Simon, Christopher. *The Irish Theatre.* London: Thames and Hudson, 1983.
Gogarty, Oliver. "A Word on Criticism and *Broken Soil.*" *United Irishman* (Dec. 1903): 6.
"The Grasshopper." *Evening Telegraph* (Oct. 25 1922): 3.

Hogan, Robert. *After the Irish Renaissance: A Critical History of the Irish Drama since The Plough and the Stars*. Minneapolis: University of Minnesota Press, 1967.

Hogan, Robert, and Richard Burnham. [1]. *The Art of the Amateur, 1916–1920*. Dublin: Dolmen (Humanities Press), 1984.

———. [2]. *The Years of O'Casey, 1921–26: A Documentary History*. Gerrards Cross, Buckinghamshire: Colin Smythe, 1992; rpt., Newark: University of Delaware Press, 1992.

Hogan, Robert, Richard Burnham, and Daniel Poteet. *The Rise of the Realists, 1910–1915*. Dublin: Dolmen (Humanities Press), 1979.

Hogan, Robert, and James Kilroy [1]. *The Abbey Theatre: The Years of Synge, 1905–1909*. Dublin: Dolmen (Humanities Press), 1978.

———. [2]. *The Irish Literary Theatre 1899–1901*. Dublin: Dolmen (Humanities Press), 1975.

———. [3]. *Laying the Foundations 1902–1904*. Dublin: Dolmen (Humanities Press), 1976.

Holloway, Joseph. [1]. *Joseph Holloway's Abbey Theatre: A Selection from His Unpublished Journal, "Impressions of a Dublin Playgoer."* 1899–1926. Carbondale: Southern Illinois University Press, 1967.

———. [2]. *Joseph Holloway's Irish Theatre*. 1926–1944. 3 vols. Ed. Robert Hogan and Michael J. O'Neill. Dixon, Calif.: Proscenium, 1968.

———. [3]. "Impressions of a Dublin Playgoer." National Library of Ireland, Unpublished ms. 1873, Oct. 26 1922. Quoted in Hogan and Burnham [2].

Hunt, Hugh. *The Abbey: Ireland's National Theatre, 1904–1978*. New York: Columbia University Press, 1979.

"Irish National Theatre Society." *Irish Times* (4 Dec. 1903): 7.

"Jacques." [1]. *"Grasshopper." Irish Independent*, (25 Oct. 1922): 4.

———. [2]. "A Workhouse Drama." *Irish Independent* (6 May 1910).

Katz Clarke, Brenda. *The Emergence of the Irish Peasant Play at the Abbey Theatre*. Ann Arbor: UMI Research Press, 1982.

Review of *The Land. Freeman's Journal* (10 June 1905): 8.

Review of *The Land. Irish Times* (10 June 1905).

"The Land Hunger." *Daily Express* (10 June 1905): 8.

Loftus, R. *Nationalism in Modern Anglo-Irish Poetry*. Madison: University of Wisconsin Press, 1964.

M. H. J. B. "The Grasshopper." *Evening Herald* (25 Oct. 1992): 3.

Malone, Andrew. *The Irish Drama*. 1929. New York and London: Benjamin Blom, 1965.

Maxwell, D. E. S. *A Critical History of Modern Irish Drama, 1891–1980*. Cambridge: Cambridge University Press, 1984.

Miller, Liam. "Three Tributes Delivered at the Graveside." *Journal of Irish Literature* 2.1 (Jan. 1973): 12–13.

"New Abbey Play." *Irish Times* (25 Oct. 1922): 6.

O'Donnell, F. Hugh. *The Stage Irishman of the Pseudo-Celtic Drama*. London: John Long, 1904.

"Royal Court Theatre." *Times* (11 June 1910): 12.

"Some Novelists and Poets Troop into the Theatre." *New York Times* (28 July 1919): sec. 4 (*Book Review*): 8.

"Spealadoir" [James H. Cousins]. "The Plays at the Molesworth Hall." *United Irishman* (12 Dec. 1903): 6.

Sternlicht, Sanford. *Padraic Colum*. Boston: G. K. Hall, 1985.

"The Theatre of Ireland." *Freeman's Journal* (23 May 1908): 8.

Weygandt, Cornelius. *Irish Plays and Playwrights*. 1913; rpt. Westport, Conn.: Greenwood, 1979.

"X." "Muskerryism." *Sinn Fein* (16 July 1910): 3.

Young, Ella. " 'Thomas Muskerry' in Court." *Sinn Fein* (9 July 1910).

BIBLIOGRAPHIES

Bowen, Zack. *Annotated Catalogue and Bibliography for the Colum Collection of the Library at State University of New York at Binghamton*. Binghamton, N.Y.: SUNY Press, 1970.

Denson, Alan. [1]. "Padraic Colum: An Appreciation with a Check-list of His Publications." *Dublin Magazine* 6.1 (Spring 1967): 50–67.

———. [2]. "Padraic Colum: Factual Additions and Corrections to a Check-list of His Publications." *Dublin Magazine* 6.2 (Summer 1967): 83–85.

Teresa Deevy
(1894–1963)

EILEEN KEARNEY

Teresa Deevy was born into a prosperous Catholic merchant's family on the outskirts of Waterford near the river Suir on 19 January 1894. She was the youngest of thirteen children (nine girls and four boys), two of whom died in infancy. Her father, Edward Deevy, who ran a successful drapery business, died when Teresa was only three. Her mother, Mary Feehan Deevy, was a deeply religious woman who passed on her staunch Catholic beliefs to her children. A strong bond developed between Teresa (or Tessa, as she was known in her family) and her mother. In Teresa's early years, her mother encouraged her to invent stories; later, she enthusiastically supported her playwriting aspirations. In appreciation of this encouragement, Deevy dedicated her two major publications, *Katie Roche* in *Famous Plays of 1935–36*, and her volume of *Three Plays*, to her mother, who had died in 1930.

Although her education, medical needs, and playwriting brought her to spend extended periods of time in Cork, London, and Dublin, Deevy lived most of her life in "Landscape." She spent her last years in Waterford, where she died alone in the Maypark Nursing Home on 19 January 1963, just two days short of her sixty-ninth birthday. Neither she nor any of her seven sisters ever married or had children.

Teresa Deevy wrote twenty-five plays, six of which were given full-scale productions at the Abbey Theatre in Dublin between 1930 and 1936. Two of her plays were televised by the BBC, and many were broadcast on Radió Éireann. Due to her subject matter and style, Deevy was called "the Irish Chekhov," and she was considered by her contemporary critics to be somewhat of an experimental playwright. She became known for her vivid characterizations and her finely individualized dialogue; the latter accomplishment is quite impressive in light of the fact that in her adult years she was totally deaf.

Deevy grew up in rather luxurious surroundings in "Landscape," where, aided by their live-in nurse-servant, Mary Ryan, she played in the spacious gardens as a child and hosted dancing parties as a young adult. She received her early education while boarding at the Ursuline Convent in Waterford. There she was active in music (piano and voice) and sports, and her literary and writing interests led her to contribute many articles to the school magazine. She aspired to be an elementary school teacher, a dream that she unwittingly was preparing to relinquish.

Shortly after entering University College, Dublin, in 1913, Deevy experienced the first signs of what would soon permanently alter the course of her life. She developed Ménière's disease, a condition that results in the loss of hearing. She transferred to University College, Cork, where she continued her studies in liberal arts. By the time she graduated with a bachelor's degree in 1917, she was completely deaf.

After her university graduation, Teresa Deevy moved to London to seek treatment for Ménière's disease and to study lipreading. Although she grew to be quite a master of lipreading (in French as well as English!), she never had the patience to learn the advanced sign language that required only one hand; she could only awkwardly use both hands to spell out each word letter by letter. When lipreading failed her, she resorted to notes written on a pad.

In London Deevy's passion for the theater was ignited. While living in Blackheath with her sister Josie, a domestic science teacher, she went to the theater as often as possible, and whenever feasible, she read the script beforehand. She was especially impressed with Chekhov and Shaw, and influences of the former would later surface in her own plays. Inspired by the wealth of theater in London, she penned her first three plays under the pseudonym of D. V. Goode: *Practice and Precept, Let Us Live*, and *The Firstborn*. She returned to Ireland in 1919 and was determined to devote her energy to playwriting and searching for a theater in which to showcase her talents. At this time she also fought desperately against censorship and repeatedly visited prisoners in her work with Cumman na mBan, a nationwide, independent women's organization committed to working for the establishment of an Irish republic.

In 1928 Teresa Deevy submitted to the Abbey a one-act play, *Reserved Ground*, which was promptly rejected. Along with the rejection notice, however, she was informed that "the author showed power and promise" (see Fox). Deevy wrote another play and submitted it as well, only to be rejected again. She was then informed that one member of the Reading Committee was especially interested in helping her. While hoping it was Lady Gregory, for whom she had the highest respect, she was surprised to find out that Lennox Robinson had voiced this enthusiasm and faith in the new playwright. Eight years later Deevy would be quoted in an Abbey Theatre Green Room interview as crediting Lennox Robinson with having taught her everything she knew (see Holloway). Years later Teresa Deevy wrote a letter to the critic Michael J. O'Neill, Robinson's biographer, reminiscing about the playwriting advice Robinson had once given her: "Remember that everything must be said three times, once for the intelligent audience, twice for the unintelligent, and the third for the critics" (see O'Neill).

After Tomorrow was Deevy's next attempt, but the Abbey Theatre board found its one-act length too short for their purposes. Deevy remained extremely receptive to criticism, and she persisted in working to improve her writing. She finally saw her script *Reapers*, a three-act play, accepted and produced at the Abbey Theatre in March 1930. Thus began her successful, if short-lived, marriage with the Abbey. Following *Reapers*, the Abbey produced Deevy's next five plays: *A Disciple* (1931), *Temporal Powers* (1932), *The King of Spain's Daughter* (1935), *Katie Roche* (1936), and *The Wild Goose* (1936). *A Disciple*, *The King of Spain's Daughter*, *Katie Roche*, *The Wild Goose*, and *Strange Birth* were all published in various periodicals and anthologies during Deevy's lifetime.

With the success of her plays in the 1930s, Teresa Deevy moved from Waterford to Dublin to be in the center of theatrical activity. She and her sister Nell, who served as Teresa's interpreter until her death in 1954, shared a flat on Waterloo Road, not far from St. Stephen's Green. The contemporary Cork playwright, critic, and journalist Robert O'Donoghue recalls meeting Deevy at various times with Ria Mooney, the talented Abbey actor and director, in Bewley's on Grafton Street, which he considered to be "the Mecca of Irish artistic life at the time." Youthful artists and writers such as he were enthralled with James Joyce, living and breathing under the spell of *Ulysses*, and they brought a pervasive bohemian ambience to the social gatherings of the Dublin literati. According to O'Donoghue, however, Teresa Deevy had little contact with such a milieu: "She belonged to a world that was passing, a Chekhovian afterglow."

Deevy's association with the Abbey ended with the production of *The Wild Goose* in 1936. Repeating a dangerous pattern of mistakes in artistic judgment that they had made with O'Casey (*The Silver Tassie*, 1928), Denis Johnston (*The Old Lady Says "No!"*), and Paul Vincent Carroll (*The White Steed*, 1938), among others, the Abbey Theatre board rejected another script from someone whom they had fostered (or, in Johnston's case, might have fostered). Deeply hurt when the Abbey rejected one of her best plays, *Wife to James Whelan*, in 1942, Deevy turned away from the stage and started writing for radio; this excellent play was later produced on radio by both the BBC and Radió Éireann and received its first stage production in Madame D. Bannard Cogley's Studio Theatre in 1956. Although Deevy's works virtually disappeared from the Abbey repertoire after 1936, the Abbey's experimental Peacock Theatre did produce another of her plays, *Light Falling*, in 1948; it was obvious, however, that her heyday at the Abbey was over.

Deevy's Catholicism was deeply rooted, and while she had continually challenged Catholic traditions in her plays of the 1930s, her own faith remained unquestioned. In her later years especially, she attended daily mass and made many pilgrimages to Lourdes (where she volunteered her services) and to Italy in honor of Padre Pio. Her later plays, in fact, have strictly religious themes.

In her later years back at "Landscape," Deevy wrote some children's stories and coauthored with Helen Staunton and Patricia Lynch a children's book called *Lisheen*. During this time, she also published several essays, short stories, and radio scripts in the *Irish Writing* magazine. In 1956, seven years before her death, Deevy was elected to the Irish Academy of Letters, a distinguished national literary honor.

Selected Biographical Sources: Dunne [1, 2]; Fox; O'Donoghue; O'Neill.

MAJOR PLAYS, PREMIERES, AND SIGNIFICANT REVIVALS: THEATRICAL RECEPTION

Six of Teresa Deevy's twenty-five plays were given major productions at the Abbey Theatre in Dublin between 1930 and 1936. Although she had several other plays produced either on stage or on television, and many scripts produced on radio, the six Abbey productions are addressed here.

Reapers. 1930. (a three-act play). Opened 18 March and ran through 23 March 1930. Lennox Robinson directed it, and the cast featured Denis O'Dea, Shelah Richards, F. J. McCormick, and Eileen Crowe. It shared the bill with Yeats' nationalistic one-act play, *Cathleen Ni Houlihan.*

In *Reapers* Deevy introduces a new avenue to Irish drama. The play, which presents Irish middle-class life in a provincial town, deals with a national theme as well as with business and family troubles; it was also written by a woman who hailed from such a setting and background.

Critical response to *Reapers* was generally favorable. Yeats wrote to Lady Gregory that this play showed great promise and was full of interesting material (see Fox). Malone wrote that while the most significant dramatic and theatrical event of the year was the opening of the Gate Theatre, "Miss T. Deevy" was "a lady who promises well" and was "probably the new dramatist from whom the most may be expected in the future."

From the available reviews, it is clear that the majority of Deevy's critics concur on three points about *Reapers*: Deevy demonstrates a gift for finely individualized characterizations ("*The Reapers*: Work of New Woman Dramatist") and "fresh, vivid, and subtle dialogue" ("Waterford Lady's First Play"), her creation of plot leaves much to be desired ("Drama Notes"), and she shows great promise for future plays. Many reviewers note Deevy's fine handling of dialogue and subtext and comment on the degree of Chekhovian reticence present in the conversations in *Reapers*, similar to that of *The Cherry Orchard* or *The Three Sisters* (see "Waterford Lady's First Play").

A Disciple. 1931. Opened 24 August at the Abbey. A one-act comedy. Directed by Lennox Robinson and starring the "baby of the Abbey," Kitty Curling.

A Disciple was formidably sandwiched in between Yeats' *Cathleen Ni Hou-*

lihan and Shaw's three-act play in blank verse, *The Admirable Bashville, or Constancy Unrewarded.* At a later date, *A Disciple* was retitled *In Search of Valour* and as such was broadcast on the radio, as well as televised in London by the BBC by Deevy's contemporary playwright/director Denis Johnston.

Literary critics praised *A Disciple*, which introduces what Dunne [1] identifies as the typical Deevy theme: the contradiction between desire and the impossibility of fulfillment. Centered around Ellie Irwin, a young domestic servant girl who romanticizes ways to escape her boring lot in life, the play presents a less than ideal view of marriage; Deevy came to instill this view in most of her female characters. Reminiscent of the peasants in Synge's *The Playboy of the Western World*, Riley observes that Ellie has the ability to make a glorious story out of a dirty deed, but only when it is reported secondhand; when she confronts the reality of these fantasies, she can see only the great gap between the two. Deevy's comic flair is best exemplified, as Jordan [1] points out, in this "preposterous gap between Ellie's illusions and their subjects."

Theater critics who reviewed the Abbey performance were less enthusiastic. Although they collectively praise her for her strong characterizations and acknowledge that "Miss Deevy has made an appreciable advance in her craft" ("A Dramatist of Hurry"), they voice similar complaints about the cluttered plot (see Hayes).

Temporal Powers. 1932. Opened at the Abbey on 12 September. It shared the bill with a revival of *Spreading the News* by Lady Gregory. Lennox Robinson directed, and the cast featured Eileen Crowe, F. J. McCormick, Arthur Shields, and Maureen Delaney.

With *Temporal Powers*, Teresa Deevy swept the theatergoing public away. Because of a dearth of good scripts, the Abbey Theatre announced "that it will produce one new play, and award a prize of fifty guineas for the best play submitted during the absence of the company on its American tour in the autumn." Under the pen name of E. Blair, Deevy submitted *Temporal Powers* to this contest. The judges, among whom was Brinsley MacNamara, found the play to be "strikingly original and of fine literary quality" ("Abbey Theatre Play Competition") and ended up awarding the prize to both *Temporal Powers* and Paul Vincent Carroll's *Things That Are Caesar's.*

The Abbey Theatre production of *Temporal Powers* was a critical success. Theater critics throughout the metropolitan Dublin area shared the enthusiasm of novelist and short story writer Frank O'Connor. Several critics echo the play competition judges in praising Deevy for the script's originality (see "At the Abbey"; "First Production"; "Irish Theatre Notes"), and while some feel the plot is too loosely knit and in need of pruning, most of the reviewers single out Deevy's gift for characterization, which is "at times brilliant" ("Irish Theatre Notes"). One critic ("At the Abbey") compliments Deevy for her "happy knack . . . of racy dialogue and a sense of irony and shrewd mother wit." Another reviewer (''New Abbey Theatre Play'') claims that *Temporal Powers* is ''easily the best work that Miss Deevy has yet done for the theatre.''

Temporal Powers deals with poverty and its effect on marriage in a moving yet unsentimental way. The play demands a reflective audience, as it presents the viewer or reader with an ethical debate about the patriarchal privileges of men and the accompanying submissiveness of women.

The King of Spain's Daughter. 1935. One-act play. Directed by Fred Johnson. The production starred Ria Mooney, Ann Clery, J. Winter, John Stephenson, and the promising young Cyril Cusack. It shared the bill with a revival of *Wrack*, a full-length peasant drama by the Donegal naturalist, Peadar O'Donnell. Revived at the Abbey on 27 July 1936, featuring much of the same cast.

The critics praised the play and production. The *Irish Times* (''The Dublin Theatres'') reports on the newest work by the ''author of a couple of unusually interesting plays'': ''[T]he entertainment was excellent. . . . without being in any way pretentious.'' O Meadhra commends the ''quiet mastery'' with which Ria Mooney played the title role and adds, ''This character study by Teresa Deevy in the Schnitzler or Molnar mode is worthy of more praise than it has received.'' Twenty-one years later Fox writes, ''Abbey enthusiasts will remember her *King of Spain's Daughter* for its poetry, its power of imagination and its glow of romance.''

On a literary note, one reviewer (''Books of the Week'') praises the play as a ''splendid example of Deevy's gift for character study and natural dialogue.'' *The King of Spain's Daughter* centers around its fickle, flighty young protagonist, Annie Kinsella, who is a first cousin of Ellie Irwin and the literary precursor of Katie Roche. Bored and frustrated with her dull, humble surroundings, Annie makes herself the center of colorful, fantastic stories; like so many of Deevy's heroines, Annie lives in her dreams. In no other play does Teresa Deevy make such a blatant statement about marriage and its mistakenly assumed panacean qualities.

Katie Roche. 1936. Hugh Hunt directed the premiere production, which opened at the Abbey on 16 March. Eileen Crowe played the title role.

The Abbey production of *Katie Roche* was hailed by the critics. One reviewer (''*Katie Roche* at the Abbey'') described it as ''well worth seeing,'' commending it for its originality and its admirable acting. Other critics repeatedly praised Deevy's gift for subtext, which was most noticeable in performance.

After opening in 1936, *Katie Roche* enjoyed several Abbey revivals, all of which were deemed at least mildly successful by the critics. In 1938 the play was performed on tour by the Abbey Players in London, Cambridge, and New York (among other American cities), where leading critic George Jean Nathan praised it highly (see Fox). It was then chosen to be part of the 1938 Abbey Festival of Plays, in which Deevy shared the program with such dramatists as Sean O'Casey, George Bernard Shaw, Frank O'Connor, George Shiels, Brinsley

MacNamara, Micheál Mac Liammóir, Paul Vincent Carroll, T. C. Murray, Lennox Robinson, and Denis Johnston. In 1949 *Katie Roche* was again revived for an eleven-week run. Two years after the tragic fire that destroyed the old Abbey in 1951, the play was again performed in 1953 at the Queen's Theatre in Dublin, the Abbey's temporary home from 1951 to 1966, where Maire Ni Dhomhnaill played Katie. Most recently, it was presented at the Abbey in 1975, twelve years after Teresa Deevy's death, under the direction of Joe Dowling, with Jeananne Crowley performing the title role. A radio version of the play was also broadcast in Sweden.

The prolific and versatile critic and playwright St. John Ervine delivered laudatory bouquets to Deevy, calling *Katie Roche* a "most remarkable" play and noting that Deevy's "dialogue . . . is uncommonly apt to the person who speaks it. . . . Miss Deevy may be a genius." For Teresa Deevy herself, such praise was particularly important, for her copy of Ervine's work, *How to Write a Play*, was one of her most treasured books and bears many marginal notes made by her.

Katie Roche presents Teresa Deevy's most thoroughly developed character study. The three-act play is essentially a multilayered, dramatic portrait of a vibrant, fiercely independent young woman who allows her romantic passions to rule her heart, while her social conditioning rules her head. Like *The King of Spain's Daughter*, *Katie Roche* presents a less than ideal picture of marriage; but while the former addresses premarital blues, the latter deals with postmarital blues.

The Wild Goose. 1936. Originally entitled *Parts Set*. Opened at the Abbey on 9 November, directed by Hugh Hunt. Fred Johnson and Ria Mooney played the leading roles. Although the Abbey never revived *The Wild Goose*, Radió Éireann broadcast a cut version of the play in the mid-1960s; this radio abridgement condensed the three-act play into a 45–minute version.

For the first time in Teresa Deevy's playwriting career, the critics (see "*The Wild Goose*") hailed her for the "brilliant" and "superb" construction evidenced in *The Wild Goose*. In a literary review of Deevy's *Three Plays*, Robinson [1] praises Deevy for "keeping herself directly in her line, never swerving for a moment from her individuality, [keeping] her integrity, [owing] nothing to anyone but herself." Theater critic Sean O Meadhra [2] focused more on the Abbey's production, particularly the marked improvement in its technical aspects. With all of the exciting technical innovations being presented concurrently by the newly established Gate Theatre, the Abbey evidently wished to raise its technical standards.

In light of the thematic and characterization patterns that Deevy had established by this time, *The Wild Goose* was a diversion. Set in 1692 after the Treaty of Limerick, this was Deevy's only attempt at a play with a blatantly political theme; it is also the farthest removed from the contemporary time frame that she ever got. Unlike her previous plays, this one has a male as its central character.

ASSESSMENT OF DEEVY'S CAREER

When the Abbey Theatre rejected Sean O'Casey's expressionistic experiment, *The Silver Tassie*, in 1928, the state of Ireland's subsidized national theater began to fade slowly in artistic standards and enthusiasm. O'Casey's departure from the Abbey's hallowed hall marked the end of an extensive first chapter in the history of the Abbey, in which William Butler Yeats, Lady Augusta Gregory, John Millington Synge, and O'Casey had all shared the limelight while establishing "the Abbey tradition." In the decade that followed, however, new voices were heard, and new playwrights surfaced in a quiet spirit of artistic rebellion.

Teresa Deevy can be considered the most significant and interesting new playwright at this time. She was a remarkable woman who holds a place second only to Lady Gregory in the gallery of Irish women dramatists. Although she was certainly recognized by her contemporaries during her heyday in the 1930s, her name rarely appears now in books about the Abbey Theatre. After Deevy's death in 1963, contemporary Waterford playwright James Cheasty wrote a moving obituary, reporting that of all Irish women dramatists whose plays have been produced "in the Abbey Theatre, Teresa Deevy was, with the exception of Lady Gregory, the most memorable." In her own silent sphere of the written word, Teresa Deevy journeyed on a highly individual artistic and spiritual pilgrimage. While many Irish authors shared those sentiments of Joyce's Stephen Dedalus, that "the shortest way to Tara was *via* Holyhead," Deevy spent the majority of her life in her native Ireland, with which she associated a deep and reverent sense of home.

Post-Treaty Ireland was, as Hunt points out, "not just a nation once again, it was a very different nation from the one about which the founders of the Abbey had written their plays." Indeed, in the 1920s and 1930s, the Abbey theatrical scene had changed utterly from Yeats' initial design for it; the center did not hold, nor did the theatergoing public want it to hold.

The afterglow of the Celtic Twilight was a thing of the past, and the new generation of Irish writers who emerged from the Troubles of 1916 to 1922 was influenced more by the modern world than by the past of Ireland. The plays of this period reflect this new Irish consciousness in that the contemporary dramatists reflected the social and political changes taking place all over the country.

The Abbey's prevalent issue became a concern for what the audience wanted and what the new dramatists might do toward broadening the scope and direction of the Irish drama. Although the realistic—sometimes comic, sometimes tragic—but always well-made model still prevailed, Abbey dramatists began presenting many new sides of Irish life on the stage. The thematic resources of the Irish city and countryside now seemed inexhaustible, and, due to the Abbey's continued popularity, for the first time in a long time Irish-born playwrights tended to remain in Ireland and write primarily for an Irish audience. Each county or region produced its own dramatist; Waterford's shining example was Teresa Deevy. In her brief but successful association with the Abbey, she brought a new voice to the evolution of modern Irish drama. When her association with it involuntarily ended in 1942, one would suspect that she shared her colleague O'Casey's sentiments that the terrible beauty was now more terrible and less beautiful.

Through the medium of drama, Deevy defines the extremely limited field of women's choices in Catholic Ireland of the early twentieth century. In her brilliant portraits of romantic, high-strung, individualistic young women in rural Ireland, she "catches them in flight at a moment in life when they put aside their youthful illusions and accept a greyer but more plausible adult reality" (Callaghan). This compromise is reached, however, only after each heroine fights the good fight. This theme, which is repeatedly woven throughout all of Deevy's plays, clearly reflects the social values prevalent in Catholic Ireland in the 1920s and 1930s and, in particular, those that dictated socially acceptable modes of behavior for middle-class women. Deevy especially points to women's options (or lack thereof) concerning marriage and childbearing. Yet in spite of her conservative Catholic semblance of Victorian respectability, Deevy was, relatively speaking, radical in her artistic endeavors. Her admittedly reserved feminist ideals quietly permeate her work. Perhaps she created her characters as vicarious vehicles of her own desire to challenge those values.

People who knew Teresa Deevy claim that she seldom complained of her deafness. It is intriguing that she progressed as far as she did in an art form that begins with written verbal expression and manifests itself in a theatrical production where the sounds of the dialogue interspersed with silences are at the very core of the performance. Deevy's colleagues and family members recall her immense appreciation of the gift of eyesight, for with her eyes Teresa Deevy studied people. She was interested in every minute detail about them, and through lipreading or with the assistance of her sister Nell, she listened intently to people's thoughts about Dublin's theatrical and cultural happenings. As Dunne [2] speculates, her impairment no doubt opened up new dimensions to her as a writer. She is also universally remembered by those who knew her for her kindness, gentleness, generosity, unworldliness, and religious faith.

As can be evidenced in her life and work, Teresa Deevy admired independence, especially in women. This may partially explain her choice to remain single all her life; it certainly explains the gallery of female dramatic characters she created. In a letter to Dunne (rpt. in Dunne [2]), Kyle Deevy, Teresa's nephew, recalls his aunt's attitude: "Anyone, especially a young girl, who struck out on her own and made good was a hero to her."

Despite her independence, which could be evidenced by all her travels alone, Teresa Deevy cannot be considered a rebel. Perhaps her deafness provided a sense of intuitive detachment, by which she further developed her already keen perception of people. It seems, in spite of her intense interest in people, that she was an onlooker, a perceiver; while not in the least bit uninvolved, she was involved most definitely from a writer's distance, and that distance opens up her work to interpretive ambiguity.

In a program note for the Abbey's 1975 revival of *Katie Roche*, Denis Johnston reflects on the accomplishments of his colleague's works, "the best of which are of young girls all drawn with humour and understanding, in which she clearly embodied much of her own ever-youthful lust for living and undefeatable romanticism." Teresa Deevy's romantic joie de vivre did indeed make its mark on the Abbey Theatre in the 1930s, and it is time she is placed in that decade's spotlight, where she belongs.

ARCHIVAL SOURCES

Teresa Deevy Estate Papers, "Landscape," Waterford, Ireland. Under the proprietorship of Teresa Deevy's nephew, Jack Deevy, and his wife, Noeleen Deevy, these papers include correspondence with critics, publishers, Abbey Theatre personnel, and literary figures of the day, as well as theater programs and newspaper reviews of Deevy's plays. Also present are numerous Deevy manuscripts, including many of the following unpublished (but not necessarily unproduced) stage or radio plays: *Light Falling, One Look and What It Led To, In the Cellar of My Friend, Dignity, Within a Marble City, Polinka, The Finding of the Ball, Holiday House, Wife to James Whelan, Supreme Dominion, Going Beyond Alma's Glory, MacConglinne, A Minute's Wait, After Tomorrow, Possession* (a ballet), *Concerning Meagher, or, How Did He Die*, and *Reserved Ground*. There are also manuscripts of three early plays that Deevy presumably wrote under the pseudonym of D. V. Goode: *Practice and Precept, Let Us Live*, and *The Firstborn*. Finally, the papers also include religious memorabilia, most likely collected later in Teresa Deevy's life.

NOTE

Parts of this essay were previously published in *The Theatre Annual* in Kearney's "Teresa Deevey: Ireland's Forgotten Second Lady of the Abbey Theatre," vol. 40 (1985): 77–90. These parts are reprinted with the editors' permission.

PRIMARY BIBLIOGRAPHY

Plays

A Disciple. In *Dublin Magazine* 1. 12 (1937).
Katie Roche. In *Famous Plays of 1935–36*. London: Victor Gollancz, 1936.
The King of Spain's Daughter. *Theatre Arts* (June 1935).

Temporal Powers. In *The Journal of Irish Literature* (A Teresa Deevy Number) 14 (May 1985): 18–75. Ed. Robert Hogan, Gordon Henderson, and Kathleen Danaher.

Anthologies

The King of Spain's Daughter and Other One-Act Plays. (Includes *The King of Spain's Daughter, In Search of Valour,* and *Strange Birth.*) Dublin: New Frontiers, 1947.
Three Plays. (Includes *Katie Roche, The King of Spain's Daughter,* and *The Wild Goose.*) London: Macmillan, 1939.

SECONDARY BIBLIOGRAPHY

"Abbey Theatre Play Competition: The Judges' Report." *Daily Express* (1931).
"Abbey Theatre: *Temporal Powers.*" *Irish Times* (13 Sept. 1932).
"At the Abbey." *Republic* (17 Sept. 1932).
Blythe, Ernest. *The Abbey Theatre.* Dublin: National Theatre Society, 1964.
"Books of the Week: The Irish Theatre, Some Notable Publications." *Irish Statesman* (1939):6.
Brady, Anne M., and Brian Cleeve, eds. *A Biographical Dictionary of Irish Writers.* Gigginstown: Lilliput, 1985.
Caherty, Therese, ed. *More Missing Pieces: Her Story of Irish Women.* Dublin: Attic, 1985.
Callaghan, Mary Rose. "Teresa Deevy." *Dictionary of Irish Literature.* Ed. Robert Hogan. Westport, Conn.: Greenwood, 1979. 192.
Cheasty, James. "Teresa Deevy: An Appreciation." *Irish Independent* (24 Jan. 1963).
Cleeve, Brian. *Dictionary of Irish Writers.* Cork: Mercier, 1967.
Doyle, Paul. *Paul Vincent Carroll.* Lewisburg, Pa.: Bucknell University Press, 1971.
"Drama Notes: *The Reapers.*" *Irish Statesman* (1930).
"A Dramatist of Hurry: First Production of *A Disciple* at the Abbey." *Irish Statesman* (25 Aug. 1931).
"The Dublin Theatres: New Play at the Abbey, *The King of Spain's Daughter.*" *Irish Times* (30 Apr. 1935).
Dunne, Sean. [1]. "Rediscovering Teresa Deevy." *Cork Examiner* (20 Mar. 1984): 10.
————. [2]. "Teresa Deevy: An Introduction." *Journal of Irish Literature* 14 (May 1985): 3–16.
Ellis-Fermor, Una. *The Irish Dramatic Movement.* 2d ed. London: Methuen, 1954.
Ervine, St. John. "At the Play: More Famous Plays." *Observer* (5 July 1936).
Fallis, Richard. *The Irish Renaissance.* Syracuse, N.Y.: Syracuse University Press, 1977.
Fay, Gerard. *The Abbey Theatre, Cradle of Genius.* Dublin: Clonmore, 1958.
"First Production of *Temporal Powers* at the Abbey: Original Prize Play." *Telegraph* (13 Sept. 1932).
Fitz-Simon, Christopher. *The Irish Theatre.* London: Thames, 1983.
Fox, Richard Michael. "From My Album: Teresa Deevy." *Irish Statesman* (Nov. 1956).
Hayes, J. J. "A Revival and Two New Ones." *The New York Times Theater Reviews 1920–1970.* Vol. 3, 1930–1934. New York: New York Times and Arno Press, 1971.

Hoehn, Matthew, ed. *Catholic Authors: Contemporary Biographical Sketches*. Newark: St. Mary's, 1952.

Hogan, Robert [1]. *After the Irish Renaissance*. Minneapolis: University of Minnesota Press, 1967.

———. [2]. *"Since O'Casey" and Other Essays on Irish Drama*. Totowa, N.J.: Barnes, 1983.

Holloway, Joseph. "Interview with Author." *Irish Times* (14 Mar. 1936).

Hunt, Hugh. *The Abbey: Ireland's National Theatre, 1904–1979*. Dublin: Gill, 1979.

"Irish Theatre Notes: Prize Play with Originality, *Temporal Powers* Enthusiasm, No Drawing-Rooms." *Irish Statesman* (Sept. 1932).

Johnston, Denis. *Abbey Theatre Program Notes* (2 June 1975).

Jordan, John. [1]. "Teresa Deevy: An Introduction." *University Review* (Spring 1956): 13–26.

———. [2]. "Mortal Longings." *Hibernia Review* (1973).

"*Katie Roche* at the Abbey." *Leader* (21 Mar. 1936).

Kavanagh, Peter. *The Story of the Abbey Theatre*. New York: Devin-Adair, 1950.

Kearney, Eileen [1]. "The Plays of Teresa Deevy: A Checklist." *Journal of Irish Literature* 14 (May 1985): 16–17.

———. [2]. "Teresa Deevy: Ireland's Forgotten Second Lady of the Abbey Theatre." *Theatre Annual* 40 (1985): 77–90.

Lane, Temple. "The Dramatic Art of Teresa Deevy." *Dublin Magazine* 21 (1946): 35–42.

Mac Liammóir, Micheál. *Theatre in Ireland*. Dublin: Three Candles, 1964.

MacNamara, Brinsley. *Abbey Plays, 1899–1948*. Dublin: Three Candles, 1950.

Malone, Andrew E. "The Irish Theatre in 1930." *Dublin Magazine* (Apr.–June 1931): 1–11.

Maxwell, D. E. S. *A Critical History of Modern Irish Drama, 1891–1980*. Cambridge: Cambridge University Press, 1984.

Monks, Julia. "The People I Meet: Lip-Reading Dramatist Acted as Dialogue Expert to German Playwright." *Irish Press* (29 Nov. 1957).

"New Abbey Theatre Play: *Temporal Powers*." *Manchester Guardian* (15 Sept. 1932).

"Obituary: Teresa Deevy." *Irish Times* (21 Jan. 1963): 7.

O'Connor, Frank. *A Short History of Irish Literature: A Backward Look*. New York: Capricorn, 1968.

O'Donoghue, Robert. "Peripheral Memories." *Cork Examiner* (20 Mar. 1984): 10.

Ó hAodha, Micheál. *Theatre in Ireland*. Oxford: Blackwell, 1974.

O Meadhra, Sean. [1]. "Murder in the Abbey." *Ireland To-day* (Sept. 1936): 63.

———. [2]. "Wild Geese—And Tame." *Ireland To-day* (Dec. 1936): 66.

O'Neill, Michael J. *Lennox Robinson*. New York: Grosset, 1964.

"*The Reapers*: First Production at the Abbey Theatre." *Irish Times* (21 Mar. 1930).

"*The Reapers*: Work of New Woman Dramatist at the Abbey." *Evening Herald* (19 Mar. 1930).

Riley, J. D. "On Teresa Deevy's Plays." *Irish Writing* 32 (Autumn 1955): 30–36.

Robinson, Lennox. [1]. Book review of Teresa Deevy's *Three Plays*. *Dublin Magazine* (June 1940).

———. [2]. *Ireland's Abbey Theatre: A History 1899–1951*. London: Sidgwick, 1951.

———. [3]. *The Irish Theatre; Lectures delivered during the Abbey Theatre Festival held in Dublin in August 1938.* New York: Haskell House, 1971 (reprint of work first published in 1939).

————. [4]. *The Irish Theatre.* London: Macmillan, 1939.

Sahal, N. *Sixty Years of Realistic Irish Drama (1900–1960).* Bombay: Macmillan, 1971.

"Studio Theatre Club Success: Fine Production of New Play by Teresa Deevy." *Irish Independent* (5 Oct. 1956).

"Sunday Review." *Irish Times* (20 Jan. 1963): 3.

"Teresa Deevy's New Play." *Evening Mail* (5 Oct. 1956).

"Waterford Lady's First Play: A Night at the Abbey Theatre." *Waterford News* (21 Mar. 1930).

"*The Wild Goose*: New Play by Miss Deevy at the Abbey Theatre." *Irish Statesman* (10 Nov. 1936).

Yeats, William Butler. *The Autobiography of William Butler Yeats.* New York: Collier, 1965.

Anne Devlin

(19?–)

LISA M. ANDERSON

Anne Devlin is probably best known for two of her scripts, her play script *Ourselves Alone* and her television script *Naming the Names*. Her script credits continue to increase as her name becomes better known both in Britain and in the United States. She has two single-author plays to her name, as well as one collaborative script, which she wrote with David Edgar and Stephen Bill, and she has also written five television scripts.

Devlin was born to a Catholic family in Belfast, Northern Ireland, and from her experiences there she draws the majority of her materials for her play and television scripts. She lived briefly in Andersontown, the setting of *Ourselves Alone*, before leaving Northern Ireland for England. She has lived in Birmingham since 1984.

Devlin's writing debut came in 1982, when she wrote *A Woman Calling* for BBC-2 Television. Soon after, she wrote *Venus de Milo Instead* and *The Long March*, her first acclaimed script based on the Troubles in Northern Ireland. Her stage debut was in 1985, when *Ourselves Alone* premiered in Liverpool at the Liverpool Playhouse Studio. An English translation of Sinn Fein, the name of the political wing of the Irish Republican Army (IRA), *Ourselves Alone* opened in October 1985 and garnered sufficient positive critical response to move the play to the Royal Court Theatre Upstairs in London in November of that year. It was produced in the United States in 1987 at the Kreeger Theatre/Arena Stage in Washington, D.C. It tells the story of three women, Frieda, Josie, and Donna, surviving in the Catholic Andersontown, a West Belfast suburb. Devlin won several awards for her script, among them the Susan Smith Blackburn Prize and the George Devine Award, both in 1985.

In the intervening years between *Ourselves Alone* and her next stage work, the collaborative *Heartlanders*, Devlin worked primarily on television and film scripts. Following the path begun with her earlier scripts, she focused on plots that grew out of her experiences in Belfast. In 1987, her most acclaimed television script, *Naming the Names*, debuted on BBC television. Set in Belfast, the script centers on a young woman who is involved with the IRA. It has been shown on Canadian television and on public television in the United States. One of her scripts has not been focused on Northern Ireland; her script for the BBC version of D. H. Lawrence's *The Rainbow* departs from her usual subject matter.

Heartlanders, Devlin's collaborative script, has one character from Belfast and is a community play conceived for Birmingham's centenary. Her most recent effort, *After Easter*, has not had as much favorable press, although Devlin returns to her signature themes in this new play.

Selected Biographical Source: Lojek.

MAJOR PLAYS, PREMIERES, AND SIGNIFICANT REVIVALS: THEATRICAL RECEPTION

Ourselves Alone. 1985. Opened 24 October at the Liverpool Playhouse Studio. Coproduced at the Royal Court Theatre Upstairs, London, where it opened on 20 November 1985. Directed by Simon Curtis.

Acclaimed by critics in England and the United States. Most critical work on Devlin centers on this play. Three women, Frieda, Josie, and Donna, who are sisters (one by marriage), must deal with the pressures of living their lives with men active in the IRA. Josie herself is also involved for a time. The women express their views of Republicanism and the way that it affects their lives and the lives of the men around them (Campbell), and, some critics argue, the play presents a feminist perspective on women dealing with what amounts to a wartime situation (Lojek, Lustig). Of course, the real presence of terrorist acts has also been examined (Greenhalgh).

Heartlanders. (with Stephen Bill and David Edgar). 1989. Opened 19 October at the Birmingham Repertory Theatre. Directed by Chris Parr.

Heartlanders was conceived as a community play for the city of Birmingham's centenary. There is a large range of characters, each of whom is involved with one of three primary stories: Aam, a young man who has come from India in search of a wife, only to find that his chosen is already living with an Englishman; Tom, who is on a business trip but is hoping to rekindle an old affair and ends up befriending Rose, a pregnant woman from Belfast; and Margaret, an upper-middle-class woman who encounters the Afro-Caribbean community while searching for her runaway daughter.

After Easter. 1994. Opened 18 May at the Other Place, Stratford, directed by Michael Attenborough.

Greta lives in England and has cut herself off from her Irish roots; when the play begins, we find her on a quest for something.

Married to a Marxist atheist, she has a breakdown, induced by what are either hallucinations or visions, depending on your perspective. Greta's sister Aoife takes her from the hospital, and Greta stays with Helen, who feigns an American accent so that she is not recognized as Irish. She finds she must return to Ireland when her father has a heart attack and, in doing so, confronts her own identity. Nightingale [1] found the play to be incoherent in parts.

TELEVISION SCRIPTS AND PREMIERE AIR DATES

The Long March. BBC television. 1984. Directed by Chris Parr; a woman returns to Ulster after years in England. She begins working for her old boyfriend and becomes involved with a young IRA member. Deals with the main character's feelings of ambivalence about the situation.

Naming the Names. BBC Radio, 1984; BBC television, 1987. Set in Northern Ireland; a young girl becomes involved in politics and inadvertently leads her English lover to his death.

The Rainbow. BBC television. 1988. A three-part adaptation of D. H. Lawrence's novel.

A Woman Calling. BBC television. 1982.

Venus de Milo Instead. BBC television.

ASSESSMENT OF DEVLIN'S CAREER

Anne Devlin, at this point in her career, offers her audiences an intimate look into the lives of women, particularly the Catholic women of Northern Ireland. She has a particular viewpoint that illuminates for her audiences the difficulties faced by women "caught up in conflict" (Greenhalgh). We see all of her primary female characters, in her dramas about the conflict, feeling ambivalence about their roles within the culture. Frieda, in the first scene of *Ourselves Alone*, refuses to sing any more songs where "the women are doormats." Josie is betrayed by the man she loves, and Donna must live her life without her husband, jailed for his role in the IRA. In *The Long March*, Helen is forced to have an opinion and take a position on the hunger strikes and Blanket protests because of the men in her life.

There is also a thorough development of her female characters, from *The Long March* to *After Easter*. While *After Easter* can be fuzzy at times, Greta is learning to come to grips with her identity in a way that Josie was only beginning to question, that Helen was unable to question, and that Frieda ran away from.

Devlin's women are also outsiders (Lojek); their refusal to accept the status quo without questioning it helps to illuminate their positions within the social and political conflicts within Northern Ireland. As Greenlaugh comments, "For the women in Devlin's plays, the history of Ireland is a suffocating dream of violence initiated and carried out by men, unsparingly revealed in the 'gradual and deliberate processes' that 'weave their way in the dark corners of all our rooms.' "

PRIMARY BIBLIOGRAPHY

After Easter. London: Faber and Faber, 1994.
Heartlanders. With Stephen Bill and David Edgar. London: Nick Hern Books, 1989.
Ourselves Alone, A Woman Calling, and *The Long March*. London: Faber and Faber, 1986.

SECONDARY BIBLIOGRAPHY

Armistead, Claire. [Review of *Heartlanders*.] *Financial Times* (24 Oct. 1989).
Barber, John. [Review of *Ourselves Alone*.] *Daily Telegraph* (25 Nov. 1985).
Billington, Michael. [Review of *Ourselves Alone*.] *Manchester Guardian* (23 Nov. 1985).
Campbell, Derek. "Ancestral Voices Prophesying War: The Impact of Tribal War on Northern Ireland's Contemporary Playwrights." *Theatre Three* (Spring 1990): 20–35.
"Fringe Life after the Death of the GLC." *Plays International* (Dec. 1986): 38–39.
Gardenr, Lyn. [Review of *Ourselves Alone*.] *City Limits* (29 Nov. 1985).
Greenhalgh, Susanne. "The Bomb in the Baby Carriage: Women and Terrorism in Contemporary Drama." In *Terrorism and Modern Drama*. Ed. John Orr and Dragan Klaic. Edinburgh: Edinburgh University Press, 1990. 160–83.
Gussow, Mel. [Review of Arena Stage production of *Ourselves Alone*.] *New York Times* (5 Apr. 1987): 61:1.
Hackett, Dennis. [Review of *The Long March*.] *Times* (21 Nov. 1984): 16e.
Hiley, Jim. [Review of *Ourselves Alone*.] *Listener* (28 Nov. 1985).
Hoyle, Martin. [Review of *Ourselves Alone*.] *Financial Times* (22 Nov. 1985).
Lojek, Helen. "Difference without Indifference: The Drama of Frank McGuinness and Anne Devlin." *Eire/Ireland* 25.2 (Summer 1990): 56–68.
Lustig, Vera. "Rising Tide." *Women's Review* 2.11 (Sept. 1986): 34–35.
Mackenzie, Susie. [Review of *Ourselves Alone*.]. *Time Out* (28 Nov. 1985).
Nightingale, Benedict. [1]. [Review of *After Easter*.] *Times* (30 May 1994).
———. [2]. Review of *Ourselves Alone*.] *New Statesman* (24 Jan. 1986).
"A Question of Confidence." *Woman's Review* 2.7 (May 1986): 8–9.
Ratcliffe, Michael. [Review of *Ourselves Alone*.] *Observer* (3 Nov. 1985).
Shulman, Milton. [Review of *Ourselves Alone*.] *London Standard* (22 Nov. 1985).
Williams, Ian. [Review of *Ourselves Alone*.] *Tribune* (8 Nov. 1985).

Brian Friel

(1929–   )

DANINE FARQUHARSON

Widely recognized as Ireland's greatest living dramatist, Brian Friel looks like a self-satisfied leprechaun. His devilish smile and elusive nature have successfully frustrated media and literary critics alike in their attempts to secure the revelational "pot o'gold" at the end of an astounding theatrical career. Their failure, in general, is due to the fact that Brian Friel is simply not finished yet. Thirty years after the international success of *Philadelphia, Here I Come!*, his latest play, *Wonderful Tennessee*, is enjoying celebrated reviews in Dublin, London, and New York.

Born on 9 January 1929 in Omagh, County Tyrone, Northern Ireland, Brian Friel was formally educated in Derry, Belfast, and County Kildare, Eire, where he received a B.A. from Maynooth College (the National Seminary) in 1948. After a postgraduate teacher-training course at Saint Joseph's College, Belfast, Friel taught for more than a decade in Derry. He retired in 1960 at the age of thirty-one to become a full-time writer. His first play, *The Enemy Within*, premiered at the Abbey Theatre in 1962, but not until 1964—after spending two months studying dramaturgy at the Guthrie Theatre in Minneapolis—did Friel achieve international acclaim with *Philadelphia, Here I Come!*, the hit of that summer's Dublin Theatre Festival.

Falling hard upon the heels of that success, *The Loves of Cass McGuire* (1966) and *Lovers: Winners and Losers* (1967) firmly established Friel as a critically acclaimed dramatist in Ireland and abroad. One of his most important achievements as both an Irishman and a playwright was the foundation of the Derry-based Field Day Theatre Company in 1980 with his close friend, actor Stephen Rea. This association led to the production of his two finest plays—*Translations* (1980) and *The Communication Cord* (1982). *Translations* has since been awarded the Ewart-Biggs Peace Prize, and film director Neil Jordan is currently working on a screen adaptation.

Some of Brian Friel's literary honors include election to the Irish Academy of Letters in 1972; membership in Aosdana, the national treasury of Irish artists; and an honorary D.Litt. from the National University of Ireland in 1982. A 1986 nomination to the Irish Senate makes Friel the first Irish writer to serve in such a capacity since W. B. Yeats. One of Friel's longtime friends once commented, however, that ''he only went once and he didn't speak.'' In 1989 BBC Radio devoted a six-play season to the work of Brian Friel, the first living playwright so distinguished.

Today, Brian Friel lives with his wife of forty years, Anne, in Greencastle on the Innishowen Peninsula, about twenty miles from the border dividing Northern Ireland and County Donegal.

Selected Biographical Sources: Maxwell [1, 2]; Pine.

MAJOR PLAYS, PREMIERES, AND SIGNIFICANT REVIVALS: THEATRICAL RECEPTION

Philadelphia, Here I Come!. 1964. Opened on 28 September at the Gaiety Theatre, Dublin.

Although it is certainly true that the 1966 Broadway production of *Philadelphia, Here I Come!* initiated Brian Friel into the international arena of theatrical success, it was a trial by fire in terms of American critical reception. Following a glorious triumph at the Dublin Theatre Festival, the Irish production under director Hilton Edwards received a cold, if not caustic, opening night review from the *New York Times*. ''There is considerable pleasantness, little poetry and insufficient power in [Friel's] play,'' writes Kauffmann, in a review that called the production naive and concluded that the play was ''appealing enough but unexciting'' (28). Despite such a lukewarm reception in print, American theatergoers must have found *Philadelphia* much more appealing than did its initial critic because it went on for 326 performances, making it the longest-running Irish play on Broadway. It was a prophetic beginning for Friel's theatrical career, as public response would often contradict critical reaction in the next twenty-five years.

The Loves of Cass McGuire. 1966. Opened 6 October at the Helen Hayes Theatre, New York.

Friel's fabulous box office success in the United States led him and Hilton Edwards to decide on opening his next play, *The Loves of Cass McGuire*, in New York at the Helen Hayes Theatre—the site of *Philadelphia*'s long run— with a mixed Irish and American cast. The combination proved to be disastrous, as nearly every reviewer remarked that the inability of Ruth Gordon as Cass to master the Irish idiom robbed the play of its essential character. As Henry Hewes noted, ''Miss Gordon seems as Irish as Levy's Rye Bread'' (quoted in Schlueter 82). Yet, Friel's Philadelphia reputation was already strong enough to carry him through three plays in three years (*Cass, Lovers, Crystal and Fox*), all receiving positive Irish reviews and warm American reception (*Lovers* was named one of Broadway's ten best plays in 1968).

The Mundy Scheme. 1969. Opened 10 June at the Olympia Theatre, Dublin.

The summer of 1969 saw an interesting division in critical response that became characteristic of Brian Friel's career in the 1970s. *The Mundy Scheme* was praised by *Irish Times'* mild-mannered theater critic, Kelly [1], who relished in Friel's parody of contemporary Irish political machinations, while Barnes panned the play as "too slight" and "incapable of decent development" and probably contributed significantly to its ill-fated Broadway run of only four shows.

The Freedom of the City. 1973. Opened 20 February at the Abbey Theatre, Dublin.

Similarly, *Freedom* was heralded in Dublin as a politically scathing attack on Britain's Bloody Sunday debacle, but the *London Times*, which, up until now, blandly endorsed New York's verdicts of Friel's plays, condescendingly ignored the anticolonial, anti-British sentiment in *Freedom*. Reviewer Irving Wardle [1] reduces the obvious political nature of the play to a Marxist struggle between rich and poor and then criticizes Friel for being apparent and "single-minded" in purpose. Wardle goes on to praise Albert Finney for saving an otherwise "docile" Irish play with an impressively "fluent" production.

Living Quarters. 1977. **Faith Healer.** 1979. *Living Quarters* opened 24 March at the Abbey Theatre, Dublin. *Faith Healer* opened 5 April at the Longacre Theatre, New York.

The 1970s, which were Friel's most experimental years as a dramatic artist, with plays such as *Living Quarters* (1977) and *Faith Healer* (1979), were not so rewarding in terms of critical response. James Mason, who played the lead in the Broadway production of *Faith Healer*, suffered the same criticism as Ruth Gordon did ten years earlier, while Eder of the *New York Times* questioned Friel's use of the monologue form and wrote that the play lacked any "poetic force." Even faithful supporter Kelly [2] was baffled by Friel's attempts to move away from engaging character portraits toward metadramatic concerns and curiously commented that *Living Quarters* left him "regretting that Friel . . . hadn't chosen to use this particular theme for a novel instead." Yet, *Faith Healer* is Friel's greatest box office success since *Philadelphia, Here I Come!*

Translations. 1980. Opened 23 September at the Guildhall, Londonderry, by the Field Day Theatre Company.

As tenacious as ever, Friel emerged from a critically disparaging decade with the formation of the Field Day Theatre Company and came home to an "electric love affair" with Irish critics and theatergoers alike (Nowlan). *Translations* marked the beginning of a stage in Friel's career that can be compared to Hollywood's glitzy, star-studded film premieres, as the details of who attended his opening nights with whom received as much press coverage in the *Irish Times* as critical analyses of the plays themselves. London and New York raved about *Translations*, probably because it, visually at least, fitted into their category of Irish drama that is linguistically compelling and powerfully tragic: "[A]ll the life of the piece is concentrated into its concern with language . . . I have never been more certain of witnessing the premiere of a national classic" (Wardle [2]). Friel's other Field Day plays maintained a certain theatrical momentum, but mostly in Ireland, as the company's cultural/political agenda followed an increasingly provocative role in Irish artistic pursuits. Field Day has become a much-talked-about theatrical phenomenon in Ireland and yet is rarely commented upon in British and American papers. In 1990, however, Friel split with Field Day—for publicly unknown reasons—and *Dancing at Lughnasa* premiered at the Abbey in Dublin and not the Guildhall in Derry.

Dancing at Lughnasa. 1990. Opened 24 April at the Abbey Theatre, Dublin.

Dancing represents many homecomings for playwright Brian Friel. He returns to Ballybeg, to poignant characters, and to international success. Even though Friel is attempting to find alternatives to linguistic communication and to express a necessity for paganism in a way of life plagued by routine, the critics seized upon the dreamy, nostalgic atmosphere of the play as its most marketable quality. *Dancing* is indeed reminiscent of *Philadelphia, Here I Come!*, even to the point of an older Donal Donnelly—who played Private Gar on Broadway in 1966—returning to the stage in the role of Father Jack.

Wonderful Tennessee. 1993. Opened 30 June at the Abbey Theatre, Dublin.

Despite the dramatic kudos heaped upon *Dancing*, if the reaction to his most recent production, *Wonderful Tennessee*, is any indication, Friel will never be able to rest upon his laurels for very long. Despite exaggerated praise for *Wonderful Tennessee* from the *Irish Times*, Rich of the *New York Times* documents "withering" attacks from the public, "divided reviews," and "snippy press in London." Never destined to be an eternal "darling" of the press, Brian Friel and his ever-expanding canon of Irish drama continue to keep the critics and the public in constant debate.

ASSESSMENT OF FRIEL'S CAREER

The Ballybeg Cycle

Although *Philadelphia, Here I Come!* is not Brian Friel's first play, it does introduce into the Friel canon the conceptual place that a reviewer for the *Economist* claims "could eventually be as famous as William Faulkner's Yoknapatawpha county or Thomas Hardy's Wessex." Writing within a literary tradition beset with postcolonial questions of space, Brian Friel cracks open the geographic map to create Baile Beag, or Ballybeg, an imaginary, microcosmic Irish realm around which arbitrarily drawn borders hold no authoritative power. Ballybeg can be considered part of that legendary fifth province that Hederman and Kerney articulated in *The Crane Bag* as "the secret centre . . . the place where all oppositions [may be] resolved."

Philadelphia, Here I Come! stages some of those oppositions in an emotional play about young Gar O'Donnell, torn between a loyalty to his Irish homeland, which is rooted in the desire for a yet undeveloped relationship with a noncommunicative father, and the lure of better (economic) opportunities in America. Gar's dilemma is familiar enough in the history of Irish literature, but Friel translates the nature of a divided people by physically splitting Gar into two separate entities: the private and the public. Other than this innovative characterization—innovative in 1964, at least—*Philadelphia, Here I Come!* is basically a realistic drama that tells, on one level, of the tragedy of Ireland's loss of youth and hope through emigration, and, on a more significant level, of the tragic inability of father and son to open up the lines of communication. The play begins to delineate oppositions within the Irish mind more so than it seeks to resolve them. In answer to private Gar's goading question in the final moment of the play: "God, Boy, why do you have to leave? Why? Why?", public Gar answers: "I don't know. I—I—I don't know."

Fifteen years and several plays after the success of *Philadelphia, Here I Come!*, Friel returns to Ballybeg with a quirky, Chekhovian-style play about a Catholic family and their collective as well as individual heartaches. *Aristocrats* is set in Ballybeg Hall, County Donegal, the crumbling homestead of District Justice O'Donnell (the name as well as the setting establishes a theatrical lineage to Gar), his three daughters, and their "peculiar" brother. The family has gathered at the Big House for sister Claire's wedding and ends up remaining for the patriarch's funeral; but celebration and mourning are not the only oppositions at play in *Aristocrats*. The architectural home of a rare and dying class of Irish Catholic aristocracy becomes a metaphor for the meeting of the inside/private and the outside/public natures of the characters, along with their respective conventionalities and eccentricities. With its moments of delightful humor and touching sadness, *Aristocrats* reads like a eulogy for a part of Ireland's past and for a family struggling with boundaries—both tangible and implicit—surrounding both the home and the homeland.

In 1980–1982 Brian Friel reached a point in an already well established theatrical career in which he was able to unite several dramatic concerns within two plays set, once again, in Ballybeg. With the formation of the Field Day Theatre Company with actor Stephen Rea in Derry, Northern Ireland, Friel found a home base for plays that now count among the very best in his career.

Set in the 1830s, when the British Army Engineer Corps carried out the mapping and renaming of Ireland under the banner of the Ordnance Survey, *Translations* portrays, on a number of dramatic levels, the crisis of dispossession: of language, of land, of identity, and of political power. Despite the fact that it depicts many aspects of Ireland's history as an oppressed nation (linguistically, culturally, and politically), *Translations* also addresses the continuing concerns of contemporary Irish men and women who struggle with questions of language and identity. *Translations*, then, is situated in a state of hesitation, oscillating between several possible meanings where language resists our efforts to take from it a single, tyrannical meaning. As Richard Pine notes, the contemporary Irish mind is ambivalent and bifurcated, and, in the case of *Translations*, we have to decide whether or not resolution matters, whether or not the conclusion of the play successfully resolves the dilemma of cultural decline under the weight of colonial repression.

Beginning with naming and the process of self-articulation, Friel weaves a drama of language and meaning that attempts to reestablish the connections between the word and its significance. He does not treat the value of names lightly, but rather with deadly seriousness. In doing so, he is asserting that language in Ireland does have power but need not be the tool of political powermongers; instead, it can be the instrument of change and progress. However, progress and change can be constructive only when the tensions involved are made clear. There is no doubt that the pressures Friel is dramatizing are English versus Irish, the public versus the private, and so on, but the fact that he chooses to dramatize these tensions as opposed to resolving them leaves the stage and political/cultural dialogue open to further debate. *Translations*, in essence, exposes more problems than it solves in order to create new space for dialogue.

In 1982, the Field Day Theatre Company staged *The Communication Cord*, a play that takes the tragic paradigm of the then critically acclaimed *Translations*—the dislocation of the Irish psyche and exploitation of the Irish language by British colonialism—and rewrites it within the genre of farce. In his own words, Friel felt that the Irish "situation has become so absurd and so . . . crass that it seems to me it might be a valid way to talk and write about it." Keeping in line with Field Day's postcolonial, revisionist mandate, Friel takes the pious version of Irish cultural and linguistic history portrayed in *Translations* and inverts/subverts it in a superbly and tightly written farce that depicts the necessity for continual rewriting and reassessment.

Many reviewer/critics blithely interpreted *Translations* as an elegy for a certain charming rusticity in rural Ireland. Friel, in a vicious attack on such sentimentality, engages his audience with fast-paced, comic dialogue that ultimately says that, indeed, the British are largely responsible for a dislocated Irish psyche, but so, too, are the unthinking responses of characters such as Tim and Senator Donovan. In fact, Friel makes an even more stinging attack on the contemporary Irishperson, as in the scene where the Senator and Nora Dan sit back and glorify the virtues of the sham cottage and, in the same breath, offer it up for sale based on their insincere descriptions of its "pietás". Initially, the artificially constructed cottage sends out smoke signals in the form of blinding chimney "blowdowns" into Tim's face, to warn against the stacking of deceptions upon deceptions until "reality" is completely lost. Not heeding such signs, not comprehending the code of the cottage, Tim plunges into a classically farcical plot until control has evaporated, and all structures—even artificial ones—completely collapse.

This is a very clear statement that some kind of apocalyptic change must occur in how the Irish perceive their past, in order to reevaluate their present condition. The term "apocalyptic" is intentional because it signifies destruction, but it also contains the belief/necessity for reconstruction. *The Communication Cord* is an extreme but effective answer to the problem of pious romanticization: through the annihilation of the hedge/school–cottage artifice, it becomes a play that literally, physically, and symbolically clears out a space and a stage, allowing for something new to be written.

After ten years of successful collaboration with the Field Day Theatre Company, Friel moved south to the Abbey and took Ballybeg with him. With the premiere of *Dancing at Lughnasa* at the Abbey Theatre in 1990, there is a noticeable distancing between the political content of the Field Day political agenda and the thematic concerns of Friel. It is a complicated shift; not only does Field Day reach beyond the geographic borders of Ireland to accommodate "foreign" contributors to its pamphlet series, but, as Deane [1] notes, Field Day is seeking to establish parallels of the Irish situation within the global community.

As Field Day shifts its emphasis, so, too, does the dramaturgy of Friel. *Dancing at Lughnasa* relinquishes the intensely ironic linguistic "play" of *Translations* and *The Communication Cord*, as well as the subversive treatment of traditional perceptions of history, mythology, and heroism in *Making History*, in favor of a more nostalgic, melancholy atmosphere that moves away from a belief in the power of the spoken or written word. Physical movement rather than verbal interaction seems to be the preferred mode of communication: in Michael's words, "it is as if language had surrendered to movement—as if this ritual, this wordless ceremony, was now the way to speak, to whisper private and sacred things, to be in touch with some otherness" (*Dancing at Lughnasa*, act 2). If Ballybeg is to be connected with that mythical center of Irish consciousness, then Friel in his dramatic quest through its landscapes has turned away from purely linguistic expression. Instead, he is experimenting with the dramatic metaphors of dance and, as in his most recent play, *Wonderful Tennessee*, music to express a connectedness to the fifth province of Ireland.

The "Other" Brian Friel

The dramatic career of Brian Friel cannot be reduced to only those plays set in the town of Ballybeg. Having a history of accomplished short story publications, Friel's canon contains a number of dramatic works that exhibit acutely sensitive constructions of character, revealing an extraordinary deftness in the portrayal of not only the dynamics of the Irish psyche but human nature in general. Beginning with a poignantly nontraditional sketch of St. Columba in *The Enemy Within*, through the musical rhapsodies of Cass and company in

The Loves of Cass McGuire, to an antiromantic, highly rhetorical picture of the Great Hugh O'Neill in *Making History*, Brian Friel demonstrates that, as an artist, he is as comfortable and as adept at working with questions of human existence as he is with tackling problems of cultural codes and communication.

The great majority of Brian Friel's plays can be labeled "realistic" in terms of theatrical presentation. There is, however, a handful of works that deserve mention for their experimental nature and self-reflexivity. *Faith Healer*, which *Irish Times* drama critic Seamus Kelly believes to be one of Friel's finest plays, is a series of four monologues by three characters that combine to create a portrait of an artist. Frank Hardy, the faith healer/traveling showman of the title, is allowed the first and the last words on stage, and Friel presents him as both artist and failed artist in an inseparable state of being. His personal questioning about the nature and effect of his "gift" to heal is parallel to Friel's own continuing journey through success and failure as playwright and artistic voice.

The metadramatic quality of Friel's work is most striking in an infrequently produced, often overlooked play—*Living Quarters*. In this provocative reenactment of the final hours before Commandant Frank Butler's suicide, Friel completely annihilates the traditional fourth wall of the theater as a character authoritatively named Sir continually interrupts the remainder of the cast to ensure that they remain faithful to the "ledger" (read "script") as he has it before him. Sir, as an onstage directorial presence, is an example of Friel's artistic self-consciousness about the nature of theater as a constructed translation of events with its own set of limitations and boundaries.

Drama as a form of fictionalized construction is a theme that Friel elaborates upon in his most overtly political play, *The Freedom of the City*, a theatrical allusion to the events of Bloody Sunday. In this instance, the fourth wall crumbles with the presence of the tribunal of inquiry into the deaths of three civil rights demonstrators shot by British troops. Friel sets up a montage of different versions of the same event, much like the monologues of the three characters in *Faith Healer*, which together examine the way in which "truth" is a construction based on often contradictory, individual perceptions.

Although Friel is theatrically most at home in Ballybeg, the diversity of his dramatic efforts establishes him as a playwright who is never entirely comfortable within a particular style, time period, or subject matter (his translations of Russian authors such as Chekhov and Turgenev are further examples of his eclecticism) and who is continually seeking new ways to grapple with questions of human nature.

PRIMARY BIBLIOGRAPHY

Plays

Aristocrats. Dublin: Gallery Press, 1981.
The Communication Cord. London: Faber and Faber, 1983.

Crystal and Fox. London: Faber and Faber, 1970.
Dancing at Lughnasa. London: Faber and Faber, 1990.
The Enemy Within. Dublin: Gallery Press, 1979.
Faith Healer. London: Faber and Faber, 1980.
Fathers and Sons, after Turgenev. London: Faber and Faber, 1987.
The Freedom of the City. London: Faber and Faber, 1974.
The Gentle Island. London: Davis–Poynter, 1973.
Living Quarters. London: Faber and Faber, 1978.
Lovers: Winners and Losers. London: Faber and Faber, 1969.
The Loves of Cass McGuire. London: Faber and Faber, 1967.
Making History. London: Faber and Faber, 1989.
The Mundy Scheme. New York: Farrar, Straus & Giroux, 1970.
Philadelphia, Here I Come! London: Faber and Faber, 1965.
Three Sisters by Anton Chekhov. Dublin: Gallery Press, 1981.
Translations. London: Faber and Faber, 1981.
Volunteers. London: Faber and Faber, 1979.
Wonderful Tennessee. London: Faber and Faber, 1993.

Anthology

Selected Plays. Introduction by Seamus Deane. (*Philadelphia, Here I Come!, The Freedom of the City, Living Quarters, Aristocrats, Faith Healer, Translations.*) London: Faber and Faber, 1984.

SECONDARY BIBLIOGRAPHY

A. W. "Introducing Brian Friel." *Acorn* 14 (Nov. 1970): 25–28.
Andrews, Elmer. *The Art of Brian Friel: Neither Reality Nor Dreams.* New York: St. Martin's Press, 1995.
Andrews, J. M. *A Paper Landscape.* Oxford: Oxford University Press, 1975.
Barnes, Clive. "The Theatre: Friel's *Mundy Scheme*." *New York Times* (12 Dec. 1969): 75.
Bertha, Csilla. "Tragedies of National Fate: A Comparison between Brian Friel's *Translations* and Its Hungarian Counterpart, Andras Suto's *A Szuzai menyegao*." *Irish University Review* 17 (Aug. 1987): 207–22.
Binnie, Eric. "Brecht and Friel: Some Irish Parallels." *Modern Drama* 31.1 (1988): 365–70.
Dantanus, Ulf. *Brian Friel: A Study.* London: Faber and Faber, 1988.
Deane, Seamus. [1]. "Brian Friel." In *Celtic Revivals.* London: Faber and Faber, 1986. 166–74.
———. [2]. "Brian Friel." *Ireland Today* 978 (1981): 7–10.
Eder, Richard. "Drama: Friel's *Faith Healer*." *New York Times* (6 Apr. 1979): C3.
Etherton, Michael. *Contemporary Irish Dramatists.* London: Macmillan, 1989.
Field Day Theatre Company. [1]. *Ireland's Field Day.* (Pamphlet Nos. 1–6.) London: Hutchinson, 1985.
———. [2]. *Nationalism, Colonialism and Literature.* (Pamphlet Nos. 13–15.) Minneapolis: Minneapolis University Press, 1990.

FitzGibbon, Gerald. "Historical Obsession in Recent Irish Drama." *The Crows behind the Plough: History and Violence in Anglo-Irish Poetry and Drama*. Ed. Geert Lernout. Amsterdam: Rodopi, 1991. 41–60.

Friel, Brian. [1]. "The Theatre of Hope and Despair." *Everyman*, no. 1 (1968).

———. [2]. "The Future of Irish Drama." *Irish Times* (12 Feb. 1970).

———. [3]. "Plays Peasant and Unpeasant." *Times Literary Supplement* (17 Mar. 1972).

———. [4]. "Self-Portrait." *Aquarius*, no. 5 (1972).

———. [5]. "Extracts from a Sporadic Diary." *The Writers: A Sense of Ireland*. Ed. Andrew Carpenter and Peter Fallon. Dublin: O'Brien Press, 1980. 39.

———. [6]. "Extracts . . ." *Ireland and the Arts*. Ed. Tim Pat Coogan. London: Quartet Books, 1982.

Gray, John. "Field Day Five Years on." *Linen Hall Review* 2 (Summer 1984): 4–10.

Grene, Nicholas. "Distancing Drama: Sean O'Casey to Brian Friel." In *Irish Writers and the Theatre*. Ed. Masaru Sekine. Totowa, N.J.: Barnes and Noble, 1987. 47–70.

Hederman, M[ark] P[atrick] and Richard Kearney, eds. *The Crane Bag Book of Irish Studies*. Vol. 1. Dublin: Blackwater Press, 1982.

Hickey, Des, and Gus Smith. *A Paler Shade of Green*. London: Leslie Frewin, 1972.

Johnston, Denis. "Brian Friel and Modern Irish Drama." *Hibernia* 7 (Mar. 1975): 22.

Kauffmann, Stanley. "*Philadelphia, Here I Come!* Arrives." *New York Times* (17 Feb. 1966): 28.

Kavanagh, Julie. "Friel at Last." *Vanity Fair* (Oct. 1991). (Interview with Brian Friel.)

Kearney, Richard. [1]. "Language Play: Brian Friel and Ireland's Verbal Theatre." *Studies* 72 (Spring 1983): 20–56.

———. [2]. "Friel and the Politics of Language." *Massachusetts Review* 28 (Fall 1987): 510–15.

Kelly, Seamus. [1]. "Friel Runs Riot in Corridors of Power." *Irish Times* (11 June 1969): 10.

———. [2]. "*Living Quarters* at the Abbey." *Irish Times* (25 Mar. 1977): 9.

King, Kimball. *Ten Modern Irish Playwrights*. New York: Garland, 1979.

Maxwell, D. E. S. [1]. *Brian Friel*. Lewisburg, Pa.: Bucknell University Press, 1973.

———. [2]. *Images: Arts and the People of Northern Ireland*. Belfast: Northern Ireland Information Office/Arts Council of Northern Ireland, n.d. (Interview with Brian Friel.)

McGrath, F. C. "Brian Friel and the Politics of Anglo-Irish Language." *Colby Quarterly* 26.4 (1990): 241–48.

Murray, Christopher. "Brian Friel's *Making History* and the Problem of Historical Accuracy." *The Crows behind the Plough: History and Violence in Anglo-Irish Poetry and Drama*. Ed. Geert Lernout. Amsterdam: Rodopi, 1991. 61–78.

Niel, Ruth. "Non-Realistic Techniques in the Plays of Brian Friel: The Debt to International Drama." In *Literary Interrelations: Ireland, England and the World II*. Ed. Wolfgang Zach and Heinz Kosok. Tübingen: Narr, 1987. 349–359.

Nowlan, David. "Electric Love Affair as Play Opens in Derry." *Irish Times* (24 Sept. 1980): 8.

O'Brien, George. *Brian Friel*. Boston: Twayne, 1990.

O'Toole, Fintan. "The Man from God Knows Where." *In Dublin* (28 Oct. 1982). (Interview with Brian Friel.)

Pine, Richard. *Brian Friel and Ireland's Drama*. London: Routledge, 1990.

Rich, Frank. "After and beyond *Lughnasa.*" *New York Times* (17 July 1993): Arts 9.

Schlueter, June. "Brian Friel." In *Dictionary of Literary Biography.* Ed. Stanley Weintraub. vol. 13. Detroit: Gale Research, 1982. 179–85.

Smith, Robert S. "The Hermeneutic Motion in Brian Friel's *Translations.*" *Modern Drama* 3 (Sept. 1991): 392–409.

Taplin, Diana. *Guardian* 1 December 1986. (Interview with Brian Friel.)

Throne, Marilyn. "The Disintegration of Authority: A Study of the Fathers in Five Plays of Brian Friel." *Colby Quarterly Review* 3 (Sept. 1988): 162–72.

Tillinghast, Richard. "Brian Friel: Transcending the National Pastime." *New Criterion* 10.2 (1991): 35–41.

Timm, Eitel F. "Modern Mind, Myth and History: Brian Friel's *Translations.*" *Studies in Anglo-Irish Literature.* Ed. Heinz Kosok. Bonn: Bouvier, 1982. 447–54.

Verstaeta, Ginette. "Brian Friel's Drama and the Limits of Language." In *History and Violence in Anglo-Irish Literature.* Ed. Geert Lernout. Amsterdam: Rodopi, 1988. 85–96.

Wardle, Irving. [1]. "Downstairs and Up at the Royal Court." *Times* (28 Feb. 1973): 13.

———. [2]. *"Translations."* *Times* (13 May 1981): 11.

Waters, John. "The Frontiersman." *In Dublin* (15 May 1986). (Interview with Brian Friel.)

Wiley, Catherine A. "Recreating Ballybeg: Two *Translations* by Brian Friel." *Journal of Dramatic Theory and Criticism* 1.2 (1987): 51–61.

Winkler, Elizabeth Hale. "'Eejitin' About: Adolescence in Friel and Keane." *Éire-Ireland* 16 (Fall 1981): 138–44.

Zach, Wolfgang. "Brian Friel's *Translations*: National and Universal Dimensions." *Medieval and Modern Ireland.* Ed. Richard Wall. Totowa, N.J.: Barnes and Noble, 1988. 74–90.

BIBLIOGRAPHIES

Mikhail, E. H. [1]. *A Research Guide of Modern Anglo-Irish Dramatists.* Troy, N.Y.: Whitston, 1979.

———. [2]. *An Annotated Bibliography of Modern Anglo-Irish Drama.* Troy, N.Y.: Whitston, 1981.

Lady Isabella Augusta Persse Gregory
(1852–1932)

TRAMBLE T. TURNER

Lady Augusta Gregory, best known as one of the founders of the Abbey Theatre of Dublin, obtained her title and much of her resources when she married Sir William Gregory on 4 March 1880. In 1897, five years after her husband's death, she began discussions with William Butler Yeats and Edward Martyn that led to their founding the Irish Literary Theatre in 1899. In addition to the thirty-six works she wrote independently, her collaborative efforts helped provide material for the Abbey Theatre. Her work included providing the plot for Douglas Hyde's Irish plays, providing dialect and revisions for Yeats, and a collaboration to complete Synge's final, incomplete play. (A discussion of dates and details of such collaborations may be found in Kohfeldt, pp. 164–65, 142–47, and 198–200; in Chapters 7 and 8 of Coxhead's study; and in Ann Saddlemyer's forewords to her editions of the complete plays.)

Isabella Augusta Persse was born on 15 March 1852 in County Galway at her family's estate, Roxborough. The twelfth child of sixteen, she was raised and influenced by her Irish-speaking nurse, Mary Sheridan. In her preface to *Cuchulain*, Gregory credited Sheridan with stirring her interest in heroic Irish tales and in the Irish people. During the 1890s, Lady Gregory began to collect the folktales and lore of her area. By 1898, she was also learning the Gaelic language. *Cuchulain of Muirthemne* (1902), one her retellings of the Irish epics, provided source material for Yeats and other writers of the Irish Renaissance. *Gods and Fighting Men*, a second work in that vein, was published in 1904. Those prose works were followed by *Poets and Dreamers* (1903) and the 1906 publication of *A Book of Saints and Wonders* and *The Kiltartan History Book* (1909; expanded version 1926). *Visions and Beliefs in the West of Ireland* (1920) provided another gathering of folklore. In those works and in her plays, Lady

Gregory perfected her own style of Irish English, which has come to be called the Kiltartan dialect.

Gregory provided her own account of the founding of the Abbey Theatre and of her collaborations with Yeats in *Our Irish Theatre* (1911). She also recounted the life of her art patron nephew in *Hugh Lane's Life and Achievement* (1921). Aside from contributing a near constant flow of plays for Abbey productions, Lady Gregory played a critical role in decisions about which plays would be produced each season.

Selected Biographical Sources: Adams; Kohfeldt; Kopper.

MAJOR PLAYS, PREMIERES, AND SIGNIFICANT REVIVALS: THEATRICAL RECEPTION

Often presented as part of an Abbey Theatre Company evening of plays, Lady Gregory's plays were frequently neglected in the critical reviews. Despite limited commentary, a pattern emerges from the reviews: her "little" plays were consistently amusing in their Irish character and dialect, the plots were often considered "thin," and critics who reviewed her work more extensively regularly compared her work favorably with that of Yeats and Synge.

Cathleen Ni Houlihan. 1902. Written in collaboration with Yeats in 1901. Irish National Theatre Society. Cathleen: Maud Gonne.

The Pot of Broth. 1902. Written in collaboration with Yeats in 1901. Irish National Theatre Society.

Twenty-Five. 14 March 1903. A one-act play. Irish National Theatre Society at Molesworth Hall, Dublin. 7 May 1903: Queen's Gate Hall, London. Christie Hernderson: W. G. Fay.

Of the London productions, Wilfred Blunt wrote that the play was " 'the most perfect work of art and the most touching play I have ever seen acted' " (quoted in Kohfeldt 164). (Blunt's affair with the playwright should be taken into account when considering his remarks.)

The Times Literary Supplement (Review of *Twenty-Five*) hailed the innovations of the Irish National Theatre Society: "We had never realized the musical possibilities of our language until we had heard these Irish people speak it. . . . But it is time to say something of the vital part of our pleasure, the pleasure of mind and mood. That, too is largely a pleasure of rest—and resignation. The mind is steeped in seriousness; the mood is uniformly sad. . . . In Lady Gregory's *Twenty-Five* there is more solid matter of fact, more of human nature's daily food."

Where There Is Nothing. 1904. (A collaboration with Yeats and Douglas Hyde). Opened at the Royal Court Theatre, London. 26 June 1904: revised as *The Unicorn from the Stars.*

Spreading the News. 1904. On the first bill of the Abbey Theatre, 27 December. 20 November 1911: Maxine Elliott's Theatre, New York. Bartley Fallon: Arthur Sinclair, Mrs. Fallon: Sara Allgood. June 1912: Court Theatre, London. Bartley Fallon: Arthur Sinclair, Mrs. Fallon: Sara Allgood.

The *Irish Times* (Review of *Spreading the News*) commented on the play's contribution to an evening that opened with Yeats' *On Baile's Strand* and *Cathleen ni Houlihan*: "It is a tripping little piece, founded on a simple idea of modern Irish life, but yielding in its short compass abundance of rich comedy." The *New York Times* (Review of *Spreading the News*) commented: "Almost continuous laughter greeted Lady Gregory's one-act comedy 'Spreading the News,' which, Irish or not, contains a pretty good lesson for this gossipy old town, as for any other town where stray bits of information are magnified and make trouble." And the *Athenaeum* observed, "It is pure farce, brilliant and forced in turn, and the whole company flung themselves into it with relish."

Kincora. 1905. Opened 25 March at the Abbey Theatre. Brian: F. J. Fay, Murrough: George Roberts, Malachi: A. Power, Gormleith: Maire Ni Shiublaigh, Sitric: P. MacShiubhlaigh, Maelmora: Seamus O'Sullivan, Brennain: Arthur Sinclair, Derrick: W. G. Fay, Rury: J. H. Dunne, Maire: Maire Ni Gharbhaigh. Aoibhell, a woman of the Sidhe: Sara Allgood.

Maud Gonne took note of the original production's reception in March 1905: "I am so glad to read of the success of Kincora" (see White 196). That reaction was not the final review from nationalist forces, however. Four years later, Gonne was to write, "I was very sorry that her Kincora was attacked in Sinn Fein when she was ill" (268).

The *Irish Times* (Review of *Kincora*) singled the work out as one of her greatest achievements: "More, perhaps, than any of its predecessors, 'Kincora' appeals not only to the small number of professed students of dramatic literature, but to a large number of the Irish people. . . . The play unfolds itself in a prologue and three acts, each of which is part of a cohesive and interesting work."

The White Cockade. 1905. Opened 9 December at the Abbey Theatre, Dublin. Matt Kelleher: W. G. Fay, Owen Kelleher: F. Walker, Mrs. Kelleher: Sara Allgood, King James: Arthur Sinclair, Sarsfield: F. J. Fay, Carter: J. H. Dunne, Old Lady: Maire Ni Shiublaigh.

Within two years of its first performance, the play was referred to as a "well-known comedy . . . a piece dealing with the troublous times in 1689" (Review of the *White Cockade*).

Hyacinth Halvey. 1906. Opened 19 February at the Abbey Theatre. 30 May 1910: Royal Court Theatre, London. 12 June 1911: Royal Court Theatre, London. 15 December 1911: the Irish National Theatre Society at Maxine Elliott's Theatre, New York. 20 August 1917: The Coliseum, London.

According to *The Irish Times* (Review of *Hyacinth Halvey*), the play "displays a keen appreciation of true humor in her treatment of the situation, which never fails to interest and amuse the audience.'' One of the most frequently reviewed of Lady Gregory's plays, the 1911 New York production garnered a review from the *New York Times* (Review of *Hyacinth Halvey*) that represents a general trend to praise the playwright's comic talents while slighting her ability to construct plot: ''[I]t is of a kind which rather eludes satisfactory description, for the reason that the characters themselves and the lines, spoken as they are in the rich and strange dialect, provide more of the actual fun than the plot itself.''

The 1910 London revival was termed an ''original and amusing little comedy'' by the *Times*, noting that the play ''has been played previously in London and has never failed to provoke mirth.'' Of the June 1912 London production, the *Athenaeum* (Review of *Hyacinth Halvey*) commented that the play ''has perhaps obtained the widest popularity of any of Lady Gregory's farces. . . . None the less, it supplies the appropriate illusion of people standing on their heads for the sheer joy of it which that accomplished discoverer of peasant drollery can impart.'' The 1917 revival was praised for providing the Abbey Theatre Players ''much better material than the sketch which they acted at the Coliseum last week'' (Review of *Hyacinth Halvey*, the *Times*), while a review of the 1939 revival referred to the play as ''an agreeably amusing anecdote'' (Review of *Hyacinth Halvey*, the *Times*).

The Gaol Gate. 1906. Opened 20 October at the Abbey Theatre, Dublin. Mary Cashel: Sara Allgood, Mary Cushin: Maire O'Neill, The Gatekeeper: Frank J. Fay. 27 November 1911, New York. An opening play for Synge's *The Playboy*.

The *Irish Times* (Review of *The Gaol Gate*) called it ''a rather unconventional, not to say unconvincing, piece of work.''

The Canavans. 1906. A three-act comedy. Opened 8 December at the Abbey Theatre, Dublin. (Revised version debuted 31 October 1907.) 1906 Cast: Peter Canavan: W. G. Fay, Antony: J. A. O'Rourke, Widow Greely: Maire O'Neill, Widow Deeny: Brigit O'Dempsey, Captain Headley: Arthur Sinclair.

The *Irish Times* (Review of *The Canavans*) observed that ''[t]he rather severe ideas with which the Society set out upon its mission have been somewhat modified, and their performances are now more attractive to what may be called the 'man in the street.' ''

The Rising of the Moon. 1907. Opened March at the Abbey Theatre, Dublin. Cast: W. G. Fay, J. A. O'Rourke, J. M. Kerrigan, Arthur Sinclair. 24 February 1908: New York, at the Savoy Theatre. Ballad Singer: W. G. Fay, Sergeant: F. J. Fay, Policeman: Dudley Digges, Policeman: J. M. Kerrigan. 20 November 1911: Maxine Elliott's Theatre, New York. Sergeant: Arthur Sinclair, Ballad Singer: J. M. Kerrigan. 20 October 1932: Martin Beck Theatre, New York. Sergeant: Arthur Sinclair, Ballad Singer: Michael J. Dolan, Policeman X: Denis

O'Dea, Policeman B: Arthur Shields. 28 August 1957: Edinburgh at the Regent Hall.

Political commentary heavily tinged the initial review of the play in the *Irish Times* (Review of *The Rising of the Moon*): " 'The Rising of the Moon,' it may safely be predicted, will ... come in for a good deal of hostile criticism, and the possibility that such a development was unforeseen reflects very little credit on the intelligence of those to whom the destinies of the Abbey Theatre are entrusted.''

The *New York Times* (Review of *The Rising of the Moon*) described the 1908 production as "a comedy-drama of the Fenian period in Irish history.... The little piece offered the novelty of a production without a single feminine character, and even without any feminine motive.'' In a 1911 review of a revival of the play, The *Times* (Review of *The Rising of the Moon*) called the play "a charming little thing with a bit of ... sentiment to it and touches of ... humor suggestive of Irish character, but not necessarily illuminative of it.'' Atkinson [1] wrote of a 1932 revival that "these wandering players came heavily freighted with the sort of plays that turn theatregoing into enchantment.... Even if you knew every turning in the plays you would have to be tone-deaf to find them familiar or uninteresting.''

The Jackdaw. 1907. Opened 23 February at the Abbey Theatre, Dublin. Mrs. Broderick: Sara Allgood, Joseph Nestor: F. J. Fay, Michael Cooney: W. G. Fay. 14 December 1911: Maxine Elliott's Theatre, New York. Sibby Fahy: Eileen O'Doherty, Timothy Ward: J. M. Kerrigan, Mrs. Broderick: Sara Allgood, Tommy Nally: J. A. O'Rourke, Joseph Nestor: Fred O'Donovan, Michael Cooney: Arthur Sinclair.

The *Irish Times* (Review of *The Jackdaw*) reports: "The amusing situation which the piece develops appeared to meet with much approval. The comedy, however, is somewhat unconvincing.'' The *New York Times* (Review of *The Jackdaw*) described the play as "an amusing satire of the effects of minding other people's business.''

Dervorgilla. 1907. Opened 31 October at the Abbey Theatre, Dublin. Dervorgilla: Sara Allgood, Mona: Maire O'Neill, Mamie: Brigit O'Dempsey, Flann: F. J. Fay, Songmaker: W. G. Fay, Boy: Arthur Sinclair.

The *Irish Times* (Review of *Dervorgilla*) noted that the play "is described as a tragedy in one act. It would give a better idea of the scope of Lady Gregory's latest work to describe it as one act of a tragedy—the final act.''

The Unicorn and the Stars. 1907. Opened 21 November at the Abbey Theatre (23 November listed in Kohfeldt). A collaboration with Yeats. Yeats wrote of the play that " 'but for the fable and the chief character it is wholly her work' " (Coxhead 109). Father John: Ernest Vaughan, Thomas Hearne: Arthur Sinclair, Andrew Hearne: J. A. O'Rourke, Martin Hearne: F. J. Fay, Johnny Bacach: W. G.

Fay, Paudeen: J. M. Kerrigan, Biddy Lally: Maire O'Neill, Nanny: Brigit O'Dempsey.

The Workhouse Ward. 1908. Opened 20 April at the Abbey Theatre, Dublin. Michael Miskell: Fred O'Donovan, Mike McInerney: Arthur Sinclair, Mrs. Donohue: Maire O'Neill. 25 October 1928: Arts Theatre Club, London. 10 April 1959: Gate Theatre, New York. Michael Miskell: Raymond Johnson, Mike McInerney: Jared Reed, Mrs. Donohue: Martha Orrick. A play derived from Gregory's collaboration with Douglas Hyde on *Tigh na mBocht* (The Poorhouse). Micheál Mac Liammóir identified the work as " 'that most subtly national and topical of one-act plays' " (Coxhead 118).

The *Irish Times* (Review of *The Workhouse Ward*) considered the play more successful than the collaboration on which it was based. "Quite recently Lady Gregory has arranged [the original] for three players only, but in doing so she found it necessary to substitute entirely new dialogue, the two men in the former play obviously being supposed to talk to an audience in the ward which has now been taken from them."

The 1910 London production presented the play in repertory with four plays by Synge and other Abbey plays, which resulted in the following comparative assessment from Archer: "In our admiration for his [Synge's] genius, however, we must not forget that the National Theatre has brought to the front a whole school of noteworthy writers [including] Lady Gregory, whose comic character sketches, 'Hyacinth Halvey' and 'The Workhouse Ward,' are full of spirit and humor."

The 1928 London production played on a bill with T. C. Murray's *Birthright* and Synge's *The Shadow of the Glen*. The *Times* (Review of *The Workhouse Ward*) reviewer was perhaps partially influenced by concepts of the Celtic Twilight. "Each in its way, they show how much we should be indebted to this shadowy Ireland, both for plays and for acting."

The 1959 revival resulted in an Atkinson [2] review that raised interesting comparisons between Lady Gregory's play and Synge's *Well of the Saints*, the other play on the double bill. "Lady Gregory's trifle also has rhythm, tone, and color. . . . Both plays are iconoclastic. What is normal is what is unbearable. . . . The freshness of Synge and Lady Gregory has lost none of its irony and bubble."

The Image. 1909. A three-act comedy. Opened 11 November at the Abbey Theatre, Dublin. Thomas Coppinger: Arthur Sinclair, Mary Coppinger: Sara Allgood, Malachi Naughton: Fred O'Donovan, Brian Hostey: Sydney J. Morgan, Peggy Mahon: Maire O'Neill, Darby Costello: J. M. Kerrigan, Peter Mannion: J. A. O'Rourke. 1 June 1910: Court Theatre, London. 21 December 1911: Maxine Elliott's Theatre, New York. Thomas Coppinger: Arthur Sinclair, Mary Coppinger: Sara Allgood, Malachi Naughton: Fred O'Donovan, Peggy Mahon: Cathleen Nesbitt.

The *Irish Times* (Review of *The Image*) reports, "Lady Gregory points a useful moral. She tells us to preach less and to practise more, and in doing so makes some sly hits at Irish life.''

Of the 1 June 1910 London premiere, the *Times* (Review of *The Image*) remarked that ''[t]he first thing that strikes one about it is that it is quite extraordinarily Irish. Its language and its accent are the Irish not of the stage, but of Ireland, far more so even than was the case in [Shaw's] *John Bull's Other Island*. And this, to the Saxon members of the audience, made some of it not at all easy to follow, a difficulty which was intensified by the fact that the plot, such as it is, is extremely nebulous.'' Nevertheless, the reviewer went on to praise the work: ''[T]he interest of the play, for it is interesting, lies in its idealism and humour, for Lady Gregory can hardly fail to be humourous when she puts her mind to it—and in the many quaint Irishisms of phrase and expression with which it is thickly sown.'' The reviewer for the *Athenaeum* (Review of *The Image*) used the occasion to reflect on Lady Gregory's career to date: ''There is no disputing Lady Gregory's mastery of the kind of one-act play which offers a study of the Irish peasant's proneness to make-believe. Within this medium, though her attitude is more that of a kindly outsider than an observer capable of projecting a sympathetic imagination into the lives of the people, her methods of comedy are singularly successful, and she gives very diverting pictures of mental indolence and love of day-dreaming among the peasantry.''

The *New York Times* (Review of *The Image*) notice about the New York production described the plot, centered on Peggy Mahon's tale, as ''an old folk story heard from his grandmother.''

Kincora. 11 February 1909. Revised version. The Abbey Theatre. Brian: Arthur Sinclair, Maelmora: Sydney J. Morgan, Malachi: Ambrose Power, Sitric: U. Wright, Gormnleith: Sara Allgood, Murrough: Fred O'Donovan, Brennain: J. M. Kerrigan, Rury: J. H. Dunne, Phelan: J. A. O'Rourke, Beggar: Maire O'Neill.

The Full Moon. 1910. A one-act play. Opened 10 November at the Abbey Theatre, Dublin. 15 June 1911: Court Theatre, London premiere. Shawn Early: J. A. O'Rourke, Bartley Fallon: Arthur Sinclair, Hyacinth Halvey: Fred O'Donovan, Mrs. Broderick: Sara Allgood, Cracked Mary: Maire O'Neill.

The *Irish Times* (Review of *The Full Moon*) viewed the play as a falling off in creativity: ''It can hardly be regarded as a valuable addition of the Abbey repertoire.''

The *Times* (Review of *The Full Moon*) reported that the premiere of ''[t]he little play introduces us again to several of our old acquaintances from Cloon.'' Calling attention to that novelty of the play and the performers, the review continued, ''There would not be so much interest in the piece if we did not know some of the characters already, and the action is rather slow in starting, but it is amusing enough when it does start.''

Coats. 1910. A one-act play. Opened 1 December at the Abbey Theatre, Dublin. Editors: J. M. Kerrigan and Arthur Sinclair. 3 March 1913: Wallack's Theatre, New York.

The *Irish Times* (Review of *Coats*) took note of the play's "wordy warfare" and a comedic structure wherein not only do the characters accidentally swap coats, but "hasty changes of language take place."

The Travelling Man. 1910. A one-act play. Opened 2 March at the Abbey Theatre, Dublin. 9 February 1912: the Court Theatre, London. 26 December 1916: Cohan and Harris Theatre, New York.

The *Irish Independent* (Review of *The Travelling Man*) noted that the premiere showed continuity with earlier Gregory plays: "In 'The Travelling Man' is presented an interesting story based on a Galway folk-lore tale."

In comparing the play with Yeats' *The Hour Glass*, which was performed on the same bill in the 1912 London production, the *Times* reviewer praised Yeats' sometimes collaborator: "It was a good thought to include in the same bill Lady Gregory's little Miracle, *The Travelling Man*, for Lady Gregory can stand comparison with Mr. Yeats better than most people." The *New York Times* (Review of *The Travelling Man*) reported, "Lady Gregory's miracle play of Christ unrecognized, is good dramatic literature, and it is represented now by an intelligent if somewhat inert performance. . . . But its place in a children's program is simpl[y] inexplicable."

The Deliverer. 1911. A one-act play. Opened 5 January (listed elsewhere as 12 January), at the Abbey Theatre, Dublin. Ard: Fred O'Donovan, Malachi: J. A. O'Rourke, Dan: Arthur Sinclair, Ard's Wife: Maire Ni Shiublaigh, Malachi's Wife: Sara Allgood, Dan's Wife: Maire O'Neill, King's Nurseling: J. M. Kerrigan.

The *Irish Times* review (Review of *The Deliverer*) of the original Abbey Theatre production was given over almost entirely to comments on Gordon Craig's set designs for Yeats' *The Hour Glass*. Nevertheless, the reviewer took time to raise a question about Lady Gregory's potential use of allegory: "[S]uffice it now to say that its central figure is Moses, with an interesting variant, however, from the Bible story. . . . The place of such a play in the Irish dramatic movement is not very clear, unless it is intended as a political parable for Irish consumption."

McDonough's Wife. 1912. (First performed as *MacDaragh's Wife.*) Opened 11 January at the Abbey Theatre, Dublin. First Hag: Mary Roberts, Second Hag: Helena Moloney, MacDaragh: Philip Guiry.

The *Irish Times* (Review of *McDonough's Wife*) considered this tale of a husband who returns home to be greeted with the news of his wife's death an unfortunate departure from comedy. "The incident treated is rather crude, and the dialogue by no means convincing."

The Bogie Man. 1912. A one-act play. Opened 8 July at the Court Theatre, London. (This premiere is sometimes listed as 4 July 1912.)

The *Times* reviewer (Review of *The Bogie Man*) generalized about Lady Gregory's past one-act comedies based on this premiere: "With Lady Gregory's little comedies it constantly occurs to one that nobody else would have thought of that, or thought of it just like that. . . . [F]uture audiences will perhaps laugh more heartily when the quaint dialogue, Theocritan in its balance, its give and take, has been pruned a little and committed a little more securely to memory." The *Pall Mall Gazette* (Review of *The Bogie Man*) faulted the play as "a disappointment. Its little joke did not quite come off."

Damer's Gold. 1912. A two-act play. Opened 21 November by the Abbey Players, London. 17 February 1913: Wallack's Theatre (NY). Delia Hessian: Sara Allgood, Staffy Kirwan: Sidney J. Morgan, Ralph Hessian: J. M. Kerrigan, Patrick Kirwan: Arthur Sinclair.

The *New York Herald Tribune* (Review of *Damer's Gold*) observed that the play "furnishes an interesting example of the comedy of lines and those comic more by implication than in essence. . . . There is very little that is amusing in the comedy—that is, amusing in the sense which the designation 'comedy' conveys to the average theatregoer. . . . The effect is rather a certain biting quality which interests instead of entertains."

The Wrens. 1914. A one-act play. Opened 1 June (listed as 18 June in the *Times*) at the Court Theatre, London. William Hevener, a ballad singer: J. M. Kerrigan, Margy Hevener: Kathleen Drago.

The *Times* (Review of *The Wrens*) review called attention to the subversive qualities of work, identifying it as "a study of political motives which has a sharp sting in it, though we should not care to guess exactly in which direction its shafts are aimed."

Shanwalla. 1915. A three-act play. Opened 8 April at the Abbey Theatre. Scarry: H. Hutchinson, Bride Scarry, the Spirit Wife: Kathleen Drago, James Brogan: Arthur Sinclair, Pat O'Malley: Fred O'Donovan, The Beggar: J. M. Kerrigan.

The *Irish Times* (Review of *Shanwalla*) noted that "speculation" had greeted the announced title but that the word "is the name of a racehorse, and it is around attempts to dope the horse that a powerful drama is built up. It is, however, in its relation to the supernatural that the play presents most novelty, and, on the whole, the introductions of a spirit are typified in an acceptable manner, and arrest the attention firmly."

The *Times* (Review of *Shanwalla*) review of the premiere noted that the "first production . . . was cordially received. . . . The play is impressive and powerful, both as drama and in its relation to the supernatural."

Hanrahan's Oath. 1918. A one-act play. Opened 20 January at the Abbey Theatre. Mary Gillis: Maureen Delaney, Hanrahan: Fred O'Donovan.

The *Irish Times* (Review of *Hanrahan's Oath*) considered the work "an excellent little comedy by Lady Gregory. One cannot but admire the ingenuity which marks the inspiration of the piece and the neatness with which its development is worked out."

The Dragon. 1919. Opened 21 April at the Abbey Theatre. King: Barry Fitzgerald, Princess Nuala: Eithne Magee. 25 March 1929: The Jitney Players, New York. The Dall Glie: Jack Rennick, The King: Harrison Dowd, The Queen: Alice B. Keating, The Princess Nuala: Elizabeth Zachary.

The *Irish Times* (Review of *The Dragon*) found this "wonder play in three acts" to be "mythical and fanciful to a large extent, and takes one back to the days when Kings reigned in Ireland."

Two *New York Times* comments suggest the "actor-proof" quality of Lady Gregory's writing and how themes in her folk material might relate to personal concerns. "It is, one imagines, a play better suited to interpretation by ambitious youngsters than the mannered, brittle Sheridan comedy which is their regular bill." And: "Those who like such extravagant departures from reality as Celtic fantasy may find the play enjoyable."

The Golden Apple. 1920. Opened 6 January at the Abbey Theatre. The cast included Hugh Nagle, Christine Hayden, Eithne Magee, F. J. McCormick, Maureen Delany, Arthur Shields, and Barry Fitzgerald.

The *Irish Times* (Review of *The Golden Apple*) highlighted the attraction of the work for children: "It is really a Hibernian version of one of Grimm's fairy tales; an adaptation of an old legend to suit Kiltartan little folk. . . . Lady Gregory has not, however, written the play for disgruntled people, who do not understand the childish joys of Kiltartan, so their opinions must be discounted."

The Bellows of Aristotle. 1921. Opened 17 March at the Abbey Theatre.

Of the play, Maud Gonne wrote, "It is a most charming fantastic little play, introducing numbers of old Irish songs. It has the good humoured gaiety & fantasy & charm of the best of Lady Gregory's work & should prove a great favorite at the Abbey" (White, p. 424). The reviewer for the *Irish Independent* (Review of *The Bellows of Aristotle*) was less favorable: "It is more than a wonder play—it is a wonderful play, the most wonderful thing about it being that anyone would have the patience and pertinacity to write three acts of it.

The Old Woman Remembers. 1923. Opened 31 December at the Abbey Theatre. Read by Sara Allgood.

The *Irish Independent*'s review praised Allgood's power and the political content of the piece: "[A]lthough the opportunity for adding effect by declamatory gestures was practically absent, her clear voice recalled with passionate emotion various phases of struggles for Irish freedom dealt with in the poem."

The Story Brought by Brigit. 1924. Opened 15 April at the Abbey Theatre.

Reviewing this three-act passion play, the *Irish Times* (Review of *The Story*

Brought by Brigit) identified Lady Gregory's stylized language as the central issue for critical response: "[An] appreciation of this new Passion Play will vary with the taste for the manner of writing to which Lady Gregory adheres. Those with whom it agrees will probably find 'The Story Brought by Brigit' a very moving and wonderful dramatic narration; and, indeed, there were moments in the production last night when no one could fail to be impressed."

Sancho's Master. 1927. Opened 14 March at the Abbey Theatre. Don Quixote: F. J. McCormick, Duchess: Shelah Richards, Sancho: Barry Fitzgerald.

The *Irish Independent* (Review of *Sancho's Master*) offered mixed praise for the three-act play: "If Lady Gregory does not achieve the impossible, she does succeed in providing an entertainment that has at least a smack of the richness of the original. . . . Lady Gregory was often more successful when she allowed Sancho or the housekeeper to describe Don Quixote's adventures at secondhand than when she selected incidents for actual presentation on the stage."

Hayes' Dublin report to the *New York Times* on this debut faulted Lady Gregory's adaptation: "In attempting to transfer 'Don Quixote' to the stage, Lady Gregory, paradoxically, has succeeded and failed. She succeeded in investing the Knight of the Rueful Countenance with all the pathos and tragedy that are his . . . but, despite the excellent work and the effort of the Abbey actor F. J. McCormick to make the figure dominate, the background of comedy and horseplay completely overwhelmed the Don and rendered him ludicrous."

Dave. 1927. A one-act wonder play. Opened 9 May at the Abbey Theatre. Dave: J. Stephenson. Also in the cast: Miss K. Curling, Maureen Delany, J. Dolan, and P. J. Carolan.

The *Irish Times* (Review of *Dave*) compared the work with the newer, urban plays of the Abbey: "It was precisely what one expected from the Kiltartan pen. There are those who like their mystical Kiltartanese as often as they can have it, and for them it's 'Dave,' the manservant, whose personal appearance is that of the toiler in a pre-O'Casey age."

ADDITIONAL PLAYS, ADAPTATIONS, AND PRODUCTIONS

Colman and Guaire. 1898. Lady Gregory's first play. Not produced. Published as *My First Play* (London: Elkin Mathew and Marrot, 1930). *A Losing Game.* Though unproduced, the play served as the basis for *Twenty-Five. The Doctor in Spite of Himself.* 16 April 1906. A translation of Molière. The Abbey Theatre. Sganarelle: W. G. Fay, Martha: Sara Allgood, Robert: Arthur Sinclair, Valere: A. Power, Luke: U. Wright, Geronte: F. J. Fay, Jacqueline: Maire O'Neill, Lucy: Brigit O'Dempsey, Leeane: Arthur Sinclair. *Interior.* 1907. A translation of Maeterlinck's play. *The Poorhouse.* 3 April 1907; a collaboration with Douglas Hyde. The Abbey Theatre. Colum: W. G. Fay, Paudeen: Arthur Sinclair, The Matron: Maire O'Neill, A Country Woman: Brigit O'Dempsey. The *Irish Times* (Review of *The Poorhouse*) reports that "it may be frankly said that the piece is hardly worthy of the collaborateurs. It is a mere trifle—

its performance did not occupy more than ten minutes—and the comedy seemed
only just to begin when the end came.''

    Teja. 19 March 1908. A translation of Sudermann's play. The Abbey Theatre.
Teja: J. M. Kerrigan, Balthilda: Maire O'Neill, Amalaberga: Sara Allgood,
Bishop Agilla: Arthur Sinclair, Theodemir: Sydney Morgan, Eurich: U. Wright,
Haribalt: J. A. O'Rourke, Ildebad: Fred O'Donovan. The review in the *Irish
Times* (Review of *Teja*) praised the translation and suggested the complexity of
some of the female characters. *The Rogueries of Scapin.* 4 April 1908. A trans-
lation of Molière's *Les Fourberies de Scapin.* The Abbey Theatre. Argante:
Sydney Morgan, Géronte: J. A. O'Rourke, Octave: Fred O'Donovan, Hyacinthe:
Maire Ni Gharbheagh, Zerbinette: Maire O'Neill, Scapin: Arthur Sinclair, Sil-
vestre: Ambrose Power, Leandre: J. M. Kerrigan, Nerine: Eileen O'Doherty,
Carle: Stuart Hamilton. 12 June 1911: Court Theatre, London. The cast changes
included Hyacinthe: Eithne Magee, Zerbinette: Sara Allgood, Carle: Brinsley
MacNamara. The other leads were the same as in Dublin. *Miser.* 21 January
1909. Another translation of a Molière play, *L'Avare.* The Abbey Theatre. Har-
pagon: Arthur Sinclair, Cleante: Fred O'Donovan, Valere: J. M. Kerrigan, An-
selme: U. Wright, Elise: Eileen O'Doherty, Marianne: Maire O'Neill, Frosine:
Sara Allgood, Master Simon: S. J. Morgan, Master Jacques: J. A. O'Rourke, La
Gleche: Eric Gorman. *Mirandolina.* 24 February 1910. A translation of Gol-
doni's play. The Abbey Theatre. Captain Ripafratta: Fred O'Donovan, Marquis
of Forlipopli: Arthur Sinclair, Count of Albafiorita: J. M. Kerrigan, Mirandolina:
Maire O'Neill, Ortensia: Eithne Magee, Fabrizio: J. A. O'Rourke, The Captain's
Servant: Sydney J. Morgan. 17 August 1925: Everyman Theatre, London. Cap
tain Ripafratta: Charles Carson, Mirandolina: Ruth Bower, Marquis of Forlipopli: J. Leslie Frite, Count of Albafiorita: Roy Byford. *Deirdre of the Sorrows.*
1910. By J. M. Synge. Gregory, Yeats, and Maire O'Neill collaborated to complete the posthumous work. *Nativity Play.* 12 January 1911. A translation of a
Douglas Hyde play. The Abbey Theatre. Cast: Sara Allgood, Maire O'Neill,
Fred O'Donovan, Arthur Sinclair, J. M. Kerrigan, Sydney J. Morgan.

    The Marriage. 11 January 1912. A translation of a Douglas Hyde play. The
Abbey Theatre. *Grania.* [1910]. Unproduced. *The Jester.* 1919. A three-act wonder play written for her grandson. *On the Racecourse.* Unproduced revision of
Twenty-Five. The Would-Be Gentleman. 4 January 1926. A translation of Molière's *Le Bourgeois Gentilhomme.* The Abbey Theatre. Mr. Jordain: Barry Fitzgerald, Mrs. Jordain: Maureen Delany, Lucile: Shelah Richards, Nicola: Eileen
Crowe, Cleonte: Arthur Shields, Coviel: Tony Quinn, Dorante: Michael J. Dolan, Dorimene: May Craig, Philosophy Master: Frank J. McCormick, Master-
Tailor: Gabriel Fallon, Fencing Master: John Breen.

ASSESSMENT OF LADY GREGORY'S CAREER

    Coxhead's excellent study of Lady Gregory's career raises issues about the
Gregory canon that merit further study. For example, Coxhead reasonably questions basing Gregory's reputation solely on her one-act successes. Of *The Rising*

of the Moon, Coxhead notes that "[i]t is revived not merely oftener than her other plays, but ten times oftener. It is the only work of hers that many people know." Yet, as with the most popular work of other authors, "[i]t is seldom the best, or ever the one over which we have worked hardest" (112). Coxhead argues that "[i]f it is generally true that she does better in the one-act than in the three-act form, still there is *The White Cockade* to prove that she had it in her to write full-length plays" (115). Though Coxhead uses *Kincora* as an example of when Gregory's "failure of nerve," encouraged by Yeats, weakened her ability to successfully create, the revised and original versions of that play provide an important basis for reexamining Gregory's dramaturgy and her technique for providing indirect political commentary on the situation in Ireland. Such a discussion of colonialist themes could develop the suggestions first made in the reviews of *The Deliverer* and *The Wrens.*

Similarly, claims for the significance of Lady Gregory's tragedies were eloquently stated by Saddlemyer in her foreword to *The Tragedies and Tragic-comedies of Lady Gregory,* the second volume of the *Collected Plays:* "Nowhere does Lady Gregory's love of country show itself more clearly than in her tragedies and the closely related history plays" (v). The playwright's "love of country" resulted in her ability to create controversy, as may be seen in the 11 March 1907 *Irish Times* review of *The Rising of the Moon.* That review, in particular, demonstrates the value of cultural studies for interpreting her works in the context of their first presentation. Her ability to construct critiques of colonialism within her tragedies, her histories, and her comic texts merits additional study.

While scholarship in the last thirty years has increasingly given Gregory credit for her active role in collaborations with Yeats, she herself said of *The Unicorn from the Stars* that she "did 'not wish to include it in her own works,' " though the play was " 'almost wholly hers in handiwork' " (White 492, n. 131.9). Yet, as FitzGerald and Coxhead have noted, Lady Gregory's tendency not to take full credit for her contribution was influenced by social ideas of the time. Coxhead, for instance, faults not only Gogarty for distorting the record in his autobiography but the preconceptions that were "unchallenged in an anti-feminist country" (105).

A tribute to Lady Gregory's ability to challege occurs in the writings of a woman who played a singular role in the founding of the republic. After Yeats sent Maud Gonne a copy of Lady Gregory's *Our Irish Theatre,* Gonne provided her own assessment of Lady Gregory's career, in a postscript to a 1914 letter: "I don't want you to think that because I don't care much for Lady Gregory's *book* on the theatre, I underrate her work—I think she has done great work & has shown great courage & *staying* power—her perseverance under difficulties has been wonderful—I also think her book on Cuchulain & Finn most valuable & most charming. I have read & reread them many times & always with delight" (White 336).

Her development of an Irish English literary dialect remains a specific aspect of Lady Gregory's contribution to Irish literature that also merits further investigation. (Coxhead offers limited but specific analysis in pages 121–23 of her study.) A potentially useful text for such a study would be Gregory's *The Kiltartan Molière* (Dublin: Maunsel, 1910). That collection could also be an impetus to new studies of Lady Gregory's career as a translator.

The focus of continuing scholarly interest, Lady Gregory's career receives a fresh examination by Waters. An extended feminist analysis of Gregory's career will be provided in a forthcoming study by Waters and Lucy McDiarmid. Kohfeldt's and FitzGerald's work provides the basis for examining Lady Gregory's ability to create positions of power and privacy for herself. Lady Gregory's ability to conduct discreet affairs with such figures as Wilfred Blunt provides a context for reading such characters as Gormleith in *Kincora*. For future studies of the plays in the context of Gregory's life and social context, feminist and semiotic analyses hold perhaps the most promise.

ARCHIVAL SOURCES

The Lady Gregory Archives of the Henry W. and Albert A. Berg Collection, New York Public Library. Special Collections Department, Robert Woodruff Library, Emory University.

PRIMARY BIBLIOGRAPHY

Unpublished Plays

The Dispensary
Heads or Harps (collaboration with Yeats)
The Lighted Window
The Meadow Gate
Michelin
The Shoelace
The Coole Edition of the Works of Lady Gregory. Ed. T. R. Henn and Colin Smythe. New York: Oxford University Press, 1970–1971. *The Collected Plays*, I–IV, ed. Ann Saddlemyer, are part of *The Coole Edition*.

SECONDARY BIBLIOGRAPHY

Adams, Hazard. *Lady Gregory*. Lewisburg, Pa.: Bucknell University Press, 1973.
Archer, William. Review of *The Workhouse Ward*. *Nation* (19 June 1909): 420.
Atkinson, Brooks. [1]. Review of *The Rising of the Moon*. *New York Times* (21 Oct. 1932): 25.
———. [2]. Review of *The Workhouse Ward*. *New York Times* (11 Apr. 1959): 15.

Review of *The Bellows of Aristotle*. *Irish Independent* (18 Mar. 1921): 40.

Review of *The Bogie Man*. *Pall Mall Gazette* (9 July 1912): 5.

Review of *The Bogie Man*. *Times* (9 July 1912): 11.

Review of *The Canavans*. *Irish Times* (10 Dec. 1906): 8.

Review of *Coats*. *Irish Times* (2 Dec. 1910): 4.

Coxhead, Elizabeth. *Lady Gregory*. London: Macmillan, 1961.

Review of *Damer's Gold*. *New York Herald Tribune* (18 Feb. 1913): 9.

Review of *Dave*. *Irish Times* (10 May 1927): 10.

Review of *The Deliverer*. *Irish Times* (6 Jan. 1911): 4.

Review of *Dervorgilla*. *Irish Times* (1 Nov. 1907): 5.

Review of *The Dragon*. *Irish Times* (22 Apr. 1919): 7.

Review of *The Dragon*. *New York Times* (26 Mar. 1929): 34.

FitzGerald, Mary. " 'Perfection of the Life': Lady Gregory's Autobiographical Writings." In *Lady Gregory, Fifty Years After*. Ed. Ann Saddlemyer and Colin Smythe. Totowa, N.J.: Barnes and Noble, 1987: 45–55.

Review of *The Full Moon*. *Irish Times* (11 Nov. 1910): 8.

Review of *The Full Moon*. *Times* (16 June 1911): 11.

Review of *The Gaol Gate*. *Irish Times* (22 Oct. 1906): 8.

Review of *The Golden Apple*. *Irish Times* (7 Jan. 1920): 5.

Review of *Hanrahan's Oath*. *Irish Times* (30 Jan. 1918): 6.

Hayes, J. J. Review of *Sancho's Master*. *New York Times* (10 Apr. 1927): sec. 8: 4.

Review of *Hyacinth Halvey*. *Athenaeum* (29 June 1912): 741.

Review of *Hyacinth Halvey*. *Irish Times* (20 Feb. 1906): 3.

Review of *Hyacinth Halvey*. *New York Times* (16 Dec. 1911): 4.

Review of *Hyacinth Halvey*. *Times* (31 May 1910): 12.

Review of *Hyacinth Halvey*. *Times* (21 Aug. 1917): 3.

Review of *Hyacinth Halvey*. *Times* (6 Dec. 1939): 12.

Review of *The Image*. *Athenaeum* (11 June 1910): 715.

Review of *The Image*. *Irish Times* (12 Nov. 1909): 8.

Review of *The Image*. *New York Times* (22 Dec. 1911): 9.

Review of *The Image*. *Times* (2 June 1910): 12.

Review of *The Jackdaw*. *Irish Times* (25 Feb. 1908): 7.

Review of *The Jackdaw*. *New York Times* (15 Dec. 1911).

Review of *Kincora*. *Irish Times* (27 Mar. 1905): 7.

Kohfeldt, Mary Lou. *Lady Gregory: The Woman behind the Irish Renaissance*. New York: Atheneum, 1985.

Kopper, Edward A. *Lady Isabella Persse Gregory*. Boston: Twayne, 1976.

Review of *McDonough's Wife*. *Irish Times* (12 Jan. 1912): 5.

Mikhail, E. H., ed. [1]. *Lady Gregory, Interviews and Recollections*. London: Macmillan, 1977.

Review of *The Old Woman Remembers*. *Irish Independent* (1 Jan. 1924): 6.

Review of *The Poorhouse*. *Irish Times* (4 Apr. 1907): 6.

Review of *The Rising of the Moon*. *Irish Times* (11 Mar. 1907): 7.

Review of *The Rising of the Moon*. *New York Times* (25 Feb. 1908): 7.

Review of *The Rising of the Moon*. *Times* (21 Nov. 1911): 9.

Saddlemyer, Ann. [1]. *In Defence of Lady Gregory, Playwright*. Chester Springs, Pa.: Dufour Editions, 1966.

———, ed. [2]. *Theatre Business, the Correspondence of the First Abbey Theatre Di-*

rectors: William Butler Yeats, Lady Gregory, and J. M. Synge. University Park: Pennsylvania State University Press, 1982.

Saddlemyer, Ann, and Colin Smythe, eds. *Lady Gregory, Fifty Years After.* Totowa, N.J.: Barnes and Noble, 1987.

Review of *Sancho's Master. Irish Independent* (15 Mar. 1927): 8.

Review of *Shanwalla. Irish Times* (9 Apr. 1915): 8.

Review of *Shanwalla. Times* (9 Apr. 1915): 11.

Review of *Spreading the News. Athenaeum* (22 June 1912): 715.

Review of *Spreading the News. Irish Times* (28 Dec. 1904): 5.

Review of *Spreading the News. New York Times* (21 Nov. 1911): 9.

Review of *The Story Brought by Brigit. Irish Times* (16 Apr. 1924): 4.

Review of *Teja. Irish Times* (20 Mar. 1908): 8.

Review of *The Travelling Man. Irish Independent* (4 Mar. 1910): 6.

Review of *The Travelling Man. New York Times* (27 Dec. 1916): 7.

Review of *The Travelling Man. Times* (10 Feb. 1912): 10.

Review of *Twenty-Five.* The *Times Literary Supplement* (8 May 1903): 146.

Waters, Maureen. "Lady Gregory's Grania: A Feminist Perspective." *Irish University Review* (Spring 1995).

White, Anna MacBride, and A. Norman Jeffares. *The Gonne-Yeats Letters, 1893–1938.* New York: W. W. Norton, 1992.

Review of *The White Cockade. Irish Times* (25 Feb. 1908): 7.

Review of *The Workhouse Ward. Irish Times* (21 Apr. 1908): 6.

Review of *The Wrens. Times* (19 June 1914): 10.

BIBLIOGRAPHY

Mikhail, E. H. [2]. *Lady Gregory: An Annotated Bibliography of Criticism.* Troy, N.Y.: Whitston, 1982.

Denis Johnston
(1901–1984)

NOEL PEACOCK

Denis Johnston was born 18 June 1901 in Dublin to Kathleen King Johnston and William Denis Johnston, an Anglo-Irish barrister and judge. In accordance with family expectation, Johnston planned a career in law, attending Christ's College, Cambridge University (1919–1923), where he received the B.A. and LL.B. degrees, and Harvard Law School (1923–1924). At Harvard his interest in drama, which for a decade he pursued in parallel with his legal career, emerged. In 1925 he was called to the bar in London's Inner Temple, while beginning an association with the Dublin Drama League and the New Players, organizations affiliated with the Abbey Theatre but dedicated to exploring plays the more conservative Abbey stage rejected. Johnston both acted and directed in these troupes. The following year he was called to the bar in Northern Ireland after receiving the M.A. and LL.M. degrees from Cambridge.

In 1928 Johnston married Shelah Richards, an actress at the Abbey, with whom he had two children, and the following year, 1929, his first play, *The Old Lady Says "No!"*, was produced by the Gate Theatre Company, after being rejected by the Abbey. Dublin theater lore has it that Johnston changed the play's original title, *Shadowdance*, to conform to the words scrawled in the margin of the manuscript upon its rejection, the old lady in question being Lady Gregory, although textual evidence reveals this as an unfounded rumor (see St. Peter [1]). His next play, *The Moon in the Yellow River*, received a more positive response from the Abbey, where it was produced in 1931.

In 1933 Johnston embarked on the first of many excursions outside the theater, collaborating with Barry Fitzgerald and Cyril Cusack, among others, on a silent film version of Frank O'Connor's short story "Guests of the Nation." The following year he acted with Fitzgerald and Sara Allgood in a film version of J. M. Synge's *Riders to the Sea*. Meanwhile, his next two plays, *A Bride for the*

Unicorn (1933) and *Storm Song* (1934), were produced at the Gate Theatre. In 1936 *Blind Man's Buff*, Johnston's adaptation of Ernst Toller's expressionistic courtroom drama *Die Blinde Göttin*, was produced at the Abbey. This was a somewhat symbolic means for Johnston to bid farewell to his original legal profession. The same year he gave up his law practice and joined the BBC in Belfast, where he was involved in a number of radio plays, including the epic *Lillibulero*. The following year he was working for BBC London, where by the early 1940s he was established as a writer, broadcaster, and producer.

Two more plays, *The Golden Cuckoo* and *The Dreaming Dust*, were produced in 1939 and 1940, respectively, although, throughout the 1940s, Johnston's time was taken up with radio and television work. Between 1942 and 1945 he was a war correspondent for the BBC in the Middle East, Italy, France, and Germany, for which he was awarded the Order of the British Empire. Out of this wartime experience emerged a memoir, *Nine River from Jordan*, which later became the basis for an opera libretto of the same name. He divorced in 1945 and married the actress Betty Chancellor, with whom he had two sons. After recording the only interview given by George Bernard Shaw on the occasion of his ninetieth birthday for BBC television in 1946, Johnston moved to America, where, after working for NBC's "Theatre Guild on the Air" for two years (1947–1949), he pursued a joint career as dramatist and academic. In 1948 his only one-act play, *A Fourth for Bridge*, was completed.

In addition to the numerous American premieres of his earlier plays, Johnston was involved in the productions of *Strange Occurrence on Ireland's Eye* at the Abbey in 1956, *The Scythe and the Sunset* in Cambridge, Massachusetts, in 1958, and two operas for which, collaborating with the composer Hugo Weisgall, he wrote the librettos: *Nine Rivers* (1955) and an adaptation of Pirandello's *Six Characters in Search of an Author* (1959). Johnston has held academic positions at numerous American universities (including Smith and Amherst Colleges, the universities of Iowa and California, and New York University). He was awarded a Guggenheim Fellowship for his research on Jonathan Swift in 1955–1956. The first volume of Denis Johnston's *Dramatic Works* was published in 1977. He died in 1984.

Selected Biographical Sources: Barnett [1, 2]; Rory Johnston.

MAJOR PLAYS, PREMIERES, AND SIGNIFICANT
REVIVALS: THEATRICAL RECEPTION

The Old Lady Says "No!". 1929. Opened 3 July. Peacock Theatre, Dublin. Produced by the Gate Theatre Studio. Directed by Hilton Edwards.

Produced by the Gate after being rejected by the Abbey, Johnston's first play, written under the pseudonym "E. W. Tocher," received sharply mixed reviews. These focused generally on the play's use of expressionistic techniques and its attack on Irish cultural patriotism. While there was general admiration for Edwards' production of a difficult work, some reviewers found this difficulty confusing. Holloway [1] found it an incomprehensible "madhouse play" and repudiated its attack on Irish society and blasphemous use of scriptural allusion. The *Irish Times* (Review of *The Old Lady Says "No!"*) judged the confusion as arising from a lack of intellectual coherence. The play's satire, it felt, while obvious, was gentle and more likely to provoke laughter than offense. The *Daily Express* (Review of *The Old Lady Says "No!"*) thought the Gate's decision to produce *The Old Lady* courageous, given the play's anti-Irishness. It acknowledged its experimental aspect but thought it too clever, "sparkl[ing] with the borrowed tinsel of quotation." The *Irish Independent* (Review of *The Old Lady Says "No!"*) admired the sincerity of its attack on Irish culture. Curran, in the play's most positive review, praised a richness and modernity unseen since Synge and admired Johnston's deployment of expressionistic devices without reducing characters to mere types. He remarks positively on the play's allusive structure, arguing that its use of Scripture never occurs in a blasphemous context.

The Moon in the Yellow River. 1931. Opened 27 April. Abbey Theatre, Dublin. Directed by Lennox Robinson.

Johnston's second play, though contrasting sharply in its realism with the expressionistic *The Old Lady*, still left Holloway [1] confused and offended at its perceived anti-Irishness. Others were more charitable. The *Irish Times* (Review of *The Moon in the Yellow River*), while noting the audience's bewilderment, regarded the play as an intellectual work that, in its reliance on discussion, recalled Chekhov, Pirandello, and Toller and that contained some "delightful studies of Irish life." Like the *Times* (Review of *The Moon in the Yellow River*), which saw similar influences, it reported an absence of story in the play. The *Times*, while predicting theater riots, nevertheless downplayed any hostile audience reaction and agreed with the *Irish Times* that the play was motivated by Johnston's "exalted patriotism." It saw *The Moon* as one of the Abbey's most thoughtful productions in years, though, while admiring Johnston's erudition and creation of character and dialogue, it complained of the play's excessive allusiveness.

A Bride for the Unicorn. 1933. Opened 9 May. Gate Theatre, Dublin.

Like *The Old Lady*, with which it was compared by the *Irish Times* (Review of *A Bride for the Unicorn*), Johnston's third play, for which the pseudonym E. W. Tocher was by now regarded as tiresomely disingenuous, was found brilliant and confusing. As with its predecessor, *A Bride* was considered a vigorous and delightful satire at the level of individual scenes, although its larger significance remained somewhat elusive. Its break from the realistic theater into what was again identified as expressionism was regarded as courageous.

Blind Man's Buff. 1936. Opened 28 December. Abbey Theatre, Dublin. Directed by Hugh Hunt.

Johnston's adaptation of Ernst Toller's *Die Blinde Göttin* (*The Blind Goddess*) was well received. Holloway [2], in the past unsympathetic to Johnston's work, found it thoroughly absorbing, a sentiment echoed by other reviewers. The *Irish*

Times (Review of *Blind Man's Buff*) praised this reworking of Toller's original play about a criminal trial, remarking that, at the levels of theme, plot, dialogue, and character, Johnston's version was a humanized improvement on what it regarded as a too-abstract German original: "Its German philosophical bones have been given an excellent covering of good Irish flesh." The *Times* agreed, noting that Johnston's version had improved an overly didactic propaganda play by rewriting it in terms of "normal" life, altering dialogue, character, and situation in a realistic direction. These comments, combined with the *Irish Times'* remark that Johnston's play, in its increase of tragic effect over Toller's, is a "contemporary . . . counterpart to Greek tragic drama," indicate a response to Johnston that departs from earlier complaints of the excessively expressionist character of his work. Comments about the play's control of suspense unanimously called it successful.

The Golden Cuckoo. 1939. Opened 25 April. Gate Theatre, Dublin.

Holloway [3] once again witnessed an incomprehensible "madhouse affair." The *Irish Times* (Review of *The Golden Cuckoo*), on the other hand, applauded the play in what were essentially positive versions of the negative criticisms that Johnston's first plays, *The Old Lady Says "No!"* and *The Moon in the Yellow River*, had received. The play's political satire, even when at times close to the bone of an Irish audience, was unerringly funny and liable to provoke laughter rather than anger. The use of local allusions was not found to damage an easy understanding of the play, and its plot, though long and slow to develop, was never boring. Johnston, previously a writer of scene-length tours de force that he was unable to sustain for the length of an entire production, was now a "very skillful dramatist." The *Times* (Review of *The Golden Cuckoo*) was less charitable, finding the play's first and third acts boring, despite the successful, if cynical, humor of the second. It also hinted at naive didacticism in its summary of the play as "a rather vague plea for justice over greed."

The Scythe and the Sunset. 1958. Opened 14 March. Poets' Theatre, Cambridge, Massachusetts.

The Irish premiere at the Abbey (19 May 1958) received enthusiastic reviews that saw the play as Johnston's return to his old form. The *Irish Times* (Review of the *Scythe and the Sunset*) described it as a sophisticated Irish history play "that should re-establish him as our most clear-sighted commentator on the new Ireland and its beginnings." Conor Cruise O'Brien praised the play for its avoidance of easy sentiment and refusal to romanticize the 1916 Easter Uprising "in favour of a comedy of argumentation and attitude" that dramatized the complex and ambiguous range of possible responses to the rebellion.

ASSESSMENT OF JOHNSTON'S CAREER

Most reviews of Johnston's first play, *The Old Lady Says "No!"*, remarked on its startling use of expressionist techniques; response to his second play, *The Moon in the Yellow River*, adjudged it a stringent, if at times confusing, exercise in traditional theatrical realism. Much of subsequent Johnston scholarship has dwelled on this formally heterogeneous nature of his dramatic output. Johnston is nothing if not inimical to catering to an audience's inherited aesthetic and political expectations, and the challenge he presented to Irish drama is evident in the artistic and moral topicality of his plays, a topicality that has permitted a clear shift in the tenor of evaluative responses. Thus, the discomfort provoked by the *The Old Lady*'s perceived confusedness and political and religious blasphemy gave way fairly swiftly to appreciation of its erudition, dramatic experimentation, and political courage (see Ellis-Fermor, Nathan, Hogan, Jordan).

The antirealistic tendency in Johnston, evident in *The Old Lady* as well as in *A Bride for the Unicorn* and his choice to write the libretto for Pirandello's *Six Characters in Search of an Author*, has drawn considerable critical attention. Johnston was for a long time regarded—either negatively, as in the case of the early reviewers, or positively, as in the case of later critics (see Canfield)—as the first authentic Irish exponent of a Strindbergian expressionism, despite Johnston's own repudiation of this label. Ronsley attributes Johnston's antipathy to the term to his rejection, later in his career, of a technique that possessed an avant-garde cachet when he was first starting out and "was evidently not so hostile to the term" (178). This is not the case, however, since Johnston's insistence that " 'The Old Lady Says "No!" ' is not an expressionist play and ought never to have been mistaken for one" ("A Note" 79) occurs in 1929, the same year in which the play premiered. Johnston's attraction to experimental European forms is obvious and has been usefully qualified in more recent criticism. O'Brien [1] argues that expressionism constitutes a technique that provided Johnston with an available means to attack the stultifying tradition of the Abbey's "peasant realism" (see O'Brien [1]) and was thus of tactical importance in his quest for adequate expression; although, as Cave [2] argues, in the "density and incisiveness of [the play's] psychological insights" it is a technique that *The Old Lady* transcends. O'Brien [2] notes as well that *The Old Lady's* literary historical significance lies in its *adaptation* of continental expressionist devices to a specifically Irish context, in the same way that he would adapt Ernst Toller's *Die Blinde Göttin*. These remarks recognize implicitly a point made by other critics, that Johnston's theatrical background lies as much in European experimental drama as it does in the traditional Irish theater, an observation that, on one hand, explains a certain initial hostility at home to his work and, on the other, argues that he be taken seriously as a world dramatist (see Barnett [2]; Jordan).

It would thus be more accurate to say that Johnston deployed expressionist technique in his first play while rejecting its accompanying ideology. Two points are worth making here: the play not only embodies expressionist method but, by means of the Emmet character's violent transition from the frame play into the central, hallucinatory play within a play, actually dramatizes the scandalous eruption of these techniques into the preceding stream of Abbey traditionalism; and this emergence of expressionist form is a paradoxical rejection of politically rebellious impulses that are usually associated with expressionism. In this respect the play regards more traditional Irish dramatic form, in its sentimentalizing of violence, as the receptacle of revolutionary politics and counters with an aesthetic experimentalism that cautions liberalism and political moderation.

Johnston's realist plays, which, like *The Old Lady*, engage in the political subject of Irish nationalism, share with his experimental work their hostility to romantic patriotism. Thus, just as hallucination in *The Old Lady* corresponds to nightmare rather than to patriotic fantasy, the realistic world of *The Moon in the Yellow River* and *The Scythe and the Sunset* eschews the didactic possibilities of political theater in favor of exposing the irreconcilable moral ambiguities of the nationalism question (see Achilles; Ferrar; Grene; O'Reilly). Kilroy, accordingly, sees Shavian influences in Johnston's realism, in the sense that "the mechanized plot and system of ideas in [*The Moon in the Yellow River*] are leavened by a delicate, touching movement in feeling." Other critics, such as O'Reilly and Robert Hogan [1], have noted the complex attention to structure and character in these works, so it is perhaps surprising to find a critic like Thomas Hogan pronouncing the play's satire "text-book Anglo-Irish stuff," especially in light of the opinions of later critics that it attacks what Johnston perceives as the more simplistic politics of a playwright like O'Casey (whose *The Plough and the Stars* the title of *The Scythe and the Sunset* parodies). The advantage to the swerve away from the dream play is in the opportunity it affords Johnston to explore the construction of character, an opportunity that, to most other accounts, he exploits effectively.

It may be to the formal variety of his oeuvre and the difficulty this variety presents to classifying him as one particular type of playwright that we can attribute Johnston's uncertain critical reputation. This uncertainty unquestionably derives as well from the tendency of Johnston scholarship, either implicitly or explicitly, to see his first two plays as his best work. Barnett [2], for example, considers the three plays following *The Moon*—*A Bride for the Unicorn*, *Storm Song*, and *Blind Man's Buff*—as Johnston's "least satisfactory" works, despite the initial positive reception of the Toller adaptation. This general feeling is shared by other critics (see Fraser and Ferrar), although persuasive individual defenses of the plays can be found (O'Reilly; Achilles; Cave; Rollins; Murray; Ronsley [4]). One reason for this decline in Johnston's later reputation may again be his penchant for variety in both the mode and the type of his theatrical writing. Thus, starting in the mid-1930s, we find among Johnston's works an adaptation of another playwright's work (*Blind Man's Buff*), an allegorical comedy (*The Golden Cuckoo*), a historical biographical drama (*The Dreaming Dust*), an experimental drama later reworked as the libretto for an opera (*Nine Rivers from Jordan*), another libretto/adaptation (*Six Characters*), a courtroom drama (*Strange Occurrence on Ireland's Eye*), and a history play about the Easter Uprising (*The Scythe and the Sunset*). The argument that Johnston's later career is, according to this varied itinerary, idiosyncratic and derivative—following up on his personal interest in Swift's life, for example, or focusing on mere adaptations—may be easily qualified in more positive terms, not just by acknowledging solid later works such as *The Scythe*. Indeed, Johnston's quest to discover new means of theatrical expression finds him crossing boundaries usually untraversed by traditional playwrights and engaging in both generic and authorial dialogism with other forms (music), the work of other writers (Toller, Pirandello, and his collaborator, Hugo Weisgall), and other media (radio and television). To the claim that his dramatic output increasingly peters out (only one play was produced in the decade of the 1940s, and only four theatrical works over the decade between 1956 and 1968), one need only adduce Johnston's extraordinary output of criticism and radio drama, the latter of which speaks not only to his versatility as an artist but to his modernity and adaptability to new media (a contemporary self-placement not unexpected, given the criticism of cultural nostalgia in his early plays). Therefore, while the decline in quality perceived in Johnston's drama since the 1930s may bespeak a deeper impasse with the available means of dramatic expression, his later career could be equally regarded as transcending this creative block in unexpected directions, directions themselves resistant to the terms of traditional dramatic scholarship.

ARCHIVAL SOURCES

The most extensive collection of Johnston manuscripts and related materials is in the library of the New University of Ulster, Coleraine, Northern Ireland. Copies of notebook, diaries, and various correspondence are available in the Mugar Memorial Library, Boston University, and the Williston Memorial Library, Mount Holyoke College. The original manuscript of an early version of *The Old Lady Says "No!"* is in the library of the University of British Columbia, Victoria.

PRIMARY BIBLIOGRAPHY

Plays

Blind Man's Buff. London: Jonathan Cape, 1938.
"The Golden Cuckoo" and Other Plays. London: Jonathan Cape, 1954.
"The Moon in the Yellow River" and "The Old Lady Says 'No!' ": Two Plays. Foreword by C. P. Curran. London: Jonathan Cape, 1932.
Nine Rivers from Jordan. Bryn Mawr, Pa.: Theodore Presser, 1968.
The Old Lady Says "No!" Ed. Christine St. Peter. Washington, D.C.: Catholic University of America Press, 1992.
"Six Characters in Search of an Author": Translated and Adapted for Opera by Denis Johnston. Bryn Mawr, Pa.: Merion Music, 1957.
"Storm Song" and "A Bride for the Unicorn": Two Plays. London: Jonathan Cape, 1938.

Anthologies

Collected Plays. 2 vols. London: Jonathan Cape, 1960.
The Dramatic Works of Denis Johnston. 3 vols. Gerrards Cross, Buckinghamshire: Colin Smythe, 1977, 1979, 1992.

Essays and Articles on Drama and Theater

"Brian Friel and Modern Irish Drama." *Hibernia* (7 Mar. 1975).
"Did You Know Yeats? And Did You Lunch with Shaw?" *Flight from the Celtic Twilight.* Ed. Des Hickey and Gus Smith. New York: Bobbs-Merrill, 1973.
"Dream Theatre." *Smith Alumnae Quarterly* (winter 1963).
"The Making of the Theatre." *The Gate Theatre.* Ed. Bulmer Hobson. Dublin: Gate Theatre, 1934.
"Needed: New Perspectives for the Theatre." *Theatre Arts* 46 (Dec. 1962).
"A Note on What Happened." *Dramatic Works.* Vol. 1. Gerrards Cross, Buckinghamshire: Colin Smythe, 1977. 76–82.
"Policy for the Abbey Theatre." *Hibernia* (15 May 1970).
"Policy in the Theatre." *Hibernia* (29 May 1970).
"Public Opinion: A National Morality Play." *Bell* 1.6 (Mar. 1941).
"Sean O'Casey: An Appreciation." *Living Age* 329.4267 (Apr. 1926).
"Sean O'Casey: Realist or Romantic?" *Listener* (17 Oct. 1946).
"Shaw: The Man and His Work." *Irish Times* (26 July 1941).
"Theatre or Cinema." *Listener* (11 Sept. 1935).
"What Has Happened to the Irish." *Theatre Arts* 43 (July 1959).
"What's Wrong with the New Theatres." *Theatre Arts* 47 (Aug.–Sept. 1963).
"Yeats as Dramatist." *Irish Times* (13 June 1935).

SECONDARY BIBLIOGRAPHY

Achilles, Joachen. "Sean O'Casey's and Denis Johnston's National Plays: Two Dramatic Approaches to Irish Society." *Studies in Anglo-Irish Literature.* Ed. Heine Kosok. Bonn: Bouvier, 1982.
Barnett, Gene A. [1]. *Denis Johnston.* Boston: Twayne, 1978.
———. [2]. "Denis Johnston." *Dictionary of Literary Biography. Vol. 10: Modern British Dramatists, 1900–1945.* Ed. Stanley Weintraub. Foreword by Sir Harold Hobson. Detroit: Gale Research, 1982.
Review of *Blind Man's Buff.* "German Play in an Irish Setting." *Times* (30 Dec. 1936): 8.
Review of *Blind Man's Buff.* "New Play at the Abbey Theatre." *Irish Times* (28 Dec. 1936): 8.
Boyd, John. "The Endless Search." *Denis Johnston: A Retrospective.* Ed. Joseph Ronsley. Totowa, N.J.: Barnes and Noble, 1981. 157–77.
Review of *A Bride for the Unicorn.* "Mr. Johnston's New Play: Expressionism at the Gate." *Irish Times* (10 May 1933): 6.
Canfield, Curtis. *Plays of Changing Ireland.* New York: Macmillan, 1936.

Cave, Richard Allen. [1]. "Dramatising the Life of Swift." *Irish Writers and the Theatre.* Ed. Masaru Sekine. Totowa, N.J.: Barnes and Noble, 1987. 17.–32.

————. [2]. "Johnston, Toller and Expressionism." *Denis Johnston: A Retrospective.* Ed. Joseph Ronsley. Totowa, N.J.: Barnes and Noble, 1981. 78–104.

Culme-Seymour, Mark. "With Denis Johnston in the Western Desert." *Denis Johnston: A Retrospective.* Ed. Joseph Ronsley. Totowa, N.J.: Barnes and Noble, 1981. 214–27.

Curran, Constantine. [Review of *The Old Lady Says "No!"*] *Irish Statesman* (13 June 1929): 374–76.

Cusack, Cyril. "Dear Denis!" *Denis Johnston: A Retrospective.* Ed. Joseph Ronsley. Totowa, N.J.: Barnes and Noble, 1981. 184–88.

Review of *The Dreaming Dust.* "Irish Drama: Two New Plays." *Times* (28 Mar. 1940): 6.

Review of *The Dreaming Dust. Irish Times* (26 Mar. 1940): 4.

Edwards, Hilton. "An Appreciation." *Denis Johnston: A Retrospective.* Ed. Joseph Ronsley. Totowa, N.J.: Barnes and Noble, 1981. 1–3.

Elliot, Maurice. " 'He Is Always Just Round the Next Corner': Denis Johnston's *In Search of Swift.*" *Denis Johnston: A Retrospective.* Ed. Joseph Ronsley. Totowa, N.J.: Barnes and Noble, 1981. 119–32.

Ellis-Fermor, Una. *The Irish Dramatic Movement.* London: Methuen, 1939.

Ferrar, Harold. *Denis Johnston's Irish Theatre.* Dublin: Dolmen Press, 1973.

Flot, Michel. "*The Moon in the Yellow River* de Denis Johnston: Texte et Représentation." *Etudes Irlandais* (11 Dec. 1986): 93–109.

Fraser, G. S. *The Modern Writer and His World.* London: Verschoyle, 1952.

Review of *The Golden Cuckoo.* "Mr. Denis Johnston's New Play." *Times* (28 Apr. 1939): 14.

Review of *The Golden Cuckoo.* "Denis Johnston's New Play." *Irish Times* (26 Apr. 1939): 8.

Grene, Nicholas. "Distancing Drama: Sean O'Casey to Brian Friel." *Irish Writers and the Theatre.* Ed. Masaru Sekine. Totowa, N.J.: Barnes and Noble, 1987. 47–70.

Hogan, Robert. [1]. *After the Irish Renaissance: A Critical History of the Irish Drama since* The Plough and the Stars. Minneapolis: University of Minnesota Press, 1967.

————. [2]. "Denis Johnston's Horse Laugh." *Denis Johnston: A Retrospective.* Ed. Joseph Ronsley. Totowa, N.J.: Barnes and Noble, 1981. 59–77.

Hogan, Thomas. "Denis Johnston: Last of the Anglo-Irish." *Envoy* 3.9 (Aug. 1950): 33–46.

Holloway, Joseph. [1]. *Joseph Holloway's Irish Theatre.* Vol. 1. Ed. Robert Hogan and Michael J. O'Neill. Dixon, Calif.: Proscenium Press, 1968.

————. [2]. *Joseph Holloway's Irish Theatre.* Vol. 2. Ed. Robert Hogan and Michael J. O'Neill. Dixon, Calif.: Proscenium Press, 1969.

————. [3]. *Joseph Holloway's Irish Theatre.* Vol. 3. Ed. Robert Hogan and Michael J. O'Neill. Dixon, Calif.: Proscenium Press, 1970.

Illiano, Antonio. *"Six Characters," An American Opera. Review of National Literatures.* 14 (1987): 136–59.

Johnston, Rory, ed. *Orders and Desecrations: The Life of the Playwright Denis Johnston.* Foreword by Hugh Leonard. Dublin: Lilliput Press, 1992.

Jordan, John. "The Irish Theatre—Retrospect and Premonition." *Contemporary Theatre.*

Ed. John Russell Brown and Bernard Harris. London: Edward Arnold, 1962. 165–84.

Kilroy, Thomas. *The Moon in the Yellow River.* Ed. Joseph Ronsley. Totowa, N.J.: Barnes and Noble, 1981. 49–58.

Mac Liammóir, Micheál. "Problem Plays." *The Irish Theatre: Lectures Delivered during the Abbey Theatre Festival Held in Dublin in August 1938.* Ed. Lennox Robinson. New York: Haskell House, 1971. 199–227.

Maxwell, D. E. S. *A Critical History of Modern Irish Drama 1891–1980.* Cambridge: Cambridge University Press, 1984.

McHugh, Roger. "The Plays of Denis Johnston." *Denis Johnston: A Retrospective.* Ed. Joseph Ronsley. Totowa, N.J.: Barnes and Noble, 1981. 178–84.

Mercier, Vivian. "Perfection of the Life or of the Work." *Denis Johnston: A Retrospective.* Ed. Joseph Ronsley. Totowa, N.J.: Barnes and Noble, 1981. 228–44.

Review of *The Moon in the Yellow River. Times* (30 Apr. 1931): 12.

Review of *The Moon in the Yellow River.* "New Play at the Abbey." *Irish Times* (28 Apr. 1931): 4.

Murray, George. "*The Golden Cuckoo*: A Very Remarkable Bird." *Denis Johnston: A Retrospective.* Ed. Joseph Ronsley. Totowa, N.J.: Barnes and Noble, 1981. 105–18.

Nathan, George Jean. *Theatre Book of the Year 1947–1948.* Intro. Charles Argoff. Cranbury, N.J.; London: Associated University Presses, 1947. 279–82.

O'Brien, Conor Cruise. [Review of *The Scythe and the Sunset.*] *Times Literary Supplement* (14 Oct. 1960): 656.

O'Brien, John. [1]. "The Abbey Theatre Saying No." *Journal of Irish Literature* 2.1 (Jan. 1991): 19–24.

———. [2]. "Expressionism and the Formative Years: Insights from the Early Diaries of Denis Johnston." *Canadian Journal of Irish Studies* 15.1 (July 1989): 35–57.

Review of *The Old Lady Says "No!". Daily Express* (10 July 1929).

Review of *The Old Lady Says "No!". Irish Independent* (Early July 1929).

Review of *The Old Lady Says "No!".* "An Irish Revue." *Irish Times* (4 July 1929): 4.

O'Reilly, Veronica. "The Realism of Denis Johnston." *Myth and Reality in Irish Literature.* Ed. Joseph Ronsley. Waterloo: Wilfrid Laurier University Press, 1977. 281–96.

Reid, B. L. "Johston in Academe." *Denis Johnston: A Retrospective.* Ed. Joseph Ronsley. Totowa, N.J.: Barnes and Noble, 1981. 203–13.

Rollins, Ronald G. "Enigmatic Ghosts of Swift in Yeats and Johnston." *Éire-Ireland: A Journal of Irish Studies* 18.2 (summer 1983): 103–15.

Ronsley, Joseph. [1]. "A Checklist of Denis Johnston's Writings." *Denis Johnston: A Retrospective.* Totowa, N.J.: Barnes and Noble, 1981. 245–62.

———, ed. [2]. *Denis Johnston: A Retrospective.* Gerrards Cross, Buckinghamshire: Colin Smythe; Totowa, N.J.: Barnes and Noble, 1981.

———. [3]. "The Difficult Debut of Johnston's *The Old Lady Says "No!"*" *Essays for Richard Ellman: Omnium Gatherum.* Kingston, Montreal: McGill-Queen's University Press, 1989.

———. [4]. " 'A Humane and Well-Intentioned Piece of Gallantry': Denis Johnston's *The Scythe and the Sunset. Denis Johnston: A Retrospective.* Totowa, N.J.: Barnes and Noble, 1981. 133–56.

Schonberg, Harold C. [Review of *Nine Rivers from Jordan.*] *New York Times* (10 Oct. 1968): 62.

Schrank, Bernice. "The Low and the Lofty: A Comparison of Sean O'Casey's *The Plough and the Stars* and Denis Johnston's *The Scythe and the Sunset.*" *Modern Language Studies* 11 (1980–81): 11–16.

Review of *The Scythe and the Sunset. Irish Times* (4 July 1951): 5.

Review of *Storm Song.* "First Production at Gate Theatre." *Irish Times* (31 Jan. 1934): 6.

St. Peter, Christine. [1]. "Denis Johnston, the Abbey and the Spirit of the Age." *Irish University Review: A Journal of Irish Studies* 17.2 (autumn 1987): 187–206.

———. [2]. "*The Old Lady*: In Principio." *Denis Johnston: A Retrospective.* Ed. Joseph Ronsley. Totowa, N.J.: Barnes and Noble, 1987. 10–23.

Taubman, Howard. [Review of *Six Characters in Search of an Author.*] *New York Times* (27 Apr. 1959): 22.

BIBLIOGRAPHY

Ronsley, Joseph. "A Check-List of Denis Johnston's Writings." *Denis Johnston: A Retrospective.* Ed. Joseph Ronsley. Totowa, N.J.: Barnes and Noble, 1981. 245–62.

John B. Keane

(1928–)

SISTER MARIE HUBERT KEALY

John B. Keane is a prominent figure in contemporary Irish theater. He owes his popularity to his acute observation of ordinary life and his ability to create authentic characters and dialogue.

John Brendan Keane was born at 45 Church Street in Listowel, County Kerry, on 21 July 1928. He is the son of William B. Keane and Hannah Purtill Keane, the fourth child in a family of five boys and four girls. After completing his education at St. Michael's College, Listowel, in 1946, Keane worked as a pharmacist's assistant until 1952, when he emigrated to Northampton. In England, he held a variety of jobs, including two years as a furnace operator at British Timken, and began to write poetry and fiction seriously. He returned permanently to Listowel in 1954. Keane married Mary O'Connor on 5 January 1955; shortly afterward, he purchased a public house at 37 William Street, which he continues to operate. The Keanes have three sons, William, Conor, and John; one daughter, Joanna; and three granddaughters.

Keane's inspiration to write for the stage resulted from his seeing the Listowel Drama Group's production of Joseph Tomelty's *All Soul's Night*, and his first play, *Sive*, was produced by the same company of amateurs on 2 February 1959. Although the play had been rejected by the Abbey Theatre, Keane entered it in the regional drama festivals, where it merited first place in the All-Ireland Drama Festival at Athlone in April 1959. The success of *Sive* launched Keane's playwriting career, but professional recognition did not come until the Cork-based Southern Theatre Group, directed by James N. Healy, acquired the rights to *Sive* and produced the play successfully in Cork, Dublin, and other cities. *Sive* has been revived frequently and remains a very popular play. Nineteen plays have followed *Sive*; most of them have appeared in the provinces before being produced in Dublin.

In addition to his plays, Keane has written poetry, essays, and fiction. His "letter" portraits of well-known Irish characters have the same earthy appeal as his plays. His most recent work includes several collections, *Love Bites* (1991), *Ram of God and Other Stories* (1992), *Letters to the Brain* (1993), and three novels, *The Bodhran Makers* (1986), *Durango* (1991), and *The Contractors* (1993). His most recent play, *Vigilantes* (1991), has not been staged at this writing. Keane regularly contributes essays to the *Limerick Leader*, the *Evening Herald* (Dublin), the *Irish Echo*, and the *Kingdom*.

Keane is a member of Aosdana, the Irish Academy of Arts, and past president of Irish P.E.N.; in 1991, he was granted life membership in the Royal Dublin Society. He has been awarded honorary degrees by Trinity College, Dublin, and Marymount Manhattan College in New York. Keane has received the *Sunday Tribune* Award for Literature (1986), the *Sunday Independent* Special Arts Award (1986), and the American-Irish Award for Literature (1988). He was named Kerryman of the year in 1989 and merited the People of the Year Award in 1990. For more than twenty years, Keane has been one of the major forces behind the annual Listowel Writers' Week.

Selected Biographical Sources: Keane, *Self-Portrait*; Feehan; Kealy [1].

MAJOR PLAYS, PREMIERES, AND SIGNIFICANT REVIVALS: THEATRICAL RECEPTION

Sive. 1959. Performed 2 February by the Listowel Drama Group in Walsh's Ballroom, Listowel. Won All-Ireland Drama Final 26 April 1959; amateur production invited by Abbey Theatre for one-week run at Queen's Theatre, Dublin, May 1959. Professional production by Southern Theatre Group, Cork, opened 29 June 1959 for six-week run; moved to Olympia Theatre, Dublin, for two weeks then toured southwest Ireland. London production: Lyric Theatre, Hammersmith, opened 25 October 1960; was poorly received chiefly because it was miscast. American premiere: Riordan High School, San Francisco, by Southern Theatre Group. Produced by Celtic Theatre Company, New Jersey, in 1984. Revival (revised two-act version), Abbey Theatre, June 1985.

The story of a young girl about to be married to an old man is a common plot in folk literature; Keane elevates it to a new category. He uses the songs of the tinkers to reinforce his commentary on the old ways, and *Sive* remains one of Keane's best plays. Although time has altered marriage customs, the economic stress that could lead to an arranged marriage is current and easily appreciated by the audience. The authentic Kerry touches—the matchmaker, the tinkers, and the recurring beat of the bodhran—provide both local color and nostalgia for simpler times.

Sharon's Grave. 1960. Opened 1 February, Father Matthew Hall, Cork, produced by the Southern Theatre Group; after a long run in Cork moved to Olympia Theatre, Dublin, for a two-week run. Off-Broadway production 8 November

1961, Maidman Playhouse, New York; Celtic Theatre Company, New Jersey production, 1977.

Sharon's Grave also springs from the folk art of rural Ireland. Here Keane uses both a local legend and physical deformity to portray warped souls and sexual frustrations. As in *Sive*, Keane's strength is in his characters and their authentic dialogue.

The Highest House on the Mountain. 1960. Opened 14 September at Gas Company Theatre, Dun Laoghaire. Presented by Orion Productions for Dublin Theatre Festival and enjoyed longest run in the festival. Opened at Olympia Theatre, Dublin, in November 1964 for two weeks; produced by Southern Theatre Group.

Loneliness in conflict with traditional sexual mores is the context for the story of two brothers and their devices for coping with their personal frustrations.

Many Young Men of Twenty. 1961. Opened 5 July at Father Matthew Hall, Cork; produced by Southern Theatre Group. Moved to Olympia Theatre, Dublin 28 August 1961 for two-week run. Revival: Gaiety Theatre, Dublin, 1966.

A musical about emigration, *Many Young Men of Twenty* reflects the economic conditions that force the people of rural Ireland to leave for the doubly foreign world of urban England. The play is rich in lively dialogue, and the title song underscores the note of nostalgia in the action.

No More in Dust. 1961. Opened 12 September at Gas Company Theatre, Dun Laoghaire. Produced by Orion Productions for Dublin Theatre Festival.

A companion piece to *Hut 42*, the play relates the misfortunes of two country girls forced by their circumstances to work in the city. It drew full houses despite lukewarm reception by critics. The play was never published; copies of the script are difficult to locate today.

The Man from Clare. 1962. Opened 1 July at Father Matthew Hall, Cork; presented by Southern Theatre Group. Produced by Abbey Theatre at the Queen's Theatre, Dublin, 5 August 1963. Revival: Abbey Theatre, 1984, to commemorate centenary of Gaelic Athletic League. Revival (revised, two-act version): Gaiety Theatre, Dublin, 1992.

Using the context of a familiar football rivalry, Keane relates the meeting of an aging athlete and a woman on the brink of middle age. Under the comedy is the recurring motif of loneliness and frustrated hopes.

Hut 42. 1962. The only Keane play to have an Abbey Theatre premiere. Opened 12 November at Queen's Theatre, Dublin.

A view of men separated from their families because of their need to work in England, the play carries Keane's criticism of an economic system that forces emigration. The play enjoyed only moderate success and has not been revived.

The Year of the Hiker. 1962. Opened 17 July, Father Matthew Hall, Cork; presented by Southern Theatre Group. Both Cork run and tour were received enthusiastically. Opened 16 November 1964 at Eblana Theatre, Dublin, presented by Gemini Productions; later moved to Gate Theatre, Dublin. American tour by Theatre of the South: June 1972, Riordan High School, San Francisco. Radio production: Tim Danaher, RTE, Dublin, 26 October 1975. Produced by Celtic Theatre Company, New Jersey, 1979. Revival (revised, two-act version): Gaiety Theatre, Dublin, 1990.

This play looks at a recurring phenomenon in Irish rural life—the wanderer; however, Keane offers a view of an individual, not a stereotype. An equally important, but sometimes overlooked, theme of the play is the father–son relationship.

The Field. 1965. Opened 1 November at Olympia Theatre, Dublin presented by Gemini Productions. Well received. Produced by both Gemini Productions and Southern Theatre Group several times in the late 1960s. Radio production: Tim Danaher, RTE, Dublin, 2 March 1972. Revival: Abbey Theatre, Dublin, 1980. Revival (revised, two-act version): Abbey Theatre, 1987, directed by Ben Barnes. Tour to Moscow and Leningrad, February 1988. Adapted for film by Jim Sheridan, 1990. Richard Harris was nominated for the Best Actor Award for his portrayal of Bull McCabe.

In this work, the land is both a major character and the motivating force of the action. Based on an actual, unsolved murder, the play probes Bull's passionate attachment to the land and the silent isolation he endures as a result of his crime. Keane's own love of the soil enables him to capture the protagonist's struggle to retain the land at any price. The film version highlights Bull's passion but misses the nuances of rural justice.

The Rain at the End of Summer. 1967. Opened 19 June at Gaiety Theatre, Dublin, produced by Theatre of the South.

The play attempts to deal with the urban middle class. Keane's work is not effective when he moves away from rural characters and themes.

Big Maggie. 1969. Opened 20 January 1969 at the Opera House, Cork, produced by Gemini Productions. Moved to City Theatre, Limerick, then to the Olympia Theatre, Dublin, 10 February 1969. Very successful play; Ireland's best actresses have played Maggie: Marie Kean, Anna Manahan, Ronnie Masterson, Brenda Fricker. Produced by Celtic Theatre Company, New Jersey, 24 May 1979. Off-Broadway production, Fall 1983, at the Douglas Fairbanks Theatre. Revival (revised, two-act version): Abbey Theatre, Dublin, 1988.

Like the characters in *Sive* and *The Field*, Maggie Polpin has a visceral force about her; she is a scheming woman who works her own will on her children while protesting that she is acting in their best interests. Maggie is a complex figure who can arouse both distaste and admiration in the audience. In the revised version, Keane has written a new ending in which Maggie sums up her position between the new and old sets of sexual values.

The Change in Mame Fadden. 1971. Opened 10 May at the Opera House, Cork; presented by Gemini Productions. Moved 24 May 1971 to Olympia Theatre, Dublin; not well received.

This play attempts to deal with the psychological problems of menopause. The title character is not as well drawn as Maggie Polpin, and the play remains less successful as a result.

Moll. 1971. Opened 1 July at Aras Phadraig, Killarney, produced by Theatre of the South. Moved to the Opera House, Cork, 26 July 1971. Moved to the Olympia Theatre, Dublin, 4 October 1971. Poorly received by critics; well received by audience in tour of southern counties. Revival: Gaiety Theatre, Dublin, 1991, produced by Groundwork. Well received, outstanding box office success.

Moll is the clever and domineering housekeeper to the local parish priest. This is a pleasant comedy that succeeds because it arouses recognition of an earlier time but does not attempt social commentary.

The Crazy Wall. 1973. Opened 27 June at Theatre Royal, Waterford; produced by Theatre of the South. Moved to Opera House, Cork, 23 July 1973. Opened 6 May 1974 at Gaiety Theatre, Dublin.

Keane considers *The Crazy Wall* his best play because he has based the major character on his own father. The theme, however, is too personal, and the characterizations do not work as well as in his other plays.

The Good Thing. 1976. Opened 1 March at City Theatre, Limerick, presented by Gemini Productions. Moved to Eblana Theatre, Dublin, 19 April 1976. Mixed reception.

Once again, Keane's gift for character and dialogue fails him when he attempts a modern problem play in an urban setting.

The Buds of Ballybunion. 1978. Opened 7 July at White Memorial Theatre, Clonmel; produced by Theatre of the South. Moved 24 July 1978 to Olympia Theatre, Dublin.

A lighthearted comedy about late-summer vacationers at the seaside, *The Buds of Ballybunion* is a pleasant diversion but not one of Keane's best plays.

The Chastitute. 1980. Opened 3 June at the Opera House, Cork; presented by Gemini Productions. Moved 16 June 1980 to Olympia Theatre, Dublin. Revival: Gaiety Theatre, Dublin, 1993.

The sexual frustrations of John Bosco McLaine have been drawn from Keane's *Letters of a Love-Hungry Farmer* (1974). The playwright fuses the comic and the tragic in this work. The protagonist's sex escapades are hilarious, but his terrible loneliness is always evident to the audience, especially in the final scene.

ADDITIONAL PLAYS, ADAPTATIONS, AND PRODUCTIONS

The Roses of Tralee. 1965. Musical. Opened 29 November at Opera House, Cork, produced by Theatre of the South. Moved to Gaiety Theatre, Dublin, 12 April 1966. *Faoiseamh.* 1970. One-act. Opened 15 October, Damer Hall, Dublin. *The One-Way Ticket.* 1972. One-act. Opened March at Plaza Theatre, Listowel. *Values.* 1973. Three one-act plays. Opened 25 April, Group Theatre, Cork. *Matchmaker.* 1975. Adapted by Ray McAnally and Barry Cassin from Keane's *Letters of a Matchmaker.* Opened at Eblana Theatre, Dublin, 1975 and toured with great success. Staged at Irish Arts Center, New Jersey. Toured by Gemini Productions, 1991.

ASSESSMENT OF KEANE'S CAREER

Since 1985, Keane has enjoyed renewed prominence and popularity. Revivals of his major plays, written between 1959 and 1980, have been attracting a second generation of playgoers. Although most of his works were popular with audiences at their first production, the revivals have brought Keane even greater box office and critical acclaim. The enduring quality of his insight into human nature has proved that the folk and rural motifs are not dated, because the truths they illustrate are perennial. Keane's association with Ben Barnes and Groundwork Productions has given his work a new look. He has permitted Barnes to tighten scenes that were overwritten, and the resulting two-act versions are more in keeping with contemporary theater practice.

The themes of Keane's early plays reflect his association with the Amateur Drama Movement, which in the 1950s reproduced the style of the Abbey Theatre. However, the National Theatre Company largely ignored Keane's plays, in spite of his popular success. Ironically, Keane, more than any other contemporary playwright, has carried on the traditional themes of land, emigration, and the trials of love in a rural environment. His continuity of the peasant play, however, is not merely a convention. Keane uses familiar contexts in order to focus on the plight of individuals in contemporary Ireland. His characters, especially female characters, offer a criticism of Irish society that would have been impossible in the 1940s and 1950s.

Keane manages to focus on the tension between the received social traditions and the struggle for individuality that marks all modern literature. His later dramas portray modern life in rural communities; these plays depend on realistic details rather than folk devices for their power. Keane's concerns range from land greed and financial security, to sexual mores and problems of personal fulfillment. He draws on his own experience and consistently expresses his impatience with the conditions that force young people to emigrate in order to find employment. His depiction of individual struggles with identity, position, and sexual frustration contributes memorable characters even in his less successful plays.

Keane has the gift of storytelling and of recapturing the full flavor of an incident. Through humor and careful characterization, Keane dresses his acute observation of the Kerry landscape with an appeal that invests traditional Irish themes with universal relevance. Keane's limitations are those of the world in which he lives; his settings and plots are typical of rural Ireland, and his plays must be examined in that context. He portrays a rural scene that is not always attractive; yet, Keane does not condemn; rather, he expends great energy in showing reasons for the sins of his characters. It is the social system Keane blames, if there is any blame to be assigned.

Keane's plays combine folk characters and realistic plots and settings with a touch of satire. Although he claims to have no message of reform, Keane's plays are documents that examine the situation of individuals struggling with modern problems in an environment of religious and social expectations. He does not touch the question of the six Northern counties, but he does attack the government for the economic conditions that force so many young people to emigrate. Keane draws on the world he knows to order his perceptions of contemporary life. He approaches his subjects with clear-eyed appraisal and a touch of nostalgia.

Keane has earned his popularity at home, but he is not well known outside Ireland. Attempts to introduce his plays to the New York audience met with little success (see *Big Maggie*, 1983); therefore, some critics contend that his work does not travel well. Keane's current success and the potential for film offers may change this assessment. The playwright's association with Groundwork Productions has resulted in a new enthusiasm for his work in Ireland and may promote a wider appreciation for his plays on the continent and in the United States.

ARCHIVAL SOURCES

Keane's personal papers and manuscripts are housed in the Trinity College Library, Dublin. Reviews and photos of some of his works are in the Billy Rose Collection of the New York Public Library.

PRIMARY BIBLIOGRAPHY

Plays

Big Maggie. Cork: Mercier, 1969.
The Change in Mame Fadden. Cork: Mercier, 1973.
The Chastitute. Cork: Mercier, 1981.
The Crazy Wall. Cork: Mercier, 1974.
The Field. Cork: Mercier, 1966.
The Good Thing. Newark, Del.: Proscenium, 1978.
The Highest House on the Mountain. Dublin: Progress House, 1961.

Hut 42. Dixon, Calif.: Proscenium, 1962.

The Man from Clare. Cork: Mercier, 1974.

The Man from Clare. Rev. ed. by Ben Barnes. Cork: Mercier, 1992.

Many Young Men of Twenty. Dublin: Progress House, 1961. (Also *Seven Irish Plays.* Minneapolis: University Press of Minnesota, 1967.)

Moll. Cork: Mercier, 1971.

Moll. Rev. ed. by Ben Barnes. Cork: Mercier, 1991.

The One-Way Ticket. Barrington, Ill.: Performance, 1972.

The Rain at the End of Summer. Dublin: Progress House, 1967.

Sharon's Grave. Dublin: Progress House, 1960. (Also *Seven Irish Plays.* Minneapolis: University Press of Minnesota, 1967.)

Sive. Dublin: Progress House, 1959.

Values: Three One-Act Plays. Cork: Mercier, 1980.

The Year of the Hiker. Cork: Mercier, 1973.

The Year of the Hiker. Rev. ed. by Ben Barnes. Cork: Mercier, 1991.

Anthology

Three Plays. (*Sive, The Field, Big Maggie.*) Rev. ed. by Ben Barnes. Cork: Mercier, 1990.

Autobiography

Self-Portrait. Cork: Mercier, 1964.

Essay on Drama and Theater

"A Last Instalment." *The World of Brendan Behan.* Ed. Sean McCann. New York: Twayne, 1965. 201–5.

SECONDARY BIBLIOGRAPHY

Brady, Seamus. "Are They Our Great Writers of Tomorrow?" *Irish Digest* 79 (1963): 9–12.

Cassin, Barry. Introduction. *The Highest House on the Mountain* by John B. Keane. Dublin: Progress House, 1961.

A Clear Eye and an Open Hand. Documentary. Prod. Muiris MacConghail. RTE television, Dublin, 1990.

Comiskey, Ray. "A Hundred Key People in Irish Theatre." *Irish Times* (20 June 1985): 12.

Csilla, Bertha. "Distortions of Character in John B. Keane's Peasant Plays." *Acta Academiae Paedagogicae Agiensis* 19 (1989): 41–55.

Dantanus, Ulf. "Time for a New Irish Playwright?" *Moderna Sprak* 71 (1977): 37–47.

"Discussion on Irish Theatre Misfired." *Irish Times* (27 Feb. 1961): 5.

Fallon, Gabriel. "Dublin's Fourth Theatre Festival." *Modern Drama* 5 (1962): 21–26.

Feehan, John M. *Fifty Years Young: A Tribute to John B. Keane.* Cork: Mercier, 1979.

Fox, R. M. "Social Criticism in the Irish Theatre." *Aryan Path* 38 (1967): 179–81.

Gaughan, J. Anthony. *Listowel and Its Vicinity.* Cork: Mercier, 1973.

Gillespie, Elgie. "The Saturday Interview: John B. Keane." *Irish Times* (19 June 1976): 5.

Healy, James N.[1]. "The Birth of *Sive.*" *Fifty Years Young.* Ed. John M. Feehan. Cork: Mercier, 1979, 9–17.

———. [2]. Foreword. *Sharon's Grave* by John B. Keane. Dublin: Progress House, 1960, vi–viii.

Henderson, Joanne L. "Checklist of Four Kerry Writers." *Journal of Irish Literature* 1 (1972): 101–19.

Hogan, Robert.[1]. "The Art and Craft of John B. Keane." *Fifty Years Young.* Ed. John M. Feehan. Cork: Mercier, 1979, 79–89.

———. [2]. "The Hidden Ireland of John B. Keane." *After the Irish Renaissance: A Critical History of Irish Drama since* The Plough and the Stars. Minneapolis: University of Minnesota Press, 1967.

———. [3]. *Seven Irish Plays.* Minneapolis: University of Minnesota Press, 1967.

———. [4]. "Where Have All the Shamrocks Gone?" *Aspects of Irish Theatre.* Ed. Patrick Rafroidi, Raymonde Popot, and William Parker. Paris: Editions universitaires, 1972, 261–71.

"John B. Keane's Listowel." *My Own Place.* Prod. John Williams. RTE television, Dublin, 7 May 1980.

Kealy, Marie Hubert.[1]. *Kerry Playwright: Sense of Place in the Plays of John B. Keane.* Selinsgrove, Pa.: Susquehanna University Press, 1993.

———. [2]. "Spirit of Place: A Context for Social Criticism in John B. Keane's *The Field* and *Big Maggie.*" *Irish University Review* 19 (1989): 287–301.

———. [3]. "Spirit of Place in the Plays of John B. Keane: A Way of Reading Contemporary Irish Drama." Ph.D. diss., University of Pennsylvania, 1986.

———. [4]. "The Wall and the Wanderer: Unresolved Domestic Conflict in the Plays of John B. Keane." *Notes on Modern Irish Literature* 2 (1990): 74–78.

Linehan, Fergus. "Four Irish Playwrights." *Irish Digest* 74 (1962): 84–87.

Moriarty, Eileen Marie. "John B. Keane: Kerry Dramatist." Ph.D. diss., University of Washington, 1980.

Moseley, Virginia. "A Week in Dublin." *Modern Drama* 4 (1961): 164–71.

Murray, Christopher. [1]. "Irish Drama in Transition 1966–1978." *Etudes Irlandaises.* (1979): 287–308.

———. [2]. "Recent Irish Drama." *Studies in Anglo-Irish Literature.* Ed. Heinz Kosok. Bonn: Bouvier, 1982, 439–46.

Ó hAodha, Micheál.[1]. Foreword. *Sive* by John B. Keane. Dublin: Progress House, 1959, 5–6.

———. [2]. "*Sive*—a Portent!" Program notes. *Sive* by John B. Keane. Dir. Ben Barnes. Abbey Theatre, Dublin, 1985.

O'Toole, Fintan. "*Sive*—The Ritual Dimension." Program notes. *Sive* by John B. Keane. Dir. Ben Barnes. Abbey Theatre, Dublin, 1985.

Pannecoucke, Jean-Michel. "John Brendan Keane and the New Irish Rural Drama." *Aspects of the Irish Theatre.* Ed. Patrick Rafroidi, Raymonde Popot, and William Parker. Paris: Editions universitaires, 1972, 137–45.

Rushe, Desmond. "Keane to Begin." *Éire-Ireland* 15 (1980): 112–15.

Ryan, Phyllis. "John B's Women." *Fifty Years Young*. Ed. John M. Feehan. Cork: Mercier, 1979, 61–72.

Smith, Gus. *Festival Glory in Athlone*. Dublin: Aherlow, 1977.

Smith, Gus, and Des Hickey. *John B: The Real Keane*. Cork: Mercier, 1992.

"Talking to John B. Keane." *Walkways*. Prod. Pat Leahy. RTE radio, Dublin, 23 September 1985.

Winkler, Elizabeth Hale. "Eejitin' About: Adolescence in Friel and Keane." *Éire-Ireland* 16 (1981): 138–44.

Hugh Leonard
(1926–   )

SANDRA MANOOGIAN PEARCE

Hugh Leonard is best known for his 1978 Tony Award–winning play *Da*, an autobiographical account of the playwright's return to the home of his youth for his father's funeral and a reconciliation with the memory of that often irascible but irresistible father. The universality of the theme and unforgettable nature of the father figure have earned Leonard a solid reputation in drama circles.

Leonard was born in Dublin on 9 November 1926. Leonard is his pen name, ironically chosen from a psychopathic character he created in his first play, *The Italian Road*, rejected by the Abbey Theatre. His original name was John Byrne, but he was adopted soon after birth and later called himself John Keyes Byrne, using the name of his adoptive father. He grew up in Dalkey, the son of Margaret and Nicholas Keyes, a gardener. He attended the local school, then went on to Harolds Boys', where he won a scholarship to Presentation College, but the "thought of [his] penal servitude being extended, not by two years, but a possible six was a pain so exquisite" that he declined the offer, as he delightfully relates in his second autobiography, *Out after Dark* (58). His first piece of autobiographical prose, *Home before Dark*, details much of his early life, including many scenes that he used in *Da*.

In 1945 he joined the Irish civil service and became involved in amateur theatricals. His marriage to Paule Jacquet, a Belgian, in 1955 and the subsequent birth of his daughter, Danielle, were followed by the production in Dublin of three of his plays: *The Big Birthday, A Leap in the Dark*, and *Madigan's Lock*. Leonard felt secure enough to quit his position with the Land Commission and take up writing professionally in 1959. During the 1960s Leonard wrote serials for sponsored radio, joined Granada television as a script writer, and worked as a freelance writer in London, earning the Italia Award for one of his television scripts in 1967. The Granada position had necessitated moving to Manchester until his move to London in 1963, and, while in England, Leonard was experiencing great success with his plays on the Dublin stage.

In 1970, Leonard returned to Ireland, where he has continued to live. From 1976 to 1977 he served as literary editor for the Abbey and a year later became program director for the Dublin Theatre Festival. In addition to the Tony Award he won for *Da*, the play also collected the New York Drama Critics' Circle Award, the Drama Desk Award, and the Outer Critics' Circle Award (all in 1978). *A Life* has received the Harvey Award. A highly prolific writer, Leonard's output has been, and probably will continue to be, nothing short of amazing, including original plays, adaptations, television plays, television series, film scripts, prose, theater criticism, book reviews, and a weekly column for the *Irish Independent*.

Selected Biographical Sources: Kosok; Rogers and Ross.

MAJOR PLAYS, PREMIERES, AND SIGNIFICANT REVIVALS: THEATRICAL RECEPTION

The Big Birthday. 1956. Opened 25 January at the Abbey Theatre, Dublin.

Leonard was a twenty-eight-year-old civil servant in the Land Commission when this play was accepted. After reading the script, the Abbey declared ("First Performance") that "a new writer of great promise had appeared." While the *Irish Times* ("First Performance") review called it Leonard's first play, indeed, it was his second, the first, *The Italian Road*, having been rejected by the Abbey. Furthermore, the play had been rewritten from an amateur production six years earlier. It was, however, Leonard's first big break, was well received, and was the beginning of his illustrious career.

Madigan's Lock. 1958. Opened at the Globe Theatre, Dublin; September 1963, at the Theatre Royal in Stratford; 23 June 1970, at the Olney Theatre, Maryland.

Leonard earned high praise at the British opening. The play, with hints of a "Dublin Barrie," was a "charming fable" that needed "a delicacy of atmosphere beyond the apparent range of Mr. Simpson's cast." Hence, the unnamed London critic ("Fable Marred by Whimsy") placed blame on the acting and not the script and declared the play an interesting follow-up to *Stephen D*, establishing Leonard as a "dramatist in his own right."

Stephen D. 1962. Opened 24 September at the Gate, Dublin; 12 February 1963, at St. Martin's Theatre, London; 1966, at the Olney Theatre, Maryland; 24 September 1967, at the East 74th Street Theatre, New York; revived 18 May 1978, at the Abbey Theatre, Dublin.

Outside of *Da, Stephen D*, Leonard's adaptation of Joyce's novels *A Portrait of the Artist as a Young Man* and *Stephen Hero*, is perhaps the most beloved play of the critics. Leonard, however, considers it his most "loathe[d] because it gave [him] a reputation as an adaptor that took an awful lot of time to shake off again" (Gillespie [1]). Smith gave it a "warm reception," with Norman

Rodway's portrayal of Stephen winning him many curtain calls. Kennedy prophesied "a major and merited success" for what he also praised as "a significant piece of theatre, brilliantly produced, acted with unanimous excellence, and received enthusiastically by a full house." Indeed, Kennedy's enthusiasm for the play could hardly contain itself as he lamented there not being enough "space to praise all the minor performances in a cast which . . . hadn't a weak link." Walsh declared it a "play of great power and intensity," complimenting Leonard's "real and imaginative vision . . . in presenting a full-length portrait of Joyce the child, the youth and the adolescent" (as cited in Smith). Atkinson judged it to be "the finest new play of the Dublin season." Its London opening brought more accolades. Fitzgerald pronounced it "by far the most stageworthy Joyce adaptation to date." The review credited the triumph to Leonard's "unfailing sense of dramatic line, and his instinct for timing episodes to complement one another," citing Stephen's abrupt announcement after a vow of purity: "Chastity, having been found a great inconvenience, was soon given up." The *New York Times* ("London Press Acclaims Play") quoted three more London papers thrilled with the production, calling it "pure genius . . . beautifully constructed . . . spellbinding." Oddly enough, when the play came to the United States, to Leonard's favorite regional theater in Maryland, Kauffmann panned it as a "disappointment" and specifically denounced the casting of George Grizzard, whose Stephen was "only a wistful, pouty, lackadaisical young fellow." Its New York engagement did not improve the reviews. Barnes [1] admitted that the "words have a fiery eloquence. . . . But something is wrong. . . . What is not included is the actual portrait of the young man's transition into an artist." Kerr [1] more generously proclaimed it one of the "brighter spots in the season's otherwise disastrous first week." Unfortunately, when revived in 1978 at the Abbey, Nowlan [1] found that the play "lived up to none" of its anticipated greatness. Nowlan confessed to being a bit confused that "so fine a play" should receive "so negative a review," attributing it, in part, to Barry McGovern's Stephen being "too nice a guy altogether."

Dublin One. 1963. Opened in September at the Dublin Theatre Festival.

Leonard's adaptation of Joyce's *Dubliners* received rave reviews. With the exception of "some ludicrous lantern slide projections," the *Times* ("Hit and Miss with Joyce") declared the production excellent, with a "number of really superb performances," and claimed that the script succeeded best with "Counterpart," "Grace," and "A Little Cloud" and succeeded least with "Two Gallants" and "An Encounter" because Leonard's narrator didn't stick wholly with Joyce's words but included some "lengthy dialogue which wanders right up to the present day and sometimes strays into revue smartalecisms which would make the apolitical and sensitive Joyce turn in his grave." Nothing could be farther from the truth: Joyce was hardly apolitical, as most astute readers now see, and Joyce loved the humor of the revue, of the music hall. More important, Leonard has succeeded on the stage with Joyce's material where Joyce did not.

The Poker Session. 1963. Opened 23 September at the Gate Theatre, Dublin; 11 February 1964, at the Globe Theatre, London; 19 September 1967, at the Martinique Theatre, New York.

Billy Beavis has just returned home from an insane asylum, a stay occasioned by the treachery of his family and friends. Our sympathies for Billy grow until we learn that he has murdered his friend Des and blamed Teddy because of Des' bluffing in a poker game. The *Times* ("Dramatist Represents Modern Middle-Class Ireland") credits Leonard with this play as "the first serious Irish dramatist to have appeared on the scene since Brendan Behan, and in many ways he is the more interesting" because he writes about modern, middle-class Ireland, cutting the "umbilical cord which has tethered so much Irish writing to the past." In this early review of the play's opening at the Gate Theatre, the same London critic went on to praise the play's "cunning first act" and Leonard's "innovations" in terms of characters, who would fit into any suburban setting, and theme, where religion and politics take second seat to American commercialism and trade. With its opening in London, Young gave the play a mixed review, citing its excellent script, "written with great sensitivity," and excellent cast, "acted very choicely," but generally admitting that this comedy-thriller did "not offer anything of the same caliber as *Stephen D* (an unfair comparison often made by drama critics, *Stephen D* being entirely Joyce's words and a completely different production by Leonard). When the play opened off-Broadway, Shepard called it an "uneven work." Shepard found the language "simple and clear . . . evocative and fitting" but suggested that Leonard's wit and humor needed to be channeled and that the cast threw away some of the lines "carelessly." Wade panned the play as a case of "dramatic thuggery" but, then again, labeled it a "new" play, "entirely lacking in innocence . . . kindliness or indeed any human feeling worth having." Since in 1969 the play was five years old in London, it was hardly a "new" play, and one can, perhaps, assume that the rest of Wade's critique was equally off the mark. In addition, in a 1993 review of Finn Gallagher's selection of Leonard's plays, Linehan bemoans the omission of *The Poker Session*.

The Au Pair Man. 1968. Opened 7 October at the Dublin Theatre Festival; 1969, at the Duchess Theatre, London; 27 December 1973, at the Vivian Beaumont Theatre, New York.

Leonard's satire on the British monarchy was first mistaken by Dublin critics as a "straight light comedy," with the ambiguities of its allegory appearing somewhat confusing (Wardle [1]). As a young, brash Irish bill collector demands payment from a patrician British lady for a room divider, the room divider quickly becomes a symbol of Ireland's colonial status, but the symbol is not clear-cut. The Irishman falls for the charms of the woman's prestigious class, acquiring polish at the expense of his independence. According to Wardle, the allegory refers "both to the assimilation of Britain's angry generation into the establishment and to Anglo-Irish history" and its controversy over the "Border."

Aside from what Wardle saw as ambiguities in the script, he thought the acting "good value." Joan Greenwood was an excellent "eccentric royal recluse" and Donal McCann an excellent "raw Irish mick" transformed into "emasculated British booby." Barnes [2] praised the acting but again had some reservations about the allegorical text: "That Mr. Leonard is trying to get somewhere is obvious, but where he is getting is less clear." Barnes questioned the choice of the play, considering the play's brief run in London's West End five years previously. Reviews of the New York opening were mixed (as cited in Cronin [1]): Douglas Watt agreed the script was not as good as the acting, feeling the play took on overtones of Shaw in Eugene's "tirade about discrimination against working class or [in] Mrs. Roger's monologue in support of a segregated society"; Richard Watts (see Cronin [1]) was more positive, placing *The Au Pair Man* between the "brilliant" *Stephen D* and "the bad comedy" of *The Patrick Pearse Motel*; Sean Cronin [1] applauded the fine acting and directing.

The Patrick Pearse Motel. 1971. Opened 15 March at the Olympia Theatre, Dublin; 17 June, at the Queen's Theatre, London.

Another Dublin Theatre Festival entry, this farce garnered good reviews. The motel is a commercial venture about to be opened in the Wicklow Mountains, south of Dublin. The rooms are named after historical Irish heroes, and it is readily apparent that Leonard is satirizing professed Irish hero worship with actual Irish materialism. The results are a good farcical romp. Roberts wrote that "author, cast, and director . . . cause the audience to laugh so attentively that it does not miss any of the local gibes." Leonard's "misanthropic wit" raises the level of this farce past "a mere technical exercise." Wardle [2], on the other hand, claimed that Leonard's script may sound "a much bitterer" play than James Grout's production of it: "If anything, Mr. Leonard puts in more verbal material and more characterization than farce can bear." Wardle, however, praised Leonard's "powerful flair for the traditional mechanics with wardrobes and incriminating underwear . . . and effective reversals of stereotype." Both critics lauded the performance of a "magnificently outraged" (Roberts) Godfrey Quigley as the jealous husband. Wardle proclaimed that Leonard "blazes off at his prey with both barrels," his satire aimed at "Irish property developers and Irish television." Years later, Leonard commented upon the play, saying: "I like to write about serious matters—like 'The Patrick Pearse Motel.' . . . I do write very serious plays but within the medium of comedy" (Shanahan).

Da. 1973. Opened 9 August at the Olney Theatre, Maryland; 9 October at the Olympia Theatre, Dublin; 8 March 1978, at the Hudson Guild Theatre, New York; 1 May, at the Morosco Theatre, New York.

McCarthy praised Leonard's efforts. In putting his past on the stage, "Leonard has discovered just where he does belong." In June 1978, *Da* won four Tony Awards: one for best play, Barnard Hughes for best actor, Lester Rawlins for best supporting actor, and Melvin Bernhardt for best direction. Berkvist quoted Barnard Hughes as loving the play as soon as he read it: "*Da* was gold."

McEldouney explained the extraordinary nature of this success: Leonard "getting a Tony Award is like a black man getting into the KKK. NY theatre is like a secret society." Back in March, 1978, Eder described the central character as "loquacious, exasperating, persistent and finally not far from irresistible." He declared the comedy "a clear-running delight" where the sentiment is "fortified with brains and bones." Gussow [1] reported in an interview with Leonard that the play is "pretty nearly totally autobiographical." Leonard explained the play's lackluster reviews from London: "English people don't like Irish plays. They feel they can't identify with them. . . . But Ireland is relatively contemporary, the same as elsewhere. I would hope that the people in 'Da' are no different from their equivalents in New York. An Irish play is bad when it is not applicable except in Ireland." Kerr [2] proclaimed that *Da* seems "the richest and wisest play we've been offered this year." Kerr eloquently added: "As the play moves like mist—and with bountiful humor—through intricately dovetailed flashbacks, we are really tracking Da down . . . putting together a salty, vagrant, violent, pitiful image that with its sheer complexity becomes unforgettable." After its opening on Broadway, Gussow [2] gave it the ultimate accolade: "By the end of the evening . . . we know these people . . . as deeply as we should know our own family."

Summer. 1974. Opened at the Olympia Theatre, Dublin.

Exclamations of "rapturous reception" (Nowlan [2]) were countered by accusations of "shallow and superficial" (Rushe [1]). This play about three couples and two of their children having two Sunday picnics—six years apart—atop a hill overlooking Dublin collected really mixed reviews. Lewsen praised director Waring's handling of the first section when "realism gives way to a series of isolated soliloquies" but did not like the slow motion of the women setting the picnic table in a later realistic passage. On the whole, Lewsen found the play very successful, though the young couple's ending duologue was "somewhat contrived." Nowlan's acclaim could barely be contained: "[F]or the Tchekov quality, writ small for a jaunty Dublin accent and for superb performances it should not be missed." Much more critical, Rushe [1] said that Leonard's concept was good, but he filled it with the wrong type of comedy when it was "or should be a painfully sad commentary on the emptiness of modern standards." Rushe's comments seem unduly harsh, more judgmental of the human condition than of Leonard's comedy. *Summer* opened off-Broadway to generally favorable reviews: Watt claimed it was predictably plotted but "beautifully balanced" (cited in Cronin [2]); Kerr [3] commended Leonard's ever "deft, forgiving hand" but was "less than ecstatic" about the play, bothered by a "random" quality: "The group as a group never really comes into focus. . . . They appear most unlikely companions." Kalem [1] and Kroll [1] both praised New York director Brian Murray for his "unerring hand" and "delicate direction," respectively. In two separate reviews, Rich [1, 2] condemned Leonard's employment of pop songs. He liked the play's opening moments but was dissatisfied with the young couple, a weakness Leonard conceded to in a recent interview.

A Life. 1979. Opened 4 October at the Abbey Theatre, Dublin; 2 November 1980, at the Morosco Theatre, New York.

In the same interview, Leonard admitted that *A Life* is his favorite, replacing *Summer.* When asked (by this author) if he liked this play even more than his Tony Award–winning *Da*, he replied that *Da* was "just a memory, but *A Life* is a creation." The story of Desmond Drumm (briefly introduced in *Da*), who is up for retirement and has been told he has six months to live, is more than the story of one man; like *Da*, its predecessor, "it disquisits upon the universality of Dalkey, though more objectively" (Gillespie [2]). Veteran Cyril Cusack played the starring role. Rushe [2] overwhelmingly lauded the "splendid writing, much superb acting, a great deal of humor, a delicately difficult constructional approach, and an involving study of a man whose stiffly cerebral attitude to living has robbed it of its humanity and fun." The *Irish Times* ("An Irishman's Diary") declared the play a "copper-bottomed smash hit" and quoted Leonard as saying that the part of Drummond had been written for the brilliant Cusack, and Leonard "acknowledged his debt" to him. The play opened in New York to similar rave reviews. In the "Critic's Notebook," Kerr [4] devoted an entire column recounting the extraordinary humor Leonard generated with only six words, as a lively redhead serves the protagonist a cup of tea, having prematurely put in a lump of sugar: "How many?" she asks. "None," he replies. "Don't stir yours," she advises, handing him the cup. In a separate review, Kerr [5] praised the tight focus and love of language that Leonard bestowed upon the play. Chaillet [1] discussed its "warm, human richness." Kalem [2] contended that despite Drumm's "razor-blade lips," we are won over because he applies "more cruelly exacting standards to himself" than to others. By contrast, Brustein bitterly panned the play, and Rich [4] disclaimed the play's greatness but did admit that it gives "us a great character," that Leonard's Drumm "is not only worth an evening; he's a man who ultimately commands our laughter, affection and compassion." Novick [1] admitted that while the play was a "conventional sentimental drama," he was interested in it because the "old selves of the characters are shrewdly dovetailed in the writing." Clive Barnes [3] called the play "a gentle triumph of retrospection," but Douglas Watt contended that the play "firmly [*sic*] refuses to come to life" (as cited in Cronin [3]). In a 1991 update, Woodworth maintained that "technically" the play may be "possibly a masterpiece."

The Mask of Moriarty. 1985. Opened December at the Gate Theatre, Dublin; 1987, at the Haymarket Theatre, London.

Begun as a Christmas show, Leonard's Sherlock Holmes adventure play was originally titled *The Face*, but then Leonard (in a three-part log on the play's conception and production) contends he changed it to "mask" for the alliterative effect, and its identity theme was born. Rushe [3] summarized the reactions of a number of Dublin papers, all generally favorable: the *Irish Independent* found it "devilishly clever," the *Irish Press* thought the complexity of the plot may have interfered with Leonard's "fabulous comic talent," and the *Irish Times* believed the opening scenes the funniest Mr. Leonard has ever written. Rushe's only complaint was a mild one, targeting that Leonard's irreverence may have gone too far in putting Watson in drag in two scenes. Leonard addressed the irreverence as being "affectionate," in an interview he granted to Peachment. In an interview in 1992 with Claran, Leonard admitted that "Act 2 didn't really work. I was rushed. It was about a year afterwards before I saw how it should be done."

Moving. 1992. Opened 21 April at the Abbey Theatre, Dublin.

In the same 1992 interview with Claire Claran, Leonard discussed his intentions for *Moving*. He set out to write "an Irish 'Our Town.' It's the old Jimmy Stewart thing in 'It's a Wonderful Life.' " Nowlan [3] called the play "dangerously subtle, socially provocative, and most skillfully constructed," urging people, "Go see." A more negative critic, Rushe [4] claimed that only the moving man remained a constant, and the rest of the play did not "have credible flesh and blood characters with whom one can identify and become emotionally involved." While Rushe did admit to Leonard's "superb skill as a craftsman and wordsmith," he felt that the "Noone family leave one untouched and unmoved in the end."

Chamber Music. 1994. Opened 24 August at the Abbey Theatre, Dublin.

Leonard's latest play garnered mixed reviews, especially since *Chamber Music* is the umbrella title for two very different pieces. The first, *Senna for Sonny*, is a farce with heavy scatological touches (which Leonard denies are allusions to Joyce's *Chamber Music*, his first volume of poems, the title supposedly punning on the tingling sound of Nora sitting on the chamberpot), and the second, *The Lilly Lally Show*, is a powerful one-woman show of an aging, lonely comedienne auditioning for one last performance. Nowlan [4] called Barbara Brennan's often funny, often bittersweet rendition a "small pearl of acerbic drama," where Brennan played "most subtly in brilliant layers of gross comedy and much darker layers of loneliness" the role of Mary Moone (alias Lilly Lally). The first part of the evening, Nowlan correctly assessed as "the swine that is cast before the pearl." Despite "energetic playing" by the cast, Nowlan believed the piece "demands a greater suspension of disbelief than [one] is able to muster." It is 1929, and Charles Mangan has returned from seven years of exile in France from the "Free State death Squads." He tries to sell some unbreakable chamberpots to his old foe General O'Horan, and full Rabelaisian humor follows. Nowlan conceded that the play "attempts . . . a most commendable and determined ambition to flush out some of the hypocrisies and dishonesties which attended the revolutionary founding of this State." However, the current dramaturge at the Abbey said they received many complaints about the play's scatological vulgarity and few praises for the political satire. In fairness to Leonard, other reviewers had different reactions: while Carr agreed with Nowlan that *The Lilly Lally Show* won "the warmest reception," she differed about the first piece, which "effectively satirise[s] the jingish political and cultural pieties of an era." McGarry enjoyed both pieces, claiming the "result is an enjoyable, undemanding evening"; and Lawlor found *Senna* to be "entertaining stuff with dollops of farce" and *Lilly*, amazingly, to be "another kettle of fish. . . . [B]ecause there's something missing in the script which fails to make it all ring true."

ADDITIONAL PLAYS, ADAPTATIONS, AND PRODUCTIONS

Plays not reviewed in this chapter (many of which remain unpublished) include the following: *The Italian Road* (1954), *A Leap in the Dark* (1957), *A Walk on the Water* (1960), *The Passion of Peter McGinty* (1961), *The Family Way* (1966), *The Late Arrival of Incoming Aircraft* (1968, adaptation of Leonard's television play), *When the Saints Go Cycling In* (1965, adaptation of Flann O'Brien's *The Dalkey Archives*), *Mick and Nick* (1966, also produced as *All the Nice People*), *The Quick and the Dead* (1967), *The Barracks* (1969, adaptation of John McGahern's novel), *Irishmen: A Suburb of Babylon* (1975; contained *Nothing Personal* and *The Last of the Mohicans*; when published in 1983, *Suburb of Babylon* also contained *Time of Wolves and Tigers*); *Some of My Best Friends Are Husbands* (1976, adaptation of play by Eugene Labiche); *Liam Liar* (1976, adaptation of Waterhouse and Hill's *Billy Liar*); *Time Was* (1981); *Pizzazz* (1986; contained *A View from the Obelisk, Roman Fever*, and *Pizzazz*).

In addition, Leonard has written and had produced numerous screenplays, television plays, and television scripts.

ASSESSMENT OF LEONARD'S CAREER

According to Heinz Kosok, the word most critics use to appraise Leonard's work is "*professional*, a description that carries connotations of criticism as well as admiration" (290). While Leonard has been universally praised for his clever and witty dialogue and his technical mastery of the stage, some contend that Leonard has become more concerned with commercial success, following the current fashions in modern drama rather than tackling the tough issues of society and his country. Leonard would have a ready answer for these critics; he sees the purpose of drama as entertainment. He has little patience for those who must have deep philosophical or political meaning for a play to be worthwhile. He is very proud of the fact that he has had many years of constant work, totally earning his comfortable living from his writing, especially writing for the stage. He has admitted that moving back to Ireland from England in 1970 meant earning less money, but it also meant doing more of what he wanted: more theater and less television (Rogers and Ross 89). While there are still those who claim a "slickness" to his work (as cited in Hogan [1]), others compare him to some of the greats. Novick [2] discusses the Chekhovian themes of *Summer* where, as in *"Uncle Vanya* rather than *The Cherry Orchard*, [we] are not swept up in social change but trapped in aimlessness and mediocrity." Kroll [2] compares *Da* to *Long Day's Journey into Night*, where O'Neill's masterpiece "raised Hibernian self-pity into universal terror and redemption," while Leonard's masterpiece "played on your heartstrings like a harp." Kosok likens *Da* to another American great, *Death of a Salesman*, and feels that Leonard succeeds better than Miller (289). Indeed, Kosok ranks Leonard with Brian Friel as one of the two most important contemporary playwrights (291). The salient word here is "contemporary"; Leonard is still living, still producing plays; hence, it is a bit early to be assessing his career and reputation. In 1979 most would have agreed with Hogan's [2] contention that in "technical expertise . . . cleverness, facility in dialogue, and plot construction, Leonard is perhaps better equipped to create great plays than any present writer in Ireland" (373). In 1995 it has become clear that Leonard is not writing "great" plays; that spot clearly has been earned by Brian Friel. Nevertheless, Leonard's prolific production over thirty years has provided the Irish stage with delightful entertainments, fulfilling easily Leonard's own goals.

As we assess Leonard's plays to date, one item can be readily agreed upon: Leonard's prolific writing for television and film has finely tuned his craft, honing his writing skills to a point where he can be called upon frequently and dependably for a script. While, of his stage plays, *Da* is clearly the one he will be best remembered for, a few others deserve more mention here—*Stephen D, The Poker Session, The Au Pair Man, The Patrick Pearse Motel, Summer*, and *A Life*—all excellent and worthy of revivals and a place in theater history.

Stephen D was Leonard's first international success, but also the beginning of a very lucrative career as an adaptor. Much as Leonard dislikes that designation, his numerous adaptations for stage, television, and film have made him a household name in the British Isles. This adaptation of Joyce was the first; many others followed—Dickens, Brontë, Conan Doyle, Maugham, Flaubert, and Dostoyesvski, just to name a few. *The Poker Session* marks the beginning of what Leonard explained to Ned Chaillet [2] was an obsession with "the theme of betrayal—its effects and its inevitability" (321). Billy Beavis is a very interesting dramatic character. Linehan feels that this play has been overlooked and is deserving of renewed attention. *The Au Pair Man* has been called "Pinteresque . . . a theatre-of-the-absurd situation composed of minute fragments of closely observed reality that becomes grotesque—simultaneously comic and frightening—through an unusual arrangement of the fragments" (Kosok 287). In addition, Leonard's play hints broadly at an underlying allegorical meaning. At this level, the play becomes an important commentary on a decaying British Empire and its ineffective colonization of Ireland: Mrs. Rogers (British) repeatedly borrows Eugene's (Irish) pen and repeatedly refuses to relinquish a room-dividing wall unit. Though somewhat simplistic in its political message, the play would still delight audiences with its comic treatment of a continuing political problem. *The Patrick Pearse Motel* also goes beyond its farcical humor to offer a political and economic theme. While its comedy can stand on its own as a typical bedroom farce, the addition of telling details makes the play even funnier: the motel's new restaurant offers the best steaks in Ireland in its Famine Room, while the drunken caretaker of this new Irish motel was a participant in the 1916 Uprising. The characters in the play all gently mock Irish mythology as each bears a name of a hero or heroine of the past while engaging in actions far from heroic.

Up to the production of *Da*, Leonard's works had been fairly objective and impersonal, and while Leonard did not leave behind his acidic wit or ironic detachment in plays to come, *Da* marked the start of a new emotionalism, even vulnerability, in Leonard's work. A highly successful fusion of the past and present, *Da* is a moving account of Leonard's coming to terms with his adoptive father's passing, while having universal import. It remains Leonard's greatest achievement, though he dismisses it as "just a memory." *Summer* used to be Leonard's favorite, but over the years he has become convinced by critics that the young couple remain a problem. It remains a good play, nevertheless, with three adult couples meeting for two picnics six years apart, exposing slowly the frustrations and failures of any (not just Irish) bourgeois existence. *A Life* returned Leonard's artistic talents to a character in *Da*, but Leonard remarks that Drumm is "pure imagination, pure creation" and hence his favorite character in his favorite play. Gill believes that it is "a measure of Leonard's skill as a playwright that we find Drumm touching and funny as well as irritating" (174). Of course, much the same was said of the irascibly annoying Da. Leonard has a particular talent for drawing these characters who evoke comedies with a heavy bittersweet tone.

Despite having undergone quadruple bypass heart surgery recently, Leonard has quickly returned to writing, with "a renewed energy surge," as he puts it. We can probably expect many more successful scripts from this very active sixty-six-year-old.

PRIMARY BIBLIOGRAPHY

Plays

The Au Pair Man. London: Samuel French, 1972.

Da. Newark, Del.: Proscenium Press (with the Society of Irish Playwrights, Dublin), 1975; rev. ed., New York and London: Atheneum, 1978; acting ed., London, 1979, New York, 1980: Samuel French.

Da, A Life, Time Was. Harmondsworth, Middlesex: Penguin, 1981.

A Life. London, 1980 and New York, 1982: Samuel French.

Madigan's Lock and Pizzazz. Dublin: Brophy Books, 1987.

The Mask of Moriarty. London: Samuel French, 1986; Dublin: Brophy Books, 1987.

Moving. London: Samuel French, 1994.

The Patrick Pearse Motel. London: Samuel French, 1972.
Pizzazz. London: Samuel French, 1986. (Containing *A View from the Obelisk, Roman Fever, Pizzazz.*)
The Poker Session. London: Evans Brothers, 1963.
Summer. Gerrards Cross, Buckinghamshire: Colin Smythe, 1991.

Prose

Home before Night. London: Andre Deutsch, 1979; New York: Atheneum, 1980; Harmondsworth, Middlesex: Penguin, 1981. (Memoir.)
Leonard's Last Book. Wicklow, Enniskerry, Co.: Egotist Press, 1978. (Essays.)
Out after Dark. London: Andre Deutsch, 1989; Harmondsworth, Middlesex: Penguin, 1991. (Memoir.)
Parnell and the English Woman. London: Andre Deutsch, 1989. (Novel.)

Dramatic Adaptations

Dublin One. (produced 1963; unpublished script at Abbey Theatre archives).
Stephen D. London and New York: Evans Brothers, 1965. (Adapted from James Joyce's *A Portrait of the Artist as a Young Man* and *Stephen Hero.*)

Unpublished Play Scripts

The Big Birthday (produced 1956; script at Abbey Theatre archives).
Chamber Music (produced 1994; script at Abbey Theatre archives).

Anthology

Selected Plays of Hugh Leonard: Irish Drama Selections 9. (The Au Pair Man, The Patrick Pearse Motel, Da, Summer, A Life, Kill.) Ed. S. F. Gallagher. Gerrards Cross, Buckinghamshire: Colin Smythe, 1992; Washington, D.C.: Catholic University of America Press, 1992.

Article

"Leonard on *The Mask of Moriarty*: A Three-Part Log." *Irish Times* (28 September 1985), (30 September 1985), (17 October 1985).

SECONDARY BIBLIOGRAPHY

Atkinson, Brooks. [Review of *Stephen D.*] *New York Times* (24 Dec. 1962).
Barnes, Clive. [1]. "Hugh Leonard Adapts Novel by Joyce." *New York Times* (25 Sept. 1967).
———. [2]. "Stage: 'The Au Pair Man' in Allegorical Guise." *New York Times* (28 Dec. 1973).
———. [3]. [Review of *A Life.*] *Irish Times* (4 Nov. 1986).

Berkvist, Robert. "Barnard Hughes—Born to Play 'Da'?" *New York Times* (11 June 1978).

Brustein, Robert. "A Passion for the Familiar." *New Republic* (6 Dec. 1980).

Carr, Mary. "Potted Performances at the Abbey." *Evening Herald* (Dublin) (24 Aug. 1994).

Chaillet, Ned. [1]. "A Life." *Times* (5 Feb. 1980).

————. [2]. "Hugh Leonard." *Contemporary Dramatists*. 4th ed. Chicago: St. James Press, 1988.

Claran, Claire. [Review of *The Mask of Moriarity*.] *Irish Times* (12 Apr. 1992).

Cronin, Sean. [1]. "Few Cheers for Leonard Play in New York." *Irish Times* (8 Jan. 1974).

————. [2]. "Leonard Play Opens in New York." *Irish Times* (3 Oct. 1980).

————. [3]. "Broadway Triumph for Leonard." *Irish Times* (4 Nov. 1980).

"Dramatist Represents Modern Middle-Class Ireland." *Times* (25 Sept. 1963).

Eder, Richard. "Da, an Irish Memory Play, Opens." *New York Times* (14 Mar. 1978).

"Fable Marred by Whimsy." *Times* (27 Sept. 1963).

"First Performance of New Play Abbey." *Irish Times* (1 Feb. 1956).

Fitzgerald, Jim. "Stageworthy Joyce Adaptation." *Times* (13 Feb. 1963).

Gill, Brendan. "The Theatre: Family Matters." *New Yorker* (10 Nov. 1980).

Gillespie, Elgy. [1]. "The Saturday Interview: Hugh Leonard." *Irish Times* (11 Dec. 1976).

————. [2]. "Cyril Cusack Appearing in 'A Life' by Hugh Leonard." *Irish Times* (3 Oct. 1979).

Gussow, Mel. [1]. "The Irish Playwright and His '*Da*.' " *New York Times* (24 Mar. 1978).

————. [2]. " 'Da' Gets a New Life on Broadway." *Times* (2 May 1978).

"Hit and Miss with Joyce." *Times* (1 Oct. 1963).

Hogan, Robert. [1]. "Leonard, Hugh." *Contemporary Literary Criticism*. Vol. 19. Ed. Sharon R. Gunton. Detroit: Gale Research, 1981.

————. [2]. "Leonard, Hugh." *Dictionary of Irish Literature*. Westport, Conn.: Greenwood Press, 1979.

"Hugh Leonard Play In London Premiere." *New York Times* (12 Feb. 1964).

"An Irishman's Diary." *Irish Times* (6 Oct. 1979).

Kalem, T. E. [1]. "Time's Toll." *Times* (13 Oct. 1980).

————. [2]. [Review of *A Life*.] *Time* (24 Nov. 1980).

Kauffmann, Stanley. [Review of *Stephen D.*] *New York Times* (5 Aug. 1966).

Kennedy, Maurice. "Stephen D." *Irish Times* (25 Sept. 1962).

Kerr, Walter. [1]. [Review of Stephen D.] *New York Times* (8 Oct. 1967).

————. [2]. ". . . a Masterful 'Da'." *New York Times* (14 May 1978).

————. [3]. "A 'Summer' Greatly in Need of Seasoning." *New York Times* (5 Oct. 1980).

————. [4]. "Critic's Notebook: How Playwrights Do—Or Don't—Make a Point." *New York Times* (4 Dec. 1980).

————. [5]. "From a Tightly Focused 'Life' to a Scattershot 'Fifth of July.' " *New York Times* (16 Nov. 1980).

Kosok, Heinz. "Hugh Leonard." *Dictionary of Literary Biography: British Dramatists since World War II*. Vol. 13. Ed. Stanley Weintraub. Detroit: Gale Research, 1982.

Kroll, Jack. [1]. "Sunday Outings." *Newsweek* (13 Oct. 1980).

———. [2]. "Master of the Harp." *Newsweek* (17 Nov. 1980).

Lawlor, David. "From Frothy Farce to an Ageing Star." *Evening Press* (Dublin) (24 Aug. 1994).

Leonard, William J. "Leonard, Hugh." *Contemporary Literary Criticism*. Vol. 19. Ed. Sharon R. Gunton. Detroit: Gale Research, 1981.

Lewsen, Charles. "Dublin Theatre Festival." *Times* (11 Oct. 1974).

Linehan, Fergus. "First Ranker." *Irish Times* (20 Feb. 1993).

"London Press Acclaims Play from Joyce Novels." *New York Times* (14 Feb. 1963).

McCarthy, Kerry. "Playwright Leonard Puts His Past on the Stage." *Irish Independent* (9 Oct. 1973).

McEldouney, Eugene. "Our Playwright Extraordinary." *Irish Times* (11 June 1980).

McGarry, Patsy. "Nice Double Humour, But Farce Is Slow." *Irish Press* (24 Aug. 1994).

Novick, Julius. [1]. [Review of *A Life*.] *Nation* (22 Nov. 1980).

———. [2]. "Summer Passione." *Nation* (18 Oct. 1980).

Nowlan, David [1]. " 'Stephen D' at the Abbey." *Irish Times* (19 May 1978).

———. [2]. "Play by Hugh Leonard at Olympia." *Irish Times* (8 Oct. 1974).

———. [3]. "Moving about in Perfect Synch." *Irish Times* (22 Apr. 1992).

———. [4]. "Small Pearl of Acerbic Drama." *Irish Times* (24 Aug. 1994).

Peachment, Chris. "Sent Up with Wildean Fun." *Times* (15 June 1987).

Power, Victor. "Leonard, Hugh." *Contemporary Literary Criticism*. Vol. 19. Ed. Sharon R. Gunton. Detroit: Gale Research, 1981.

Rich, Frank. [1]. "Play: Hugh Leonard's 'Summer'." *New York Times* (29 Sept. 1980).

———. [2]. "Fake Happy Endings and Pop-Song Mania." *New York Times* (23 Oct. 1980).

———. [3]. "Stage: Dotrice in Hugh Leonard's 'A Life.' " *New York Times* (3 Nov. 1980).

———. [4]. [Review of *A Life*.] *Irish Times* (4 Nov. 1980).

Roberts, Peter. [Review of *The Patrick Pearse Motel*.] *Times* (19 Mar. 1971).

Rogers, Cynthia, and Jean W. Ross. "Byrne, John Keyes." *Contemporary Authors*. Vol. 102. Ed Francis Locher. Detroit: Gale Research, 1981. (Interview.)

Rushe, Desmond. [1]. "Unwanted Comedy Spirits Summer." *Irish Independent* (8 Oct. 1974).

———. [2]. "Life Is a Happy 21st for Hugh Leonard." *Irish Independent* (6 Oct. 1979).

———. [3]. "Leonard Spoof of Sherlock." *New York Times* (8 Oct. 1985).

———. [4]. "Leonard Promise Unfulfilled." *Irish Independent* (22 Apr. 1992).

Shanahan, Kate. "Love, Life and the Whole Damn Thing." *Irish Times* (3 Sept. 1987).

Shepard, Richard. "Play by Hugh Leonard Seen at Martinique." *New York Times* (20 Sept. 1967).

Smith, Hugh. "Joyce's 'Stephen' Staged in Dublin." *New York Times* (25 Sept. 1962).

Taylor, John Russell. "Leonard, Hugh." *Contemporary Literary Criticism*. Vol. 19. Ed. Sharon R. Gunton. Detroit: Gale Research, 1981.

Wade, David. "A Little Kindness." *Times* (15 Feb. 1969).

Wardle, Irving. [1]. "Dublin Satire on the Monarchy." *Times* (8 Oct. 1968).

———. [2]. [Review of *The Patrick Pearse Motel*.] *Times* (18 June 1971).

Watt, Douglas. [Review of *A Life*.] *Irish Times* (4 Nov. 1986).

Woodworth, Paddy. "Long Life of Leonard." *Irish Times* (10 Aug. 1991).

Young, B. A. "Hugh Leonard Play in London Premiere." *New York Times* (12 Feb. 1964).

Christine Pakenham, Lady Longford
(1900–1980)

KATHLEEN A. QUINN

Christine Patti Pakenham, Countess of Longford, was born Christine Patti Trew in Cheddar, Somerset, England, on 6 September 1900, to Richard and Amy Trew. Her parents separated when she was a child, and she lived with her mother, who was forced to take in lodgers. When she was fourteen, she moved to Oxford with her mother, and Christine attended Oxford Wells High School. She received a classical scholarship to Somerville College, Oxford, where she studied Latin, Greek, philosophy, and ancient history. There she met Edward Pakenham, the elder son of the Earl of Longford, in 1922, and they were married in 1925. They lived at Pakenham Hall (now called Tullynally Castle), Castle-pollard, County Westmeath, Ireland.

In 1928, two events set the pattern for her professional life: she published her first book, *Vespasian and Some of His Contemporaries*, a light biography of the Roman emperor; then she and Edward saw an impressive production of *Peer Gynt* by Hilton Edwards and Micheál Mac Liammóir at the Peacock Theatre. In 1930, they purchased a substantial number of shares in Edwards and Mac Liammóir's Dublin Gate Theatre Company, which opened that year in the Rotunda, thus beginning their long association with that theater. That same year Christine wrote her first novel, *Making Conversation*, a semiautobiographical account of her early life. It was published in 1931, the year in which Edward became a member of the Board of Directors of the Gate Theatre, and they immediately became involved in theater business after years of being inveterate playgoers.

The year 1932 saw the publication of Christine's second novel, *Country Places*, and the production of her first play, *Queens and Emperors*, for the Edwards-Mac Liammóir company. She describes it as ''better forgotten except for the kindness of Hilton and Micheál and all concerned'' (quoted in Cowell 89). She and Edward translated Aeschylus' *Oresteia*, with Christine translating

The Furies. Although their version, called *Agamemnon*, played to somewhat empty houses in 1933, it is important as the first of her many translations and adaptations. Her play *Mr. Jiggins of Jigginstown*, adapted from her novel of that name, quickly followed and was well received; the only thing the *Irish Times* reviewer criticized was the title.

Tensions within the Gate company, particularly between Lord Longford and the Edwards-Mac Liammóir partnership, increased in 1934, and her only play staged at the Gate that year was a one-act called *The New Girl*. In 1935, her translation of *Antigone* was performed by students at All Hallows College in Dublin, and her novel *Printed Cotton* was published. The Longfords broke official association with Edwards and Mac Liammóir in 1936, starting their own company, Longford Productions. The split occurred over a proposed company production in Egypt: Edwards and Mac Liammóir wanted to make the trip; Lady Longford described her husband's position as "Not an inch, no surrender, don't shut the Gate! Like the Old Lady, Edward said no" ("Touring" 9). As a result, Edwards and Mac Liammóir agreed to share the Gate Theatre with Longford Productions, each using it for six months. In *Enter Certain Players*, she explains that Longford Productions "was started by Edward in 1936 and ceased with his death twenty-five years later" (53), saying that it began when he joined the board at the Gate, "and when he started his Longford Productions, from then to the end of his life he was faithful to their traditions" of bringing the classics to the Irish people (56). When not playing in the Gate, the Longfords took their company on tour, performing in small theaters or alternate venues in cities and towns throughout Ireland as well as in England. As Lady Longford says in her memoirs, "Why didn't the Abbey do Farquhar and Congreve and Sheridan? Never mind, the Gate would" ("Talk" 9). The list of Irish towns to which they brought their classical and their original productions is impressive: Athlone, Ballina, Belfast, Birr, Boyle, Cahir, Carlow, Castlepollard, Castlereagh, Cavan, Clonmel, Cobh, Cork, Drogheda, Dundalk, Dungarven, Ennis, Fermoy, Galway, Kilkenny, Killarney, Limerick, Longford, Mallow, Mullingar, Navan, Nenagh, Roscommon, Sligo, Thurles, Tralee, Tuam, Tullamore, Waterford, Westport, Wexford, and Youghal.

With their hectic schedule, Lady Longford did not have as much time for her writing as she later admitted she would have liked. In 1937, her adaptation of Jane Austen's *Pride and Prejudice* was performed at the Gate with James Mason as Darcy, and her play *Anything but the Truth* played to full houses, although it was not acclaimed critically. It was included in the Longford Productions repertoire at the Westminster Theatre, London, later that season. This was closely followed by *The Absentee*, her adaptation of the Maria Edgeworth novel. During the early 1940s, she began writing historical dramas, most notably, *Lord Edward* (1941), *The United Brothers* (1942), and *Patrick Sarsfield* (1943). She also wrote other plays at this time: *Sea Change* (1940), *The Watcher* (an adaptation from J. Sheridan Le Fanu, 1942), and *The Avenger* (1943).

Her prolific playwriting continued with *The Earl of Straw* (1944), *John Donne*

(1945), *Uncle Silas* (another adaptation from Le Fanu, 1947), *Tankardstown; or, A Lot to Be Thankful For* (1948), and *Mr. Supple; or, Time Will Tell* (1949). More plays were written and produced during the following decade: *The Paragons* (1950), *Witch Hunt* (1952), *The Hill of Quirke* (1953), *Stop the Clock* (1955), *La Dame aux Camelias* (a translation from Dumas the younger, 1956), and *Mount Lawless* (1957).

Christine's final play, *Stephen Stoney*, was produced in 1960, the year before her husband's death. After Lord Longford's death in 1961, her professional life changed drastically. No longer did she help manage Longford Productions. However, from 1961 to 1964 she was manager of the Gate Theatre and became a member of their Board of Directors in 1969. During the 1960s Lady Longford became a regular book reviewer for the Saturday edition of the *Irish Times*, and she was a regular panelist on the RTE arts program "Survey." In 1967, she was awarded life membership in the Irish Actors' Equity Association, and the following year she was elected a member of the Irish Academy of Letters. In 1970, her novel *Making Conversation* was reissued.

In April 1980, the newly revived Longford Productions—with Lady Longford on its Board of Directors—staged its first play. On 25 April 1980, Christine received an honorary D. Litt. from the National University of Ireland; the citation praised her as a "playwright, novelist, patron of the arts, dedicated servant of theatre in Ireland" (quoted in "Honorary" 13). She died on 14 May 1980. After her death, her memoirs, covering her life from 1918 to 1939, were discovered; they were published serially in the *Irish Times* in May 1981.

Selected Biographical Sources: Cowell; Lord Pakenham.

MAJOR PLAYS, PREMIERES, AND SIGNIFICANT REVIVALS: THEATRICAL RECEPTION

Queens and Emperors. 1932. Opened 15 March at the Dublin Gate Theatre. Produced by Edwards-Mac Liammóir Dublin Gate Theatre Productions.

Her first play, though not a critical success, showed her talent for dialogue and gave audiences a sample of her wit.

Agamemnon. 1933. Opened 15 February at the Dublin Gate Theatre. Produced by Edwards-Mac Liammóir Dublin Gate Theatre Productions.

This translation of *The Oresteia*, by Aeschylus, was done by the earl and countess of Longford. *The Furies*, the third play in the trilogy, was translated by Lady Longford. Although it played to empty houses, the work was, according to a reviewer, "dignified and vigorous."

Mr. Jiggins of Jigginstown. 1933. Opened 28 March at the Dublin Gate Theatre. Produced by the Edwards-Mac Liammóir Dublin Gate Theatre Productions. Directed by Hilton Edwards. Revivals: Killarney town hall, 20 August 1939; Mullingar, September 1939.

An adaptation of her own novel, this play's title character is loosely based on a County Westmeath man, Adolphus Cooke, who, according to Cowell, "disappointed the expectations of his pretentious relatives by leaving his fortune to found a nondenominational school for boys" (94). The *Irish Times* (Review of *Mr. Jiggins of Jigginstown*) praised the characterization, saying it must "be the result of personal characterization and a clever pen," and Hogan commends it for displaying her "highly competent craftsmanship" (127).

Pride and Prejudice. 1937. Opened 25 January at the Dublin Gate Theatre. Produced by Longford Productions.

This adaptation of Jane Austen's novel, according to the *Irish Times* (Review of *Pride and Prejudice*), "charmed the audience into a close attention to every picturesque phase of an unexciting story. . . . A high degree of art is shown in the delicate handling of the verbal difficulties of the old-time stilted language." Particularly notable was the performance of James Mason as Darcy; already a cinema star, he had been temporarily released from his movie contract to play this role. In a personal interview (1991), the playwright Séamus De Búrca said that this was her best play.

Anything but the Truth. 1937. Opened 25 May at the Dublin Gate Theatre. Directed by Peter Powell. Produced by Longford Productions. Revival October 1937 at Westminster Theatre (London).

Cowell, who had a minor role in the Dublin production, said that it "was frightfully sophisticated, with sparkling Coward-like dialogue," yet he admits that reviews, like that in the *TCD Miscellany*, did not accept it as well as the audience did (118). The *Irish Times* (Review of *Anything but the the Truth*) did praise its entertainment value: "If judgment were to be based upon the number of laughs produced in the audience . . . Lady Longford will be accounted a benefactor of humanity."

Lord Edward. 1941. Opened 10 June at the Dublin Gate Theatre. Produced by Longford Productions. Directed by John Izon.

This, her first historical drama, delineates the exploits of Lord Edward Fitz-Gerald. Hogan praises the dialogue while admitting the technical weaknesses of the play, calling it, finally, "painless educational theatre" (127–28). The *Irish Times* (Review of *Lord Edward*) suggested that, although it had some weaknesses, it was important for rescuing the image of Lord Edward "from the oblivion of a now forgotten melodrama." Pádhraig Óg Ó Conaire translated it into Irish in 1944: *An Tiarna Éadbhárd.*

The United Brothers. 1942. Opened 4 April at the Dublin Gate Theatre. Was held over for a third week. Produced by Longford Productions. Directed by John Izon.

A historical drama about John and Henry Sheares, the 1798 rebels who had been immortalized in a poem by Lady Wilde, this drama—of the brothers, their sister, and the man who betrayed them—was, according to the *Irish Times* (Review of *The United Brothers*), full of "charm and grace," brought "the Dublin of 1798 as near to us as the Dublin of to-day,'' and showed ''the nobility'' of the brothers as well as their ''simplicity of heart.''

Patrick Sarsfield. 1943. Opened 18 May at the Dublin Gate Theatre. Produced by Longford Productions. Directed by John Izon.

Written to mark the 250th anniversary of Sarsfield's death, this play combines the history of the famous battles between King William of Orange and King James II with the portrayal of the faithful Sarsfield. The *Irish Times* (Review of *Patrick Sarsfield*) praised the richness and depth of the play's texture while acknowledging some weaknesses in Sarsfield's portrayal; however, he acknowledged the difficulties in depicting a historical figure who has become a folk figure. The play's relevance to the current Troubles in Northern Ireland, particularly in terms of the mythic recitation of history, would interest contemporary readers.

The Earl of Straw. 1944. Opened 10 October at the Dublin Gate Theatre. Produced by Longford Productions. Directed by John Izon.

This play, which dramatizes the early seventeenth-century rebellion of Tyrone against Queen Elizabeth, marks a movement from historical drama to historical comedy as it depicts the Sugaun Earl of Desmond. Hogan calls this her finest history play, commending its ''vivid glimpse into the rebellion and the reasons for its failure'' and suggesting that, onstage, it would have ''the excitement of a swashbuckling movie,'' finally saying ''this is as vivid and accomplished a historical play as any dramatist has written in modern Ireland'' (129). The *Irish Times* (Review of *The Earl of Straw*), however, suggests that the play, although it has many interesting comic reversals, suffers from lack of historical accuracy. In addition, he accuses it of being derivative of Bernard Shaw's *John Bull's Other Island*; as such, it works only as a parody of Shaw.

Tankardstown; or, A Lot to Be Thankful For. 1948. Opened 13 July at the Dublin Gate Theatre. Produced by Longford Productions. Directed by John Izon. Also in Cork and Wexford. Revival: Arts Theatre, Salisbury, England, January 1949.

Maxwell says this play has dialogue that ''ambles along pleasantly enough . . . [but without] defining a space where the varied themes might speak to each other'' (133). Hogan admits it is slightly dated and somewhat thinly plotted but again admires ''the absolute rightness of her dialogue'' (130). The *Irish Times* (Review of *Tankardstown*), however, ranked it as one of the top three Irish comedies in the past ten years, seeing the characters as ''mouthpieces for the dramatists' brilliantly satirical topical commentary on the playground of the Western world.''

Mr. Supple; or, Time Will Tell. 1949. Opened 4 October at the Dublin Gate Theatre. Produced by Longford Productions. Directed by Dan O'Connell. Extended for a seven-week run.

Lady Longford's dialogue in this play, according to Hogan, ''deftly exposes the faults and foibles of . . . well-chosen Irish types'' (130). The *Irish Times* (Review of *Mr. Supple*) said that Lady Longford ''has rarely indulged her talent for deflationary light satire to better effect'' than in this play.

The Hill of Quirke. 1953. Opened 6 October at the Dublin Gate Theatre. Produced by Longford Productions. Directed by Dan O'Connell.

Robert Hogan calls it ''Lady Longford's best contemporary play'' (130). In a review of the first production, however, the *Irish Times* (Review of *The Hill of Quirke*) said that it would work better as a farce; as such, it ''could be one of the funniest dramatic commentaries on tostalitarianism [*sic*] in Ireland yet written.'' It later appeared as a radio production.

ADDITIONAL PLAYS, ADAPTATIONS, AND PRODUCTIONS

Aside from *The Furies* (part of *Agamemnon*), Lady Longford translated *Antigone* (1935) from Sophocles and *La Dame aux Camelias* (1956) from Dumas the younger. The former received an amateur production by clerical students at All Hallows College, Dublin; the latter opened at the Dublin Gate Theatre for Longford Productions.

She also wrote well-received adaptations besides *Pride and Prejudice*. *The Absentee* (1938) was based on the Maria Edgeworth novel. The works of Joseph Sheridan Le Fanu seemed to hold a particular fascination for her, and three of her plays were adapted from his works: *The Watcher* (1942), based on ''The Familiar''; *Uncle Silas* (1947), based on the novel, which she had edited that year; and *The Avenger* (1943), based on ''Ultor de Lacy.''

Her only one-act play, *The New Girl* (February 1934) was produced by Edwards-Mac Liammóir Dublin Gate Theatre Productions. In addition, several full-length plays, all from Longford Productions, opened at the Dublin Gate Theatre: *Sea Change* (1940), *John Donne* (1945), *The Paragons* (1950), *Witch Hunt* (1952), *Stop the Clock* (1955), *Mount Lawless* (1957), and *Stephen Stoney* (1960).

ASSESSMENT OF LONGFORD'S CAREER

Frequently, Longford's plays have been considered to have only slight value. D. E. S. Maxwell, for instance, says that her plays—as well as those of her husband—''passed their hour agreeably and urged no greater claim.'' He compares their plays to Lady Gregory's, ''though they took their work less solemnly than their predecessor did hers. The plays are an upstaged version of the Abbey's . . . 'kitchen comedy' '' (Maxwell 133). Hilton Edwards suggests that Lady Longford lacked seriousness of purpose as a dramatist, yet admits, ''Her wit was always unexpected and needle-sharp, with a cut and a thrust that would lay a dragon low, but the most apparently banal cliché that she uttered concealed a perfection and an evaluation which were frightening in their penetration'' (9).

Hogan says that her plays were "notable for their ease of dialogue and deftness of construction," asserting that her "contemporary plays generally reflect the foibles of Irish life with an accuracy hardly matched since the comedies of Lennox Robinson" (126). Pine seems to concur when he discusses her first three plays: "Typical of Lady Longford's cutting style, these were satirical comedies displaying the author's deep psychological insight and ability to expose the ridiculous by means of social comedy" (56). Ó hAodha commends the Longfords' original plays and particularly their adaptations of Le Fanu's stories (125).

Most contemporary reviewers, however, praised her plays in general even when they criticized specific problems or weaknesses. The *Irish Times'* review of *The Hill of Quirke* observed, "Lady Longford has established herself as a playwright with a shrewd eye and a sharp pen for topical satire on many previous occasions." Similarly, its review of *Tankardstown* praises her mastery of social comedy: "Lady Longford is a jump ahead of the rest of us in seeing the fun behind the knavishness and folly that makes us wince." Her knowledge of both England and Ireland gave her the freedom "to prick the bubble of national self-conceit on either side of the Irish Sea as maliciously as she like[d]" (Review of *Mr. Supple*). Other contemporary reviewers praised her insights, dialogue, and form. One applauds her "management of the twelve scenes" and her "delicate handling" of language in her adaptation of *Pride and Prejudice* (Review of *Pride and Prejudice*) (8). Even the reviewer of her first play, *Queens and Emperors*, mentions "witty dialogue" and "memorable" lines while criticizing the play itself: "[T]here is no conflict, no climax, no tragedy, and only the very thinnest of comedy" (Review of *Queens and Emperors*).

One area that has been neglected by early reviewers as well as modern critics is her nationalism. Both she and Lord Longford were ardent nationalists; they studied the Irish language, they wrote about historical figures, and, generally at their own expense, they worked untiringly to bring theater to Irish people, even those who could not travel to the established theaters in cities. Yet in Lady Longford's plays, her nationalism shines forth most clearly. From *Mr. Jiggins of Jigginstown*, with the greedy Anglo-Irish relatives vying for the inheritance, to such historical dramas as *Patrick Sarsfield* and *The United Brothers*, her love for her adopted country predominates. Contemporary reviewers often acknowledged this. For instance, the reviewer of *The United Brothers* said, "In the last words of John Sheares, as spoken by his no less noble sister, the spirit of 1798 and that of Easter Week 1916, come together as one" (2).

Although she is best known for her plays, she excited much interest as a novelist, and discussions about her often stress her achievements in this genre, sometimes giving it precedence over her plays. Pakenham's autobiography, *Born to Believe*, mentions her primarily as a novelist; in their brief discussion of the Longfords, McHugh and Harmon describe her first as a novelist (332). More than half of her plays have never been published, yet her novel *Making Conversation* was reissued in 1970, following Johnson's 1968 article on it in the

Times Literary Supplement. Cowell suggests that, if she had continued writing novels rather than plays, the novels "might well have proved to be her greater achievement." Yet, he says, her love of the theater and Edward's encouragement caused her to focus on drama: "She churned out plays, almost to order, and always under pressure from Edward. . . . Capable of infinitely greater heights in the drama than she attained, Christine's talent was neglected, undisciplined, wasted" (Cowell 77).

Lady Longford was, perhaps, her own harshest critic. In her memoirs, she mentions the success of *Pride and Prejudice* but immediately dismisses it with, "Then we did a real play" ("Touring" 9). When discussing *Anything but the Truth*, she claims that it "was not very good" because it lacked depth: "The audience laughed very loud and we had good houses. Still, what was the point? What was the idea, if any? I imagined I had one, and somehow it failed to emerge" ("Touring" 9). She had a talent, but, because of time restraints and other obligations, it never fully emerged. Yet audiences and readers have been, and will continue to be, delighted with the talent and material that did emerge from the pen of Christine Pakenham, countess of Longford.

ARCHIVAL SOURCES

The archives of Longford Productions disappeared in 1970 when the Gate Theatre was being modernized.

PRIMARY BIBLIOGRAPHY

Plays

The Earl of Straw. Dublin: Hodges Figgis, 1945.
The Hill of Quirke. Dublin: P. J. Bourke, 1958.
Lord Edward. Dublin: Hodges Figgis, 1941.
Mr. Jiggins of Jigginstown. London: Gollancz, 1933; rpt., *Plays of Changing Ireland*. Ed. Curtis Canfield. New York: Macmillan, 1936. 269–320.
Mr. Supple; or, Time Will Tell. Dublin: P. J. Bourke [1950?]; rpt., [1958?].
The Oresteia. Translated into English Verse by the Earl of Longford and Christine Longford. Dublin: Hodges Figgis, 1933.
Patrick Sarsfield. Dublin: Hodges Figgis, 1943.
Tankardstown; or, A Lot to Be Thankful For. Dublin: P. J. Bourke, [1948?]; rpts., [1950? 1958?].
An Tiarna Éadbhárd [Lord Edward]. Trans. Pádhraic Óg Ó Conaire. Dublin: Oifig an tSolátair, 1944.
The United Brothers. Dublin: Hodges Figgis, 1942.

Novels

Country Places. London: Gollancz, 1932. Dublin: Parkside Press, [1945].
Making Conversation. London: Stein and Gollancz, 1931; rpt., Faber and Faber, 1970.

Mr. Jiggins of Jigginstown. London: Gollancz, 1933.
Printed Cotton. London: Methuen, 1935.

Essays and Articles on Drama and Theater

A Biography of Dublin. London: Methuen, 1936.
"Essay." *Enter Certain Players: Edwards–MacLiammóir and the Gate, 1928–1978*. Ed. Peter Luke. Dublin: Dolmen Press, 1978, 53–56.
Introduction. *Uncle Silas* [abridged]. By Joseph Sheridan Le Fanu. With an introduction and edited by Christine Longford. Harmondsworth; New York: Penguin, 1940.
Introduction. *Uncle Silas*. By Joseph Sheridan Le Fanu. With an introduction and edited by Christine Longford. West Drayton; New York: Penguin, 1947.
"Ireland For Ever: The Longford Memoirs—2." *Irish Times* (14 Mar. 1981).
"The Longford Memoirs—1." *Irish Times* (7 Mar. 1981).
"Talk and Theatre: The Longford Memoirs—3." *Irish Times* (21 Mar. 1981).
"Touring the Country: The Longford Memoirs—4." *Irish Times* (28 Mar. 1981).
Vespasian and Some of His Contemporaries. Dublin: Hodges, Figgis, 1928.

SECONDARY BIBLIOGRAPHY

Review of *Agamemnon*. *Irish Times* (16 Feb. 1933): 5.
Review of *Anything but the Truth*. *Irish Times* (26 May 1937): 5.
Review of *Anything but the Truth*. *Times* (19 Oct. 1937): 14.
"Christine Lady Longford Dies." *Irish Times* (15 May 1980): 1.
Cowell, John. *No Profit but the Name: The Longfords and the Gate Theatre*. Dublin: O'Brien Press, 1988.
"Death of Christine Longford." *Irish Press* (15 May 1980): 3.
Review of *The Earl of Straw*. *Irish Times* (11 Oct. 1944): 3.
Edwards, Hilton. "Christine Lady Longford: A Unique Talent." *Irish Times* (16 May 1980): 9.
Fitz-Simon, Christopher. *The Irish Theatre*. London: Thames and Hudson, 1983.
Fitzgerald, Marion. "Lady of the Theatre." *Word* (Dec. 1969): 17–19.
Review of *The Hill of Quirke*. *Irish Times* (7 Oct. 1953): 5.
Hogan, Robert. *After the Irish Renaissance: A Critical History of the Irish Drama since The Plough and the Stars*. Minneapolis: University of Minnesota Press, 1967, 126–32.
"Honorary Degree for Christine Lady Longford." *Irish Times* (25 Apr. 1980): 13.
Johnson, Pamela H. "Christine Longford's *Making Conversation*." *Times Literary Supplement* (28 Nov. 1968): 1332–33.
"Lady Longford Dies in Dublin Hospital." *Irish Times* (15 May 1980): 7.
[Longford, Lord (Edward Pakenham)]. *Longford Productions*. Dublin: Gate Theatre, [1939].
Review of *Lord Edward*. *Irish Times* (11 June 1941): 6.
Luke, Peter, ed. *Enter Certain Players: Edwards–Mac Liammóir and the Gate, 1928–1978*. Dublin: Dolmen Press, 1978.
Lyons, J. "Play-Going in the 40s." *Dublin Magazine* 9.4 (Autumn 1972): 80–86.

Maxwell, D. E. S. *A Critical History of Modern Irish Drama 1891–1980*. Cambridge: Cambridge University Press, 1984.

McHugh, Roger, and Maurice Harmon. *A Short History of Anglo-Irish Literature: From Its Origins to the Present Day*. Dublin: Wolfhound Press, 1982.

Review of *Mr. Jiggins of Jigginstown*. *Irish Times* (29 Mar. 1933): 4.

Review of *Mr. Supple; or, Time Will Tell*. *Irish Times* (5 Oct. 1949): 5.

Nowlan, David. [Review of *Three Sisters*.] *Irish Times* (9 Apr. 1980): 8.

Ó hAodha, Micheál. *Theatre in Ireland*. Oxford: Basil Blackwell, 1974.

Pakenham, Lord [Frank]. *Born to Believe: An Autobiography*. London: Jonathan Cape, 1953.

Review of *Patrick Sarsfield*. *Irish Times* (19 May 1943): 3.

Pine, Richard. With Richard Cave. *The Dublin Gate Theatre 1928–1978*. Cambridge: Chadwyck-Healey, 1984.

Review of *Pride and Prejudice*. *Irish Times* (26 Jan. 1937): 8.

Review of *Queens and Emperors*. *Irish Times* (16 Mar. 1932): 6.

Review of *Tankardstown; or, A Lot to Be Thankful For*. *Irish Times* (14 July 1948): 3.

Review of *The United Brothers*. *Irish Times* (6 Apr. 1942): 2.

Watkinson, Eve. *Irish Times* (22 Feb. 1978): 9. (Letter to editor.)

Donagh MacDonagh
(1912–1968)

GORDON M. WICKSTROM

Donagh MacDonagh was born in Dublin in 1912 into the very thick of Irish nationalist revolutionary politics and insurrection. His father, poet and university lecturer Thomas MacDonagh, was one of the leaders and martyrs of the Easter Rising of 1916; one of the last to surrender, he was executed by the British in Kilmainham Gaol in the predawn hours of 3 May of that year of such "terrible beauty."

His mother, Muriel, née Gifford, was also deeply embroiled in Irish nationalism, not alone by her marriage to her patriot husband but through her own prominent family. The six Gifford sisters, but not the six brothers, were intimately tied to the nationalist cause and to the revolutionary events of that momentous spring of 1916.

The notorious execution of his father and his mother's subsequent death by drowning while swimming at sea the next year, only her thirty-first, left him and his sister Barbara helpless amid the struggles for custody by various unfeeling relatives. The children got little or no useful education, affection, or real care. They grew up lonely and deprived, but not without a sense of who they were or who their parents were in the great scheme of Irish things. It was a legacy both to support and to burden the children.

In 1917, the four-year-old Donagh was given a vaccine containing live tuberculosis. It struck him down and had him in and out of the hospital for much of his younger boyhood. But recovery had its penalty: he was to be quite a small man, barely five feet two inches tall, and with a slight hump on his neck and upper left back that, for many, always singled him out.

Only late, at age twelve, did MacDonagh begin to get his first real education, when he entered Belvedere College in Dublin, the Jesuit school that was also James Joyce's. Soon he was turning his hand to writing little stories and developing the literary interests that were to determine his future. After Belvedere he matriculated at University College, Dublin (UCD), in 1932, where he quickly became a student *literateur* and literary ringleader. His M.A. thesis at UCD on T. S. Eliot was the beginning of an important period of mutual interest and appreciation between poets: the celebrated Anglo-American and the young Irish comer.

MacDonagh then read law at Kings Inn and was called to the bar in 1935, the year of his marriage to Maura Smyth, with whom he had two children, Breifne and Iseult. He practiced in the Western Law Circuit, where he was often called upon to try cases in Irish, at which he was expert. In 1941 he was made a district court justice. He insisted that the work as both barrister and judge was rewarding and agreeable, a happy complement to his other life in literature and music. The stories he told of his work as judge, especially in the West, were often the hit of the town.

But then another terrible death struck the young family when his wife, Maura, died at twenty-three in a drowning accident at home in 1939. Eventually, in 1943, MacDonagh married Maura's sister Nuala; and two children, Niall and Barbara, were born. Then again, as though the Furies had not had enough of the MacDonaghs, Nuala, in her turn, died an accidental death by choking in 1970. The family wonders that all three of the "MacDonagh women" were wearing the same diamond ring at the times of their otherwise gratuitous, senseless deaths.

MacDonagh began writing poetry at about fourteen and was intensely interested in all matters literary. At the university he was at the center of a gifted generation of creative young people. He edited and contributed to the college magazine and saw his first professionally published poems in the *Irish Times* in 1934. Soon after, Eliot took several poems for the *Criterion Magazine* in London. But in that same seminal year of 1934, with his by now close friend Niall Sheridan, he published *Twenty Poems*, ten each from the young poets and at their own expense. These attracted great attention and launched them, like young mandarins, into Dublin's literary life.

In 1939 MacDonagh began his highly successful broadcasting career on Radió Éireann. He had grown deeply interested in ballads and all folk music and collected widely and passionately. His regular broadcasts of such music were always popular. His devoted listeners aided him in his ever-growing collection. His radio work continued with the greatly successful quiz program "Information Please," modeled on the American prototype.

He was by then a successful playwright as well, his earthy yet bright comedies in verse tapping into every Dubliner's consciousness with their ironic, verbal lyricism, wit, and generous use of song.

There was little in Dublin's literary or cultural life that MacDonagh did not touch upon. While at UCD, he was responsible for the first production in Ireland of Eliot's *Murder in the Cathedral*, which Eliot attended and greatly admired, even if partly from backstage, where he helped out as a stagehand. MacDonagh was everywhere and in everything—or so it seemed. Everybody knew him, and he knew everybody. It was a lively time for poetry, which he fiercely loved and practiced—and so not at all unusual that he should turn to verse for his plays (discussed in particular later), verse plays being part or the scheme of things in British drama at the time, with Eliot their great exponent.

Iseult McGuinness, MacDonagh's daughter and literary executor, does not disdain to speak of her father as a "Dublin character" and all that that has come to mean in the richness of Irish life and letters. He was an impatient man, sometimes irritable, always determined, intense and possessive on behalf of poetry and song. He was a noted raconteur, a wit, a great friend, and generous. He was famous like his father before him, patriots both, in their own ways. He remarked that while Joyce required exile from Ireland in order to write, he nevertheless had to take Dublin with him into exile. MacDonagh, on the other hand, was more than happy to keep to Dublin and live it, as it were, in the flesh.

Donagh MacDonagh died suddenly and unexpectedly at fifty-five on 1 January 1968.

Biographical Sources: FitzGerald; Sheridan [1, 2]; "Talking to Donagh MacDonagh."

MAJOR PLAYS, PREMIERES, AND SIGNIFICANT REVIVALS: THEATRICAL RECEPTION

Fading Mansions. 1945. Opened at the Duchess Theatre, London, in September 1945. Directed by Laurence Olivier, with Siobhan McKenna in the cast.

Fading Mansions is MacDonagh's only play not in verse. A treatment of Anouilh's *Romeo and Jeanette*, it was a "disaster" and never played again.

Happy as Larry. 1947. Comedy in verse. First produced with great success by Austin Clarke and the Lyric Theatre Company at the rented-for-the-occasion Abbey Theatre in May 1947, after the Abbey management had rejected it.

Happy as Larry was widely produced and translated. Maxwell called the play "a linguistically spirited romp. . . . [s]omewhat in the manner of John Gay's 'Beggar's Opera' " (222). He adds, though, that the verse "has a thinness that does not long survive its performance" (222). In New York, Burgess Meredith took it up, gave it a Broadway musical structure, and produced and acted in it at the Coronet Theatre, opening on 6 January 1950. The music was by Mischa and Wesley Portnoff. It was a quick and costly failure, providing MacDonagh with his "New York experience." Atkinson, for example, noted Meredith's enthrallment with the play but concluded that "it is impossible to share his taste." MacDonagh's daughter Iseult remembers calling it "the year we were rich."

Down by the Liffey Side. 1949–1950. First produced by the Sundrive Players of Dublin (amateur) as part of the Kilmuckridge Drama Festival on 29 March 1976.

This verse comedy-musical spectacle included music by Adrian Beecham, son of the conductor, Sir Thomas.

God's Gentry. 1951. First produced in 1951 at the Belfast Arts Theatre, Belfast. The second production was at Mount Holyoke College, South Hadley, Massachusetts in December 1951. Later that same month, Hilton Edwards directed it with Micheál Mac Liammóir's settings at the Gate Theatre, Dublin, on 26 December.

This verse comedy held the Gate stage longer than any Irish play to that date had held any stage, and since then, it has been a favorite play with amateur groups.

Step-in-the-Hollow. 1957. The first production opened at the Gaiety Theatre, 11 March 1957, in a production by the Gate Theatre Company, directed by Hilton Edwards, who also played Justice Redmond O'Hanlon.

The production of this verse comedy was highly successful.

Lady Spider. 1959. Given its first stage performance on 18 September, by Orion Productions in the Gas Company Theatre in Dun Laoghaire. Under an earlier title, *The Last Hero*, it was first produced as a radio play by the BBC Home Service, Belfast, on 12 October 1953, with Siobhan McKenna as Deirdre. Radio productions from Dublin and London followed soon after.

Careless Love. 1960. Performed in the 1960 season, 11–13 April, by the Irish National Ballet at the Olympia Theatre, Dublin. This ballet included music by A. J. Potter.

Let Freedom Ring. 1963. Produced by the Dublin Council of Trade Unions in October at the Olympia Theatre, Dublin, commemorating the fiftieth anniversary of the 1913 labor lockouts.

A masque.

Patrick. 1965. For Telefis Eireann. First broadcast in 1965.

This libretto for an opera included music by A. J. Potter. This was MacDonagh's last major undertaking.

ASSESSMENT OF MacDONAGH'S CAREER

MacDonagh's plays are all of a piece with his entire literary career. Verse is the essential ingredient of the way in which this artist looked at the life around him. Whether he was telling stories, broadcasting ballads, writing plays, poems, or criticism, the poet's vision defined his work.

His verse is unfailingly clear, sharp, surprising, colloquial, speedy, genial, ironic, and mostly joyful. He works in and out of rhyme with remarkable ease. But the *music* of it all is perhaps its most singular quality, unless it be the ease with which it seems to flow. His plays take on local, folk situations and characters with affection and zest, and he is fond of letting them sing their songs. *Lady Spider*, his ''Deirdre'' play, differs from his other plays, as it differs with the other Deirdre plays of AE, Yeats, and Synge. *Lady Spider* is a deeply skeptical, if not cynical, play, disabused of the romantic trappings that have tended to surround this Irish heroine who so troubled Ireland of legend. It represents a trend in MacDonagh's work toward an ironic, critical posture in the face of the Ireland of that day's romantic tendencies.

Of course, MacDonagh's ''verse plays'' in that postwar period were part of a greater movement in British drama led by T. S. Eliot and Christopher Fry. It is important to recall, and often not noted, that MacDonagh's *Happy as Larry* (1946) preceded Eliot's *The Cocktail Party* (1950) and Fry's *The Lady's Not for Burning* (1949). It was a movement that threw up some singular and successful plays but failed to have any lasting impact on the future of the drama or theater. So MacDonagh's plays have had no influence; nor could they be kept alive for future production in the theater by anything like a steady interest in ''poetic drama.'' The theater found another idol to pursue, and in England, in 1957, he was Jimmy Porter in *Look Back in Anger*. In Ireland there were Jimmy Porters aplenty with their embittered stories to tell of a different Dublin—of the north side and the social deprivations that O'Casey had hinted at but finally romanticized in his own special way.

So it was the destiny of Donagh MacDonagh's plays to be neglected, their excellence passed over by different cultural agendas, by a new theater, and surely by a *new music* alien to MacDonagh and his compatriots' imagination. On the other hand, the plays may yet be read with pleasure, the poems remain full of life and heart, and few have matched MacDonagh as a commentator on the life of the fabled city that he so dearly loved.

A biography of MacDonagh seems necessary, as does recognition of his place in the abbreviated history of modern verse drama and his contribution to the dramatizations of Irish legend (as seen in *Lady Spider*).

ARCHIVAL SOURCES

Inquiries about MacDonagh's works should be addressed to Iseult McGuiness, MacDonagh's daughter, at 11 College Drive, Dublin 6, Ireland.

PRIMARY BIBLIOGRAPHY

Plays

Happy as Larry. Dublin: Hour Glass Press, 1946; also in *Four Modern Plays*. Harmondsworth: Penguin, 1957.

Lady Spider. Ed. Gordon M. Wickstrom. *The Journal of Irish Literature* 9 (Sept. 1980): 3–82.

Step-in-the-Hollow. In *Penguin Plays.* Ed. E. Martin Browne. Harmondsworth: Penguin, 1959.

Articles and Essays on Drama and Theater

"Behans Abroad, Being the Subject Matter of a Talk from Radio Eireann." *Kilkenny Magazine* 12–13 (Spring 1965): 55–60.

"The Lass of Aughrim or the Betrayal of James Joyce." *The Celtic Master.* Ed. Maurice Harmon. Dublin: Dolmen Press, 1969. 17–25.

SECONDARY BIBLIOGRAPHY

Atkinson, Brooks. "Burgess Meredith Appears in a Musical Fantasy Entitled 'Happy as Larry' at the Coronet." *New York Times* (7 Jan. 1950): 11.

"Donagh MacDonagh Looks at His Dublin." *Evening Press* (29 Oct. 1962): 10.

FitzGerald, Marion. "Marion FitzGerald Talking to Donagh MacDonagh: The Man of Law and of Letters." *Sunday Radio Times* (14 Apr. 1963).

Hogan, Robert, and Michael J. O'Neill. *Joseph Holloway's Irish Theatre, vol. 2, 1932–1937.* Dixon, Calif.: Proscenium Press, 1969.

Maxwell, D. E. S. *A Cultural History of Modern Irish Drama.* Cambridge: Cambridge University Press, 1984.

Sheridan, Niall.[1]. "District Justice Donagh MacDonagh Dies in Dublin." *Irish Times* (2 January 1968).

———.[2]. "Donagh MacDonagh." *RTE Guide* (12 Jan. 1968).

"Talking to Donagh MacDonagh." *Irish Times* (25 Aug. 1962): 10.

Wickstrom, Gordon M. Introduction to *Lady Spider. Journal of Irish Literature* 9 (Sept. 1980): 4–6.

"Widow and Children of Thos. MacDonough [*sic*], Executed at Dublin." *New York Evening Journal* (16 May 1916): 3.

Micheál Mac Liammóir

(1899–1978)

R. J. CLOUGHERTY, JR.

While Micheál Mac Liammóir will perhaps be remembered most for founding the Dublin Gate Theatre in conjunction with Hilton Edwards, the numerous talents he possessed and functions he performed within the theater are overwhelming. Mac Liammóir's role at the Gate included not only his actings, settings, costume designs, and lighting designs but also his abilities as a playwright.

In any attempt to research Mac Liammóir's life or career, one faces the immediate difficulty of separating the persona from the person. This is caused by Mac Liammóir's ability not only to create a persona for himself but to sustain it throughout his life. This is further exacerbated by the fact that Mac Liammóir wrote and published numerous memoirs and autobiographies that sustain that persona, including *All for Hecuba, Each Actor on His Own Ass, Enter a Goldfish, Put Money in Thy Purse*, and *An Oscar of No Importance*. This myth is further reinforced by Hilton Edwards' *Mantle of the Harlequin*. The result is that many texts about Mac Liammóir convey as much, if not more, myth than fact.

The most basic element of the Mac Liammóir persona is his Irish identity. Many accept Mac Liammóir's claim that he was born in Blackrock, a suburb of Cork (Richard Pine claims Limerick as the family origin); however, his birth certificate, reprinted in the appendix of Ó hAodha's *The Importance of Being Micheál*, records that he was, in fact, born in the Willesden section of London. He was born as Alfred Lee Willmore. As Micheál Mac Liammóir, he died on 6 March 1978. While his birth may have been English, he must always be considered an Irish writer, for that was the literary tradition into which he was born and in which he performed, wrote, and died.

As Alfred Willmore, he began as a child actor at the age of ten in a play entitled *The Goldfish* (also included in the cast was another child actor, Noël

Coward); he also appeared in Beerbohm Tree's production of *MacBeth* (doubling as MacDuff's son and the apparition of the bloody child), *Peter Pan* (as Michael), and the title role in *Oliver Twist*. Despite his success, he chose to study art at the Slade School, where he first established himself as an artist when some of his sketches appeared in *Punch*.

Two major events that contributed to the creation of the Mac Liammóir persona occurred while he was at the Slade School. The first was his studying Irish through courses offered by the London branch of the Gaelic League. Mac Liammóir had always had a fascination with the Irish based on his love of the works of Oscar Wilde and W. B. Yeats. While neither of them spoke or wrote in Irish, Mac Liammóir saw the language as a vehicle into the culture.

The other significant event is his relationship with a fellow student named Maire O'Keefe. The two developed an inseparable, but seemingly not romantic, relationship. They eventually moved to Dublin and took up residence on Howth, and there his Irish identity truly began to develop. He was selling sketches and drawings at this time, and the signatures reflect a variety of spellings as he attempted to find a Gaelicized form of his name.

While in Ireland, Mac Liammóir did some acting and set design; however, when Maire developed consumption and had to leave for the continent, Mac Liammóir went with her. Following her death, he decided to return to acting full-time by joining the company of his brother-in-law, Anew McMaster. In McMaster's theater company he came to know Hilton Edwards.

The meeting itself marks a significant event for Irish theater, yet, like so many significant events, it occurred through a series of strange twists and events. One of the leading actors of McMaster's company became ill, and McMaster took on Edwards to temporarily replace him in the role of Iago. While they were touring Ireland, Edwards developed pneumonia, and he and Mac Liammóir stayed in Cork while the company moved on. At this time the two began to discuss the possibilities of opening a theater together; McMaster's later refusal to perform a Mac Liammóir play with Edwards as producer reinforced their desire.

Their first work as a partnership was in the opening of the Taibhdhearc na Gaillimhe—the Irish-language theater. It was agreed that the first play to be performed would be *Diarmuid agus Gràinne*, a play that Mac Liammóir claimed he had written in Irish and later translated into English (he, in fact, had first written it in English and then translated it into Irish). Edwards, who spoke no Irish, nevertheless directed the play; however, the significance to Mac Liammóir is that this is the first of his plays to be produced. The Taibhdhearc has revived the play many times, as the Gate Theatre has done with the English-language version.

In founding the Gate Theatre in Dublin, Mac Liammóir and Edwards were attempting to establish a theater that produced the best available dramas in the world; the perception was that the Abbey was completely focused on producing Irish dramas. They were not unique in this aspect. When the Abbey was originally the Irish National Theatre Company, this was a part of its aim; to this day, the Abbey produces non-Irish plays (the Abbey Company performed Shakespeare in the 1993 Galway Arts Festival). In addition, the Dublin Drama League had held the same mission for ten years prior to the opening of the Gate. The Gate differed primarily, however, in its founders; while under the direction of Yeats, the Abbey had developed the image of being a writer's theater, whereas the Gate, with the technical and production abilities of Mac Liammóir and Edwards, developed the reputation of being a director's theater. Undoubtedly, these are generalizations with numerous exceptions. In its original season, the Gate Theatre began with Ibsen's *Peer Gynt* and included O'Neill's *The Hairy Ape* and *Anna Christie*, Nicolai Evreinov's *The Theatre of the Soul*, Wilde's *Salome*, and Elmer Greensfelder's *Six Stokers Whop Own the Bloomin' Earth*, in addition to Mac Liammóir's *Diarmuid agus Gràinne*.

Selected Biographical Sources: Luke; Ó hAodha.

MAJOR PLAYS, PREMIERES, AND SIGNIFICANT REVIVALS: THEATRICAL RECEPTION

Diarmid Agus Gràinne. 1928. The Irish version was first performed in 1928 and saw revivals in 1931, 1953, and 1978. The Gate performed the English version first in its opening season (1928), with revivals in 1929 and 1930.

Mac Liammóir's play was also very successful in English. According to Ó hAodha, the reviews were somewhat mixed, but C. P. Curran gave it a favorable notice in the *Irish Statesman* (see Ó hAodha), and Lady Gregory noted of the production in the Peacock: "I felt far more in sympathy with it than with The Big House at the Abbey, going on next door" (quoted in Ó hAodha 71). Thus, Mac Liammóir was fulfilling his Irish persona, both in meeting Irish expectations and in shaping the very definition of Irishness.

The Ford of the Hurdles. 1929. The Gate's third season; opened on 9 September 1929.

This work has often been termed a masque or a pageant and has been facetiously known as "Mac Liammóir through the Ages." In this play, Mac Liammóir covered seven scenes of Irish history up to the 1916 Rising—playing Pearse in the final scene; this scene was later changed into a play in itself entitled *Easter 1916*, which was performed in the same season, opening with David Sears' *Juggernaut* on 21 April 1930.

Where Stars Walk. 1940. Opened at the Gaiety Theatre, Dublin, on 19 February 1940.

Fitz-Simon refers to the play as "an outstanding commercial success [which] . . . may have been the reason for the kind of recognition which made Edwards and Mac Liammóir into national figures" (180). While Fitz-Simon notes that the critics of the 1940s did not quite discern the significance of the play, he argues that it is most significant for its unification of the Anglo-Irish and Gaelic traditions in Irish theater.

Dancing Shadow. 1941. Opened 17 February. Directed by Hilton Edwards at the Gaiety Theatre to open the new year.

The previous year had ended with a production of seven smaller pieces, two by Mac Liammóir (*Dublin Blues* and *To Be Quite Frank*). Ó hAodha argues that, at this time, Denis Johnston, who had had many of his plays produced by the Gate, was beginning to turn away from Edwards-Mac Liammóir and toward the Longfords and the Abbey (133). Thus, at this point, Mac Liammóir developed a responsibility for writing new plays for the theater. In the case of *Dancing Shadow*, in particular, the minor nature of the play can be seen in that there is little record of it except that it was produced. However, even Hilton Edwards omitted it from his list of plays produced, in the *Mantle of the Harlequin*.

ADDITIONAL PLAYS, ADAPTATIONS, AND PRODUCTIONS

The relationship between the Longfords and Edwards and Mac Liammóir need not be conveyed here; however, once a split had occurred, the Longfords operated the Gate and used its name for six months of the year while Edwards and Mac Liammóir used it for the other six months. In the eleventh season of the Gate, during the time when the Longfords had the theater, Mac Liammóir and Edwards used the Opera House in Cork and the Grand Opera House in Belfast prior to their departure for their third international tour. The repertoire of the opera houses included Marcel Achard's *Le Corsaire* (translated to *Hollywood Pirates*) and Henri-Rene Lenormand's *Les Rates* (translated as *Juliet in the Rain*), both of these translated and adapted by Mac Liammóir. He was quite prolific in creating adaptations for the Gate's stage. Beyond those already listed, Mac Liammóir wrote adaptations of Charlotte Brontë's *Jane Eyre*, Charles Dickens' *A Tale of Two Cities*, George du Maurier's *Trilby*, Jules Romains' *An Apple a Day*, and Wilde's *Picture of Dorian Gray* and a translation of Pirandello's *Henry IV*.

Many plays, including *Ill Met by Moonlight* (opened 8 April 1946), *Portrait of Miriam* (22 September 1947), *The Mountains Look Different* (27 September 1948), and *Home for Christmas* (26 December 1950), were written to meet the needs and abilities of the Gate. This, however, should be considered not a reflection of Mac Liammóir's talent but the reality of the conditions in Ireland during and after the National Emergency.

In the 1950s, the Gate produced two other minor Mac Liammóir plays, *Slipper for the Moon* (26 December 1954) and *Pageant of Saint Patrick* (8 May 1957). However, with the coming of the 1960s came the major phase of Mac Liammóir's career as a playwright with his solo performances that he both wrote and performed.

ASSESSMENT OF Mac LIAMMÓIR'S CAREER

The success and power of Mac Liammóir's later works were such that one wonders if another actor could perform these successfully, as so much of the plays rested within the persona and skill of Mac Liammóir. His writing plays to fit the talents and needs of an entire company of players undoubtedly sharpened his abilities to write a play for himself. The significance here is that Mac Liammóir is not only the actor but the playwright; thus, one level of interpretation was removed between playwright and author.

Perhaps of more significance here is the fact that each of these plays, *The Importance of Being Oscar*, *I Must Be Talking to My Friends*, and *Talking about Yeats*, focuses specifically on writers and literature. Thus, what Mac Liammóir, in essence, does is use the theater as a vehicle for literary criticism, as his selection of text and authors and his presentation of them present Mac Liammóir's reading of these authors. In his introduction to the printed edition of *The Importance of Being Oscar*, Hilton Edwards notes: ''Mac Liammóir's contribution, both as a writer and an actor, not only confirms Wilde's stature as an artist, but relates his artistry to the now historic facts of his life; achieving what a distinguished drama critic has best described as: 'a new form: oral biography' '' (5).

The Importance of Being Oscar can be seen as an act of criticism in its nature; it is passages of Wilde's work for which Mac Liammóir arranged and wrote transitions. The difficulty of identifying or categorizing such a text is seen in Edwards' reaction, quoted by Mac Liammóir in *An Oscar of No Importance*: ''A recital, not a play. But don't bill it as a recital. Fundamentally, it will be an entertainment. But we can't call it that either'' (quoted in Ó hAodha 163).

The play itself features Mac Liammóir as himself, a reader of Wilde, not attempting to imitate Wilde; thus, the play reveals itself as an interpretation that depends on Mac Liammóir. Edwards confirms this in the introduction to the play in printed form: ''Now *The Importance of Being Oscar* appears in print, unassisted by the voice or presence of its *interpreter*. In this form it must necessarily have an effect altogether different from that of the theatrical performance for which it was intended'' (6; italics added).

Ironically, the play was first performed as a private entertainment in the Gaelic Hall, Curragh Camp, County Kildare, on 15 September 1960 and then opened to the public at the Gate on 19 September as a part of the Dublin Theatre Festival. The success of the reviews was overwhelming not only in Dublin but throughout the world as this show toured the globe, moving to London and New York, but also being performed in Helsinki, Stockholm, Paris, South America, and Australia, to superb review everywhere. Its final performance, which occurred at the Gate Theatre in December 1975, was broadcast by RTE and recorded by CBS records.

When first developing *The Importance of Being Oscar*, Mac Liammóir had considered performing an anthology of Irish writers. He returned to this project next, which emerged as *I Must Be Talking to My Friends*. This play was first performed as part of a tribute to stage manager Tom Jones in 1962. The play in its fully developed form opened at the Gate on 15 April 1963. For the centenary of Yeats' birth, Mac Liammóir wrote *Talking about Yeats*, which premiered on 20 June 1965. These latter two did not enjoy the success of *The Importance of Being Oscar*, but Ó hAodha notes that the plays did well with academic audiences.

The last original Mac Liammóir show was *Prelude in Kazbek Street*, which opened at the Gate on 9 October 1973. Fitz-Simon refers to the play as "a propaganda play which came rather too late in the history of the campaign for homosexual equality to strike an original note" (180).

NOTE

I would like to thank Christopher Townley and Eileen Joyce of the Taidhbhearc and Mary Rooney of the Gate Theatre for their invaluable assistance.

PRIMARY BIBLIOGRAPHY

Plays

Dancing Shadow
Diarmuid agus Gràinne. Baile Atha Cliath: Oifig Dialta Foilseachain, Dublin, 1935.
Ford of the Hurdles. Dublin, 1929.
Home for Christmas
Ill Met by Moonlight. Dublin: J. Duffy, 1954.
The Importance of Being Oscar. Dublin: Dolmen Press, 1963.
I Must Be Talking to My Friends
The Mountains Look Different
Prelude in Kazbek Street
A Slipper for the Moon
Talking about Yeats
Where Stars Walk. Dublin: Progress House, 1962.

Prose Works

All for Hecuba. 1st American ed., Boston: Brandon, 1967.
Designs and Illustrations: 1917–1972. Foreword by Hilton Edwards. Cataloged by Richard Pine and Orba Murphy. Dublin: Dublin Arts Festival, 1973.
Each Actor on His Ass. London: Routledge and K. Paul, 1961.
Fairy Nights. 1922. Dublin: O'Brien Press, 1984.
An Oscar of No Importance. London: Heinemann, 1968.
Put Money in Thy Purse. 2d ed. London: Methuen, 1976.
Theatre in Ireland. Dublin: Cultural Relations Committee, 1964.
W. B. Yeats and His World. With Eavan Boland. London: Thames and Hudson, 1977.

SECONDARY BIBLIOGRAPHY

Edwards, Hilton. *Mantle for the Harlequin*. Dublin: Progress House, 1958.

Fitz-Simon, Christopher. *The Irish Theatre*. London: Thames and Hudson, 1983.

Luke, Peter, ed. *Enter Certain Players: Edwards, Mac Liammóir, and the Gate, 1928–1978*. Dublin: Dolmen, 1978.

Ó hAodha, Micheál. *The Importance of Being Micheál: A Portrait of Mac Liammóir*. Cooleen: Brandon, 1990.

Pine, Richard, ed. *All for Hecuba: An Exhibition to Mark the Golden Jubilee. 1928–1978, of the Edwards-Mac Liammóir Partnership and of the Dublin Gate Theatre*. Dublin: Organising Committee, 1978.

Brinsley MacNamara
(1890–1963)

DAWN DUNCAN

Recognized for his realistic and satirical literary portraits of life in the Irish Midlands, MacNamara's reputation as a dramatist has always been over-shadowed by his hard-edged novels. However, he deserves recognition for his theatrical contributions to Ireland both as a playwright and as a director/actor/social figure associated with the Abbey.

MacNamara was born John Weldon in Ballinacor, Hiskenstown, County Westmeath, 6 September 1890, one of seven children of the local schoolmaster, James Weldon. In 1905 the Weldon family moved to Delvin, a nearby Midlands town, where young John grew interested in the political possibilities of drama as he attended melodramas staged by traveling troupes.

In 1908 John Weldon launched his theatrical career by staging and playing the title role in Henry C. Mangan's *Robert Emmet*. In 1909 Weldon moved to Dublin and shortly thereafter joined the Abbey Theatre Company as an actor. Adopting the stage name Brinsley MacNamara, the same pseudonym that he would use for the preponderance of his writing career, MacNamara made his acting debut on 29 September 1910 as Denis Barton in R. J. Ray's *The Casting Out of Martin Whelan*. On the basis of this promising performance, MacNamara was included in the 1911–1912 Abbey touring company, playing minor roles and understudying Sydney Morgan across the United States.

MacNamara began his writing career in 1912, concentrating on poems, articles, and plays, including a three-act play, *The Clerk of the Union*, which the Abbey rejected. By 1913 MacNamara was back in Ireland. After his essay "The Abbey Theatre—Is It on the Decline?" was published in the *Irish Independent*, a disillusioned MacNamara returned to Delvin, where he remained until 1918.

The year 1918 marks a turning point in MacNamara's career and life. With the publication of his controversial but acclaimed novel, *The Valley of the*

Squinting Windows, MacNamara leaped to artistic prominence as a leader in the new realism movement. However, his realistic portrayals did not go over well in his hometown, forcing him to leave Delvin once again. The novel's success led MacNamara also to write his first successful play for the Abbey, *The Rebellion in Ballycullen* (1919). The same year, his second novel, *The Clanking of Chains*, was published. His third novel, *In Clay and in Bronze* (1920), quickly followed, also published as *The Irishman* under a different pseudonym, "Oliver Blyth." On 25 June 1920, MacNamara married Ellen Degidon, a schoolteacher, and the couple settled in Quin, County Clare, where their only child, Oliver, was born on 16 May 1921. MacNamara continued to write, producing a second drama for the Abbey, *The Land for the People* (1921), and a fourth novel, *The Mirror in the Dusk* (1921). MacNamara moved back to Dublin for at least a portion of each year starting in 1922, leaving his wife to rear their son in Quin. By 1925, his move had become permanent.

Between 1923 and 1945, MacNamara wrote seven more plays, all of which were produced at the Abbey. These include three dramas that continued his bitter look at life in the Midlands: *The Master* (1928), *Margaret Gillan* (1933)— winner of the Casement Prize as best Irish play of the year and recipient of the Harmsworth Literary Award, and *The Grand House in the City* (1936), a play that mixes drama and comedy and shifts locales between the Midlands and Dublin. In addition, MacNamara wrote four romantic comedies: *The Glorious Uncertainty* (1923), *Look at the Heffernans!* (1926), *The Three Thimbles* (1941), and *Marks and Mabel* (1945).

MacNamara also continued to publish novels and short stories. His remaining novels include *The Various Lives of Marcus Igoe* (1929), *Return to Ebontheever* (1936), and *Michael Caravan* (1946). He also published two collections of short stories, *The Smiling Faces* (1929) and *Some Curious People* (1945), as well as a novella, *The Whole Story of the X.Y.Z.* (1951).

In addition to his literary career, MacNamara was involved in the Dublin artistic scene on a number of levels. In 1924 he became registrar of the National Gallery of Ireland, a position he retained until 1960. In 1932 MacNamara became a founding member of the Irish Academy of Letters. He was also a member of the Board of Directors for the Abbey Theatre for a short time in 1935.

In 1960 MacNamara's health deteriorated, causing him to resign his post at the National Gallery. He died while in Sir Patrick Dun's Hospital, Dublin, on 4 February 1963 and is buried in Dean's Grange Cemetery, Dublin.

Selected Biographical Sources: Boylan; McDonnell; Christopher Murray.

MAJOR PLAYS, PREMIERES, AND SIGNIFICANT REVIVALS: THEATRICAL RECEPTION

The Rebellion in Ballycullen. 1919. Opened 11 March at the Abbey Theatre, Dublin, for 6 performances.

Responding to the painful effects of the publication of his novel *The Valley of the Squinting Windows*, MacNamara dramatically explores how and why artistic expression and political action are irreconcilable in nature. Malone [2] considers this a powerful first play, demonstrating a promising potential. Christopher Murray thinks the play was a courageous effort. However, he faults it for its static position, its rhetorical style, and its thin characterization. Lawrence notes that the play indicated promise on the part of the author, who managed to avoid pleading his case despite the autobiographical nature. However, he agrees basically with Murray that the play lacked wit and emotion, striking the audience as merely an "academic" conflict. There is some indication that the performance itself may have been to blame and that production should have been postponed. Evidently, memory problems abounded, and the prompter could be heard from the stage, with resulting weak performances of characters who should have been much more forceful and emotional.

The Land for the People. 1920. Opened 30 November at the Abbey Theatre, Dublin, for 6 performances; revised version opened 26 April 1927 at the Abbey for 6 performances. Directed by Lennox Robinson. Revived many times (see Malone [2]).

An unflinching satire of land-grabbers who betray their own, Christopher Murray credits this play with providing a true picture of MacNamara's vision and a solid treatment of the themes of greed and self-importance. However, he regards the play as political propaganda, given the Irish situation at the time of its staging. The revised version in 1927 was well received. Malone [2] admires the bitter satire and vivid realism of the revised version.

The Glorious Uncertainty. 1923. Opened 27 November at the Abbey Theatre, Dublin, for 6 performances. Revived frequently (see Malone [2]).

MacNamara departed from his trademark realism to write a romantic comedy revolving around a favorite Irish pastime, horse racing, and the gamble for fortune and love. T. C. Murray praises the good humor of the writing, the realistic atmosphere of the pub and turf, and the delightful roguery of the characters. Malone [2] records that after its opening, the rollicking comedy enjoyed an annual revival for numerous years at the Abbey, always serving to delight the Irish audiences. As Christopher Murray notes, this practice stopped with the opening of the new Abbey in 1966.

Look at the Heffernans! 1926. Opened 12 April at the Abbey Theatre, Dublin, for 7 performances. Revival: John Golden Theatre, New York. Opened 16 November 1934. Produced by the Abbey Theatre in association with Elbert A. Wickes; directed by Lennox Robinson. Translated to Gaelic by Frank Dermody.

This romantic comedy revolves around the intrigues of a local matchmaker bent on marrying off the solidly single middle-aged members of the Heffernan family. T. C. Murray notes that, despite the use of well-worn stage conventions, the writing remains fresh and vigorous. Christopher Murray cites the brilliance of the company performing the opening production and praises MacNamara for providing diversionary delight for a stressed community. Joseph Holloway records that the house was packed and that the audience responded enthusiastically. Malone [2] praises the characterization that takes types to a level that not only evokes individual laughter but also provides a "tonic" for Irish society. The play was so successful that it became an established piece in the Abbey repertory, having been staged 175 times in MacNamara's lifetime.

The New York revival also gained accolades for the performances of the Abbey players, but the text did not fare so well. Robert Garland of the *New York World-Telegram* thought the play itself overly long and lacking in excitement, though the actors did their best to infuse the thin work with energy.

The Master. 1928. (Originally called *The Boycott*.) Opened 6 March at the Abbey Theatre, Dublin, for 6 performances.

This play calls to mind the problems MacNamara's father experienced as headmaster at Ballinvalley National School in 1918. Yeats thought the first act was the best he had seen in years. Malone [3] claimed it was the most interesting play to be staged at the Abbey since *The Plough and the Stars*. Gaffney admires MacNamara's bitter but delicate handling of controversial material and insists that future historians will turn to this play for insight into the period and the place. Christopher Murray admires the tightness of the story but warns that the master is so aggressive as to become unsympathetic. Holloway notes that the old master's oratory becomes a nuisance. T. C. Murray agrees that the schoolmaster comes across as overly arrogant, but he defends the individuality of the characters drawn. He also claims that the conflict supersedes its Irishness, making the issue interesting to any audience, if the audience can find a way to sympathize with the powerful personality of the schoolmaster. However, Curran faults MacNamara for creating flat, typical characters who merely speak his long-winded manifesto.

Margaret Gillan. 1933. Opened 17 July at the Abbey Theatre, Dublin, for 7 performances. Produced by Arthur Shields.

A classically styled tragedy of frustrated love and obsessive jealousy, this award-winning drama compels praise from critics Kavanagh and Hogan for both its emotional intensity and strange power, especially in the person of the title character. Hogan warns that to carry off the relentless tragedy, the actress in the title role must give "a virtuouso performance," or the play may devolve into melodrama. T. C. Murray concurs regarding the protagonist's role and suggests that the Abbey company was not able to explore the depths of the written play in performance.

The Grand House in the City. 1936. Opened 3 February at the Abbey Theatre, Dublin, for 6 performances.

A symbolic portrayal of the past, present, and future of Ireland, two houses—one in the city and one in the country—help the owners maintain an illusion of grandness. Joseph Holloway attended opening night and records that the house was full and the audience enthusiastic. Though he doubted whether it would sustain full houses for the run, his later notes indicate that he was wrong in his first assessment and that the audience continued to appreciate what he himself agreed were delightful character studies given in witty dialogue, even if the play did seem a bit "talky." In a review signed A.E.M. (indicating probably Andrew E. Malone), the critic calls this MacNamara's best play and compares it to a Chekhovian comedy. He does admit that the first and fourth acts could use some tightening but describes the second and third acts as brilliant. Oddly, this reviewer calls this MacNamara work "a man's play" despite the interesting female characters.

The Three Thimbles. 1941. Opened 24 November at the Abbey Theatre, Dublin, for 6 performances.

A complicated comedy based on the metaphor of the carnival game with a pea under one of three thimbles. In this case, the invisible object is money, which may or may not be in the possession of one of three men, who also may or may not use the money to acquire or maintain ownership of the Big House, Coolraney. Everything is a gamble or an illusion, as Martin, the main character, both explains and symbolizes. He is the returned black-sheep member of the family that originally owned Coolraney. Having once lost the estate because of gambling debts, he now seems to have been bequeathed a large sum from a jilted lover, and with his newfound wealth comes a tangle of friends and relations in need. The illusory funds have the potential to make some or all of their dreams come true.

Marks and Mabel. 1945. Opened 6 August at the Abbey Theatre, Dublin, for 31 performances.

Wonderful possibilities for a feminist reading of this sequel to *Look at the Heffernans!* The women are now in control, to the chagrin of the one bachelor holdout. However, the married men seem, for the most part, happy with the arrangement. Certainly, the women, even when at odds with one another, exercise their wits far beyond the abilities of the solid male folk. Through the women's machinations, a whole new Heffernan success story via business is born, and the future unfolds with an end to fortune-hunting men and the rise of satisfied, power-wielding women.

ADDITIONAL PLAYS, ADAPTATIONS, AND PRODUCTIONS

The most interesting manuscript is *Lost in the Years* (1937), also titled *Swift's Secret Way.* According to Michael McDonnell, MacNamara collaborated with Violet A. Pearn on a play about Swift that successfully opened on 11 May. However, since he notes *Lost in the Years* separately, these two plays may or may not be related. Hogan records that a play entitled *The Uncrowned King*, written by V. A. Pearn and MacNamara, was staged by Longford Productions (also known as one portion of the Gate Theatre) in the late 1930s. A manuscript of a one-act farce, *The Ballycullen Band* (also called *The Band*), is also housed at the Ransom Center at the University of Texas. Another seemingly unproduced MacNamara work is *The House in Park Avenue*, which MacNamara terms "a Victorian drama of Dublin in three acts." Also at the Ransom Center is an incomplete play script, *The Local Journalist*. There have been two adaptations of MacNamara plays, the Irish television version of *The Glorious Uncertainty* in 1970 and a musical version of *Look at the Heffernans!* for the Dublin Theatre Festival of 1973.

ASSESSMENT OF MACNAMARA'S CAREER

Brinsley MacNamara has been identified as one of Ireland's leading playwrights of the 1920s (see Courtney). Malone [1] describes MacNamara as the author who delineated Ireland for the first quarter of the century to English-speaking audiences. Christopher Murray places MacNamara at the center of realism, the movement of the 1920s, thereby crediting him with influencing Lennox Robinson, T. C. Murray, and Sean O'Casey. While critics differ on how to label MacNamara—novelist or playwright—the label may be less important than the actual contribution MacNamara made to both forms.

Though in 1913 MacNamara had left the Abbey and Dublin publicly disappointed, describing Yeats and his theater as having given way to common tastes, neither Yeats nor any of his colleagues exercised a vindictive memory when it came to MacNamara's plays. During the 1920 season, seeking a new vision and voice for the Abbey, Lennox Robinson produced plays by relatively unknown writers. Kavanagh notes that the best of the playwrights promoted by Robinson was MacNamara and that the best of the plays produced by Robinson in 1920 was MacNamara's *The Land for the People*. However, Kavanagh's praise is limited, as, he contends, were the selections and talent pool. Yet Kavanagh acknowledges that, as a playwright, MacNamara showed definite potential. Interestingly, though Robinson continued to promote MacNamara's works, the playwright remained dissatisfied with the direction Robinson gave the Abbey.

Perhaps part of MacNamara's dissatisfaction with the Abbey was his desire to do more than the limited realism with which he has been associated. From the beginning his dramas were thickly layered, more than mere representations of reality. Jeffares claims that MacNamara's dramas are laced with Gothicism, connecting him to the likes of Maturin, Sheridan Le Fanu, and Bram Stoker. Considering the focus on the isolated individual struggling for identity against broad social disapproval, MacNamara's tragedies indeed have a Gothic feel, and his tales of the small, closed Irish communities do evoke an undercurrent that, if not quite terror, is at least menacing.

However, Malone [2] sees the portraits of Midlands villages provided by MacNamara as not Gothic horror but as unrelenting realism. Malone especially praises the description of village political life provided in *The Master* (1928), a play Malone claims is tighter than those by O'Casey and more realistic. Hogan agrees that MacNamara was a master of realism but adds that his plays never managed to shock audiences into self-recognition. Because MacNamara contrasts idealism with political realities, Malone [2] confirms MacNamara's connection to Ibsen. He goes so far as to compliment Ireland that it could produce and provide a place for one such as MacNamara, who never needed to exile himself from the island in order to write, despite the social commentary he provided. In 1929 Malone predicted, wrongly in retrospect, that MacNamara would write the great Irish plays of his time, knowing, as he did, both the rural Midlands and the Dublin salons. He praised MacNamara's style for both its somberness and grace, claiming his technique could stand up to any test MacNamara might make of it, be it for purposes of comedy or drama.

Most critics claim MacNamara's tragedies are imbued with far greater power than any of his comedies. T. C. Murray summarizes MacNamara's contribution to the theater as being one of a great tragedian, able to bring his audiences to a catharsis based on the combination of "pity and terror" in his plays. McDonnell singles out the tragic *Margaret Gillan* as the best of MacNamara's plays, the consensus of most critics who prefer the tragedies and MacNamara's Ibsen-like attacks on society.

McDonnell, among others, sees MacNamara's chief foe as the Catholic Church and its tyrannical clergy. However, such a view is overly narrow, given the works that serve up the landowners, both the tradition-bound, downward spiraling Ascendancy class and the land-grabbing merchants attempting upward mobility, as the objects of harshest criticism. McDonnell does rightfully identify MacNamara as a writer who does for the Midlands what Joyce does for Dublin—both men forever affected by, and affecting, the view of these places that gave rise to their lives and their writings. Certainly, MacNamara's personal life experience shapes his plays with more literal correlation than many a dramatist. *The Rebellion in Ballycullen* is a re-creation of the horrified home response to his novel *The Valley of the Squinting Windows*. Alan Forde and his family are mere fictional substitutes for the Weldon family, allowing MacNamara free rein in his telling of the "truth." Or are they?

In an address to a gathering of teachers from the Midlands in Mullingar, MacNamara both explained and defended his position as writer of social criticism. In reference to Ibsen, he called himself "a kind of enemy of his people" because, rather than writing about the vices of the colonizer and the virtues of the native, he provides realistic (not real) portraits of the natives. Stressing that his characters are not actual people from real life, though they are realistic, he insisted that his own imagination should be credited for the portraits he provides. As a case in point, he gives the history of his writing of *The Master*, widely believed to be a factual account of an actual event. He claims that the first draft was written in 1917, a year before the events it supposedly dramatizes. MacNamara says that he imagined what an altruistic nationalist teacher with the courage of his character, James Clinton, would face and that he wrote and revised accordingly.

MacNamara's literary fame tends to rest on his ability to truthfully portray the rural and small village life of Irish Midlanders, people who forced him out of his own hometown with their narrowly defined social acceptabilities. Malone tagged him as the originator of Irish realistic fiction, a style called, for MacNamara's first novel, the fiction of "squinting windows" (see McDonnell). MacNamara's writing obsessively paints a portrait of Irish Midlanders trapped by tradition and unwilling or unable to break the societal chains that bound them. T. C. Murray credits MacNamara with a natural gift for writing—a vivid imagination that enabled him to create memorably real characters and dialogue, a result of his continual study of life (137). He also notes that MacNamara's stint as an actor with the Abbey reinforced his playwriting ability. Murray goes on to compare MacNamara's writing spirit to the satire of Swift, striking at the petty jealousies and politics of village life that have embittered and wearied his own spirit. This comparison may be more accurate than that to Ibsen, given MacNamara's feelings about his people and his penchant for satire. MacNamara may have been subconsciously aware of his link to the great Irish satirist because Swift became the subject of two of his plays, the unproduced *Lost in the Years* and *The Uncrowned King*, coauthored with V. A. Pearn.

In one play, *The Grand House in the City*, MacNamara attempted to combine his dramatic realism with comedy, his knowledge of the Midlands with his life in Dublin. This play also helps clarify the target of MacNamara's social criticism—not the clergy, nor only the Midlands, but all of Ireland. Both the city and country houses are facing financial disaster that may be avoided only by marriage to merchant money in the form of a deplorable land-grabber or his amazingly innocent daughter. The declining gentry, the land-grabbing merchant, the socialist worker are all represented and embroiled, legally and emotionally, in a battle for the estate. The characters are both real and ridiculous, the situations and dialogue laughable and frightening. Unfortunately, the play does not hold up well, perhaps because of its overly ambitious attempt to symbolically dramatize Ireland's complex history. The satire has somehow been diffused by the mixed forms.

Critics split into two camps with regard to which are MacNamara's stage masterpieces, his comedies or his tragedies. MacNamara's best-known comedies are *The Glorious Uncertainty* and *Look at the Heffernans!*, both of which were successes at the Abbey. While critics, for the most part, tend to favor MacNamara's tragedies and realistic dramas, there is something to be said for his comedic ability. The popularity of his comedies helped turn the Abbey from a theater for the elite into a theater where average Dublin people could feel at home and be entertained, and thus these plays brought the Abbey back to financial stability during the 1940s (see Kavanagh). His lighthearted comedies, not his bitter satires, are ultimately what have made MacNamara memorable to audiences. He achieved a popularity with these works that has kept his name among recognizable Irish playwrights. Malone refers to MacNamara's turn to comedy not as capitulation to a desire for social success but as "a pleasant surprise" when compared to his other works.

Regardless of whether MacNamara was writing bitterly or comically, the one strain that runs true throughout his works is his faithfulness to portraying the various types of Irish Midlanders—farmers, priests, publicans, bookies, teachers, and others—and an accurate depiction of rural life. Rather than contrasting MacNamara's tragic or comic plays, Fallis places MacNamara among those playwrights capable of producing consistently good work that compelled viewers to observe rural Ireland's "meanness." While certainly such a negative connotation might privilege the tragic tellings of Midlands life, the comedies—as they have since the days of Aristophanes—do as much to show the small-mindedness that absorbed MacNamara's imagination.

Because of MacNamara's clear-sighted descriptions of the small-mindedness of his country folk, one might expect such an author to exercise a liberalness of artistic imagination that would not allow him to conform to societal standards. Unfortunately, such was not the case, and MacNamara's seeming capitulation in the face of social pressure created conflicts in both his life and his work.

The striking example of MacNamara's own narrow-mindedness was his response to the work of Sean O'Casey. When the Abbey produced *The Silver Tassie* while MacNamara served on the board, the newest director parted ways with his colleagues in a publicly embarrassing manner for all concerned. In the midst of the uproar, MacNamara published an article in the *Irish Independent* (see Kavanagh) denouncing the production, his fellow directors, any audience that would appreciate such a work, and O'Casey—especially O'Casey— roundly. MacNamara did not stop at attacking this one O'Casey play but declared all of the popular playwright's works "vulgar and worthless" (see Kavanagh). Yeats stepped in and called for MacNamara's resignation, which MacNamara refused to give willingly on the grounds that his own voice was needed to save the Abbey. Kavanagh confirms that MacNamara was forced from his position.

Hogan acknowledges that MacNamara's personality may have been problematic, but he judges his playwriting abilities to show a strong sense of workmanship. Hogan comments on the equal division of material devoted to good-natured, lightweight comedy and depressing dramatic realism. However, he also blames the success of MacNamara's comedies for diluting, perhaps even destroying, the realism for which the Abbey was known, a realism with which MacNamara himself has been associated as an originator.

While MacNamara's theatrical output was sparse, nine plays between 1919 and 1945, a few of his works, though a bit dated for contemporary production, remain noteworthy. Both *The Glorious Uncertainty* and *Look at the Heffernans!* set a standard for comedy and commercial success at the Abbey. T. C. Murray recognizes the irony in the popularity of MacNamara's comedies, two plays that he tags "less important" than the dramas, regardless of widespread appeal. *Margaret Gillan*, on the other hand, deserves its place among those brave artistic efforts that, though not as financially viable, have made the Abbey world-renowned as a place from which playwrights of unusual power emerge. Unfortunately, for whatever reasons, MacNamara abandoned his prophetic realism in favor of commercial comedy and a socially recognizable position as a man of the arts and letters. O'Casey, in his letter of defense regarding *The Silver Tassie*, may have accurately perceived MacNamara's real problem when he suggests that MacNamara sought popularity, to his lasting misery. Perhaps, in the end, the pressures of society won out over the sharp artistic edge.

Like a prophet who will not be accepted in his hometown, MacNamara remains a voice worth hearing for anyone who would understand the intricacies of life in the Irish Midlands during the first half of the century, perhaps even now. While MacNamara may not have looked clearly enough through the lens of realism at himself, the central content of all his literary work, regardless of form, remains social criticism. His plays cannot be said to have a universal or timeless quality, but the appeal is in the realistic village portraits drawn with a satirical pen, portraits that illuminate a specific place and time. Scholars and critics, rather than concentrating on either his tragedies or comedies, would do well to look at the common context and social concerns shared by all of MacNamara's works. A study of his unproduced works, both those that are complete and the numerous fragments, would reveal a greater imagination than has been heretofore credited as well as throw light on the produced works. Finneran suggests that a collection of MacNamara's plays is overdue, a suggestion that should be heeded.

ARCHIVAL SOURCES

Manuscripts, typescripts, and fragments—of both published and unpublished works—are located in the Brinsley MacNamara Collection and the W. R. Rodgers Collection, both housed in the Harry Ransom Research Center, University of Texas at Austin.

PRIMARY BIBLIOGRAPHY

Plays

The Glorious Uncertainty. Dublin and Cork: Talbot Press, n.d.; Dublin: P. J. Bourke, 1957.
Look at the Heffernans! Dublin and Cork: Talbot Press, n.d.
Margaret Gillan. London: Allen and Unwin, 1934.
Marks and Mabel. Dublin: James Duffy, 1945.

Essays and Articles about Drama and Theater

''The Abbey in America.'' *Freeman's Journal* (2 May 1913).
Abbey Plays, 1899–1948. Dublin: At the Sign of the Three Candles, 1949.

"The Abbey Theatre: Is It on the Decline?" *Irish Independent* (9 May 1913).
"On Actors: Their Peculiar Calling." *Irish Independent* (28 July 1913).
"The Author and His Characters." Address to teachers from Midlands, Mullingar, Ireland. Brinsley MacNamara's Works, Ransom Center, University of Texas at Austin.
"Resignation of Abbey Director." *Irish Independent* (4 Sept. 1935).
"Revelation by a Director of the Theatre." *Irish Independent* (29 Aug. 1935).
"The Skin of Our Teeth." *Irish Times* (9 Oct. 1945). (Review.)

Novels

The Clanking of the Chains. New York: Brentano's, 1919; Dublin: Maunsel, 1920.
In Clay and in Bronze. New York: Brentano's, 1920.
The Irishman. (under pseudonym, "Oliver Blyth.") London: Everleigh Nash, 1920.
Michael Caravan. Dublin: Talbot Press, 1946.
The Mirror in the Dusk. Dublin and London: Maunsel and Roberts, 1921.
Return to Ebontheever. London: Jonathan Cape, 1930. Reissued as *Othello's Daughter*, 1942.
The Valley of the Squinting Windows. Dublin: Maunsel, 1918; London: Sampson Low, Marston, 1918; New York: Brentano's, 1919.
The Various Lives of Marcus Igoe. London: Sampson Low, Marston, 1929.
The Whole Story of the X.Y.Z. Belfast: H. R. Carter, 1951. (Novella.)

Short Story Anthologies

The Smiling Faces. London: Mandrake, 1929.
Some Curious People. Dublin: Talbot, 1945.

SECONDARY BIBLIOGRAPHY

Boyd, Ernest. *Ireland's Literary Renaissance.* 1916. New York: Barnes and Noble, 1968.
Boylan, Henry. *A Dictionary of Irish Biography.* New York: St. Martin's Press, 1988.
Brady, Anne M., and Brian Cleeve. *A Biographical Dictionary of Irish Writers.* New York: St. Martin's Press, 1985, 152–53.
Courtney, Richard. *Outline History of British Drama.* Totowa, N.J.: Littlefield, Adams, 1982.
Curran, Constantine P. "Review of 'The Master.' " *Irish Statesman* (10 Mar. 1928).
Fallis, Richard. *The Irish Renaissance.* Syracuse, N.Y.: Syracuse University Press, 1977.
Farrell, James T. *On Irish Themes.* Philadelphia: University of Pennsylvania Press, 1982.
Finneran, Richard J. *Anglo-Irish Literature: A Review of Research.* New York: Modern Language Association, 1976.
Gaffney, Gertrude. "Review of 'The Master.' " *Evening Herald* (7 Mar. 1928).
"The Grand House in the City." Signed A. E. M. Brinsley MacNamara's Works, Ransom Center, University of Texas at Austin.
Gregory, Lady Augusta. *Lady Gregory's Journals.* Vol. 2, Books Thirty to Thirty-Four: 21 February 1925–9 May 1932. Ed. Daniel J. Murphy. New York: Oxford University Press, 1987.

Hartnoll, Phyliss, ed. "MacNamara, Brinsley." *The Oxford Companion to the Theatre*. 4th ed. Oxford: Oxford University Press, 1983. 515.

Hogan, Robert. *After the Irish Renaissance: A Critical History of the Irish Drama since* The Plough and the Stars. Minneapolis: University of Minnesota Press, 1967.

Holloway, Joseph. *Joseph Holloway's Abbey Theatre: A Selection from His Unpublished Journal*. Impressions of a Dublin Playgoer. Ed. Robert Hogan and Michael J. O'Neill. Carbondale: Southern Illinois University Press, 1967.

Hunt, Hugh. *The Abbey: Ireland's National Theatre, 1904–1978*. New York: Columbia University Press, 1979.

Jeffares, A. Norman. *Anglo-Irish Literature*. New York: Schocken Books, 1982.

Kavanagh, Peter. *The Story of the Abbey Theatre from Its Origins in 1899 to the Present*. New York: Devin-Adair, 1950.

Kiely, Benedict. *Modern Irish Fiction*. Dublin: Golden Eagle Books, 1950.

Lane, Denis, and Carol McCrory Lane, eds. "MacNamara, Brinsley (1890–1963)." *Modern Irish Literature*. New York: Ungar, 1988.

Lawrence, W. J. "Review of 'The Rebellion in Ballycullen.' " *The Stage* (20 Mar. 1919).

Malone, Andrew E. [1]. "Brinsley MacNamara: An Appreciation." *The Dublin Magazine* (July 1929): 46–56.

———. [2]. *The Irish Drama*. 1929. New York: Benjamin Blom, 1965.

———. [3]. [Review of *The Master*.] *Irish Times* (7 Mar. 1928).

McDonnell, Michael. "MacNamara, Brinsley." *Dictionary of Irish Literature*. Ed. Robert Hogan. Westport, Conn.: Greenwood, 1979, 418–21.

Meehan, Donnchadh A. "Of Four Fantasies." *Bookman* (Dec. 1948).

Murray, Christopher. "Brinsley MacNamara." *Modern British Dramatists, 1900–1945*. Part 2: M–Z. *Dictionary of Literary Biography*. Vol. 10. Ed. Stanley Weintraub. Detroit: Gale, 1982, 3–8.

Murray, T. C. "George Shiels, Brinsley MacNamara, etc." *The Irish Theatre: Lectures Delivered during the Abbey Theatre Festival Held in Dublin in August 1938*. Ed. Lennox Robinson. 1939. New York: Haskell House, 1971, 117–46.

O'Casey, Sean. *The Letters of Sean O'Casey*. Vol. 1, 1910–1941. Ed. David Krause. New York: Macmillan, 1975.

BIBLIOGRAPHY

McDonnell, Michael. "Brinsley MacNamara (1890–1963): A Checklist." *Journal of Irish Literature* 4 (May 1975): 79–88.

Gerald MacNamara

(1865–1938)

KATHLEEN DANAHER

Gerald MacNamara's plays were among the most popular contributions to the Ulster Literary Theatre, which was formed in Belfast in the early 1900s in emulation of the Abbey and as part of the greater movement, the Irish Literary Renaissance. MacNamara's significance is probably best summed up by his longtime colleague Rutherford Mayne:

[W]ith the decline in recent years of the Theatre he served so loyally, and the scanty material left in print, there is little showing nowadays of this courageous old Irish jester, whose modesty and dislike of publicity should not deny him the recognition he is justly entitled to, as one of the finest comic geniuses that the Irish dramatic revival has produced (53).

While Mayne, as a lifelong friend and colleague, may have exaggerated his genius, MacNamara certainly was a brilliant man who delighted audiences with boisterous satires so unlike the conventional realistic drama of the time.

Very little is known of MacNamara's personal life. He gave no interviews. His son, a journalist and playwright, is no longer living, and his granddaughter remembers very little of him. He was born Henry (Harry) Cooke Morrow on 27 August 1865. He took his pseudonym when he began working with the Ulster Literary Theatre, as did all members of the group at the outset. His mother was a MacNamara, from a Gaelic-speaking and thus probably Catholic family, which moved from Galway to County Down. His father was a Protestant from Comber, County Down, who started a family business in Belfast—George Morrow and Son, Ltd., House Painters, Decorators and Renovators—of which Harry Morrow eventually became the head. There were several Morrow brothers, and two of them, Fred and Jack, applied their knowledge of the family business to costuming, stage production, and design. Harry Morrow assisted his brothers, but writing and acting were his main interests. In 1910 he was president of the Ulster Arts Club, an association of actors, artists, painters, and musicians; his photograph is still on the wall of the Arts Club today. From 1912 until his death he adjudicated in the *Belfast Telegraph's* children's drawing competition. Reporting on some of the other brothers, the *Belfast Telegraph* writes that "Norman was a fine poster artist, Eddie was a black and white artist on *The Bystander*, and George became famous for his illustrations of a series of books by E. V. Lucas and for his many cartoons in *Punch*." James Devlin, a freelance actor who knew Gerald MacNamara's son, says the family was liberal and nationalist, as well as artistic and intellectual. Beyond that it is difficult to reconstruct Harry Morrow's life. Mainly through his work is the essence of this remarkable man revealed.

Although MacNamara's main interest was political satire, he also wrote a one-act play satirizing the style of J. M. Synge. Its title, *The Mist That Does Be on the Bog*, has passed into common currency. His two sketches, "Cuchulain II" and "A Crank from the U.S.A.," are satirical as well, but they do not succeed so well as his plays. He wrote four closet dramas, all of which appeared in *The Dublin Magazine* between 1923 and 1925. "Stage Directions for a Play Called *William John Jamieson*" is a vehicle for his humorous observations on the theater; "The Babes in the Wood" is a satire of a popular Christmas pantomime and of the William Archer translations of Ibsen; "Tcinderella" is a vehicle for jokes about Russian writers such as Chekhov, Turgenev, and Gorky; and "Little Devil Dought" or "If Ye Don't Give Me Monic I'll Swccpc Ye All Out" is a satire on the revenge tragedy. All of the pieces are well done, and the jokes are obvious, broad, and funny.

MacNamara is credited with a total of eleven stage plays, several of which were repeated throughout his lifetime. But after his death only two revivals are known: *No Surrender* by the Ulster Group Theatre in 1960 and *Thompson in Tir-na-n-Og* by the Lyric Players Theatre in 1961. However, there were probably many amateur revivals in the North, especially of *Thompson in Tir-na-n-Og*.

Only two of MacNamara's stage plays ever reached print, *Thompson in Tir-na-n-Og* and *Who Fears to Speak?* Only five typescripts are extant: *Suzanne and the Sovereigns, The Mist That Does Be on the Bog, Thompson in Tir-na-n-Og*, and two versions of *No Surrender*. MacNamara's lost plays include *An August Day, The Throwbacks, Sincerity, Fee-Faw-Fum*, and *Thompson on Terra Firma*. Another lost play, *The Spurious Sovereign*, has been attributed to MacNamara, although he never acknowledged authorship. Reviews of some of these lost plays are so tantalizing that one can only hope there is a box marked MacNamara still hidden somewhere in the corner of a dusty room.

Reviews of MacNamara's acting are just as tantalizing and make us wish to have seen the actor, as well as his plays, on the stage. A short, unprepossessing man, MacNamara delighted audiences with his comic character parts for well over thirty years. "As a student in Paris," Mayne writes, "he had taken a deep interest in the work and technique of the Coquelins reflected afterward in his own exquisite art as an actor.''

Gerald MacNamara died on 11 January 1938 at the age of seventy-two.

Selected Biographical Sources: Sam Hanna Bell; Mayne.

MAJOR PLAYS, PREMIERES, AND SIGNIFICANT REVIVALS: THEATRICAL RECEPTION

Suzanne and the Sovereigns. 1907. (An Extravaganza in Four Acts). A collaboration with Lewis Purcell. Opened 26 December for a week at the Belfast Exhibition Hall; a repeat success the following year during the week of 11 January; produced again the week of 28 November, 1910 at the Grand Opera House, Belfast; revived for Dublin audiences at the Gaiety the week of 7 March 1914 and the week of 27 November 1916.

A fantastic burlesque unlike anything previously produced in Belfast or Dublin, this play became the Ulster Literary Theatre's first popular success. MacNamara and Purcell mocked Orange tradition and reduced the Battle of the Boyne to a minor incident in a satire of history and romance. With Ulster in ferment at the time over the Home Rule issue, the play could have caused a first-class riot. Instead, it charmed audiences with its bold but lighthearted good spirits. *Nomad's Weekly* (Review of *Suzanne and the Sovereigns*) called its first revival "one huge gargantuan gigantic giggle from start to finish." With the 1910 revival the *Ulster Guardian* (see Sam Hanna Bell) was amazed not to "learn from some frightened official that the theatre was besieged," but the play was still greeted with delight. The 1914 production, however, apparently lacked the spirit and comedy of the earlier performances. The 1916 press notices were enthusiastic, but the play was never revived after that.

The Mist That Does Be on the Bog. 1909. (A Fog in One Act). Opened by the Ulster Literary Theatre at the Abbey on 26 and 27 November. Produced the following year at the Grand Opera House, Belfast, the week of 7 March. Revived at the Grand Opera House the week of 14 September 1914, the week of 25 March 1918, and the week of 3 April 1922.

This simple, refreshing curtain-raiser was one of the Ulster Literary Theatre's most popular plays. Its title has become a familiar, satiric phrase to describe people who write like Synge. David Kennedy claims the play mocks not only Synge and his *Playboy* but also the whole movement toward poetic drama and the Celtic Twilight into which Yeats led his followers. There were some kinks in the first production, and when it was last performed in 1922, Holloway [1] thought the satire had "become stale." But in its prime, the *Irish Times* (Ulster Players at the Abbey Theatre") thought it "neatly constructed and genuinely amusing," and *Nomad's Weekly* (Review of *The Mist That Does Be on the Bog*) thought it "uproariously funny and splendidly acted."

The Spurious Sovereign. 1910. (A Burlesque-Melodrama in a Prologue and Four Acts). Produced by the Theatre of Ireland at Molesworth Hall, Dublin, on 28 March.

Maire Nic Shiubhlaigh, a Theatre of Ireland actress, wrote that this play was MacNamara's, although its only signature is "J. O'E" (205). While no other sources confirm his authorship, the evidence points to her being correct. First, she knew the Morrow brothers well, for "Fred and Jack, especially Fred, 'made' the Theatre of Ireland, much as the Fays had made the original National Theatre Society" (88). It is unlikely she would have been mistaken about their brother Harry's contribution. Also, the play is MacNamara's type: a parody of historic and romantic melodrama, combined with a mockery of popular stagecraft. Arthur Griffith's review suits MacNamara well: the parody was wild, the audience delighted. Indeed, one character made the house "shriek with laughter in his tragic speeches and asides to the audience."

Thompson in Tir-na-n-Og. 1912. (A Comedy in One Act). First produced at the Grand Opera House, Belfast, the week of 9 December. Produced regularly by the Ulster Theatre in subsequent years: 1913: 31 January and 1 February at the Abbey, Dublin, 1914: week of 14 September at the Grand Opera House, Belfast, and week of 14 December at the Gaiety, Dublin, 1916: week of 27 November at the Gaiety and week of 4 December at the Grand Opera House; 1917: 10 December at the Gaiety and 21 May at the Grand Opera House; 1918: 9 and 10 January in Dundalk, week of 27 May at the Gaiety, and 9 December at the Gaiety; 1919: 2 June and 10 November at the Grand Opera House; 1921: 21 December at the Gaiety; 1923: week of 4 September at the Liverpool Playhouse and also at the Scala Theatre in London; 1926: week of 4 October at the Cork Opera House. Revived by the Lyric Players Theater in 1961. Published in 1918 by the Talbot Press, Dublin.

This play, originally in three acts, was written on request for the Gaelic League, which rejected it because it ridiculed Gaelic heroes. MacNamara then condensed it to a one-act and gave it to the Ulster Literary Theatre (see Sam Hanna Bell). Actually, the play burlesques both Gaels and Orangemen, their heroes and heroines. But the lovable Orangeman Thompson bears the brunt of the satire when he can't explain to Cuchulain why Ulstermen aren't Hibernians, don't speak Irish, prefer foreign to Home Rule, and revere a Dutch prince rather than an Irish king.

The *Irish Times* ("The Ulster Players," 13 December 1922) described the play as a "gentle satire." In 1912, anything bolder would have provoked a city already tense over the passing of a Home Rule bill in the House of Commons. Winston Churchill had been burned in effigy, and on Covenant Day, almost 500,000 people had signed their names in opposition to Home Rule, some in their own blood, at desks lined up for a third of a mile, allowing 540 signatures at once. But MacNamara was not placative. Thompson compromises himself as not many Orangemen, even in desperation, ever would: "Ach, don't burn me, and I'll learn Gaelic, and I'll make the childer learn it—I will sowl, and I have a parrot at home that my uncle brought from foreign parts; it can only whistle 'Dolly's Brae,' but be heavens I'll learn it Gaelic, too.''

Poor Thompson is so frazzled that he'd have his own parrot switch to Gaelic, when his specialty is a tune about the knocking of "five hundred papishes right over Dolly's brae." For such comedy, the play "won golden opinions from the experienced critic as well as from the man in the pit and gallery" (*Nomad's Weekly*, Review of *Thompson in Tir-na-n-Og*). MacNamara's subject was volatile, but his handling of it so diverting that, according to the *Northern Whig* ("Grand Opera House"), "for three quarters of an hour . . . the audience rocked and roared as one has seldom heard theatre-goers in these degenerate days." Rivets and bolts ready to be thrown were forgotten in the gaiety.

Acclaim for *Thompson in Tir-na-n-Og* continued throughout its production history. In 1914, the *Irish Times* ("The Gaeity Theatre") praised it as "one of the most amusing pieces that has ever been written in connection with the Irish dramatic movement." In 1922, Reid, reviewing the work of the Ulster Theatre, said that "one must mention Gerald MacNamara's brilliant and fantastic farce . . . a little masterpiece of its kind. . . . The comic power displayed in it is quite individual." As late as 1927 *Thompson in Tir-na-n-Og* continued to draw crowds. Rutherford Mayne (see Sam Hanna Bell) thought the Ulster Theatre languished because the Opera House turned down all new plays in favor of *Thompson*. It was actually Mayne's own very popular play, *The Drone*, that was so often produced at the expense of other works. But *Thompson* was undoubtedly second in popularity.

The Throwbacks. 1917. (A Supernatural Comedy in Three Acts). First produced on 3 December at the Opera House, Belfast; then on 10 December at the Gaiety, Dublin. Revived the following year on 7 and 8 January in Newry. A rewritten version was produced five years later the week of 14 December.

This play's motif is the same as *Thompson*'s, an audacious mixture of past and present, with a militant feminist and four quarrelsome chieftains from North, South, East, and West. "As can easily be imagined from these elements," writes the *Northern Whig* ("Public Amusements"), "the author extracts a great amount of fun and plants many shrewd hints amongst present-day Irish factions. The audience relished these hugely and roared with laughter." Although critics noted some deficiencies, an especially alluring review in *The Freeman's Journal* (see Sam Hanna Bell) sharpens one's disappointment that this play remains lost:

The satirist in Ireland treads no primrose path, more especially if, like the author of *The Throwbacks*, his shafts are winged at all parties. Where others who have tried the same course move as gingerly as a ship in a mine-field, Mr. MacNamara drives riotously ahead, with a gale of laughter from his victims filling the sails of his craft.

Productions of the rewritten version were also well received. The *Irish Times* ("The Ulster Players," 15 December 1922) was unqualified in its praise, saying

MacNamara "improves by geometrical progression . . . for *The Throwbacks* is as much better than *Thompson* as *Thompson* is than *The Mist That Does Be on the Bog* . . . an advance in technique and in stage craft . . . fine comedy and real poetry of idea." With such acclamation, it is unfortunate *The Throwbacks* was never published. Hogan and Burnham have seen the manuscript and believe the play's success would depend a good deal on the acting. "Nevertheless," they add, "as a full-length variation on *Thompson in Tir-na-n-Og*, the play indicates what an interesting satiric fantasist MacNamara was."

Sincerity. 1918. (A Play in One Act). First produced the week of 27 May at the Gaiety in Dublin. Never revived.

This comedy's theme is religious tolerance: a boy raised by Protestant guardians develops an interest in Christianity and Confucianism, is claimed by his Catholic father, and then is married by the Chief Rabbi. *Sincerity* was not well received. Joseph Power, a Dublin critic and Ulster Theatre partisan, wrote (Hogan and Burnham) that he did not want to say much about *Sincerity* because it was entirely unworthy of an inimitable humorist like MacNamara. However, Jacques thought the players in the opening scene "made a sad hash of the author's work" and didn't quite "get the hang of the author's meaning." Also, Hogan and Burnham suggest that until the manuscript turns up, "it would be well to reserve judgement on *Sincerity*; for, when MacNamara is good, he is very good."

Fee-Faw-Fum. 1923. (A Play in One Act). First produced during Easter week by the Ulster Players at the Opera House in Derry. Produced again the week of 4 September at the Liverpool Playhouse and then again the week of 26 November at the Gaiety in Dublin.

Fee-Faw-Fum is based on an ancient Irish legend. It features Conn Ligg, an Ulster giant, whose goal in life is to rest on his laurels. The price of doing so involves some slapstick and stratagem that kept audiences well entertained. As with *The Throwbacks*, reviews of this play can only make one regret that the manuscript has not been found. In *The Belfast Newsletter* ("The Ulster Theatre," 24 January 1928): "one of the most laughable that has ever been submitted by the company, and the large audience expressed their appreciation wholeheartedly." In the *Irish Times* ("Ulster Players at the Gaiety Theatre"): "[It] is packed with keen humour from beginning to end. . . . The play is well-constructed and worked out. There is a laugh in every phase." In the *Irish Statesman* ("Drama in Dublin"): "[T]he play has the vintage quality of the inimitable *Thompson*. . . . Few dramatists would have had the courage to compound such a mixture, and perhaps nobody but Mr. MacNamara could have seasoned it with such irresistible fun and unending laughter."

No Surrender. 1928. (A Play in Three Acts with a Prologue). First produced the week of 23 January at the Grand Opera House, Belfast. Revived the following year the week of 14 December at the Gaiety, Dublin. With some revisions to the text, the Group Theatre in Belfast revived it in 1960.

This play was first written as a farce in two acts and then expanded. It brings past and future together in hilarious conflict. Set in 1990, King William III decides to visit Belfast with the understanding that all "old Order" Orangemen are dead. The play's climax is the unexpected arrival and subsequent death of the "last" Orangeman from Bambooza Island, Australia. The anticlimax is the arrival of his die-hard son, causing the weary king to wire this message to purgatory: "Have my bed well-aired—am coming home tonight. William Rex." *No Surrender* was well received, with the *Belfast Newsletter* ("Belfast Theatres and Cinemas") calling it "amusing, fanciful, and witty . . . one of the finest plays yet produced by the Ulster Players." The Group Theatre production of 1960 places the play further in the future, in 2090.

Who Fears to Speak? 1928. (A Play in One Act). Produced the week of 21 January at the Grand Opera House, Belfast. Never revived. Published in 1929 in *The Dublin Magazine.*

Unlike MacNamara's other political plays, which are set in the future or the mythological past, *Who Fears to Speak?* is a scene from Ireland's history. The year is 1797, and the play's title refers to the poem "Who Fears to Speak of '98?" written in memory of the rebellion of 1798, impressed so indelibly on Irish consciousness. The play lacks the dramatic conflict of *No Surrender*, but it is a neat comic skit. Its well-drawn characters taunt each other and show their blind sides but finally manage to pool their resources for the cause of a United Ireland. The *Belfast Newsletter* ("The Ulster Theatre," 25 January 1929) wrote, "There may be some subtle meaning in the play, but, if so, the subtlety is so extreme that a Belfast audience is not likely to discover it." Napper Tandy's disguise in the end does seem to lack a plausible motivation, yet the meaning of his announcement that he is off to Wexford is certainly not a puzzle.

The Ulster Literary Theatre was formed for the purpose of using drama to spread the principles of Wolfe Tone and the United Irishmen. Usually, MacNamara supports those principles by mocking the failure to reach for them. In this play, however, he honors men who do aim for liberty, equality, and fraternity. Mere "Muddlers," they barely succeed, and their bungling of fraternity is the comic essence of the play.

Thompson on Terra Firma. 1934. (A Play in One Act). First produced at the Grand Opera House, Belfast. No later productions.

Here Thompson returns to earth after his visit to Tir-na-n-Og and becomes an ardent nationalist, Gaelic leaguer, and scholar. The play's crux is how to restore his sanity. *Thompson on Terra Firma* did not achieve the success of some of MacNamara's other works. Rutherford Mayne explains why: "[T]hough it contained some of his finest flashes of wit, the humour was too intermittent and some of the incidents too long drawn out."

ADDITIONAL PLAYS, ADAPTATIONS, AND PRODUCTIONS

An August Day 1908. (A Play in Two Acts). Submitted to the Abbey but apparently rejected. Unmentioned by Mayne in his tribute to MacNamara and by historians of the Ulster Theatre. For knowledge of this play's existence we must be thankful to Holloway, that indefatigable recorder of Dublin's theatrical affairs. Hogan and Kilroy report that Synge and Abbey secretary W. A. Henderson opposed production.

ASSESSMENT OF MACNAMARA'S CAREER

Gerald MacNamara was one of the most important writers and actors for the Ulster Literary Theatre, which began in 1902, excited by both the aestheticism and nationalism of Dublin theater and politics. In 1915 the group, Sam Hanna Bell tells us, "became modest and blacked out 'Literary.' " The group was modest, too, at the start of its endeavors, as it sought help from Dublin in its attempt to use drama as a vehicle of propaganda. But after being snubbed by Yeats, who apparently suspected more interest in politics than art, the Ulster Literary Theatre decided to venture out on its own. On the way back to Belfast, Bulmer Hobson struck the arm of his seat and announced to David Parkhill, "Damn Yeats, we'll write our own plays!" (see Sam Hanna Bell). Their first act of defiance was to publish *Uladh* [1], a literary review, with a manifesto designed as a rebuff to Yeats. They claimed a "broad difference between the Ulster and Leinster schools . . . a talent more satiric than poetic." In the next issue they allowed James Cousins, using the pen name "Connla," to upbraid them for immodesty and provincial self-consciousness for defining a "school," while the elements of a possible "school" were still in a state of flux. Cousins (see *Uladh* [2]) urged, "Let us labour patiently at our own material. If the product be really good, it will then be time enough to philosophise." But philosophize they would (see *Uladh* [3]): "We have not attempted to define a school, but merely stating what may be, and indeed is, a ruling characteristic. . . . No; we shall have our own way, though the differences will always be within the generous circle of one nationality."

As for the claim to satire, these men knew, one might say, what they had in their pockets. Parkhill's satire, *The Enthusiast*, was to become standard fare in the Ulster Theatre's repertoire. The Morrow brothers' Christmas burlesque, *Suzanne*, produced before a small audience of friends, would eventually become the celebrated *Suzanne and the Sovereigns*, a collaboration between MacNamara and Parkhill, whose pseudonym was Lewis Purcell. As it turned out, Gerald MacNamara was to become the consistent satirist for the group, providing so often with his "genius for caricature . . . a riot of fun" ("The Ulster Theatre." *The Belfast Newsletter* 19 October 1922). His one separately published play, *Thompson in Tir-na-n-Og*, was constantly revived and was rivaled in popularity only by Rutherford Mayne's *The Drone*. His other most popular satires were

The Mist That Does Be on the Bog and *Suzanne and the Sovereigns*. But in both the Ulster Theatre and the Abbey, the rural comedy prevailed. As few followed Yeats in writing poetic drama, few followed MacNamara in writing satire.

Like his colleague Rutherford Mayne, Gerald MacNamara was a brilliant amateur actor, and he excelled in comic character parts. *Nomad's Weekly* (Rev. of *If*) found him "so unctuously funny" as Tom the waiter in Mayne's comedy, *If*, "that he only had to purse his lips to call forth a roar of responsive laughter." He pleased Dublin playgoers as well. In 1907 the Ulster Literary Theatre paid its first visit to the city with Purcell's *The Pagan* and Mayne's *The Turn of the Road*; MacNamara played, respectively, the humorous Falstaffian Cellach and John Graeme, the farmer. His acting, Mayne says, "won an appreciative tribute from W. J. Lawrence, the well-known critic." Lawrence also noted Mac-Namara's appeal in Dolly Byrne's *The Land of the Stranger*: "Mr. MacNamara, though somewhat unequal, was greatly helped by his curiously individual, half-jerky, hair-explosive methods in striving to give illusion to a character operating on the outer edge of reality." Another reviewer, Susan L. Mitchell, called MacNamara a "rarely accomplished actor." Holloway [2] thought "old Gerald MacNamara as Pat McCann was a delightful old soul." The *Dublin Evening Mail* ("Ulster Players in Dublin") wrote: "Indeed it must be said that he is an actor of undoubted qualifications. One might even go further and say that if he is an amateur the profession could very easily take a lesson from his book."

It is this praise for his outstanding ability that one reads time and time again, and the inevitable conclusions emerge: he was invaluable as an actor as well as a writer; he generated success. Not a year went by that he did not add to the Ulster Theatre's distinction by acting in its productions. MacNamara was not only excellent; he was also memorable. Rutherford Mayne believed the character of Dan Murray in his own play, *The Drone*, would ever remain associated with MacNamara. The *Londonderry Sentinel* ("Visit of the Ulster Players") found all the acting in that play "so delightful that it would be almost invidious to make distinctions" yet thought MacNamara's "truly delightful characterization . . . so effectively done that it simply could not be excelled." The *Times* ("Mr. H. C. Morrow"), in its obituary of MacNamara, actually described him as "the creator of the character Dan."

Again and again the word appears in reviews of MacNamara's writing and acting: "delightful." If he conveyed such a quality through his work, one can't help but think he was delightful himself. Indeed, Mayne's tribute begins, "That loveable personality known as Harry Morrow." If we may repeat a *Freeman's Journal* critic (see Sam Hanna Bell), "Where others who have tried the same course move as gingerly as a ship in a mine-field, Mr. MacNamara drives riotously ahead, with a gale of laughter from his victims filling the sails of his craft."

We do not know exactly what MacNamara thought he might accomplish. He certainly must have been pleased to hear the laughter and to find out that the rivets and bolts ready to be thrown during *Thompson in Tir-na-n-Og* never left men's pockets. It also must have been satisfying to learn that the same play attracted a special guest, Lord Birkenhead, speaker of those frightening lines: "There is no length to which Ulster would not be entitled to go, however desperate or unconditional" (MacEoin). Still, Mayne's remarks make us think MacNamara must have hoped to accomplish even more. He probably wished, as George Bernard Shaw did, to influence the times; and Orangeism was as intractable an issue as any Shaw addressed. Shaw had high goals for humanity and believed his comedy would forward those goals. Indeed, in Shaw's late revision of Shakespeare's *Cymbeline*, Iachimo claims that laughter "saves the world many thousand murders" (see Gassner). Although MacNamara probably never expected such results, he still must have been discouraged to see, toward the end of his life, a continuation of the sectarian strife and violence he had witnessed since childhood.

Shaw (see Gassner) consoled himself with the reflection, "We have no reason to believe we are the Creator's last word." MacNamara, too, must have had his consolations. If he grew weary with mankind, as indeed he must have, it did not show in his plays. He brought to the stage, time and again, the ideal of humane tolerance, educating and engaging his audiences through a rare combination of sharp but benevolent satire. Amid what has been described (J. Bowyer Bell; Mayne) as a "tragedy in endless acts," the example of "that courageous old Irish jester" served Ulster well.

ARCHIVAL SOURCES

Typescripts of some of MacNamara's works are housed at the Belfast Public Library. The two-act version of *No Surrender* is from the private library of Robert Hogan.

PRIMARY BIBLIOGRAPHY

Play

Thompson in Tir-na-n-Og. Dublin: Talbot Press, 1918.
Who Fears to Speak? The Dublin Magazine, new series 4.1 (1922): 30–52.

Burlesques

"The Babes in the Wood." *The Dublin Magazine* 1.8 (1924), 684–98.
"Little Devil Dought; or, If Ye Don't Give Me Monie I'll Sweepe Ye All Out." *The Dublin Magazine*, Part I: 2.5 (1924): 312–21; Part II: 2.6 (1925): 376–85.
"Stage Directions for a Play Called *William John Jamieson*." *The Dublin Magazine*:

"Characters" 1.3 (1923): 212–18; "Scenery" 1. 4 (1923): 263–71; "Production" 1.7 (1924): 598–605.

"Tcinderella." *The Dublin Magazine* 2.2 (1924): 118–28.

Sketches

"A Crank from the U.S.A." *Christmas Lady of the House* (1919): 22–23, 52.

"Cuchulain II, A Belfast Idyll." *Christmas Lady of the House* (1918): 17–18. Repr. *Irish Tatler and Sketch* (Christmas 1935): 9–11.

SECONDARY BIBLIOGRAPHY

"Belfast Theatres and Cinemas, Grand Opera House." *Belfast Newsletter* (24 Jan. 1928): 11.

Bell, J. Bowyer. "The Chronicles of Violence in Northern Ireland: A Tragedy in Endless Acts." *Review of Politics* 38.4 (1976): 310.

Bell, Sam Hanna. *The Theatre in Ulster*. Dublin: Gill and Macmillan, 1972.

"Drama in Dublin." *Irish Statesman* (8 Dec. 1923): 406.

"The Five Brothers." *Belfast Telegraph* (20 Sept. 1954).

"The Gaiety Theatre." *Irish Times* (17 Dec. 1914): 7.

Gassner, John. "Bernard Shaw and the Making of the Modern Mind." *Bernard Shaw's Plays*. Ed. Warren S. Smith. New York: W. W. Norton, 1970, 299–301.

"Grand Opera House." *Northern Whig* (10 Dec. 1912): 3.

Griffith, Arthur. "This Week." *Sinn Fein* (Easter Week 1910): 3.

Hogan, Robert, and Richard Burnham. *The Art of the Amateur: 1916–1920*. Vol. 5 of *The Modern Irish Drama*. Dublin: Dolmen Press, 1984.

Hogan, Robert, and James Kilroy. *The Abbey Theatre: The Years of Synge 1905–1909*. Dublin: Dolmen Press, 1978.

Holloway, Joseph. [1]. *Impressions of a Dublin Playgoer*. 23 Aug. 1922. National Library of Ireland MS. 1872: 357–58.

———. [2]. *Impressions*. 8 Dec. 1924. MS. 1890: 1163–66.

Review of *If*. Nomad's Weekly and Belfast Critic (20 Nov. 1913): 13.

Jacques. "Home Talent Doing Well." *Evening Herald* (1 June 1918): 2.

Kennedy, David. "The Drama in Ulster." *The Arts in Ulster: A Symposium*. Ed. Sam Hanna Bell, Nesca A. Robb, and John Hewitt. London: George G. Harrap, 1951.

Lawrence, W. J. "Irish Production." *Stage* (11 Dec. 1924).

MacEoin, Gary. *Northern Ireland: Captive of History*. New York: Holt, Rinehart and Winston, 1974; 143.

Mayne, Rutherford. "Gerald MacNamara." *The Dublin Magazine*, new series 13.2 (1938): 53–56.

Review of *The Mist That Does Be on the Bog*. Nomad's Weekly and Belfast Critic (12 Mar. 1910): 17.

Mitchell, Susan L. "Drama Notes." *Irish Statesman* (13 Dec. 1924): 436.

"Mr. H. C. Morrow." *Times* (12 Jan. 1938): 12.

Nic Shiubhlaigh, Maire. *The Splendid Years*. Dublin: James Duffy, 1955.

"Public Amusements." *Northern Whig* (4 Dec. 1917): 3.

Reid, Forrest. "Eighteen Years' Work—The Ulster Players." *Irish Times* (5 Dec. 1922): xviii.

Review of *Suzanne and the Sovereigns. Nomad's Weekly and Belfast Critic* (16 Jan. 1909): 8.

Review of *Thompson in Tir-na-n-Og. Nomad's Weekly and Belfast Critic* (21 Dec. 1912): 13.

Uladh. [1]. No. 1 (1904).

———. [2]. No. 2 (1905).

———. [3]. No. 2 (1905).

"The Ulster Players." *Irish Times* (13 Dec. 1922): 4.

"The Ulster Players." *Irish Times* (15 Dec. 1922): 8.

"Ulster Players at the Abbey Theatre." *Irish Times* (27 Nov. 1909): 8.

"Ulster Players at the Gaiety Theatre." *Irish Times* (28 Nov. 1923): 4.

"Ulster Players in Dublin." *Dublin Evening Mail* (1 Feb. 1913): 6.

"The Ulster Theatre." *Belfast Newsletter* (19 Oct. 1922): 6.

"The Ulster Theatre." *Belfast Newsletter* (20 Apr. 1923): 11.

"The Ulster Theatre." *Belfast Newsletter* (25 Jan. 1929): 6.

"Visit of the Ulster Players." *Londonderry Sentinel* (3 Apr. 1923): 4.

Edward Martyn
(1859–1923)

WILLIAM J. FEENEY

Edward Martyn had a distinctive way of saying, "Let no man write my epitaph." As directed in his will, his body was dissected in a Dublin hospital and interred in a pauper's grave. Had there been a tombstone, it should have been inscribed: "Here lies a minor dramatist, a pioneer of Irish theater, a patron of the arts, a lovable eccentric whose reach ever exceeded his grasp."

He was born on 30 January 1859, at Loughrea, County Galway. In 1860 his father died, leaving him to be raised by a socially conscious mother. Martyn was educated at Belvedere College, Dublin, and Beaumont College, Windsor, both Jesuit schools; and briefly at Oxford. With his cousin George Moore he traveled to Europe, then divided his time between London and his estate, Tulira, Ardrahan, Galway. The last of his line, Martyn ignored his mother's demands that he marry. Ireland's cultural advancement became his mission. He endowed the Palestrina Choir in Dublin's pro-Cathedral, financed church building and decoration, encouraged Irish manufacture of stained glass and the revival of Irish music, dance, and language.

The Irish Literary Theatre was inaugurated in 1899, after months of planning by W. B. Yeats, Lady Gregory, and Martyn. Moore became involved while the first plays were in rehearsal. To this three-year experiment in creating native Irish drama, Martyn contributed two plays, *The Heather Field* and *Maeve*, and covered any financial losses. Another play, *The Tale of a Town*, was rejected by Moore and Yeats. Rewritten, mostly by Moore, it was staged as *The Bending of the Bough* in 1900. This transmogrification of his play, added to philosophical differences with Yeats, caused Martyn to withdraw from the group, which later established the Abbey Theatre.

He briefly served as president of the Theatre of Ireland when it was created in 1906. Lacking leadership and successful plays, it withered into extinction in

1912. Joined by Thomas MacDonagh and Joseph Plunkett, Martyn organized the Irish Theatre in 1914 and directed it alone when his young partners died following the 1916 Easter Rising. From November 1914 to January 1920 the theater, a whimsical 100–seat house in an unfashionable Dublin neighborhood, offered nonpeasant Irish plays, several by Martyn; contemporary European masterpieces; and, infrequently, plays in the Irish language. Martyn's degenerating health and financial state and disturbances caused by the War of Independence brought about the collapse of the theater. On 5 December 1923, Martyn died at Tulira.

Selected Biographical Sources: Courtney; Gwynn; Hall; Malone.

MAJOR PLAYS, PREMIERES, AND SIGNIFICANT
REVIVALS: THEATRICAL RECEPTION

The Heather Field. 1899. A three-act play. Opened on 9 May in the Antient Concert Rooms, Dublin. On 6 June it was staged at Terry's Theatre, London, and in New York on 19–21 April 1900 at the Carnegie Lyceum. Later presentations were by the Players Club at the Queen's Theatre, Dublin, in the final week of June 1903; at the Abbey on 15 April 1909; and at the Irish Theatre, Dublin, on 5–11 November 1916 and 1–6 April 1918. In Zurich the English Players, organized by James Joyce and Claude Sykes, performed *The Heather Field* in March 1919. Radió Éireann broadcast the play on 19 January 1947.

Against the advice of friends and the entreaties of his wife, Grace, Carden Tyrrell attempts reclamation of a heather field. Under pressure of expense, Grace's opposition, and outbreak of wild heather in the cultivated field, Tyrrell lapses into madness.

With the exception of the *Irish Times* (Review of *The Heather Field*, 10 May 1899), Dublin reviewers commended the premiere: the *Evening Mail* (Review of *The Heather Field*) called it a triumph; the *Evening Herald* (Review of *The Heather Field*), a fine and wholesome drama. Beerbohm and Holloway thought the play acted better than it read. Abroad it fared less well. The *London Daily Telegraph* (Review of *The Heather Field*), like the *Irish Times*, sniffed at it as an Ibsenite drama of drainage. The *New York Times* (Review of *The Heather Field*) labeled Tyrrell a raving maniac. Evidently, in 1906 the Abbey considered a revival. A. E. F. Horniman, its benefactress, wrote to Yeats (Hogan [3]) her opinion that *The Heather Field* was dull and immoral and, more sensibly, that it would be difficult to cast nine-year-old Kit Tyrrell. For the 1909 revival the *Daily Independent* wondered why Dublin literati ever saw merit in the play. Frank Fay questioned the revival as, at best, a poor choice for a company not geared to drawing-room drama (Hogan [3]). The 1918 revival was judged a success, particularly for the acting, by O'Lonain, the *Irish Times* (Review of *The Heather Field*, 2 April 1918), and *Freeman's Journal* (Review of *The Heather Field*, 2 April 1918). James Joyce, in program notes for the Zurich performance, named *The Heather Field* Martyn's masterwork and said that Martyn, as an Ibsenite, occupied a unique position in Irish letters; other playwrights were concentrating on peasant drama.

Maeve. 1900. In two acts. Performed at the Gaiety, Dublin, on 19 February, revived at the Abbey by the Theatre of Ireland on 22 May 1908.

Colman O'Heynes, impecunious Prince of Burren, offers his daughter Maeve in marriage to a wealthy Englishman, Hugh Fitz Walter. Maeve's true love is cold, ideal Celtic beauty. To avoid a loveless union, she wills her own death.

Yeats [1] and Lady Gregory feared that *Maeve* was too poetical and remote, but the audience was appreciative. The *Irish Times* (Review of *Maeve*) was not: *Maeve* appealed only to the mind; it was not genuine theater. Lady Gregory [1] was surprised to find that some of the audience thought the play was "political." Holloway heard laughter during the premiere and the revival, despite the fact that *Maeve* contains no intentional humor. In critiques of the revival, the *Freeman's Journal* (Review of *Maeve*) and *Sinn Fein* (Review of *Maeve*) complimented the actors on rising above the inadequacies of the play.

The Place-Hunters. 1902. A one-act sketch. Printed in the *Leader* of 26 July; not performed or critically evaluated.

Unionist barristers and landowners are angry because Dublin Castle is mollifying nationalists with patronage. Attorney General Steppingstone Feathernest retains their loyalty with lavish promises, including an audience with the king when he visits Dublin.

An Enchanted Sea. 1904. A tragedy in four acts. Presented by the Players Club in the Antient Concert Rooms on 18–19 April.

Aside from the catastrophic ending, the play resembles Ibsen's *The Lady from the Sea.* The Font estate has reverted to fifteen-year-old Guy Font, who shares a fascination for the sea with an older friend, Lord Mask. Needing the estate as dowry for a match between her daughter and Mask, Guy's aunt Rachel Font murders him. Mask drowns, possibly a suicide, and as police move in, Rachel hangs herself.

Griffith [1] observed in Rachel a formidable, if crudely drawn, character; the play was ably constructed but not emotionally appealing. *All-Ireland Review* (Review of *The Place-Hunters*) commented on the churchlike, though attentive, stillness of the audience. Holloway wrote the play off as dreary and improbable. Fay regarded as unactable the role of elfin Guy Font. Martyn himself soured on the play after Moore interpreted Mask and Guy as homosexuals [Feeney].

The Tale of a Town. 1905. In five acts. Performed by the National Players Society (Martyn was its vice president), a branch of the Gaelic League, at Molesworth Hall (Dublin), on 31 October.

An English town, Anglebury, deprives an unnamed Irish town of its share of a business arrangement. Jasper Dean campaigns for redress but is defeated by pro-Britishers in social and political control of the Irish town.

Griffith [2] extolled the play as a revelation of the unscrupulous methods by which England dominated Ireland.

Grangecolman. 1912. In three acts. Played by the Independent Theatre Company at the Abbey on 25–27 January and revived at the Irish Theatre on 18–23 June 1917.

To prevent the marriage of her father, reclusive widower Michael Colman, and his young amanuensis, Clare Farquhar, Catharine Devlin dresses as the family ghost, a figure in white, knowing that Clare has made a casual vow to shoot the legendary ghost if it appears.

The 1912 presentation was commended, especially the performance of Countess Markievicz as Catharine, in the *Evening Telegraph* (Review of *Grangecolman*). *Sinn Fein* (Review of *Grangecolman*) found too much Ibsen in the strong women and weak men (Colman and Catharine's husband). Reviews in 1917 praised the acting. *The Leader* (Review of *Grangecolman*), however, detected similarities in the Grangecolman ménage and the occupants of Grangegorman Mental Hospital in Dublin.

The Dream Physician. 1914. A five-act comedy. Performed on 2–7 November in the Little Theatre, 40 Upper O'Connell Street, Dublin.

Audrey Lester's quarrel with her husband causes a breakdown in which she thinks he is dead. Psychotherapy practiced by Sister Farnan (Lady Gregory) convinces Audrey that she has been dreaming. The nurse introduces her to George Augustus Moon (Moore) and Beau Brummell (Yeats); creatures so weird could exist only in dreamland. In a secondary plot Otho Gerrard (Joyce) ignores his sensible uncle (Martyn) and worships an imaginary poetess.

Aside from the knockabout comedy of Moon and Brummell, the *Irish Times* (Review of *The Dream Physician*) frowned on the play as wildly improbable, an unfortunate mixture of comic and potentially tragic elements. The feminist *Irish Citizen* (Review of *The Dream Physician*) faulted Martyn for lead-footed satire and a bias against womankind. Reviewing the published text for *New Ireland*, O'Dempsey, an admirer of Moore, disliked the work. Peter McBrien, in *Studies*, was pleased to see Moore ridiculed, as was the reviewer for the *Daily Independent* (Review of *The Dream Physician*).

The Privilege of Place. 1915. An unpublished three-act comedy. Staged in the Irish Theatre on 8–14 November.

Owen Hort, son of bureaucrat Sir Matthew Hort, faces a difficult civil service examination. Social-climbing Peter O'Keeffe arranges for his son Terence to take the test posing as Owen; in exchange Sir Matthew must consent to the marriage of Terence and Maggie Hort. The scheme explodes when Owen confesses the fraud, and spirited Maggie weds a policeman.

Because the play was set in 1902, the *Freeman's Journal* (Review of *The Privilege of Place*, 9 November 1915) and *New Ireland* (Review of *The Privilege of Place*) dismissed it as dated. The *Evening Mail* (Review of *The Privilege of Place*) scented Ibsenism in the pitting of idealist Owen against materialist Sir Matthew (as in *Pillars of Society*). The *Irish Citizen* (Review of *The Privilege of Place*) rejoiced that Martyn finally had created a likable woman. The *Daily Independent* (Review of *The Privilege of Place*, 9 November 1915) lauded the political intent and the writing.

Romulus and Remus. 1916. In one act. Presented at the Irish Theatre on 18–23 December.

Denis D'Oran (Martyn) and his assistants, Romulus Malone (Moore) and Remus Delaney (Yeats), operate a beauty parlor (theater). The shopgirl, Daisy Hoolihan (Lady Gregory), has been enticed by Remus into helping him collect dead flies, from which he extracts an odorless perfume (peasant drama). Cornucopia Moynihan, whom Romulus has loved and left (a jab at Moore's boasting of "affairs"), traces him to the shop and creates a noisy scene.

The *Daily Independent* (Review of *Romulus and Remus*, 19 December 1916) and *Freeman's Journal* (Review of *Romulus and Remus*, 19 December 1916) identified the characters. Holloway said the comedy misfired. *Irish Opinion* (Review of *Romulus and Remus*), after deducting points for grotesquery, was moderately amused.

Regina Eyre. 1919. An unpublished play in four acts. Performed at the Irish Theatre for six days beginning 28 April.

It is gender-reversed *Hamlet*. Regina, studying in Germany, returns to her County Kerry home upon her mother's death and her father's marriage to his widowed sister-in-law Dympna. A confidante informs Regina that Dympna may have poisoned her husband and Magnus Eyre's first wife. The moment of truth (borrowed from Ibsen's *When We Dead Awaken*) takes place on Carrantuohill, Ireland's highest mountain. Evil Dympna falls to her death, and pure-souled Regina gains the summit. (The set was designed by Micheál Mac Liammóir.)

The *Evening Telegraph* (Review of *Regina Eyre*), *Daily Independent* (Review of *Regina Eyre*), *Freeman's Journal*, (Review of *Regina Eyre*), *The Leader* (Review of *Regina Eyre*), and New Ireland (Review of Regina Eyre), unanimously declared *Regina* weird, talky, and unconvincing. There were only a dozen in the audience on opening night, and even fewer after the reviews were printed.

ASSESSMENT OF MARTYN'S CAREER

Edward Martyn always has stood in the shadow of flamboyant, successful contemporaries such as Yeats, Moore, and Lady Gregory. He remains the comic figure of *Hail and Farewell*, of Yeats' patronizing memoirs, part-Quixote, part-Simon Stylites. So it will be until his full epitaph is written. Gwynn's is admittedly a memoir; Courtney's is not definitive. It is possible, however, to document Martyn's ideas and evaluate his plays.

Those who founded the Irish theater agreed that Irishmen generally were considered, at best, good-hearted ignoramuses, and, at worst, dangerously at the mercy of easily aroused emotions. Their theater would create a truer image, but where to find the truth? Yeats turned to Irish mythology and to rural Ireland, that part of the country least infected by alien culture. Martyn saw more to Ireland than peasants and pre-Christian heroes. His drama would be psychological, intellectual, representing (though not always approving of) nonpeasant Ireland: politicians, professionals, Big House gentry, persons who thought and felt, as distinguished from folks who merely reacted to physical environment.

There was no precedent for either type of theater. As Joyce wrote, Ireland had not produced even a miracle play; authors had to look abroad for models. He and Martyn found them in Ibsen. Yeats [1] and Synge considered the Norwegian an unsuitable influence; he delineated a society devoid of passion or poetry. Ellis-Fermor, indeed, calls the Irish drama movement a reaction against Ibsen.

It may seem odd that scrupulous Martyn should be drawn to someone whose work had been described as, among other things, a loathsome sore unbandaged. Actually, by the time Martyn began to write, Ibsen and his paladins had overpowered the opposition. All his important plays had been staged in London; even Queen Victoria had seen *Ghosts*. *An Enemy of the People* was brought to Dublin in 1894, and *A Doll's House* in 1897. Hostile criticism had been reduced to complaints of dullness and incomprehensibility.

Martyn borrowed Ibsen's stagecraft, characters, and themes and bypassed his iconoclasms. *The Heather Field* is a paradigm of what is and is not Ibsenite. It offers meticulous descriptions of set and characters, precise stage directions. One is aware (as in, for instance, *Rosmersholm*) of the world immediately beyond the Big House. Grace Tyrrell is an unwomanly woman; her husband, an unmanly man, dreamy, reclusive, obsessed with an unattainable goal, like John Gabriel Borkmann's mining scheme. Reminiscences of Carden Tyrrell and his brother Miles on their joyous youth and travel to Europe, though they parallel Martyn's own excursions, echo the happy childhood recalled by Asta and Alfred Allmers in *Little Eyolf*. Catharine Devlin makes a similar comparison of gracious past and bleak present in *Grangecolman*. A cryptic statement by Old Ekdal in *The Wild Duck*, "The woods avenge themselves," constitutes the theme of *The Heather Field*. Tyrrell violates the natural order by cultivating the heather field, his wife by forcing a naturally reclusive man into Big House society, and there are painful consequences.

Martyn's play, however, does not rely on conspiracy of silence or exfoliation of guilty secrets, nor does it hint at infidelity. Unlike some later plays, it does not challenge the establishment. Lord Shrule, Tyrrell's neighbor, is a kindly friend whose sound advice goes unheeded. Grace does not seek dominance for its own sake, in the fashion of Hedda Gabler-Tesman or Hilde Wangel in *The Master Builder*. Interference with Tyrrell's impossible dream is a matter of survival for herself and their young son.

Although his political plays may have been influenced by *An Enemy of the People*, Martyn did not need to go beyond Ireland for subject matter. *The Tale of a Town* was based on the finding of a Royal Commission in 1896 that Ireland had paid a disproportionate share of taxes levied by the United Kingdom. Irish leaders, hopelessly divided after the fall of Parnell, were unable to secure an adjustment. Actual English and Irish political figures are recognizable in the cast of characters. The "haves" and social climbers in *The Place-Hunters* and *The Privilege of Place* represent socioeconomic types rather than well-known individuals. Martyn's own politics changed gradually from conservatism to ostentatious nationalism. For a time he was president of Sinn Fein, which advocated unilateral, yet nonviolent, separation of Ireland from the United Kingdom.

Irish history enters the plays both allegorically and literally. In *Maeve* the marriage arrangement reflects a twelfth-century event. Dermot MacMurrough, fugitive King of Leinster, obtained military assistance from Richard Fitzgilbert, Earl of Pembroke, in recovering his kingdom. In return MacMurrough's daughter Eva was pledged in marriage to Fitzgilbert, and England secured a foothold in Ireland. A side issue in *The Heather Field* is the demands of tenants that Tyrrell reduce their rents. Similar demands were made of Martyn and other landowners by the Irish Land League.

Martyn, Moore, and Yeats satirized each other, sometimes so outrageously that it is difficult to decide if this was retribution or recreation. Moore often introduced a Martyn-type into his fiction, for example, John Norton in *A Mere Accident* (1887), a blindly devout, woman-shunning Catholic. Yeats and Martyn are quasi-comic figures in *Hail and Farewell* (1911–1914). Yeats' reminiscences [1,2] portray Moore and Martyn, especially the latter, as dressed-up Catholic peasants. In *The Cat and the Moon* (1917) he dramatizes them as saint and sinner companions. The Moore and Yeats personages in Martyn's comedies are gross caricatures. Sister Farnan and Daisy Hoolihan, the Lady Gregory types, are sensible women until they are mesmerized by the Yeats character. (Martyn and Lady Gregory were friendly neighbors in Galway.) Mockery of Joyce, as Otho Gerrard, seems philosophically, not personally, motivated. Courtney, McFate in the introduction to the 1972 reprint of *The Dream Physician*, and Setterquist note a shift in attitude underlying the personal satire: once sympathetic to dreamers, Martyn now makes fun of those who hide from reality.

Malone, O'Connor, Courtney, Ellis-Fermor, Yeats [2], Moore, Setterquist, and Weygandt rank *The Heather Field* and, perhaps, *Maeve* as important contributions to Irish drama. These plays are permeated by a sense of tragic joy, of escape, through madness or death, from a world too full of weeping. Structure is coherent, the conflict of idealism and practicality is carefully developed, and dialogue, despite some creakiness, is forward-moving. *Maeve* is valued by Weygandt and Malone primarily for its unearthly atmosphere and cold beauty. Robinson writes that if the characters are not distinctively Irish, the setting is.

Of the later plays, two were unpublished, one was never staged, and only *Grangecolman* was revived. Martyn himself said [Feeney] that no matter what he wrote afterward, people always harked back to *The Heather Field*. Ryan, who had access to the typescript of *Regina Eyre*, metaphorically traces Martyn's output from the mountains of *The Heather Field* to the plains of *The Tale of a Town*, the swamps of *The Dream Physician*, the subterranean obscurity of *Romulus and Remus*, and the abyss of *Regina*. Malone sees the characters of *The Tale of a Town* as puppets; Weygandt, as personifications in a morality play. Martyn is at his best, Weygandt declares and Setterquist agrees, in small-cast plays, in the quiet intensity of drawing-room confrontations, and fails in crowded scenes. Boyd [1] partially dissents: *The Tale of a Town* may be artistically inferior to Moore's variation, but it far better interprets sociopolitical conditions in Ireland, of which Moore had limited knowledge. *An Enchanted Sea* is marred, in the judgment of Weygandt and Ellis-Fermor, by the clumsy characterization of Rachel Font. *Grangecolman*, while not a strong work, is, in Boyd's [1] estimation, a departure from the mistiness of the earlier plays, the dialogue is less marmoreal, and there is an air of intense reality. The female characters [Feeney] undergo subtle shifts in personality as the play progresses, in contrast to the largely static figures of Martyn's other works. But beyond observations such as these, scholars rarely venture.

Martyn's deficiencies are not in creation. According to Yeats [1], Moore said that Martyn was better at conceiving plots than he was. Usually dismissive of Martyn, Yeats [2] approved his taste, intellect, and patience; regrettably, he could not transfer thoughts to paper. Gwynn observes that Martyn was imbued with the classical Renaissance spirit but not with the craft of Renaissance artists. Ellis-Fermor, acknowledging Martyn as a trailblazer in Irish drama of ideas, attributes the firmness of his early plays to guidance from his friends Moore and Arthur Symons. On his own he faltered. Boyd [2] and Ellis-Fermor think that Martyn's satirical gifts were better suited to the novel than to the stage. In evaluating the political satires, Setterquist is of the opinion that Martyn's indignation flew out of control and turned the characters into freaks. As early as 1901, Joyce [1], dissenting from favorable opinions of Martyn, contended that he was crippled by incorrigible style. Malone describes his dialogue as literary, hence unfitted to theater. In the same vein Weygandt remarks that the dialogue creates spokespersons for philosophies, not individuals with whom an audience can empathize. Ryan considers the mannered dialogue the weakest element in Martyn's work.

Aside from these shortcomings, Martyn's drama of ideas came at an unpropitious time. Ireland then needed a theater that could make Irishmen proud or angry. Hogan [4] states that from the beginning, Martyn bored his audiences. A worldview gloomy as that of Ecclesiastes—Yeats [1] called it hatred of life— was not the right stuff.

As a rallying point for Irish theater, neither "Ibsen with an Irish accent" nor Celtic Twilight prevailed. Freethinking creative writers and box office realities demanded recognition. The Abbey survived, especially after Horniman's subsidy ended, by making concessions to the actual world. Yeats may have shuddered fastidiously at the grittiness of the Cork realists or the broad comedy of William Boyle and George Shiels, but the drama's laws the drama's patrons give. Martyn clung disastrously to "fitt audience tho' few" dogma. The Irish Theatre defiantly presented such outré entertainment as *Uncle Vanya* and Maeterlinck's *The Intruder*, and a full house was a rarity.

For Martyn, however, there was a measure of vindication. The Dublin Drama League, founded in 1918 by Lennox Robinson and others, attempted the sophisticated, world-embracing art envisioned by Martyn. Then the Gate Theatre, with adequate facilities, professional players (Martyn insisted on dedicated amateurs), and culturally evolving audiences, shaped these principles into durable being. Micheál Mac Liammóir, one of its originators, graciously credited Martyn and the Irish Theatre for pointing the way. The first production at the Gate, on 14 October 1928, was *Peer Gynt*—a choice Martyn would have approved.

ARCHIVAL SOURCES

A typescript of Martyn's unpublished and unperformed *The Playboy of the Eastern World*, a satirical allegory in one act, is in the University College Dublin archives. Its theme is the conflict between two matriarchs, Britannia and Hibernia, and their offspring. There are Martyn and Martyn-related documents in the Berg Collection in the New York Public Library. Joseph Holloway's monumental manuscript diary, in the National Library of Ireland, is a storehouse of information, gossip, and opinion concerning Martyn. A large body of Martyn's papers (Ryan, letter to Setterquist) reportedly disappeared when the Carmelite priory in London was destroyed during an air raid in 1941.

PRIMARY BIBLIOGRAPHY

Plays

The Dream Physician. Dublin: Talbot, 1917; repr., Vol. 7, Irish Drama Series. Intro. Patricia McFate. Chicago: De Paul University Press, 1972.
Grangecolman. Dublin: Maunsel, 1912.
The Heather Field and *Maeve.* Intro. George Moore. London: Duckworth, 1899. *The Heather Field* reprinted Vol. 1, Irish Drama Series, 1966; *Maeve* in Vol. 2, 1967.
The Place-Hunters. The Leader 26 July 1902.
Romulus and Remus. The Irish People (21 Dec. 1907): 1–2; repr., *Lost Plays of the Irish Renaissance*, Vol. 2, *Edward Martyn and the Irish Theatre.* Newark, Del.: Proscenium, 1980.
Selected Plays by George Moore and Edward Martyn. Ed. David Eakin and Michael Case, Washington, D.C.: Catholic University of America Press, 1995.
The Tale of a Town and *An Enchanted Sea.* Kilkenny: Standish O'Grady; London: Fisher Unwin, 1902.

Essays and Articles on Drama and Theater

"Astorea Redux." *Banba* (May 1921): 57–59. (On the vanities of actors.)
"*The Cherry Orchard* of Tchekoff." *New Ireland* (21 June 1919): 108–9.

"Little Eyolf." *Sinn Fein* (13 July 1912): 3.
"A Plea for a National Theatre in Ireland." *Samhain* (Oct. 1901): 14–15.
"A Plea for the Revival of the Irish Literary Theatre." *Irish Review* (Apr. 1914): 79–84.

Novel

Morgante the Lesser. London: Swan Sonnenschein, 1890.

SECONDARY BIBLIOGRAPHY

Beerbohm, Max. "In Dublin." *Saturday Review* (13 May 1899): 587–88.
Boyd, Ernest. [1]. *The Contemporary Drama of Ireland.* Boston: Little, Brown, 1928.
———. [2]. "The Work of the Irish Theatre." *Irish Monthly* (Feb. 1919): 71–78.
Courtney, Marie-Therese. *Edward Martyn and the Irish Theatre.* New York: Vantage, 1956.
Review of *The Dream Physician. Daily Independent* (21 Jan. 1918).
Review of *The Dream Physician. Irish Citizen* (7 Nov. 1914): 194.
Review of *The Dream Physician. Irish Times* (3 Nov. 1914): 194.
Egan, Michael, ed. *Ibsen, the Critical Heritage.* London: Routledge and Kegan Paul, 1972.
Ellis-Fermor, Una. *The Irish Dramatic Movement.* London: Methuen, 1939.
Fallis, Richard. *The Irish Renaissance.* Syracuse, N.Y.: Syracuse University Press, 1977.
Fay, William G., and Catherine Carswell. *The Fays of the Abbey Theatre.* London: Rich and Cowan, 1935.
Feeney, William J. *Drama in Hardwicke Street: A History of the Irish Theatre Company.* Cranbury, N.J.: Associated University Press, 1984.
Review of *Grangecolman. Evening Telegraph* (26 Jan. 1912).
Review of *Grangecolman. Freeman's Journal* (26 Jan. 1912).
Review of *Grangecolman. Leader* (30 June 1917): 485.
Review of *Grangecolman. Sinn Fein* (3 Feb. 1912).
Gregory, Lady Isabella. [1]. *Our Irish Theatre.* New York: Putnam, 1913.
———. [2]. *Seventy Years, 1852–1922, An Autobiography.* New York: Macmillan, 1974.
Griffith, Arthur. [1]. [Review of *An Enchanted Sea.*] *United Irishman* (23 Apr. 1904): 1.
———. [2]. [Review of *The Tale of a Town.*] *United Irishman* (4 Nov. 1905): 1.
Gwynn, Denis. *Edward Martyn and the Irish Revival.* London: Jonathan Cape, 1930.
Hall, Wayne. *Shadowy Heroes: Irish Literature of the 1890's.* Syracuse, N.Y.: Syracuse University Press, 1980.
Review of *The Heather Field. Daily Independent* (16 Apr. 1909).
Review of *The Heather Field. Daily Telegraph* (7 June 1899).
Review of *The Heather Field. Evening Herald* (10 May 1899).
Review of *The Heather Field. Evening Mail* (10 May 1899).
Review of *The Heather Field. Freeman's Journal* (10 May 1899).
Review of *The Heather Field. Freeman's Journal* (2 Apr. 1918).
Review of *The Heather Field. Irish Times* (10 May 1899).
Review of *The Heather Field. Irish Times* (2 Apr. 1918).
Review of *The Heather Field. New York Times* (20 Apr. 1900).

Hogan, Robert, and James Kilroy. [1]. *The Irish Literary Theatre, 1899–1901, The Modern Irish Drama*. Vol. 1. Dublin: Dolmen, 1976.

Hogan, Robert. [2]. *Laying the Foundations, 1902–1904. The Modern Irish Drama*. Vol. 2. Dublin: Dolmen; Atlantic Highlands, N.J.: Humanities, 1975.

Hogan, Robert, and James Kilroy. [3]. *The Abbey Theatre: The Years of Synge, 1905–1909. The Modern Irish Drama*. Vol. 3. Dublin: Dolmen; Atlantic Highlands, N.J.: Humanities, 1978.

Hogan, Robert, Richard Burnham, and Daniel J. Poteet. [4]. *The Rise of the Realists. The Modern Irish Drama. Vol. 4*. Dublin: Dolmen; Atlantic Highlands, N.J.: Humanities, 1979.

Hogan, Robert, and Richard Burnham. [5]. *The Years of O'Casey, 1921–1926*. Newark: University of Delaware Press; Gerrards Cross, Buckinghamshire: Colin Smythe, 1992.

Holloway, Joseph. *Joseph Holloway's Abbey Theatre*. Ed. Robert Hogan and Michael J. O'Neill. Carbondale: Southern Illinois University Press, 1967.

Ibsen, Henrik. [1]. *A Doll's House, The Wild Duck, The Lady from the Sea*. London: J. M. Dent, 1966.

————. [2]. *The Last Plays*. Trans. and intro., William Archer. New York: Hill and Wang, 1964.

Joyce, James. *The Critical Writings of James Joyce*. Ed. Ellsworth Mason and Richard Ellmann. New York: Viking, 1959.

MacDonagh, John. "Edward Martyn." *Dublin Magazine* (Jan. 1924): 465–567.

Mac Liammóir, Micheál. *Theatre in Ireland*. Dublin: Cultural Relations Committee of Ireland, 1950.

Review of *Maeve. Freeman's Journal* (23 May 1908).

Review of *Maeve. Irish Times* (20 Feb. 1900).

Review of *Maeve. Sinn Fein* (30 May 1908).

Malone, Andrew. *The Irish Drama*. London: Constable, 1930.

McBrien, Peter. "The Dream Physician." *Studies* (June 1918): 362–63.

McFate, Patricia. "The Bending of the Bough and the Heather Field: Two Portraits of the Artist." *Éire-Ireland* (Spring 1973): 52–61.

Moore, George. *Hail and Farewell*. Ed. R. A. Cave. Gerrards Cross, Buckinghamshire: Colin Smythe, 1976.

Nolan, J. C. M. "Edward Martyn and Guests at Tulira." *Irish Arts Review* (1994): 167–73.

O'Connor, Ulick. *All the Olympians*. New York: Atheneum, 1984.

O'Dempsey, Michael. "A Very Open Letter." *New Ireland* (9 Mar. 1918): 291–92.

O'Lonain, Michael. [Review of *The Heather Field*.] *Young Ireland* 13 (Apr. 1918): 2.

Review of *The Place-Hunters. All-Ireland Review* (23 Apr. 1904): 200.

Review of *The Privilege of Place. Daily Independent* (9 Nov. 1915).

Review of *The Privilege of Place. Evening Mail* (9 November 1915).

Review of *The Privilege of Place. Freeman's Journal* (19 Dec. 1916).

Review of *The Privilege of Place. Irish Citizen* (13 Nov. 1915): 165.

Review of *The Privilege of Place. New Ireland* (20 Nov. 1915): 29.

Review of *Regina Eyre. Daily Independent* (29 Apr. 1919).

Review of *Regina Eyre. Evening Telegraph* (29 Apr. 1919).

Review of *Regina Eyre. Freeman's Journal* (29 Apr. 1919).

Review of *Regina Eyre. Leader* (10 May 1919): 317.

Review of *Regina Eyre*. *New Ireland* (17 May 1919): 29–30.

Robinson, Lennox. *Ireland's Abbey Theatre, A History 1899–1951*. London: Sidgwick and Jackson, 1951.

Review of *Romulus and Remus*. *Daily Independent* (19 Dec. 1916).

Review of *Romulus and Remus*. *Freeman's Journal* (9 Nov. 1915).

Review of *Romulus and Remus*. *Irish Opinion* (23 Dec. 1916): 2.

Ryan, Stephen. "Edward Martyn's Last Play." *Studies* (Summer 1958): 192–99.

Setterquist, Jan. *Edward Martyn. Ibsen and the Beginnings of Anglo-Irish Drama*. Vol. 2. Uppsala: Uppsala Irish Studies, 1960.

Weygandt, Cornelius. *Irish Plays and Playwrights*. Boston: Houghton Mifflin, 1913.

Yeats, William Butler. [1]. *The Autobiography of William Butler Yeats*. New York: Macmillan, 1953.

———. [2]. *Memoirs*. Ed. Denis Donoghue. New York: Macmillan, 1973.

Frank McGuinness

(1953–   )

HELEN LOJEK

One of Ireland's foremost contemporary dramatists, Frank McGuinness is best known for his Dublin and London success with *Observe the Sons of Ulster Marching towards the Somme* (1986) and for *Someone Who'll Watch over Me* (1992), which (following a successful run in London) became his first major New York production.

McGuinness was born in Buncrana, County Donegal, in 1953. The northern-most county of the republic and part of the province of Ulster, Donegal protrudes like a thumb to the west and north of Northern Ireland. Donegal's border with Northern Ireland gives a particular immediacy to the tensions that inform so much of Irish life and of McGuinness' drama, and its geographic isolation from the rest of the republic makes it an appropriate birthplace for a playwright who so often employs outsider perspectives and themes of marginalization and separation.

In 1972 McGuinness was a student at University College, Dublin (UCD), when Bloody Sunday again riveted attention on Irish political and religious conflicts. He was also a student at UCD when he attended his first theater production, at the age of nineteen. In the 1970s he published poems and stories on the New Irish Writing page of the *Irish Press*, but his first real literary success came in 1982, when Patrick Mason directed *Factory Girls* at the Abbey's "little" theater, the Peacock. McGuinness has since had a productive relationship with both Mason and the Peacock.

Throughout the 1980s McGuinness lectured in English at St. Patrick's College Maynooth (part of the National University of Ireland but often thought of as Ireland's "seminary"), appeared regularly at a variety of literary conferences, and wrote a wide range of theatrical pieces. McGuinness' academic interests in linguistics, history, and medieval literature often show in his plays, where they intersect with such popular culture forms as movies, songs, jokes, slang, political slogans, and melodrama. History, literature, and popular culture all often serve as distancing devices—filters through which, paradoxically, McGuinness allows us to see contemporary Ireland more clearly. In 1983 TEAM Theatre (a Theatre in Education company) commissioned McGuinness to write a play for use in its tour of Irish secondary schools. The result was *Borderlands*, set in McGuinness' home region and produced by TEAM in 1984. In 1985 TEAM produced *Gatherers*, which later became part of the 1985 Dublin Theatre Festival. In 1985 *Baglady* premiered at the Peacock and was then paired with *Ladybag* for a double bill at the Dublin Theatre Festival and a tour of Ireland in early 1986.

Observe the Sons of Ulster Marching towards the Somme, which premiered at the Peacock in 1985, toured Northern Ireland, opened in a new production at England's Hampstead Theatre in 1986, and gained McGuinness his first major recognition, winning a variety of Irish and English prizes. McGuinness' participation (with director Joe Dowling) in a 1986 Derry workshop, *Making a Play*, sponsored by a variety of Northern Irish arts associations, marked his continued involvement in public arts education projects. In 1986 McGuinness wrote *Innocence*. In 1987 his adaptations of Lorca's *Yerma* and Ibsen's *Rosmersholm* (commissioned by the National Theatre of Great Britain) opened in the same week; three one-acts (collectively titled *Times in It*) premiered at the Peacock; and *Scout*, a television drama, showed on BBC2. In 1988 *Carthaginians* and McGuinness' adaptation of Ibsen's *Peer Gynt* were both part of the Dublin Theatre Festival, and McGuinness directed a production of Brian Friel's *The Gentle Island* (1971) for the Peacock. In 1989 the Royal Shakespeare Company produced *Mary and Lizzie*, and *The Hen House* appeared on BBC2.

In the 1990s McGuinness continues to live in Dublin, to teach at St. Patrick's, to serve on the board of the Abbey Theatre, and to produce an astonishing variety of works. In 1990 his adaptation of Chekhov's *Three Sisters* was produced in Dublin. *The Bread Man*, part of the 1990 Dublin Theatre Festival, is set in a small town in northeast Donegal in 1970 and is the only McGuinness play to approach his own experience directly. In 1991 his adaptation of Brecht's *Threepenny Opera* was produced, and he was selected for membership in Aosdana. The fruitful intersection of McGuinness' academic and artistic interests is indicated by his 1991 analysis of Thomas Kilroy's version of Chekhov's *The Seagull* and by two as yet unproduced plays: *The Beautiful Lie* (about Oscar Wilde) and a version of Ibsen's *Hedda Gabler*. In 1992–1993 he was writer in residence for the Abbey Theatre. Receipt of the American Ireland Fund Literary Award in 1992 freed McGuinness to do travel and research for a work in progress, but the impressive London and New York successes of *Someone Who'll Watch over Me* that year did the most to broaden his reputation.

Selected Biographical Sources: Lojek [1]; O'Dwyer; O'Toole [2]; Pine.

MAJOR PLAYS, PREMIERES, AND SIGNIFICANT
REVIVALS: THEATRICAL RECEPTION

Factory Girls. 1982. Opened 11 March at the Abbey's Peacock Theatre, Dublin. Directed by Patrick Mason. Revival: 1988, with a slightly recast scene 8, Druid Theatre Company, Galway. The Druid then took the production to Riverside Studios, London, where it opened in May. Directed by Garry Hynes. Most revisions, undoubtedly a result of McGuinness' increasing theatrical experience, seem designed to shorten scene 8 and tighten its focus.

In a Donegal shirt factory based on the one in which McGuinness' mother and aunts labored, five women respond to the challenge of exorbitant quotas and potential redundancy with a wildcat strike and barricade themselves inside the factory office. The focus on work (as opposed to politics, history, terrorism, family, or love) and the largely female cast (the two male roles are relatively minor) separate this play from the usual in contemporary Irish drama—or, for that matter, the usual in contemporary English-language drama. Emelie Fitzgibbon [1] found the "overall theme quite effective but, strangely, inadequacy in the creation of the male characters militated against a total credible dramatic conflict in terms either of equal opportunity, agitation or workers' rights" (41). Craig [3] praised the 1988 production as "impressive" and lauded McGuinness' "good use of the racy and self-assertive manner associated with factory girls. . . . The mood veers from comedy to ferocity, with the odd poignant moment thrown in."

The play's premiere began a series of successful relationships between McGuinness and director Patrick Mason (who took *Factory Girls* on tour in Australia) and between McGuinness and the Peacock.

Borderlands. 1984. Opened 8 February at the Dominican Convent, Dun Laoire, Ireland. Commissioned and produced by TEAM (a Theatre in Education company). Directed by Martin Drury.

Written for presentation to second-level (fifteen- to seventeen-year-old) students, *Borderlands* announced itself as a "theatre-parable for 1984" designed to "challenge" the audience to think more deeply about Irish political issues. A workshop/discussion followed each performance. Four young men (two Protestants and two Catholics) sidestep their religious/political differences and go on a charity walk from Derry across the border. As it finally emerged, the play was far from the focus originally suggested by Drury, who had invited McGuinness to do a "piece on language" as "a response to the dawning of Orwell's year of dread." Writing for a company that uses no lights, drapes, or makeup and that typically performs in nontheater spaces (often without even a raised platform), McGuinness relied on the basics of drama and on a thoughtful awareness of the relationship of the actors to the audience. Cast and audience joined in the postperformance discussion of issues.

Gatherers. 1985. Produced by TEAM Theatre Company in the autumn. Remounted for the 1985 Dublin Theatre Festival.

The 1932 Eucharistic Congress held in Dublin and the 1979 papal visit to Ireland provide the contexts for discussions of religion, nation, and personal destiny by generations of Irish.

Observe the Sons of Ulster Marching towards the Somme. 1985. Opened in February at the Peacock Theatre, Dublin. Directed by Patrick Mason. The production toured Ireland and was part of the 1985 Belfast Theatre Festival. It returned to Dublin for a three-week run at the Abbey, where it opened 2 December 1985. In July 1986 a new production opened at the Hampstead Theatre, London, under the direction of Michael Attenborough.

This play, about eight young Protestant volunteers in the Great War (a play without women), was widely acclaimed in both Ireland and England and propelled McGuinness into the position of promising young Irish playwright. Billington described it as a "play which transcends immediate politics to deal with permanent truths" and pronounced it "one of the finest Irish plays I have seen in years." Jeffery called it a "powerful and subtle play." Coveney called it "a stunning play . . . poetic and powerful." Reviewers almost universally praised the compassionate insight that McGuinness (a Catholic) brought to Ulster Protestantism. The play won the 1985 Harvey's Best Play Award, the Rooney Prize for Irish Literature, the *London Standard* Most Promising Playwright Award, the Cheltenham Literary Prize, an Arts Council bursary, the 1986 Plays and Players Award for Most Promising Playwright, and the 1986 London Fringe Awards for Best Play and Best Playwright New to the Fringe. *Observe the Sons of Ulster Marching towards the Somme* also marked McGuinness' departure from traditional realism into a mixture of dream, fantasy, and realism—and his increasing use of evocative light and sound.

Baglady. 1985. One-act. Opened in March at the Peacock Theatre (Dublin). Directed by Patrick Mason. *Baglady* and *Ladybag* (one act, unpublished) were both part of the 1985 Dublin Theatre Festival. The two one-acts were remounted as a double bill at the Peacock in March 1986, with the same cast and director. In September 1992 *Baglady* was produced by Scena Theatre at the Woolly Mammoth Theatre, Washington, D.C., as part of the New European Play Festival/Sense of Ireland Festival.

The dramatic monologue *Baglady* was written for actress Maureen Toal, who had appeared in *Factory Girls* and to whom *Baglady* is dedicated. Together, especially with Toal appearing in both, the plays revealed McGuinness' dramatic range and emphasized his sense of the symbiotic tie between laughter and tears.

Mahony found the 1992 Washington, D.C., production disappointing, deciding that *Baglady* is "an underdeveloped play . . . not representative of [McGuinness'] considerable range and achievement as a playwright" and "should not be sent abroad to audiences who know nothing more of his work."

Innocence, the Life and Death of Michelangelo Merisi, Caravaggio. 1986.
Opened 7 October at the Gate Theatre, Dublin. Directed by Patrick Mason.

This play about Renaissance Italian painter Caravaggio is the first of Mc-
Guinness' original stage plays to be set outside Ireland and marks his most
extensive use of light and music to effect theatrical transformations. Ger Fitzgibbon praised it for using "the beat of local idiom in a terse, theatrical way"
and found the "marriage of localized ritualistic idiom with a kind of vertiginous
nightmare expressionism" effective. Etherton reveals that McGuinness has acknowledged the influence of Fugard's *Demetos* on *Innocence* (47). Like *Observe
the Sons of Ulster*, the play uses history, homosexuality, and artistry as perspectives from which to examine issues of continuing importance in Ireland.

Scout. September 1987. (BBC2.) Produced by Danny Boyle.

The script was one of three commissioned by the BBC from Irish writers
(Anne Devlin and John McGahern wrote the others). Seeking nonstereotypical
treatments of Ireland, the BBC stipulated that the scripts should not deal with
either armed conflict or cross-cultural love affairs (Sheehan 405). Nokes found
McGuinness' tale of a football scout for Manchester United (which starred Frank
McAnally and Stephen Rea) a "fable" about religion that, "in striving to avoid
the violent reality of Ulster politics," opted instead for a "set of sentimental
myths."

Carthaginians. 1988. Opened 26 September at the Peacock Theatre as part of
the Dublin Theatre Festival. Directed by Sarah Pia Anderson. Opened in July
1989 at the Hampstead, London, with a largely new cast, also directed by Anderson.

Seven people waiting in a Derry cemetery for the dead to rise tell their own
stories and the stories of Derry, a focal point for Irish tensions. O'Toole [1]
found the play's "interweaving of the political, the visionary and the sexual . . .
difficult and elusive," but he praised the play as "desperately funny and wonderfully flowing" and written with "astonishing skill." Craig [2] wished this
"haphazard" play had a more definite shape, though she praised some of its
parts. Schneider found "music and light . . . used to good effect" (89) and approved the play's "quick change of registers, the absurd and the farcical, the
language of prayer and ritual, reminiscences of the American Civil Rights Movement, and snippets from the mass media" (92). Ger Fitzgibbon found "the
marriage of classical myth and contemporary scene . . . neither compelling nor
purposeful," but Pine described it as "arguably, McGuinness's most successful
play because it indicates how the ritual process can change one's view of oneself" (30).

Many subsequent commentators (e.g., O'Dwyer and Pine) have seen the play,
which explores Northern Catholic feelings, as a companion piece to *Observe the
Sons of Ulster*, which concentrates on Northern Protestants. *Carthaginians* continues McGuinness' inventive mixture of classical references and popular cul-

ture, his use of homosexuality to create an outsider perspective from which to view Irish society, and his exploration of ritualized drama incorporated as a kind of play within the play.

Mary and Lizzie. 1989. Workshopped by members of the Royal Shakespeare Company at Stratford-upon-Avon in July 1988. Opened 27 September 1989 by the Royal Shakespeare Company in the Pit at the Barbican. Directed by Sarah Pia Anderson.

McGuinness' tale of the two Irish sisters who loved Friedrich Engels met with a lukewarm reception. Taylor regarded it as "a play of ideas" that, "because McGuinness eschews both poetic language and dramatic interaction," never quite succeeds dramatically.

The Hen House. September 1989. (BBC2) Directed by Danny Boyle.

With Sinead Cusack as a widow who imprisons a retarded child in a henhouse, the production explores the constrictions of life in Donegal in the 1950s. It won the Prix de l'Intervision and the Prix de l'Art Critique at the 1990 Prague International Television Festival.

The Bread Man. 1990. Opened 2 October at the Gate Theatre as part of the Dublin Theatre Festival. Directed by Andy Hinds.

In "a town in North-East Donegal" in the 1970s, a man's difficulties come to a head when he is accused of theft, but from that point on, he begins to rise. Set in the Ireland of McGuinness' youth, the play establishes a parallel between public and private crises. McGuinness has referred to his effort in the play "to get 'home' . . . to return to the landscape of my birth, to the language of my birth, and to listen to it." Pine observes, "There are a lot of questions that one brings away from the play—'Where is home?'—the idea of loss of place, displacement; the word tramp was used interestingly" (29).

Someone Who'll Watch over Me. 1992. Opened 4 July at the Hampstead Theatre, London. Directed by Robin Lefevre. Starring Alec McCowen, Hugh Quarshie, and Stephen Rea. Moved in September to the Vaudeville Theatre, London, with James McDaniel replacing Hugh Quarshie. Produced by Noel Pearson. Opened 22 November at the Booth Theatre, New York, with the same cast, director, and producer; ran at the Booth until 13 June 1993. Opened in April 1993 at the Abbey Theatre, Dublin, with a new cast directed by Robin Lefevre.

The play was a serious contender for the New York Drama Critics Circle Award for Best Play and won the Critics Circle Award for Best Foreign Play. It was nominated for the Laurence Olivier Award for Best Play, given by the Society of West End Theatres (London).

In London this depiction of three cellmates (an Irishman, an Englishman, and an American) chained to the wall of a windowless Beirut room by captors who never appear on stage, won general acclaim. Nightingale found it "sensitive, absorbing, if somewhat underwritten." Theodores noted the contrast of "the starkness and deprivation" of the captives' situation to the "firing line of cheap jokes and cross-cultural cliches which take on a gorgeous innocence and clarity.''

The New York production's early reviews were lukewarm. Rich, for example, declared the play had "the artificial tone of an acting class exercise" and found the characters "schematically and sometimes stereotypically drawn." Later reviews were more positive. Oliver found this a "beautiful play . . . beautifully performed" and noted its "unfashionable" focus, "barely touching on the men's sexuality, though not avoiding it, either." Barnes noted the play has "a heart, a soul and a sense of humor. It is admittedly, in places, both sentimental and manipulative, and it doesn't probe deeply into the hostage psyche." He praised McGuinness' "overriding concern . . . with the theatricality of the situation, and the chances it offers for gallows humor." Simon decided the play was "too good for note-taking," and though he "chafed" at the absence of women, he admired the "glory of McGuinness's invention: It draws its substance from every part of the geographical, historical, cultural map; it welds disparateness into solidarity; it compensates for the fettered body with a larkingly unfettered spirit."

In Dublin, Nowlan praised the play as "sparely and elegantly written: at once highly literate and easily accessible, its references immediately topical, its content timeless. It is a highly comic and deeply serious work of dramatic art."

In addition to the play's own merits, the success of the New York production was undoubtedly helped by the excellence of the cast and the skill of the producer, who timed its New York opening to coincide with the opening of Neil Jordan's film *The Crying Game*, which also starred Stephen Rea. The 1992 success of Brian Friel's *Dancing at Lughnasa* (also produced by Pearson) helped prepare New York audiences for another Irish play, and *Someone Who'll Watch over Me*—which includes McGuinness' first American character—demands less specific understanding of Irish history and politics than some earlier McGuinness plays and is therefore more accessible to American audiences.

ADDITIONAL PLAYS, ADAPTATIONS, AND PRODUCTIONS

Rosmersholm. 1987. McGuinness' "adaptation" of Ibsen's play was commissioned by the National Theatre of Great Britain and opened at the Cottesloe Theatre, London, in May. Directed by Sarah Pia Anderson. A new production, also directed by Anderson but with a largely new cast, opened at La Mama, New York, in December 1988.

Rosmersholm elicited little response in either London or New York. Meyer dismissed the London performance as "sadly misguided" and McGuinness' script as "stilted and often obscure." Gussow responded more positively to the New York performance and noted that McGuinness' adaptation "somewhat alleviated" the "rhetorical excess" of the original. The script was the first of a number of significant adaptations by McGuinness.

Yerma. 1987. McGuinness' version of Federico Garcia Lorca's play opened 5 May at the Peacock Theatre, Dublin. Directed by Michael Attenborough.

McGuinness ("Alone Again") has described the play as "an examination of hope abandoned" and indicated that he identified with Yerma, the woman who longs for, but is unable to have, a child and whose despair leads her to kill her husband. Coveney related McGuinness' version "to a local peasant drama tradition" and noted the "startling contrast" between the "extraordinary Catholic image" Yerma has of herself and the "secular reality of [her] physical condition."

Peer Gynt. 1988. An adaptation of Ibsen's play. Opened 4 October at the Gate Theatre as part of the Dublin Theatre Festival. Directed by Patrick Mason.

Roche praised McGuinness' version for bringing "home just how much the young Peer anticipates Synge's Christy Mahon in making himself a mighty man through the power of a lie" (42–43).

Three Sisters. 1990. An adaptation of Chekhov's play. Opened 28 March at the Gate Theatre, Dublin. Directed by Adrian Noble. Reopened with the same cast and director in December at the Royal Court Theatre, London.

Aside from the masterful stroke of casting Cyril Cusack as Chebutykin and Cusack's daughters (Sorcha, Niamh, and Sinead) as Chebutykin's daughters, the play elicited little critical commentary, though Binyon found "the pervasive hint of a brogue" effective as "a constant reminder that here we are in the provinces, yearning for the unattainable metropolis."

Threepenny Opera. 1991. An adaptation of Brecht's play that moves the setting to London in the 1950s. Opened in July at the Gate Theatre, Dublin. Directed by Patrick Mason.

Munk found the production, which starred Marianne Faithfull, "almost though not totally awful" but praised its true understanding of the original and its willingness to address "class as a real subject." McGuinness' "version of the dialogue has a raw lilting crudity that's echt Brecht however unliteral."

ASSESSMENT OF McGUINNESS' CAREER

The challenge for critics of McGuinness' work is to respond adequately to a career that is still in midcourse and to plays that have not been widely tested outside Ireland. That challenge is increased by the unusually slight body of interpretive analysis focusing on McGuinness' work. In many ways, both the lack of foreign productions and the critical neglect are surprising. McGuinness is one of the foremost playwrights in Ireland, where he is both well known and admired and where his plays are almost universally well received. Irish critics are, of course, generally kind to their own playwrights, but McGuinness' popular and critical successes place him in the same rank with Brian Friel and Tom Murphy—both of whom have received far more attention from both critics and non-Irish theaters. The recent West End and Broadway success of *Someone*

Who'll Watch over Me (1992) should be an impetus for change in both areas, since it gained McGuinness an audience he had not previously reached.

McGuinness has cited Spanish playwright Federico Garcia Lorca as a model for writers who want "to inform their work with political thinking, while at the same time keeping it concrete and keeping it specific, and not using jargon and sloganeering, and not calling for easy forms of thinking or easy labelling" ("Alone Again" 16). Not surprisingly, that description fits McGuinness' work precisely. The realities of his troubled country are never far from the center of his plays, but they are not dealt with polemically or simplistically. His belief that "[w]ith any culture you respect, you have to respect its complexities" ("Alone Again" 16) informs his work and makes it difficult to categorize his responses. History, myth, emotional imbalance, classical literature, sexual orientation—all at various times become distancing filters through which contemporary Ireland is seen.

In keeping his work concrete and specific as well as political, McGuinness often matches private agonies and public disruptions, making the interior turmoil of his characters parallel the external turmoil of their world. He regularly positions audiences to see things from perspectives not his own. A man, he has written plays (*Factory Girls, Baglady*) that focus on the experience of women; a Catholic from the republic, he has written about Ulster Protestants (*Observe the Sons of Ulster*); childless, he has written about the experience of fatherhood (*Bread Man*); a twentieth-century Irishman, he has written about sixteenth-century Italy (*Innocence*). His appreciation for the complexity of his culture is matched by his appreciation for the complexity of human nature: "[F]or those men [the *Sons of Ulster*] to come to a full appreciation of what they were fighting for, they had to learn what is conventionally called the female side of themselves. To know they were fighting for whole human beings, for full human beings"; for the breadman to come back to sanity, he must move beyond the inherited terms of politics and religion to his own experience as conceiver of a child; he must learn that "his history is personal" (McGuinness, quoted in White 8).

McGuinness' first play, *Factory Girls*, operates within the bounds of conventional realism with which twentieth-century audiences are comfortable. Since then he has moved to nonnaturalistic drama and increasing experimentation with expressionistic and symbolic uses of sound and light. The worlds of dream, imagination, hallucination, and reality mingle and resonate against each other. His latest play, *Someone Who'll Watch over Me*, moves back toward naturalistic staging, and the simplicity of its set and cast, combined with the diminished "Irishness" of its themes, makes it McGuinness' most exportable play. McGuinness' willingness to write both realism and nonnaturalism (often bordering on expressionism), his willingness to explore both prosaic sunlight and poetic moonlight make his continuing interest in Ibsen (whose works span a similar range) understandable and revealing.

McGuinness' plays also touch a full scale of cultural notes, from classical, to medieval, to religious, to contemporary pop culture. His characters leap playfully from references to Dido to references to Wimbeldon. (The implication in *Someone Who'll Watch over Me* that there are odd parallels among the American spiritual "Amazing Grace," the Bible's tale of Ruth, and the classical tale of Orpheus is vintage McGuinness.) Pain and tragedy elicit laughter. Sanity and insanity are inextricable.

In praising Thomas Kilroy's version of *The Seagull*, McGuinness identified it as a "significant turning point in Irish theatre." "At the instigation of an English theatre, an Irish playwright is given an opportunity to use a major European play as a metaphor for his own country's intellectual history.... We could begin to claim international contact, translating key texts into our own speech" ("A Voice from the Trees" 3). The description fits much of McGuinness' own work as well, and it indicates the importance he attaches to breaking through the isolation that has frequently both protected and limited Irish playwrights. McGuinness' use of settings and themes that are unusual in Irish drama, the range of his allusions, and the variety of influences evident in his works move him well beyond the comfortable limits of Irish peasant drama.

McGuinness' familiarity with Chekhov and Ibsen (and the close attention to their texts necessitated by his adaptations) has grounded him in realistic drama with a social/political thrust. His academic involvement with medieval literature has grounded him in writing that takes its religion and its visions as seriously as its everyday reality. His interest in linguistics has heightened his awareness of language and ambiguity. His love of play and song and popular culture has freed him to infuse his work with a sometimes antic disposition. His love of a country with a history and present of pressing problems has shaped his themes. As a whole his work is among the most far-ranging, complex, and vital in contemporary Irish drama. Its continued evolution promises continued enrichment to the field—and continued challenges to the critics, who have much work to do.

PRIMARY BIBLIOGRAPHY

Plays

Baglady. (with *Carthaginians*). London: Faber and Faber, 1988.
Borderlands. In *Three Team Plays.* Ed. Martin Drury. Dublin: Wolfhound Press, 1988.
Carthaginians. (with *Bag Lady*). London: Faber and Faber, 1988.
The Factory Girls. Dublin: Monarch Line, 1982. (Also Dublin: Wolfhound Press, 1988.)
Innocence, The Life and Death of Michelangelo Merisi, Caravaggio. London: Faber and Faber, 1987.
Mary and Lizzie. London: Faber and Faber, 1989.
Observe the Sons of Ulster Marching towards the Somme. London: Faber and Faber, 1986.
Someone Who'll Watch over Me. London: Faber and Faber, 1992.

Adaptations

Peer Gynt by Henrik Ibsen. 1988. London: Faber and Faber, 1990.
Rosmersholm by Henrik Ibsen. 1987.
Threepenny Opera by Bertolt Brecht. 1991.
Three Sisters by Anton Chekhov. London: Faber and Faber, 1990.
Yerma by Federico Garcia Lorca. 1987.

Television Scripts

Scout BBC-2 (1986).
The Hen House BBC-2 (1989).

Essays and Articles on Drama and Theater

"Alone Again, Naturally." *In Dublin* (14 May 1987): 15–18. (Interview with John Wa-
    ters.)
"The Artist as a Young Pup." *Irish Literary Supplement* (Fall 1987): 9.
"A Popular Theatre?" With Patrick Mason. *The Crane Bag* 8.2 (1984): 109–10.
"Something Natural, Something Wonderful." *Irish Literary Supplement* (Spring 1989):
    24.
"A Voice from the Trees: Thomas Kilroy's Version of Chekhov's *The Seagull*." *Irish
    University Review* (Spring/Summer 1991): 3–14.

Interview

[Interview with Charles Hunter.] *Irish Times* (15 Feb. 1985).

SECONDARY BIBLIOGRAPHY

Barnes, Clive. "Three Most Captivating Hostages." *New York Post* (24 Nov. 1992):
    Travel Section: 25.
Billington, Michael. "Orange March to Destruction." *Manchester Guardian* (17 Nov.
    1985): 20.
Binyon, T. J. "The Cry from the Provinces." *Times Literary Supplement* (3 Aug. 1990):
    825.
Burke, Patrick. "Dance unto Death." *Irish Literary Supplement* (Fall 1987): 45.
Coveney, Michael. "Sex and Moral Hypocrisy." *Weekend Financial Times* (London)
    (10 May 1987).
Craig, Patricia. [1]. "A Backward Boy." *Times Literary Supplement* (15–21 Sept. 1989):
    1005.
———. [2]. "A Graveside Manner." *Times Literary Supplement* (28 July 1989): 824.
———. [3]. "Getting Shirty." *Times Literary Supplement* (27 May–2 June 1988): 585.
deJongh, Nicholas. "Winning Wimbledon from a Cell in Beirut." *London Evening Stan-
    dard* (13 July 1992): 7.

Etherton, Michael. *Contemporary Irish Dramatists.* New York: St. Martin's Press, 1989, 45–51 and passim.

Feingold, Michael. "Free and Uneasy." *Village Voice* (1 Dec. 1992): 87.

Fitzgibbon, Emelie. [1]. "All Change: Contemporary Fashions in the Irish Theatre." *Irish Writers and the Theatre.* Ed. Masaru Sekine. Totowa, N.J.: Barnes and Noble, 1986, 33–46.

———. [2]. "Three TEAM Plays." Ed. Martin Drury. *Irish Literary Supplement* (Spring 1989): 13.

Fitzgibbon, Ger. "Sex, Politics and Religion." *The Irish Literary Supplement* (Spring 1989): 15.

Gussow, Mel. "An Enemy of the People, with Personal Problems." *New York Times* (14 Dec. 1988): C21.

Hewison, Robert. "Spirits Rise above Less than Zero." [Review of *Someone Who'll Watch over Me.*] *Sunday Times* (19 July 1992): sec. 7: 8.

Jeffery, Keith. "Under the Blood-Red Hand." (22 Nov. 1985): 1326.

Lojek, Helen. [1]. "Difference without Indifference: The Drama of Frank McGuinness and Anne Devlin." *Éire-Ireland* (Summer 1990): 56–68.

———. [2]. "Myth and Bonding in Frank McGuinness's *Observe the Sons of Ulster Marching towards the Somme.*" *Canadian Journal of Irish Studies* (July 1988): 45–53.

Mahony, Tina. "Irish Drama in the City of Double-Speak." *Irish Literary Supplement* (Spring 1993): 24.

Meyer, Michael. "The Weight of Tradition." *Times Literary Supplement* (15 May 1987): 518.

Munk, Erika. "Caught in the Crossfire: In the Shadow of Gunmen." *American Theatre* (Dec. 1991): 34–35, 66–67.

Nightingale, Benedict. "Held Hostage to Old Misfortunes." *Times* (13 July 1992): Life and Times: 2.

Nokes, David. "Dreaming Dreams without Drama." *Times Literary Supplement* (18–24 Sept. 1987): 1018.

Nowlan, David. "An Elegant Work of Art." *Irish Times* (15 Apr. 1993): 8.

O'Dwyer, Riana. "Dancing in the Borderlands: The Plays of Frank McGuinness." In *The Crows behind the Plough: History and Violence in Anglo-Irish Poetry and Drama.* Amsterdam: Rodopi, 1991.

Oliver, Edith. "Cellmates." *New Yorker* (7 Dec. 1992): 154.

O'Mahony, John. "Back on Broadway." *Irish Echo* (25 Nov. 1992): 1, 38.

O'Toole, Fintan. [1]. "A Leap beyond the Dark." *Irish Times* (1 Oct. 1988): Weekend: 11.

———. [2]. "You Don't Think I'm as Stupid as Yeats, Do You?" *Irish Times* (24 Sept. 1988): Weekend: 3. (Interview with Frank McGuinness.)

Penny, Liz. "In the Forbidden City." *Theatre Ireland* 12 (1986): 62.

Peyser, Marc. "Working Both Ends of the Terrorist's Gun." *Newsweek* (8 Feb. 1993): 83.

Pine, Richard. "Frank McGuinness: A Profile." *Irish Literary Supplement* (Spring 1991): 29–30.

Rich, Frank. "Coping with Incarceration, Or, the Lighter Side of Beirut." *New York Times* (24 Nov. 1992): C13.

Roche, Anthony. "Ghosts in Irish Drama." *More Real than Reality: The Fantastic in*

Irish Literature and the Arts. Ed. Donald E. Morse and Csilla Bertha. New York: Greenwood Press, 1991. 41–66.

Schneider, Ulrich. "Staging History in Contemporary Anglo-Irish Drama: Brian Friel and Frank McGuinness." In *The Crows behind the Plough: History and Violence in Anglo-Irish Poetry and Drama.* Amsterdam: Rodopi, 1991, 79–98.

Sheehan, Helena. *Irish Television Drama: A Society and Its Stories.* Dublin: Radio Telefís Eireann, 1987.

Simon, John. "Stout Fellow, McGuinness." *New York* (7 Dec. 1992): 68, 89.

Taylor, Neil. "Wandering Lives." *Times Literary Supplement* (13 Oct. 1989): 1124.

Theodores, Diana. "Beirut? Well, It Sure Beats Strabane." *Sunday Tribune* (London) (13 Sept. 1992): B4.

White, Victoria. "Irish Dramatists: In Fear of the Female?" *Irish Times* (18 June 1991): 8.

Winer, Linda. "A Look at Hostages, Very Neat and Tidy." *New York Newsday* (24 Nov. 1992): II: 39.

Wolf, Matt. "Two Vehicles Carry an Irish Actor to America." *New York Times* (22 Nov. 1992): 21.

Thomas Murphy

(1935–   )

JOSÉ LANTERS

Although Tom Murphy has been called "Ireland's greatest living playwright" (Waters), his work has also been called undisciplined and melodramatic; the extreme reactions evoked by his plays are reflected in the many ups and downs of his career.

Thomas Bernard Murphy was born in Tuam, County Galway, on 23 February 1935, the youngest of ten children. At the age of fifteen, Murphy left Tuam Christian Brothers School, where he was very unhappy, and spent the following two years at the Technical College, after which he worked as an apprentice fitter-welder at Tuam's sugar factory. In 1955 a scholarship took him to a training college for vocational teachers in Dublin, where he qualified as a metalwork teacher in 1957. He taught for almost five years at Mountbellew Vocational School, County Galway.

Between 1951 and 1962 Tom Murphy developed his interest in theater and engaged in amateur dramatics with the Tuam Little Theatre Guild. His first play, *On the Outside*, jointly written in 1959 with his childhood friend Noel O'Donoghue, won the manuscript prize at the All-Ireland Amateur Drama Competition; likewise, *The Iron Men* (revised as *A Whistle in the Dark*) won script competitions in 1960 and 1961. The Irish professional stage was not ready for his brand of theater, however—the Abbey Theatre's rejection of *The Iron Men* came in the form of a derogatory letter from its managing director, Ernest Blythe, who subsequently also rejected *The Fooleen*—and in 1962 Tom Murphy moved to London to write full-time for the stage and television. He married Mary Hippisley in 1966; they have three children, Brennan, Nell, and John. He returned to Ireland in 1970.

One of the things Murphy came back to confront was the Catholic background that had left him bitter and disillusioned with institutionalized religion. His wish for some form of reconciliation led him in 1971 to accept the invitation to join the International Advisory Committee on the Use of English in the Liturgy. The two-year experience did not bring back his faith in the church but helped focus his own spiritual concerns, many of which were later expressed in his highly controversial play *The Sanctuary Lamp* (1975).

Although Ireland had begun to recognize Murphy's talent by the late 1960s— he received the award for distinction in literature from the Irish Academy of Letters in 1972 and became a member of the Abbey Theatre's Board of Directors in 1973 (a function he held until 1983)—his career remained uneven. While the Irish productions of such plays as *Famine* (1968) and *The Morning after Optimism* (1971) were well received, *The Orphans* (1968) was a failure, and after the tumultuous reception of *The Sanctuary Lamp* (1975) and the disaster of *The J. Arthur Maginnis Story* (1976), Murphy decided to stop writing for two years. The responses to his comeback play, *The Blue Macushla* (1980), were discouraging, but any doubts as to Murphy's genius were dispelled by *The Gigli Concert* (1983), *Conversations on a Homecoming* (1985), and especially *Bailegangaire* (1985), the latter two produced while Murphy was writer in association at the Druid Theatre, Galway (1983–1985). In 1986 he joined the Abbey Theatre in a similar position. With *Too Late for Logic* (1989), Murphy seemed to be looking for new directions; his only subsequent play to date, *The Patriot Game* (1991), is a reworking of a twenty-five-year-old television script. In 1994 Tom Murphy published his first novel, *The Seduction of Morality*.

For his plays Murphy has received the Independent Newspapers Award (1983), two Harvey's Awards (for *The Gigli Concert* and *Bailegangaire*) and the *Sunday Tribune* Award (1985–1986). He has been a member of the Irish Academy of Letters since 1982 and of Aosdana since 1984.

Selected Biographical Sources: "Murphy, Thomas (Bernard)," *Contemporary Authors*, Murray [3]; O'Toole [2]; Waters.

MAJOR PLAYS, PREMIERES, AND SIGNIFICANT REVIVALS: THEATRICAL RECEPTION

On the Outside. 1961. One act. Amateur production, Cork, 1961. Broadcast by Radió Éireann, 1962. First professional production (double-billed with *On the Inside*, written 1974) at the Project Arts Centre, Dublin, on 30 September 1974, directed by Tom Murphy; transferred to the Abbey Theatre on 18 November 1974. Both one-acts were also performed at the Long Wharf Theater, New Haven, Connecticut, in March 1976.

Barnes [1], writing about the American production, saw *On the Outside* as "simply an evocative recording of life" and found it "not quite interesting enough." Coleby, however, reviewing the printed version of the plays, emphasized the timelessness and universality of the pieces: "Mr. Murphy spins his stories in masterly fashion, making no concessions and striking not one false note."

A Whistle in the Dark. 1961. Three acts. Opened 11 September at the Theatre Royal, Stratford East, London, produced by Joan Littlewood; transferred to the Apollo Theatre, London, 17 October 1961. First Irish performance at the Olympia Theatre, Dublin, 13 March 1962. Revivals: Long Wharf Theater, New Haven, Connecticut, February 1968, and Mercury Theatre, Off-Broadway, October 1969, both directed by Arvin Brown; Abbey Theatre, October 1986 and July 1987; Royal Court Theatre, London, July 1989 (Abbey Theatre production directed by Garry Hynes); South Street Theatre, New York, November 1989 (Irish Repertory Theatre directed by Charlotte Moore).

The *Times* critic ("A Terrifying Play") called *A Whistle in the Dark* "a quite terrifying play." Misguided by prejudice, several reviewers chose to see the play's violent characters as accurate depictions of all Irishmen: O'Toole [2] cites comments by Baker (who urged everyone to see "just what bog vipers we are nursing in our bosom"), Shulman ("The Most Anthropoidal Family of the Year"), and Tynan ("What blights this play is something endemic in the Irish temperament"). The negative Irish response to the play was, in part, a defensive reaction: "Many Irish were to take the play as the latest national insult from one of Ireland's writers, who, according to popular prejudice, make money by exhibiting our weaknesses to the world" (Griffin). Subsequent American reviewers were more appreciative. Barnes [2] called *A Whistle in the Dark* a "strange, ugly, impressive play" and saw in it the "horror, complexity and final catharsis of Greek tragedy." *Variety* (Review of *A Whistle in the Dark*) called it "a consistently absorbing, blisteringly powerful theatre piece," while *Time* magazine (Review of *A Whistle in the Dark*)—which later nominated it Play of the Year—praised its "strength, wisdom and broody disconcerting beauty." The 1989 revivals in both London and New York drew high praise from critics, who stressed the play had not dated at all.

A Crucial Week in the Life of a Grocer's Assistant. 1967. Twelve scenes; an earlier version of the play was called *The Fooleen.* First broadcast by BBC television, March 1967. A revised version directed by Alan Simpson opened at the Abbey Theatre, 10 November 1969, and reopened in August 1970.

The play is set in a small town in rural Ireland in 1958 and is thematically very close to *On the Outside* in its depiction of the frustrations of young people facing emigration. O'Toole [2] comments, "The play ends hopefully rather than triumphantly" (71). Seamus Kelly [1] was less convinced by the play's ending and saw the "wickedly squalid picture" painted by Murphy as "a sombre rubbing of a coin that has no bright side."

Famine. 1968. Twelve scenes. Opened at the Peacock Theatre, Dublin, 21 March, and transferred to the Abbey stage, 24 June 1968. Directed by Tomás Mac Anna. Revivals: Royal Court Theatre, London, 1969; Lyric Theatre, Belfast, January 1973; Project Arts Centre, Dublin, 1978 (directed by Tom Murphy); Druid Theatre, Galway, 1984; Abbey Theatre, October 1993.

Enthusing about *Famine* in the *Irish Times*, Henry Kelly described an "enthralled Peacock house" applauding the author of a play "that is perhaps the most powerful and brilliant work that the Dublin stage has had for years. . . . [T]his play provokes one to superlatives." According to Murray [2] *Famine* is "one of the great experiences in the modern Irish theatre." Walshe [1] expresses the opinion of many when she calls *Famine* one of Murphy's most powerful dramas.

The Orphans. 1968. Three acts. Opened at the Gate Theatre, Dublin, 7 October, as part of the Dublin Theatre Festival. Directed by Vincent Dowling. Subsequently staged at Loyola University, Chicago, August 1969, and Newark, Delaware, 1971.

Foley and O'Toole ([2], 103), while acknowledging that the play's depiction of the secularized, technological world of the 1960s was, in many ways, true to life, considered the play generally undramatic and one of Murphy's least successful works. Several reviewers commented on the Chekhovian feel of the play and on Murphy's attempt to move away from Irish topics, although Wardle found the play's themes of physical disgust and religious sentimentality "more Irish than ever."

The Morning after Optimism. 1971. Ten scenes. Originally subtitled *Grief*. First performed during the Dublin Theatre Festival at the Abbey Theatre, 15 March 1971, directed by Hugh Hunt; reopened Abbey Theatre, 12 July 1971. Revivals: Manhattan Theatre Club, New York, June 1974; Abbey Theatre, June 1977; Project Arts Centre, Dublin, May 1983.

The Morning after Optimism is a radical departure into psychological symbolism and the idiom of fairy tale. The strangeness of the play left audiences and reviewers alike divided as to its merits. Thomas Kilroy confessed to reveling in its "great lunatic monologues," although he, like others, felt that the play could be pruned. Nowlan [2] commented that "it must surely be the most original and one of the most moving and impressive plays to have been presented by the Abbey in the past quarter century." American reviewers were more reserved in their praise; *Variety* (Review of *The Morning after Optimism*) found the Dublin production "satisfying"; Gussow saw the American premiere and felt that "By the end of two extremely long acts, one's tolerance for adult fairy tales is stretched."

The White House. 1972. Two acts, later rewritten as *Conversations on a Homecoming*. Opened at the Abbey Theatre, 20 March. Also broadcast by RTE television, February 1977.

The first act, subtitled "Conversations on a Homecoming," was set in the early 1970s; the second ("Speeches of Farewell"), a decade earlier at the time of the Kennedy assassination. The play was structurally unsatisfactory and remained so even after the order of the acts was reversed; "nevertheless," wrote Lewsen, "this is a resonant work by a writer of passion." Nowlan [4] called it "the bleakest dramatic statement ever made in, or about, this country."

The Sanctuary Lamp. 1975. Two acts. First performed during the Dublin Theatre Festival, Abbey Theatre, 7 October, directed by Jonathan Hales. Revivals: Abbey Theatre, July 1976; Open Space Theatre, New York, June 1980, directed by Lynn Michaels; the revised version of the play opened at the Abbey Theatre in November 1985.

This highly controversial play about man's search for solace in the face of fear and loneliness and the failure of organized religion to provide spiritual sustenance provoked strong statements from both admirers and enemies. Some audience members considered it blasphemous and walked out in protest. The *Education Times* called it ''an immoral piece of art'' (cited by Griffin). Among the play's admirers were Nowlan [4], who called it ''likely the most anti-clerical play ever staged by Ireland's national theatre'' but also ''a most profoundly religious play,'' and then-Irish president Cearbhall O Dalaigh, who declared *The Sanctuary Lamp* one of the greatest Abbey plays ever (cited by Griffin). English reviewers were, on the whole, bemused by the play and the reactions it evoked in Ireland. The American production was marred by bad diction, which rendered some of the speeches unintelligible: ''[T]his is a flawed production of an interesting play'' (Corry).

The J. Arthur Maginnis Story. 1976. Irish Theatre Company touring production directed by Joe Dowling. Opened Pavilion Theatre, Dun Laoghaire, 9 November; from there it moved to Wexford and Galway.

Announced as a ''musical extravaganza,'' *The J. Arthur Maginnis Story* is a send-up of various sacred Irish cows, including nationalism, religion, folklore, and the national brew, Guinness. Responses were unfavorable: describing it as ''wearisome,'' Seamus Kelly [2] found it ''full of sound and brewery, signifying nothing.'' Murphy concedes that the piece was carelessly written.

The Blue Macushla. 1980. Two acts. Opened at the Abbey Theatre, 6 March. Directed by Jim Sheridan. Revived during the Dublin Theatre Festival, 1983.

Murphy's attempt to apply the idiom of American gangster movies to the stage as a metaphor for corruption and terrorism in contemporary Ireland fell flat, partly because the Abbey production was flawed and partly because ''its central device of gangster idiom is not used with enough suppleness and discrimination'' (O'Toole [2], 127), causing the play to lose some of its satirical edge. Nowlan [1] blamed both the play, whose ''allegory is not clear,'' and the ''inept and very unsure'' production for the theatrical failure.

The Gigli Concert. 1983. Eight scenes. Opened at the Abbey Theatre, 29 September. Directed by Patrick Mason. Revivals: South Coast Repertory Theatre, Costa Mesa, California, December 1984; Abbey Theatre, April 1984 and March 1991; Almeida Theatre, London, January 1992, directed by Karel Reisz.

The Gigli Concert was generally felt to have secured Murphy's reputation as a master of the theater both in Ireland and abroad. Claudia Harris notes that, while generally positive, ''the reviews of the Abbey premiere agreed on one thing—the three-hour play was too long." Murray [2] found it "hard to imagine a finer production than that given at the Abbey. . . . It made for stunning theatre." Calling *The Gigli Concert* "a work of immense power and creative vision," Hadfield criticized the 1984 Abbey production for failing to capitalize on the symbolic landscape of the play. The ecstatic reaction of Britain's theater critics to the 1992 Almeida production was summarized by Meany: many reviewers emphasized the play's spiritual dimension, and there was universal praise for actors Tony Doyle, Barry Foster, and Ruth McCabe. Kellaway spoke of a "thrilling and intense experience," while Pitman called the play "an impressive mind-bender, frustrating but fascinating."

Conversations on a Homecoming. 1985. Opened at the Druid Theatre, Galway, 16 April, directed by Garry Hynes. Revivals: SUNY, Purchase, New York, July 1986 (Druid Theatre Company); Donmar Warehouse, London, October 1987; Abbey Theatre, February 1992, directed by Garry Hynes.

Conversations on a Homecoming is the substantially rewritten first half of *The White House*; the past explicitly depicted in the earlier version is now evoked in the form of characters' reminiscences, making the action more dramatically effective and coherent. Although not everybody was convinced— Simon called it "a dreadful play"—most reactions were favorable: "The wonder of this intermissionless play is that Murphy maintains our fascination for two hours and leaves us, not in despair, but oddly exhilarated" (Tierney).

Bailegangaire. 1985. Two acts. Opened at the Druid Theatre, Galway, 5 December, directed by Garry Hynes. Revival: London, February 1986; Gaiety Theatre, Dublin, May 1986; New Haven, Connecticut, 1987.

Bailegangaire (literally, "town without laughter") is subtitled *The Story of Bailegangaire and How It Came by Its Appellation.* McArdle praised the Druid production (with Siobhan McKenna as Mommo), in which "the careful orchestration of voices and moods which makes Murphy's plays so theatrically poetic was achieved magnificently." Murray [3] observes that "some English reviewers . . . could make sense of it only as allegory, with Mommo as Ireland obsessed with her history." Nightingale saw the London production and found the play "not the most theatrically pulsating of pieces . . . but one written with unerring grace and wit." Walshe [2] sums up general opinion when she states that "*Bailegangaire* remains in print what it was acclaimed at the time of performance: the single most powerful expression in theatre in recent years."

A Thief of a Christmas. 1985. Two acts. Opened at the Abbey Theatre, 30 December. Directed by Roy Heayberd.

Subtitled *The Actuality of How Bailegangaire Came by Its Appellation*, the play essentially dramatizes the story of the laughing competition told by Mommo in *Bailegangaire*. Some reviewers criticized Murphy for losing sight of dramatic shape and coherence: "But the risks are taken in the cause of a fiercely courageous, unblinking vision" (Woodworth).

Too Late for Logic. 1989. Eight scenes. Opened at the Abbey Theatre, 3 October, directed by Patrick Mason.

The work was generally greeted as a major new play by Murphy, albeit a difficult and unsettling one. Nowlan [6] called it "one of his most disturbing, most affecting and most subjective works," adding up to "an important event in Irish theatre." Kingston praised both the "superb production" (a sentiment not shared by O'Toole [1]) and Murphy's "beautifully imagined" scenes, which "ache with feeling and flower into incidents of piercing sadness or absurd laughter." O'Toole [1] saw this "complex, rich and often tormented" and yet "somewhat unsatisfying" play as the work of a writer in transition.

The Patriot Game. 1991. Twenty-four scenes. Originally written as a BBC television play in 1966 but never produced. Opened at the Peacock Theatre, Dublin, 15 May. Directed by Alan Gilsenan. Revived at the Tramway Theatre, Glasgow, 4 September 1991.

Although Dublin's *Evening Press* apparently called this documentary drama about the 1916 Easter Rising "incredibly moving and engaging," general opinion was unfavorable. Gerry Colgan found the play lacking in dramatic or intellectual excitement and the view of the Rising conventional and idealized, although O'Toole ([2], 115) found the script "remarkable for its view of the Rising as a bizarre ritual." Walshe [1] calls the play an "all-time low."

ADDITIONAL PLAYS, ADAPTATIONS, AND PRODUCTIONS

The Vicar of Wakefield, Murphy's adaptation of Goldsmith's novel, was produced at the Abbey Theatre in 1974. In August 1979 Murphy directed J. M. Synge's *The Well of the Saints*; he also wrote and directed the play's companion piece, *Epitaph under Ether*, a compilation based on Synge's life and works (Abbey Theatre, August 1979). Murphy's adaptation of Liam O'Flaherty's novel *The Informer*—"in many ways closer to being an original Murphy play than it is to O'Flaherty" (O'Toole [2], 118)—was staged in 1981 at the Olympia Theatre, Dublin, under Murphy's direction, and at the Actors Theater, Louisville, Kentucky, in April 1982. *She Stoops to Conquer* (Abbey Theatre, 1982) is Murphy's version of Goldsmith's play set in an Irish context.

ASSESSMENT OF MURPHY'S CAREER

Brian Friel has said of Tom Murphy that he is "the most restless, the most obsessive imagination at work in the Irish theatre today" and that what distinguishes him from his comtemporaries is the "pure theatricality" of his language. Murphy himself has stressed that his plays are formed out of a mood, not plot or character, in a tortured process of writing and rewriting (O'Toole [3]). His commitment to theater as performance and to the belief that each play changes as he changes himself means that no work is ever finalized until it reaches the rehearsal stage and that the revision process continues with each new production or publication. The changes to some plays are extensive: for example, the second act of *The White House* was rewritten as a new play, *Conversations on a Homecoming*; *The Sanctuary Lamp* was substantially revised between its two Abbey productions; and the published version of *Too Late for Logic* differed considerably from the Abbey production.

Reviewers of Murphy's early play *A Whistle in the Dark* frequently compared it to Pinter's *The Homecoming*, which it predates. Since then Murphy has more often been likened to Beckett, an influence he denies; he acknowledges an affinity with Tennessee Williams, Synge, and Lorca. With the latter two he shares the creation of a unique theatrical language: torrents of words (leading some critics to remark that his plays are overwritten) that are both startlingly poetic and rooted in contemporary idiom, notably Tuam "lingo" (see Carney). Murphy is a devotee of opera, and the organization of speech in his works is often musical or operatic; Murphy himself speaks of his interest in the "spoken aria" (Boland). Speaking out or singing is connected with the quest to overcome tragedy and despair and attain spiritual wholeness, as is testified by the endings of *A Crucial Week*, *The Gigli Concert*, and *Bailegangaire* and by the central image of the confessional in *The Sanctuary Lamp*. Singing is, in Murphy's words, "yourself alive in time. . . . As somebody said to me, 'Great singing is prayer' " (O'Toole [3]).

Murphy's plays, while not autobiographical in the narrow sense (" 'The play has to transcend me,' " he told Victoria White), are deeply rooted in personal experience. Boland quotes Murphy as saying that " 'all the types and characters in my work have been filtered through people I knew in Tuam.' " The recurring "doubles" in his plays—the two couples in *The Morning after Optimism*, Harry and Francisco in *The Sanctuary Lamp*, the "twins" Michael and Tom in *Conversations on a Homecoming*, Man and King in *The Gigli Concert*, and the brothers Michael and Christopher and their wives Patricia and Cornelia in *Too Late for Logic*—while reflecting the Jungian notion that one integrated personality may be made up of two contradictory halves, may ultimately have their origin in the younger twin brother Murphy invented for himself in his childhood. Likewise, while stressing that John Connor and Mother in *Famine* are not his parents, Murphy admits that some aspects of the play are derived from his early sense of being underprivileged, of being starved of affection and generosity: " 'I felt that famine in the environment of Tuam in the late 1940s and the 1950s' " (O'Toole [3]).

Murphy's themes revolve around the quest for transcendence and spiritual renewal; its realization often involves a leap of faith or a feat of magic—the "possibilizing" of the impossible—as in *The Gigli Concert* when King accomplishes what was initially the Irish Man's desire by singing like Gigli. Murray [3] stresses that the redemptive process is not moral but happens "through human fellowship alone" and has nothing to do with casting off a burden of guilt. In one interview Murphy declared, " 'We're all victims. . . . All my violent characters are people frustrated in love' " (Purcell).

During his career Tom Murphy's plays have focused on societal, institutional, familial, and personal crisis and breakdown against the backdrop of a changing world. *On the Outside, On the Inside*, and *A Crucial Week* reflect the economic stagnation of the 1950s; the socioeconomic changes and the struggle for personal liberation of the 1960s and 1970s form the background to *The Orphans* and *The Sanctuary Lamp*; and the dark side of the materialism and individualism of the past two decades is revealed in such plays as *The Blue Macushla, The Gigli Concert*, and *Too Late for Logic*. In his best work, however, the themes are universal, harking back to Greek tragedy (the Oresteia in *The Sanctuary Lamp*), myth (Orpheus in *Too Late for Logic*, Faust in *The Gigli Concert*), folktale (*Bailegangaire*), or fairy tale (*The Morning after Optimism*); Murphy's most narrowly "Irish" plays (*The Blue Macushla, The J. Arthur Maginnis Story, The Patriot Game*) have been among his least successful.

Tom Murphy has not thus far achieved the international recognition that has time and again been predicted for him. Most commentators explain this by pointing to the uncompromising and demanding nature of his work for audiences, actors, and producers alike (some plays are extremely long; some require a huge cast; *Conversations on a Homecoming* requires one actor to drink seven pints of beer; all plays are emotionally taxing); other critics mention that his plays are obscure and hard to read without the benefit of a performance. In the face of such criticism Murphy has remained defiant: "The risks have sometimes left me with injured legs, but sometimes they've paid off. My motto is, 'If you can do it, why bother?' " (quoted in White).

PRIMARY BIBLIOGRAPHY

Plays

Bailegangaire. Dublin: Gallery Press, 1986.
Conversations on a Homecoming. Dublin: Gallery Press, 1986.
Famine. Dublin: Gallery Press, 1977.
The Fooleen. Dixon, Calif.: Proscenium Press, 1968. Revised as *A Crucial Week in the Life of a Grocer's Assistant*. Dublin: Gallery Press, 1978.
The Gigli Concert. Dublin: Gallery Press, 1984.
The Morning after Optimism. Cork/Dublin: Mercier, 1973.
On the Inside (with *On the Outside*). Dublin: Gallery Press, 1976.
On the Outside (with *On the Inside*). Dublin: Gallery Press, 1976; New ed. Dublin: Gallery Press, 1984.
The Orphans. *The Journal of Irish Literature* 3 (1974): 39–44; Newark, Del.: Proscenium Press, 1974.
The Sanctuary Lamp. Swords: Poolbeg Press, 1976; Rev. ed. Dublin: Gallery Press, 1984.
Too Late for Logic. London: Methuen, 1990.

A Whistle in the Dark. New York: Samuel French, 1970; New ed. Dublin: Gallery Press, 1984; London: Methuen, 1990.

Anthologies

After Tragedy. Three Irish Plays by Tom Murphy. (The Gigli Concert, Bailegangaire, Conversations on a Homecoming.) London: Methuen, 1988.

Plays: One. (Famine, The Patriot Game, The Blue Macushla.) London: Methuen, 1992.

Plays: Two. (Conversations on a Homecoming, Bailegangaire, A Thief of a Christmas.) London: Methuen, 1993.

A Whistle in the Dark and Other Plays. (A Whistle in the Dark, A Crucial Week in the Life of a Grocer's Assistant, On the Outside, On the Inside.) London: Methuen, 1989.

SECONDARY BIBLIOGRAPHY

Barnes, Clive. [1] [Review of *On the Outside/On the Inside*.] *New York Times* (9 Mar. 1976): 27.

————. [2]. " 'A Whistle in the Dark' Opens at the Mercury." *New York Times* (9 Oct. 1969): 55.

Boland, John. "Back to Broad Strokes." *Hibernia* (6 Mar. 1980): 21.

Carney, Jim. "A Conversation on Tom Murphy's Homecoming." *Herald* (Tuam) (7 Dec. 1985): 3.

Coleby, John. Review of [*On the Outside/On the Inside*.] *Drama* 128 (Spring 1978): 81.

Colgan, Gerry. " 'The Patriot Game' at the Peacock." *Irish Times* (16 May 1991): 8.

Corry, John. "Spiritual Refugees." *New York Times* (24 June 1980): 14.

Foley, Donal. "Theme on Family Life." *Irish Times* (8 Oct. 1968): 8.

Friel, Brian. "Exiles." Program Note for *The Blue Macushla*, Abbey Theatre (6 Mar. 1980).

Gillespie, Elgy. [1]. "Elgy Gillespie Talked to Tom Murphy." *Irish Times* (8 Mar. 1980): 14.

————. [2]. "Elgy Gillespie Talks to Tom Murphy about 'The Sanctuary Lamp,' His New Play at the Abbey." *Irish Times* (10 Oct. 1975): 10.

Griffin, Christopher. "Produced, Praised, and Hammered: The Career of Thomas Murphy." *Theatre Ireland* 4 (Sept./Dec. 1983): 17–19.

Gussow, Mel. " 'Morning After' Set in Irish Whimsy." *New York Times* (28 June 1974): 24.

Hadfield, Paul. " 'The Gigli Concert.' " *Theatre Ireland* 5 (1984): 78–80.

Harris, Claudia. "Prize-Winning Play by Murphy." *Irish Literary Supplement* 4.1 (1985): 39.

Irish University Review 17.1 (1987). (A Tom Murphy Special Issue.)

Kellaway, Kate. "Through a Glass, Darkly." *Observer* (12 Jan. 1992).

Kelly, Henry. "Applause for Play by Thomas Murphy." *Irish Times* (22 Mar. 1968): 8.

Kelly, Seamus. [1]. "Bitter Comedy Well Played at the Abbey." *Irish Times* (11 Nov. 1969): 10.

————. [2]. "New Tom Murphy Play at Pavilion." *Irish Times* (10 Nov. 1976): 11.

Kent, Kay. "Festival Faces: Thomas Murphy and Dan O'Herlihy." *Irish Times* (20 Mar. 1972): 10.

Kilroy, Thomas. "Heroes and Villains." *Hibernia* 36.6 (19 Mar. 1971):9.

Kingston, Jeremy. "Too Late for Logic, Abbey, Dublin." *Times* (5 Oct. 1989): 20.

Lewsen, Charles. "An Exile's Return to the Past." *Times* (22 Mar. 1972): 9.

McArdle, Kathy. "Two Murphy Plays about Homecomings." *Irish Literary Supplement* 6.1 (1987): 28.

Meany, Helen. " 'The Gigli Concert' Sets London Critics Singing." *Irish Times* (10 Jan. 1992).

Review of *The Morning After Optimism*. *Variety* (19 May 1971): 76.

"Murphy, Thomas (Bernard)." *Contemporary Literary Criticism* 51 (1989): 299–308.

"Murphy, Thomas (Bernard)." *Contemporary Authors* 101 (1981): 336–37.

Murray, Christopher. [1]. "Coming Home Again." Program Note to *Bailegangaire*, Druid (5 Dec. 1985).

———. [2]. [Review of *Famine, The Gigli Concert*, and *The Sanctuary Lamp*.] *Irish University Review* 14.2 (1984): 280–82.

———. [3]. "Thomas Murphy." *Contemporary Dramatists*. 4th ed. Ed. D. L. Kirkpatrick. Chicago and London: St. James Press, 1988, 391–92.

Nightingale, Benedict. "Shaw Line." *New Statesman* (28 Feb. 1986): 31.

Nowlan, David. [1]. " 'The Blue Macushla' at the Abbey." *Irish Times* (7 Mar. 1980): 10.

———. [2]. "Impressive Revival at Abbey." *Irish Times* (15 July 1971): 10.

———. [3]. " 'Morning after Optimism' at the Abbey." *Irish Times* (16 Mar. 1971): 10.

———. [4]. "Small-Town Ireland Is Theme of Abbey Play." *Irish Times* (21 Mar. 1972): 12.

———. [5]. "Tom Murphy's 'The Sanctuary Lamp' at the Abbey."*Irish Times* (8 Oct. 1975): 10.

———. [6]. " 'Too Late for Logic' at the Abbey Theatre." *Irish Times* (4 Oct. 1989): 12.

O'Toole, Fintan. [1]. "Murphy in the Underworld." *Irish Times* (7 Oct. 1989): Weekend: 5.

———. [2]. *The Politics of Magic: The Work and Times of Tom Murphy*. Dublin: Raven Arts Press, 1988. Exp. and rev. ed. 1994.

———. [3]. "Tribute Portrait: Tom Murphy." *Sunday Tribune* (1 May 1983): 5–6.

Pitman, Jack. [Review of *The Gigli Concert*.] *Variety* 27 (Jan. 1992): 57, 60.

Purcell, Deirdre. "Into the Dark." *Sunday Tribune* (19 Oct. 1986): 17.

Simon, John. "Sodden Old Sod." *New York* (11 Aug. 1986): 56.

"A Terrifying Play." *Times* (12 Sept. 1961): 14.

Tierney, Jim. [Review of *Conversations on a Homecoming*.] *Variety* (9 Mar. 1992): 61.

Walshe, Eibhear. [1]. "The Best and the Worst." *Irish Literary Supplement* 12.1 (1993): 21.

———. [2]. "Tom Murphy's Word-Plays." *Graph* 2 (1987): 5–6.

Wardle, Irving. "Irish Residents and Exiles." *Times* (12 Oct. 1968): 21, 23.

Waters, John. "The Frontiersman." *In Dublin* (15 May 1986): 24–29.

"What's On in the Arts." *Irish Times* (1 Mar. 1971): 12.

Review of *A Whistle in the Dark*. *Variety* (15 Oct. 1969): 64.

Review of *A Whistle in the Dark*. *Time* (17 Oct. 1969): 71.

White, Victoria. "Drama of Music and Madness." *Irish Times* (16 Mar. 1991): Weekend: 5.

Woodworth, Paddy. "The Laughter of the Deprived." *Sunday Independent* (5 Jan. 1986): 15.

T. C. Murray
(1873–1959)

PATRICK BURKE

One aspect of the Irish Literary Revival has received little study: while the world depicted in the acknowledged masterpieces of earlier Irish drama—the best-known work of Synge, O'Casey, Beckett—is often rural in setting and Catholic in ethos, those authors do not themselves originate in, or greatly respect, that world. That artistic interface and the tension implied by it require further study. Precisely because the dramatists referred to enjoy a somewhat intimidating reputation, a larger group of playwrights, who both, for the most part, originate in biographically, and take as raw material artistically, the rural, Catholic, conservative world of pre-1960s Ireland, is less well known, especially outside their country of origin. The principal members of this group are Padraic Colum, Lennox Robinson, Paul Vincent Carroll, and, preeminently, T. C. Murray.

Thomas Cornelius Murray was born in Macroom, County Cork, on 17 January 1873. (When characters in such renowned plays of Murray's as *Maurice Harte, Autumn Fire,* or *Michaelmas Eve* refer to "the town," that can invariably be understood to be Macroom.) In 1891, he won a Queen's Scholarship and went to Dublin to St. Patrick's College, Drumcondra, a training college for national (primary) teachers. At the end of the two-year course, he came back to County Cork in 1893 and taught successively in Carrignavar, Cork City, Carrigtwohill, and, from 1900, in Rathduff, where he was principal teacher. In 1915, partly as a consequence of local clerical disapproval of his *Maurice Harte* (1912), Murray, by then married, with five children, moved to Dublin, to become headmaster of the Model Schools at Inchicore. (That conflict with the clergy may have influenced Murray's pseudonymous *The Serf* of 1920.) He remained there until his retirement in 1932. Murray enjoyed a very distinguished reputation in his own lifetime; at various periods in the 1930s, he was president of the Irish Playwrights' Association, president of the Irish Academy of Letters (which he had joined initially on Yeats' invitation), and director of the Authors' Guild of Ireland. In 1949, the National University of Ireland awarded him an honorary D. Litt. He died on 7 March 1959, at his home in Ballsbridge, Dublin.

Selected Biographical Sources: Maxwell; Weygandt.

MAJOR PLAYS, PREMIERES, AND SIGNIFICANT REVIVALS: THEATRICAL RECEPTION

The Wheel o'Fortune. 1909. First presented by the Cork Dramatic Society at the Dun Theatre in the city on 2 December.

The Dun took its inspiration from visits to Cork in 1907 and 1909 of the Abbey Theatre, which had itself been founded in 1904. Set up in 1909 by the writer Daniel Corkery, a businessman, Tom O'Gorman, and Terence Mac-Swiney (later to be lord mayor of Cork and, in nationalist protest, to die on hunger strike in 1920), An Dun aimed broadly to be for Cork and its writers what the Abbey was to the country as a whole. Presented as part of a triple bill with Corkery's *The Hermit and the King* and *The Lesson of His Life* by S. L. Robinson (later to be better known as Lennox Robinson, playwright and play producer), *The Wheel o'Fortune*, a slightly chilling comedy about an "arranged" marriage, made quite an impact on its Cork audiences and was repeated in later years, though Murray revised it as *Sovereign Love* in 1913 (see later). *The Cork Constitution* (Review of *The Wheel o'Fortune*) was prophetically perceptive: "[O]ne cannot expect perfection at a first attempt. . . . Mr. Murray has done very well. He manages dialogue with considerable skill, and the emotions and feelings he wants to make evident are not to be mistaken."

Birthright. 1910. Murray's first notable claim to prominence as an Irish dramatist came with the two-act *Birthright*, which premiered at the Abbey on 27 October.

It is a play of sibling rivalry, given focus by that most Irish of dramatic concerns, land inheritance. In a reversal of the character patterning so familiar from the Christian parable of the Prodigal Son, *Birthright* presents Hugh Morrissey, the elder of the two sons of Bart and Maura, as fun-loving, athletic, a lover of verse and song, in contrast to his brother, Shane, who is serious, diligent, and careful. Bart's misgivings about Hugh's suitability to replace him as landowner—Hugh's *birthright* as the older son—and his clear preference for Shane, contrasting with Maura's more pronounced emotional closeness to Hugh, pave the way for the powerful climax of *Birthright*, in which, unintentionally, Shane kills Hugh in a fight.

Though quite warmly received in 1910—"[Murray] has given us a work of high merit" (Review of *Birthright, Freemans' Journal*); "Mr. Murray can take his place in the front rank of Abbey Theatre dramatists" (Review of *Birthright, Irish Independent*)—the revised version presented at the Abbey on 16 February 1911 won its author unprecedented critical acclaim. The revision, mainly to the second act, tightened the play's structure and intensified the tragic ending. The *Daily Express* critic's comment, that "it is a vivid picture in which the characters are vividly drawn but yet with a perfect truth," was representative of the response. *Birthright* was part of the program of the first Abbey visit to the United States in 1911, opening at the Plymouth Theatre, Boston, on 23 September. Weygandt cites opinion that it was the "best play new to America" that year, though its starkness initially shocked sentimental Irish-American sensibilities.

Maurice Harte. 1912. For many audiences, prior to *Autumn Fire* in 1924, the most memorable Murray play was *Maurice Harte*, first presented by the Abbey Company at the Royal Court Theatre, London, on 20 June.

Its title character, a student for the Catholic priesthood, confesses to his farming-stock parents in act 1 that he believes he has no vocation. From social embarrassment and what they believe is Maurice's lack of appreciation of the money spent on his education, they prevail on him to continue as a seminarian. He reluctantly agrees, to please them, but has cracked under the nervous pressure by the end of the second act.

Maurice Harte reflects Murray's deep interest in Catholicism; as Weygandt observes, "It is a play at the very heart of Irish Catholic life." The premiere was faulted by some critics on grounds of repetition and theatrical redundancy: "In each act, we are taken through the same series of emotional states in the same order" (Review of *Maurice Harte*). There was general agreement on the power, even the painfulness, of the play's ending, the latter perspective rather amusingly reflected in the diaries of that inveterate Dublin theater first-nighter over a period of forty years, Joseph Holloway (Hogan and O'Neill [1]), when *Maurice Harte* was revived in the Abbey in August 1923: "Sean O'Casey . . . doesn't like Murray's plays because they take too much out of him." Nonetheless, at a revival in the Abbey just a year later (July 1924), Holloway [1] quotes O'Casey as believing "*Maurice Harte* a great play greatly acted." The play formed part of the second Abbey Theatre tour to Boston, New York, and Chicago in 1913.

Sovereign Love. 1913. On 11 November the redrafted *The Wheel o'Fortune* was presented as *Sovereign Love* at the Abbey.

It appeared to work in its stated genre, even if the victory that its plot discomfitingly accords to economic forces over romantic forces, in *one* interpretation of the play's title, reverses classical comic patterns.

A revival of *Sovereign Love*, from 12 to 14 April 1923 at the Abbey, formed part of a double bill with the premiere of O'Casey's *The Shadow of a Gunman*.

Spring. 1918. Murray's next *performed* play was the one-act *Spring*, first produced at the Abbey Theatre on 8 January.

To this day it is a firm favorite with amateur societies in Ireland, regularly winning the one-act sections at drama festivals. Set in 1908, in a "remote bogland" in West Cork, *Spring* focuses on the economic vicissitudes of Seamus and Jude, their seven children, and Andreesh, the father of Seamus, who lives with them. Just when it seems that penury will require the old man to leave the home and end his days in the misery of a workhouse, news breaks that the Liberal government at Westminster (at that time in charge of administration in Ireland) has introduced the Pensions Act and that, as a consequence, Andreesh will have his own independent source of income. The death of Andreesh— probably because, like his prototype, King Lear, his heart ''cracked with joy''— supplies the very moving ending to the play.

The credibility and integrity of Murray's characters, together with the muted poetry of the language he gives them, were recognized immediately: ''The human interest is sustained to the end of a play of fine emotional intensity'' (Review of *Spring*, *The Leader*); ''The players got their audience all right, and, as usual, the Abbey audience became actors too'' (Review of *Spring*, *Evening Herald*).

The Serf. 1920. Premiered at the Abbey 5 October.

Because, no doubt, of its theme—the conflict between one of what the *Irish Times* (Review of *The Serf*) called ''the vast army of aggrieved teachers'' and his tyrannical priest school-manager—Murray's next play, *The Serf*, was presented under a pseudonym, ''Stephen Morgan.''

Aftermath. 1922. Premiered at the Abbey 10 January.

The premiere of *Aftermath*, Murray's next full-length play at the Abbey, marked a number of departures for its author. He moves away—somewhat unsuccessfully, in the opinion of critics such as W. J. Lawrence and Dorothy Macardle—from the rural that which he had so often endowed with a quiet poetry in such plays as *Birthright* and *Spring*, toward a more urbanized, educated speech. *Aftermath*, a better play than the paucity of its revivals suggests, also introduces, by means of the character of Doctor Manning, the element of sexual potency, which Murray was to ambivalently treat in such later plays as *Autumn Fire*, *Michaelmas Eve*, and *Illumination*.

The ''aftermath'' of the play's title derives from the wrong life choices of Myles O'Regan, a young, sensitive teacher, and Grace Sheridan, who should have married each other: instead she marries the middle-aged Doctor Manning. Myles, at his strong mother's behest and, for economic and property motives, marries the decent but intellectually obtuse Mary Hogan. At the end, Myles leaves Mary: ''There's a voice crying to me all hours 'Go! Go!' and I dare not disobey.''

Contemporary response was, in general, very enthusiastic. Frank Hugh O'Donnell (a name forever linked to the controversy attendant on Yeats' *The Countess Cathleen* in 1899) believed that *Aftermath* was ''a greater tragedy than perhaps either that of *Maurice Harte* or *Birthright*'' and that Murray was ''our greatest living Irish dramatist.'' ''Jacques'' [1] followed his positive review with a more considered and very perceptive piece [3], which included the following: ''*Aftermath* is not a great play. It has not the strength and sweeping onwardness of *Birthright*, but it is a splendid example of untheatrical, progressive development in which realism is so natural, and the results so inevitable that we are left almost stunned at the last.''

Negative responses, in the minority, had to do with either what Ervine, himself a playwright, believed was lack of dramatic *force* in *Aftermath* or what the very perceptive Macardle, herself an admirer of Murray, felt was unease in the language: ''*Aftermath,* in which the characters do not use dialect, is the least moving and revealing of his plays.''

Autumn Fire. 1924. Premiered at the Abbey on 8 September.

Autumn Fire is the most enduring of Murray's works, by consensus both critical and popular. A three-acter, it depicts the love of Owen Keegan, a middle-aged, prosperous farmer, for Nance Desmond, less than half his age, and the opposition to that love of Ellen, Keegan's daughter, who feels (correctly, as it happens) that she will lose inheritance rights to Nance, and of Michael, Keegan's son, who loves Nance himself. (It is a notable coincidence that a few months after *Autumn Fire*, Eugene O'Neill was to write *Desire under the Elms*, which has the same theme and character dynamics.) Soon after his marriage to Nance, Keegan is maimed in an accident and is bedridden. Seeing his young wife and son in an embrace that he takes to be quasi-incestuous and adulterous, though, in reality, they are bidding farewell to each other, Owen Keegan banishes his son and faces a dismal future for the life remaining to him, living, as he believes, with a faithless wife and a malicious daughter. The words with which *Autumn Fire* concludes, as Keegan attempts to pray, are some of the best known in Irish drama: ''They've broken me—son, wife, daughter. I've no one now but the Son of God.''

In the light of its subsequent reputation, contemporary critical response to *Autumn Fire* was less than euphoric. Lady Gregory, in her journal entry for 2 March 1924, had noted that the play was ''rather heavy and machine made, but good enough to put on.'' ''Jacques'' [2] commented: ''[T]he general effect is not impressive. One serious fault is a lack of humour.'' (The latter remark is quite unfair to at least the second act of the play.) Mitchell was disappointed by what she believed was an anticlimactic ending.

Joseph Holloway was both enthusiastic and prophetic: ''Murray's great play *Autumn Fire* . . . Murray has written a very strong drama full of effective characterization'' (quoted in Hogan [4]). He was impressed, too, with the acting of Eileen Crowe (an actress who gave over fifty years to the Abbey) as Nance Desmond and with Michael J. Dolan's Owen Keegan, one of the legendary performances in the Irish theater.

Autumn Fire has been often revived, notably in London in April 1926, at the Abbey in May 1926, and in Boston in April 1932; it is surprising, therefore, that, notwithstanding its enduring popularity with Irish amateurs, the play has not been performed professionally in Ireland since 1953—there was a version in Irish in 1973—though, at the time of this writing, the Abbey retains a one-year option on performance rights.

The Pipe in the Fields. 1927. Premiered at the Abbey on 3 October.

This play marked a return by Murray to the one-act format, in which, as in *Spring* and *The Briery Gap*, he had shown himself a master. (Murray dedicated the play to a young nephew, "T. H.," as a play "with a very happy ending.") The central character in this beautifully written piece is Peter Keville, whose status as a figure of both religious and artistic sensibility is imaged in his untutored playing on a fife, given him by a tramp whose "soul had gone into that instrument," of a strange, very beautiful music in harmony with the rhythms of nature. Partly on the advice of a kindly priest, Father Moore, Peter's parents' suspicions are dispelled (they had tried to remove the fife from him), and, unusually in Murray, the play ends happily. In theme, setting, and, in particular, the use of music and, at the ending, of a dancer ("as of a spirit dimly revealed"), *The Pipe in the Fields* shows the influences of Yeats's drama on Murray. Apart from a rather censorious review by J. W. G.—"Had he made it a fine piece of fantasy I think he would have had a better chance"—the play was very well received, occasioning some of the most enthusiastic reviewing ever accorded Murray, of which the *Irish Times* (Review of *The Pipe in the Fields*) was most eloquently representative: "a play that puts the seal on the already established reputation of a notable dramatist. A quickening of the heartbeat, a catching at the throat, a feeling of pleasure that the world is very good—all that, and some indefinable more, was what the people experienced. . . . The happy ending . . . through its natural, easy, simple accomplishment, is perhaps the greatest thing in a piece of dramatic writing that grips from start to finish." There was unanimity among the reviewers on the quality of the acting, especially that of F. J. McCormick as Peter, and of the production by Lennox Robinson.

ADDITIONAL PLAYS, ADAPTATIONS, AND PRODUCTIONS

The remainder of Murray's oeuvre, with one indisputable exception, has not stood the test of time as strenuously as *Birthright, Spring, Autumn Fire,* or *The Pipe in the Fields.* This holds even for such plays as *The Blind Wolf* or *Illumination,* which were enthusiastically received on first production. *The Blind Wolf* (premiered at the Abbey on 30 April 1928) is Murray's unevenly powerful version of the old Hungarian folktale of the old parents, half-crazed with poverty, who kill a wealthy stranger, only to discover in the final act that he is their own long-absent son. (The story is found also in George Lillo's verse play, *Fatal Curiosity* (1736), and, among many other versions in many languages, in an earlier Abbey play, *The Homecoming* by Gertrude Robins, presented in 1913.) *The Blind Wolf* has not been published.

A Flutter of Wings. 1930. This play, Murray's attempt at a suburban comedy, was, in fact, rejected by the Abbey—Murray's first rejection by them and a source of indignation to him and his admirers such as Holloway—and, in the words of Robert Hogan [2], "ill-advisedly snapped up" by the new Gate Theatre in Dublin, where it premiered on 10 November 1930, directed by the young Hilton Edwards.

Michaelmas Eve. 1932. This is the exception referred to earlier. It premiered at the Abbey on 27 June 1932, believed by Yeats, according to Holloway (Hogan and O'Neill [3]), to have been "the best play Murray has written since *Maurice Harte*." Hugh Kearns, a young farm laborer, marries his older employer, Mary Keating, thereby giving precedence to wealth and security over the passion he feels for Moll Garvey, Mary's serving girl, whose strong erotic feelings equal his. As in *Autumn Fire*, the play builds to a powerfully unsettling conclusion: Moll has finally lost Hugh, Hugh is tiring of the overprotective Mary, and Mary will never be sure of the veracity of Moll's claim that Hugh's desire for *her* is still ardent.

Holloway (Hogan and O'Neill [3]), who had attended a reading of the play by Murray in April and formed the conclusion then that "it is one of the most artistic things that Murray has as yet done, if not the most artistic," was highly enthusiastic on opening night: "The dialogue was ever apt and always poetic. . . . The critics were . . . delighted that Murray had come back into his own" (3). D. S., while very impressed with acting levels, expressed dissatisfaction with the ending of the play—"My quarrel with Mr. Murray is that he offers no solution"—and with what he believed was Murray's failure to distinguish between sociological and dramatic truth.

A Spot in the Sun. 1938. This one-act Ibsenite piece in which an overloving husband supports his wife's mistaken estimation as to her creative ability as a novelist, with disastrous results, was given a listlessly acted premiere at the Abbey, on 14 February 1938, directed by Hugh Hunt.

Illumination. 1939. This was Murray's last major play, a kind of reversed *Maurice Harte*, in which Brian Egan, a successful solicitor's son, declines to follow his father's career, opting instead for the ascetic life of a monk in Melleray. It premiered at the Abbey on 31 July 1939 in a production by Lennox Robinson. Because it is a very Catholic play and because its implied Catholic values have themselves been redefined, especially since the Second Vatican Council, *Illumination* is disablingly dated.

The Briery Gap. 1948. Reference has to be made to *The Briery Gap*, which, although published (*Spring* and *Other Plays*) in 1917, having been written in 1914, was not performed until 1948, at the Abbey Experimental Theatre, essentially because it presented a young girl, Joan, pregnant out of wedlock by her lover, Morgan. Faced with clerical condemnation, social stigmatization, and, finally, abandonment by Morgan, Joan, in at least one ending to the play (of which there are three variants), takes her own life. As numerous amateur productions have demonstrated, *The Briery Gap* is a taut one-act in which writing and characterization are as resonant and involving as anything in Murray. It was last staged professionally (at the Abbey) in 1973.

ASSESSMENT OF MURRAY'S CAREER

T. C. Murray was deeply impressed by his reading of Racine (the relationship of *Phèdre* to *Autumn Fire* is transparent) and, in his early years as a national teacher in Cork, by performances by the Frank Benson Company of Shakespeare; *Spring*, directly, and *Birthright*, indirectly, show the influence of *King Lear* and, in the case of the latter, of *The Winter's Tale*; *Aftermath*, of *Hamlet*; and *The Blind Wolf*, of *Macbeth*. From Synge, as Macardle (whose brief assessment of Murray in 1925 is still the most penetrating) has pointed out, Murray learned something "of the power and beauty of . . . English moulded on the Gaelic phrase," notwithstanding his significant differences from, as well as with, the slightly older playwright. The impact of Yeats' *Plays for Dancers* on *The Pipe in the Fields* has been noted, and there is more than a suggestion of Ibsen in the nuancing of psychic conflicts in *Aftermath* (*John Gabriel Borkman*), *A Spot in the Sun* (*A Doll's House*), and *Illumination* (*Ghosts*).

Murray's temperamental gentleness and modesty and his unswerving commitment to an orthodox, if somewhat puritanical, Catholicism did not inhibit him from severely, even captiously, criticizing the first productions of his plays, as Holloway (passim) has pointed out—the costuming in *Birthright* and *Sovereign Love*, the casting of *Aftermath* and *Autumn Fire* (where he was totally wrong about M. J. Dolan's unsuitability as Owen Keegan!), the "lack of subtlety" in the interpretation of *Maurice Harte*. He was critical, too (in general, with artistic astuteness), of his own writing—the rather weak second acts of *Aftermath* and *A Flutter of Wings*, the incompleteness of *A Spot in the Sun*, the superiority to the rest of the third act of *Autumn Fire*.

Essentially, with due allowance for differences of emphasis, language, and tone, Murray's plays consistently rehearse a series of starkly contrasted oppositions and their impact on human destiny. On one hand, there are the powerful presences of passion and eroticism (in *Autumn Fire*, *Michaelmas Eve*, *Maurice Harte*, *Illumination* and *The Briery Gap* [in which it is described as a "madness"]); of the natural world (*Spring*, *The Pipe in the Fields*); of poetry and music (*Birthright*, *Aftermath*, *The Pipe in the Fields*, the first act of *The Blind Wolf*); of ineluctable calling (*Aftermath*, *The Pipe in the Fields*, *Illumination*, the parodic instance of *Maurice Harte*); of the joyful play of human energy (*Birthright*, *Autumn Fire*). Those powerful presences find themselves opposed by philistinism (*Aftermath*, *A Spot in the Sun*); the yearning for untroubled security (*The Briery Gap*, *Michaelmas Eve*); the demands of social conformity (*Maurice Harte*, *The Briery Gap*), or, more insidiously, economic possession (*Maurice Harte*, *Sovereign Love*, *Spring*, *The Blind Wolf*, *Michaelmas Eve*) and land ownership (*Birthright*, *The Briery Gap*, *Aftermath*, *Autumn Fire*, *Michaelmas Eve*). In some plays, the familially crucial figure of the mother moves between these oppositions, an advocate of destructive compromise (Mrs. O'Regan in *Aftermath*, Mrs. Kearns in *Michaelmas Eve*), a figure of supportive wisdom (Mrs. Morrissey in *Birthright*, Mrs. Egan in *Illumination*), or an embodiment of moral myopia (Mrs. Harte). There is corresponding movement of the socially significant priest, either enhancing understanding (Father Moore in *The Pipe in the Fields*) or championing constraint of individuals (Father Coyne in *The Briery Gap*, the unnamed priests of *Autumn Fire*). In one play only, *The Pipe in the Fields*, do the resolutions of conflicts make for unqualified human fulfillment; elsewhere, for the most part, we behold compromise, disappointment, waste, or death, the characters presented as hapless victims of a cold fate or of ungenerous fellow beings. Hogan [4] suggests that "what seriousness and honesty and craft could accomplish, Murray did accomplish; and, when totting him up, it is necessary to define his limitations by the accomplishments of the greatest Irish plays." Maxwell, more enthusiastically, believes that Murray's work possesses "a life beyond its contemporary relevance." The truth, in one view, belongs to Macardle, where she sums up the playwright's achievement: his drama is a "criticism of the life of Ireland"; it is also a "criticism of life."

ARCHIVAL MATERIAL

The following unpublished plays are held in manuscripts and on microfilm in the National Library of Ireland: *The Serf, The Blind Wolf, A Spot in the Sun, Illumination*.

PRIMARY BIBLIOGRAPHY

Aftermath. Dublin: Talbot Press, 1922.
Autumn Fire. London: Allen and Unwin, 1925; Boston and New York: Houghton Mifflin, 1926.
Birthright. Dublin: Maunsel, 1911; rpt., London: Allen and Unwin, 1928.
Birthright (with a brief introduction and biographical note on Murray by D. E. S. Maxwell). Ed. Seamus Deane. *The Field Day Anthology of Irish Writing*. Vol. 2. Derry: Field Day Publications, 1991, 659–74, 717.
The Green Branch. *Dublin Magazine* 15 (July–Sept. 1943).
Maurice Harte. Dublin: Maunsel, 1912.
Maurice Harte (with an introduction to Murray). Ed. Coilin D. Owens and Joan N. Radner. *Irish Drama: 1900–1980*. Washington, D.C.: Catholic University of America Press, 1990, 167–208.
Michaelmas Eve. London: Allen and Unwin, 1932.
The Pipe in the Fields (with *Birthright*). London: Allen and Unwin, 1928.
Spring and Other Plays. (*Sovereign Love* and *The Briery Gap*.) Dublin: Talbot Press, 1917.

SECONDARY BIBLIOGRAPHY

Review of *Birthright*. *Daily Express* (17 Feb. 1911).
Review of *Birthright*. *Freeman's Journal* (28 Oct. 1910).
Review of *Birthright*. *Irish Independent* (28 Oct. 1910).

D. S. [Review of *Michaelmas Eve.*] *Irish Independent* (28 June 1932).

Ervine, St. John. [Review of *Aftermath.*] *Observer* (7 Jan. 1923).

Fitzgibbon, T. G. "The Element of Conflict in the Plays of T. C. Murray." *Studies* 64 (1975): 59–65.

Hogan, Robert, and J. Kilroy. [1]. *The Abbey Theatre: The Years of Synge 1905–1909*. Dublin: Dolmen Press; Atlantic Highlands, N.J.: Humanities Press, 1978.

Hogan, Robert, R. Burnham, and D. P. Poteet. [2]. *The Abbey Theatre: The Rise of the Realists 1910–1915*. Dublin: Dolmen Press; Atlantic Highlands, N.J.: Humanities Press, 1979.

Hogan, Robert, and R. Burnham. [3]. *The Art of the Amateur 1916–1920*. Mountrath, Portlaoise: Dolmen Press; Atlantic Highlands, N.J.: Humanities Press, 1984.

Hogan, Robert, and R. Burnham. [4]. *The Years of O'Casey 1921–1926*. Gerrards Cross, Buckinghamshire: Colin Smythe, 1992.

Hogan, Robert, and M. J. O'Neill eds., [1]. *Joseph Holloway's Abbey Theatre*. Carbondale and Edwardsville: Southern Illinois University Press, 1967.

———. [2]. *Joseph Holloway's Irish Theatre, Volume One, 1926–1931*. Dixon, Calif.: Proscenium Press, 1968.

———. [3]. *Joseph Holloway's Irish Theatre, Volume Two, 1932–1937*. Dixon, Calif.: Proscenium Press, 1969.

———. [4]. *Joseph Holloway's Irish Theatre, Volume Three, 1938–1944*. Dixon, Calif.: Proscenium Press, 1970.

"Jacques." [1]. [Review of *Aftermath.*] *Evening Herald* (11 Jan. 1922).

———. [2]. [Review of *Autumn Fire.*] *Irish Independent* (9 Sept. 1924).

———. [3]. "Music and Drama." *Evening Herald* (14 Jan. 1922).

J. W. G. [Review of *The Pipe in the Fields.*] *Irish Independent* (4 Oct. 1927).

Macardle, Dorothy, "The Dramatic Art of T. C. Murray." *Dublin Magazine* (Jan. 1925): 393–98.

Review of *Maurice Harte. Westminster Gazette* (21 June 1912).

Maxwell, D. E. S. *A Critical History of Modern Irish Drama 1891–1980*. Cambridge: Cambridge University Press, 1984.

Mitchell, Susan. [Review of *Autumn Fire.*] *The Irish Statesman* (13 Sept. 1924).

O'Donnell, Frank Hugh. [Review of *Aftermath.*] *Gael* (16 Jan. 1922).

Ó hAodha, M. "T. C. Murray and Some Critics." *Studies* 47 (1958): 185–91.

Review of *The Pipe in the Fields. Irish Times* (4 Oct. 1927).

Review of *The Serf. Irish Times* (6 Oct. 1920).

Review of *Spring. Evening Herald* (9 Jan. 1918).

Review of *Spring. Leader* (2 Feb. 1918).

Weygandt, C. *Irish Plays and Playwrights*. Boston: Houghton Mifflin, 1913; rpt., Westport, Conn.: Greenwood Press, 1979.

Review of *The Wheel o' Fortune. Cork Constitution* (3 Dec. 1909).

Sean O'Casey
(1880–1964)

BERNICE SCHRANK

Sean O'Casey was born into an Irish Protestant family in Dublin in 1880. Poverty dominated his childhood and early manhood. He went to work at an early age and held many menial, low-paid jobs. In his early twenties, O'Casey committed himself to the nationalist struggle to free Ireland from English domination. Gradually, however, O'Casey was caught up in another process of radicalization. He joined and became increasingly active in the Irish Transport and General Workers Union. The Dublin Lockout and General Strike of 1913 was for him a watershed event during which he came to believe that working-class interests were of paramount importance, and these were not served by Irish nationalism. As a result, O'Casey did not participate in the Easter Rising of 1916. From the period of the Troubles to the establishment of the Irish Free State in 1921, O'Casey's politics moved further leftward. He ultimately embraced communism.

At this time, O'Casey began to write plays, channeling his political energy away from direct action and into creating a politically engaged theater in which to advance his ideological concerns. He was not an instant success. In 1920, his first two efforts, *The Frost in the Flower* (now lost) and *The Harvest Festival* (published posthumously and never produced), were rejected by the Abbey Theatre. Undeterred, during 1922, he submitted to the Abbey three more efforts, *The Seamless Coat of Kathleen* (lost), which the Abbey rejected, *The Crimson and the Tri-Colour* (lost), which the Abbey also rejected, and *The Shadow of a Gunman* (originally entitled *On the Run*), which the Abbey successfully produced in April 1923. O'Casey was now forty-three and still working at menial jobs. In October 1923 the Abbey produced O'Casey's one-act allegory, *Cathleen Listens In*. In March 1924 the Abbey staged *Juno and the Paycock*, and like *Gunman*, it was popular at the box office; indeed, O'Casey's successes rescued the Abbey from near bankruptcy. Based on these successes, O'Casey gave up manual labor and devoted himself to writing. By the autumn of 1924, he had another playlet for the Abbey, *Nannie's Night Out*. Despite the general popularity of his plays, there was some unease that O'Casey was dramatizing a view of Irish life that was unnecessarily sordid. In 1925–1926, he completed *The Plough and the Stars*, his third full-length play, which, with *Gunman* and *Juno*, became known as the "Dublin Trilogy." Taken together, these plays provide a devastating critique of the new nation's public pieties, arguing that Irish nationalism was not merely irrelevant to Dublin's slum dwellers but also dangerous, increasing the toll of death and destruction without any compensatory benefits. With the presentation of *The Plough and the Stars* at the Abbey in February 1926, what had been muted criticism of O'Casey became, on the fourth night, a riot as nationalists tried to prevent the play from being performed.

The opportunity to go to England in 1926 to receive the Hawthornden Prize (for *Juno and the Paycock*) must have seemed a godsend to O'Casey, who regarded the disturbance at *The Plough* as an ill omen of what life in the new Free State was likely to entail for a political and artistic gadfly like himself. The relocation allowed him to participate in the staging of the British premiere of *The Plough and the Stars* and, in the following year, the British premiere of *The Shadow of a Gunman*. During rehearsals for *Gunman*, O'Casey met and fell in love with the young and beautiful actress Eileen Carey, who played the role of Minnie Powell. They were married on 23 September 1927. While enjoying considerable success in London, O'Casey completed a new play, *The Silver Tassie*, which he submitted to the Abbey in 1928. The Abbey directors were not impressed, and the play was rejected. An acrimonious public debate ensued over the merits of the Abbey decision. When the dust settled, the Abbey lost their most promising playwright. More seriously, O'Casey lost a theater and was confirmed in his English exile. His loss was not at first apparent. *The Silver Tassie* found a producer in London, Charles B. Cochran, who spared no expense to stage the play. It was an immediate success.

The onset of the depression created serious financial hardship for O'Casey and his family. To raise money, he sold to Samuel French, Ltd., half the amateur rights to the "Dublin Trilogy." Meanwhile he completed a new play, *Within the Gates*, which was published in 1933 and had an early 1934 production in London. In the autumn of 1934, it opened on Broadway with an impressive cast that included Lillian Gish as the Young Whore, and it was a box office success. When the play was taken to Boston, however, the mayor banned it because of its criticism of religion and its advocacy of sexual fulfillment. In 1938, O'Casey and his family moved to Devon, where they resided until his death. Throughout this period, O'Casey worked on his autobiography and continued to publish volumes intermittently from 1939 until 1954, when the work was completed. The American royalties from the autobiography were an important source of income for O'Casey.

In the 1940s O'Casey wrote a series of works sometimes referred to as his "colored plays," *The Star Turns Red, Purple Dust, Red Roses for Me*, and *Oak Leaves and Lavender*, in which, more explicitly than elsewhere in his drama, he presented the dynamics of change at moments of historical crisis from a socialist perspective. Critical response to these "colored" plays has been largely negative. By the end of the 1940s, with the publication of *Cock-a-Doodle Dandy* (1949), O'Casey moved into his most technically innovative phase. In 1954, he completed *The Bishop's Bonfire*, and in 1955 it opened in Dublin amid another public controversy in which the work was attacked for being anti-Catholic. Early in 1957, O'Casey was in the process of completing *The Drums of Father Ned* when he was invited by the Dublin Tostal [Festival] Council to submit a play to be performed as part of the International Theater Festival to be held the following year in Ireland. O'Casey submitted *Drums*. Before long, it was clear that there was clerical objection to the play. In 1958, it was withdrawn. O'Casey reacted to this new attack on his work by banning all professional productions of his plays in Ireland. The ban was lifted in 1964.

By the 1960s, O'Casey had become a worthy subject of academic scrutiny, particularly in the United States. Two seminal studies in 1960, one by Krause and the other by Hogan [1], were early indications of the kind of scholarly interest that O'Casey's work would increasingly attract. Indeed, that scholarly interest assured the production of several of the later plays. Like *Drums, Behind the Green Curtains* and *Figuro in the Night* had their world premieres at American university theaters. O'Casey died in 1964, assured that his place in the history of twentieth-century drama was secure.

Selected Biographical Sources: Kosok; Krause; Jack Mitchell; Scrimgeour.

MAJOR PLAYS, PREMIERES, AND SIGNIFICANT REVIVALS: THEATRICAL RECEPTION

The Shadow of a Gunman. 1923. Premiered on 12 April 1923 at the Abbey and ran for the last three nights of the season. When the Abbey reopened at the end of August, it was once again staged and proved a great success, playing to capacity houses. It had its English premiere on 27 May 1927 at the Court Theatre, London and ran for 64 performances. The first American production, directed by Whitford Kane at the Kenneth Sawyer Goodman Memorial Theatre, Chicago, opened on 10 April 1929. In Britain there were several important productions, among them the Mermaid Theatre, London, revival in April 1967, directed by, and starring, Jack MacGowran as Seumas Shields, and the Royal Shakespeare Company revival in 1980 at the Other Place, directed by Michael Bogdanov. In 1991, the O'Casey Theater Company performed the play in Newry (Northern Ireland) and then took it on tour in the United States.

The earliest reviews applauded the play's quality. O'Donnell [2] captured the general view: "Not for a very long time has such a good play come our way." The London and Chicago reviewers were less impressed. Critics for the *Daily*

Mail ("Irish Players") and the *Observer* (H[orsnell?]) thought *Gunman* inferior to *Juno* and *Plough*. Donaghey did not think the play was O'Casey at his best.

Cathleen Listens In. 1923. First performed at the Abbey in October 1923, it was revised by O'Casey and revived by the Abbey in 1925. There have been no subsequent revivals.

Reviewers for the *Evening Telegraph* ("Notes and News"), *Freeman's Journal* (McH.), *Evening Herald* (O'Donnell [1]), and *Irish Times* (Prior) all complained that the topical references were hard to follow. Only S[usan] M[itchell] thought it was unnecessary to explain the allusions when the heroine was named Cathleen ni Houlihan (one of the names for Ireland), and the characters included a Free Stater, a Republican, a Farmer, and a Business Man (various factions in postrevolutionary Ireland).

Juno and the Paycock. 1924. *Juno* opened at the Abbey on 3 March 1924 to universal acclaim.

Joseph Holloway [1] thought the play intensely moving and was particularly impressed by the last act. The English premiere was at the Royalty, London, on 16 December 1925. In March 1926, the play transferred to the Fortune. It had a successful run, with over 200 performances, and reviewers were effusive in their praise. The American premiere at the Mayfair, New York on 15 March 1926 was less successful. Woollcott's harsh judgment that the performance was "chaotic, spasmodic and generally destructive" was shared by D. W. B. and Krutch. *Juno* has been one of O'Casey's most popular plays, and scarcely a year goes by without a production of it somewhere. Important later revivals include the Trevor Nunn production at the Aldwych, London, in 1980, with Judi Dench as Juno, and the Joe Dowling production at the Gate, Dublin, in 1986.

Nannie's Night Out. 1924. First performed by the Abbey in 1924 as the afterpiece for Shaw's *Arms and the Man*, there does not appear to have been another production until 1961, when Robert Hogan staged it at the Little Theatre, Lafayette, Indiana. There is no record of a British professional production.

Joseph Holloway [1] complained that the play had too much talk. Buggy suggested that the introduction of tragic realities after a heavy dose of merriment was disconcerting. The reviewer for the *Irish Times* ("New Comedy"), however, found that, despite the comedy, tragedy in the figure of Nannie dominated the play.

The Plough and the Stars. 1926. Opened at the Abbey on 8 February 1926, directed by Lennox Robinson with Barry Fitzgerald as Fluther, F. J. McCormick as Jack Clitheroe, and Shelah Richards as Nora.

Although the first few nights were tranquil, on the fourth night there was an organized disturbance by nationalists offended at what they regarded as O'Casey's hostile presentation of the sacrifices made by the heroes of the Easter Rebellion. Members of the audience mounted the stage to prevent the play from continuing. Barry Fitzgerald was reported to have knocked at least one of the rioters off the stage. The curtain came down for some ten minutes while police were called to restore order. Yeats made a splendid speech in defense of O'Casey but was not heard. Anticipating the problem, he distributed a written copy of it to the newspapers. When order was eventually restored, the play resumed. There were no further disturbances in the theater, although for many weeks after the riot, Dublin newspapers carried articles and letters to the editor, many of them hostile to O'Casey. The riot and the resultant publicity were, however, good for the box office. For a fuller treatment of the riot, see Hunt, Lowery [2], and Hogan and Burnham [2]. Nearly three months after the disturbances in Dublin, *The Plough* had its English premiere at the Fortune Theatre under the direction of J. B. Fagan. Agate [2] found greatness in O'Casey's ability to create realistic characters. Brown [2] praised the play's Shakespearean moments. Ervine heralded O'Casey as an Irish Chekhov. The reviewer for the *London Times* (''Fortune Theatre'') was less impressed and worried about mixing comedy and tragedy. On 28 November 1927, the play opened in New York at the Hudson Theatre with an Irish cast. The reviews were almost exclusively laudatory, ranging from extravagant panegyric (Nathan [1]) to cautious praise (Atkinson [1, 3]). There have been many revivals of the play. Perhaps the most original was at the Abbey in 1991, directed by Garry Hynes in a Brechtian manner. The pace was slow, and the tragic elements of the play overshadowed the comedy. The Dublin critics (Rushe [1], Nowlan and McGarry) applauded Hynes' brilliance.

The Silver Tassie. 1929. Rejected by the Abbey, it opened in London in 1929 at the Apollo Theatre, directed by Raymond Massey.

The setting for the expressionist second act was designed by the artist Augustus John and was universally praised. Charles Laughton starred as Harry Heegan. Besides not being completely credible as an Irish footballer, his voice failed in act 1. He recovered in the final two acts, and, according to Agate [1], ''he laid bare the heart of the play.''

The London critics were nearly unanimous in praising both the play and the production. Brailsford wrote that the production ranked ''among the great events of our generation, perhaps the greatest event since the war.'' Shipp commented that even if the play fell short of perfection, ''in its enormous sweep it can carry a hundred . . . blemishes and yet remain a work of genius.'' Morgan indicated that O'Casey's ''attempt to make his play take wings from naturalistic earth succeeds; we move in a new plane of imagination.'' In 1969, there was a highly regarded revival by the Royal Shakespeare Company at the Aldwych, London. As Wardle astutely noted, in 1928 *The Silver Tassie* was ahead of its time, but by 1969, it spoke to the times. The Irish playwright Hugh Leonard best captured the critical consensus when he commented that the play was muddled and yet profoundly moving, a work of genius that glowed on the stage.

Within the Gates. 1934. Premiered in London at the Royalty Theatre on 7 February 1934 to mixed reviews.

Most critics recognized the difficulties inherent in O'Casey's challenge to the prevailing conventions of stage realism. Some were sympathetic. For example, Grein [1, 2] found the play and the production faultless, heralded its poetic and lyrical qualities, and applauded its abandonment of naturalism. Disher shared Grein's uncritical enthusiasm. For most of the other London critics, the play was a disaster. Agate [4] blamed the style. J. G. B. found "the mixture of poetry, music and realism . . . unendurable as drama." The critic of the *Scotsman* ("London Theatres") dismissed the play as an "odd mixture of symbolism and venom." The play did not survive long in the West End.

It opened in New York at the National Theatre on 22 October 1934 and was an immediate box office success. Atkinson [2, 5] showered verbal confetti over both the play and the production. Nathan [2] found the play an enriching theatrical experience, and Isaacs praised it as poetry's gift to the theater. While these critics applauded the performance, they were equally interested in establishing the play as a successful poetic challenge to the prevailing orthodoxies of stage realism. Critics for whom the a priori benefits of poetic drama were less obvious were somewhat more reserved in their praise. Ruhl, for example, found the production spotty. Whitney thought it was a vastly overrated poetic drama that had some moving moments. John Mason Brown commented that it was a tiresome jumble of muddy symbolism. Young and Alexander complained that it was banal. The play had a successful New York run, closing on 12 January 1935 after 101 performances. After the play was banned in Boston, it reopened in New York for 40 additional performances.

The End of the Beginning. 1937. Premiered at the Abbey in 1937.

Although the audience apparently enjoyed the fun, Holloway [3] was not amused, and none of the reviewers thought much of the play or the production. In 1953, there was a successful London revival at the Unity Theatre. Douglas characterized the play as "sheer exuberance." Harle advised her readers not to miss the show, and the critics for the *Times* ("Unity Theatre") and *Stage* ("The Unity") thought the play delightful.

Pound on Demand. 1939. The first production was in 1939 at the Q Theatre in London, directed by Beatrix Lehmann. It was paired with the other O'Casey playlet written around the same time, *The End of the Beginning*, and a one-acter by Strindberg.

Whereas Brown [1] did not find the spectacle of two sodden workers unable to withdraw money at a post office particularly funny, the reviewer for *Stage* ("The Q") thought the piece extremely diverting. The most successful revival of the play was the Mermaid, London, production in 1967, starring Jack MacGowran, who gave a spectacular performance as a wobbly drunk. According to O'Riordan, this production established the comic potential of the play.

The Star Turns Red. 1940. The play premiered at the Unity Theatre, London.

Reviews were mainly lukewarm, although Agate [3] called it a great play and a "*magnum opus* of compassion." In his last effort as artistic director of the Abbey, Tomás MacAnna, in 1978, revived *Star*. Gus Smith praised MacAnna's attempt to keep O'Casey's late plays in front of Dublin audiences. Chaillet was extremely impressed. Other critics were more cautious. Although many reviewers thought the play distinctly inferior O'Casey, they were taken with the quality of the production and the emotional power of the play. O'Connor advised his readers that both play and production were well worth crossing the Irish Sea to attend. Kelly [2] noted that the play stood up better than most of O'Casey's later works.

Purple Dust. 1943. It premiered at the People's Theatre, Newcastle upon Tyne, on 16 December, directed by Peter Trower. In 1944, it had its American premiere at the Tributary Theatre, Boston, directed by Eliot Duvey. In 1962, it was presented at the Mermaid, London, as part of their O'Casey Festival.

The critics were underwhelmed. D. F. B. called the production "dull and tiresome." Rutherford suggested that the problem with the production was that the play was inadequate. Tynan [2] characterized the play as a "tenuous one-joke jape." In 1973, Tomás MacAnna successfully directed the play at the Lyric, Belfast.

Red Roses for Me. 1943. Shelah Richards directed the world premiere at the Olympia Theatre, Dublin.

The reaction of the Dublin critics was mixed. The reviews in the *Evening Herald* ("*Red Roses for Me*") and the *Irish Independent* (D. S.) were enthusiastic; Fallon and the *Irish Times* ("Olympia Theatre") were disturbed by the play's confusing mixture of styles. The production was a box office success, playing to capacity audiences, with heavy advance booking. The first English production was also in 1943 at the People's Theatre, Newcastle upon Tyne. The first American production was in 1944 at the New England Mutual Hall, Boston, produced by Eliot Duvey and the Tributary Theatre. In 1946, *Red Roses* was revived at the Embassy Theatre in London with an Irish cast under the direction of Ria Mooney. The reviews were generally laudatory. The reviewer for the *London Times* ("New Theatre"), for example, took pleasure in the poetic language. Hope-Wallace wrote that "O'Casey gives his slum-dwellers such a raiment of eloquence that gorgeous notions infect all things both great and small." Trewin [2, 3] likewise praised the splendid sound of the words. The play was so popular that, after some five weeks at the Embassy, the play transferred to a larger theater in Hammersmith (Lyric), and then, six weeks later, it went to the West End. The 1962 production at the Mermaid as part of an O'Casey Festival and the Abbey production directed by Tomás MacAnna in 1967 were less successful.

Oak Leaves and Lavender. 1946. The world premiere was in Sweden. There does not appear to have been a production in either Ireland or the United States.

The English premiere, at the Lyric, Hammersmith, London, in 1947 played to a packed house. By the end of the evening, however, the *Irish Independent* ("London Greets") reported that the enthusiasm of the audience had dampened. It was panned by the critics. Williams, for example, experienced it as "one long blush of embarrassment."

Cock-a-Doodle Dandy. 1949. The play had its world premiere at the People's Theatre, Newcastle upon Tyne, directed by Peter Trower.

Frank Holloway found the production disappointing. More combative than the local reviewer, Kelly [1] angrily denounced the play as a slander on the Irish people. In early 1950, the play premiered in the United States at the Theatre-in-the-Round, Dallas, Texas, codirected by Margo Jones and Jonathan Seymour. In 1959, it was revived at the Royal Court, London, after previews in Newcastle and at the Edinburgh Festival. Most responses ranged from the rhapsodic to the enthusiastic. For example, in *Stage and Television Today*, the reviewer ("Triumph") thought the production dwarfed "every other play now in London in scope of ideas, passionate feeling and imaginative mastery." B[aker] thanked O'Casey for providing a breath of fresh air to liven up the West End. The play had its Abbey premiere in 1977, directed by Tomás MacAnna. Critical opinion was divided. MacAvock disliked the play's crude Mack Sennet slapstick, but Colgan and Finegan [2] were delighted.

Hall of Healing. 1952. The world premiere of *Hall of Healing* was at the Yugoslav-American Hall in New York, directed by Joseph Papirofsky (Joe Papp).

Atkinson [4] could find nothing good to say about it. The following year, the play had its London premiere at the Unity Theatre, directed by David Dawson. The reviews were favorable. Douglas appreciated the didactic quality of the play, which, he felt, effectively dramatized the consequences for the poor of not organizing. Trewin [1] was impressed with the way O'Casey handled the dialogue. The play was first produced at the Abbey in 1966, directed by Tomás MacAnna.

Time to Go. 1952. It was first performed at the Yugoslav-American Hall, New York, directed by Albert Lipton with music by Earl Robinson. On the same bill were two other one-act plays by O'Casey, *Bedtime Story* and *Hall of Healing*.

Atkinson [4] was unenthusiastic. The next year, the play had its London premiere at the Unity Theatre, directed by Ivor Pinkus. The reviewer for the *London Times* ("Unity Theatre") thought the work an excellent comedy in which small-town tradespeople were criticized. The reviewer for *Stage* ("The Unity") noted that the play effectively combined symbol, fantasy, and comedy.

Bedtime Story. 1952. The first production was at the Yugoslav-American Hall, New York, directed by Joseph Papirofsky (Joe Papp). It premiered with two other O'Casey one-acters, *Hall of Healing* and *Time to Go*. In 1972, it was workshopped by the Abbey at the Peacock. There have been two recent London revivals, one in 1985 and another in 1992, directed by Shivaun O'Casey.

The Bishop's Bonfire. 1955. Premiered at the Gaiety Theatre, Dublin, produced by Cyril Cusack and directed by Tyrone Guthrie.

There was great excitement on opening night, since this was the first O'Casey play to have a world premiere in Dublin since the 1937 production of *The End of the Beginning*. Reaction was mixed, and there was a disturbance in the theater as the play ended. Irish reviewers condemned the play. The reviewer for the *Irish Tatler and Sketch* (''Between''), X., and Finegan [1] claimed that, because O'Casey did not live in Ireland, he was ignorant about Ireland. Another persistent complaint was that the play was anticlerical. The Catholic *Standard* led a campaign to discredit the play. English reviewers were far more impressed with the play's achievement. Tynan [1] lauded the play as vintage O'Casey. Wilson praised the play's poetry. Barber appreciated the play as ''an old man's lyrical salute to the sensuous beauty of life.'' It reached the Mermaid (London) in 1961. The production was well received by critics and audience. Shulman's comment was typical: despite an uncertain production, the play, he wrote, ''reveals enough of the great O'Casey to make us grateful that he can still be writing works like this in his middle seventies.'' In 1988, there was an American production at the Lyric Stage, Boston.

The Drums of Father Ned. 1959. The play had its world premiere at the Little Theatre, Lafayette, Indiana, directed by Jeanne Orr and Robert Hogan.

Writing for the *Saturday Review of Literature*, Hewes commented that, if the production did not fully realize the lyricism of the play, it nevertheless succeeded in creating an entertaining theatrical evening. The play had its European premiere at the Queen's Theatre in Hornchurch, Essex, in 1960, directed by David Phethean. In 1966, under the direction of Tomás MacAnna, it was performed in Dublin at the Olympia Theatre. It reached the Abbey in 1985, directed by MacAnna.

When they were not hostile, the Dublin critics were dismissive. Sheridan disposed of the play and production thusly: ''*The Drums of Father Ned* is a classic example of how even the great may fail, and Tomás MacAnna's overplayed and pompous production cannot rescue the diaphanous material.''

Behind the Green Curtains. 1962. The play premiered in December at the Strong Auditorium of the University of Rochester, New York directed by Robert Hogan. In 1975, it had its first Irish production at the Project Arts Centre, Dublin, directed by Frank Murphy.

Rushe [2] found the play a total embarrassment. Martin thought the play interesting but faulted the director for not forging a unity out of the play's divergent styles.

The Moon Shines on Kylenamoe. 1962. The play had its premiere at the Kirby Memorial Theater of Amherst College, Massachusetts. Under the direction of Tomás MacAnna, it was staged at the Peacock Theatre, Dublin in 1975.

Figuro in the Night. 1962. The play premiered on 11 May at the Hofstra Play-house, Hofstra College, New York, directed by Miriam Tulin. In 1975, Tomás MacAnna brought it to the Peacock (Dublin), along with *The Moon Shines on Kylenamoe.*

The Dublin critics were underimpressed. Mac Goris thought the productions entertaining, but MacInerney found both plays "tired, rambling, inchoate things that may most charitably be thought of as unpromising drafts."

ASSESSMENT OF O'CASEY'S CAREER

A popular and pernicious perception of O'Casey's work is that the realistic "Dublin Trilogy" represents the high point of his achievement, and everything after *Plough* is one long, embarrassingly bloated falling away from his initial greatness. Despite its popularity, this view is gradually yielding to a more ac-curate assessment of O'Casey's achievement as a premature practitioner of the art of "total theater." A typical O'Casey play, in fact, combines in varying proportions vaudeville turns, melodramatic discoveries, sentimental song, strange noises, tired clichés, poetic speeches, angry polemics, romantic encoun-ters, circling dancers, flamboyant costumes, and miraculous transformations.

Much recent criticism has exerted itself to show that this inclusivity is as true of O'Casey's early efforts as it is of the later work. Critics have indeed dem-onstrated that even in the three Dublin plays, realism is only one technique among many that O'Casey used (Innes; Kosok; Schrank [2]; Templeton). Klei-man's study of *The Silver Tassie* and *Red Roses for Me* in relation to both the expressionist theater and the theater of the absurd, along with Ayling's analysis [1, 2] of O'Casey's distancing effects, have, moreover, encouraged a view of O'Casey not as a wayward genius who could not control his material but as a theatrical intelligence of the highest order who rejected stage realism in favor of an all-embracing theater to express his profound sense of the palpable richness of life.

While there is growing acceptance of O'Casey's radical reinvention of the stage, there is less willingness to deal with O'Casey's ideological commitments. Krause, for example, stressed O'Casey's affirmative vision, while Hogan [1] emphasizes his technical achievement. Neither specifically addresses the political implications of O'Casey's plays. Other criticism focuses on selected aspects of O'Casey's plays, such things as the types and uses of characters (Benstock, Scrimgeour) or their satirical targets and effects (Bobby Smith). Despite the importance and value of these later studies, their methodologies, like those of the earlier critics, devalue O'Casey's political concerns. The work of Lowery [1], Jack Mitchell, and Schrank [1] takes up directly and unapologetically O'Casey's left-wing politics, but they are lonely voices.

This general reluctance to deal with O'Casey's socialism is unfortunate be-cause it artificially isolates O'Casey's technical achievements from his political concerns. O'Casey's advocacy of life's richness through the techniques of "total theater" is balanced by his recognition that social and political conditions (often conveyed by the intrusive world outside) frequently prevent that richness from being realized. So, in the early plays (from *The Shadow of a Gunman* to *Within the Gates*), O'Casey examines the inadequacy of loving hearts and comic idiosyncracies alone to redirect the forces of history in a manner that addresses the deepest needs of the poor. In the middle plays (from *The Star Turns Red* to *Purple Dust*), O'Casey presents the challenge to entrenched power by inevitable and radical change. In the late plays (from *Cock-a-Doodle Dandy* to *Figuro in the Night*), O'Casey dramatizes the anarchic force of sexuality to subvert and, in some cases, to overthrow the repressive authority of the establishment.

Indeed, O'Casey's entire dramatic output consistently explores both the ways by which society may be transformed and humanized to accommodate the expansive needs of the human spirit and also the reasons such social change is often frustrated. His plays, moreover, encourage audiences to take offense at the unfolding spectacle of disempowerment during which his already economically and politically marginalized characters are overwhelmed by hostile events that are, by and large, not of their making. O'Casey's plays do not, however, offer characters and audience the easy consolation of defeat by immutable forces. Either implicitly or explicitly, O'Casey's plays suggest mechanisms for amelioration, so that the oppressive conditions he dramatizes may be understood, by the audience if not by the characters, as neither necessary nor permanent. In fact, taken as a whole, O'Casey's drama demonstrates that, inherent in the life of his impoverished but resilient characters, there is the possibility for revolutionary change. While their personal weaknesses as well as their objective conditions may delay the realization of that possibility, these circumstances cannot permanently defeat them.

ARCHIVAL SOURCES

Extensive manuscripts are housed in the Berg Collection of the New York Public Library at the 42nd Street Library. Cast lists and reviews are available in the Billy Rose Collection of the New York Public Library. The Theatre Museum, London, has noncirculating, production-related material, including reviews and cast lists of O'Casey's plays, primarily those staged in London. The National Library, Dublin, houses a collection of Abbey cast lists.

PRIMARY BIBLIOGRAPHY

Plays

Behind the Green Curtains. London: Macmillan, 1961.
The Bishop's Bonfire. London: Macmillan, 1955.
Cock-a-Doodle Dandy. London: Macmillan, 1949.

The Drums of Father Ned. London: Macmillan; New York: St. Martin's Press, 1960.
The Harvest Festival: A Play in Three Acts. Introduction by John O'Riordan. New York: New York Public Library, 1979; Gerrards Cross, Buckinghamshire: Colin Smythe, 1980.
Juno and the Paycock. London: Macmillan, 1928.
Oak Leaves and Lavender or A World on Wallpaper. London: Macmillan, 1946.
The Plough and the Stars. London: Macmillan, 1926.
Purple Dust. London: Macmillan, 1940.
Red Roses for Me. London: Macmillan, 1942.
The Silver Tassie. London: Macmillan, 1928.
The Star Turns Red. London: Macmillan, 1940.
Two Plays. (*The Shadow of a Gunman* and *Juno and the Paycock.*) London: Macmillan, 1925.
Within the Gates. London: Macmillan, 1933.

Anthologies

Collected Plays I. (*Juno and the Paycock, The Shadow of a Gunman, The Plough and the Stars, The End of the Beginning, A Pound on Demand.*) London: Macmillan, 1949.
Collected Plays II. (*The Silver Tassie, Within the Gates, The Star Turns Red.*) London: Macmillan, 1949.
Collected Plays III. (*Purple Dust, Red Roses for Me, Hall of Healing.*) London: Macmillan, 1951.
Collected Plays IV. (*Oak Leaves and Lavender, Cock-a-Doodle Dandy, Bedtime Story, Time to Go.*) London: Macmillan, 1951.
The Complete Plays of Sean O'Casey 1. London: Macmillan, 1984. Reissue of *Collected Plays I.*
The Complete Plays of Sean O'Casey 2. London: Macmillan, 1984. Reissue of *Collected Plays II.*
The Complete Plays of Sean O'Casey 3. London: Macmillan, 1984. Reissue of *Collected Plays III.*
The Complete Plays of Sean O'Casey 4. London: Macmillan, 1984. Reissue of *Collected Plays IV.*
The Complete Plays of Sean O'Casey 5. (*The Bishop's Bonfire, The Drums of Father Ned, Behind the Green Curtains, Figuro in the Night, The Moon Shines on Kylenamoe, The Harvest Festival, Kathleen Listens In, Nannie's Night Out.*) London: Macmillan, 1984.
Five Irish Plays. (*Juno and the Paycock, The Shadow of a Gunman, The Plough and the Stars, The End of the Beginning, A Pound on Demand.*) London: Macmillan, 1935.
Five One-Act Plays. (*The End of the Beginning, A Pound on Demand, Hall of Healing, Bedtime Story, Time to Go.*) London: Macmillan, 1958.
Selected Plays of Sean O'Casey. (*The Shadow of a Gunman, Juno and the Paycock, The Plough and the Stars, The Silver Tassie, Within the Gates, Purple Dust, Red Roses for Me, Bedtime Story, Time to Go.*) Introduction by John Gassner. New York: George Braziller, 1954.

Three More Plays. (*The Silver Tassie, Purple Dust, Red Roses for Me.*) London: Macmillan; New York: St. Martin's Press, 1965.

Three Plays. (*Juno and the Paycock, The Shadow of a Gunman, The Plough and the Stars.*) London: Macmillan, 1957.

Essays and Articles on Drama and Theater

Blasts and Benedictions. Selected and Introduced by Ronald Ayling. London, Melbourne, and Toronto: Macmillan; New York: St. Martin's Press, 1967.

Feathers from the Green Crow. Sean O'Casey, 1905–1925. Ed. Robert Hogan. Columbia: University of Missouri Press, 1962.

The Flying Wasp. London: Macmillan, 1937.

The Green Crow. New York: George Braziller, 1956.

Under a Colored Cap. London: Macmillan; New York: St. Martin's Press, 1963.

Windfalls. Stories, Poems and Plays. London: Macmillan, 1934.

SECONDARY BIBLIOGRAPHY

Agate, James. [1]. "Apollo. *The Silver Tassie.*" *London Observer* (13 Oct. 1929): 6.

———. [2]. "Fortune: *The Plough and the Stars.*" *Sunday Times* (16 May 1926): 3.

———. [3]. "A Masterpiece. Unity: *The Star Turns Red*—A Play by Sean O'Casey." *Sunday Times* (17 Mar. 1940): 3.

———. [4]. "Royalty. *Within the Gates.* By Sean O'Casey." *London Observer* (11 Feb. 1934): 6.

Alexander, Leon. "Sean O'Casey Tilts a Dull Lance against Puritanism in Play *Within the Gates.*" *Daily Worker* (New York) (27 Oct. 1934): 5.

Atkinson, Brooks. [1]. "O'Casey and the Irish Players: *The Plough and the Stars.*" *New York Times* (29 Nov. 1927): 30.

———. [2]. "The Play: Fantasy of the Seasons in Hyde Park in Sean O'Casey's *Within the Gates.*" *New York Times* (23 Oct. 1934): 23.

———. [3]. "Sean O'Casey's *The Plough and the Stars* Performed by the Irish Players." *New York Times* (4 Dec. 1927): sec. 10: 1.

———. [4]. "Three New One-Act Plays by Sean O'Casey Put On by an Off-Broadway Group of Actors." *New York Times* (8 May 1952): 35.

———. [5]. "*Within the Gates.* Sean O'Casey's Fantasy of Hyde Park—Drama of Life as They Lead It Out-of-Doors." *New York Times* (28 Oct. 1934): sec. 9: 1.

Ayling, Ronald. [1]. "Character Control and 'Alienation' in *The Plough and the Stars.*" *James Joyce Quarterly* (Fall 1970): 29–47.

———. [2]. *Continuity and Innovation in Sean O'Casey's Drama.* Salzburg: Institute fur Englische Sprache und Literatur; New York: Humanities Press, 1976.

B., D. F. "Mermaid: *Purple Dust.*" *Theatre World* (Sept. 1962): 32.

B., D. W. "Broad Comedy; Stark Realism out of Dublin. O'Casey's Play of *Juno and the Paycock.*" *Boston Evening Transcript* (26 Mar. 1926): 8.

B., J. G. "An Irish Man's General Grouse: Sean O'Casey's Play on a London Park Theme." *London Evening News* (8 Feb. 1934): 9.

B[aker], F. G. "*Cock-a-Doodle Dandy.*" *Plays and Players* (London) (Oct. 1959): 15.

Barber, John. "O'Casey Turns Up with a Shocker." *Daily Express* (1 Mar. 1955): 3.

Benstock, Bernard. *Paycocks and Others*. Dublin: Gill and Macmillan, 1976.

"Between the Acts." *Irish Tatler and Sketch* (Apr. 1955): 66.

Brailsford, H. N. " 'This Was the War': The Ruthless Courage of O'Casey's Great Play of Revolt." *New Leader* (1 Nov. 1929): 8.

Brown, Ivor. [1]. "*Q: A Pound on Demand. The End of the Beginning* by Sean O'Casey." *London Observer* (22 Oct. 1939): 11.

———. [2]. "The Theatre. Stout and Bitter. *The Plough and the Stars* by Sean O'Casey. The Fortune Theatre." *Saturday Review* (22 May 1926): 614–15.

Brown, John Mason. "*Within the Gates*." *New York Post* (23 Oct. 1934): 17.

Buggy, Bertha. "From the Back Seats." *Irish Statesman* (18 Oct. 1924): 8.

Chaillet, Ned. "Sean O'Casey's Train to Revolution. *The Star Turns Red*. Abbey, Dublin." *Times* (8 Feb. 1978).

Colgan, Gerry. "Cockshots." *Hibernia* (19 Aug. 1977): 21.

Disher, Willson M. "A New Sort of Play. Sean O'Casey's Genius. Raw Life." *London Daily Mail* (8 Feb. 1934): 17.

D[onaghey], F[rederick]. "Theatre." *Chicago Daily Tribune* (11 Apr. 1929): 33.

Douglas, Donald. "O'Casey Smashes His Targets." *London Daily Worker* (29 May 1953):2.

E[rvine] St. J[ohn]. "At the Play. *The Plough and the Stars*. By Sean O'Casey." *London Observer* (16 May 1926): 4.

Fallon, Gabriel. "Red, Red Roses." *Dublin Standard* (26 Mar. 1943): 3.

Finegan, John.[1]. "O'Casey Out of Touch." *Evening Herald* (1 Mar. 1955): 6.

———. [2]. " 'Pantomime' by Sean O'Casey." *Evening Herald* (12 Aug. 1977): 7.

"Fortune Theatre: *The Plough and the Stars* by Sean O'Casey." *Times* (14 May 1926): 4.

Grein, J. T. [1]. "The World of the Theatre." *Illustrated London News* (3 Mar. 1934): 320.

———. [2]. "The World of the Theatre." *Illustrated London News* (31 Mar. 1934): 498.

Harle, Eve. "Irish Life on London Stage." *Challenge* (6 June 1953): 2.

Hewes, Henry. "The Green Crow Flies Again." *Saturday Review of Literature* (9 May 1959): 22.

Hogan, Robert [1]. *The Experiments of Sean O'Casey*. New York: St. Martin's Press, 1960.

Hogan, Robert, and Richard Burnham [2]. *The Years of O'Casey, 1921–1926: A Documentary History*. Newark: University of Delaware Press, 1992.

Holloway, Frank. "*Cock-a-Doodle Dandy* Sean O'Casey." *Tyne-side Phoenix* (Newcastle upon Tyne) (Spring 1950): 9–10.

Holloway, Joseph. [1]. *Joseph Holloway's Abbey Theatre*. Ed. Robert Hogan and Michael J. O'Neill. Carbondale and Edwardsville: Southern Illinois University Press; London and Amsterdam: Feffer and Simons, 1967.

———. [2]. *Joseph Holloway's Irish Theatre. Volume One—1926–1931*. Ed. Robert Hogan and Michael J. O'Neill. Dixon, Calif.: Proscenium Press, 1968.

———. [3]. *Joseph Holloway's Irish Theatre. Volume Two—1932–1937*. Ed. Robert Hogan and Michael J. O'Neill. Dixon, Calif.: Proscenium Press, 1969.

———. [4]. *Joseph Holloway's Irish Theatre. Volume Three—1938–1944*. Ed. Robert Hogan and Michael J. O'Neill. Dixon, Calif.: Proscenium Press, 1970.

Hope-Wallace, Philip. "*Red Roses for Me*. Sean O'Casey. Embassy." *Time and Tide* (9 Mar. 1946): 224.

H[orsnell?], H[orace?]. "Court: *The Shadow of a Gunman*, by Sean O'Casey." *London Observer* (29 May 1927): 15.

Hunt, Hugh. *The Abbey: Ireland's National Theatre 1904–1979.* New York: Columbia University Press, 1979.

Innes, Christopher. "The Essential Continuity of Sean O'Casey." *Modern Drama* 33 (1990): 419–33.

"Irish Players Back: Sean O'Casey's Humour and Tragedy." *London Daily Mail* (28 May 1927): 9.

Isaacs, Edith. "Playhouse Gates. Broadway in Review." *Theatre Arts Monthly* (New York) (Dec. 1934): 894–99.

Kelly, Seamus. [1]. "Play to Arouse Anger and Pity." *Irish Times* (14 Dec. 1949): 7.

———. [2]. "*The Star Turns Red* at the Abbey." *Irish Times* (3 Feb. 1978): 9.

Kleiman, Carol. *Sean O'Casey's Bridge of Vision: Four Essays on Structure and Perspective.* Toronto: University of Toronto Press, 1982.

Kosok, Heinz. *O'Casey the Dramatist.* Gerrards Cross, Buckinghamshire: Colin Smythe; Totowa, N.J.: Barnes and Noble, 1985.

Krause, David. *Sean O'Casey: The Man and His Work.* New York: Macmillan, 1960.

Krutch, Joseph Wood. "A Dublin Success." *Nation* (31 Mar. 1926): 348.

Leonard, Hugh. "Aldwych. *The Silver Tassie.*" *Plays and Players* (Nov. 1969): 20–23.

"London Greets New O'Casey Play." *Irish Independent* (14 May 1947): 6.

"London Theatres: *Within the Gates.*" *Scotsman* (8 Feb. 1934): 8.

Lowery, Robert G. [1]. "O'Casey, Critics, and Communism." *Sean O'Casey Review* (Fall 1974): 14–18.

———, ed. [2]. *A Whirlwind in Dublin: "The Plough and the Stars" Riots.* Westport, Conn.: Greenwood Press, 1984.

MacAvock, Desmond. "Slapstick at Its Most Crude. *Cock-a-Doodle Dandy.*" *Evening Press* (12 Aug. 1977): 4.

Mac Goris, Mary. "O'Casey's Funny One-Actors." *Irish Independent* (15 Aug. 1975): 7.

MacInerney, John. "The Later O'Casey Exhumed." *Irish Press* (15 Aug. 1975): 4.

Martin, Augustine. "Play Reviews. *Behind the Green Curtains* at the Project." *Sean O'Casey Review* (Fall 1975): 78–81.

McGarry, Patsy. "Tenement Dublin As We Have Never Seen It." *Irish Press* (8 May 1991): 3.

McH., M. F. "Abbey Theatre: New One-Act Phantasy Produced. A Witty Play." *Freeman's Journal* (2 Oct. 1923): 4.

Mitchell, Jack. *The Essential O'Casey.* New York: International; Berlin: Seven Seas, 1980.

M[itchell], S[usan] L. "Dramatic Notes." *Irish Statesman* (6 Oct. 1923): 122.

Morgan, Charles. "Apollo Theatre. *The Silver Tassie*, a Tragic Comedy by Sean O'Casey." *Times* (12 October 1929): 8.

Nathan, George Jean. [1]. "Judging the Shows." *Judge* (17 Dec. 1927): 18.

———. [2]. "Nathan Digests the Plays. *Within the Gates.*" *American Spectator* (Dec. 1934): 12.

"New Comedy at the Abbey: *Nannie's Night Out.*" *Irish Times* (30 Sep. 1924): 4.

"New Theatre. *Red Roses for Me* by Sean O'Casey." *Times* (29 May 1946): 6.

"Notes and News of Dublin Productions." *Evening Telegraph* (6 Oct. 1923): 4.

Nowlan, David. "Hynes Puts Emphasis on Expressionism. *The Plough and the Stars* at the Abbey Theatre." *Irish Times* (8 May 1991): 8.

O'Connor, Evin. "On This Week at Dublin." *Stage and Television Today* (23 Feb. 1978): 22–23.

O'D[onnell], F[rank] J. H[ugh]. [1]. "*Cathleen Listens In*: Topical Extravaganza at the Abbey Theatre." *Evening Herald* (2 Oct. 1923): 2.

———. [2]. "Treat at the Abbey: *The Shadow of a Gunman*." *Evening Herald* (13 Apr. 1923).

"Olympia Theatre. *Red Roses for Me*." *Irish Times* (16 Mar. 1943).

O'Riordan, John. *A Guide to O'Casey's Plays*. London: Macmillan, 1984.

Prior. "Abbey Theatre: *Cathleen Listens In*." *Irish Times* (2 Oct. 1923): 4.

"The *Q*: One-Act Plays. *A Pound on Demand. The End of the Beginning*." *Stage* (19 Oct. 1939): 8.

"*Red Roses for Me*." *Evening Herald* (16 Mar. 1943): 2.

Ruhl, Arthur. "The Theatres: *Within the Gates* by Sean O'Casey." *New York Herald Tribune* (23 Oct. 1934): 14.

Rushe, Desmond. [1]. "A Mould Breaking Debut of Courage." *Irish Independent* (8 May 1991): 8.

———. [2]. "O'Casey in Decay." *Irish Independent* (23 July 1975): 11.

Rutherford, Malcolm. "Dust to Dust." *Spectator* (24 Aug. 1962): 272.

S., D. "New O'Casey Play." *Irish Independent* (16 Mar. 1943): 2.

Schrank, Bernice. [1]. "Class Acts: Radical Politics and the Plays of Sean O'Casey." *"Standing in Their Shifts Itself . . .": Irish Drama from Farquhar to Friel*. Ed. Eberhard Bort. Bremen: Verlag für E.S.I.S. Publikationen Holger Beyer, 1993, 89–102.

———. [2]. "The Naturalism in O'Casey's Early Plays." *Sean O'Casey Review* 4 (1977): 41–48.

Scrimgeour, James R. *Sean O'Casey*. Boston: Twayne, 1978.

Sheridan, Michael. "Father Ned's Drums Hollow at the Abbey." *Irish Press* (10 May 1985): 4.

Shipp, Horace. "*The Silver Tassie*." *English Review* (Nov. 1929): 639.

Shulman, Milton. "O'Casey in His Seventies: Unquenchable As Ever." *Evening Standard* (27 July 1961): 4.

Smith, Bobby H. *O'Casey's Satiric Vision*. Kent, Ohio: Kent State University Press, 1978.

Smith, Gus. "Abbey Braves the Red Flag." *Sunday Independent* (5 Feb. 1978): 2.

Templeton, Joan. "Sean O'Casey and Expressionism." *Modern Drama* (May 1971): 47–62.

Trewin, J. C. [1]. "Five Plays." *London Observer* (24 May 1953): 11.

———. [2]. "*Red Roses for Me*." *London Observer* (London) (3 Mar. 1946): 2.

———. [3]. "Roses for Sean O'Casey." *John O'London's Weekly* (22 Mar. 1946): 254.

"Triumph of Living Is Celebrated in *Cock-a-Doodle Dandy*." *Stage and Television Today* (18 Sep. 1959): 17.

Tynan, Kenneth. [1]. "Irish Stew." *London Observer* (6 Mar. 1955): 11.

———. [2]. "Theatre: *Purple Dust* (Mermaid)." *London Observer* (19 Aug. 1962).

"Unity Theatre. Sean O'Casey's Short Plays." *Times* (23 May 1953): 8.

"The Unity: Three in a Row." *Stage* (28 May 1953): 9.

Wardle, Irving. "Welcome Revival. Aldwych Theatre: *The Silver Tassie* by Sean O'Casey." *Times* (11 Sep. 1969).

Whitney, John. "Broadway Last Night. Sean O'Casey's *Within the Gates* Is Beautifully Written Play, But—." *Newark Evening News* (23 Oct. 1934): 10.

Williams, Stephen. "Where Land Girls Sing." *Evening News* (14 May 1947): 2.
Wilson, Cecil. "O'Casey Explodes a Stick of Dramatic Dynamite." *Daily Mail* (1 Mar. 1955): 8.
Woollcott, Alexander. "The Stage. The Latest from Dublin." *New York World* (17 Mar. 1926).
X. "Sean O'Casey." *Leader* (12 March 1955): 17–18.
Young, Stark. "Theatre Gates. *Within the Gates* by Sean O'Casey. National Theatre." *New Republic* (7 Nov. 1934): 369.

BIBLIOGRAPHIES

Ayling, Ronald, and Michael J. Durkan. *Sean O'Casey: A Bibliography*. London: Macmillan, 1978.
Mikhail, Edward H. *Sean O'Casey and His Critics: An Annotated Bibliography, 1916–1982*. Metuchen, N.J.; London: Scarecrow Press, 1985.

Seumas O'Kelly

(ca. 1880–1918)

BRENDAN O'GRADY

Seumas O'Kelly was a career journalist, a minor poet, a prominent fictionist, and a respected playwright. As several of O'Kelly's contemporaries and successors in the Irish dramatic movement won international renown for the brilliance of their productions, his own star receded. So short was O'Kelly's celebrity that, in 1929, ten years after the publication of his last play, Morton wrote of him as "a neglected talent." In 1971 Saul [2, 1] was still referring to O'Kelly as "Ireland's most neglected genius" and as "one of the most undervalued—and tragic—figures of the Irish Renaissance." Boyd [1] and Malone [2] were among the theater critics who acknowledged that O'Kelly was a "natural dramatist." O'Kelly's plays, long ignored by many critics and historians, have been saved from oblivion mainly because they have been cherished by a few.

Seumas O'Kelly was born about 1880 (possibly as early as 1875) in Loughhrea, a town in eastern Galway. Edward Martyn lived there in Tulira Castle, Lady Gregory's residence was several miles away at Coole Park, and poets Anthony Raftery and J. J. Callanan were buried nearby. There, O'Kelly's father ran a corn mill and handled grains, and young Seumas immersed himself in the actualities of rural Ireland: poverty, hard labor, gombeenism, agrarian agitation, evictions, the Land War. Fascinated with storytelling, folklore, and animal lore and gifted with an ear sensitive to distinctive dialect and an eye ever alert to local mannerisms, O'Kelly discovered among the lonely people of the Connacht countryside lively emotions and hidden drama. His intimate acquaintance with farmers, fishermen, shopkeepers, tradesmen, and local gentry is reflected in his realistic fiction and peasant plays.

About his twenty-fifth year O'Kelly accepted the editorship of the Skibbereen *Southern Star*, the first in a series of newspaper positions that provided his livelihood and enabled him to pursue his literary ambitions. By 1916 he was editor of the *Leinster Leader* in Naas, County Kildare, and contributor to other publications in England and Ireland. Though he was a competent newspaperman, his large journalistic output was in no way memorable. The best of his creative writings, however, were outstanding; and seventy-five years after it was published, his classic novelette *The Weaver's Grave* continues to be admired. In the dozen years beginning in 1906 O'Kelly composed two full-length novels, two novelettes, four volumes of short stories, a collection of verse, and nine produced plays. Six of those plays were one-acters, one was a two-act drama, and two were three-act dramas.

All the while, O'Kelly was an ardent nationalist who was active in the Gaelic League and the Sinn Fein movements. During his last months he served as deputy editor of *Nationality* in Dublin while Sinn Fein founder Arthur Griffith was under arrest. Unfortunately, after an altercation with a band of rowdy British soldiers who had invaded the newspaper office and caused some damage, O'Kelly suffered a fatal hemorrhage and died on 14 November 1918. Dublin accorded him the funeral of a national hero.

Selected Biographical Sources: Cavanagh; Grennan; Malone [4]; O'Hanlon [1, 2]; Ó hAodha [2]; O'Sullivan [2, 4, 5]; Saul [2].

MAJOR PLAYS, PREMIERES, AND SIGNIFICANT REVIVALS: THEATRICAL RECEPTION

The Matchmakers. 1907. This one-act comedy was first staged on 13 December at the Abbey Theatre, by the Theatre of Ireland, a company of talented, dedicated amateurs.

The play's popularity was immediate and lasting. Actress Mary Walker recalls how a potentially disapproving audience was won over by the hilarity of the piece, and the *Freeman's Journal* (14 December 1907) relates that the house was "kept in continuous outbursts of laughter." A slightly grotesque comedy about a "made marriage," *The Matchmakers'* perennial appeal to amateur theatrical groups accounts for the frequent reprintings of the script. Several years after the auspicious opening performance, O'Kelly was pleased to relate that his little play had been staged in every county of Ireland.

The Stranger. 1908. Under its original title, *The Flame on the Hearth*, this one-act drama was produced by the Theatre of Ireland group at the Abbey Theatre on 14 November and again at the Rotunda on 19 March 1909. Dissatisfied with that version (which was lost), O'Kelly rewrote and retitled the play in 1912. There is no record of a professional production of *The Stranger*.

The plot involves an incident in the dangerous career of Michael Dwyer, the legendary Wicklow insurgent of 1798. The conflict focuses on the family with whom Dwyer seeks refuge while fleeing from his British pursuers: the family's allegiance is divided, and the loyalties of the parents are severely tested. Though the nationalistic theme may be too explicitly presented, O'Kelly's portrayal is evidently based on the known character and views of Michael Dwyer.

The Shuiler's Child. 1909. This drama in two acts was first staged by the Theatre of Ireland players at Dublin's Rotunda, and a year later it was added to the Abbey Theatre's peasant repertoire. In the Irish translation, *Mac na Mna Deirce*, it was produced onstage in May 1913.

The original cast featured Mary Walker and Constance Markievicz and included (under the alias Stephen James) a promising actor-writer named James Stephens. O'Kelly told Mary Walker that his play had been inspired by an incident in Henrik Ibsen's *Brand*. When the play was revived in April 1948 for the Masque Theatre at Ozanam Hall, Dublin, Walker came out of retirement to play the lead. In her view, *The Shuiler's Child* was "undoubtedly the most successful play" presented by the Theatre of Ireland company.

The Shuiler's Child is the O'Kelly play that has best stood the test of time. In 1971 Saul [2] wrote that this play (along with *The Bribe*) established O'Kelly's "real claim to significance as a dramatist." In 1977 Richard Fallis called this play "a fine essay in dramatic realism, melodramatic but effective in its presentation of a poverty-stricken woman's efforts to provide a decent upbringing for her son." Among the play's virtues Fallis lists honesty, sympathy, and "fine command of ordinary speech." In 1982 McHugh and Harmon were still able to speak of "the considerable power" of *The Shuiler's Child*. A. E. Malone [4], in 1930, had gone so far as to predict that this play "should come as near immortality as can be achieved."

The Home-Coming. 1910. The Theatre of Ireland staged this one-act play at Molesworth Hall, Dublin. The playwright himself regarded this drama as a "curtain-raiser," an assessment echoed by G. B. Saul [2], who thought that it was "slight in every way" and labeled it "a triviality" indebted to Lady Gregory's *The Gaol Gate* and William Boyle's *The Building Fund*.

A peasant play, *The Home-Coming* celebrates an elderly woman's restoration to the ancestral cottage and land from which her family had been harshly evicted. Though the theme is dated, and the dialogue is sometimes sentimental, Radió Éireann dramatized this short play on 16 November 1943, the twenty-fifth anniversary of Seumas O'Kelly's death. Gabriel Fallon produced the program, and the cast included Peg Monaghan, Patricia Clancy, Liam Redmond and Robert Mooney. Fine acting aside, O'Kelly's attempt to dramatize the old agrarian grievances is overtly propagandistic.

Lustre. 1913. This stark tragedy in one act is considered to have been a collaborative effort in 1913 (or earlier) between O'Kelly and Count Casimir de Markievicz; however, O'Kelly's literary impress is evident throughout. Production data for *Lustre* are scarce: at least one amateur production was documented in February 1930, and there probably were others; but professional producers for

English audiences seem to have bypassed it, even though translators made it available for the Polish theater and a Russian film.

Set in a simple peasant cabin in the West of Ireland, the action reveals how a crude young Private Soldier in the Connaught Rangers kills his elderly, widowed mother during his mean act of stealing her prized dishes. The realistic setting and characterization, the authentic dialogue, and the symbolic and ironic value of the widow's lusterware are among the strengths of this compressed tragedy. The moving portrayal of peasant poverty and pathos makes *Lustre*, for Saul [2] and others, an "effective," if not an "overwhelming," achievement.

The Bribe. 1913. One of O'Kelly's most successful plays made its debut at the Abbey Theatre, 18 December. Lennox Robinson directed a highly proficient cast in an impressive staging of this three-act drama. The cast included Nora Desmond, Kathleen Drago, Eileen O'Doherty, Fred O'Donovan, and Arthur Sinclair.

The Bribe deals with the tragic consequences of bribery and corruption under the old system of selecting dispensary doctors in a small town. In essence it is a drama of consciences in crisis.

The 1913 production was roundly applauded. Saul [2] cites such diverse publications as *Irish Life, Tuam News, Irish Times, The British Review,* and *Irish News and Belfast Morning News,* all praising O'Kelly's work. *The Stage Year Book* for 1914 designated *The Bribe* "the play of the year." Another enthusiast crowned it "the play of the Abbey."

On the twenty-fifth anniversary of O'Kelly's death, the Abbey Players again presented *The Bribe*. By that time, the administration of medical posts had undergone reforms, and the play had lost its immediacy. The critical response to the drama was, therefore, more reserved. Lennox Robinson [1], though, still called it "a moving and subtle play."

In a 1969 retrospective Grennan declared, "The simple moral symmetries of plot [of *The Bribe*] rob it of all subtlety and in general it is a poor performance." On the other hand, two years earlier, Saul [3] had acclaimed *The Bribe* "a play that will stand with the finest products of the [Irish] Renaissance."

Driftwood. 1915. Annie E. F. Horniman commissioned this one-act society comedy, and Douglas Gordon staged it on 11 October at the Gaiety Theatre in Manchester, and on 10 January 1916 at the Duke of York's Theatre, London.

The *Manchester Guardian* reviewer criticized *Driftwood* for its "talkiness," and *The Stage* was displeased with the dialogue. Saul [2] labeled this effort "clearly second-rate, however successful in production." To some critics O'Kelly seemed to be out of his normal element when he turned from interest in rural themes to domestic discord among suburban sophisticates. However, as Saul [2] indicates, ten reviews in the British press generally approved of the play, and George Bernard Shaw even sent O'Kelly a complimentary letter.

The Parnellite. 1917. On 24 September the Irish National Theatre Society staged this three-act tragedy at the Abbey Theatre. The producer was Fred O'Donovan. In early drafts, the play was entitled *Kilmacshane.*

The Parnellite depicts Stephen O'Moore, ardent supporter of Charles Stewart Parnell's 1881 "No Rent" Manifesto, who returns to his Connacht cabin after eighteen months in prison (for having resisted eviction), only to find that his once-sympathetic neighbors have turned against Parnell because of indiscretion in his personal life, and now they show their wrath by stoning Stephen O'Moore to death. The drama has been seen as an indictment of the anti-Parnell forces in Irish politics.

In 1917 *The Parnellite* still had contemporary significance, not—as for audiences today—mere historical associations. Whether or not O'Kelly's audiences were chafed in conscience, they certainly were concerned about the moral questions behind Parnell's downfall and the political consequences of their desertion of their leader.

Politics in abeyance, the style of the play is uneven and diffuse, the characterization is weak, and the second act (a travesty on the court system) is too farcical. Replete with nationalist symbolism and New Testament parallels, the play borders on overt propaganda. Saul [2] relates that the opening night audience gave the play a "genuine ovation." Reviews in the press, however, were more reserved: The *Irish Times* (25 September), *Irish Life* (28 September), and *Dublin Saturday Post* (29 September) were mainly favorable, while the *Freeman's Journal* (25 September) said the play was "the creation of a novelist rather than a dramatist" and that it needed "a great deal of pruning." A. E. Malone [3], attempting to be both kind and just, assessed *The Parnellite* as "effective rather than thrilling, but much above the average Irish play."

Meadowsweet. 1919. This is the only one-act play by O'Kelly that the Irish National Theatre Society produced at its own Abbey Theatre. Staged 7 October, it was very well received. The play was revived in 1969 at Dublin's Peacock Theatre.

The underlying issue of land acquisition—and the importance the Irish people attach to land ownership—allows room for the essential comedy enacted by four country characters. Traces of satire and grotesquerie blend with farcical actions and witty dialogue, leading critic Saul [2] to assess the play as "a lightly amiable brevity whose 'Kiltaran' lingo happily lacks the exaggeration of Lady Gregory's." Stephen Gwynn praised *Meadowsweet* for its "humour of country life," enriched with O'Kelly's "command of picturesque idiom." At the Dublin Theatre Festival in 1969, Ó hAodha [2] reports, *Meadowsweet* again "delighted audiences."

ASSESSMENT OF O'KELLY'S CAREER

During the pre–World War I phase of the Irish Literary Awakening, more emphasis was placed on drama than on the other genres. At that time, Seumas O'Kelly, who always aspired to be a playwright, was actually better known for his plays than for the works of fiction that posthumously secured his reputation.

As a dramatist, O'Kelly's inventory consisted of nine produced plays. The most meritorious works are the two charming one-act comedies that have retained their value as pleasant entertainments, *The Matchmakers* (his first play) and *Meadowsweet* (his final play); and the two full-length, well-wrought tragedies that effectively dramatize unhappy conditions and concerns in late nineteenth-century Ireland, namely, *The Bribe* and *The Shuiler's Child*. All of these plays (and four others as well) have their setting in rural Ireland.

The Irish theater of O'Kelly's era, as Brenna Katz Clarke explains, gave rise to the subgenre known as the peasant play. Among the writers who established the peasant play's respectability were J. M. Synge, Lady Gregory, and Douglas Hyde. T. C. Murray, Padraic Colum, George Fitzmaurice, and a host of others also wrote plays on peasant themes. As a rural realist, therefore, O'Kelly was in good company. He deserves recognition as an authentic voice of the Irish countryside.

O'Kelly was also a clear voice of Irish nationhood. Patriotic drama flourished in Dublin early in this century, and O'Kelly joined W. B. Yeats, Lady Gregory, Sean O'Casey, and many others who dramatized nationalistic themes. O'Kelly's personal convictions were reflected in at least three of his plays; but whether those convictions were deftly transmuted into fine art is arguable: *The Home-Coming* and *The Stranger* are rather obvious propaganda pieces, and *The Parnellite* is not notably successful as art. Moreover, the political issues raised in these plays have lost the immediacy they had for their original audiences.

In the writing of several one-act plays, O'Kelly was following the trend that prevailed in the Abbey Theatre during its first forty years. From the outset W. B. Yeats, George Russell, George Moore, Lady Gregory, Edward Martyn, and J. M. Synge all composed one-acters. The small stage was, no doubt, a factor; but the short play (like the short story) also appealed to many writers and playgoers. O'Kelly's one-act plays ranged from acceptable to extremely popular. Though he created no masterpieces, O'Kelly proved adept at this demanding art form.

For the modest but solid body of his playwriting, O'Kelly has attained appreciative recognition, but not fame. Time—and the double scrutiny of theatergoers and drama readers—has relegated O'Kelly to the secondary order of Irish playwrights. Though often neglected by critics and literary historians, he has not been entirely forgotten. After all, during his short career, Seumas O'Kelly moved with unassuming dignity among the most celebrated dramatists of the Irish Literary Renaissance and contributed worthily to Dublin's reputation as a great center for drama.

PRIMARY BIBLIOGRAPHY

Plays

The Bribe. Dublin and London: Maunsel, 1914; Dublin: James Duffy, 1952.

Driftwood. Dublin Magazine 1.4 (Sept. 1923): 287–306.

His Father's Son. Sinn Fein (Dublin) (15 Dec. 1906, 5 Jan. 1907, 12 Jan. 1907).

The Home-Coming. Sinn Fein (28 Aug. 1909); *Three Plays*. Dublin: M. H. Gill and Son, 1912; *Waysiders*. Dublin: Talbot, 1917; London: Unwin, n.d.

Lustre (collaboration with Casimir de Markievicz). *Irish Weekly Independent* (Christmas 1920); *Éire-Ireland* 2.4 (Winter 1967): 53–71.

The Matchmakers. Dublin: Talbot, 1908; *Three Plays*. Dublin: M. H. Gill and Son, 1912; Dublin: James Duffy, 1950, 1977.

Meadowsweet. Naas: Leinster Leader, 1919; Dublin: Talbot, 1922.

The Parnellite. Naas: Leinster Leader, 1919.

The Shuiler's Child. Dublin: Maunsel, 1909; Dublin: Oifig Diolta Foillseacain Rialtais, 1913; (Translated into Irish by Miceal Mac Rauidri and Sean Mac Giollarnat, under the title *Mac Na Mna Deirce*.) Chicago: DePaul University, 1971 (Introd. George Brandon Saul).

The Stranger. Three Plays. Dublin: M. H. Gill and Son, 1912.

Anthology

Three Plays by Seumas O'Kelly. (*The Home-Coming, The Matchmakers*, and *The Stranger*.) Dublin: M. H. Gill and Son, 1912.

SECONDARY BIBLIOGRAPHY

Boyd, Ernest A. [1]. *The Contemporary Drama of Ireland*. Dublin: Talbot, 1918; London: Unwin, 1918.

————. [2]. *Ireland's Literary Renaissance*. New York: Knopf, 1922.

Cavanagh, Mary Anne Francis. "The Two Voices of Seumas O'Kelly: A Study of the Man and His Work. Diss., University College, Dublin, 1968.

Clarke, Brenna Katz. *The Emergence of the Irish Peasant Play at the Abbey Theatre*. Ann Arbor: UMI Research Press, 1982.

Colum, Padraic. "Introduction." *The Leprechaun of Kilmeen* by Seumas O'Kelly. Dublin: Gill and Macmillan, 1968.

Cronin, Colm. "Introduction." *Ranns and Ballads* by Seumas O'Kelly. Dun Laoghaire: Seumas O'Kelly Society, 1968.

"Death of Seumas O'Kelly." *Leinster Leader* (16 Nov. 1918).

Fallis, Richard. *The Irish Renaissance*. Syracuse, N.Y.: Syracuse University Press, 1977.

Gregory, Lady Augusta. *Our Irish Theatre*. New York: Putnam's Sons, 1914.

Grennan, Eamon, ed. "Introduction." *A Land of Loneliness and Other Stories* by Seumas O'Kelly. Dublin: Gill and Macmillan, 1969.

Gwynn, Stephen. "Modern Irish Literature." *Manchester Guardian Commercial* (15 March 1923).

Hogan, Robert, and Michael J. O'Neill, eds. [1]. *Joseph Holloway's Abbey Theatre: A Selection from His Unpublished Journal, Impressions of a Dublin Playgoer.* Carbondale: Southern Illinois University Press, 1967.

Hogan, Robert, Richard Burnham, and Daniel P. Poteet. [2]. *The Rise of the Realists 1910–1915. The Modern Irish Drama, a Documentary History.* Vol. 4. Atlantic Heights, N.J.: Humanities Press, 1979.

Hogan, Robert, and James Kilroy. [3]. *The Abbey Theatre: The Years of Synge 1905–1909.* Atlantic Heights, N.J.: Humanities Press, 1978.

Hogan, Robert. [4]. *Lost Plays of the Irish Renaissance.* Newark, Del.: Proscenium Press, 1970.

Hunt, Hugh. *The Abbey, Ireland's National Theatre 1904–1978.* New York: Columbia University Press, 1979.

Kavanagh, Peter. *The Story of the Abbey Theatre.* New York: Devin-Adair, 1950.

Malone, Andrew E. [1]. "The Decline of the Irish Drama." *Dublin Magazine* (May 1924).

———. [2]. *The Irish Drama.* London: Constable, 1929; New York: Benjamin Blom, 1965.

———. [3]. "The Rise of the Realistic Movement." *The Irish Theatre* by Lennox Robinson. New York: Haskell House, 1971.

———. [4]. "Seumas O'Kelly." *Dublin Magazine* (July–Sept. 1930): 39–46.

McHugh, Roger, and Maurice Harmon. *Short History of Anglo-Irish Literature from Its Origins to the Present Day.* Totowa, N.J.: Barnes and Noble, 1982.

Morton, David. "Literature and Life: A Neglected Talent." *Irish Statesman* (31 Aug. 1929).

Ó hAodha, Micheál. [1]. *The Abbey—Then and Now.* Dublin: Abbey Theatre, 1968.

———. [2]. "Seumas O'Kelly: Voice of the Countryside." *Irish Times* (10 Nov. 1978): 10.

———. [3]. *Seumas O'Kelly's The Weaver's Grave, Adapted by M. Ó hAodha; Being Volume 5 of the New Abbey Theatre Series.* Newark, Del.: Proscenium Press, 1984.

O'Hanlon, Aidan. [1]. "Literary Musings: The Man Who Wrote 'Deer-park': Sad Neglect of a Gifted Irish Author." *Irish Independent* (1 Mar. 1947): 4.

———. [2]. "Seumas O'Kelly 1888–1918." *Capuchin* Annual, 1949.

O'Kelly, M. "Preface." *The Parnellite.* Naas: Leinster Leader, 1919.

O'Sullivan, Seumas. [1]. *Essays and Recollections.* Dublin: Talbot, 1944.

———. [2]. "The Late Mr. Seumas O'Kelly." *Leinster Leader* (23 Nov. 1918): 3.

———. [3]. *The Rose and the Bottle and Other Essays.* Dublin: Talbot, 1946.

———. [4]. "Seumas O'Kelly." *Irish Times* (13 Nov. 1943).

———. [5]. "Seumas O'Kelly. His Work and His Personality." *Sunday Independent* (17 Nov. 1918).

Reid, Forrest. *Retrospective Adventures.* London: Faber and Faber, 1942.

Robinson, Lennox. [1]. *Ireland's Abbey Theatre: A History 1899–1951.* Port Washington, N.Y.: Kennikat Press, 1968.

———, ed. [2]. *The Irish Theatre.* New York: Haskell House, 1971.

Saul, George Brandon. [1]. "Introduction." *The Shuiler's Child* by Seumas O'Kelly. Chicago: DePaul University Press, 1971.

———. [2]. *Seumas O'Kelly.* Lewisburg, Pa.: Bucknell University Press, 1971.

————. [3]. "The Verse, Novels and Drama of Seumas O'Kelly." *Éire-Ireland* (Spring 1967): 48–57.

"Seumas O'Kelly." *The Gael*, Literary Supplement (28 Aug. 1922): 3.

Walker, Mary [Maire Nic Shiubhlaigh]. *The Splendid Years*. Dublin: Duffy, 1955.

Stewart Parker
(1941–1988)

CLAUDIA W. HARRIS

Stewart Parker was born 20 October 1941 to George Herbert, a tailor's cutter, and Isabel Lynas Parker. He described his Unionist/Protestant family as "not hardline." The family lived in East Belfast near the shipyards and the aircraft factory and had links to both Harland Wolff and Shorts, where Parker's older brother, George Herbert, still works. Parker claimed that this Sydenham/Bally-macarrett area was good fostering for a writer: "You had to struggle with the place because you were told you were British with an allegiance to a monarch, yet there was a feeling that you were Irish. If you managed to get through it, there was a great advantage to draw from such a background and be able to write British as well as Irish characters. It gave me a wider canvas on which to paint" (Allen). Like most Northern Irish playwrights, Parker's background frequently surfaces in his plays.

The family moved away from this smoggy industrial area to a housing estate in Hollywood when Parker was eight, in part, because he had pleurisy; that disease caused him to miss an entire year of school as well as his Eleven Plus exam. He then attended Ashfield Boys Intermediate School with students who had failed the exam. But Parker's misfortune turned around, because John Malone taught English at Ashfield and introduced the thirteen-year-old Parker to theater; Malone cast Parker as Everyman in the 1955 school play. After grammar school in Hollywood, Parker went to Queen's University to study English and, during his years there, participated in Philip Hobsbaum's Poetry Groups with, among other students, Seamus Heaney, Seamus Deane, James Simmons, Bernard McLaverty, Michael Longley, Derek Mahon, and Paul Muldoon. Parker helped create the literary magazine *Interest* and was active in the Drama Society as a director, writer, and actor, usually playing old men, he said, because of his height and deep voice. He founded the New Stage Club with playwright Bill

Morrison in 1963. At Queen's, Parker completed both a B.A. in English and an M.A. in poetic drama; Hobsbaum supervised his thesis—"The Modern Poet as Dramatist: Some Aspects of Non-Realistic Drama, with Special Reference to Eliot, Yeats, and cummings." Parker the writer was always a scholar as well.

When Parker was nineteen and in his second year at university, his leg became very painful. After he had been on crutches for months with increasing pain, the doctors at the Royal Victoria Hospital diagnosed Ewing's tumor, a type of bone cancer, and amputated his leg.

Frank McGuinness [2] believes that "the wound inflicted played its part in his writing, not in self-pity or cynicism, but in a joyous determination to celebrate sweet life in all its struggles and defeats. The ability to transcend suffering first requires the courage to confront it." Assessing whether Parker's celebrated sunny disposition developed working through this crisis or was always a personality trait is less important than acknowledging that he was renowned for his wry wit, his fun-loving nature, his "Stewartwear," and his refusal to begrudge anyone else's success. To know Parker was almost inevitably to love him. Anyone who did know him recognizes Stewartwear as an apt designation for his personal style: he would show up decked out in a nubby tweed, wide-striped jacket, a jaunty cap, outlandish scarf, gaudy socks, or unusual shoes, or, as he was dressed for the opening of *Pentecost* (1987) in Derry, in a white linen suit, a dapper white hat, and bright red shoes.

After a chance meeting with an American professor in London, Parker was invited to teach at Hamilton College in Utica, New York, and lectured there in English from 1964 to 1967; then from 1967 to 1969 he taught literature and writing at Cornell University. He married actress Kate Ireland in 1964 just before leaving for America. After thoroughly enjoying his five years in America and despite loving scholarly pursuits, he decided, however, to return to Belfast and write full-time; lecturing left little time for writing, although he had certainly honed his own style by teaching writing. He returned to Cornell for several more summer sessions until 1974, when his career began to take hold. While in America, he began writing *Iceberg*, the play that gave him his real start, working on it during 1969 and 1970. *Iceberg* became a major breakthrough and was the first play he liked well enough to keep. But politics as well as art caused him to question teaching as a career path; news reports of the 1969 Belfast riots propelled him home to Northern Ireland. No longer able to remain in America while the headlines screamed—"Flames Engulf Belfast," "Belfast Burns"— and yet not knowing what would be left of the city they loved, Parker and his wife sailed August 1969 aboard the *Queen Elizabeth II*.

In December 1971, Parker was given a bursary of three hundred pounds by the Northern Ireland Arts Council. Many of his radio plays were produced by BBC radio in Belfast. Nonetheless, *Spokesong*, which he began writing while he was living in America, was refused in 1974 both in Belfast and in Edinburgh. The play was a sensation, however, at the Dublin Theatre Festival in 1975 and continued to pay the bills as late as 1987. Parker won the *London Evening*

Standard Award as the most promising playwright of 1976 for *Spokesong*. Glenda Jackson presented the award, 2 February 1977, at a ceremony in London, where Parker made a short speech. The prospect of meeting Glenda Jackson and speaking at such an occasion led Parker to write in a letter, "It's too hysterical for words. I'm trying to pretend that it's going to happen to somebody else, a distant acquaintance. Which is true, in a way." During the decade that followed, he fulfilled the promise that the award recognized.

In 1977, he was awarded a £1,750 bursary from Thames Television to work as playwright in residence at the King's Head and traveled regularly from Belfast to London while writing *Kingdom Come* (1978) for the theater. After moving to Edinburgh in 1978, he did extensive work for television. In 1979, he received the Christopher Ewart-Biggs Memorial Prize of £1,500 for his television play *I'm a Dreamer, Montreal*—given in memory of the British ambassador who was killed by a car bomb to the writer whose "work seems best to embody ideals of greater understanding in England of the real nature of the Irish problem; of showing the sterility of violence; of creating a bond between the countries of the EEC." In 1985, he won the Banff International Television Festival prize. In 1987, he was presented with the Harvey's Irish Theatre Award for *Pentecost* as the year's best play. He and his wife had divorced in 1982. The requirements of his work then caused him to move to London, where he was living with his partner, playwright Lesley Bruce, when he died of cancer 2 November 1988.

Upon his death, Parker's friends established the Stewart Parker Trust to encourage emerging Irish playwrights with an annual award of £7,500 during the period they are deemed most vulnerable—the two years following the first professional production of their initial play. The trustees are Brian Friel, Seamus Heaney, Jennifer Johnston, Frank McGuinness, and Stephen Rea, and the secretary is John Fairleigh, Queen's University, Belfast.

Selected Biographical Sources: Allen; Carty; Lesniak; McGuinness [2]; Purcell; Walsh; letters to Alfred Gingold and Beatrice MacLeod.

MAJOR PLAYS, PREMIERES, AND SIGNIFICANT REVIVALS: THEATRICAL RECEPTION

Spokesong or The Common Wheel. 1975. Opened 6 October at the John Player Theatre, Dublin, for a one-week run during the Dublin Theatre Festival, directed by Michael Heffernan. Produced by the King's Head, opening 13 September 1976 (previews from 7 September) and running to the end of the year, directed by Robert Gillespie. Reopening 16 February 1977 at the Vaudeville Theatre, London, West End. Produced by the Long Wharf Theatre, New Haven, Connecticut, the American Premiere, opening 2 February 1978, directed by Kenneth Frankel and starring John Lithgow. The production reopened 15 March 1979 at the Circle in the Square, New York.

Spokesong, in an extended metaphor, tells the history of Belfast through telling the development of the bicycle—"Spokesong, spokesong / Music of the spheres / How magically it evokes song / Spinning along through the gears. ... Whispering down through the years.'' Parker uses the fact that John Boyd Dunlop reinvented pneumatic tires in his veterinary establishment in Belfast in 1888 and attached them to the newly invented safety cycle. W. Hume of the Belfast Cruisers Cycling Club repeatedly beat English cyclists by using this new tire, thus wiping the smiles off his opponents' faces and ensuring these balloon tires' popularity, especially since Hume opened a factory in Dublin for their manufacture in 1889. *Spokesong or The Common Wheel* spans the years from the opening of a Belfast cycle shop in 1890 to the present development-scheme threat against its existence.

Jimmy Kennedy, who was then well over eighty, wrote the music; he had moved to Ireland because of the tax laws for artists and was famous for "South of the Border," "Harbour Lights," "April in Portugal," and "Red Sails in the Sunset." But he had never written music for a stage play and would not have worked on this one except that in 1974 Parker interviewed him for his music column in the *Irish Times*. Parker published their interview and then "nervously" sent Kennedy the *Spokesong* script. "The lyrics were a joy," says Kennedy, "and it was a special joy to me that they were already written, so all I had to think about was the music" (Morley).

Of the 1975 festival production, Archer says that this "excruciatingly funny" play exceeded his "wildest anticipation," calling it the best play the "festival has to offer" and the "best statement yet made by a playwright of the tragedy of a torn people."

Willox, reporting that the 1976 King's Head production of *Spokesong* broke box office records on the London fringe before moving into the West End and into the awards, predicts that it "could be hailed as the best dramatic work ever to come out of Ulster." Ironically, it was a year before it would be performed in Belfast. Parker expresses amazement that there were virtually no negative reviews: "I think they must be grateful for a laugh, since they have to sit through so many gloomy plays."

A new production by the Irish Theatre Company directed by Patrick Mason opened 13 March 1978 at the Arts Theatre, Belfast; the *Belfast Telegraph* ("Spokesong") reviewer, although claiming not to be particularly "enamoured" by the play, says, "Parker, being the master craftsman that he is, can in turn be very lighthearted and very serious in his treatment of the Ulster problem as the wheels of his bicycles spin the time away." As a first play, *Spokesong* was an amazing phenomenon. A summary of a few openings testifies to its broad appeal: December 1979, Centaur Theatre in Montreal; 13 May 1983, Theatre Gael, Atlanta, Georgia; 7 November 1983, Denver Theatre Center; 17 July 1985, Body Politic, Chicago; 4 February 1986, Old Globe Theatre, San Diego; 14 July 1986, Pasadena Playhouse; 27 June 1989, Rough Magic, Tivoli Theatre, Dublin; 6–30 September 1989, Lyric Theatre, Belfast; September to October 1991, Stage One tour of England.

In fact, by March 1978, less than three years after it opened in Dublin, *Spokesong* was playing in Denmark, Finland, Germany, Australia, Canada, and America. In a 29 January 1977 letter, Parker reports on a November 1976 French version called *Les Rayons Qui Chantent*, which was performed in Brussels by the National Theatre of Belgium, saying, "Alas, it did not set Belgium alight. Possibly a combination of bicycles and urban violence would not appeal to the Belgian national character in any guise, but the contributions of an aged and humourless academic translator and a non-French speaking English director didn't help much. The show was ingenious and slick but almost entirely lacking in reality or coherence, and it quite properly got the thumbs-down. I learnt from the experience!" In 1977, *Cyklernes Sang*, produced by Det Konglelige Teater, played in Copenhagen. Irene Lewis of the Hartford Stage Company competed with Long Wharf for *Spokesong*; Lewis even sent it to the Manhattan Theatre Club, which caused Parker to muse, "I hope this doesn't end with drawn bicycle pumps at dawn."

The reviews of the 1978 Long Wharf production are glowing: Eder calls *Spokesong* "a most funny and piercingly intelligent play," and Barnes labels it a "dazzling play."

Catchpenny Twist. 1977. Opened 25 August at the Peacock Theatre, Dublin, directed by Patrick Laffan. Produced by the Hartford, Connecticut Stage Company, opening 6 October 1978, directed by Irene Lewis. Produced at the King's Head, London, opening 21 February 1980, directed by Robert Gillespie. Produced by Soho Rep., New York, February 1984.

Written with composer Shaun Davey, *Catchpenny Twist*, subtitled *A Charade in Two Acts*, features a songwriting duo—a Protestant composer and a Catholic lyricist—churning out catchpenny songs alternately for loyalist or for republican buddies while hoping for their big break, winning the Euorovision Song Contest. These former teachers find they can't run far enough, fast enough when the warring factions discover their double game. The play hilariously reflects the Parker/Davey creative duo but, according to Parker, also "presupposes some kind of interest in the commercial pop music industry, which turned out to be wholly lacking amongst the critics, who mainly just complained that the band was too loud."

Nowlan [1], of the Peacock production, asserts that since pop music is boring, the play is boring and "fails to convey indifference without being indifferent," although he also acknowledges that the "show bursts with flashes of brilliance."

Writing about the 1980 King's Head production, Peter calls it a "hard, ribald and hilarious little play." Cushman says Parker writes with "smouldering joviality." Billington [1] claims the show has high entertainment value as well as making a crucial point about there being no such word as "apolitical" in Northern Ireland. The off-off-Broadway production at the Soho Rep. New York, February 1984, garnered quite good reviews, as well, in the *New York Post* and the *Village Voice*.

Kingdom Come. 1978. Opened 10 November at the King's Head Theatre, London, directed by Tony Tanner. Opened 10 November 1982 at the Lyric Player's Theatre, Belfast, produced by the Lyric Player's Theatre.

Collaborating again with composer Shaun Davey, Parker bases this musical on the happy accident of the Caribbean island Montserrat, settled in the seventeenth century by an Irish adventurer whose black slaves intermingled with his Irish indentured servants.

Kingdom Come was not well received in London. Shulman [2] asserts that "the Northern Ireland situation stubbornly resists efforts to be amusing, flippant or satirical about it." Billington [2] complains that the whole concept is fundamentally flawed, making "a confusing situation almost wholly impenetrable." Wardle, though, says that if you can put the story out of your head, you can enjoy the songs, which "include some of the wittiest and most agile lyrics I have heard since the last Sondheim." Although kindly lauding the play's whimsical fun, Coveney [1] is not "convinced that the slight dramatic content can justify such a militant punch-line." The negative reviews brought Conor Cruise O'Brien to the rescue; calling the play a tour de force, he says that "to have made great fun out of good sense about Northern Ireland is something which I should have thought impossible."

Nightshade. 1980. Opened 9 October at the Peacock Theatre, Dublin, directed by Chris Parr. Produced by Birmingham Rep., June 1983. Produced by the King's Head, London, February 1984. Produced by Rough Magic, Project Arts Centre, Dublin, opening 2 February 1987, directed by Lynne Parker.

Nightshade features Quinn, the unlikely combination of a professional mortician and amateur magician. The play is a macabre romp that treats coffins like Chinese boxes, family as expendable, sanity as fleeting, grief as avoidable, and death as the ultimate illusion.

The play opened during the same Dublin Theatre Festival as Brian Friel's *Translations*, which made for tough comparisons. In fact, Parker expected the critics to pan the play and prepared a speech for the 10 October 1980 festival press conference. Parker was on the boat to England when his director met the press; Parr read Parker's tribute to the Abbey for "indulging him," then folded the statement and put it in his pocket with the comment: "I won't read the rest of it because he anticipated a very hostile response." Considering *Nightshade*'s subject, the reviews were surprisingly positive. Only Houlihan's comments are wholly negative. Sheridan [1], in an otherwise less than enthusiastic review, ends by saying: "*Nightshade* is to be admired. It is tough on the constitution, but then, so was *Ulysses*." Smith calls it "an extremely clever piece of theatre." McKenna says the play "infiltrates the mind and emotions," becoming a "lively" part of you, and then characterizes it as "a swirl of verbal and visual images, fairy stories, magical tricks and chocolate-box coffins." Nowlan [2] declares the play Parker's best and says it is "a surrealistic amalgam of parable and reality, of the prosaic and the scarcely imaginable, of the comic and of the profoundly sad." Proclaiming the play "a reviewer's nightmare and an audience's delight," Toibin declares *Nightshade* "a mixture of experiment, inventiveness, wit, sheer theatricality, obscure motifs and elements that are deeply moving."

Despite these reviews, *Nightshade* has a troubled history. Although the Dublin production successfully played in the Belfast Festival, a planned Doris Abrahams' production on Broadway fell through the spring of 1980 because of a disagreement between Parker's New York and London agents over British rights to the play. In a 4 June 1980 letter, Parker tells of a luncheon in New York with Abrahams where the play had been discussed as *"a fait accompli"*: "I have learned enough by now to order the most expensive thing on the menu at these luncheons, since the chances are good that that's the extent of what you're going to get. So it turned out." In a 15 December 1981 letter, Parker professes to still be hoping for a London production. Then, 6 June 1983, Parker declares "the first night in Birmingham last Wednesday to be very smooth." Of the King's Head production, he writes, 31 March 1984: "It was done well and a lot of people expressed pleasure to me regarding it, but alas the critics were at best respectful and at worst derisive, and that hurt attendances badly. I'm afraid it's an ill-fated piece. Never mind. Perhaps it'll be rediscovered in a hundred years and proclaimed a masterpiece." Parker refers to *Nightshade* as his fondest play because he suffered most for it and says, "Death in Ireland is part of the farce of life" (Allen).

Pratt's Fall. 1983. Opened January, at the Tron Theatre, Glasgow. Produced by Western Union during the Dublin Theatre Festival, Eblana Theatre, opening 26 September 1983, directed by Patrick Mason.

The play in its simplest form is the 10–minute reverie of geographer Godfrey Dudley as he rehearses his wedding speech and thinks of his bride, Serena Pratt, a travel agent who lost a party of chartered accountants to the headhunters.

In a 30 November 1982 letter, Parker describes the difficulties of working with small companies like Tron: "The theatre is an 18th Century church building which has been adapted and is a very good space indeed for the show, but the people running it are well-intentioned novices, clueless about the nuts and bolts of actually doing plays."

The Dublin production, however, also had many strikes against it. Unlike the Tron, the Eblana Theatre in the basement of the bus station was a thoroughly unsatisfactory space for the play—small but dead acoustically. Hard to hear, the actors conveyed confusion about what they were doing and why. Nowlan [8] clearly doesn't like the play, saying it is "too intellectually discursive to provide emotional satisfaction in the personal struggle between George and Victoria," but then Nowlan makes it seem quite appealing by calling it a "cross between a West-End comedy, a sub-Wildean conversation, and a minor Shavian dissertation." Inventive as usual, Parker certainly gave more in this instance than the productions gave back.

Northern Star. 1984. Opened 7 November at the Lyric Player's Theatre, Belfast, directed by Peter Farago. Revived for the Dublin Theatre Festival, opening 24 September 1985 at the Olympia.

Northern Star begins with the downfall of the 1798 Uprising and then, in a series of flashbacks, explains what led up to its failure through telling the story of Henry Joy McCracken, the Presbyterian Ulsterman who led the Republican uprising.

Nearly everyone associated with the Lyric, which commissioned the play, from the poet John Hewitt to Ciaran McKeown, anticipated that *Northern Star* would make a political difference in Northern Ireland because it would show a time when Catholics and Protestants worked together for reform. Although Parker was somewhat bemused by these expectations, he was nonetheless pleased with the reaction to the play; as he writes, 13 December 1984, "I was embroiled in the usual neuroses of getting a new play on, but I'm glad to say it was all worth it this time. *Northern Star* has had the warmest reception of all my work in Ireland. Which was especially gratifying since it was the first one ever to be premiered in Belfast . . . the show engendered real political controversy and debate and was extremely well attended."

O'Toole [2] declares that "there is no past tense in Irish history" and heralds "wry, tough-minded, funny" *Northern Star* as "the best new Irish play of 1984." Bell, saying the play is "lyrical" and "alive with humour," explains that "tribalism, superstition, catalogues of atrocities and counter-atrocities haunt the play, just as they do our society"; however, she wonders if the introspective quality of the play explains the audience's "understated response." Nowlan [4], declaring the play Parker's best, says, "Seldom has Irish history been so provocatively or so entertainingly drawn on the stage." Reviewing the revival for the Dublin Festival, Nowlan [5] says the play is "as cynically, as realistically and as sorrowfully true a picture of Irish political history as has ever been seen on the stage." Cropper [1] claims Parker provides "exactly the right mirror in which to reflect the agony of 18th-century Ireland" and finds "the perfect technique for his purpose." William A. Henry III, in a *Time Magazine* report on the festival, says that "this ambitious and risky pastiche spoke with mounting power" and identifies the play as "the high point of the festival."

Heavenly Bodies. 1986. Opened 21 April at the Birmingham Repertory Theatre, directed by Peter Farago.

Heavenly Bodies begins with the death of Queen Victoria's favorite playwright, Dion Boucicault (1820–1890), and then, through speeded-up flashbacks, shows the story of this Irishman's fall.

The reviews are largely negative. The *What's On* critique is one of the more positive: "Parker's script is often excellent; poignant and brash by turns, laced with many powerful, stark images and emotional strength and yet equally adept at fluent burlesque as mood and expression demands. Unfortunately, while sharp, little actually draws blood and one remains impressed but largely unmoved." One review refers to it as a "prolonged tedious tale," and another, as a three-hour piece that "contains too much of everything." Cropper [1] says the "piece lacks both affective distance and historical resonance" and is "self-conscious and rather flat." Peter claims it is "more fun to lead that sort of life than to read about it"—or to see it performed, apparently. Parker rewrote and shortened the play in preparation for its publication.

Pentecost. 1987. Opened 23 September at the Guildhall, Derry, produced and toured by Field Day Theatre Company, directed by Patrick Mason. Produced by Tricycle Theatre Company at the Lyric Hammersmith Studio, London, January 1989, directed by Nicolas Kent. Produced by the Round House Theatre, Washington, D.C., October 1992. Produced and toured by Tinderbox, November 1994. Produced by Rough Magic, Dublin, October 1995, directed by Lynne Parker.

Pentecost takes place during the Ulster Workers Council strike in 1974 and the fall of the power-sharing executive; the setting is a derelict, terraced house where four diverse people collect to escape the chaos of Belfast.

In a 30 October 1987 letter, Parker writes accurately that the play received "terrific notices and a full-throated audience response." Holland [1] says, "Of all his plays, this is the most intimate and the most daring in the way he articulates a hope for spiritual regeneration through personal grace." Keyes finds that "the richness and complexity of Stewart Parker's language create a vivid dramatic experience." O'Toole [3] gives the most cautious assessment, saying Parker doesn't quite manage to find the transcendence he's seeking. But Rushe says it is "Parker's best play to date," and Downey says it "shows Mr. Parker at his best." Moloney finds in it a rare "message of hope" for Northern Ireland. Nowlan [6] finds the play "works on all levels: comic, touching and truthful" and says [7] that the play "is the richest and deepest drama yet to come from this ever-intelligent and entertaining playwright." Coyle [2] believes, based on this play, that Parker "is at the peak of his considerable talents when writing for the theatre." The London production mounted soon after Parker's death was also reviewed favorably: Billington [3] calls it a "Belfast Heartbreak House"; Kemp says it is "grippingly close" to reality; Kingston finds Parker's "dialogue, tense, passionate or witty, commands belief."

ADDITIONAL PLAYS, ADAPTATIONS, AND PRODUCTIONS

An early project of Parker's was editing and seeing to the publication of fellow Ballymacarrett playwright Sam Thompson's play *Over the Bridge* (1960) in December 1970; Thompson had died 15 February 1965. Parker credits working-class Thompson with being the first to give a shattering reflection of the Protestant "lost tribe." In his introduction to this influential, controversial play about the shipyards, Parker compares the play in its commonsense decency to *Everyman* and explains: "In Northern Ireland we have neither religion nor politics, but only a kind of fog of religi-otics which seeps in everywhere. To be a writer is to be a public figure, up there in the trenches with the captains and the clergymen."

When Parker returned to Belfast in 1969, he decided to write anything anyone would pay him to write. So he wrote scripts for school broadcasts, reviews, interviews, documentaries; he even wrote pamphlets on milk marketing and egg production.

Iceberg was produced as a radio play for BBC Belfast, directed by Robert Cooper and broadcast January 1975. However, before that, it was given a staged reading at Cornell University, 5 August 1974. The play was performed for the university's Sunday Circus in the black-box Drummond Theatre.

I'm a Dreamer Montreal was commissioned by BBC radio April 1975, and even though Parker says it was interesting enough work, he writes in a 22 February 1976 letter: "I'm finding it unabsorbing because my mind keeps straining at the leash to get into another stage play."

Parker's first television play, *Private Grounds*, was broadcast 21 November 1975. The play is about an Ulster family picnic and, as Parker says, "could be described as a comedy, but it does reflect some of the tension and fear in present day Ulster society."

The Kamikaze Ground Staff Reunion Dinner was broadcast on BBC radio, Edinburgh, 16 December 1979 and on BBC television in 1981. The play is set in 1980, when, at the yearly reunion dinner, Kamiwashi declares the unthinkable—the real heroes were the kamikaze pilots who came home again.

Parker's *The Traveller*, a radio play broadcast in 1985, is an 80–minute study of a travel writer having a slow breakdown on a nightmare trip around Britain and may have some relationship to his own mad dashing around Britain.

ASSESSMENT OF PARKER'S CAREER

When dealing with a sadly foreshortened career like Stewart Parker's, the temptation is to concentrate on the work lost rather than the work achieved. Yes, the honesty, riskiness, and excellence of his plays do heighten the sense of loss over the Irish epic Parker planned in collaboration with Trevor Nunn or the nineteenth-century Irish western set in Donegal and Connaught or all the other projects, for that matter, that can be only imperfectly imagined. But during a professional writing career spanning less than twenty years, Parker wrote and saw produced eight full-length plays, three short plays, including *Iceberg*, eight television plays, a six-part television series, ten radio plays, a ten-episode adaptation of a novel for radio, and, at the very least, two radio documentaries. He published three collections of poetry and one book of children's stories and wrote at least one novel. To this list must be added his published criticism, articles, reviews, interviews, prefaces, and program notes; his unpublished M.A. thesis; and his radio and television interviews, reviews, and arts commentary. Seen as a whole, the volume of work makes "prolific" seem an inadequate description; and, in addition, the consistently high quality of the work makes Kennedy's [3] classification of Parker as a "major-league" or "first-division" writer seem apt: "Anyone who knew him can vouch for the fact that he was brimming with the best sort of paradoxes: a first-division writer who steadfastly refused to project himself as a first-division writer, and who ceaselessly pushed his work into new territories; a ferociously disciplined and focused worker who nonetheless did not allow his work to stand as a barrier between himself and the rest of the world; a very private man who took a genuine, unselfish delight in people, and who considered friendship to be one of the truly great pleasures of life.''

Parker would, no doubt, argue with Kennedy's phrase "ferociously disciplined and focused worker.'' Although Parker was truly collaborative, thriving in creative surroundings and sincerely enjoying what actors and directors brought to his work, he also discusses freely the blind panic he felt each time he was faced with that awesome piece of blank white paper and asked himself, How do you write a play? When a writer is as prolific as Parker, the temptation is to assume the work came easily. Nevertheless, Parker knew his procrastination was not laziness: "There's the awful knowledge that no matter what you write, it's going to be a million miles from what you've intended. You know it's going to disappoint you. As long as you don't write anything, it's going to be great'' (Purcell). Despite Parker's understandable writer's fears, Kennedy's assessment stands, because, once Parker got past that blank page, he would work tirelessly to learn, to adapt, to revise. When a critic said the title was the best thing about *The Kamikaze Ground Staff Reunion Dinner*, Parker's response was not anger but a determination to concentrate on writing better plays and not worrying so much about their titles. The temptation is to believe someone as modest and self-deprecating as Parker. For instance, he claimed that lyrics "are what I write on the back of a cigarette packet when I go to bed. I do them for relaxation.'' But Shaun Davey, who was his composer for *Catchpenny Twist* and *Kingdom Come*, asserts that Parker's "lyrics contain all the deftness and playful invention of the great American songwriters.'' When a writer was as genuinely liked and admired as Parker, the temptation is to dismiss the praise as somehow tainted by his early death. Although Kennedy's earlier statement was published the year after his death, the following statement was published nearly two years before his death and before he was even ill. If anything, this earlier assessment of Parker's work is even stronger than Kennedy's later one: "Stewart Parker is one of the most intrepid writers to have emerged from this island in the past fifteen years. Never content with resting on his considerable laurels, he is that rare breed of playwright who has successfully resisted being pigeon-holed, and has therefore produced a formidable body of work which is as diverse as it is challenging and inventive'' (Kennedy [1]).

In his drama, Parker brilliantly uses such happenstance as the Irish-influenced Montserrat or the invention of the pneumatic tire in Belfast or the sinking of the unsinkable *Titanic* as opportunities to address his real concerns with injustice and hypocrisy. That Parker uses comedy and music to explore life and death issues is often misunderstood outside Ireland. But music, according to Mc-Guinness [2], offers Parker "the power to analyse and illuminate the complexities of division in Irish history''; Parker's lyrics then are often most revealing of his artistic aims. His multifaceted style, as Andrews [1] points out, also makes Parker's work universal: "Parker's is an adventurous, flexible, ambitious talent. It travels well—from one country to another, from one medium to another. His success rests on that rare combination of popularity and integrity, and an exciting experimentalism." Claiming that educating in an entertaining way is the primary goal of drama, Parker constantly plays with both language and situations. Always a strong advocate of fun, Parker believes that for the word "drama" should be substituted the word "play": "Play is how we test the world and register its realities. Play is how we experiment, imagine, invent, and move forward. Play is above all how we enjoy the earth and celebrate our life upon it" (*Dramatis Personae*). As Carty says, "Playing with effects is as important to Parker as anything he has to say: his theatre is a brilliantly inspired blend of form and content."

Never easy on either his audience or his culture, Parker demonstrates with his highly entertaining but challenging work just how adventurous an artist and commentator he is. Often referred to as the Irish Tom Stoppard, Parker is, without doubt, the most consistently experimental contemporary Irish playwright. Heaney supports this assessment: "On the one hand, he had a sure grip on the folk wisdom and collective life of his hometown and a natural sense of the northern downbeat. On the other hand, as if to complement this indigenous streak, he made himself into a writer with a developed experimental attitude. There was always an edge of risk in his work, a chance deliberately taken in the treatment. And this was all of a piece with his fine inclination to keep displacing himself from every easy option and predictable move." Seeing himself as a poet, Parker explores in his M.A. thesis his belief that the poet has a special claim on the theater: "If every great poet is not a dramatist, every great dramatist is, in the broadest sense, a poet." Calling realism a spectrum and naturalism the dominant theatrical convention of the present age, Parker instead focuses on playwrights who deliberately violate "the first premise of the convention—that the audience should be as convinced as possible that what it is witnessing is actuality, not artifice." As if mapping a strategy for his own later work, Parker professes interest in playwrights who not only do not conceal artifice but also use techniques that make artifice "part of the play's whole meaning. These techniques—like verse, the use of masks, the use of actors as symbols rather than flesh-and-blood people, the introduction of dreams or imagined events into the play's narrative—are essentially as old as drama itself." In this early analysis of poetic drama are the seeds of Parker's dramatic techniques: ghosts, white-face, magic, verse, lyrics, music, history, myth—all the aspects of artifice that he exploits with such verve.

His sense of the central place for the poetic Parker carries with him into his work for the theater. Beatrice MacLeod, theater critic for the *Ithaca Journal* and Parker's landlady when he taught at Cornell, describes her visit to Parker's

Putney home when, for the first time, she saw videos of his television work: "My feeling about that evening was an awareness of a burgeoning creativity which I couldn't keep up with. So vivid and so full of his passion was each piece of work that I didn't think of them as separate works. Everything I saw was exciting and attached to Stewart; his work came out of him, the Stewart that I knew. He wanted very much to have me see these things, and I as a critic was absent completely. I had no way of looking at a piece of work which I should make a judgment on. I was just experiencing a wonderful night of revelation that he was a poet of the theatre, that I was privileged to know him." Parker was a playwright because he had something to say and because he possessed rare dramatic skills with which to say it. He welcomed acute assessment; he valued critical insight; he was a scholar as well as an artist.

Since Parker wrote persuasively about what theater could and should do, looking at *Dramatis Personae*, where he lays out his dramatic theory, provides a helpful gloss on his own work. Unlike some of his countrymen, Parker never claims to be apolitical: "Art amplifies and distorts, seeking to alter perceptions to a purpose. A play which reinforces complacent assumptions, which confirms lazy preconceptions, which fails to combine emotional honesty with coherent analysis, which goes in short for the easy answer, is in my view actually harmful." Yet, he believes, "if ever a time and place cried out for the solace and rigour and passionate rejoinder of great drama, it is here and now. There is a whole culture to be achieved." Since politicians have retreated into sectarian stockades, Parker says artists must "construct a working model of wholeness by means of which this society can begin to hold up its head in the world." Parker was devoted to creating this model of wholeness, believing that "new forms are needed, forms of inclusiveness. The drama constantly demands that we re-invent it, that we transform it with new ways of showing, to cater adequately to the unique plight in which we find ourselves." Parker's experimentalism, therefore, is his effort to reinvent drama and, in turn, to transform his culture. Feeling the urgency of this process, Parker claims that "writing from within a life-experience of this place, at this time, the demands could not be more formidable or more momentous." Believing firmly in the power of drama to change perceptions, Parker wants to help his countrymen stop "picking over the entrails of the past, and begin to hint at a vision of the future," to move from pastness to wholeness. Parker's goal, then, is to create a dynamic, life-changing drama, one that redefines art, politics, religion, culture, and even historical narrative. In discussing *Northern Star*, Brown says, "The myth of an exacting and perennial siege cautions that community against raising the gates to liberalism, fraternity and political trust. In both the Nationalist and Unionist versions of the Irish past there is therefore a profound sense of history as a nightmare from which it is impossible to awake. . . . So when Stewart Parker reads the past as a continuous present he confirms what Irish people, Unionist and Nationalist feel about their differing histories. To be Irish is to endure the nightmare of historical stasis."

An image Parker employs to good effect is of the world as a stage, which is a particularly pervasive metaphor in Ireland. In *Northern Star*, Henry Joy McCracken says: "Haven't we always been on a stage, in our own eyes? Playing to the gods. History, posterity. A rough, hard audience. Thundering out our appointed parts." Parker's worst hell is endlessly repeating performances, but alone, without an audience and with no escape from the stage. That may be the worst hell, as well, for artists and politicians in Ireland. Parker shows in his work how rough it is to be caught in the loneliness of that thundering self-performance, of the endlessness of the poses and of the masks. Parker tries to offer his audiences redemption from that isolation, from that particular hell, by offering a new image of wholeness, a new way to reach out to each other in mercy. Andrews [2] asserts that "what makes him such a marvelous force for good and such an exciting playwright is his basic dynamic outlook, the depth and completeness of his interrogation of the lives and conditions of his characters, Catholic and Protestant, without fear and without compromise, so that between author and audience common recognition emerges, a supervening bond above and beyond ideas." His drama, then, is truly dangerous; it might actually create change. Parker requires forgiving rather than remembering, giving rather than withholding, loving rather than hating. The Fall of man and his hoped-for redemption are the universal theme uniting all of Parker's work; his art sings redemption but with an antiheroic, antimartyr tone. Redemption for Parker clearly lies not in religion but in humanity, in the mercy, belief, forgiveness, and love his people can offer each other. Marian in *Pentecost* declares, "We have committed sacrilege enough on life, in this place, in these times." Parker's righteous anger at the sins perpetrated in Northern Ireland in the name of religion is clear not only in the words he writes for his characters but in his personal conversation. Parker, while seeing the faults of Northern Ireland, believes firmly in redemption; he challenges his audiences to give up worn-out symbols, to get past animosities, to believe that an image of wholeness is possible.

Parker's work reflects the only possible hope—the warmth and wittiness and humanity of Northern Irish individuals—and will be seen as a major contribution to a new image for Northern Ireland. With an appropriate Parkerean irony, his final image is Pentecostal fire, that fire of the spirit. Seamus Heaney remembers with "vicarious pride" when Parker first rose to read at Philip Hobsbaum's poetry group soon after his leg was amputated: "He lurched formally and significantly to his feet, a move which in retrospect gains great symbolic power. It was a signal of personal victory, of the triumph of artistic utterance over demeaning circumstances, of the possibility of genial spirits in the face of destructive events. As such it had a meaning not only for himself but for the imaginative and spiritual life of Northern Ireland as a whole over the two decades that were to come. . . . He stood for that victory over the negative aspects of Ulster experience which everybody wants to believe is possible." Universally liked in a society known for its divisiveness, Parker spent his lifetime entertaining and cleverly communicating meaningful stories, but he also delivered a tough message: the need to eliminate prejudice, to bridge cultures, to reconcile differences. As Parker says in *Dramatis Personae*, his Queen's lecture in honor of John Malone, his first theater mentor, he wants "to substitute vibrant and authentic myths for the false and destructive ones on which we have been weaned." Stewart Parker shared his life in a personal, ongoing way with friends and audiences that demonstrates a compelling need to have his work understood and performed, an abiding desire to express honestly what he valued most—the power of theater both to celebrate life and to change lives.

ARCHIVAL SOURCES

Parker scholarship is hindered because no designated, public archive of his work exists at present, although Lesley Bruce, his executor, is considering depositing his papers in a Belfast library. If Parker's radio and television work is the research focus, Thames Television in London might prove helpful, or the BBC Radio Archive at the Ulster Folk and Transport Museum in Belfast, which has recordings of some plays and interviews.

PRIMARY BIBLIOGRAPHY

Plays

Catchpenny Twist. Dublin: Gallery Press, 1980; New York: Samuel French, 1984.
Heavenly Bodies. In *Three Plays for Ireland.* Birmingham: Oberon Books, 1989.
Nightshade. Dublin: Co-Op Books, 1980.
Northern Star. In *Three Plays for Ireland.* Birmingham: Oberon Books, 1989.
Pentecost. In *Three Plays for Ireland.* Birmingham: Oberon Books, 1989.
Spokesong. Plays and Players 24.3 (Dec. 1976): 43–50 and 24.4 (Jan. 1977): 43–50 (one act in each issue); also London: Samuel French, 1980.

Anthology

Three Plays for Ireland: Northern Star, Heavenly Bodies, Pentecost. Birmingham: Oberon Books, 1989.

Essays and Articles on Drama and Theater

"Belfast's Woman: A Superior Brand of Dynamite." *Evening Standard* (2 Nov. 1976): 13.
"Buntus Belfast." *Irish Times* (28 Jan. 1970): 9.
Dramatis Personae. John Malone Memorial Lecture. Belfast: Queen's University, 1986.
"Me and Jim." *Irish University Review: A Journal of Irish Studies* 12.1 (Spring 1982): 32–34.
"The Modern Poet as Dramatist: Some Aspects of Non-Realistic Drama, with Special

Reference to Eliot, Yeats, and cummings." Master's thesis, Department of English, Queen's University, Belfast, 1964.

"School for Revolution." *Irish Times* (7 Apr. 1970): 11.

"State of Play." *Canadian Journal of Irish Studies* 7.1 (June 1981): 5–11.

"The Tribe and Thompson." *Irish Times* (18 June 1970): 11.

"An Ulster Volunteer." *Irish Times* (6 Mar. 1970): 11.

SECONDARY BIBLIOGRAPHY

Adams, Anne. [Review of *Heavenly Bodies*.] "Play Should Be Heard Not Seen." *Daily News* (24 Apr. 1986).

Allen, Robert. "Stewart Parker: Playwright from a Lost Tribe." *Irish Times* (31 Jan. 1987): 9.

Andrews, Elmer. [1]. "The Power of Play." *Theatre Ireland* 18 (Apr.–June 1989): 21–28.

———. [2]. "The Will to Freedom." *Theatre Ireland* 19 (July–Sept. 1989): 19–23.

———. [3]. "The Will to Freedom: Politics and Play in the Theatre of Stewart Parker." *Irish Writers and Politics*. Savage, Md.: Barnes and Noble, 1990. (Reprint of two *Theatre Ireland* articles.)

Archer, Kane. [Review of *Spokesong*.] " 'Spokesong' Turns Up a Few Surprises." *Irish Times* (7 Oct. 1975): 15.

Barnes, Clive. [Review of *Spokesong*.] "Dazzling 'Spokesong' Rewarding." *New York Post* (13 Feb. 1978).

"Belfast Playwright Stewart Parker." *Chicago Tribune* (5 Nov. 1988): sec. 1: 12.

Bell, Jane. [Review of *Northern Star*.] "Reflective Star." *Belfast Telegraph* (8 Nov. 1984): 7.

Berkvist, Robert. [Review of *Spokesong*.] "Play about Irish History." *New York Times* (11 Mar. 1979).

Billington, Michael. [1]. [Review of *Catchpenny Twist*.] *Guardian* (22 Feb. 1980).

———. [2]. [Review of *Kingdom Come*.] *Guardian* (18 Jan. 1978).

———. [3]. [Review of *Pentecost*.] "Hope in Heartbreak House." *Guardian* (11 Jan. 1989).

Binchy, Maeve. "Enthusiastic London Premiere for Parker Play." *Irish Times* (10 Jan. 1989).

Blake, Douglas. [Review of *Kingdom Come*.] " 'Kingdom Coming' at the King's Head." *The Stage* (26 Jan. 1978).

Brennan, Brian. [Review of *Spokesong*.] "Splendid Spin in a Land of Whimsy." *Sunday Independent* (2 July 1989).

Brogan, Treasa. [1]. [Review of *Nightshade*.] "Nightshade No Sleeping Beauty." *Evening Press* (5 Feb. 1987).

———. [2]. [Review of *Spokesong*.] "Spokesong Is the Best Ever." *Evening Press* (28 June 1989).

Brown, Terence. "History's Nightmare: Stewart Parker's *Northern Star*." *Theatre Ireland* 13 (Fall 1987): 40–41.

Carey, Brian. [Review of *Spokesong*.] "Wheels of good fortune." *Irish Press* (28 June 1989).

Carty, Ciaran. "Northern Star Rising on the Tide." *Sunday Tribune* (29 Sept. 1985).

Review of *Catchpenny Twist*. "Irish Stew." *Sunday Telegraph* (24 Feb. 1980).

Clines, Francis X. [Review of *Pentecost*.] "Theater Crosses Borders in Ireland, Fueled by the Troubles and a Love of Language." *New York Times* (27 Sept. 1987).

Colgan, Gerry. [Review of *Spokesong*.] " 'Spokesong' at the Tivoli." *Irish Times* (28 June 1989).

Collins, Gail. "Partisan Position on Pizzas." *Stewart Parker*. Ed. John Fairleigh. Supplement to *Fortnight* 278 (Nov. 1989): 6.

Cooper, Robert. "Riveting Exchanges." *Stewart Parker*. Ed. John Fairleigh. Supplement to *Fortnight* 278 (Nov. 1989): 5.

Coveney, Michael. [1]. [Review of *Kingdom Come*.] *Financial Times* (18 Jan. 1978).

———. [3]. [Review of *Pentecost*.] *Financial Times* (10 Jan. 1989).

Coyle, Jane. [1]. [Review of *Nightshade*.] *Guardian* (19 Mar. 1987).

———. [2]. [Review of *Pentecost*.] *Guardian* (26 Sept. 1987).

Crawford, Dan. "Warmth, Humour, Humanity." *Stewart Parker*. Ed. John Fairleigh. Supplement to *Fortnight* 278 (Nov. 1989): 8.

Cropper, Martin. [1]. [Review of *Heavenly Bodies*; includes mention of *Northern Star*] *Times* (24 Apr. 1986).

Curtiss, Thomas Quinn. "Best of New Offerings." *International Herald-Tribune* (16 Oct. 1980): 7.

Cushman, Robert. [Review of *Catchpenny Twist*.] "Belfast Songsters." *Observer* (24 Feb. 1980): 15.

Davey, Shaun. "Well-Crafted Cigarette Packets." *Stewart Parker*. Ed. John Fairleigh. Supplement to *Fortnight* 278 (Nov. 1989): 3–4.

"Death of Playwright Stewart Parker." *Irish Times* (3 Nov. 1988).

Dewhurst, Keith. "Uniting Irishman." *Guardian* (5 Nov. 1988).

Downey, Gerard. [Review of *Pentecost*.] " 'Pentecost' Shows Parker at his Best." *Belfast Telegraph* (24 Sept. 1987).

Drake, Sylvie. [1]. [Review of *Spokesong*.] *Los Angeles Times* (4 Feb. 1986): 6: 1, 6.

———. [2]. [Review of *Spokesong*.] *Los Angeles Times* (14 July 1986): 6: 1, 4.

Eder, Richard. [1]. [Review of *Spokesong*.] " 'Spokesong,' by Stewart Parker, Belfast Drama, at Long Wharf." *New York Times* (11 Feb. 1978): 12.

———. [2]. [Review of *Spokesong*.] "Stage: 'Spokesong' Spins Cycle of Belfast." *New York Times* (16 Mar. 1979): C3.

Edwardes, Jane. "On Stewart Parker." *Time Out* (4 Jan. 1989).

Edwards, Christopher. [Review of *Pentecost*.] "Up to Snuff." *Spectator* 262. 8374 (14 Jan. 1989): 40–41.

Finegan, John. [Review of *Spokesong*.] "Bicycle Made for You." *Evening Herald* (28 June 1989).

Gingold, Alfred. "Valuing the Individual Moment." *Stewart Parker*. Ed. John Fairleigh. Supplement to *Fortnight* 278 (Nov. 1989): 1–2.

Gismondi, Paul. [Review of *Pentecost*.] *Tablet* (14 Jan. 1989): 45–46.

Hanna, Jack. [Review of *Spokesong*.] *Alpha* (6 July 1989).

Harding, Tim. [1]. [Review of *Nightshade*.] *Sunday Press* (8 Feb. 1987).

———. [2]. [Review of *Spokesong*.] "Wheel Men and Real Women." *Sunday Press* (2 July 1989).

Harris, Claudia W. [1]. "A Living Mythology: Stewart Parker." *Theatre Ireland* 13 (Fall 1987): 15–17.

———. [2]. "The Flame That Bloomed: A Memorial to Stewart Parker." *Irish Literary Supplement* 8.1 (Spring 1989): 4.

———. [3]. "From Pastness to Wholeness: Stewart Parker's Reinventing Theatre." *Colby Quarterly* 27.4 (Dec. 1991): 233–41. Reprinted in *"Standing in Their Shifts Itself . . ." Irish Drama from Farquhar to Friel.* Vol. 1. Ed. Eberhart Bort. Germany: Verlag, 1993: 281–93.

———. [4]. [Review of *Three Plays for Ireland.*] "The Last Plays of Stewart Parker." *Irish Literary Supplement* 9.1 (Spring 1990): 9.

———. [5]. "The Tip of the Iceberg: Assessing the Work of Stewart Parker." *Graph: Irish Literary Review* 13 (Winter 1992, Spring 1993): 10–12.

Haywood, Bob. [Review of *Heavenly Bodies.*] "Our Barry Just Won't Play Dead." *Sunday Mercury* (27 Apr. 1986): 15.

Heaney, Seamus. "Victorious Ulsterman." *Sunday Independent* (Ireland) (6 Nov. 1988): 18.

Review of *Heavenly Bodies. Birmingham Post* (23 Apr. 1986).

Henderson, Lynda. "The Spokesman." *Stewart Parker.* Ed. John Fairleigh. Supplement to *Fortnight* 278 (Nov. 1989): 2.

Hennegan, Tony. [Review of *Nightshade.*] "Death as a Sinister Illusion." *Irish Independent* (10 Oct. 1980).

Henry, William A. III. "Acts of History: Dublin Revives Its Festival." *Time Magazine* (21 Oct. 1985).

Hewison, Robert. [Review of *Pentecost.*] "Home Truths That Give the Irish Question an Eloquent Resolution." *Sunday Times* (15 Jan. 1989).

Hill, Niki. "The Way We Were: Pentecost Time for Playwright." *Sunday News* (11 Oct. 1987).

Hobsbaum, Philip. "Belfast Letter: Nobody's Province." *Spectator,* no. 7207 (12 Aug. 1966): 208–9.

Holland, Mary. [1]. [Review of *Pentecost.*] "The Belfast Bible." *Observer* (27 Sept. 1987).

———. [2]. "Such Goodness Demands That We Respond." *Irish Times* (9 Nov. 1988): 14.

Houlihan, Con. [Review of *Nightshade.*] "Thought of What Might Have Been . . ." *Evening Press* (10 Oct. 1980).

Hurren, Kenneth. [Review of *Pentecost.*] "Ulster's Hopeless Comedy of Terrors." *Mail on Sunday* 15 Jan. 1989.

Review of *Iris in the Traffic, Ruby in the Rain.* "Belfast Revisited." *Radio Times* (21 Nov. 1981).

"Irish Spokes Person." *Guardian* (6 Oct. 1984).

Itzin, Catherine. "Three New Plays." *Plays and Players* 24.3 (Dec. 1976): 32.

Johnstone, Robert. [Review of *Three Plays for Ireland.*] "Playing for Ireland." *Honest Ulsterman* 86 (Spring/Summer 1989): 59–64.

Jones, D.A.N. [Review of *Pentecost.*] "Prods versus Popeheads." *Sunday Telegraph* (15 Jan. 1989).

Kemp, Peter. [Review of *Pentecost.*] "Walking Wounded." *Independent* (11 Jan. 1989).

Kennedy, Douglas. [1]. Program Note to Rough Magic 1987 production of *Nightshade.*

———. [2] [Review of *Pentecost.*] "Ireland's Fatal Attraction." *New Statesman and Society* 2.31 (6 Jan. 1989): 45–47.

———. [3]. Program Note to Rough Magic 1989 production of *Spokesong.*

———. [4]. "Stewart Parker: An Appreciation." *Irish Times* (4 Nov. 1988).

Kennedy, Maev. "Tortoise at Work." *Irish Times* (17 Sept. 1985).

Kent, Nicholas. "A Wonderfully Brave Ending." *Stewart Parker*. Ed. John Fairleigh. Supplement to *Fortnight* 278 (Nov. 1989): 10–11.

Keyes, John. [Review of *Pentecost*.] "Contested Territory." *Fortnight* (Nov. 1987).

Kidel, Mark. "Shades of Parker: Provos, Prods and Plays." *Observer Magazine* 4 Dec. 1977: 34.

Review of *Kingdom Come*. *Observer* (22 Jan. 1978).

Review of *Kingdom Come*. "This Mixture of Irish-Caribbean Makes a Brilliant Show." *West Indian World* (3–9 Feb. 1978): 10.

Kingston, Jeremy. [Review of *Pentecost*.] "Final Possibility of Hope." *Times* (11 Jan. 1989).

Lesniak, James G. *Contemporary Authors: A Biobibliographical Guide*. New York: Gale Research, 1991, 325.

McCracken, Kathleen. "Fractures and Continuities: Melodramatic Elements in Stewart Parker's *Nightshade*." *Notes on Modern Irish Literature* 2 (1990): 68–73.

McFerran, Ann. "Putting His Spoke In." *Time Out* (3 Sept. 1976).

McGuinness, Frank. [1]. "Dear Stewart." *Stewart Parker*. Ed. John Fairleigh. Supplement to *Fortnight* 278 (Nov. 1989): 4.

———. [2]. "Stewart Parker." *Independent* (England) (5 Nov. 1988).

McKenna, David. [Review of *Nightshade*.] *In Dublin* (17–30 Oct. 1980).

Meyers, Kevin. "An Irishman's Diary." *Irish Times* (3 Feb. 1987): 11.

Moloney, Eugene. [Review of *Pentecost*.] "Parker Gives a Ray of Hope." *Irish News* (24 Sept. 1987).

Morley, Sheridan. "Speaking of Spokesong." *Times* (15 Feb 1977).

Review of *Nightshade*. *Sunday Independent* (8 Feb. 1987).

Nowlan, David. [1]. [Review of *Catchpenny Twist*.] " 'Catchpenny Twist' at the Peacock." *Irish Times* (26 Oct. 1977): 9.

———. [2]. [Review of *Nightshade*.] " 'Nightshade' at the Peacock." *Irish Times* (10 Oct. 1980).

———. [3]. [Review of *Nightshade*.] " 'Nightshade' at the Project." *Irish Times* (5 Feb. 1987).

———. [4]. [Review of *Northern Star*.] " 'Northern Star' at Belfast Lyric Theatre." *Irish Times* (8 Nov. 1984): 12.

———. [5]. [Review of *Northern Star*.] " 'Northern Star' at the Olympia." *Irish Times* (24 Sept. 1985): 10.

———. [6]. [Review of *Pentecost*.] " 'Pentecost' at the Guildhall, Derry." *Irish Times* (24 Sept. 1987).

———. [7] [Review of *Pentecost*.] " 'Pentecost'' Comes to Dublin." *Irish Times* (29 Sept. 1987).

———. [8]. [Review of *Pratt's Fall*.] " 'Pratt's Fall' at the Eblana." *Irish Times* (27 Sept. 1983): 10.

Nurse, Keith. [Review of *Kingdom Come*.] *Daily Telegraph* (18 Jan. 1978).

O'Brien, Conor Cruise. [Review of *Kingdom Come*.] "A Song of Disembafflement." *Observer* (29 Jan. 1978).

O'Brien, Simon. "Spokesong." *New Cyclist Magazine* (Sept./Oct. 1991).

O'Donnell, Mary. [Review of *Spokesong*.] "Taking Taboos for a Comic Ride." *Sunday Tribune* (2 July 1989).

O'Toole, Fintan. [1]. [Review of *Nightshade.*] "Rough Magic Cast a Spell." *Sunday Tribune* (8 Feb. 1987).

———. [2]. [Review of *Northern Star.*] "Tensions in Past and Present Tense." *Sunday Tribune* (2 Dec. 1984): 18.

———. [3]. [Review of *Pentecost.*] "Death and the Insurrection." *Sunday Tribune* (27 Sept. 1987): 19.

Parker, Lynne. "Wrestling with Flesh and Blood." *Stewart Parker.* Ed. John Fairleigh. Supplement to *Fortnight* 278 (Nov. 1989): 7.

"Parker's 'Spokesong' Comes Full Cycle." *Belfast Telegraph* (14 Mar. 1978).

Parkin, Andrew. "Metaphor as Dramatic Structure in Plays by Stewart Parker." In *Irish Writers and the Theatre.* Ed. Masaru Sekine. Gerrards Cross, Buckinghamshire: Colin Smythe, 1986, 135–150.

Review of *Pentecost.* "Play Strips Ulster Bare." *Belfast Newsletter* (24 Sept. 1987).

Peter, John. [Review of *Catchpenny Twist.*] "Innocents in an Irish Minefield." *Sunday Times* (2 Mar. 1980): 43.

Peterson, Maureen. "Author Happy Writing for the Stage." *Gazette* (Montreal) (15 Dec. 1979.

Purcell, Deirdre. "The Illusionist." *Sunday Tribune* (27 Sept. 1987).

Raby, David Ian. [Review of *Heavenly Bodies.*] *Plays and Players*, no. 394 (July 1986): 30.

Rafferty, Gerard. "Parker, Playwright." *Belfast Telegraph* (25 Jan. 1980).

Richards, Shaun. "To Bind the Northern to the Southern Stars: Field Day in Derry and Dublin." *Irish Review* 4 (Spring 1988): 52–58.

Roche, Lorcan. [Review of *Spokesong.*] "Parker Play Near Perfect." *Irish Independent* (28 June 1989).

Rothstein, Mervyn. "Stewart Parker, 47, a Playwright on Irish Troubles, Dies in London." *New York Times* (4 Nov. 1988): B4.

Rushe, Desmond. [Review of *Pentecost.*] "Optimistic Pentecost Is Parker at His Best." *Irish Independent* (29 Sept. 1987).

Sheridan, Michael. [1]. [Review of *Nightshade.*] "Heavy Dose of Deadly 'Nightshade.' " *Irish Press* (10 Oct. 1980).

———. [2]. [Review of *Pentecost.*] "Comic Spirit in Pentecost." *Irish Press* (29 Sept. 1987).

Shulman, Milton [1]. [Review of *Catchpenny Twist.*] "No escape . . ." *Evening Standard* (22 Feb. 1980): 15

———. [2]. [Review of *Kingdom Come.*] "The Irish Limbo." *Evening Standard* (18 Jan. 1978).

———. [3]. [Review of *Pentecost.*] "Hope in Faith." *Evening Standard* (10 Jan. 1989).

Simpson, David. "The Prolific Pen of Mr. Parker." *Belfast Telegraph* (3 Nov. 1984): 7.

Smith, Gus. [Review of *Nightshade.*] "Enter McKenna—the Magician." *Sunday Independent* (12 Oct. 1980).

Smith, Sid. [Review of *Spokesong.*] *Chicago Tribune* (18 July 1985): 8.

Smyth, Damian. "Descent, Dissent, 'Tradition.' " *Stewart Parker.* Ed. John Fairleigh. Supplement to *Fortnight* 278 (Nov. 1989): 9–10.

Sommers, Pamela. [Review of *Pentecost.*] "Tongues Aflame in *Pentecost.*" *Washington Post* (8 Oct. 1992).

" 'Spokesong.' " *Belfast Telegraph* (6 Sept. 1976).

"Stewart Parker." *Daily Telegraph* (4 Nov. 1988).

Thompson, Peter. [Review of *Nightshade*.] *Irish Press* (5 Feb. 1987).

Toibin, Colm. [Review of *Nightshade*.] "Parker Pens a Rare Delight." *Hibernia* (16 Oct. 1980).

Walsh, Caroline. "The Saturday Profile: Stewart Parker." *Irish Times* (13 Aug. 1977).

Wardle, Irving. [Review of *Kingdom Come*.] "Witty and Agile Lyrics among Exotic Foliage." *Times* (18 Jan. 1978).

Watt, Douglas. [Review of *Spokesong*.] "*Spokesong* Lets the Air out of Its Tires." *Daily News* (16 Mar. 1979).

Willox, Bob. [Review of *Spokesong*.] "Parker Pens a Great Play." *Newsletter* (21 Feb. 1977).

Christina Reid

(1942–   )

CARLA J. McDONOUGH

Christina Reid came to prominence in the 1980s, thanks to the writer-in-residence program at the Lyric Theatre, Belfast. She held that position for the 1983–1984 season, and at the Lyric, *Tea in a China Cup* was first performed. Positive notices for that play have led to a proliferation of theater work that has focused largely upon the lives and conflicts experienced by the women of Northern Ireland, specifically, within Reid's own Protestant background. In sorting through ideologies from family and state, Reid's characters tend, more than anything else, to be searching for a coherent self-vision—oftentimes finding themselves in conflict with the beliefs of their families and of their historical positioning within Irish culture.

Reid's roots are in Ardoyne, where she recalls that her strongest influences were the women in her family: "All the greatest influences on my life were women—women talking, telling stories and jokes, all the sort of uninhibited humour that happens where there are no men about" (Campbell). Reid tells of spending much of her time on Coolderry Street off Donegall Road, where her grandmother lived. Her mother was often with her grandmother, reflecting the generational connections within families that Reid presents often in her plays. Her holidays were usually spent in Donaghadee with her aunts and cousins, a matriarchal core that was visited by their men only on the weekends when they were free from work (Campbell).

The portrait that Reid offers of her childhood may explain, in part, why she came to playwriting rather late. Her background is working-class Protestant, leaving little time for the leisure usually needed for a writing career. She left school at fifteen, soon working a series of unfulfilling jobs and eventually marrying. She did not return to university until many years later. Her stint with the Lyric came while she was working on an English degree at Queen's Univirsity as an older return student, already a mother in her late thirties. The Lyric position, funded and partly selected by Thames Television, offered Reid the chance to devote herself full-time to developing her playwriting. After seeing productions of *Tea in a China Cup* (1983), *Joyriders* (1986), *Did You Hear the One about the Irishman?* (1984), and *The Last of a Dyin' Race* (1986) performed in both Ireland and London, as an outgrowth of the position at the Lyric, Reid moved to London in 1987, bringing along her three daughters. The following year, she became writer in residence at the Young Vic in London. Under their auspices, her former radio play, *My Name? Shall I Tell You My Name?* (1987), was produced on stage, in addition to *Lords, Dukes and Earls* (1989). *The Belle of Belfast City* (1989) followed shortly after, having its premiere back at the Lyric in Belfast.

Most of Reid's plays deal in some way with family issues, particularly with the younger generation's trying to cope in the face of prejudice and economic disadvantage, which has been institutionalized not only by the politics outside the family but more significantly by the politics of the family. Most of her plays are written from the viewpoint of a Protestant family in Belfast, no doubt reflecting, to some extent, the families among whom Reid grew up. Reid's work also pays homage to the social realist plays of Sean O'Casey. *Joyriders* even opens with its characters watching the end of *Shadow of a Gunman* and echoes that play's plot as well. Reid comments about O'Casey, "I love what he does, particularly in those early plays: he breaks your heart while making you laugh" (Wolf).

Similarly, Reid's plays tend to blend humor into generally humorless conflicts and struggles. The humor often stems from the absurdity of the situation in which, as Reid makes clear, characters Protestant and Catholic are suffering similar blows but insisting on maintaining their differences as a way to vilify each other. Her portrait of the teenagers in *Joyriders*, who piece together a semblance of adolescence with its flirting and banter amid the devastations of poverty and the dangers of drugs and violence, emphasizes their vitality and humor even as it highlights their sense of realism, that their lives are headed nowhere. Humor becomes, for many of her characters, a survival tactic.

A recurrent theme within Reid's plays is that of confronting one's past (whether represented by familial, national, regional, or religious history) and trying to come to terms with it in order to move beyond it. Again and again, she shows us that characters unable to rethink their beliefs, to adapt, to change, and to show understanding or compassion for others are the ones who become destructive forces in their own lives and in the lives of those around them. *Did You Hear the One about the Irishman?* documents how violence begets more violence, even as the two love interests manage to forge an alliance between Catholic and Protestant. But the play leaves the audience with the potent image of the joking comedian who tells one too many "dumb Irishman" jokes to an Irishman, leading that Irishman to infer he must turn to a gun in order to gain respect. *My Name? Shall I Tell You My Name?* shows us a granddaughter's memories of her grandfather, whom she loves, even though she disagrees with his values and prejudices. So, too, in *Belle of Belfast City* and *Tea in a China Cup* we witness female characters trying to work their way through the maze of misleading, entrapping ideologies instilled in them by their well-meaning families.

Reid's plays have been deemed by one critic in an article about Irish "political" theater not to be of political interest (Maxwell). Reid herself would no doubt agree, in that she dislikes labels such as "political" playwright or "feminist" playwright, arguing that "I think labels diminish good art. I don't make political statements, I present words and images that are open to interpretation" (Campbell). However, it seems feasible for plays that straightforwardly examine the traditions, prejudices, and stereotypes that fuel political party lines to qualify for possible political interpretations. In this way, Reid's plays excel, offering insight into the everyday lives of the people of Belfast. She also offers the dramatic world a first-rate look into the lives of women and of the young—two groups often overlooked by male playwrights of greater fame. Reviewers of her plays tend to agree that her treatment of her characters is balanced and unsentimental. Wolfe has even called *Tea* and *Joyriders* "two of the best Northern Irish plays of the Eighties."

In addition to the stage plays, Reid continues to work with radio and television in the fertile ground provided there for British playwrights. With five major plays to her credit, Reid has surely not exhausted her reservoir of stories and will no doubt continue to be a strong female voice in Irish drama.

Selected Biographical Sources: Griffiths and Llewellyn-Jones; Wilmer.

MAJOR PLAYS, PREMIERES, AND SIGNIFICANT REVIVALS: THEATRICAL RECEPTION

Tea in a China Cup. 1983. Premiered at Lyric Player's Theatre, Belfast, 9 November. Directed by Leon Rubin. Toured Northern Ireland in 1983. Riverside Studios, London, 1984. Perth Theatre, 1985. Volkstheater, Vienna, 1986. Redgrave Theatre, Farnham, 1986. Community Theatre, Terre Haute, Indiana, 1989.

This play confronts the assumptions and stereotypes that keep Protestants and Catholics apart in Ireland even as their economic plight would logically seem to be the thing that should bring them together. *Tea* traces a Protestant family in Belfast between 1939 and 1972, focusing particularly on the relationship between the dying Sarah and her daughter Beth. Sarah's die-hard Protestant loyalty to Ulster is reflected in the family's contribution of sons to fight for England. The repetition of dialogue between the World War I departure of Sarah's brother and the departure of her son into the English army in the 1970s (one of the few jobs open to him) gives an ominous tone to the ideal of Ulster loyalty to England. Other than working as soldiers for England, the men offer little in support of the family, becoming, instead, burdens for their women, who are left to support and to cover up for the drinking and gambling of their men. The family's assumption that being Protestant is associated with keeping up certain appearances or symbols of "culture," such as a fine china teacup, indicates their disgust at what they view as "dirty" Catholics. Beth's friendship with the Catholic girl Theresa counterpoints these stereotypes as the two girls share similar questions and confusion regarding the ideologies their families pass on to them. The glorification of the Protestant past also demonstrates the inflexibleness that serves to destroy the very people it supposedly upholds. Beth's family's insistence upon "keeping up appearances" keeps her in a bad marriage, covering up for her husband's "gambling" in stocks, which she has learned is no different from her father's betting on the dog races. Only in losing her mother does Beth begin to realize the mistakes she has made, and the play indicates that she intends, in selling her husband's house, to move beyond the old ways while maintaining some of the strengths she learned from her mother, as represented by the china cup she keeps. *Tea* has been Reid's best-received and best-known play, earning her first break into professional theater with the Lyric Belfast as well as several awards. The play was runner-up in the *Irish Times/ Dublin Theatre Festival/Women's Play Competition* of 1982, and it won the Thames Television Playwright Scheme Award for 1983. The critical reception of the play has generally been positive, although Peter [1] finds the "absence" of male characters to be both "the play's theme as well as its weakness," a criticism that comes off as rather phallocentric, especially since the play's theme is not about "male absence" but about women, their lives, their mistakes, and their strengths. Masters calls the play "lovely," "moving," and "passionate," while Rosenfield of the *Irish Times* describes it as "finely judged, [having] beautifully written scenes with well-drawn characters."

Did You Hear the One about the Irishman? 1985. Rehearsed reading by the Royal Shakespeare Company in the United States. Premiere performance at the King's Head Theatre, London, 1987. Directed by Caroline Sharman.

This play borrows from the vaudeville stage as a way of examining the clichés, stereotypes, and misrepresentations of the Irish. The juxtapositioning of the comedian's monologues and the news reports with the story of the two families, the Protestant Clarkes and the Catholic Raffertys, who both have sons in Maze Prison, creates a Brechtian effect that serves to counter any moves toward sentimentalizing the star-crossed love story between Brian Rafferty and Allison Clarke. The play leaves us with the same ethnic jokes with which it began but ultimately serves to show how such degrading humor leads to anger and ultimately to violence. The relationship between Brian and Allison, who try to bridge the gap between Catholic and Protestant by recognizing the similarities of their situations, is a move that will be attempted by many of Reid's subsequent characters. Their failure is rather spectacular, but in later plays both the attempts toward reconciliation and the failures will be much more incremental.

The play won the Ulster Television Drama Award in 1980, which led to its subsequent productions and helped to bring Reid to the notice of the Lyric Theater in Belfast.

Joyriders. 1986. Commissioned by Paines Plough, the Writers Company. Opened at the Tricycle Theatre, London, 13 February. Directed by Pip Broughton. Tour of England and Northern Ireland, 1986. Yew Theatre Company Tour of S. Ireland, 1988. Jugendtheater, Dortmund, 1989. National Theatre, Mannheim, 1989. Radio Berne, Switzerland, 1987. Crucible Theatre, Sheffield, 1991. Project Theatre, Dublin, 1991.

   Joyriders is perhaps the most striking of Reid's play in its social realism. The play presents us with four Belfast youths who, as a probationary measure, are being forced to take part in a government-run Youth Training Program, supposedly created as an attempt to keep them off the streets and direct them into more productive lives. The program, however, is woefully inadequate in the face of the actual problems encountered by these teenagers, as the social worker Kate is all too well aware. For instance, in Belfast, a "joyrider" who steals a car and drives it around for a lark is subject to being not merely arrested but gunned down by the police. After a year of learning how to knit sweaters and cook meals, these teenagers will be back on the streets with no real prospect of employment. Although Reid borrows from O'Casey's *Shadow of a Gunman* and grounds her characters in a gritty realism that stems from personal contact with the teenagers from the slum housing of Belfast's Divis Flats, the play avoids any feeling of being derivative. The characters' lives may be representative of the lost youth, the dead-end lives of too many Belfast youth enmeshed in political and economic systems that destroy their future, but they nevertheless come off as individuals rather than as "cases." Denselow comments that the play "never attempts to shove politics down our throats . . . nor is it in any way sectarian nor indulgent nor melodramatic." However, Mackenzie criticizes the first act for not showing enough of the political situation "outside" the Youth Training Program. Reid herself emphasizes that her focus is less on the "issue" of how to treat troubled teens who face seemingly insurmountable problems due to economic disadvantage, and more on the people themselves, particularly their amazing resiliency (Donovan). Maureen and Arthur still have the capacity for hope, despite being orphaned and permanently maimed, respectively, by the political fighting in their city. The general critical consensus on the play is overwhelmingly positive, although Hewison, in a dissenting view, finds it "a bit preachy."

The Last of a Dyin' Race. 1986. BBC Radio 4, 14 January 1986. Directed by Susan Hogg. UTV/Channel 4, 1987.

   Written as a radio play and later performed on television, *The Last of a Dyin' Race* explores the passing of old traditions in regard to treatment of the dead. The play opens with the death of a woman whose daughter-in-law insists on taking her to an undertaker and having her cremated, instead of the usual ritual of a three-day laying out at home and a full wake, which the woman's half-sister manages to conduct at the funeral home. The action of the play demonstrates how the old ways bond the family together, give respect for the dead, and give the living a chance for reminiscing. Yet, the younger people's attitude toward the dead indicates how this tradition is passing, even as the neighbors support Agnes, the half-sister, in upholding the tradition of the wake in spite of the daughter-in-law. The passing of the traditional wake is part of a larger movement in which, one of the mourners notes, men are taking over the "wemmin's work" not only of laying out the dead (in becoming funeral directors) but also of bringing babies into the world by taking over the midwife's role. The division of women's and men's work is noted several times in the play and recognized as an important part of the traditions of the town. Reid has noted in an interview that her family adhered to such divisions of labor not, she indicates, out of sexism but because such a division was logical and orderly (Campbell). Offering a rich view of the rituals and traditions that create a sense of community, *The Last of a Dyin' Race* also shows how the passing of such traditions also seems inevitable. The play won the Giles Cooper Award for radio plays, which led to its original production.

My Name? Shall I Tell You My Name? 1987. BBC Radio 4. Yew Theatre Company (Dublin Theatre Festival, 1989). Young Vic Studio, London, 1990.

Written originally as a radio play "for two voices," the adaptation to the theater caused more than one critic to remark on the static quality, which was countered in performance by riveting acting and effective lighting techniques. The granddaughter and grandfather are isolated on stage as much as they are isolated ideologically from each other. Grandpa Andy's fierce Protestant loyalty to Ulster, epitomized by his memory of the Battle of the Somme, in which he fought for King and Country, stands in contrast to his granddaughter Andrea's break from that world. Andrea's love for her family is complicated by her differing beliefs. The memory play shows her coming to terms with her past (and her grandfather's past) while struggling not to be overcome by it. James finds the play "overloaded with Loyalism v Republicanism, sectarianism, racism, feminism," while Kingston [2] praises the "fierce" poignancy of the work. Thematically, the coming-of-age story of the young woman reflects the issues that have appeared often in Reid's work, the necessity (and difficulty) of balancing love for family with one's own beliefs and values.

The Belle of Belfast City. 1989. Premiered at Lyric Player's Theatre Belfast on 3 May. Contact Theatre, Manchester, 1990. Radio 4, 1990. The Orange Tree Theatre, Richmond, Surrey, June/July 1993.

Belle has in its background the vaudeville stage upon which the family's mother/grandmother, Dolly, earned her name as "the Belle of Belfast City." Dolly's love of song and laughter provides a sharp contrast to the zealous prudishness of her nephew Jack. Jack's political connections with fascists and racists who wish to secure a Protestant Ulster for England are presented in contrast to the liberal views of his cousin Rose, whose illegitimate daughter is half black. The closeness of the family of women, who support each other regardless of personal foibles, presents a strength and honesty that make all the more ludicrous Jack's concepts of women as temptresses and whores. The terrorist methods and gangsterism of both the Irish Republican Army (IRA) and the National Front are pointed out in the course of the play, as the family finds itself between the clashing political views of Rose and Jack. Fanaticism, whether religious or political, is ultimately under attack in this play, which shows the women (sisters, daughters, mothers) working toward compromise and compassion above all else. Family solidarity and the need for understanding and compassion are the themes that this play shares with its predecessors. *Belle*, however, is a bit uneven in comparison. Nowlan complains that the "stilted" dialogue and the unresolved conflicts cause the story to "fail to come together as a piece of theater." Peter [2] too, finds the play a bit "over-rhetorical" at times but praises its "humorous elements" and "lack of self-righteousness." *Belle* won its author the George Devine Award in 1986.

ASSESSMENT OF REID'S CAREER

Although Reid has been criticized for her focus on women and the "domestic" rather than the political life in Northern Ireland, it is precisely for this focus that her work is so valuable. As DiCenzo has noted in her recent study of women in Northern Irish theater, women dramatists and actors—in short, women's stories—have been overlooked in Northern Irish drama, which is overwhelmingly voiced and staged by men. Women are too often the long-suffering wife or the overprotective mother, such as we see stereotyped in so many Irish plays. While Reid looks at wives and mothers who could be said to fit this stereotype, her portraits of women are much more rounded, and her women much more self-aware than the stereotype would allow. Above all, they are survivors who forge strong bonds with their daughters, bonds that Reid's daughters cherish but that those daughters question as well. Reid gives to Northern Irish drama a bevy of strong-minded young women who are aware of their mother's (and father's and grandfather's) mistakes, even as they sometimes repeat them, but who forge new paths for themselves that become thoughtful critiques of received values and prejudices. Reid's career is only a decade old, and we can assume that her work will continue to enrich a national drama that has tended to overlook the personal and political lives of its women. As the slim bibliography available about Reid's plays makes clear, much critical work is also still needed to do her drama justice.

PRIMARY BIBLIOGRAPHY

Plays

The Belle of Belfast City and *Did You Hear the One about the Irishman?* London: Methuen, 1989.

Joyriders and *Tea in a China Cup*. London: Methuen, 1987.
The Last of a Dyin' Race. In *Best Radio Plays of 1986*. London: Methuen/BBC, 1986.

SECONDARY BIBLIOGRAPHY

Barber, John. [Review of *Tea in a China Cup*.] *Daily Telegraph* (15 Oct. 1984).
Campbell, Kerry. "Cuppas and Corpses: Kerry Campbell Talks to Chris Reid." *Belfast Review* (Oct. 1983): 24–25.
Connor, John. [Review of *Joyriders*.] *City Limits* (21 Feb. 1986).
Coveney, Michael. [Review of *Joyriders*.] *Financial Times* (19 Feb. 1986).
de Jongh, Nicholas. [Review of *Joyriders*.] *Guardian* (19 Feb. 1986).
Denselow, Anthony. [Review of *Joyriders*.] *BBC Radio London* (22 Feb. 1986).
DiCenzo, Maria R. "Charabanc Theatre Company: Placing Women Center-Stage in Northern Ireland." *Theatre Journal* 45 (1993): 175–84.
Donovan, Katie. "Joyriding with Christina Reid." *Irish Times* (8 Apr. 1991): 10.
Griffiths, Trevor R., and Margaret Llewellyn-Jones, eds. *British and Irish Women Dramatists since 1958: A Critical Handbook*. Buckingham; Philadelphia: Open University Press, 1993.
Hewison, Robert. "Irish Dimension Takes the Stage." *Sunday Times* (23 Feb. 1986): 39.
Hoyle, Martin. [Review of *Tea in a China Cup*.] *Financial Times* (15 Oct. 1984); repr., *London Theatre Record* 4 (1984): 926.
James, John. [Review of *My Name? Shall I Tell You My Name?*] "Deep South to Far North." *Times Educational Supplement* (16 Mar. 1990): 30a.
Kingston, Jeremy. [1]. "Sing-Song Repetition of the Old Bitterness." *Times* (9 June 1993) : 38d.
———. [2]. "Touching the Heart of the Matter." *Times* (9 Mar. 1990): 16.
Mackenzie, Suzie. [Review of *Joyriders*.] *Time Out* (20 February 1986).
Masters, Anthony. "A Play That Never Raises Its Voice." *Times* (15 Oct. 1984): 12.
Maxwell, D. E. S. "Northern Ireland's Political Drama." *Modern Drama* 33 (1990): 1–14.
McFerran, Ann. [Review of *Tea in a China Cup*.] *Time Out* (18 Oct. 1984).
Murdin, Lynda. [Review of *Tea in a China Cup*.] *Standard* (15 Oct. 1984).
Nathan, David. [Review of *Joyriders*.] *Jewish Chronicle* (21 Feb. 1986).
Nowlan, David. "*The Belle of Belfast City* at the Lyric Theatre." *Irish Times* (5 May 1989): 12.
Peter, John. [1]. "The Keepers and the Kept." *Sunday Times* (21 Oct. 1984): 39.
———. [2]. "Theatre 1." *Sunday Times* (14 May 1989): C9.
Ratcliffe, Michael. [Review of *Joyriders*.] *Observer* (23 Feb. 1986).
Roll-Hansen, Diderik. "Dramatic Strategy in Christina Reid's *Tea in a China Cup*." *Modern Drama* 30 (1987): 389–95.
Rosenfield, Ray. "*Tea in a China Cup* at the Lyric, Belfast." *Irish Times* (14 Nov. 1983): 10.
Wardle, Irving. "Theatre: *Joyriders*." *Times* (20 Feb. 1986):15.
Wilmer, Steve. "Women's Theatre in Ireland." *New Theatre Quarterly* 7 (1991): 353–60.
Woddis, Carole. [Review of *Tea in a China Cup*.] *City Limits* (19 Oct. 1984).
Wolf, Matt. "Out of the Shadow of the Gunman." *Times* (8 Mar. 1990): 20.

Lennox Robinson
(1886–1958)

KURT EISEN

When Lennox Robinson was installed in 1909 as director-manager of the Abbey Theatre, Dublin, he was a fledgling twenty-three-year-old writer with just three produced plays and no directing or managerial experience. Amid the artistic and political upheaval of the next five decades, Robinson dedicated himself to learning his craft as both playwright and director and played a key role in bringing modern Irish drama to American audiences.

Esmé Stuart Lennox Robinson was born 4 October 1886 in Douglas, County Cork, the seventh and youngest child in the staunchly Protestant, Anglo-Irish family of Andrew Craig and Emily Jones Robinson. Schooled mostly at home because of his poor health, Robinson immersed himself in literature and music. Following an abortive attempt at teaching, Robinson completed his move away from his family's Unionist sympathies after seeing Yeats' *Cathleen Ni Houlihan* at the Cork Opera House in August 1907—also the decisive spur to Robinson's career in the theater. Within two months he began work on his first play, *The Clancy Name*, accepted by Yeats and Lady Gregory for the Abbey in 1908. In 1909 two more of Robinson's plays reached the stage, *The Cross Roads* and *The Lesson of His Life* (in Cork). Early the next year, Yeats, whom Robinson always acknowledged as the dominating force in his life, offered him the job of running the Abbey, apparently on the basis of Robinson's literary talent and his potential as protégé. After a brief tutelage in London under George Bernard Shaw, Robinson took charge and began to steer the Abbey away from the poetic drama favored by Yeats and toward the critical realism of T. C. Murray and Sean O'Casey.

In the spring of 1910 Robinson brought out *Harvest*, which, like his earlier plays, drew heated criticism for its harsh, pointedly unsentimental view of life in rural Ireland. Shortly afterward, Robinson's inexperience as manager caused the Abbey to lose its English patron, A. E. F. Horniman, when he kept the Abbey open following the sudden death of Edward VII. Protected by Yeats from dismissal, Robinson joined Lady Gregory for the American tour of the Abbey company in 1911–1912—a financial and critical success despite riots over Synge's *The Playboy of the Western World*. Later in 1912 he directed the first of his three overtly political plays of the period, *The Patriots*. After the unprofitable third tour of the United States in 1914, Robinson, under pressure from Lady Gregory, resigned his post as director-manager.

For the next four years his new work as organizing librarian for the Carnegie Trust allowed him to tour the Irish countryside, during which time Robinson wrote two more political dramas, *The Dreamers* (1915) and *The Lost Leader* (1918), and an autobiographical novel, *A Young Man from the South* (1917). Meanwhile, Robinson also wrote a comedy that proved to be his biggest critical and commercial success, *The Whiteheaded Boy* (1916), and founded the Dublin Drama League as a venue for international theater. In 1919, despite Lady Gregory's reluctance, she and Yeats invited Robinson to resume his old position at the Abbey. Appointed to the Board of Directors in 1923, he maintained his association with the Abbey until his death.

In the 1920s, besides his directing duties at the Abbey, Robinson served as drama critic for the London *Observer* (1924–1925), founded the experimental Peacock Theatre, started the Abbey School of Acting, wrote short fiction, and edited several volumes of poetry. His own plays included *The Round Table* (1922), the well-received short play *Crabbed Youth and Age* (1922), *Never the Time and Place* (1924), *Portrait* (1925), *The White Blackbird* (1925), *The Big House* (1926), and *The Far-Off Hills* (1928). In the 1930s Robinson split his time between the Abbey and teaching at various American colleges and universities, including Amherst and Michigan. In 1931 he adapted Sheridan's *The Critic* for the Abbey; later that year he married Dorothy Travers Smith in London, then sailed to America to present advance lectures for the touring Abbey company.

His interest in Strindberg and O'Neill led him to attempt an expressionistic style in such less-successful plays as *Ever the Twain* (1929), *Give a Dog—* (1929), and *All's Over Then?* (1932). In 1933 Robinson parodied his own tendency toward aesthetic cosmopolitanism in *Drama at Inish* (renamed *Is Life Worth Living?* for its 1934 London premiere), followed by the Pirandellian one-act *Church Street* (1934). In 1935, his effectiveness diminished by heavy drinking, Robinson was replaced by Hugh Hunt as the Abbey's chief play director. The works of his later period, including *When Lovely Woman* (1936), *Killycreggs in Twilight* (1937), *Bird's Nest* (1938), *Roly Poly* (1940), and *Forget-Me-Not* (1941), reveal declining creative powers, though he continued to be prolific as a writer and editor. His radio play *Let Well Enough Alone* was broadcast on Radió Éireann in 1940; his authorized history of the Abbey appeared in 1951. In 1954, he produced his final play, *The Lucky Finger*, at Bowling Green

State University. Lennox Robinson died of heart failure on 14 October 1958 and was buried in Dublin at St. Patrick's Cathedral.

Selected Biographical Sources: Murray; O'Neill; Starkie.

MAJOR PLAYS, PREMIERES, AND SIGNIFICANT REVIVALS: THEATRICAL RECEPTION

The Clancy Name. 1908. (one act). Opened 8 October at the Abbey Theatre (a revised version premiered 30 June 1909). Opened 19 June 1911 at the Court Theatre, London.

Robinson's first play, antisentimental in its portrait of Irish farm life, was taken by critics and others as a libelous assault on every Clancy in Ireland. The *Freeman's Journal* (Review of *The Clancy Name*) denounced the play as "a blot on the stage" and suggested more vigilant censorship. Holloway noted misplaced laughter from the audience, inferior acting, and no calls for the author. Reviewers for the *Daily Express,* the *Dublin Evening Mail,* and *The Peasant and Irish Ireland* (see Hogan and Kilroy) likewise decried the play as a contrived melodrama with repellent themes.

The Cross Roads. 1909. Opened 1 April at the Abbey Theatre; a revised version opened 3 February 1910. Opened 20 June 1910 at the Court Theatre, London.

In the second of Robinson's three early plays of rural Irish life, the *Evening Herald*'s (Review of *The Cross Roads*) reviewer saw potential in Robinson as a new Synge, and the *Freeman's Journal* (Review of *The Cross Roads*) praised the writing and acting. The *Dublin Evening Mail* (Review of *The Cross Roads*) likened the performance to Coleridge's Ancient Mariner holding his audience rapt and praised Robinson's uncompromisingly grim ending, which Holloway described as "the saddest tragedy I have ever witnessed." The *Freeman's Journal* noted improvement in the 1910 revised version, approving the elimination of the prologue and the "more intensely dramatic" effect. More recently, however, O'Neill has called this the author's least successful work.

Harvest. 1910. Opened 19 May at the Abbey Theatre. Directed by Lennox Robinson. Opened 7 June at the Court Theatre, London.

This study of how excessive education can hurt the rural poor was blasted in such Dublin newspapers as the *Irish Independent* ("Beneath Criticism"), which called it "nauseating," and the *Evening Telegraph* ("An Outside Criticism"), whose reviewer found it intellectually cold and gratuitously shocking. An unsolicited "Outside Criticism" in the *Evening Telegraph* warned decent theatergoers to avoid this "seething pot of vice, filth, meanness, dishonour, dishonesty, depravity and duplicity." Lawrence [2], though, found the situations—especially the concluding irony—convincing and compelling. The *Irish Times* (Review of *Harvest*) acknowledged its shock value but found the characters strongly conceived and developed and the situation interesting, anticipating Emma Goldman's praise for Robinson's image of the fighting "true Irishman." In 1911 the

New York Times ("Bitter Irony") faulted the Abbey's touring production for spotty acting as well as weak writing, but in 1913 Weygandt defended this play (along with the hotly attacked *Harvest* and *The Clancy Name*) as sympathetic, if, at times, severe in its depictions, of "the Irish peasant."

Patriots. 1912. Opened 11 April at the Abbey Theatre. Directed by Lennox Robinson. Opened 10 June at the Court Theatre, London.

Reviewers for the *Evening Herald* (Reverend of *Patriots*) and the *Daily Express* (Review of *Patriots*) judged this—the first of three plays about Irish nationalism and its leadership—Robinson's best play to date, praising especially its tautness of dialogue and plotting. The *Evening Telegraph* had general praise but faulted the imputation of apathy among Ireland's nationalists. Stronger detractors included the *Irish Independent* (Review of *Patriots*), whose reviewer thought the play pretentious, and Lawrence [2], who disliked the satire and discerned political anachronism. Both Palmer and the *New York Times* (Review of *Patriots*) reviewer endorsed the play's central idea but found the execution unfocused and dramatically diffuse, Palmer noting his preference for *Harvest*.

The Dreamers. 1915. Opened 10 February at the Abbey Theatre. Directed by A. Patrick Wilson.

This dramatization of Robert Emmet's 1803 rebellion filled Holloway with despair for Ireland's future. Several critics found the play simply too long, including Lawrence and the *Irish Times* reviewer (see Hogan, Burnham, and Poteet). Lawrence [2] called the play essentially "a dramatic pamphlet" but acknowledged the forcefully realistic crowd scenes and perceived "the manner of the kinematograph" in its episodic plotting. Mrs. Cruise O'Brien likewise observed a profusion of external incident that diminished the play's psychological interest and tragic effect. More caustically, the *Evening Herald* (Review of *The Dreamers*) reviewer deemed the whole production "a thing of love, laughter, and blather."

The Whiteheaded Boy. 1916. Opened 13 December at the Abbey Theatre. Directed by J. Augustus Keough. Revivals: Gaiety Theatre, Manchester, England, 13 September 1920; Henry Miller's Theatre, New York, 15 September 1921; Civic Theater, Detroit, November 1929; Abbey Theatre, 25 March 1974.

This comedy of Irish upward mobility and sibling rivalry, written in only two weeks, is now widely considered Robinson's most successful play but came in for some early criticism. Holloway had scathing opening-night words for the play's chaotic final act and the playwright's postcurtain speechifying. Cruise O'Brien, though admitting his own enjoyment, compared the comedy unfavorably to the playwright's earlier plays and pondered a potentially deeper meaning beneath the laughter. Robinson himself called his play "political from beginning to end." Woollcott [2], reviewing the 1921 New York production, echoes this in likening the coddled but dependent young hero to Ireland itself: the child, as O'Neill has remarked, of the British Empire. Hackett more heartily approved the play's good humor and its seeming avoidance of overt social or political critique, while Boyd [2] and Malone [1] singled out the ease and authenticity of both dialogue and situation. More recently, critics such as Starkie and Murray have continued to praise Robinson's deft comic writing, though none so warmly as Archer [1] in 1923: "the perfection of peasant comedy" with "not its rival in the English language"; indeed, "a work of which any literature might be proud."

The Lost Leader. 1918. Opened 19 February at the Abbey Theatre. Opened 10 June 1919, at the Court Theatre, London, and 11 November 1919 at the Greenwich Village Theatre, New York.

Capitalizing on the current legend that the great nationalist Charles Parnell was still alive, this return to explicit political drama moved Holloway to record in his diary "a big night at the Abbey": a superbly executed, ambitiously conceived tragedy performed to a large and enthusiastic house. The *Irish Times* (Review of *The Lost Leader*) reviewer generally agreed with these judgments; however, the *Evening Telegraph* (Review of *The Lost Leader*) found the dialogue limp, the characters lifeless, the plot unconvincing, and the use of Parnell almost cynical. The *Evening Herald* (Review of *The Lost Leader*) critic praised the play's involving action and occasional humor but did not rank it among Robinson's best work. Of the Court production the *Athenaeum* (Review of *The Lost Leader*) reviewer had mild praise for the first two acts but chided the finale as blatant sermonizing, but Archer [2] declared the play "the best thing the Irish movement has given us" since Synge; he later [1] called it "one of the most imaginative plays of our time." Woollcott's response to the New York premiere was mixed: like other critics he noted a diminishing power toward the end as well as some implausibilities but judged its greatest merit the ability to absorb even an audience that did not already revere Parnell.

The Round Table. 1922. Opened 31 January at the Abbey Theatre. Directed by Lennox Robinson. Opened 16 March 1925, at the Q Theatre, London; 11 May at Wyndham's Theatre, London. Revised version opened 16 March 1927, at the Playhouse Theatre, Liverpool; 8 July 1927, at the Abbey Theatre; 27 February 1930, at the Gansevoort Theatre, New York.

Here Robinson's characteristic theme of frustrated idealism is manifest in a young Dublin woman, Daisy Drennan, who awakens finally to a new life. Of the first version of the play, the *Evening Telegraph* (Review of *The Round Table*) reviewer found the psychological exposition too experimental and the sober conclusion incongruent with the often humorous tone of earlier scenes. The *Evening Herald* (Review of *The Round Table*) critic likewise found unintended humor in the quasi-expressionistic devices, and O'Donnell [3] observed that the idea worked better as a story than a play. Among London reviewers MacCarthy and Agate chided theatergoers for ignoring a play better than most West End offerings. Of the revised version Foley and Hayes [4] noted much improvement, though both also expressed hope for yet another, even better version. Atkinson [10] faintly praised the New York production as good "bourgeois playgoing" but called the performances amateurish.

Crabbed Youth and Age. 1922. (one act). Opened 14 November at the Abbey Theatre. Directed by Lennox Robinson. Opened 15 October 1924 at the Dramatic Art Centre, London. Revival: Martin Beck Theatre, New York, November 1932.

This brief comedy, in which a charming mother outshines her unmarried daughter, was well received by veteran Dublin critics such as Lawrence [1], who applauded the vivacious characterization and dialogue as well as the amusing irony of the situation. Holloway and the *Evening Telegraph* (Review of *Crabbed Youth and Age*) critic shared Lawrence's views, though in much briefer form. Later, Malone [1] declared it "probably the most delightful one-act play of the contemporary theatre in any country" and Robinson's best play to date. In the 1932 New York production Atkinson [4] saw only "an amusing trifle," however, and more recently, O'Neill has judged the play merely "very competently developed," and Murray fails to mention it at all—even while arguing that Robinson was most successful in writing comedies.

The Big House. 1926. Opened 6 September at the Abbey Theatre. Directed by Lennox Robinson. Opened 4 January 1933 at the Martin Beck Theatre, New York; 22 February 1934, at the Playhouse (London).

The rapid decline of the Anglo-Irish landed class following World War I forms the center of this play, set in Robinson's native County Cork; the Alcock family finds itself trapped between the two sides in the civil war, and their house is destroyed. Malone [1] saw a lost chance for greatness in this play, which he blamed on Robinson's own mixed political sentiments. Following the 1933 New York premiere Atkinson [2] noted a weakness of construction and too much Irish political history for American audiences. In 1934 the *New York Times* (" 'The Big House' Stirs a London Audience") reported a "furor" at the London premiere, noted the author's own prophecies of further conflict in Ireland and Europe, and quoted the *Times*' criticism of the play's violent sensationalism. Charles Morgan [2] faults Robinson for focusing too much on the idealistic Alcock daughter instead of her father. Later assessments by Starkie and Murray share Malone's opinion that the play, like the Alcock house itself, collapses from its own political ambivalence.

The Far-Off Hills. 1928. Opened 22 October at the Abbey Theatre. Directed by Arthur Shields. Opened 30 March 1929 at the Q Theatre, London; opened 18 October 1932 at the Martin Beck Theatre, New York. Revivals: Ambassador Theatre, New York, October 1937; Peacock Theatre, Dublin (as *Is Glas iad na Cnuic*), September 1969; Peacock Theatre, Dublin, 29 April 1970.

Regarded by many as second only to *The Whiteheaded Boy* among Robinson's successes (and written almost as rapidly), *The Far-Off Hills* seems almost a self-satire on his trademark theme of frustrated idealism. Delighted by the

Dublin premiere, Hayes [2] ranked it among the best Irish comedies ever, approving its lack of a parochially Irish setting and predicting its success in London and New York. The *New York Times* (Review of *The Far-Off Hills*) reviewer, however, dismissed the 1932 New York production as a "diverting trifle" and noted its determined avoidance of all difficult themes. At the 1937 New York revival Atkinson [7] showed more enthusiasm, praising both the empathic characters and the graceful performances of the Abbey players. More recent valuations have also been favorable, though O'Neill notes the play's "uneven" construction.

Drama at Inish. 1933. Opened 6 February at the Abbey Theatre. Directed by Lennox Robinson. Revised as *Is Life Worth Living?*; opened August 1933 at the Ambassador Theatre, London; 9 November 1933 at the Masque Theatre, New York. Revivals: Golden Theatre, New York, as *Drama at Inish*, November 1934.

Robinson's most clearly self-parodic work directs its humor at the pretentions of the European art theater by placing it in farcical conflict with the citizenry of a small Irish town. At the Dublin premiere, the *New York Times*' ("Robinson Comedy Delights Dublin") correspondent apparently missed this point in seeing Irish rural life as the chief object of the satire (see Krause for a similar view). Reviewing the London production, Charles Morgan [3] discerned a playful joke on theater audiences, finding nothing harsh in its humor. Atkinson [8] liked the idea better than the play itself but especially faulted the "cluttered performance" of company at the New York premiere, though he praised the Abbey players in their 1934 New York revival [6].

ADDITIONAL PLAYS, ADAPTATIONS, AND PRODUCTIONS

The Cork Dramatic League staged *The Lesson of His Life* in 1909, Robinson's only non-Dublin premiere until *Give a Dog—* opened at the Strand Theatre in London in 1929. His other plays of 1924–1925 included the brief farce *Never the Time and Place, Portrait*, and *The White Blackbird*; the latter two reflect Robinson's increasing interest in psychological exposition at the time. A comedy, *The Red Sock* (1927), was produced in Dublin under the pseudonym "Jim Barry" by an offshoot of the Dublin Drama League called the New Players. Neither his American play *Ever the Twain* (1929) nor the Strindbergian *All's Over Then?* (1932) inspired critical favor, though two others, *Church Street* (1934) and *Killycreggs in Twilight* (1937), were well received. Other Abbey premieres were *Bird's Nest* (1938) and *Forget-Me-Not* (1941). Non-Abbey premieres among his later plays include *When Lovely Woman* (1936) and *Roly Poly* (1940), both at the Gate Theatre, Dublin; *The Lucky Finger* (1948), which premiered at Bowling Green State University in Ohio before moving (after revisions) to the Abbey; and *The Demon Lover* (1954), which opened at the Gaiety Theatre, Manchester. A radio play, *Let Well Enough Alone*, was broadcast by

Radió Éireann on Christmas Day, 1940. A final comedy, *Speed the Plough* (1953), is apparently unproduced. Fergus Linehan and Jim Doherty adapted *Drama at Inish* as the musical *Innish*, which premiered 8 September 1975 at the Abbey.

ASSESSMENT OF ROBINSON'S CAREER

In the best concise overview of Robinson's plays, Murray distinguishes three phases: the "grim realism" of such early plays as *The Clancy Name* and *Harvest*; the overt political thrust of *Patriots, The Lost Leader*, and *The Dreamers*; and the winsome satire of *The Whiteheaded Boy, The Far-Off Hills*, and *Crabbed Youth and Age*. Hogan includes a fourth group: the technical experimentation of *Ever the Twain* and *Church Street*. However, as Murray, Starkie, O'Neill, and others have recognized, to understand Robinson's wide-ranging contributions to Irish theater requires a consideration of the three key aspects of his career: as a playwright, certainly, but also as the Abbey's director-manager and, more generally, as an exponent of the Irish Literary Revival on both sides of the Atlantic.

Robinson's plays must form the center of this career triptych, not only because of their intrinsic value but as a matrix of Irish culture and society. He conspicuously failed to realize Yeats' vision of the Abbey as a temple of modern poetic drama; instead, Robinson provocatively confronted various social and political ideologies prevalent in Ireland before World War II. In 1913 Weygandt looked forward to more of the "sane and cleansing satire of pretension" evident in Robinson's early plays; in 1922 O'Conor declared, "No Irish writer more faithfully interprets this time"; and in 1929 Malone [1] called Robinson "certainly the most important of the younger [i.e., post-Synge] Irish dramatists." More recently, though, Robinson is seen as a chief keeper of the Irish theatrical flame between the death of Synge in 1909 and the emergence of O'Casey in the mid-1920s, a skilled practitioner "when genius was absent" (Maxwell).

Critics and scholars have been virtually unanimous in citing satiric comedy as Robinson's strength, while conceding the craftsmanship or sociological interest of his other plays. Though not himself a major modern dramatist, Robinson had a keen sense of what kind of plays and which themes were worth trying at crucial points in the development of Irish drama. By comparing *The Clancy Name* with *The Whiteheaded Boy* or comparing *All's Over Then?* with *Drama at Inish*, one sees that Robinson's evolution as playwright may follow a pattern noted by poet Patrick Kavanagh, that "tragedy is underdeveloped comedy"; or, in Robinson's own phrase, that tragedy is best realized "in terms of comedy." For instance, even in the otherwise harsh melodramatic realism of *Harvest*, when a character calls the farmhouse interior "just like a scene in the Abbey Theatre," Robinson reveals a satirical self-consciousness and an awareness of Irishness—especially the image of the Irish peasant—as a deliberate cultural construct. A comparative study of Robinson's comic and tragic modes would yield a stronger sense of his own satirical practices and how they constitute "this strange Irish thing" that Robinson himself called "the commanding force" in his own life and, by implication, the life of his times.

Perhaps even more useful would be a full-length study building on O'Neill's 1964 monograph (the only scholarly book on Robinson to date), a critical biography that places Robinson at the center of Irish drama as it reached the international stage before and following World War I. As Murray points out, despite his much-chronicled obsequiousness toward Yeats and timidity toward Lady Gregory, Robinson deserves credit for formulating the peculiar mix of idealism, romanticism, sentimentality, melodrama, realism, and hard-nosed satire that became the dominant mode among Abbey plays for several decades. His work as a lecturer, critic, fiction writer, poet, and historian also distinguishes Robinson as a highly versatile man of letters. If Robinson may not be ranked among the great creators of Irish drama, as writer and director he must be placed high among those who fashioned the medium in which great creators could flourish. Even in his calamitous rejection of *The Silver Tassie* in 1928, Robinson acknowledged O'Casey's need to push the limits of realism, a need he felt at the time in his own writing.

Accounts vary of Robinson's skills as director-manager, but at the very least his guidance lent continuity during years dominated by political upheaval and uncertain financial backing. Disputing the charge by Robinson's contemporaries that he failed to visualize performances adequately (O'Neill), Murray emphasizes Robinson's "unobtrusive" manner of harmonizing the script with all other aspects of the production. Furthermore, despite audience revolts and some red ink, to Robinson must go much of the credit for bringing the works of Synge, Yeats, Colum, and Lady Gregory across the Atlantic (see Everson [1, 2]) and for fostering the careers of O'Casey, Shiels, Brinsley MacNamara, Deevy, and T. C. Murray, among others. Moreover, Robinson helped establish the Dublin Drama League so the Abbey could showcase the drama of other nations while maintaining its primary goal of fostering the playwrights of Ireland.

To dismiss Robinson as "a competent and predictable playwright" (Krause) is accurate but misleading. Worley and Phillips are more apt in calling him "the major-minor figure of the Anglo-Irish theatre in the first half of this century." The conscious craftsmanship of his work did more than merely bide time between Synge and O'Casey: it made available a model and a medium for the working Irish dramatist and helped bring this new Irish drama to the world.

ARCHIVAL SOURCE

Manuscripts of Robinson's plays, essays, journalism, fiction, lectures, speeches, and music are housed in the Irish Collection at the Morris Library, Southern Illinois University at Carbondale. Also included are literary manuscripts of Æ (George Russell), Lady Gregory, and W. B. Yeats and his correspondence with Yeats, Lady Gregory, Sean O'Casey, George Bernard Shaw, and others associated with the Abbey Theatre.

PRIMARY BIBLIOGRAPHY

Plays

The Big House. London: Macmillan, 1928. (Also *Irish Drama, 1900–1980*. Washington, D.C.: Catholic University Press, 1990.)

Church Street. Belfast: Carter, 1955. (Also *Plays of a Changing Ireland*. New York: Macmillan, 1936.)

Crabbed Youth and Age. London, New York: Putnam, 1924.

The Cross Roads. Dublin: Maunsel, 1909.

The Dreamers. Dublin: Maunsel, 1915.

Ever the Twain. London: Macmillan, 1930.

The Far-Off Hills. London: Chatto, 1931. New York: Macmillan, 1932. (Also *Twentieth Century Plays, British*. New York: Ronald, 1941.)

Give a Dog—. London: Macmillan, 1928.

Is Life Worth Living? London: Macmillan, 1933. (Published as *Drama at Inish*. Dublin: Duffy, 1953.)

The Lost Leader. Dublin: Eigeas, 1918.

The Lucky Finger. New York: French, 1949.

Patriots. Dublin: Maunsel, 1912; New York: French, 1912; Boston: Luce, 1912.

Portrait (with *The White Blackbird*). Dublin: Talbot, 1926.

The Red Sock. *Journal of Irish Literature* 9 (1980): 34–68.

The Round Table. London, New York: Putnam, 1924.

The White Blackbird (with *Portrait*). Dublin: Talbot, 1926.

The Whiteheaded Boy. London, New York: Putnam, 1921; Dublin: Talbot, 1922.

Collections

"Four Lost Comedies by Lennox Robinson". (Edited texts and critical analysis of *The Lesson of His Life, The Red Sock, When Lovely Woman, Speed the Plough*.) Ed. Lloyd Douglas Worley. Diss., Southern Illinois University, 1979.

Killycreggs in Twilight; and Other Plays. (*Is Life Worth Living?* and *Bird's Nest*.) London: Macmillan, 1939.

More Plays. (*All's Over, Then?, Church Street*.) New York: Macmillan, 1935.

Plays. (*The Round Table, Crabbed Youth and Age, Portrait, The White Blackbird, The Big House, Give a Dog—*.) London: Macmillan, 1928.

Selected Plays of Lennox Robinson. (*Patriots, The Whiteheaded Boy, Crabbed Youth and Age, The Big House, Drama at Inish, Church Street*.) Ed. Christopher Murray. Gerrard's Cross, Buckinghamshire: Colin Smythe, 1982. Washington, D.C.: Catholic University Press, 1982.

Two One-Act Comedies. (*Never the Time and Place, Crabbed Youth and Age*.) Belfast: Carter, 1953.

Two Plays. (*Harvest, The Clancy Name*.) Dublin: Maunsel, 1911.

Writings on Drama and Theater

Curtain Up: An Autobiography. London: Michael Joseph, 1942.
Foreword. *The Irish Theatre.* Ed. Lennox Robinson. London: Macmillan, 1939.
I Sometimes Think. Dublin: Talbot, 1956.
Ireland's Abbey Theatre: A History, 1899–1951. London: Sidgwick and Jackson, 1951.
"Lady Gregory." *The Irish Theatre.* Ed. Lennox Robinson. London: Macmillan, 1939.
Pictures in a Theatre. Dublin: Sign of the Three Candles, 1947.
Scattering Branches. London: Macmillan, 1940.
Three Homes (with Tom Robinson and Nora Dorman). London: Michael Joseph, 1938.
Towards an Appreciation of the Theatre. Dublin: Metropolitan, 1945.

SECONDARY BIBLIOGRAPHY

Agate, James. [Review of *The Round Table.*] *The Contemporary Theatre, 1925.* London: Chapman and Hall, 1926, 119, 121–22.
Archer, William. [1]. *The Old Drama and the New.* New York: Dodd, Mead, 1929, 370–74.
———. [2]. "Parnell Redivivus." *The Review* (26 July 1919): 238–39.
Atkinson, Brooks. [1]. "Abbey Odds and Ends." *New York Times* (20 Nov. 1934): 24.
———. [2]. [Review of *The Big House.*] *New York Times* (5 Jan. 1933): 19.
———. [3]. [Review of *Church Street.*] *New York Times* (10 Feb. 1948): 27.
———. [4]. [Review of *Crabbed Youth and Age.*] *New York Times* (4 Nov. 1932): 25.
———. [5]. " 'Drama at Inish' Acted by the Abbey Troupe." *New York Times* (15 Nov. 1934).
———. [6]. [Review of *Drama at Inish.*] *New York Times* (15 Nov. 1934): 24.
———. [7]. [Review of *The Far-Off Hills.*] *New York Times* (11 Oct. 1937): 26.
———. [8]. [Review of *Is Life Worth Living?*] *New York Times* (10 Nov. 1933): 24.
———. [9]. "Lennox Robinson's 'The Far-Off Hills' Appears in the Abbey Theatre Repertory." *New York Times* (12 Oct. 1937).
———. [10]. [Review of *The Round Table.*] *New York Times* (28 Feb. 1930): 20.
"Beneath Criticism." *Irish Independent* (20 May 1910).
" 'The Big House' Stirs a London Audience." *New York Times* (22 Feb. 1934): 24.
"Bitter Irony in This Irish Play." *New York Times* (18 Dec. 1911): 11.
Boyd, Ernest. [1]. *The Contemporary Drama of Ireland.* Boston: Little, Brown, 1917. 164–68.
———. [2]. *Ireland's Literary Renaissance.* 1922. New York: Barnes and Noble, 1968. 352–54.
Brighouse, Harold. [Review of *Killycreggs in Twilight.*] *Manchester Guardian* (12 May 1939): 8.
Review of *Church Street. New York Times* (23 May 1934): 15.
Review of *The Clancy Name. Freeman's Journal* (9 Oct. 1908): 10.
Review of *Crabbed Youth and Age. Evening Telegraph* (15 Nov. 1922): 6.
Review of *The Cross Roads. Dublin Evening Mail* (2 Apr. 1909): 2.
Review of *The Cross Roads. Evening Herald* (1 Apr. 1909): 4.
Review of *The Cross Roads. Freeman's Journal* (2 Apr. 1909): 9.
Review of *The Cross Roads* (rev. version). *Freeman's Journal* (4 Feb. 1910).

Review of *The Dreamers. Evening Herald* (11 Feb. 1915): 2.

Review of *Ever the Twain. New York Times* (17 Dec. 1933): sec. 9: 4.

Review of *Ever the Twain. New York Times* (20 Oct. 1929): sec. 3: 3.

Everson, Ida G. [1]. "Lennox Robinson and Synge's *Playboy* (1911–1930): Two Decades of American Cultural Growth." *New England Quarterly* 44 (1971): 3–21.

———. [2]. "Young Lennox Robinson and the Abbey Theatre's First American Tour." *Modern Drama* 9 (1966): 74–89.

Review of *The Far-Off Hills. New York Times* (19 Oct. 1932): 22.

Foley, Maurice. "The Round Table Re-Polished." *Irish Statesman* (23 July 1927): 476.

Goldman, Emma. "Lenox [sic] Robinson: *Harvest*." *The Social Significance of Modern Drama.* Boston: Badger, 1914, 261–66.

Hackett, Francis. [Review of *The Whiteheaded Boy.*] *New Republic* 5 Oct. 1921: 161.

Review of *Harvest. Academy* (24 June 1911): 785–86.

Review of *Harvest. Irish Times* (20 May 1910): 5.

Hayes, J. J. [1]. [Review of *Ever the Twain.*] *New York Times* (27 Oct. 1929): sec. 9: 1.

———. [2]. [Review of *The Far-Off Hills.*] *New York Times* (11 Nov. 1928): sec. 10: 4.

———. [3]. [Review of *Give a Dog—*.] *New York Times* (9 June 1929): sec. 8: 3.

———. [4]. [Review of *The Round Table.*] *New York Times* (28 Aug. 1927): sec. 7: 1.

Hogan, Robert. *After the Irish Renaissance.* Minneapolis: University of Minnesota Press, 1967. 21–27.

Hogan, Robert, and Richard Burnham. [1]. *The Art of the Amateur, 1916–1920.* Vol. 5 of *The Modern Irish Drama: A Documentary History.* 6 vols. Dublin: Dolmen, 1984.

Hogan, Robert, and Richard Burnham. [2]. *The Years of O'Casey, 1921–1926.* Vol. 6 of *The Modern Irish Drama: A Documentary History.* 6 vols. Newark: University of Delaware Press, 1992.

Hogan, Robert, Richard Burnham, and Daniel P. Poteet. *The Rise of the Realists, 1910–1915.* Vol. 4 of *The Modern Irish Drama: A Documentary History.* 6 vols. Dublin: Dolmen, 1979.

Hogan, Robert, and James Kilroy. *The Abbey Theatre: The Years of Synge, 1905–1909.* Vol. 3 of *The Modern Irish Drama: A Documentary History.* 6 vols. Dublin: Dolmen, 1978.

Holloway, Joseph. *Joseph Holloway's Abbey Theatre: A Selection from His Unpublished Journal, Impressions of a Dublin Playgoer.* Ed. Robert Hogan and Michael J. O'Neill. Carbondale: Southern Illinois University Press, 1967.

"Inish Again." *New York Times* (14 Dec. 1937): 33.

Isaacs, Edith. [Review of *Is Life Worth Living?*] *Theatre Arts Monthly* 18 (1934): 13–14.

Review of *Killycreggs in Twilight. Times Literary Supplement* (1 Apr. 1939): 800.

Krause, David. *The Profane Book of Irish Comedy.* Ithaca, N.Y.: Cornell University Press, 1982. 195–201.

Lawrence, W. J. [1]. [Reviews of *Crabbed Youth and Age, The Round Table.*] *Journal of Irish Literature* 18.2 (1989): 28–29.

———. [2]. [Reviews of *Harvest, Patriots, The Dreamers.*] *Journal of Irish Literature* 18.1 (1989): 5–6, 16–18, 30–32, 45–47.

Review of *The Lesson of His Life. Cork Constitution* (3 Dec. 1909): 6.

"A Look round the White Blackbird." *Evening Herald* (13 Oct. 1925): 2.

Review of *The Lost Leader. Athenaeum* (20 June 1919): 500–501.

Review of *The Lost Leader. Evening Telegraph* (20 Feb. 1918): 4.

Review of *The Lost Leader. Evening Herald* (20 Feb. 1918).

Review of *The Lost Leader. Irish Times* (27 Feb. 1918): 68.

" 'Lucky Finger' Bows." *New York Times* (21 Jan. 1948): 30.

Malone, Andrew. [1]. *The Irish Drama*. London: Constable, 1929, 174–85.

———. [2]. [Review of *Portrait*.] *Dublin Magazine* (May 1925): 631–33.

Maxwell, D. E. S. *A Critical History of Modern Irish Drama, 1891–1980*. Cambridge: Cambridge University Press, 1984. 73–75.

MacCarthy, Desmond. [Review of *The Round Table*.] *New Statesman* (30 May 1925): 198.

Mitchell, Susan L. [Review of *Portrait*.] *Irish Statesman* (4 Apr. 1925): 114–15.

Morgan, A. E. *Tendencies of Modern English Drama*. London: Constable, 1924, 207–21.

Morgan, Charles. [1]. [Review of *All's Over, Then?*] *New York Times* (10 June 1932): sec. 9: 1.

———. [2]. [Review of *The Big House*.] *New York Times* (18 Mar. 1934): sec. 9: 2.

———. [3]. "Lennox Robinson Plays a Prank." *New York Times* (17 Sept. 1933): sec. 10: 1.

Murray, Christopher. "Lennox Robinson: The Abbey's Anti-Hero." *Irish Writers and the Theatre*. Ed. Masaru Sekine. Totowa, N.J.: Barnes and Noble, 1986. 114–34.

Review of *Never the Time and Place. Irish Times* (20 Feb. 1924): 6.

"A New Play by Mr. Lennox Robinson." *Manchester Guardian* (10 Apr. 1925).

O'Brien, Cruise. "Restraint in Comedy." *New Ireland* (23 Dec. 1916): 118.

O'Brien, Cruise, Mrs. [Review of *The Dreamers*.] *Irish Citizen* (20 Feb. 1915): 311.

O'Conor, Norreys Jephson. "A Dramatist of Changing Ireland." *Sewanee Review* 30 (1922): 277–85.

O'Donnell, F. J. H. [1]. "Fortune-Telling at the Abbey." *Evening Herald* (20 Feb. 1924): 4.

———. [2]. [Review of *Portrait*.] *Evening Herald* (1 Apr. 1925): 4.

———. [3]. [Review of *The Round Table*.] *Gael* (1 May 1922).

O'Neill, Michael J. *Lennox Robinson*. New York: Twayne, 1964.

"An Outside Criticism" *Evening Telegraph* (20 May 1910).

Palmer, John. [Review of *Patriots*.] *Saturday Review of Politics, Literature, Science and Art* (15 June 1912): 744.

Review of *Patriots. Daily Express* (12 Apr. 1912): 12.

Review of *Patriots. Evening Herald* (12 Apr. 1912): 2.

Review of *Patriots. Evening Telegraph* (12 Apr. 1912): 4.

Review of *Patriots. Irish Independent* (12 Apr. 1912): 10.

Review of *Patriots. New York Times* (12 Feb. 1913).

Peake, Donald James. "Selected Plays of Lennox Robinson: A Mirror of the Anglo-Irish Ascendancy." Ph.D. diss., Southern Illinois University, 1972.

Peterson, Richard F. "The Crane and the Swan: Lennox Robinson and W. B. Yeats." *Journal of Irish Literature* 9 (1980): 69–76.

Review of *Portrait. Irish Times* (1 Apr. 1925): 9.

"Robinson Comedy Delights Dublin." *New York Times* (12 Feb. 1933): sec. 2: 2.

Review of *The Round Table. Evening Herald* (1 Feb. 1922): 3.

Review of *The Round Table. Evening Telegraph* (1 Feb. 1922): 4.

Review of *The Round Table. Times* (17 Mar. 1925): 12.

Smith, C. B. "Unity in Diversity: A Critical Study of the Drama of Lennox Robinson." Diss., Trinity College Dublin, 1960.

Spinner, Kaspar. *Die Alte Dame Sagt: Nein! Drei Irische Dramatiker: Lennox Robinson, Sean O'Casey, Denis Johnston.* Bern: Francke, 1961.

Squires, Tom. [Review of *The Far-Off Hills.*] *Theatre Arts Monthly* 21 (1937): 928.

Starkie, Walter. "Lennox Robinson, 1886–1958." *Theatre Annual* 16 (1959): 7–19.

Vernon, Grenville. [Review of *Drama at Inish.*] *Commonweal* (31 Dec. 1937): 272.

Weygandt, Cornelius. "Mr. S. Lennox Robinson." *Irish Plays and Playwrights.* 1913. Port Washington, N.Y.: Kennikat, 1966, 222–32.

Review of *The White Blackbird. Irish Times* (13 Oct. 1925): 3.

Review of *The Whiteheaded Boy. Evening Herald* (14 Dec. 1916): 3.

Woollcott, Alexander. [1]. [Review of *The Lost Leader.*] *New York Times* (12 Nov. 1919): 11.

———. [2]. [Review of *The Whiteheaded Boy.*] *New York Times* (16 Sept. 1921).

Worley, Lloyd. "Robinson's Great Hoax." *Journal of Irish Literature* 9 (1980): 17–29.

Worley, Lloyd, and Gary Phillips. "A Lennox Robinson Number." *Journal of Irish Literature* 9 (1980). (Special issue; contains script of *The Red Sock.*)

Worth, Katharine. "A Place in the Country." *Times Literary Supplement* (2 Sept. 1983): 929.

George Bernard Shaw
(1856–1950)

TRAMBLE T. TURNER

G.B.S., the persona created by Bernard Shaw, was as well known in 1950 for his involvement in Fabian politics (and as a waspish writer of letters to newspapers) as for his forty-eight plays. (Shaw chose not to use George in signing himself, a practice that some critics believe resulted from his antipathy toward his father, George Carr Shaw.) While such plays as *Pygmalion* (1912, produced 1913) gained renewed fame through film (1938) and later adaptations such as *My Fair Lady* (1956), Shaw himself credited three plays with establishing his career. Curiously, the first of the three that gave Shaw his earliest commercial success, *John Bull's Other Island* (1904), had received little attention in America until the mid-1970s work of Norma Jenckes [1, 2]. The play remains one of Shaw's most popular plays in England and Ireland.

Shaw was born to Lucinda Elizabeth (Bessie) Gurly Shaw and George Carr Shaw on 26 July 1856 in Dublin. Though connected to a wealthy family (and perhaps married for her financial expectations), Lucinda Gurly was disinherited by her wealthy, unmarried aunt mainly as a result of her marriage to the improvident George Shaw. (The declining fortunes of Joyce's and Shaw's Anglo-Irish fathers provide an interesting basis for comparisons.) Two years after his mother left Ireland—and her husband—for London, Shaw followed. Having completed his first novel, *Immaturity*, on 28 September 1879, Shaw went on to write four more novels (*The Irrational Knot, Cashel Byron's Profession, Love Among the Artists*, and *An Unsocial Socialist*) that were, at the time, not accepted for publication.

After working as a music and art reviewer for papers such as the *World*, Shaw went on to become a drama critic at the *Saturday Review*. That forum enabled him to champion original, sparse stagings for Shakespearean revivals; to advocate the Ibsen productions of the Independent Theatre; to push for the establishment of a National Theatre; and to encourage a climate favorable to his own experiments in drama. His opportunity to write as a reviewer came when his mother's former voice teacher and companion, George John Vandeleur Lee, asked the young Shaw to write the reviews that Lee had contracted to write for the *Hornet*.

Shaw was an effective Hyde Park speaker, and his political involvement led to his appointment to the Executive Committee of the Fabian Party on 2 January 1885. In that role Shaw can be credited with helping to found the British Labour party. His political involvements led to a trip to Russia in 1931. During his last decade Shaw was increasingly attracted to dictators and totalitarian leaders (such as Joseph Stalin) due to a growing discouragement with the abilities of democracy to bring about social reform. Nevertheless, in his ongoing efforts to redefine communism, he was capable of claiming that more social communism existed in England during the 1930s than in Russia.

Though such works as *Widowers' Houses, Arms and the Man, The Devil's Disciple*, and *Candida* were staged by innovative companies in England and the United States from 1892 to 1900, Shaw's position as the preeminent English-language dramatist of his time was assured in 1904 and 1905 through his collaborations with the Vedrenne-Barker company. The company's successful 1904 performance of *John Bull's Other Island* led to a command performance for King Edward VII in 1905. That same year the company scored again with productions of *Man and Superman* and *Major Barbara*. In later prefaces Shaw was to cite these three plays as the basis for his burgeoning career. Noteworthy for first staging Shaw's plays, however, were the actress Florence Farr (*Arms and the Man*) and Miss Annie Horniman, who financed the enterprise as discreetly as she was later to do with the Abbey Theatre of Dublin. (Indeed, Shaw's works were often chosen for production by female directors in the first half of the century.)

Shaw's plays written during World War I (*The Inca of Perusalem, Heartbreak House, Augustus Does His Bit*, and *Annajanska*) reflect an increasingly clouded optimism about the efficacy of social and political organizations. By 1921, when he completed *Back to Methuselah*, Shaw's faith in the power of Creative Evolution and the Life Force to regenerate the world was projected increasingly further into the future with a millennial aspect. In 1926 he received the Nobel Prize for Literature for the year 1925.

The establishment of the Malvern Festival in 1929 served notice that Shaw was regarded as a national asset similar to the Bard, about whom Shaw wrote so much. Thirty-three years later North America paid Shaw the same tribute when the Shaw Festival was established in Ontario by Brian Doherty at Niagara-on-the-Lake. The Shaw Festival at Niagara-on-the-Lake has served as both a research center and an arena for maintaining popular interest in Shaw's topicality.

For example, of the 1983 production of *The Simpleton of the Unexpected Isles*, Martin Knelman wrote in Toronto's *Saturday Night*, "It was the Falklands war that triggered [Denise Coffey's] interest in *Simpleton*, which features in its bizarre plot the arrival of fleets from all over the British Empire to threaten battle over a tiny island. . . . *Simpleton* gleefully lampoons the sort of crackpot Victorian reform Shaw himself so often seemed to personify" (quoted in Margery Morgan 95). Trussler has suggested another basis for the ongoing Shavian commercial success, as well as the ongoing critical analysis: "[A]t his best . . . [Shaw] can peel away the thin veneer of national sensibilities and inhibitions so as to reveal both their deep emotional subtext and (another paradox) a profound sense of the closeness of the naturalistic and surreal" (6). Shaw died on 2 November 1950 after sustaining injuries on Sunday, 10 September, when he fell while pruning a tree in his garden at Ayot St. Lawrence.

Selected Biographical Sources: Bertolini; Carr; Henderson [1, 2]; Holroyd [1]; Rosset; Stanley Weintraub [1, 2, 3, 4, 5].

MAJOR PLAYS, PREMIERES, AND SIGNIFICANT REVIVALS: THEATRICAL RECEPTION

Widowers' Houses. 1892. Opened 9 December at the Royalty Theatre, Aberdeen. A private production directed by Herman de Lange. First American production at Herald Square Theatre, New York, 7 March 1907. Directed by Lee Shubert. First public English production: Miss Annie Horniman's Company at Midland Theatre, Manchester, 7 June 1909. Revivals: Abbey Theatre, 9 October 1916. Directed by Milton Rosmer; Stage Society at the Malvern Festival, 19 August 1930. Directed by H. K. Ayliff; Theatre Royal, Stratford-upon-Avon, 15 March 1965. Directed by Ronald Eyre; Bristol Old Vic, September 1981. Directed by John Love.

Walkley [2] observed that the play had "considerable literary qualities" but added that "Mr. Shaw's people are not dramatic characters at all, they are embodied arguments."

Arms and the Man. 1894. Opened 21 April at the Avenue Theatre, London. Directed by G. Bernard Shaw. Revivals: Savoy Theatre, London, 30 December 1907. Directed by G. Bernard Shaw and Granville-Barker; Abbey Theatre, 25 October 1916; Old Vic Theatre, 16 February 1931. Directed by Harcourt Williams, with John Gielgud as Saranoff, Ralph Richardson as Bluntschli, Marie Ney as Raina; Old Vic Company, September 1944 at the New Theatre, London. Directed by John Burrell. Cast: Laurence Olivier, Ralph Richardson, Margaret Leighton, Sybil Thorndike; Gaiety Theatre, Dublin, 1947.

Archer [1], writing about the original production, argued that it was "impossible, in short, to accept the second and third acts . . . as either 'romantic comedy' or coherent farce." Billington observes in 1970, "How well the play has stood the test of time, despite the claim of so many critics that the targets of Shaw's satire are happily obsolete."

Candida. 1894. Opened 30 July 1897, at the Independent Theatre, Aberdeen. Directed by Charles Charrington. Revivals: Browning Society, South Broad St. Theatre, Philadelphia, 18 May 1903; Court Theatre, London, 26 April 1904, Vedrenne-Barker Company. Directed by Harley Granville-Barker, Malvern Festival, 18 August 1930. Directed by H. K. Ayliff, Abbey Theatre, Dublin, 30 September 1935; Roundabout Theatre, New York, 2 February 1969. Directed by Gene Feist, Longacre Theatre, New York, 6 April 1970. Directed by Laurence Carr, Albery Theatre, London, 23 June 1977. Directed by Michael Blakemore; King's Head, 1987. Directed by Frank Hauser, production revived at the Arts Theatre, 12 January 1988. Boulevard Theatre, Soho, London, 21 September 1988. Directed by Rob Kennedy.

Howlett reports in 1977, "Michael Blakemore's production of *Candida* confirms the impression that it is a consistently unsatisfactory play." Of the 1987 revival David Nice wrote that "what Frank Hauser makes us realize is the presence of abysses threatening to open beneath order and logic" (quoted in Margery Morgan 30).

The Devil's Disciple. 1897. Opened 1 October at Harmanus Bleeker Hall, Albany, New York. Directed by Richard Mansfield. Revivals: Coronet Theatre, Notting Hill Gate, London, 7 September 1900. Directed by Shaw, Savoy Theatre, London, 14 October 1907. Directed by Shaw and Harley Granville-Barker, the production moved to the Queen's Theatre, London, on 23 November 1907; Abbey Theatre, London, 10 February 1920. Directed by Lennox Robinson; Old Vic Company at Buxton Festival, 31 August 1939 and at the Streatham Hill Theatre, 4 October 1939; Old Vic Company at the Golders Green Hippodrome, 10 June 1940. Directed by Milton Rosmer; the production moved to the Piccadilly Theatre, London, on 24 July 1940; Opera House, Manchester, 20 February 1956. Directed by Noel Willman, the production moved to the Winter Garden Theatre, London, on 18 November 1956, Shaw Theatre, 5 July 1971. Directed by Michael Croft, RSC (Royal Shakespeare Company) at the Aldwych Theatre, 13 July 1976. Directed by Jack Gold, Malvern Festival Theatre, August 1981, with Anthony Quayle as Burgoyne.

The Times (Review of *The Devil's Disciple*) found that the work "cannot be called a sympathetic play. It is full of that mordant satire with which we are familiar in Mr. Shaw's work and full, too, of that sense of insincerity, of mere posing which mars so much of it." Gilbert calls it "a kind of existential play."

Captain Brassbound's Conversion. 1899. Opened at the Strand Theatre, London, 16 December 1900 in a private performance. Directed by Charles Charrington. Revivals: Court Theatre, London, 20 March 1906. Directed by Shaw and Harley Granville-Barker, Little Theatre, London, 15 October 1912. Directed by Shaw; Cambridge Theatre, 18 February 1971. Directed by Frith Banbury; the production moved to the Ethel Barrymore Theatre, New York, 17 April 1972. Directed by Stephen Poster; Haymarket Theatre, London, 10 June 1982. Directed by Frank Hauser.

Mrs. Warren's Profession. 1902. Opened 5 January by the Stage Society, London, in a private performance. First licensed production: Prince of Wales's Theatre, Birmingham, 27 July 1925, by the Macdona Players. Directed by Esmé Percy. Revivals: Royal Court Theatre, London, 24 July 1956. Directed by Terence O'Brien, Gaiety Theatre, Dublin, 1961. Directed by Gerald Healy, National Theatre Company at the Old Vic Theatre, 30 December 1970. Directed by Ronald Eyre, Abbey Theatre, Dublin, 27 July 1977, National Theatre at the Lyttleton, 10 October 1985. Directed by Anthony Page; Harrowgate Theatre, London, 23 February 1989. Directed by Andrew Manley.

The 1902 private production by the Stage Society prompted Grein to object that if "Shaw had fully understood the nature of Mrs. Warren's profession he would have left the play unwritten or have produced a tragedy of heartrending power." By 1985, however, opinion had shifted. The writer for *Time Out* found the play to be an "uncompromising, progressive, political piece, full of passionate conviction. And, sadly, it has a lot to say which is as great an indictment of our society as it is testament to Shaw's power as dramatist. It is so rare to see such a serious and strong play about women" (quoted in Margery Morgan 19, 21).

John Bull's Other Island. 1904. Opened 1 November at the Royal Court Theatre, London, performed by the Vedrenne-Barker Company. Directed by Shaw and Harley Granville-Barker with Granville-Barker playing Father Keegan. Revivals: Abbey Theatre, Dublin, 26 September 1916, with annual revivals until 1931; Abbey Theatre, 10 March, 1969; Irish Theatre Company, 1980. Directed by Patrick Mason, with Cyril Cusack as Keegan.

Beerbohm's [2] enthusiastic review included the comment that "[m]ost of the fun comes of a slight exaggeration on the things that the character actually would say. But Mr. Shaw has also the art of extracting a ridiculous effect from every scenic situation."

Man and Superman. 1905. (Written 1901–1903). Opened 21 May at the Court Theatre, London, in a private performance by the London Stage Society (with act 3, *Don Juan in Hell* scene omitted). Directed by Shaw with Harley Granville-Barker and Lillah McCarthy in the cast. The same production was opened for public performance on 23 May 1905 by the Vedrenne-Barker company. Shaw directed with Granville-Barker's assistance. Revivals without act 3, scene ii: Hudson Theatre, New York, 5 September 1905. Presented by Charles Dillingham; Abbey Theatre, Dublin, 26 February 1917; Everyman Theatre, London, 23 May 1921. Directed by Edith Craig, Birmingham Theatre, 14 August 1945. Directed by Peter Brook, Gate Theatre, Dublin, 1951. Directed by Dan O'Connell, Theatre Royal, Bristol, 11 March 1968; Bristol Old Vic Company. Directed by John Moody, with Peter O'Toole; Malvern Festival Theatre, August 1977; Birmingham Repertory Theatre, 27 September 1982. Directed by Patrick Dromgoole, with Peter O'Toole; the production moved to the Haymarket Theatre,

London, 16 November 1982. Revivals of act 3, scene ii alone: Arts Theatre, 24 March 1943, 3 July 1946, and 8 September 1952; Coronet Theatre, Los Angeles, July 1947. The production toured fifty-two American cities, including a Carnegie Hall, New York, performance, 22 October 1951. Directed by Charles Laughton, with Laughton as the Devil, Agnes Moorehead, and Sir Cedric Hardwicke. Revivals with act 3 included: Little Theatre, London, 27 January 1928. Directed by Esmé Percy; moved to the Garrick Theatre, London, 13 February 1928. Old Vic, 31 November 1938. Directed by Lewis Casson, starring Anthony Quayle; RSC (Royal Shakespeare Company) at the Savoy Theatre, 16 August 1977. Directed by Clifford Williams; National Theatre at the Olivier, London, 2 January 1981. Directed by Christopher Monahan.

Of the 1905 production Walkley [1] complained that the "action-plot is well-nigh meaningless without the key of the idea-plot; . . . it is because of this parasitic nature of the action-plot, because of its weakness, its haphazardness, its unnaturalness . . . that one finds the play as a play unsatisfying." Similarly, Archer [3] wrote that the play was evidence of "one of the main reasons why Mr. Shaw will never be an artist in drama. It is that his intellect entirely predominates over, not only his emotions, but his perceptions."

Major Barbara. 1905. Opened 28 November at the Royal Court Theatre, London, by the Vedrenne-Barker company. Directed by Shaw and Harley Granville-Barker. Revivals: Court Theatre, London, 1 January 1906. Directed by Granville-Barker, Wyndham's Theatre, London, 5 March 1929. Directed by Lewis Casson and Charles Macdona, with Sybil Thorndike; Old Vic Theatre, 4 March 1935. Directed by Henry Cass, Theatre Royal, Bristol, 26 June 1956. Directed by John Moody, cast included Peter O'Toole as Peter Shirley; the production moved to the Old Vic Theatre on 16 July 1956; Martin Beck Theatre, New York, 30 October 1956. Directed by Charles Laughton, who played Undershaft. The cast included Glynis Johns, Cornelia Otis Skinner, and Eli Wallach; Royal Court Theatre, London, 28 August 1958. Directed by George Devine. Cast included Joan Plowright, Vanessa Redgrave; RSC (Royal Shakespeare Company) at the Aldwych Theatre, London, 19 October 1970. Directed by Clifford Williams. The cast included Judi Dench and Richard Pasco; National Theatre at the Lyttleton, 27 October 1982. Directed by Peter Gill, with Sian Phillips as Lady Britomart.

The *Pall Mall Gazette* (Review of *Major Barbara*) greeted the play with the observation that it contained "wit enough to make the fortune of half-a-dozen ordinary plays. The question is whether there is wit enough to save a three hours' discussion in the theatre. We doubt it." Similarly, Archer [2] complained that "[t]here are no human beings in *Major Barbara*: there are only animated points of view."

The Doctor's Dilemma. 1906. 20 November at the Royal Court Theatre, London. Directed by Shaw and Harley Granville-Barker. Revivals: St. James's Theatre, 6 December 1913. Directed by Granville-Barker, with Lillah McCarthy;

Everyman Theatre, London, 2 April 1923. Directed by Norman Macdermott. Starring Claude Rains and Cathleen Nesbitt; Haymarket Theatre, London, 4 March 1942. Directed by Irene Hentschel. Starring Vivien Leigh and Cyril Cusack; Gaiety Theatre, Dublin, 1947, with Cyril Cusack; Haymarket Theatre, 23 May 1963. Directed by Donald MacWhinnie; Chichester Festival Theatre, 17 May 1972. Directed by John Clements. The cast included Joan Plowright and John Neville.

Beerbohm [1] observes: "The pathos here is real. I defy you not to be touched by it, while it lasts. But I defy you, when it is over, to mourn."

Caesar and Cleopatra. 1906. (Written 1898). Opened, in German, 31 March at Neues Theater, Berlin. Produced by Max Reinhardt; directed by Hans Olden. Moved to the Deutsches Theater, 15 June 1906. First English-language production: New Amsterdam Theatre, New York, 30 October 1906. Directed by Shaw and Johnston Forbes-Robertson; moved to the Grand Theatre, Leeds, 16 September 1907, and to the Savoy Theatre, London, 25 November 1907 (with act 3 omitted). Revivals: Theatre Royal, Drury Lane, London, 14 April 1913. Directed by Shaw and Forbes-Robertson; Birmingham Repertory Theatre, 9 April 1925. Directed by H. K. Ayliff; moved to the Kingsway Theatre, London, 1925; Abbey Theatre, 24 October 1927; Malvern Festival Theatre, 24 August 1929. Directed by Ayliff; Old Vic Theatre, 19 September 1932. Directed by Harcourt Williams, with Peggy Ashcroft; Opera House, Manchester, 24 April 1951. Directed by Michael Benthall, with Laurence Olivier and Vivien Leigh; the production moved to St. James's Theatre, 10 May 1951. Birmingham Repertory Theatre, 12 June 1956. Directed by Douglas Seale, with Geoffrey Bayidon, Doreen Aris, and Albert Finney; the production moved to the Old Vic Theatre on 30 July 1957; Palace Theatre, New York, 24 February 1977. Directed by Ellis Rabb, with Rex Harrison as Caesar; Shaw Festival Theatre, Niagara-on-the-Lake, 1983.

The Times (Review of *Caesar and Cleopatra*) commented on how Shaw "uses the play as a means of giving out to you everything that happens to come at the moment into his head. Well, fortunately, it is Mr. Shaw's head, and the things that happen to come into it are generally amusing things."

The Philanderer. 1907. (written 1893). Opened 5 February at the Royal Court Theatre, London. Directed by Shaw and Harley Granville-Barker. Revivals: Royal Court Theatre, 20 January 1930. Directed by Esmé Percy; Mermaid Theatre, London, 27 January 1966. Directed by Don Taylor; National Theatre at Lyttleton, 7 September 1978. Directed by Christopher Monahan.

Shaw observed that the play "is a dangerous play with a clever but ignominious lead" (*Collected Letters*, vol. 1, p. 486). Wardle [3] observes that the 1978 revival demonstrates that the play reveals "embryonic Shavian themes . . . thoroughly integrated in a brilliantly funny play."

Getting Married. 1908. Opened 12 May at the Haymarket Theatre, London. Directed by Shaw. Revivals: Booth Theatre, New York, 6 November 1916. Directed by William Faversham; Birmingham Repertory Theatre, 18 October 1923. Directed by H. K. Ayliff; Everyman Theatre, London, 9 July 1924. Directed by Norman Macdermott, cast included Claude Rains and Edith Evans; Malvern Festival Theatre, 1982.

MacCarthy [2] observed that "[t]he play is all talk; but it is brilliant talk."

The Shewing-Up of Blanco Posnet. 1909. Opened 25 August at the Abbey Theatre, Dublin. Directed by Sara Allgood and Lady Gregory. Revivals: Everyman Theatre, London, 14 March 1921. Directed by Edith Craig; production moved to the Queen's Theatre, London, 20 July 1921; Mermaid Theatre, London, 3 October 1961. Directed by Frank Dunlop.

Fanny's First Play. 1911. Opened 19 April at the Little Theatre, London; production moved to the Kingsway Theatre, London, 1 January 1912 for a total of 622 performances. Revival: 1915, a production that failed to garner interest or reviews.

The 1911 production is often credited as Shaw's first commercial success. However, see the reference to the success of *John Bull's Other Island* in the introduction to this chapter.

Androcles and the Lion. 1912. Opened 25 November in German, at the Kleines Theater in Berlin. Produced by Max Reinhardt; moved to Hamburg in July 1913. Revivals: Abbey Theatre, Dublin, 4 November 1919; Old Vic Theatre, 24 February 1930. Directed by Harcourt Williams, with John Gielgud as the Emperor; Gaiety Theatre, Dublin, July 1956, starring Cyril Cusack; Malvern Festival Theatre, 29 August 1966. Directed by Bernard Hepton.

MacCarthy [1] observes, "An English audience has not as a rule sufficient emotional mobility to follow a method which alternates laughter with pathos, philosophy with fun, in such rapid succession."

Pygmalion. 1912. Opened in German at the Hofburgtheater in Vienna, 16 October 1913. Directed by Hugo Thimig. Revivals: His Majesty's Theatre, London, 11 April 1914. Directed by Shaw, with Herbert Beerbohm Tree and Mrs. Patrick Campbell; Aldwych Theatre, London, 10 February 1920. Directed by Shaw, with Mrs. Patrick Campbell; Court Theatre, London, 30 December 1929 and 13 April 1931. Directed by Esmé Percy (who also played Higgins); Old Vic Theatre, 21 September 1937. Directed by Tyrone Guthrie; Theatre Royal, Bristol, 12 March 1957. Directed by John Harrison. With Wendy Williams and Peter O'Toole as Doolittle; Albery Theatre, London, 15 May 1974. Directed by John Dexter. Cast: Diana Rigg, Alec McCowen, Bob Hoskins; Malvern Festival Theatre, August 1978, Shaftesbury Theater, London, 10 May 1984. Directed by Ray Cooney, with Peter O'Toole; production revived at the Plymouth Theatre, New York, 1987, with Sir John Mills as Doolittle.

Reviews of the 1974 production that starred Diana Rigg praised the return of the play, which had been held off the boards due to an agreement with the producers of *My Fair Lady.* Wardle [4] reported: "Great musical though it was, *My Fair Lady* has much to answer for in keeping this masterpiece off the stage for so long. And among the pleasures of John Dexter's magnificent revival (the first in the West End since 1953) is that of rediscovering how musical Shaw's own work is without any outside assistance."

Heartbreak House. 1920. (written 1916). Opened 10 November 1920 by the New York Theatre Guild. Directed by Dudley Digges. Revivals: Royal Court Theatre, London, 18 October 1921. Directed by Shaw and J. B. Fagan; Birmingham Repertory Theatre, 3 March 1923. Directed by H. K. Ayliff; Queen's Theatre, London, 23 April 1932. Directed by H. K. Ayliff, with Cedric Hardwicke, and Edith Evans as Ariadne (repeating her role in the English premiere); Cambridge Theatre, 18 March 1943. Directed by John Burrell; National Theatre at the Old Vic Theatre, 25 February 1975. Directed by John Schlesinger. Cast included Colin Blakely and Kate Nelligan; Malvern Festival Theatre, August 1981, with Anthony Quayle; Haymarket Theatre, London, 10 March 1983. Directed by John Dexter, with Rex Harrison and Diana Rigg.

Tracing Shaw's dramatic heritage, Agate [1] wrote that "[y]ou have to get Ibsen thoroughly in mind if you are not to find the Zepplein at the end of Shaw's play merely monstrous." In reviewing the 1983 revival, Nightingale dismissed previous complaints about the lack of structure in Shaw's plays: "Never mind the plot, which barely exists: feel the passion, which indisputably does."

Back to Methuselah. 1922. (written 1920). Produced by the New York Theatre Guild, 27 February, 13 March 1922: Parts 1 and 2, 27 February; Parts 3 and 4, 6 March; Part 5, 13 March. Directed by Philip Moeller. Revivals: Birmingham Repertory Theatre, 9–12 October 1923 with one part performed each day except for 11 October: Part 3 (matinee), Part 4 (evening). Directed by H. K. Ayliff. Cast: Edith Evans, Cedric Hardwicke, and Gwen Ffrangcon-Davies; moved to the Court Theatre, London, 18–22 February (with Caroline Keith taking the Edith Evans role); Malvern Festival Theatre, 20–22 August 1929. Directed by H. K. Ayliff; National Theatre at Old Vic Theatre, 31 July–1 August 1969. Directed by Clifford Williams and Donald Mackochnie, with Joan Plowright as the Voice of Lilith; Shaw Theatre, 18–19 June 1984. Directed by Bill Pryde; Shaw Festival, Niagara-on-the-Lake, 15 August 1986. Directed by Denise Coffey.

Responses to contemporary revivals of this alternative creation tale that Shaw termed a "Metabiological Pentateuch" have been varied. Wardle [1] wrote that the work was "[w]ithout dramatic life or coherence." The 1984 production, however, led Hay to write that "Bill Pryde and his accomplished team of nine actors have already scotched the notion that it's an intractable masterpiece."

Saint Joan. 1923. Opened 28 December at the New York Theatre Guild. Directed by Philip Moeller. Revivals: New Theatre, London, 26 March 1924. Directed by Shaw and Lewis Casson, with Sybil Thorndike and Ernest Thesiger; Regent Theatre, London, 14 January 1925. Directed by Lewis Casson, with Sybil Thorndike and Ernest Thesiger; Lyceum Theatre, London, 24 March 1926; His Majesty's Theatre, London, 6 April 1931; Old Vic Company at New Theatre, 3 December 1947. Directed by John Burrell, with Celia Johnson and Alec Guinness; Arts Theatre, Cambridge, 20 September 1954. Directed by John Fernald, with Siobhan McKenna and Kenneth Williams; production moved to Arts Theatre, London, 29 September 1954, and on to the St. Martin's Theatre, London, 9 February 1955; National Theatre at the Chichester Festival Theatre, 24 June 1963. Directed by John Dexter. Cast: Joan Plowright, Robert Stephens, and Max Adrian; production moved to the Old Vic Theatre, 30 October 1963; Abbey Theatre, Dublin, 5 December, 1972; National Theater at the Olivier, 16 February 1984. Directed by Ronald Eyre, with Frances de la Tour, Cyril Cusack, and Michael Bryant.

Pirandello emphasized the audience's reaction to the play (which he perhaps overidealized): "I noted with great satisfaction the rapt attention, the shrewd and intelligent smiling, the hearty laughter and the sincere applause [during the first three acts] with which every shaft of wit or irony in this admirable and inimitable Shavian dialogue was welcomed by an audience keenly aware of the artistic treat that was spread before it."

The Apple Cart. 1929. Opened 14 June at the Polish Theatre (Teatr Polski), Warsaw, in Polish. Directed by Karel Borowski. Opened 19 August 1929 at the Malvern Festival Theatre. Directed by H. K. Ayliff, cast included Cedric Hardwicke and Edith Evans; production moved to the Queen's Theatre, London on 17 September 1929. Revivals: Theatre Guild at the Martin Beck Theatre, New York, 24 February 1930; Garrick Theatre, Melbourne, 9 October 1933. Directed by Gregan McMahon, who played Magnus, with Coral Browne as Orinthia; Cambridge Theatre, 25 September 1935. Directed by Cedric Hardwicke, Haymarket Theatre, 7 May 1953. Directed by Michael Macowan, cast included Noël Coward, Margaret Leighton as Orinthia, and Margaret Rawlings as Lysistrata; Haymarket Theatre, London, 20 February 1986. Directed by Val May, cast included Peter O'Toole, Susannah York, and Dora Bryan as Amanda.

Sometimes subject to charges of writing star vehicles, Shaw found a forgiving attitude in Ervine: "*The Apple Cart*, which is as disconnected as a revue, is not, of course, a play, but who cares whether it is or not? . . . what an entertainment!"

Too True to Be Good. 1932. Opened 29 February by the Theatre Guild at the National Theatre, Boston. Directed by Leslie Banks, cast included Beatrice Lillie and Claude Rains; production moved to the Guild Theater, New York, 4 April 1932; opened at the Malvern Festival Theatre on 6 August 1932. Directed by H. K. Ayliff, cast included Ellen Pollock, Cedric Hardwicke, and Ralph Richardson; moved to the New Theatre, London on 13 September 1932. Revivals: Lyric Theatre, Hammersmith, 31 October 1944. Directed by Ellen Pollock, Lyceum Theatre, Edinburgh, 6 September 1965. Directed by Frank Dunlop. Production moved to the Strand Theatre, London, on 22 September 1965; Riverside Studios, 5 November 1986. Directed by Mike Alfreds.

Based on the original production, Peter Noble renewed the career-long response to Shaw's experimentalism and success: "Shaw breaks all the rules of the theatre, yet none can be said to break them more successfully" (quoted in Margery Morgan 89). Charles Morgan was less sympathetic: "Mr. Shaw's present work has, as a document, the interest and, as a play, the tedium, of an undigested notebook. Being formless, it produces neither dramatic illusion nor intellectual tension." The 1965 revival resulted in Wardle's calling for a reevaluation of the last phase of Shaw's career: "This is a good deal more than a star production of a minor Shaw play. It is a well calculated act of revaluation [*sic*] designed to open up his neglected last phase" (quoted in Margery Morgan 89).

On the Rocks. 1933. Opened 25 November at the Winter Garden Theatre, London. Directed by Lewis Casson. Revivals: Abbey Theatre, Dublin, 9 July 1934; Daly's Theater, New York, 15 June 1938; Mermaid Theatre, London, 21 August 1975. Directed by Bernard Miles; Chichester Festival Theatre, 5 May 1982. Directed by Patrick Garland and Jack Emery.

A play that sometimes resulted in charges of fascism received a more sympathetic review from Martin, who observed that it "warns rather than advocates. Make up your mind, he [Shaw] says, that Parliament, as you now know it, cannot be the instrument of salvation." The 1982 revival garnered a balanced assessment from Wardle [2], who argued that the play "shows his anarchic comic gift doing spirited battle with his authoritarian opinions."

The Simpleton of the Unexpected Isles. 1935. (written 1934). Opened 18 February 1935 at the New York Theatre Guild. Directed by Henry Wagstaffe Gribble; the Malvern Festival Theater, 29 July 1935. Directed by Herbert M. Prentice, the Comedy Theatre, London, October 1935. Directed by Gregan McMahon. Revivals: Arts Theatre, London, 7 March 1945. Directed by Judith Furse, Manchester Green Room, 30 January 1953; Shaw Festival, Niagara-on-the-Lake, June 1983. Directed by Denise Coffey.

After publication of the play, the *Times Literary Supplement* (Review of *The Simpleton of the Unexpected Isles*) termed the play "the most interesting that Mr Shaw has written since *The Apple Cart.*" The original Australian production at the Comedy Theatre, Melbourne, in October 1935, and the 1983 revival resulted in mixed praise. The *Sydney Bulletin* (Review of *The Simpleton of the Unexpected Isles*) called the play "a magnificent confusion."

The Millionairess. 1936. (Written 1934). Opened 4 January 1936 in Vienna at the Burgtheater. (Carr cites the production as opening at the Akademie Theater.)

Directed by Herbert Warnick, Opened 7 March 1936 at the King's Theatre by the McMahon Players, Melbourne, Australia. Directed by Gregan McMahon, starring Enid Hollins. Revivals: Malvern Festival Theatre, 26 July 1937. Directed by Herbert M. Prentice, the Globe Theatre, 11 September 1940. Directed by George Devine, the production starred Edith Evans; New Theatre, London, 27 June 1952. Directed by Michael Benthall, cast included Katharine Hepburn, Robert Helpmann, and Cyril Ritchard; production moved to the Shubert Theatre, New York, on 17 October 1952; Haymarket Theatre, London, 14 December 1978. Directed by Michael Lindsay-Hogg.

The *Times Literary Supplement* (Review of *The Millionairess*) identified the play's connection with Shaw's political development: "[A]mid all the bombast of assertion incidental to its author's style, we are permitted to watch Mr. Shaw feeling his way towards new territory and to understand the nature of his present confusion . . . he has delivered a genuinely constructive criticism of the excesses of democracy." The Melbourne critic for the *Argus*, however, called the play a "superb comedy—impudent, pungent, and devastating" while also attributing to the play "[l]ess preaching and dogmatizing . . . than in anything Shaw has written in ten years" (quoted in Margery Morgan 97).

Geneva. 1938. Opened 1 August at the Malvern Festival. Directed by H. K. Ayliff; moved to the Saville Theatre, London, on 22 November 1938; moved again to the St. James's Theatre on 27 January 1939. Revivals: Comedy Theatre, Melbourne, 10 July 1939. Directed by Gregan McMahon, Henry Miller's Theatre, New York, 30 January 1940. Produced by the Colbourne-Jones Company; Mermaid Theatre, London, 4 November 1971. Directed by Philip Grout.

While praising the playwright, Dent faulted the reception of the audience: "[I]t let out indiscriminate whoops of laughter at things which Mr Shaw obviously meant for serious statements. The shrug with which this political exposition concludes is a genuinely despairing one." The 1971 revival resulted in a basically enthusiastic review from Lambert, who commented that "[t]he old man's impatient anarchy wore surprisingly well, despite one or two wincingly insensitive lines." The New York opening prompted Atkinson to lament that "Mr. Shaw is not improving in his playwriting . . . he makes logic and wisdom about great matters very difficult to listen to."

In Good King Charles' Golden Days. 1939. Opened 12 August at the Malvern Festival. Directed by H. K. Ayliff; moved to the Streatham Hill Theatre, 15 April 1940 and then to the New Theatre, London, 9 May 1940. Revivals: King's Theatre, Melbourne, 9 December 1939. Directed by Gregan McMahon, People's Palace, London, 25 October 1948. Directed by Matthew Forsyth; Malvern Festival Theatre, 11 August 1949. Directed by Ernest Thesiger, Downtown Theatre, New York, 24 January 1957.

Of the Malvern opening, Agate [2] wrote that "this play's business is the affair of the men. Is it long? Yes. Too long? No. . . . Will anybody miss the lack of action? Yes, the witless and the idle."

ADDITIONAL PLAYS, ADAPTATIONS, AND PRODUCTIONS

The Admirable Bashville, or Constancy Unrewarded (1903). Opened 7 June at the Imperial Theatre, London, by the Stage Society. Directed by Shaw and Harley Granville-Barker. First public staging at the Theatre Royal, Manchester, 22 September 1905. Directed by Harold V. Neilson. Revivals: Matinee Theatre at His Majesty's Theatre, London, 26 January 1909. Directed by Shaw.
Little Theatre, Philadelphia, 8 February 1915; Malvern Theatre, 18 August 1930. Directed by H. K. Ayliff; Abbey Theatre, Dublin, 8 June 1931; Old Vic Theatre, 13 February 1933. Directed by Harcourt Williams, Arts Theatre, London, 26 April 1951. Directed by Judith Furse.

How He Lied to Her Husband (1904). Opened 26 September at the Berkeley Lyceum Theatre, New York. Directed by Arnold Daly, who starred in the production; opened in London at the Court Theatre by the Vedrenne-Barker company on 28 February 1905. Directed by Granville-Barker. Revivals: the Vedrenne-Barker production moved to the St. James's Theater on 21 March 1905 and to the Savoy Theatre, London, on 8 May 1905; Everyman Theatre, Hampstead, London, 14 March 1921. Directed by Edith Craig, Fortune Theatre, London, 26 January 1970. Directed by Michael Denison; Redgrave Theatre, Farnham, 24 May 1983.

Passion, Poison and Petrification; or, The Fatal Gazogene (1905). Opened 14 July, at the Theatrical Garden Party, Regent's Park. Directed by Cyril Maude. Produced on radio, the first of Shaw's plays to be so presented, on 15 January 1928. Shaw designated that all royalties from performances be given to the Actors' Orphanage Fund.

Press Cuttings (1909). Opened September at the Gaiety Theatre, Manchester. Directed by B. Iden Payne. Shaw directed a private performance of the play at the Court Theatre on 9 and 12 July 1909.

The Dark Lady of the Sonnets (1910). Opened 24 November at the Haymarket Theatre, London, (2 performances) as a charity benefit for the Shakespeare Memorial Theatre. Directed by Shaw and Granville-Barker. Revivals: Everyman Theatre, London, 14 March 1921. Directed by Edith Craig, moved to the Queen's Theatre, London, on 20 July 1925; American National Theatre and Academy at the Ziegfeld Theater, New York, 29 January 1930; Old Vic Theatre, 24 February 1930. Directed by Harcourt Williams, St. Martin's Theatre, 3 April 1951. Directed by Ellen Pollock, cast included Ellen Pollock as Queen Elizabeth and Griffith Jones; Open Air Theatre, Regent's Park, 17 July 1978. Directed by Richard Digby Day.

Overruled (1912). Opened 14 October at the Duke of York's Theatre, London. Directed by Shaw. *Great Catherine* (1913). Opened 18 November at the Vaudeville Theatre, London. Directed by Shaw. *The Music-Cure* (1914). Opened 28 January at the Little Theatre, London. Direction credited to "Everybody Concerned." Revival: Arts Theatre, London, 27 June 1951. Directed by John Fernald. *The Inca of Perusalem* (1916). Opened 7 October at the Repertory Theatre,

Birmingham. Directed by John Drinkwater. *Augustus Does His Bit*. 1917. Opened 21 January at the Royal Court Theatre, London. Produced by the Stage Society. Directed by Shaw. Revival: Arts Theatre, London, 20 June 1951. Directed by Roy Rich. *Annajanska, the Bolshevik Empress*. 1918. Opened 21 January under the title *Annajanska, The Wild Grand Duchess*, at the Coliseum, London. Directed by Shaw, with Lillah McCarthy. Revivals: Torch Theatre, 10 January 1939. Directed by Stewart Granger; Arts Theatre, 20 June, 1951. Directed by John Fernald.

O'Flaherty, V. C. 1920. Opened 21 June, at the 39th Street Theatre, New York, performed by the Deborah Bierne Irish Players. Opened 19 December 1920 by the Stage Society at the Lyric Theatre, Hammersmith. The first production, by amateurs, occurred on 17 February 1917 on the Western Front. The performance was given by Officers of the 40th Squadron, R.F.C., at Treizennes, Belgium. *Jitta's Atonement*. 1924. A free adaptation and translation of *Frau Gittas Sühne* (a play by Shaw's German translator, Siegfried Trebitsch). Staged at the Grand Theatre, Putney Bridge and in Leicester. Produced by Violet Vanbrugh. *The Glimpse of Reality* (1927). Written in 1909. Opened 20 November at the Arts Theatre Club, London. Directed by Maurice Browne. *The Fascinating Foundling*. 1928. Subtitled, *A Disgrace to the Author*. Opened 28 January at the Arts Theatre. Directed by Henry Oscar, starring Peggy Ashcroft. The play was originally written and staged for a charity benefit performance.

Village Wooing. 1934. Opened 17 April at the Little Theatre, Dallas. Directed by Charles Meredith; opened 19 June at the Little Theatre, London. Directed by Shaw, with Sybil Thorndike as "Z." Revivals: Abbey Theatre, 30 September 1935; Lyric Theatre, Hammersmith, 28 November 1944. Directed by Ellen Pollock, who played "Z"; Arts Theatre, 20 June 1951. Directed by Roy Rich; Royal Court Theatre, 26 July 1952. Directed by Ellen Pollock, who repeated her performance as "Z"; Fortune Theatre, 26 January 1970. Directed by Nigel Patrick; Theatre at New End, Hampstead, 8 October 1981. Directed by Frank Hauser. Cast: Judi Dench and Michael Williams; in a double bill with *Overruled*, Theatre Museum, London, 29 January 1989. *The Six of Calais*. 1934. Opened 17 July at the Open Air Theatre, Regent's Park, London. A one-act play. Directed by Maxwell Wray. *Cymbeline Refinished*. 1937. Originally titled, *Cymbeline Up to Date: A Happy Ending*. Opened 16 November at the Embassy Theatre, Swiss Cottage, London. Directed by Ronald Adman. The three-week run starred Joyce Bland as Imogen.

Bouyant Billions. 1948. Opened 21 October, at the Schauspielhaus, Zurich. Directed by Berthold Viertel. English premiere at the Malvern Festival, 13 August 1949; reopened at the Princes Theatre, 10 October 1949, London. Directed by Esmé Percy. Cast: Frances Day and Denholm Elliott. *Shakes versus Shav*. 1949. A puppet-play commissioned by Waldo Lanchester and first performed by the Waldo Lanchester Marionette Theatre at Malvern 9 August 1949. *Farfetched Fables*. 1950. A play written for amateurs. Opened at the Watergate Theatre in the fall of 1950. Directed by Esmé Percy. A Shaw Society production that ran for 30 performances. *Why She Would Not.* 1950. A comedy that Shaw was writing in the year of his death.

ASSESSMENT OF SHAW'S CAREER

While theater companies have relied on Shaw's plays from 1904 to the present for commercial success, that aspect of his reception led Susan Todd to complain that "it seems unpleasantly ironic that he should have been, for so long now, appropriated by the richest, glossiest, most commercial production companies for what is called 'revival' " (quoted in Margery Morgan 115). Nevertheless, Holroyd and others have credited the Niagara-on-the-Lake Shaw Festival with nurturing a new seriousness in Shaw studies. Aside from noting the "[f]ringe of seminars, special tours, and projects for young people" that are a part of the festival, Holroyd [1] commented that "[w]hat had begun at Malvern in the 1930s was accomplished in Niagara fifty years later" (4: 77).

From the first productions of Shaw's work, a repeated complaint has been, as Walkley [2] argued, that plays like *Widowers' Houses* are "not dramatic. I only see a number of people arguing round a table. Indeed, Mr. Shaw's people are not dramatic characters at all, they are embodied arguments." Walkley [2] indicated the reputation of G. B. S. at the century's end: "You have Mr. Shaw the musical critic, and Mr. Shaw the novelist, and Mr. Shaw the Ibsenite exegete, and Mr. Shaw the Fabian, and Mr. Shaw the vegetarian, and Mr. Shaw the anti-vivisectionist—and now there is Mr. Shaw the dramatist."

Recent trends in Shaw criticism have returned to some of those other facets of Shaw and include studies of the significance of Shaw's music and art criticism and of him as a controversialist (witness Stanley Weintraub [2]). Shaw himself encouraged analysis of his plays in terms of a musical structure: "My plays bear very plain marks of my musical education. My deliberate rhetoric, and my reversion to the Shakespearian feature of long set roles for my characters, are pure Italian opera. My rejection of plot and denouement, and my adoption of a free development of themes, are German symphony" (Shaw, *Collected Letters*, 3:374).

Gainor demonstrated how a feminist reading of the Shavian canon can produce new perspectives on such aspects of Shavian dramaturgy as cross-dressing roles and implied homoeroticism.

That Jorge Luis Borges—a writer often mentioned among "other postmodern writers from Joyce and Borges to Beckett and Calvino" (Kearney [2], 303)— described Shaw as a major influence suggests the validity of reconsidering Shaw as a postmodernist. In an interview with Seamus Heaney and Richard Kearney, Borges spoke often of the influence Shaw had on his thinking, recalling how when "I read George Bernard Shaw's *The Quintessence of Ibsenism*, I was so impressed that I went on to read all of his plays and essays and discovered there a writer of deep philosophical curiosity and a great believer in the transfiguring power of the will and of the mind" (quoted in Kearney [1], 51–52). While his comment pointed toward the elements of Barthian jeu and Bakhtinian carnival present in Shaw's works, Borges also repeatedly stressed the significance of Shavian metaphysics.

To Kearney's question "[D]o you think it is just a happy accident that your early discovery of the creative power of the mind coincided with your admiration for Irish writers and thinkers such as Berkeley, Shaw, Wilde and Joyce, who had also made such a discovery?" Borges replied:

[A]s an outsider looking on successive Irish thinkers I have sometimes been struck by unusual and remarkable repetitions. Berkeley was the first Irish philosopher I read. . . . Then followed my fascination for Wilde, Shaw and Joyce. And finally there was John Scotus Erigena, the Irish metaphysician of the 9th century. . . . In short, what Shaw calls the life-force plays the same role in his system as God does in Erigena's. . . . [T]he coincidence of thought is there. I suspect it has less to do with nationalism than with metaphysics (quoted in Kearney [1], 53–54).

Such issues of repetition, of "rewriting and rebeginning," involve what Kearney considered a critical turn in the conception of the postmodernist enterprise. "Postmodernism would thus refuse to view itself as a mere afterword to modernity. Instead it assumes the task of reinvestigating the crisis and trauma at the very heart of modernity" (Kearney [2], 32). By placing postmodernism as a recursive movement that reexamines and reinterprets basic cruxes within modernism, Kearney provided a basis for examining Shaw's work as an example of the roots of postmodernism in modernism. Stanley Weintraub [1] has recently called for such a reexamination of traditional Shaw scholarship.

Indeed, not only does *John Bull's Other Island* question concepts of Irish identity, but the Abbey Theatre's rejection of that work suggests the relevance to Shaw's response of one definition of modernism: "Modernism is, consequently, suspicious of attempts to reestablish national literatures or resurrect cultural traditions" (quoted in Kearney [2], 12). However, just as Joyce has been cited as both a high modernist and a postmodernist (depending on the critic's definitions and choice of examples), so Shaw can be situated as an early postmodernist. While also taking into account Borges' praise of Shaw, Holroyd [1] paired his tribute with that of another author in order to emphasize Shaw's dramaturgic complexity: "Borges praised him for creating superb characters on stage, Brecht for subverting character and introducing the spirit of alienation" (4:78). To Kearney's question about the "relationship with philosophy" of Borges' "works [that] are peppered with metaphysical allusions," Borges returned to Shaw's importance. His response speaks to the basis of Shaw's ongoing interest for critics: "For me Schopenhauer is the greatest philosopher. He knew the power of fiction in ideas. This conviction I share, of course, with Shaw. Both Schopenhauer and Shaw exposed the deceptive division between the writer and the thinker" (quoted in Kearney [1], 52).

ARCHIVAL SOURCES

Extensive manuscripts are housed at the Harry Ransom Humanities Research Center at the University of Texas, Austin; at the British Library Shaw Archive; and in the Shaw Collection at the University of North Carolina at Chapel Hill. The latter includes Shaw's correspondence with Malvern Festival Theatre director H. K. Ayliff and with a number of actresses. The collection also contains Shaw corrections to page proofs for biographies of Shaw by Archibald Henderson (a Chapel Hill math professor).

PRIMARY BIBLIOGRAPHY

Agitations: Letters to the Press 1875–1950. Ed. Dan H. Laurence and James Rambeau. New York: Frederick Ungar, 1985.

Bernard Shaw. *Collected Letters.* Ed. Dan H. Laurence. 4 vols. London: Max Reinhardt. 1965–1988.

The Bodley Head Bernard Shaw. London: Bodley Head, 1970–74. (Considered the standard edition.)

SECONDARY BIBLIOGRAPHY

Agate, James. [1]. [Review of *Heartbreak House.*] *Saturday Review* (21 Oct. 1921).

———. [2]. [Review of *In Good King Charles' Golden Days.*] *Sunday Times* (13 Aug. 1939).

Archer, William. [1]. [Review of *Arms and the Man.*] *World* (25 Apr. 1894).

———. [2]. [Review of *Major Barbara.*] *World* (5 Dec. 1905).

———. [3]. [Review of *Man and Superman.*] *World* (30 May 1905).

Atkinson, Brooks. [Review of *Geneva.*] *New York Times* (31 Jan. 1940): 15.

Beerbohm, Max. [1]. [Review of *The Doctor's Dilemma.*] *Saturday Review* (24 Nov. 1906).

———. [2]. [Review of *John Bull's Other Island.*] *Saturday Review* (12 Nov. 1904).

Bertolini, John A. *The Playwrighting Self of Bernard Shaw.* Carbondale: Southern Illinois University Press, 1991.

Bevan, E. Dean. *A Concordance to the Plays and Prefaces of Bernard Shaw.* 10 vols. Detroit: Gale Research, 1971.

Billington, Michael. [Review of *Arms and the Man.*] *Plays and Players* (Sept. 1970): 32.

Bloom, Harold, ed. [1]. *George Bernard Shaw: Modern Critical Views.* New York: Chelsea, 1987.

———. [2]. *Major Barbara: Modern Critical Views.* New York: Chelsea, 1988.

———. [3]. *Man and Superman: Modern Critical Views.* New York: Chelsea, 1987.

———. [4]. *Pygmalion: Modern Critical Views.* New York: Chelsea, 1988.

———. [5]. *Saint Joan: Modern Critical Views.* New York: Chelsea, 1987.

Bloomfield, Z. "American Response to George Bernard Shaw, a Study of Professional Productions, 1894–1905." *Theatre Studies* 36 (1991): 5–17.

Review of *Caesar and Cleopatra. Times* (26 Nov. 1907).

Carr, Pat M. *Bernard Shaw.* New York: Frederick Ungar, 1976.

Dent, Alan. [Review of *Geneva.*] *Spectator* (5 Aug. 1938).

Review of *The Devil's Disciple. Times* (27 Sept. 1899).

Dukore, Bernard F. [1]. *Bernard Shaw, Director.* Seattle: University of Washington Press, 1971.

———. [2]. *Bernard Shaw, Playwright.* Columbia: University of Missouri Press, 1973.

———, ed. [3]. *The Collected Screenplays of Bernard Shaw.* London: George Prior, 1980.

Ervine, St. John. [Review of *The Apple Cart.*] *Observer* (25 Aug. 1929).

Evans, T. F., ed. *Shaw: The Critical Heritage.* London: Routledge and Kegan Paul, 1976.

Gainor, J. Ellen. *Shaw's Daughters.* Ann Arbor: University of Michigan Press, 1991.

Gibbs, A. M. *Shaw: Interviews and Recollections.* New York: Macmillan, 1990.

Gilbert, W. Stephen. [Review of *The Devil's Disciple.*] *Plays and Players* (Sept. 1976): 24.

Gordon, David J. *Bernard Shaw and the Comic Sublime.* New York: St. Martin's Press, 1990.

Grein, J. T. [Review of *Mrs. Warren's Profession.*] *Sunday Special* (12 Jan. 1902).

Grene, Nicholas. [1]. *Bernard Shaw, a Critical View.* New York: St. Martin's Press, 1984.

———. [2]. "The Maturing of Immaturity, Shaw's First Novel." *Irish University Review* 20.2 (1990): 225–38.

Harrison, W. "*Geneva*, A Postwar Approach." *Journal of Irish Literature* 19.2 (1990): 52–57.

Hay, Malcolm. [Review of *Back to Methuselah.*] *Time Out* (21 June 1984).

Henderson, Archibald. [1]. *Bernard Shaw: Playboy and Prophet.* New York: Appleton, 1932.

———. [2]. *George Bernard Shaw: Man of the Century.* New York: Appleton-Century-Crofts, 1956.

Holroyd, Michael. [1]. *Bernard Shaw.* 4 vols. New York: Random House, 1988–1992.

———, ed. [2]. *The Genius of Shaw.* New York: Holt, Rinehart and Winston, 1979.

Howlett, Ivan. [Review of *Candida.*] *Plays and Players* (Aug. 1977): 25.

Hummert, Paul A. *Bernard Shaw's Marxian Romance.* Lincoln: University of Nebraska Press, 1973.

Jenckes, Norma Margaret. [1]. "John Bull's Other Island: A Critical Study of Shaw's Irish Play in Its Theatrical and Socio-Political Context." Ph.D. diss., University of Illinois, Urbana-Champaign, 1974.

———. [2]. "The Rejection of Shaw's Irish Play: *John Bull's Other Island.*" *Éire-Ireland* 10.1 (1975): 38–53.

Kearney, Richard. [1]. *Transitions, Narratives in Modern Irish Culture.* Manchester: Manchester University Press, 1988.

———. [2]. *The Wake of Imagination.* Minneapolis: University of Minnesota Press, 1988.

Lambert, J. W. [Review of *Geneva.*] *Drama* (Spring 1972): 27.

Laurence, Dan H., and Nicholas Grene, eds. *Shaw, Lady Gregory, and the Abbey.* Gerrards Cross, Buckinghamshire: Colin Smythe, 1993.

MacCarthy, Desmond. [1]. [Review of *Androcles and the Lion.*] *New Statesman* (6 Sept. 1913).

―――. [2]. [Review of *Getting Married.*] *New Statesman and Nation* (8 Apr. 1922).

Review of *Major Barbara*. *Pall Mall Gazette* (29 Nov. 1905).

Martin, Kingsley. [Review of *On the Rocks.*] *New Statesman and Nation* (2 Dec. 1933).

Meisel, Martin. *Shaw and the Nineteenth-Century Theater*. Princeton, N.J.: Princeton University Press, 1963.

Review of *The Millionairess*. *Times Literary Supplement* (28 Mar. 1936).

Morgan, Charles. [Review of *Too True to Be Good.*] *Times* (8 Aug. 1932).

Morgan, Margery. *File on Shaw*. London: Methuen, 1989.

Nightingale, Benedict. [Review of *Heartbreak House.*] *New Statesman* (18 Mar. 1983).

Pirandello, Luigi. [Review of *Saint Joan.*] *New York Times* (13 Jan. 1924).

Rosset, B. C. *Shaw of Dublin: The Formative Years*. University Park: Penn State University Press, 1964.

Review of *The Simpleton of Unexpected Isles*. *Sydney Bulletin* (16 Oct. 1935).

Review of *The Simpleton of Unexpected Isles*. *Times Literary Supplement* (28 Mar. 1936).

Smith, Warren Sylvester. *Bishop of Everywhere*. University Park: Penn State University Press, 1982.

Trussler, Simon. "Introduction." In *File on Shaw,* by Margery Morgan. London: Methuen, 1989.

Walkley, A. B. [1]. [Review of *Man and Superman.*] *Times Literary Supplement* (26 May 1905).

―――. [2]. [Review of *Widowers' Houses.*] *Speaker* (17 Dec. 1892).

Wardle, Irving. [1]. [Review of *Back to Methuselah.*] *Times* (4 Aug. 1969).

―――. [2]. [Review of *On the Rocks.*] *Times* (6 May 1982): 15.

―――. [3]. [Review of *The Philanderer.*] *Times* (8 Sept. 1978).

―――. [4]. [Review of *Pygmalion.*] *Times* (17 May 1974).

Weintraub, Rodelle, ed. *Fabian Feminist: Bernard Shaw and Woman*. University Park: Penn State University Press, 1977.

Weintraub, Stanley. [1]. *Bernard Shaw, a Guide to Research*. University Park: Penn State University Press, 1992.

―――. [2]. *Bernard Shaw on the London Art Scene, 1885–1950*. University Park: Penn State University Press, 1989.

―――. [3]. *Journey to Heartbreak: The Crucible Years of Bernard Shaw, 1914–1918*. New York: Weybright and Talley, 1971.

―――, ed. [4]. *Bernard Shaw: An Autobiography 1856–1898*. New York: Weybright and Talley, 1969; rpt., London: Max Reinhardt, 1970.

―――, ed. [5]. *Bernard Shaw: An Autobiography 1898–1950, The Playwright Years*. New York: Weybright and Talley, 1970; rpt., London: Max Reinhardt, 1971.

Weintraub, Stanley, and Rodelle Weintraub, eds. *Arms and the Man and John Bull's Other Island*. New York: Bantam, 1993.

BIBLIOGRAPHIES

G. B. Shaw: An Annotated Bibliography of Writings about Him. Vol. 1. (1871–1930). Ed. J. P. Wearing; Vol. 2 (1931–1956). Ed. Elsie B. Adams and Donald C. Haberman, 1987; Vol. 3 (1957–1978). Ed. Donald C. Haberman, 1986. DeKalb: Northern Illinois University Press, 1986–87.

George Shiels
(1881–1949)

BERNARD McKENNA

Once when I visited him, I found he was an invalid confined to his room in a wheelchair, and I learned from him that all his characters were drawn from people who came to see him and ask his advice on a great many problems. Alternatively they were drawn from characters and situations his visitors told him about. His own dramatic imagination supplied the rest. I gathered from him that he had sufficient knowledge of the law to give advice on legal questions, and, of course, his main work for his friends was to write letters for them. (Mooney [2], 88–89).

In her brief reminiscence Mooney manages to capture the essence of George Shiels' character, whom she described as ''the Molière of Ireland.'' He was a sensitive, although not sentimental, caring observer of human nature. He had a gentle and generous disposition, was deeply committed to both his family and his privacy—he possessed a disability that he did not want widely known and that he refused to let limit his achievement—and was a remarkable playwright who, although probably not a Molière, has not received the critical recognition his work merits.

George Shiels was born on 24 June 1881 in Ballybrake, County Antrim, to a Catholic family in what would become Northern Ireland. A generation after the Famine, two generations removed from Catholic Emancipation, Shiels was born at the height of the Land War and grew up in a household in which his father, Robert Shiels, and mother, Elizabeth Sweeny Shiels, told stories of the horrors of the Famine and agrarian abuses—stories that informed his *Tenants at Will*. It is remarkable that his life would coincide with much that troubled Ireland, not only the abuses of colonial rule but partition, emigration, the civil war, Free State neutrality, the German firebombs in Belfast. Emigration he would experience firsthand. After a few years of primary education at the school beside the Church of Our Lady and Saint Patrick, he, like most of his six brothers, left Ireland for North America. Stories of his life in exile tell of a young Shiels recently arrived in America spending a large percentage of his money to see a production of *Faust* and traveling to the American West working on the railroads and in the mines of Canada, the Black Hills of the Dakotas and the Indian Territory, and California. Then in 1904, while working on the Canadian Pacific Railroad somewhere between Regina and Prince Albert, he was injured and was permanently confined to a wheelchair. He returned to Ireland in 1908, establishing a fairly successful business that specialized in traveling and shipping. However, as immigration declined, so did his profits. Shiels was to make his reputation and his living as a writer.

His first attempts appeared as stories and poems painting the American West for readers of newspapers and periodicals in Northern Ireland. He had trained as a writer through a correspondence school called the Pelham Institute of the Mind. His first plays, under the pseudonym George Morshiel, were produced by the Ulster Literary Theatre, a company founded in 1902 by Bulmer Hobson and David Parkhill that produced the plays of Bernard Duffy, Rutherford Mayne, and Gerald MacNamara, among others. In 1921, the Abbey Theatre staged its first Shiels play—*Bedmates*. As was the case with much of his work, the audience responded with great enthusiasm. The Abbey staged seven more of his plays in the 1920s, even taking a production of *Professor Tim* to London. Early critics blasted Shiels for creating ''mere entertainments.'' Subsequent critics, both contemporary with Shiels and later academic scholars, base their assessment of Shiels' work on these productions. In the case of academic scholars this treatment is rather disingenuous, as he would grow as a writer in the next nineteen years. In addition, these plays do show some startlingly powerful scenes that tend to comment subtly and indirectly on contemporary conditions in Ireland, such as Ulster Free State relations and avarice. In truth, though, these early Shiels works *are* mainly entertainments showing only occasional signs of social comment or intense dramatic power.

The portrait of George Shiels as writer is of an industrious and dedicated professional. Kennedy [1], reports Shiels' incredible industry. Despite his regimen, drawing on ''boyhood memories of Ballymoney'' and the tales of his brother and sister and ''regular visitors, such as the barber, the baker and the postman'' (Kennedy [1], 53), he ''appeared a browner, healthier-looking man than'' Lady Gregory ''expected'' (Gregory 124) when Shiels drove to a friend's house to meet her. That visit coincided with the Abbey's touring of *Professor Tim*. While the players staged the play in Belfast, Shiels watched from the wings. It was the only production of any of his plays he would see. Later, he wrote to Lady Gregory that he ''used to tug at my chain for freedom, but now I am almost a willing prisoner'' (Letter of George Shiels to Lady Gregory, dated December 1929, University of Ulster at Coleraine). His discipline of work, the few regular visitors, and privacy was punctuated in 1932 by a move to Carnlough and a house with gardens and a view of the sea.

His continuing popular success enabled him to afford the move, and his development as a playwright continued in the 1930s. The Abbey staged ten of his plays (seven original productions and three revivals) during those ten years, taking *The New Gossoon* to London and America in financially lucrative tours. Their popular success helped to sustain the theater during the depression and gave actors like Sara Allgood, Barry Fitzgerald, and F. J. McCormick roles that drew the attention of the Hollywood studios. These works resemble the style of his earlier entertainments, but, also in the 1930s, Shiels began to develop his skills producing better-quality plays. Rather than simply superficial entertainments, his work began to manifest a latent pathos. On the surface, characters would laugh and involve themselves in ridiculous circumstance, but "irony is his weapon and he points it home with a smile—sometimes a savage one" (Bell [2], 81). In addition, after a 1951 Lyric Theatre revival of Shiels' 1936 *The Passing Day*, a critic commented that it "may throw too much emphasis on the sinners" (Review of *The Passing Day, Belfast Telegraph*).

In addition, in a startling move for a Northern writer, Shiels' work begins to search for a postcolonial Irish identity. Critics like Feeney, Kennedy, and Casey point out that plays from this period, like *The Rugged Path*, tell the audience "the message" is "that the Irish, without the props of British authority, must fashion their own laws and, more importantly, once they have fashioned them, they must learn to live by them" (Casey 35). Feeney writes that "with the end of British authority, at least in the Republic, the old conditioned reflexes must loose their hold" (Feeney 45). The move is startling not only because Shiels still lived under British authority but because of the prejudices against writers from the "Black North" (see Hayes [1]). It was commonly believed even by residents of the twenty-six counties that "Northern Ireland" was "destined, it may be, for temperamental reasons, always to play dramatic second to the more imaginative South" (Allen 467); writers and individuals from the North, even Catholics, were marginalized by prejudice and custom. However, it does not seem that Shiels' efforts came from some unconscious motivation to be considered a "Southern" writer. He was very conscious of his identity and had a sense of rootedness in, and awareness of, his home; in the 1940s, he again wrote plays for Northern theaters, and after the Abbey's tour in the late 1920s he wrote Lady Gregory that "your visit and that of the Abbey Company to Belfast has stirred things up in the North, there is much talk of a little theatre for Belfast" (Letter to Lady Gregory, January 1930, University of Ulster at Coleraine), anticipating the rise of the Ulster Group Theatre and, later, the Lyric Players Theatre. He maintained an awareness of the trends in Northern drama, a sensitivity that would have eluded a casual observer. Further, the movement in his plays is so subtle as to be nothing more than a genuine desire to create a new Irish identity for all Irishmen, including those in the six counties. He wrote of the "next step" for the people of Ireland. The previous generation of playwrights and authors helped define Ireland and Irish identity in opposition to British rule. Now, the Irish needed to define themselves as a nation not only independent of Britain but independent of distinctions between North and South, a necessary and logical process in nation building. However, it is important to remember that many of his plays of this and his later period reflect the complexities of Ulster–Free State relations. He functions under no delusions. He appreciates not only the difficulty in creating a national character but the necessity in maintaining within that creation distinct regional identities, distinctions made even clearer because of Partition. In the end, he seems conscious of his identity as a Northerner yet unwilling to allow that identity to purge him of his Irish identity despite the latent and sometimes manifest bias against the North.

This trend continued into the 1940s. He began to write plays—*Macooks Corner* (1942), revised from the Abbey production of *Neal Maquade, The Old Broom* (1944), *Borderwine* (1946), and *Mountain Post* (1948), and the posthumous production of *Slave Drivers* (1949)—for the Ulster Group Theatre, an organization comprising three companies—the Ulster Theatre, the Jewish Institute Dramatic Society, and the Northern Irish Players—that consolidated acting, administrative, technical, and production staff in the winter of 1939–1940. These plays continued Shiels' trend toward comic pathos and the discomfort of utilitarian morality. Further, they solidified his identity as a Northern writer. David Kennedy observes that his plays "have nowhere been better interpreted than in Belfast. It is not a matter of acting and production only—these are often better done in Dublin—but that of invisible cooperation between audience and stage: nuances of expression and character arousing overtones of feeling, emotional harmonics, in the audience" (Kennedy [1], 54). But most of Shiels' energy was spent producing scripts for the Abbey, which staged seven of his plays, including *The Rugged Path*, which proved the most successful production, in terms of a long run, in the Abbey's history. Thematically, the plays carried forward his themes of dark pathos underlying a comic surface, and they continued his earlier tendency to begin to define a new Irish identity. *The New Regime* and *The Fort Field* speak of the contrast between old and new Irish conceptions of self. Another piece, *Tenants at Will*, reaches back into Irish history, into his father's stories of the Famine and colonial agrarian abuses, to give a context for the new postcolonial identity. However, it is possible to make too much of Shiels' dark or more political side. As Ria Mooney suggests, he is, like Molière, primarily a writer of comedies and a master creator of comic characters and situations. Audiences enjoyed and demanded his plays. His naturalistic style and subtle social commentary made him a favorite of Dublin and Belfast houses. On 19 September 1949, George Shiels died at his home in Carnlough, County Antrim. He failed to see what is considered the best of his work, *Slave Drivers*, produced by the Ulster Group Theatre, but he did live to become one of the most important playwrights of the second generation of Abbey writers, the generation after Yeats and Gregory. His importance can be measured in the subtle themes of his work, but it is best measured in how his popular work and dynamic characters sustained the Abbey and the Northern houses through difficult times of Partition, depression, and the Second World War.

Selected Biographical Sources: Bell [1, 2]; Casey; Feeney; Gregory; Hogan, *After the Renaissance*; Kennedy [1, 2].

MAJOR PLAYS, PREMIERES, AND SIGNIFICANT REVIVALS: THEATRICAL RECEPTION

Productions for the Ulster Literary Theatre under the Name George Morshiel

Away from the Moss. 1918. Opened 25 November at the Grand Opera House in Belfast, County Antrim. The cast included Walter Kennedy, Norman Gray, Irene Boyd, Maire Reynolds, and Gerald MacNamara.

The critics found the play amusing but also found some fault with the quality of its construction. "The plot is very frail, and there is a great deal too much talk and too little concentration of purpose. The audience were apparently greatly amused by last night's performance. . . . To put it briefly, the play is a broad farce, and only when it is acted in that spirit does it make any appeal" ("This Week's Amusements").

Felix Reid and Bob. 1919. (originally called *The Simpleston.*) Opened 12–13 November at the Grand Opera House in Belfast, County Antrim. The cast included Charles Ayre.

Critics found fault, in part, with parts of the play's construction and found in it the portrait of Northern Irish characters that Shiels would pursue in his later work. "The scene . . . is laid in an Ulster rural environment, and the dialogue . . . represents one of the best achievements so far in the reproduction of the real Ulsterspeak in stage interchanges. It does not pretend to any intensity or to elaborate effects, but it is a singularly pleasant picture (or rather the dramatic equivalent to a pencil sketch) of Northern Irish country people and their ways" ("Ulster Theatre").

Shiels also wrote *The Tame Drudge* around 1920 for the Ulster Literary Theatre, although critics find no record of its production, nor do the holdings at Coleraine reveal a production date. In 1930, the theater also staged a revival of *Cartney and Kevney.*

Productions of the Abbey Theatre (National Theatre Society)

Bedmates. 1921. Opened 6 January at the Abbey Theatre, Dublin. The cast included Barry Fitzgerald, Tony Quinn, Michael J. Dolan, and Maureen Delany.

The rather sparse critical commentary mentions that the play was well received—"[T]he audience was vastly amused and highly delighted. Mr. Barry Fitzgerald was the ideal Irish tramp, and Mr. Tony Quinn acted the simple Ulsterman to the life" ("The Abbey Theatre" [7 January 1921]).

Insurance Money. 1921. Opened 13 December at the Abbey Theatre, Dublin. The cast included Peter Nolan, Gabriel Fallon, Eileen O'Kelly, Tony Quinn, Michael J. Dolan, Eileen Crowe. Lennox Robinson directed the production.

The critics were unanimous in their disapproval. ''The new play is poor as a dramatic work and as a comedy; the acting last night was likewise of almost consistently poor quality'' (''New Play at the Abbey''). The *Evening Herald* (''New Abbey Play'') found it ''not . . . overburdened with much complexity of plot [or] marked by any great display of dramatic achievements.''

Paul Twyning. 1922. Opened 3 October at the Abbey Theatre, Dublin. The cast included Barry Fitzgerald, Gabriel Fallon, Michael J. Dolan, P. J. Carolan, and May Craig. Lennox Robinson directed.

Critics found the production the best of Shiels' work. The reviewer for the *Evening Telegraph* (''At the Abbey'') wrote, ''It's a rather highly-coloured comedy, properly speaking; but it has good action throughout, some excellent characterisation and plenty of humour. . . . The play lends itself to some fine character acting.''

First Aid. 1923. Opened 26 December at the Abbey Theatre, Dublin. The cast included Eileen Crowe, Arthur Shields, Tony Quinn, Maureen Delany, F. J. McCormick, and Michael J. Dolan. Michael J. Dolan also directed.

The critics recorded the piece's popularity and also made note of the latent pathos that would mark Shiels' later work. ''*First Aid*, a one-act play by George Shiels, had a successful first production at the Abbey Theatre, Dublin, last night. Although the audience laughed pretty continuously, the subject of their merriment is a bitter, almost gruesome presentation of a modern Irish outlook on life, which, judging from all that one heard and read during the past couple of years, is no mere stage exaggeration'' (''The Abbey Theatre'' [27 December 1923]).

The Retrievers. 1924. Opened 12 May at the Abbey Theatre, Dublin. The cast included Michael J. Dolan, Shelah Richards, Arthur Shields, Sara Allgood, Ria Mooney, F. J. McCormick, P. J. Carolan, Maureen Delany, and May Craig. Michael J. Dolan directed.

Some critics were impressed with the production. ''I do not know of any writer to-day whose wit is so pungent, so satiric, so conducive to satisfied chuckling as Mr. Shiels'. He absolutely gleams and glitters and explodes with epigrams and loquacity'' (O'Donnell). Other critics found the piece less than successful. ''It is less a play than a succession of amusing incidents and occasional witty dialogue. It is obviously intended to be political and to point a moral, but its construction is so poor that the moral is lost'' (Mitchell [1]).

Professor Tim. 1925. Opened 14 September at the Abbey Theatre, Dublin. The cast included Eric Gorman, Sara Allgood, Eileen Crowe, F. J. McCormick, Peter Nolan, Christine Hayden, Barry Fitzgerald, P. J. Carolan, Arthur Shields, Maureen Delany, and J. Stephenson. Michael J. Dolan directed.

Critics enjoyed the play and admired the actors but, on the whole, were disappointed in the merit of the play. "Laughter could hardly have been out of place anywhere during its three Acts.... *Professor Tim* is rather a series of rough-and-tumble incidents than a play" (Mitchell [2]).

Cartney and Kevney. 1927. Opened 29 November at the Abbey Theatre, Dublin. The cast included Michael J. Dolan, Barry Fitzgerald, F. J. McCormick, Eric Gorman, P. J. Carolan, Maureen Delany, Peter Nolan, and Eileen Crowe. Arthur Shields directed.

Critics commented on the play's popularity and the high quality of acting. "The Abbey was thronged for the first night of George Shiels' comedy in three acts, *Cartney and Kevney*.... The audience liked the piece and were enthusiastic at the end, giving the actors many calls.... Barry Fitzgerald was amusing as 'Cartney,' though often hesitating in his text, and F. J. McCormick was an excellent companion in idleness as 'Kevney'.... Eileen Crowe played the role of 'Mrs. Cartney' very well, and all the rest of the cast was good in colourless parts" (quoted in Hogan and O'Neill, vol. 1: 29). Hayes [1] agreed with Holloway. "With two such clever comedians as Barry Fitzgerald and F. J. McCormick in the title roles, *Cartney and Kevney* should prove irresistible."

Mountain Dew. 1929. Opened 5 March at the Abbey Theatre, Dublin. The cast included Michael J. Dolan, May Craig, Eileen Crowe, May Bonass, Barry Fitzgerald, Maureen Delany, Hindle Mallard, F. J. McCormick, and P. J. Carolan. Arthur Shields directed.

Critics thought the play had merit but also felt that it ultimately disappoints. "The play—it can hardly be described as a comedy in view of one or two serious and dramatic situations which develop—is excellent entertainment. In his more recent plays Shiels has flecked his work with satire, and in *Mountain Dew* he gives the impression that, possessing greater experience, he would have brought the play to an end on a note of intense irony" (Hayes [2]).

The New Gossoon. 1930. Opened 19 April by the Abbey Theatre, Dublin. The cast included Maureen Delany, Denis O'Dea, Michael J. Dolan, P. J. Carolan, Frolie Mulhern, F. J. McCormick, Eileen Crowe, Arthur Shields, and Shelah Richards. Arthur Shields directed.

Critics were pleased with the production and told stories of Shiels' reaction to the play's warm reception. "A full house enjoyed *The New Gossoon* at the Abbey, and at the end called and recalled the players several times, and Arthur Shiel[d]s came forward and thanked them in behalf of the absent author. He felt pleasure in producing the piece, and the players felt pleasure in playing in it, and he was sure the audience had felt pleasure in witnessing it. The invalid author was waiting at the other end of the telephone to hear the verdict of the house" (quoted in Hogan and O'Neill, vol. 1: 60). Hayes [3] agreed with Holloway. "George Shiels . . . surpassed his every previous effort as a weaver of comedy. Moreover, he has made a contribution to the lighter side of Irish dramatic literature which, of certainty, places him in the front rank of native writers for the theatre."

The Passing Day. 1936. Opened 13 April at the Abbey Theatre in Dublin. (Originally titled *His Last Day in Business*.) The cast included F. J. McCormick, Eileen Crowe, May Craig, Denis O'Dea, Arthur Shields, Michael J. Dolan, P. J. Carolan, Eric Gorman, Barry Fitzgerald, Cyril Cusack, and Maureen Delany. Hugh Hunt directed.

Critics speak of a well-acted and entertaining piece. "The theatre was crowded, and many first nighters were present. . . . Shiels' play turned out a most interesting one and gripped the audience's interest from the start. It was enacted in half-stage settings and starts with the waiting room in a hospital, and we learn that old 'John Fibbs' has met with an accident" (quoted in Hogan and O'Neill, vol. 2: 53–54).

The Jailbird. 1936. Opened 12 October at the Abbey Theatre, Dublin. The cast included F. J. McCormick, Eileen Crowe, Shelah Richards, Frolie Mulhern, Michael J. Dolan, May Craig, P. J. Carolan, Arthur Shields, and Maureen Delany. Hugh Hunt directed.

Holloway wrote, "The audience was intensely interested in it right up to the end and if some thought Shelah Richards' portrait of 'Martha,' the country dressmaker's daughter, over-affected, I imagine that both the author and producer were partly to blame. . . . Great enthusiasm followed the ending, and as I hurried out into Abbey Street by the pit entrance, I could hear round after round of applause" (quoted in Hogan and O'Neill, vol. 2: 60–61).

Quin's Secret. 1937. Opened 29 March at the Abbey Theatre, Dublin. The cast included P. J. Carolan, Michael J. Dolan, Arthur Shields, and Cyril Cusack.

Robert Hogan, writing in the mid-1960s, analyzed the play. "*Quin's Secret* also examines chicanery in business, though its real interest lies in the characterisation of the honest young clerk, the drunken manager, and the rascally foreman. . . . The play does not sufficiently suggest that its story is a crucial symptom rather than an isolated instance, but it is a craftsmanlike job" (35). Holloway noted that the show "played before a packed house and a thoroughly amused one. It is more or less a study of characters hung together by a very slender plot. His comedy is full of good conversation which the Abbey Players interpreted to perfection. . . . I imagine that *Quin's Secret* will prove another of George Shiels' popular successes" (quoted in Hogan and O'Neill, vol. 2: 67).

Give Him a House. 1939. Opened 30 October at the Abbey Theatre, Dublin. The cast included Cyril Cusack, Ria Mooney, Brid Ni Loingsigh, Shela Ward, Gertrude Quinn, and Eric Gorman. Frank Dermody directed.

Hogan thinks "*Give Him a House* is Shiels' most tough-minded play up to this time—perhaps a bit too sardonic for the theatre. It depicts a morality as actually practised by men of no more than ordinary good will, rather than the morality we have become accustomed to from pulpits, editorials, and conventional plays. . . . [Men] always willing to sacrifice a principle to attain a profit. This not implausible view of human nature is still quite opposed to the platitudinous morality of most plays. Still, Shiels does make his case fairly and without overstatement. Predictably, the piece has not been popular'' (36). However, Holloway thought ''[t]he play . . . very rambling and moved much too slowly as almost to become boring at times. The dialogue was often sparkling and nearly always witty and to the point, and many of the characters were alive and full blooded'' (quoted in Hogan and O'Neill, vol. 3: 37).

The Rugged Path. 1940. Opened 5 August at the Abbey Theatre, Dublin. The cast included F. J. McCormick, Ria Mooney, Denis O'Dea, May Craig, and Kathleen Murphy. Michael J. Dolan directed.

Hogan analyzes the importance of the play. ''*The Rugged Path* was a milestone for the Abbey. Considering Dublin's size, its twelve-week run would be the equivalent of a smash hit in London or New York. The discovery of how profitable a long run could be helped to form the theatre's present policy of keeping plays on as long as they draw'' (36). Kavanagh, with deep sadness, comments: ''The audience, not the poet, was in control now, and it demanded to be flattered. . . . Even the standard of acting had to be lowered to suit the tastes of the public'' (181). Holloway countered by observing that ''Kavanagh didn't think *The Rugged Path* such as [*sic*] good play that it could attract so many people. There must be some real merit in it to do so, though he could not fathom it'' (quoted in Hogan and O'Neill, vol. 3: 52). He went on to say, ''It was a piece that gripped one's interest early in its development and kept one guessing to the very end. The final episode of the play was abrupt, and when the curtain fell the audience could not realise that it was over and remained silent for quite awhile. . . . I overheard the young girl who sat next to me saying in a whisper to her male companion, 'I'm dying to know how it will end' '' (quoted in Hogan and O'Neill, vol. 3: 45–46).

The Summit. 1941. Sequel to *The Rugged Path.* Opened 10 February at the Abbey Theatre, Dublin. The cast included John Macdarby, May Craig, Denis O'Dea, Brid Ni Loingsigh, Michael J. Dolan, Ria Mooney, Eileen Crowe, Kathleen Murphy, and F. J. McCormick, among others. Frank Dermody directed.

Holloway enjoyed the production and noted that he ''found the vestibule full on my arrival. . . . The sequel proved a successful solution to the problem set in *The Rugged Path*. . . . F. J. McCormick still retained some of the rougueish travelling man, 'Marcy's' sweetness of disposition, despite his inebriety. The cast fitted into their parts, and Fred Johnson as the good fairy of the sequel waved his wand with ease and effect'' (quoted in Hogan and O'Neill, vol. 3: 56).

Tenants at Will. 1945. Originally titled *The Brink of Famine.* Opened 24 September at the Abbey Theatre, Dublin. The cast included Michael J. Dolan, Cyril Cusack, Fred Johnson, Eric Gorman, F. J. McCormick, Harry Brogan, Eileen Crowe, and Denis O'Dea. Frank Dermody directed.

Hogan tells us that "*Tenants at Will*, in its original version, which was rejected by the Abbey, is reported to have been a broadly panoramic play. The revision, which the theatre produced, is a too simple, optimistic view of the plight of the small farmer a few years before the Great Famine" (38). However, Shiels thought the play "two-thirds creative and one-third documentary" and that he "could probably have done a better job with a purely creative play. . . . Anyway it's my small contribution to the literature of the period" (Shiels' papers, University of Ulster at Coleraine).

The Caretakers. 1948. Opened 16 February at the Abbey Theatre, Dublin. Ria Mooney directed.

"[A]lthough most of the characters are mean, grasping, and ruthless, this play remains a curiously broad and almost bright comedy. The reason is that many of the characters are such fine humours that it is difficult to take the plot as seriously as its savage motivations demand; instead, one is seduced into enjoying its twists, reversals, and counterturns for their own complexity" (Hogan, *After the Renaissance* 38). Ria Mooney [2] felt that "though the play wasn't the best of Shiels' work, it was like those he had written constructed with workmanlike efficiency, and enriched by his unquenchable sense of humour" (88).

ADDITIONAL PLAYS, ADAPTATIONS, AND PRODUCTIONS

In addition, the Abbey staged *Grogan and the Ferret* (13 November 1933), *Neal Maquade* (17 January 1938), *Cartney and Kevney* (8 November 1937), *Insurance Money* (9 May 1939), *The New Gossoon* (15 August 1938), *The Fort Field* (13 April 1942), *The New Regime* (6 March 1944), and *The Old Broom* (25 March 1946). The Abbey staged revivals of *The Jailbird* on 3 November 1949, of *Professor Tim* on 27 November 1950, and of *The Passing Day* on 19 October 1952 as *Ag Baint lae* (trans. Sean Toibin) and in its original form in 1981 under the direction of Tomás MacAnna. The Abbey also staged *Macook's Corner* (2 June 1969). In addition, the Peacock Theatre staged *Grogan and the Ferret* on 27 May 1970.

The following is a list of other significant productions: *Professor Tim* (British Tour), 1927. *The New Gossoon* (Apollo Theatre–London), 8 April 1931. *The New Gossoon* (American Tour), 21 October 1932. *The New Gossoon* (American Tour), 13 November 1934. *The New Gossoon* (American Tour), 29 November 1937. *Macook's Corner*, 1942. *Amanda McKittrick Ros: Author* (adaptation), 25 July 1943. *Irene Iddlesleigh* (adapted from a McKittrick novel), 1943. *The Old Broom*, 1944. *Borderwine*, 1946. *The Man of the World* (adapted from Charles Macklin), 1948. *Moodie in Manitoba*, BBC Radio, 24 June 1948. *Mountain Post*, 1948. *Slave Drivers* (originally titled *Master William*), 1950. *The Passing Day* (Festival of Britain), 1951. *Tully's Experts*, BBC Radio, 13 December 1951. *The Old Broom* (Grove Theatre), 1964. *The Passing Day* (Lyric Theatre), 1969–1970. *Macook's Corner* (Lifford Players at the Hawk's Well Theatre), 12 January 1981. *Macook's Corner* (Lifford Players at the Peacock Theatre), 1982. *Moodie in Manitoba* (Lyric Theatre), 1986–1987.

ASSESSMENT OF SHIELS' CAREER

A modern critic, with a modern sensibility, reads early reviews of George Shiels' plays with a certain degree of amusement.

Praise be to God. (It is a hard thing surely to review an Irish play without embezzling a phrase or two of their speech.) Some bigwig once confessed that he could never tell whether an Irish play was good or bad; as soon as the richness of Irish voices began to brush across the lines his critical capacity was paralysed altogether, and the most hackneyed piece of stage claptrap sounded like a poem to him (Atkinson).

At other times, however, amusement and the gentle, misguided comments of Atkinson give way to the bitterness and racial bias of a London critic who wrote of Shiels that "he has one quality—good temper—which, when found in an Irish playwright, is peculiarly endearing to an Englishman. . . . There is refreshment in an Irish play that contains neither bitterness nor propaganda (Morgan). Modern critics express frustration over what they identify as tendencies toward blank and mindlessly pleasing humor in Shiels' writings. Krause, writing in the early 1980s, finds "that unmistakable streak of bourgeois benignity in his [Shiels'] nature" (135). He goes on to speculate that "perhaps Shiels' dilemma was that he was too prolific and too popular for his own good" (135). Krause does concede, however, that Shiels "can be a richly inventive and entertaining artist of comic desecration" (135). However, he condemns, perhaps too earnestly, Shiels as a "fatalistic Irishman whose country had been exposed to 700 years of British injustice" (153) and speculates that "the aging Shiels, perhaps confined too long to chronic illness in a *Northern* Ireland village, failed to understand" (153; italics added) his nation's need for "political or comic rebellion" (153). Shiels would have railed at such an accusation that his disability somehow limited his perceptions and created a languid, old man, out of touch with the realities of Irish life. In 1930, he wrote the *Irish Times* ("Letter") that "I am not a 'bedridden invalid' . . . when I make up my mind to go to the theatre or elsewhere, I can always get there without calling an ambulance." Further, in the early twentieth century, the act of a Catholic playwright, especially a Catholic from the minority population in a small *Northern* Irish village in County Antrim, writing plays for the Abbey Theatre was an act of rebellion in self-assertion. T. C. Murray [1] writes:

One hears from time to time much talk of our Celtic sensibility to what is fine and beautiful. But no comment was necessary other than the queue at the doors of the Theatres. Ask those Catholic people why they are there, . . . they will tell you that the production they are so patiently waiting to see has had a run of heaven knows how many hundred nights in some London theatre.

Critics who are too ready to condemn Shiels for his lack of political activism should consider that Murray goes on to number Shiels, even in 1922, among those playwrights who did well to overcome racial and political and cultural bias to write plays and have English audiences pay to see them and should consider his work, however subtle, to build a postcolonial Irish identity in his later plays and should consider his efforts to build and sustain, through script writing, an indigenous theater in Belfast.

Critics who confine their comments to Shiels' creative work generally fall into two categories. There are those, like Malone, writing in the late 1920s, who see that Shiels "achieved considerable popularity as a purveyor of amusement in Dublin and in London" (237) but that "his plays have a rigidity of structure" (238) and that "in all his plays the author tends to repeat himself, there is little variation in plot or characterisation" (239). Kavanagh, writing in his history of the Abbey, tends to agree. "Shiels was a dramatic journalist rather than a playwright. His work proved vastly amusing to audiences interested only in the superficialities of life" (147). Much of this assessment is correct if one restricts readings of Shiels' plays to those works written before 1930.

However, critics who focus on the totality of his achievement find much that is valuable in Shiels' work. Considering the comments of Kavanagh and Malone, Casey writes that

it was Shiels' popularity and productivity that damned him among the less imaginative critics who seemed to dismiss his plays as lightweight entertainments. They remembered him as a writer of Ulster kitchen comedies or as a bread-and-butter playwright who kept audiences in the Abbey stalls between geniuses, but not as a first-rate dramatist in his own right (17).

Casey goes on to say that "Shiels is rightly viewed as the saviour of the Abbey. . . . In the lean depression period, it was Shiels and Lennox Robinson who provided the main fare for the company" (18). Kennedy discerns one of the most important contributions of Shiels' work, his latent pathos—"even a play which seems on the surface to be an innocuous comedy can be stripped of the muffling laughter to reveal a hard and bitter world" (Kennedy [1], 52). Lyons speaks of the movement in the early part of the twentieth century when "there began to appear a homely, rustic drama depicting Ulster men and women in ordinary situations and using everyday speech" (132). This type of depiction for the first time gave the Northern Irish a representation, not a represencing, on the stage, and this sense of identity that he gave to Ulster Catholics and Irish people in general is, perhaps, the most enduring legacy of Shiels' work.

ARCHIVAL SOURCES

The most extensive collection of George Shiels' material, including correspondence, manuscripts, play scripts, notebooks, typescripts, cuttings, and photographs, is housed in the archives of the University of Ulster at Coleraine in Northern Ireland. The Berg Collection of the New York Public Library also houses some of Shiels' letters. Playbills and some manuscripts are housed in the National Library in Dublin. Some playbills and posters are also contained in the archives of the Linen Hall Library in Belfast and the Theatre Ireland Archive in Dublin.

NOTE

I would like to thank the library staff of the University of Ulster at Coleraine, the National Library in Dublin, the Linen Hall Library in Belfast, An Leabharlann Colaiste na hOllscoile Gaillimh, the Theatre Ireland Archive, the Bodleian Library of Oxford University, the New York Public Library, the University of Delaware Library, and the Sterling Memorial Library at Yale University for their kindness and patience and generous assistance in the production of this article.

PRIMARY BIBLIOGRAPHY

Bedmates: A Play in One Act. Dublin: Gael Cooperative Society, 1922.
The Caretakers: A Play in Three Acts. Dublin: Golden Eagle Books, 1948.
The Fort Field: A Play in Three Acts. Dublin: Golden Eagle Books, 1947.
Give Him a House: A Comedy in Three Acts. Dublin: Golden Eagle Books, 1947.
Grogan and the Ferret: A Comedy in Three Acts. Dublin: Golden Eagle Books, 1947.
"Letter." *Irish Times* (23 April 1930).
The New Gossoon. In *Plays of a Changing Ireland*. Ed. Curtis Canfield. New York: Macmillan, 1936.
The Old Broom: A Comedy in Three Acts. Dublin: Golden Eagle Books, 1948.
The Passing Day: A Play in Six Scenes and The Jailbird: A Comedy in Three Acts. London: Macmillan, 1937.
Professor Tim and Paul Twyning: Comedies in Three Acts. London: Macmillan, 1927.
Quinn's Secret: A Comedy in Three Acts. Dublin: Golden Eagle Books, 1947.
The Rugged Path: A Play in Three Acts and The Summit: A Play in Three Acts. London: Macmillan, 1942.
Tenants at Will: A Play of Rural Ireland in the Young Ireland Period. Dublin: Golden Eagle Books, 1947.
Three Plays (Professor Tim, Paul Twyning, The New Gossoon). London: Macmillan, 1945.

Two Irish Plays: Mountain Dew, a Play in Three Acts and Cartney and Kesney, a Comedy in Three Acts. London: Macmillan, 1930.

SECONDARY BIBLIOGRAPHY

"The Abbey Theatre." *Irish Times* (7 Jan. 1921): 6.

"The Abbey Theatre." *Irish Times* (27 Dec. 1923): 4.

Allen, Percy. "The Theatre in Ulster." *The Living Age* (22 May 1926): 467–69.

"At the Abbey." *Evening Telegraph* (4 Oct. 1922): 4.

Atkinson, Brooks. "The New Gossoon." *New York Times* (30 Nov. 1937): 26.

Bell, Sam Hanna. [1]. *The Arts in Ulster: A Symposium.* London: Harp, 1951.

———. [2]. *The Theatre in Ulster: A Survey of the Dramatic Movement in Ulster from 1902 until the Present Day.* Dublin: Gill and Macmillan, 1972.

Casey, Daniel J. "George Shiels: The Enigmatic Playwright." *Irish Renaissance Annual* 4 (1983): 17–41; rpt., *Threshold* 33 (1983).

Ellis-Fermor, Una. *The Irish Dramatic Movement.* London: Methuen, 1964.

Feeney, William J. "The Rugged Path: A Modern View of Informers." *Éire-Ireland* 2.1 (Spring 1967): 41–47.

Gregory, Augusta Persse. *Lady Gregory's Journals.* Ed. Lennox Robinson. London: Macmillan, 1947.

Hayes, J. J. [1]. [Review of *Cartney and Kevney*.] *New York Times* (1 Jan. 1928): sec. 8: 2.

———. [2]. [Review of *Mountain Dew*.] *New York Times* (31 Mar. 1929): sec. 8: 4.

———. [3]. [Review of *The New Gossoon*.] *New York Times* (11 May 1930): sec. 9: 2.

Hogan, Robert. *After the Renaissance: A Critical History of Irish Drama since* The Plough and the Stars. Minneapolis: University of Minnesota Press, 1967.

Hogan, Robert, and Richard Burnham. [1]. *The Modern Irish Drama—Vol. 5. The Art of the Amateur 1916–1920.* Mountrath, Portlaoise: Dolmen Press, 1984.

———. [2]. *The Modern Irish Drama—Vol. 6: The Years of O'Casey, 1921–1926.* Gerrard's Cross, Buckinghamshire: Colin Smythe, 1992.

Hogan, Robert, and Michael J. O'Neill, eds. *Joseph Holloway's Irish Theatre.* 3 vols. Dixon, Calif.: Proscenium Press, 1968–1970.

Kavanagh, Peter. *The Story of the Abbey Theatre.* New York: Devin-Adair, 1950.

Kelly, J. J. "George Shiels as the Exponent of Modern Irish Comedy." Master's thesis, National University of Ireland, Dublin, 1950.

Kennedy, David. [1]. "George Shiels: A Playwright at Work." *Threshold* 25 (1974): 50–58.

———. [2]. "Ulster Books and Authors, 1900–1953." *Rann* 20 (1953).

Krause, David. *The Profane Book of Irish Comedy.* Ithaca, N.Y.: Cornell University Press, 1982.

Lyons, F. S. L. *Culture and Anarchy in Ireland 1890–1939.* Oxford: Clarendon Press, 1979.

MaCardle, Dorothy. "Experiment in Ireland." *Theatre Arts* 18.1 (Feb. 1934): 124–32.

Malone, Andrew E. *Irish Theatre.* London: Benjamin Blom, 1929.

Maxwell, D. E. S. *A Critical History of Modern Irish Drama.* Cambridge: Cambridge University Press, 1984.

Mitchell, Susan L. [1]. "Drama Notes." *Irish Statesman* (17 May 1924): 303.

———. [2]. "Drama Notes." *Irish Statesman* (19 Sept. 1925): 50.

Mooney, Ria. [1]. "Players and Painted Stage, the Autobiography of Ria Mooney, Part One." Ed. Val Mulkerns. *George Spelvin's Theatre Book* 1.2 (1978): 3–121.

———. [2]. "Players and Painted Stage, the Autobiography of Ria Mooney, Part Two." Ed. Val Mulkerns. *George Spelvin's Theatre Book* 1.3 (1978): 65–121.

Morgan, Charles. "London Letter." *New York Times* (17 Apr. 1927): sec. 7: 1.

Murray, T. C. [1]. "Catholics and the Theatre." *Evening Herald* (12 Oct. 1922): 1.

———. [2]. "George Shiels, Brinsley MacNamara, etc." *The Irish Theatre*. Ed. Lennox Robinson. London: Macmillan, 1939.

"New Abbey Play." *Evening Herald* (14 Dec. 1921): 4.

"New Play at the Abbey." *Freeman's Journal* (16 Nov. 1921): 4.

O'Connor, Frank. BBC Northern Ireland Home Service (2 Dec. 1948).

O'Donnell, Frank J. Hugh. "A Look round the Retrievers." *Evening Herald* (13 May 1924): 2.

O'Malley, Conor. *A Poet's Theatre*. Dublin: Elo Press, 1988.

———. Review of *The Passing Day. Belfast Telegraph* (21 Mar. 1951): 4.

Sahal, N. *Sixty Years of Realistic Irish Drama (1900–1960)*. Bombay: Macmillan, 1960.

"This Week's Amusements." *Belfast News-Letter* (26 Nov. 1918): 3.

"Ulster Theatre." *Irish News and Belfast Morning News* (14 Nov. 1919): 6.

Wintegest, Marianne. "Die Selbstdarstellung der Iren: eine Untersuchung zum Modernen Anglo-Irischen Drama. Ph.D. Diss. Munich University, 1973.

BIBLIOGRAPHIES

Canfield, Curtis. *Plays of a Changing Ireland*. New York: Macmillan, 1936.

Casey, Daniel J. "George Shiels: The Enigmatic Playwright." *Irish Renaissance Annual* 4 (1983): 37–39.

Feeney, William J. "George Shiels." *Dictionary of Irish Literature*. Ed. Robert Hogan. Westport, Conn.: Greenwood Press, 1980.

Hogan, Robert. "The Modern Drama." *Anglo-Irish Literature. A Review of Research*. Ed. Richard J. Finneran. New York: Modern Language Association of America, 1976.

John Millington Synge
(1871–1909)

RICHARD JONES

John Millington Synge may be more famous for the riots engendered by the original production of his *The Playboy of the Western World* than for his works per se. Still, despite chronic ill health and death shortly before his thirty-eighth birthday, Synge scripted two acknowledged masterpieces and at least two other plays that remain in the repertoire of regional and university theaters around the English-speaking world. Further, his creation of plays that met both the literary standards of W.B. Yeats and the theatrical (''playability'') standards of the Fay brothers was crucial to the development of the indigenous Irish theater.

John Millington Synge was born on 16 April 1871 in Newton Little, near Dublin, the eighth child of Kathleen (Traill) Synge and John Hatch Synge, a barrister. Educated in private schools in Dublin and Bray, Synge spent his summer holidays in County Wicklow. He entered Trinity College, Dublin, in 1888 and earned his B.A. in 1892. While at Trinity, Synge earned awards or scholarships in a variety of disciplines, including Hebrew, Irish, and music. After college, Synge moved to Germany to study music, but he abandoned this pursuit in 1894, when he went to Paris and began to entertain thoughts of becoming a writer. In 1896 he visited Italy and, far more significantly, made his first visit to the Aran Islands, where he began early drafts of *The Aran Islands*, a journal of his experiences there. Convinced by Yeats in 1898 or 1899 to return to Aran to study the life there, Synge, in fact, made several trips to the islands over the next few years.

From 1899 to 1902 Synge divided his time between Paris and Ireland. During this time, he worked on further drafts of *The Aran Islands* (which would finally be published in 1907), as well as his early one-act plays, *In the Shadow of the Glen, Riders to the Sea*, and *The Tinker's Wedding*. The first of these to be produced, *In the Shadow of the Glen*, opened on 8 October 1903, on the first bill of the newly founded Irish National Theatre Society, a hybrid of the leading Dublin acting company, the Ormonde Dramatic Society, headed by W. G. and Frank Fay, and the leading figures of contemporary Irish dramatic literature, represented by W. B. Yeats and Lady Gregory of the now-defunct Irish Literary Theatre. *Riders to the Sea* followed in February 1904, and by the end of the year, Synge was on hand for the opening of the new Abbey Theatre, which opened its doors on 27 December. Synge's *The Well of the Saints* premiered at the Abbey a few weeks later. Synge was to become a director of the Abbey company.

The year 1905 marked both the presentation of Synge's first full-length play, *The Well of the Saints*, and the restructuring of the Abbey company into the National Theatre Society, Ltd., creating a professional acting company (although keeping many of the actors from before the changeover) and formalizing the role of A. E. F. Horniman, the Abbey's patroness.

While Synge's early plays all drew continuing criticism from fervent nationalists for failing to present what they perceived as an accurate portrayal of Irish life, the protests were mild compared to the furor that accompanied the opening of *The Playboy of the Western World* early in 1907. Both sides—the theater and the most ardent nationalists—organized claques to shout down what they perceived as the opposition, leading ultimately to a number of arrests; the ''Playboy Riots'' were not a peculiarly Irish phenomenon: similar disturbances greeted the company in several cities on their American tour.

Playboy, as it happened, was the last of Synge's plays to be produced in his lifetime. Although he spent as much time as he could working on *Deirdre of the Sorrows*, his health, never robust, decayed further. Major surgery in May 1908 was unsuccessful in removing a cancerous growth, and Synge never completed his revisions. Still, the manuscript with which we are left is both interesting and playable even in its current state and was indeed produced in 1910, directed by his fiancée, Molly Allgood (stage name: Maire O'Neill). Conversely, *The Tinker's Wedding*, completed some years earlier, is a relatively minor work; probably because of the possibility of further uproar, this time for alleged insults against the priesthood, the play was not produced until November 1909 (in London), several months after Synge's death to Hodgkin's disease in the Elpis Nursing Home in Dublin on 24 March of that year.

Selected Biographical Sources: Hogan and Kilroy; Hogan, Burnham and Poteet; Hunt; Masefield; Skelton [2]).

MAJOR PLAYS, PREMIERES, AND SIGNIFICANT REVIVALS: THEATRICAL RECEPTION

In the Shadow of the Glen. 1903. (one-act). Opened 8 October at Molesworth Hall, Dublin, on the bill with W. B. Yeats' *The King's Threshold* and *Cathleen Ni Houlihan*, the initial productions of the Irish National Theatre Society. Revived repeatedly by the Abbey, 1968, 1973).

Though it was not the first play Synge wrote, *In the Shadow of the Glen* was the first of his works to be performed. The premiere performance is important historically, as it represents the first joint venture of the two most significant strands of Irish theater: the literary work of W. B. Yeats, Lady Gregory, and their recent Irish Literary Theatre project, on one hand, and the production orientation of the Ormonde Dramatic Society, on the other. The central roles of Nora Burke, the quintessential "young wife of an old man," and the poetic but pragmatic Tramp, for whose company Nora leaves her gruff and abusive husband, were played by two of the Ormonde's best actors, Maire Nic Shiubhlaigh and W. G. Fay, respectively.

The opening caused some disturbances in the theater, prompted by advance speculation that the play represented an attack on Irish womanhood. The *Irish Times* ("Irish National Theatre") reported "mingled cheers and hissing" and suggested that "morality which could be injured by witnessing [the play] must have been . . . excessively weak-kneed to start with." Still, while praising the acting and the cleverness of the dialect, the *Irish Times* found the play "exceedingly distasteful." The *Daily Express* ("Irish National Theatre Society") described the play as "most agreeable fooling," praised the acting, and concentrated on the positive responses of the audience. In contrast, Griffith [1] called the play "a corrupt version of the old-world libel on woman-kind," decried Synge as "utterly a stranger to the Irish character," and proclaimed [4]: "If the Theatre be solely an Art Theatre, then its plays can only be fairly criticized from the standpoint of Art. But whilst it calls itself Irish National its productions must be considered and criticized as Irish National." Griffith went so far as to write (and publish) a short play entitled *In a Real Wicklow Glen;* Maud Gonne, Dudley Digges, Maire Quinn, and Douglas Hyde all withdrew from the theater in protest, and the criticism continued for many months, resurfacing every time the play was revived. Meanwhile, both the play and its author were championed by W. B. Yeats and indeed by his father, the painter John Butler Yeats, who called the attacks on the play "largely dishonest." The play was subsequently one of five plays of the Irish National Theatre Society to be presented by the London Irish Literary Society in 1904 and was on the program with Yeats' *On Baile's Strand* and *Cathleen Ni Houlihan* and Lady Gregory's *Spreading the News* for the opening of the Abbey Theatre, although it was not on the bill for the first evening's performances.

Riders to the Sea. 1904. (one-act). Opened 25 February at Molesworth Hall, Dublin. Produced by the Irish National Theatre Society; directed by J. M. Synge. Revived frequently by the Abbey Theatre, 1907, 1971, and by many other professional companies.

This tragedy of a woman who loses her sons to the sea has come to be regarded as one of the greatest one-act plays ever written. In its original production, however, the response was far less enthusiastic. The *Irish Daily Independent* ("Irish National Theatre"), for example, declared it a "trifle," compared it negatively to *In the Shadow of the Glen*, and yearned for the more expansive productions for which the Irish National Theatre Company had become known. Both the *Irish Times* ("Irish National Theatre Society") and Griffith [2] objected to the presentation of a dead body on the stage. But support within the company was very strong: Fay, for example, noted that the play had indeed met with some popular success and in private correspondence declared the work "a masterpiece." The play ultimately enjoyed some measure of popular success: it received warm applause in 1907, when it served to open the evening concluded by the fateful first productions of *The Playboy of the Western World*.

The Well of the Saints. 1905. Opened 4 February at the Abbey Theatre, Dublin. Produced by the Irish National Theatre Society; directed by W. G. Fay. Revived by the Abbey Theatre in 1969.

This wistful comedy of a blind couple miraculously restored to sight only to choose blindness met with what had become by now a predictably mixed response. Reviewers decried everything from the subject matter to the scenery: Griffith [3] was predictably brutal, but he was not alone. The *Freeman's Journal* ("Irish National Theatre, Mr. Synge's New Play"), for example, criticized the play for profanity, declaring that Synge "knows nothing of Irish peasant religion." There were more balanced assessments: M'Quilland, for example, while objecting to "the squalor of the play's human nature," also praises the "many beautiful and poetic lines." An autumn tour to Oxford, Cambridge, and London brought more favorable reviews, "L" writing in London's *Sunday Sun* that the play "is an affair of European importance."

The Playboy of the Western World. 1907. Opened 26 January at the Abbey Theatre, Dublin. Produced by the National Theatre Society; directed by W. G. Fay. Often revived by the Abbey, 1968, 1971, 1990, and other professional and university companies around the world.

This comedy of a young man lionized by peasants for claiming (erroneously) to have killed his father set off some of the most violent responses in the history of the theater. Critical response was little different from that for Synge's earlier plays: praise for the acting, dialogue described in the *Daily Express* ("The Abbey Theatre") as "sparkling and witty," but also condemnation for, in the words of the *Freeman's Journal*, an "unmitigated, protracted libel upon Irish peasant men and, worse still, upon Irish peasant girlhood" (see Hogan and Kilroy [1]). But this type of commentary was hardly anything new, and indeed the opening performance elicited only some hissing from its detractors, primarily at the mention of the word "shift," a term for a woman's undergarment.

Subsequent crowds were less restrained, however: on the show's second night, hissing quickly gave way to shouting, booing, and groaning; the police were called in, later to leave at the request of W. B. Yeats and Lady Gregory, who realized their presence was more likely to instigate violence than prevent it. The play received loud applause as well as loud booing at the final curtain. The following night, the pattern continued. This time, Yeats tried to preempt the impending trouble by making a curtain speech, vowing to have a full discussion of the play with anyone interested but that the play should be allowed to stand or fall on its merits in the meantime. The play then began, but early in the first act Yeats was forced to try to quiet the crowd again. His efforts afforded little, however, as stamping, shouting, and tin trumpets soon made it impossible to hear the play. This time, the police did make arrests, and tension within the crowd escalated as the majority of the patrons had come with the express purpose either to disrupt the play or to cheer it. At the final curtain, the boos outnumbered the cheers, and the police were forced to clear the building. The protests continued, at the theater and in print, but had begun to die out by the show's closing performance, which played to a near-capacity house with little incident. It is important to note, as pointed out by Hogan, Burnham, and Poteet that the protests were, in fact, generated by a rather small group of people: indeed, the entire house for the play's second performance numbered only about eighty, many of whom were not involved in the "riots." Yeats, in fact, fulfilled his promise, and an open discussion of the play's merits was held a week to the day after the trouble started on the play's second performance. The evening was lively and spirited, but without incident: the *Daily Express* ("The Abbey Theatre Disturbances") declared it "a night not so much tinged with rowdyism as with boisterous foolery." But Yeats and Lady Gregory made it clear throughout the incident that they, and not the public, would decide the season at the Abbey: "[I]t is," said Lady Gregory, "the fiddler who chooses the tune."

This is not to suggest that the play was without supporters outside the company. For example, Roberts proclaimed *Playboy* "an extraordinarily complex and complete representation of Irish life."

In 1908 the play was produced in London (where, according to Lennox Robinson, "it was immediately recognized as a masterpiece" [see Hogan and Kilroy (1)]), Glasgow, Manchester, Birmingham, Cambridge, and Oxford: probably the first Irish company to visit Oxford in well over two hundred years. An American tour in 1911 was predictably reminiscent of the Dublin premiere: Irish Americans in Boston, Philadelphia, and Chicago were perhaps even less interested in Synge's uncompromising portrayal than were their brethren in the homeland; in Philadelphia, the cast was charged with producing "immoral and indecent plays" and arrested, although charges were later dropped (Fitz-Simon).

***The Tinker's Wedding* and *Deirdre of the Sorrows*.** Both plays were produced posthumously: the former premiered in London in November 1909; the latter, in Dublin in January 1910.

ASSESSMENT OF SYNGE'S CAREER

The facets of Synge's dramaturgy that have attracted the most positive attention from critics are indeed almost exactly those elements that generated most of the controversy surrounding the original productions of many of Synge's plays. Foremost among these is the extent to which the playwright failed, consciously or otherwise, to show the Irish character in terms some nationalists perceived as positive. In retrospect, it seems unlikely that Synge had any intention of alienating the likes of Arthur Griffith or Maud Gonne, yet it is just as certain that he did not shy away from the controversy his works engendered, albeit he allowed Yeats to be rather more vociferous than he was himself in their defense. Certainly, it is undeniable, as many critics have pointed out (see especially Williams), that Synge was Ireland's first representative of dramatic modernism: his characters are not only multifaceted but also alienated from the larger society they inhabit: Synge's central characters are either women (see Templeton), itinerants (tinkers, tramps, the prodigal Christy Mahon), or both. The antagonists, by contrast, are inexorable forces (Conchubor, the sea), the religious elite (the Saint, the Priest), or indeed—as in the case of the two major full-length plays—society itself.

Nationalists also criticized Synge's dialogue, arguing that the dialect of Synge's characters bears little resemblance to that of true Irish men and women. In one sense, this observation has some validity: Synge unquestionably tightened phrasings and enhanced the rhythms of peasant speech. Still, he wrote in his preface to *Playboy* that he used "one or two words only that I have not heard among the country people of Ireland, or spoken in my own nursery before I could read the newspapers" and that when writing *In the Shadow of the Glen*, he "got more aid than any learning could have given me from a chink in the floor of the old Wicklow house where I was staying, that let me hear what was being said by the servant girls in the kitchen." Indeed, as Howe and King, among others, point out, the similarities are manifold between the vocal patterns of Synge's characters and those that Synge transcribed, presumably word for word, in his journals and notebooks of Aran, Kerry, and Wicklow. Yet it is also true that Synge's characters do *not* speak exactly as do Irish peasants, a point noted by King, Skelton [2], and others: Synge's dramatic language, then, is a hybrid of authentic peasant speech, exaggerated vocal patterns, and dramatic license.

Third, Synge creates a physical world that is formidable and inexorable. The power of the sea, the fog rolling up and down the glen, the violent rainstorm are all part of Synge's dramatic vocabulary. The characters mirror this stark, amoral cruelty: Synge's characters inhabit a world in which the blind are objects of ridicule, in which madmen who too much identify themselves with natural forces roam the hillsides, in which hanging a squealing dog to death merits only passing mention and no real concern. Even in those moments in which the natural world is glorified, and they are manifold in Synge's plays, the playwright provides us always with an ironic twist: Nora Burke immediately undercuts the Tramp's idealized vision of his nomadic life; the Douls' lyrical description of the countryside is available to them only through their blindness.

Finally, Synge plays major changes on the structural expectations of, especially, comedy. Classical comedy, and indeed comedy throughout the nineteenth century, culminated in marriage, generally that of the central characters but occasionally (as in *The Misanthrope*) of the more sensible supporting characters. In Synge, however, this convention is thrown on its ear. *In the Shadow of the Glen* concludes not only with the disintegration of the Burke marriage but also in the abandonment of any hope for Nora's remarriage to Micheal Dara. *The Well of the Saints* does indeed conclude with a marriage, but between two pedestrian young people who differ from the central characters not by being more sensible but by their total lack of imagination. *The Playboy* closes with Pegeen Mike's not only having "lost the only Playboy of the Western World" but also quite likely having lost all ability to comfortably return to the insipid and cowardly Shawn Keough. The eponymous event of *The Tinker's Wedding* not only does not occur but is replaced by the calling down of God's holy wrath on the prospective wedding couple. Yet these four plays are undeniably comedies, rich in humor and engendering comic expectations, if only subsequently to invert them.

Dramatic structure plays an important role in the success of the tragedies, as well, although these works are clearly far more traditional in these terms. Both *Riders to the Sea* and *Deirdre of the Sorrows* exhibit all the standard Aristotelian elements of tragedy except, in the case of the former, the idea that tragic characters are, by nature, among the privileged classes, socially and/or economically. Certainly, the family of Mary, Michael, and Bartley does not meet this criterion, but the play, like *Deirdre of the Sorrows*, is dominated by another Aristotelian tenet, inevitability. Indeed, because the ultimate resolution of the plot of both these plays is so transparent so early, Synge's structural precision becomes all the more central, both in creating a dramatically interesting work and in creating that very sense of inevitability.

Finally, while the majority of Synge's plays tend to be lumped together under the general rubric of realism, such categorization is ultimately self-defeating. Like his Russian contemporary Chekhov, Synge succeeded in creating a dramatic universe in which perceptions of reality are as important as reality itself, in which naturalism and symbolism, pragmatism and idealism, coexist. Synge's world, reliant on sensory perceptions of sight and sound, is more impressionistic than realistic while, at the same time, even in the mythological *Deirdre of the Sorrows*, staying closer to a foundation in realism than did Yeats or even Martyn. Indeed, the relationship of Synge to concepts of the modern and the realistic would seem to be a particularly fruitful area for further critical research.

Ultimately, however, Synge's contributions to the development of Irish theater and drama cannot be reduced to specific elements of dramaturgy. His importance is more accurately assessed by noting that he was the first truly great playwright of the Irish Literary Renaissance, that he brought together (literally and figuratively) the theatrical desires of the Fay brothers and the dramatic expectations of Yeats and Lady Gregory, and that *The Playboy of the Western World* and *Riders to the Sea* remain among the most frequently produced Irish plays throughout the English-speaking world. Despite failing health, Synge never seems to have backed down from a controversial and career-threatening belief in the dramatist's obligation to speak his or her own truth, and the encomiums he received after his untimely death, even from those nationalists most critical of his iconoclasm, may serve as a more valuable indication of his significance than could any modern critic's evaluation.

ARCHIVAL SOURCES

Extensive manuscript resources are available at the Library of Trinity College, Dublin (cataloged in *The Synge Manuscripts in the Library of Trinity College, Dublin*, Dublin: Dolmen Press, 1971) and at the National Library of Ireland.

PRIMARY BIBLIOGRAPHY

Plays

Deirdre of the Sorrows. Churchtown: Cuala Press, 1910.
In the Shadow of the Glen. New York: John Quinn, 1904. Also (with *Riders to the Sea*), Vigo Cabinet Series, no. 24. London: Elkin Mathews, 1905.
The Playboy of the Western World. Dublin: Maunsel, 1907. Often reprinted and widely anthologized.
Riders to the Sea (with *In the Shadow of the Glen*). Vigo Cabinet Series, no. 24. London: Elkin Mathews, 1905. Also widely anthologized.
The Tinker's Wedding. Dublin: Maunsel, 1908.
The Well of the Saints. With an introduction by W. B. Yeats. London: A. H. Bullen, 1905. Also ed. with intro. by Nicholas Grene, Washington, D.C.: Catholic University Press of America, 1982.

Anthologies

The Complete Plays of John M. Synge. New York; Modern Library, 1935.
J. M. Synge: Collected Works. 4 vols. New York and London: Oxford University Press, 1962–1968.
Plays by John M. Synge. London: Allen and Unwin, 1932.
The Works of John M. Synge. 4 vols. Dublin: Maunsel, 1910; lib. ed., 5 vols., 1912.

Essays and Articles on Theater

Autobiography of J. M. Synge. New York: Columbia University Press, 1965.
"A Celtic Theatre." *Freeman's Journal* (22 Mar. 1900): 4.

Letters

Collected Letters of J. M. Synge. 2 vols. Ed. Ann Saddlemyer. Oxford: Clarendon Press and New York: Oxford University Press, 1983–1984.

J. M. Synge to Lady Gregory and W. B. Yeats. Ed. Ann Saddlemyer. Dublin: Cuala Press, 1971.

Letters to Molly: John M. Synge to Maire O'Neill. Ed. Ann Saddlemyer. Cambridge: Belknap Press of Harvard University Press, 1971.

Some Unpublished Letters and Documents of J. M. Synge. Ed. Lawrence Wilson. Montreal: Redpath Press, 1959.

"Synge to MacKenna: The Mature Years." Ed. Ann Saddlemyer. In *Irish Renaissance.* Ed. Robin Skelton and David R. Clark. Dublin: Dolmen Press, 1959.

Theatre Business: The Correspondence of the First Abbey Theatre Directors. Ed. Ann Saddlemyer. University Park: Pennsylvania State University Press, ca. 1982.

To the *United Irishman* re *In the Shadow of the Glen* (11 February 1905): 1.

To the *Irish Times* re *The Playboy of the Western World* (31 January 1907).

SECONDARY BIBLIOGRAPHY

"The Abbey Theatre." *Daily Express* (28 Jan. 1907): 6.

"The Abbey Theatre Disturbances." *Daily Express* (5 Feb. 1907): 8.

Benson, Eugene. *J. M. Synge.* London: Macmillan, 1982.

Bickley, Francis Lawrence. *J. M. Synge and the Irish Dramatic Movement.* 1912. Repr., New York: Russell and Russell, 1968.

Bourgeois, Maurice. *John Millington Synge and the Irish Theatre.* London: Constable, 1913.

Bushrui, S. B., ed. *Sunshine and the Moon's Delight: A Centenary Tribute to J. M. Synge.* Gerrards Cross, Buckinghamshire: Colin Smythe, 1979.

Clarke, Brenna Katz. *The Emergence of the Irish Peasant Play at the Abbey Theatre.* Ann Arbor: UMI Research Press, 1982.

Corkery, Daniel. *Synge and Anglo-Irish Literature.* New York: Russell and Russell, 1965.

Coxhead, Elizabeth. *J. M. Synge and Lady Gregory.* London: Longmans, Green, [1962].

"Disturbance at the Abbey Theatre." *Daily Express* (29 Jan. 1907): 5.

Ellis-Fermor, Una. *The Irish Dramatic Movement.* London: Methuen, [1954].

Fay, Frank. Letter to Joseph Holloway, 1 March 1904. Ms. No. 13,267, National Library of Ireland.

Fitz-Simon, Christopher. *The Irish Theatre.* London: Thames and Hudson, 1983.

Frazier, Adrian. *Behind the Scenes: Yeats, Horniman, and the Struggle for the Abbey Theatre.* Berkeley: University of California Press, ca. 1990.

Gerstenberger, Donna. *John Millington Synge.* Boston: Twayne, 1990.

Greene, David Herbert, and Edward M. Stephens. *J. M. Synge, 1871–1909.* New York: Macmillan, 1959.

Gregory, Lady Augusta. *Our Irish Theatre.* New York: Putnam, 1913.

Grene, Nicholas. *Synge: A Critical Study of the Plays.* London: Macmillan, 1975.

Griffith, Arthur. [1]. "All Ireland." *United Irishman* (17 Oct. 1903): 1.

———. [2]. "All Ireland." *United Irishman* (5 Mar. 1904): 1.

———. [3]. "All Ireland." *United Irishman* (11 Feb. 1905): 1.

————. [4]. Untitled note appended to W. B. Yeats, "The Irish National Theatre and Three Sorts of Ignorance." *United Irishman* (24 Oct. 1903): 2.

Gwynn, Stephen. *Irish Literature and Drama in the English Language*. London: T. Nelson and Sons [1936].

Hogan, Robert, and James Kilroy. *The Modern Irish Drama, a Documentary History II: Laying the Foundations, 1902–1904*. Dublin: Dolmen Press; Atlantic Highlands, N.J.: Humanities Press, 1976.

Hogan, Robert, Richard Burnham, and Daniel Poteet. *The Modern Irish Drama, a Documentary History III: The Abbey Theatre: The Years of Synge, 1905–1909*. Dublin: Dolmen Press; Atlantic Highlands, N.J.: Humanities Press, 1978.

Howe, P. P. *J. M. Synge: A Critical Study*. New York: Mitchell Kennerley, 1912.

Hunt, Hugh. *The Abbey: Ireland's National Theatre, 1904–1979*. New York: Columbia University Press, 1979.

"The Irish National Theatre." *Irish Times* (9 Oct. 1903): 8.

"The Irish National Theatre." *Irish Daily Independent and Nation* (26 Feb. 1904): 5.

"Irish National Theatre, Mr. Synge's New Play." *Freeman's Journal* (6 Feb. 1905): 5.

"Irish National Theatre Society." *Daily Express* (9 Oct. 1903): 5.

"Irish National Theatre Society." *Irish Times* (26 Feb. 1904): 5.

Johnson, Toni O'Brien. *Synge: The Medieval and the Grotesque*. Gerrards Cross, Buckinghamshire: Colin Smythe; Totowa, N.J.: Barnes and Noble, 1982.

Johnston, Denis. *John Millington Synge*. New York: Columbia University Press, 1965.

Kavanaugh, Peter. *The Irish Theatre*. Tralee: Kerryman, 1946.

Kiberd, Declan. *Synge and the Irish Language*. Totowa, N.J.: Rowman and Littlefield, 1979.

Kilroy, James. *The "Playboy" Riots*. Dublin: Dolmen Press, [1971].

King, Mary C. *The Drama of J. M. Synge*. Syracuse, N.Y.: Syracuse University Press, 1985.

"L." [Review of *The Well of the Saints*.] *Sunday Sun* [London] (3 Dec. 1905).

Masefield, John. *John M. Synge: A Few Personal Recollections with Biographical Notes*. New York: Macmillan, 1915; Letchworth: Garden City Press, 1916.

Mikhail, E. H., ed. *J. M. Synge: Interviews and Recollections*. New York: Barnes and Noble, 1977.

M'Quilland, L. J. "Mr. Synge's New Play: Pinero by the Liffey." *Belfast Evening Telegraph* (14 Feb. 1905).

O'Connor, Ulick. *Celtic Dawn: A Portrait of the Irish Literary Renaissance*. London H. Hamilton, 1984 (published in America as *All the Olympians: A Biographical Portrait of the Irish Literary Renaissance*. New York: Henry Holt, 1984).

O'Driscoll, Robert, ed. *Theatre and Nationalism in 20th Century Ireland*. London: Oxford University Press, 1971.

Price, Alan. *Synge and Anglo-Irish Drama*. London: Methuen, 1961.

Roberts, George. "A National Dramatist." *Shanchie* (1907): 57–60.

Saddlemyer, Ann. [1]. *J. M. Synge and Modern Comedy*. Dublin: Dolmen Press, [1968].

————. [2]. "A Share in the Dignity of the World: J. M. Synge's Dramatic Theory." In *The World of W. B. Yeats*. Ed. Robin Skelton and Ann Saddlemyer. Dublin: Dolmen Press; Seattle: Washington University Press, 1965.

Sekine, Masaru. *Irish Writers and the Theatre*. Totowa, N.J.: Barnes and Noble, 1986.

Setterquist, Jan. *Ibsen and the Beginnings of Anglo-Irish Drama*. New York: Oriole Editions, 1973.

Skelton, Robin. [1]. *J. M. Synge and His World*. New York: Viking; London: Thames and Hudson, [1971].

———. [2]. *The Writings of J. M. Synge*. Indianapolis, New York: Bobbs-Merrill, 1971.

Skelton, Robin, and David R. Clark, eds. *Irish Renaissance: A Gathering of Essays, Memoirs, and Letters from the Massachusetts Review*. Dublin: Dolmen Press, 1965.

Stephens, Edward. *My Uncle John: Edward Stephens's Life of J. M. Synge*. Ed. Andrew Carpenter. London: Oxford University Press, 1974.

Strong, L.A.G. *John Millington Synge*. New York: Haskell House, 1975.

Templeton, Joan. "The Bed and the Hearth: Synge's Redeemed Ireland." In *Drama, Sex and Politics*. Ed. James Redmond. Cambridge: Cambridge University Press, 1985. 151–57.

Williams, Simon. "John Millington Synge: Transforming the Myths of Ireland." In *Facets of European Modernism: Essays in Honour of James McFarlane Presented to Him on His 65th Birthday, 12 December 1985*. Ed. Janet Garton. Norwich: University of East Anglia, 1985. 79–98.

Worth, Katharine. *The Irish Drama of Europe from Yeats to Beckett*. Atlantic Highlands, N.J.: Humanities Press, ca. 1978.

Yeats, J. B. "The Irish National Theatre Society." *United Irishman* (31 Oct. 1903): 7.

Yeats, W. B. *Dramatic Personae, 1896–1902; Estrangement; The Death of Synge . . .* London: Macmillan, 1936.

———. *Synge and the Ireland of His Time*. Churchman, Dundrum [Ireland]: Cuala Press, 1911. Repr. Shannon: Irish University Press, 1970.

BIBLIOGRAPHIES

Kopper, Edward A., Jr. *Synge: A Review of the Criticism*. Lyndora, Pa.: E. A. Kopper, ca. 1990.

Mikhail, E. H. [1]. *An Annotated Bibliography of Modern Anglo-Irish Drama*. Troy, N.Y.: Whitston, 1981.

———. [2]. *A Research Guide to Modern Irish Dramatists*. Troy, N.Y.: Whitston, 1979.

Sam Thompson

(1916–1965)

JAMES McALEAVEY

Sam Thompson was born in Belfast in 1916. He grew up in the working-class district of Ballymacarret under the shadow of the gantries of the shipyard. A painter by trade, he gained an intimate knowledge of its working environment, which he dramatized in *Over the Bridge,* the play for which he is best known. He came to writing relatively late, through the encouragement of the novelist and radio producer Sam Hanna Bell. Bell became aware of Thompson's potential after hearing him hold forth about the shipyards and Ballymacarret in the Elbow Room, a bar near the BBC's Northern Ireland headquarters and Thompson's home. After listening to Thompson, he is reported to have said, "If you could write that as well as you tell it it would make a fine radio feature" (Mengel [2], 213). Thompson obliged, and his writing career began in 1956 with the broadcast of *Brush in Hand,* a documentary piece about apprenticeship in the shipyards, touching on labor issues on which he elaborated in later works.

Between 1955 and 1957 Thompson was engaged in writing the stage play *Over the Bridge*, which dealt with the lethal effects of sectarianism in the shipyards and, by extension, in Northern Irish society as a whole. Thompson knew that this was a potentially explosive theme, approaching James Ellis, the young and progressive director of the Ulster Group Theatre, with the words, "Hi, you! I got a play you wouldn't touch with a bargepole!" (Devlin [1], 122). Ellis took up his challenge. Although accepted by the Ulster Group Theatre in 1957, it was withdrawn under pressure from the theater's Board of Directors and was not produced until 1960. The play and the controversy surrounding it became a landmark in the cultural history of Northern Ireland and were later seen as prophetic of the Troubles to follow: "The row that started over attempts to stage the play was one of the first shock waves that ultimately heralded the earthquake which subsequently engulfed us" (Devlin [2], 276).

Although Thompson was critical of the BBC, which he saw as part of the Unionist establishment in Northern Ireland, he kept up his association with Sam Hanna Bell. In 1957 *Tommy Baxter, Shopsteward* was broadcast on radio, dealing with management's victimization of a trade union official. In 1958 *The General Foreman* was transmitted, a radio piece that dealt with the difficulties attending the ambivalent position of foreman, representing the interests of management in the workplace. *The Long Back Street*, an autobiographical piece describing his early life in Ballymacarret, its poverty, and occasional sectarian violence, was transmitted the next year. Thompson also wrote a radio serial, *The Fairmans*, subtitled *Life in a Belfast Working Family*, which was produced by Sam Denton and broadcast on BBC Northern Ireland between 1960 and 1961. It was not as successful as its predecessor in that genre, *The McCooey's* by Joseph Tomelty, being perceived as too preoccupied with problematic social issues.

The Evangelist, Thompson's only other stage play to see production, opened at Belfast's Grand Opera House on 3 June 1963. Although this play also had as its theme another contentious issue in the Northern Ireland of its time, the exploitation of evangelical fervor, neither the controversy nor the success of *Over the Bridge* was to repeat itself.

Thompson also became involved in television, writing *The Teabreakers*, for which there is no record of transmission, and the play *Cemented with Love*. This piece dwelt on underhand electoral practices (this was the time of widespread gerrymandering of electoral boundaries), such as personation, and cast Unionist and nationalist parties in a poor light. With shades of the wranglings with the Board of Directors of the Group Theatre, the broadcast of *Cemented with Love* was repeatedly delayed and finally went out on BBC Northern Ireland in April 1965, two months after the death of Thompson from his second heart attack. He left behind him the manuscript of a complete first draft of a play, *The Masquerade*, which indicated new departures in treatment, setting, and theme.

Selected Biographical Sources: Hogan; Mengel [1], [2].

MAJOR PLAYS, PREMIERES, AND SIGNIFICANT REVIVALS: THEATRICAL RECEPTION

Over the Bridge. 1960. Opened at the Empire Theatre, Belfast, 26 January for six weeks; Olympia Theatre, Dublin, 14 March for four weeks; King's Theatre, Glasgow, 11 April for one week; Lyceum, Edinburgh, 18 April for one week; Theatre Royal, Brighton, 25 April for one week; Prince's Theatre, London, 4–7 May, withdrawn. Produced jointly by Ulster Bridge Productions and London Orion Productions. Directed by James Ellis. Revivals: Lyric Players Theatre season of 1969–1970; Arts Theatre (abridged by Paddy Devlin from two and a half hours to 105 mins.) 1985; major revival, Lyric, November/December 1990.

The controversy created by the attempted censorship of *Over the Bridge* (discussed in more detail later) generated huge public interest. Its success with the Belfast public was unprecedented: the play was seen by 42,000 people in its run at the Empire and was received enthusiastically. Carson greeted the play with a mixture of praise for its realism and criticism for its lack of artifice. While coming out on the side of the play, he is kind to its would-be censors, perpetuating their myth of its unsuitability for the Group Theatre. The *Newsletter* ("First Night of *Over the Bridge* at Empire Theatre") emphasized the atmosphere of expectancy surrounding the play and the positive response of the audience to a "forthright" and well-acted play. It was well received in Dublin, the drama critic of the *Irish Times* ("*Over the Bridge* at Olympia") praising its "sincerity and force" and drawing attention to the fact that its engagedness was a refreshing change from "most of the inanities that are offered as 'slices of Irish life.'" The issues that stirred such interest in *Over the Bridge* in Belfast and, to some extent, in Dublin seemed much more remote in London. The critic of the *Times* ("Successful Climax to *Over the Bridge*"), while praising the dramatic climax of the mob scene, was unimpressed by the play's "documentary" qualities and a consequent shallowness of characterization: "[M]ost of the characters are no more than walking principles." Alvarez makes the same criticism in more scathing fashion: "In principle, Sam Thompson's play is impressive. Unfortunately, very little is involved except principles." The play's major revival in November/December 1990 attracted some publicity, but little critical attention. Love described the play as a "minor classic" and pointed out that its relevance has increased through the years, also calling for a production of the "underrated" *The Evangelist*. McFadden felt that the play retained its "shock value" but made the criticism that "Thompson's message was drummed home without much subtlety," a quality that isn't given much premium in Thompson's play and not normally employed when the desire is to shock.

The Evangelist. 1963. Opened 3 June at the Grand Opera House, Belfast, for a fortnight; Gaiety Theatre, Dublin, 19 June for two weeks, directed by Hilton Edwards. Revived briefly in 1978 by the Lyric Theatre.

While the authenticity of the gospel hall scenes were praised, Lowry considered the characterization shallow and the fundamental conflict between Manser Brown and the gospelers "not dramatic enough," the whole play "never reach[ing] the heights—or depths—of tragedy." The reviewer for the Catholic and nationalist paper the *Irish News* ("*The Evangelist* Really Good Entertainment") also praised the gospel scenes, vividly acted by Ray McAnally as Pastor Earls, their immediacy assisted by an extension of the stage into the audience. While accepting its critique of "jackboot religion" (Thompson's phrase), the reviewer finds the play's antireligious tendencies unpalatably bleak. Several reviewers praise the gospel scenes for their authenticity and power, a testament to the research Thompson had carried out in the company of James Ellis, touring such meetings in Belfast.

ASSESSMENT OF THOMPSON'S CAREER

Thompson is remembered in Northern Ireland as being the author of the controversial play *Over the Bridge*. Its setting is the shipyard, at one time the jewel in Belfast's industrial crown, the major source of employment for the men in the surrounding Ballymacarret district and beyond. The shipyard, with its values of craftsmanship, hard work, and loyalty to the Union, is part of the fabric and identity of Protestant Ulster. Jobs at the shipyard were regarded by its overwhelmingly Protestant workforce as theirs by right, and the small percentage of Catholics employed were tolerated rather than welcomed. At times of political tension, such as the riots of 1864 and 1920, this grudging tolerance was replaced by murderous expulsion. Socialists, too, were the objects of mistrust, being expelled along with Catholics in the 1920 riots; loyalist shipwrights also prevented a Labour meeting from taking place in the Ulster Hall during the first Northern Ireland elections in 1921. In the late 1950s, with Unionist power secure under Brookeborough and with the imminent failure of the Irish Republican Army's (IRA) unsuccessful and unpopular border campaign, civil strife was beginning to be thought of as a thing of the past. Of course, with its underlying causes remaining intact, this complacency proved fatally wrong.

Thompson's shipyard is an icon of, and a metonym for, the Northern Ireland of his time. If his play was meant to shine an unforgiving light on the sectarianism prevalent in that society, the controversy surrounding it was to prove revealing of how that sectarianism was policed and encouraged by those in power in Northern Ireland.

Over the Bridge had been accepted by Ellis and scheduled for performance in April 1959 and was announced as part of a program of new plays. Ritchie McKee, chairman of the Board of Directors, requested a copy for his perusal. Ellis, detecting interference with his freedom as director, refused. McKee acquired a script, which was allegedly pilfered from a set prepared for rehearsal. After reading it, McKee had rehearsals stopped and the performance of the play postponed. He insisted on major changes that would have drawn the teeth of Thompson's attack on sectarianism. Thompson refused to make the changes.

Lord Brookeborough, the prime minister of Northern Ireland, presided over a government that ruled Northern Ireland like a one-party state. It maintained Unionist control in all areas of public life through loyal appointees like McKee. J. Ritchie McKee, apart from being the chairman of the Board of Directors of the Ulster Group Theatre, was also joint administrator of the Arts Theatre; he was also on the Board of Directors of BBC Northern Ireland and one of Northern Ireland's largest estate agents and property owners. He was head of the CEMA, the government body responsible for the patronage of the arts. His predecessor in that post, Dame Dehra Parker, was a renowned bigot (she was in the habit of crossing off names from shortlists if they were Catholic-sounding)and reputedly Brookeborough's mistress. She relinquished the post only when she knew McKee would be appointed. His brother was lord mayor of Belfast. When

Thompson made his criticisms of the violent and intolerant aspect of Unionism, the Unionist state replied by trying to silence him, feigning concern that the play itself might excite mob violence.

Thompson, with Ellis and Henry Lynch-Robinson, set up their own company, Ulster Bridge Productions, and the play was accepted for performance by the variety theater, the Empire, "providing that the play itself is as both Mr. Ellis and yourself stated neither a partisan, nor has in it any religious bias" (quoted in Mengel [2], 310).

Significantly, *Over the Bridge* is not a partisan play. Its attack on Unionist rabble-rousing does not constitute a nationalist polemic, and this undoubtedly contributed greatly to its public success. The review that appeared in the *News-letter*, a Protestant and Unionist paper ("First Night of *Over the Bridge* at Empire Theatre"), draws attention to Thompson's careful dramatization of big-otry as "a two-way traffic." Thompson's politics were of a trade union socialist disposition. *Over the Bridge* advocates the brotherhood of workers over the false brotherhoods of Unionism, nationalism, and religious sect. Thompson joined the Northern Ireland Labour Party in the early 1960s within a climate of optimism that cross-sectarian working-class unity could be built around bread-and-butter issues.

Consequent on Thompson's political attitudes, the tragic hero of the play is Davy Mitchell, the veteran union activist, who sacrifices his life in order to uphold this brotherhood by working alongside his Catholic workmate. His work-mate, Peter O'Boyle, has been threatened by a Protestant mob that if he contin-ues to work, he will come to harm. Thompson is careful to diminish any tragic glory that may fall on O'Boyle by portraying his decision to work on as the result of a kind of hysterical obstinacy, rather than principle, a mirror image of the mob's unreason. Significantly, while Mitchell is killed in the subsequent attack, O'Boyle is only injured. Thompson's critique of the false consciousness of nationalism and Unionism and his desire to appear impartial by manipulating the character of O'Boyle put some strain on the play's realism. Its setting, a bastion of Unionist privilege, appears to address the imbalances of power in Northern Ireland, but Thompson eschews a criticism of the fundamental ineq-uities in that society for a nonpartisan plague on all houses.

Despite the popularity of Thompson's play and the palatability of its mes-sage—who could argue against the condemnation of irrational hatred?—the trade union movement in Northern Ireland failed to become the major nonsec-tarian political force it aspired to be. Its acceptance of the constitutional status quo led it to be perceived as Unionist by Catholics, its radicalism was suspect to the conservatism inherent in Unionist ideology, and its socialism was consid-ered irreligious by the churches on both sides.

Thompson's only other stage play to see production, *The Evangelist*, also involves the confrontation between a deluded sectarianism and a skeptical and rational socialism. Pastor Earls, a Billy Graham-style American preacher, whips up a frenzy of evangelical fervor in a working-class Protestant community with his gospel road show. He is allied to Finlay Bradford, a local businessman who owes his success to corrupt practices. They form a partnership of business and religion designed to exploit the local community. This more than hints at the confluence of religion and politics exemplified by the Orange Order and the prominent members of the business community who represented the Unionist parties of the time. Against these conspiring forces stands the agnostic socialist, Manser Brown, Bradford's brother-in-law, who lives in Bradford's house in order to be near Bradford's invalid son, Johnny. Johnny provides the battleground for the opposing forces, Bradford and Earls claiming Johnny's temporary remission as a miracle and using him for publicity for a mass evangelical rally, Manser Brown and the nurse, Norah, attempting to persuade the deluded Johnny to return to hospital. Manser Brown, in a long scene near the end of the play, tells Johnny of his father's attempt to have him adopted to hide the fact that he was conceived outside marriage. This revelation of Finlay Bradford's hypocrisy precipitates a physical collapse in Johnny, and at the end of the play he dies, leaving all his survivors compromised.

The Evangelist was structurally more complex than *Over the Bridge*: it failed to match the climax of the latter's mob scene, being most powerful in its depiction of Pastor Earls' theatrical meetings in the first half. Consequently, it was less enthusiastically received. It is a subtler play, and, to an extent, it can be taken as an allegory for the broader political situation in the North, examining as it does the manipulation by combined forces of church and business of the ignorant. Oblique references to Ian Paisley, who was at the time building his political and ecclesiastical empire, also crop up in the play. It is tempting to think that Thompson's allegorical or parabolic technique was developed as a response to the censorship of the earlier play and that, far from its less immediate impact being a deficiency, its message was designed to be subtler, more insidious, and more resonant than that of *Over the Bridge*. By isolating the action in one small community and by making the proponents of the false brotherhood of sect both a fringe group and, in Earls' case, foreign, Thompson minimized offense to his audience. Nevertheless, Thompson's critique of the exploitation of religious fervor, which had been so expertly practiced by the political figures of the past, such as the Reverend Hugh "Roaring" Hanna and his twentieth-century incarnation, the Reverend Ian Paisley, stood. That or Thompson's *Evangelist* is fatally evasive. As the reviews of the play show, there was no controversy surrounding *The Evangelist*, nor was there the same huge public interest. If Thompson's technique in the play was to write a deceptively uncontroversial parable, a time bomb to the earlier play's incendiary, the play may have been a victim of its own success.

Thompson's achievement would have been remarkable for any Irish playwright of the time, the more so because of his lack of formal education and his class background. Driven by a profoundly moral vision and a work ethic that the shipyard undoubtedly helped nurture, Thompson took risks with both the Unionist establishment and his own community. In Thompson's own streets, people have been murdered for much less. He has been seen by some as the inheritor of the Dissenter tradition in Irish history that produced the secularist United Irishmen. Thompson's priority was to provide engaged theater, diagnostic of the ills of his society. There is evidence in the draft of his last play, *The Masquerade*, that he wished to extend his range, with its pathology of fascism set in London. His objective was not to produce the liberal humanist *transcendent* art, which Alvarez might have preferred to see on the London stage, and, in his haste, to sketch the dynamics of his milieu his characterization may have suffered, but Thompson will be remembered for laying bare the atavisms in the Northern Irish state in a quiet time in its history and being a prophet of the Troubles, which were their consequence. His contribution to Northern Irish drama was recognized by Thompson's friend, the broadcaster Martin McBirney:

George Shiels, St. John Ervine and many lesser lights had dominated the Ulster theatre for over thirty years. They were skilful technicians whose dramas were enacted in the kitchen and the drawing-room by people whose ideas were oldfashioned and a little remote from reality by today's standards. *Over the Bridge* knocked down the kitchen wall and brought the streets and the shipyard onto the stage.... All the uglier aspects of our communal life were brought to the surface and the Ulster theatre could never be quite the same again (quoted in Mengel [2], 249).

Whatever the harshness of McBirney's characterization of theater before Thompson, it is difficult to imagine some of the politically engaged community theater of later years, such as the plays of Martin Lynch, without him.

ARCHIVAL SOURCES

The Sam Thompson Collection, including manuscripts, letters, journalism, and so on, organized by Stewart Parker, can be consulted in Belfast's Central Library, with the permission of its guardians, Thompson's widow, May, and son, Warren. It is an invaluable resource, as only *Over the Bridge* has been published. Mengel has a description of its contents, box by box, in his book on Thompson.

PRIMARY BIBLIOGRAPHY

Over the Bridge. Ed. and introduced by Stewart Parker. Dublin: Gill and Macmillan, 1970.

SECONDARY BIBLIOGRAPHY

Alvarez, A. "Negative Feedback." *New Statesman* (14 May 1960).
Bell, Sam Hanna. *The Theatre in Ulster: A Survey of the Dramatic Movement in Ulster from 1902 until the Present Day.* Dublin: Gill and Macmillan, 1972.

Burnside, Sam. "Not Water under the Bridge." *Fortnight* 292 (July/Aug. 1991): 16–17.

Carson, Tom. "Sincere, but Wordy, Play Brings Strife to Stage." *Belfast Telegraph* (27 Jan. 1960).

Devlin, Paddy. [1]. "First Bridge Too Far." *Theatre Ireland* 3 (June/Sept. 1983): 122–24.

———. [2]. *Straight Left: An Autobiography*. Belfast: Blackstaff Press, 1993.

"*The Evangelist* Really Good Entertainment." *Irish News* (4 June 1963).

"First Night of *Over the Bridge* at Empire Theatre." *Newsletter* (27 Jan. 1960).

Hogan, Robert. *After the Irish Renaissance*. Minneapolis: University of Minnesota Press, 1967.

Love, Hugh. "Over the Bridge." *Fortnight* (Dec. 1990).

Lowry, Betty. "Evangelical Fervour Leaves Questions Unanswered." *Belfast Telegraph* (4 June 1963).

McFadden, Grania. "Drumming Home a Message." *Belfast Telegraph* (16 Nov. 1990).

Mengel, Hagal. [1]. "A Lost Heritage: Ulster Drama and the Work of Sam Thompson." *Theatre Ireland* 1 (Sept./Dec. 1982): 18–19 and 2 (Jan./May 1982): 80–82.

———. [2]. *Sam Thompson and Modern Drama in Ulster*. Frankfurt am Main, Bern, New York: Verlag Peter Lang, 1986.

"*Over the Bridge* at the Olympia." *Irish Times* (15 Mar. 1960).

"Successful Climax to *Over the Bridge*." *Times* (5 May 1960).

Oscar Wilde
(1854–1900)

AVERIL GARDNER

Oscar Wilde once said that he had put his genius into his life but only his talent into his work. This statement, like many of Wilde's, is less true than it is witty. Some might agree with the second half without therefore agreeing with the first. Others, whatever their feelings about Wilde's life, might well think that at least some of his work revealed genius; of these, most would probably agree that Wilde's last play, *The Importance of Being Earnest*, was the outstanding exception to his dictum. Whatever may be said by scholars in favor of *Salomé, The Picture of Dorian Grey*, and *The Soul of Man under Socialism*, it is certainly true that *The Importance of Being Earnest* is Wilde's most famous work, as well as his most frequently revived play.

Oscar Wilde was born on 16 October 1854, in Dublin, the son of William Wilde, a celebrated eye surgeon who was knighted in 1864, and Jane Francesca Elgee, niece of the novelist Charles Maturin and herself a well-known poet of Irish nationalist sentiments who published under the pen name ''Speranza.'' Wilde was brought up amid the elegance of Georgian Dublin and given his first education at Portora Royal School, Enniskillen, where he won a scholarship to study classics at Trinity College, Dublin, from 1871 to 1874. The next few years Wilde spent as a scholar at Magdalen College, Oxford. There he gained a first-class degree in classics and, in 1878, won the prestigious Newdigate Prize for poetry with a poem entitled ''Ravenna,'' the firsthand knowledge for which had been obtained during a visit to Greece and Italy.

Moving to London in 1878, Wilde set himself to win both fame and well-placed friends, carrying with him the air of celebrity he had gained as an undergraduate at Oxford, where he had come under the potent aesthetic influence of Ruskin and Walter Pater. Asked in later life what he most enjoyed about being a playwright, Wilde replied: ''the immediate applause''; but it took him well over a decade to receive as much of it as he wanted, though a visit on 28 November 1879 to Henry Irving's production of *The Merchant of Venice* brought him the acquaintance of Irving and of Ellen Terry, who played Portia. Possibly, Wilde's ambitions to succeed as a dramatist sprang from his young man's passion for the fashionable actresses of the day: certainly he paraded, in sequence, his admiration for Ellen Terry, Lily Langtry, Helena Modjeska, and Sarah Bernhardt.

To some of these actresses, in 1880, Wilde showed his first completed play, *Vera: or, The Nihilists*, set in a contemporary Russia, which soon proved dangerously to resemble the world conjured up by Wilde's drama. The play attracted the interest of another actress, Mrs. Bernard Beere, who intended to present it in London on 17 December 1881; but the assassination that year of Tsar Alexander II and the political feeling this produced in England obliged Wilde to cancel the production. Wilde spent most of 1882 lecturing in North America, where his play was finally put on, with the American actress Marie Prescott in the role of Vera, for one week in August 1883. While in North America, Wilde conceived the notion of writing a play for another American actress, Mary Anderson: this was the pastiche-Jacobean costume drama in verse, *The Duchess of Padua*, which was finally produced in New York in 1891, Mary Anderson having presciently declined it because of its lack of appeal for contemporary audiences.

After finishing *The Duchess of Padua* in March 1883, Wilde attempted no more plays for the rest of the decade. The 1890s saw his emergence as a famous dramatist, this time of contemporary English life and manners—with the notable exception of his one-act biblical tragedy, *Salomé*, written mostly in Paris and in French, in 1891. This was refused a performing license in June 1892 by the lord chamberlain and was first produced in Paris on 11 February 1896. By this time, Wilde was in prison, and his plays were no longer running on the English stage, but between 1892 and 1895 he had achieved enormous success with three seriocomedies and one final comic masterpiece. In order of composition and of performance, they were *Lady Windermere's Fan, A Woman of No Importance, An Ideal Husband*, and *The Importance of Being Earnest*. The last two, in production in London in 1895, were taken off when Wilde was tried, then convicted, for homosexual practices and sentenced to two years' imprisonment.

Released from prison in May 1897, Wilde sailed for France, spending the rest of his life there and in Italy. In his last years his major work, prompted by his prison experiences, was the poem, *The Ballad of Reading Gaol* (1898); but he also hoped to write two plays, *Pharaoh* and *Ahab and Isabel*, of which only the titles remain, and he may have done further work on *A Florentine Tragedy*, a blank-verse play in one act begun in 1894/1895. Only twelve pages of this survive. Oscar Wilde died in Paris on 30 November 1900. *A Woman of No Importance* had been given, by Mr. and Mrs. Lewis Waller, a matinee performance in London exactly a year earlier; a month before Wilde's death, *Lady Windermere's Fan* was revived there; and within five years of his death not only had his two other social comedies reappeared on the London stage, but *Salomé* had received its first English performance.

Selected Biographical Sources: Ellmann [1]; Fido; Morley; Pearson.

MAJOR PLAYS, PREMIERES, AND SIGNIFICANT REVIVALS: THEATRICAL RECEPTION

Vera: or, The Nihilists. 1883. Opened 20 August at the Union Square Theatre, New York, with Marie Prescott as Vera and Lewis Morrison as Alexis; produced by Marie Prescott. The play ran for only one week, despite its advertisement that "the interior of the Tsar's palace represented in this play will be the most gorgeous piece of stage setting ever seen in this country." Subsequently, Marie Prescott went on an American tour with it (Detroit Opera House, 28 December 1888, and elsewhere).

Reviews of *Vera*, boosted in newspapers as "the greatest play of the day," were mixed. The *New York Mirror* called it a "triumph" and "the noblest contribution to its literature the stage has received in many years," but other reviews were hostile: "unreal, long-winded and wearisome" (*New York Times*); "little better than a fizzle" (*New York Tribune*); "long-drawn dramatic rot" (*New York Herald*). The *Pilot* blamed the actress, not the author: "We have read *Vera*, and we believe that if well acted, it would be a great success. Mr. Wilde has entrusted his play to an inferior actress, who can only scold on the stage and off it" (See Stuart Mason).

The Duchess of Padua: A Tragedy of the XVI Century. 1891. Under the title *Guido Ferranti*, opened 26 January 1891 at the Broadway Theatre, New York, with Lawrence Barrett as Guido Ferranti and Minna K. Gale as the Duchess; produced by Lawrence Barrett. Ran for 21 performances; was withdrawn 14 February. The play was first announced without Wilde's name, but reviewers the following day recognized the play as *The Duchess of Padua* and the author as Oscar Wilde. Thereafter, Wilde's name was attached to the advertisements.

The play (with others) was taken on tour by Minna K. Gale (Lawrence Barrett having died 20 March 1891). She opened her tour with it (now billed as *The Duchess of Padua*) on 31 August 1891 at the Chestnut Street Theatre, Philadelphia. Other performances were given, including one on 14 November at the Harlem Opera House, New York.

The play was revived as *The Duchess of Padua*, in translation, in Germany in 1904 (Hamburg) and 1906. A copyright performance was given on 18 March 1907 at the St. James's Theatre, London.

The *New York Tribune* stated that the play "had a success of esteem, and perhaps a little more. Mr. Barrett has certainly been justified in bringing it forward" (quoted in Stuart Mason).

Lady Windermere's Fan. 1892. Announced as *A Good Woman*, the play opened 20 February 1892 as *Lady Windermere's Fan* at St. James's Theatre, London,

with George Alexander as Lord Windermere, Lily Hanbury as Lady Windermere, and Marion Terry as Mrs. Erlynne; produced by George Alexander. The
play ran until 29 July, then toured the provinces, returning to the St. James's
Theatre on 31 October. It was also performed at Palmer's Theatre, New York,
in February 1893. It was revived, after Wilde's death, at three London theaters
all under the management of Robert Arthur, without Wilde's name being used:
Prince of Wales's Theatre, Kennington, 1 October 1900 (5 performances); Camden Theatre, Camden Town, 18 February 1901 (7 performances); Coronet
Theatre, 4 March 1901 (7 performances). For these three runs, Marion Terry
was the star and "draw," playing her original part of Mrs. Erlynne. The play
had three further revivals at St. James's Theatre: 7 January 1902; 19 November
1904; 14 October 1911. Since 1930 and especially after World War II, the play
has enjoyed a degree of popularity, the most notable postwar revival being at
the Royal Court Theatre, London, from 21 August 1945: the play was produced
and directed by John Gielgud, with decor by Cecil Beaton.

Wilde's first social play was extremely popular—"the hit of the season," as
Sheridan Morley has termed it—though the many reviews devoted to its first
performance were mixed. A number of critics, including Thomas, objected to
the concealment, until the end, of Mrs. Erlynne's precise relationship to Lord
Windermere; from the second night onward the fact that Mrs. Erlynne was Lady
Windermere's mother was made clear in act 2. Scott [1] was shocked that Lady
Windermere was prepared to abandon her child; *Black and White* found the play
"a pepper-box of paradoxes . . . improbable without being interesting" but conceded that it was "very amusing" and "exceedingly diverting." In a long review in the *Speaker*, Walkley [2] combined an intelligent but unmalicious
awareness of the play's faults ("glaring" ones, in his view, involving contri-
vance and implausibility) with strong appreciation of its main virtues—a witty,
sparkling, and paradoxical style and an ability to keep the audience interested:
"[I]t carries you along from start to finish without boring you for a single
moment."

A Woman of No Importance. 1893. Opened 19 April at the Haymarket Theatre,
London, with Mrs. Bernard Beere as Mrs. Arbuthnot and Herbert Beerbohm
Tree as Lord Illingworth; produced by Herbert Beerbohm Tree. Ran until 16
August, with a break of three nights (20–22 July), when the theater offered
Ibsen's *An Enemy of the People*. A touring company organized by Beerbohm
Tree, which included Mr. and Mrs. Lewis Waller, took the play to the North of
England, opening in Birmingham on 14 August 1893. The Wallers gave a single
matinee performance, in a theater unknown, on 30 November 1899; a cutting
with this information (at the Theatre Museum, Covent Garden, London) referred
to the play as being "by a certain author whom no play-bill now mentions."
The play, again presented without Wilde's name, had 2 performances (23 and
25 September 1903) at the Balham Empire; it was revived on 22 May 1907 at
His Majesty's Theatre, London. Significant revivals since World War II took

place at the Royal Court Theatre, Liverpool, one week, from 30 October 1967, with a cast that included Phyllis Calvert as Mrs. Arbuthnot, Tony Britton as Lord Illingworth, and Marie Lohr (whose first London appearance was 1901) as Lady Hunstanton; and at the Barbican Theatre, London, from 26 September 1991, directed by Philip Prowse, with Barbara Leigh-Hunt as Lady Hunstanton and a black actress, Julia Saunders, as Hester Worsley.

Reviews of the play were mainly favorable, though the *Illustrated Sporting and Dramatic* (Review of *A Woman of No Importance*) dismissed it in a headline as "a play of no importance." The *Sketch* (Review of *A Woman of No Importance*) found it "nought" as a play ("it merely consists of a few scenes borrowed from French drama, dropped into an impossible social milieu"), but judged it "a success" as an entertainment. The *Illustrated London News* (Review of *A Woman of No Importance*) had a similarly mixed view but praised the "central conception" as "worthy of intelligent discussion," greatly admired the character of Lady Hunstanton, and found Mrs. Allonby's description of the ideal husband so good that "it alone would make the reputation of a writer of dialogue." Archer [4] reviewed the play in the most glowing terms, praising its "intellectual calibre, artistic competence and dramatic instinct" alike and placing it alone "on the very highest plane of modern English drama." The 1991 revival at the Barbican, by the Royal Shakespeare Company, directed by Philip Prowse (a Wilde enthusiast), was considered a "very impressive" performance by Rutherford. Nightingale called the play's aphorisms "a load of rhinestones hanging off old rope"; Gross thought the play "oddly moving while it lasts, but, the performance over, you realise that it is the stilted period piece that you always thought it was."

A Florentine Tragedy. 1894. Possibly resumed in 1897. Incomplete one-act verse play. First performed in England 10 June 1906, King's Hall, London, with an opening scene written by T. Sturge Moore; a curtain-raiser for a production of *Salomé* directed and designed by Charles Ricketts. Further performances: Edinburgh, 19 September 1908 with Mrs. Patrick Campbell as Bianca; Birmingham Repertory Theatre, 1914–1915; Kingsway Theatre, London, 22 February 1922; Arts Theatre, Great Newport Street, London, 26 June 1927. First performed in the United States on 1 February 1927 by the Grand Guignol Players, at Grove St. Theatre, New York.

An Ideal Husband. 1895. Opened 3 January at the Theatre Royal, Haymarket, London, with Lewis Waller as Sir Robert Chiltern, Julia Nielson as Lady Chiltern, Florence West as Mrs. Cheveley, and Charles Hawtrey as Lord Goring; produced by Lewis Waller and H. H. Morell. Ran until 6 April; transferred to the Criterion Theatre on 13 April, and withdrawn on 27 April. The play opened in the United States on 12 March 1895 at the Lyceum Theatre, New York; after Wilde's arrest on 5 April, the management removed Wilde's name from the playbills and programs. The play was revived at the Coronet Theatre, Notting Hill Gate, London, on 25 September 1905, but without Wilde's name; then at the St. James's Theatre, London on 14 May 1914 (with George Alexander as Lord Goring). Further revivals in London and the provinces have been mounted since World War II: the first, from 16 November 1943 at the Westminster Theatre, London, presented by Robert Donat and with scenery and costumes by Rex Whistler; the most recent, from 4 November 1992, at the Globe Theatre, London, under the direction of Peter Hall and with a notable cast, including Michael Denison and Dulcie Grey as Lord Caversham and Lady Markby, Hannah Gordon as Lady Chiltern, Anna Carteret as Mrs. Cheveley, and Martin Shaw as an excellent Lord Goring.

The first performance of the play in 1895 appears to have been very favorably received, the Prince of Wales (the future Edward VII) being present and declaring himself well satisfied. Reviews, however, were mixed. George Bernard Shaw [1] called Wilde "our only thorough playwright" but meant by his remark that Wilde played with every aspect of the drama and had to work hard to make his wit "pleasant to this comparatively stupid audience." Of the play itself, Shaw felt it was "useless to describe a play which has no thesis," though he added one illuminating, if idiosyncratic, comment: "The modern note is struck in Sir Robert Chiltern's assertion of the individuality and courage of his wrong-doing as against the mechanical idealism of his stupidly good wife, and in his bitter criticism of a love that is only the reward of merit." H. G. Wells [1] felt that, in *An Ideal Husband*, Wilde was beginning to reveal a new seriousness, was "working his way to innocence, as others work towards experience"; nevertheless, the play was "decidedly disappointing" after its predecessors, a view shared by the *Sketch* (Review of *An Ideal Husband*), which found it "a mere play of intrigue," with "hardly a character . . . in whom one detects any signs of life." The *Black and White* (Review of *An Ideal Husband*) felt that Wilde had a serious purpose but quickly abandoned it, by using a trick of plot (Lord Goring's discovery of Mrs. Cheveley's theft of the diamond brooch) to avoid confronting the problems raised by Sir Robert Chiltern's less than ideal past. The *Daily Telegraph* (Review of *An Ideal Husband*), while sarcastically prophesying success for a play "so smart and so characteristic of the author," had nothing good to say about it, finding its subject rather "commonplace where it is not artificial" and Lady Chiltern entirely untrue to nature in her hostility to her husband's youthful insider speculation. If Sir Robert was not an ideal husband, no more was Lady Chiltern an ideal wife; instead she was "a veritable dragon of virtue," a "female puritan" being, in the reviewer's opinion, worse than a "male prig." Critical comment on the 1943 revival was less searching. The *Times* (Review of *An Ideal Husband*) indicated that the play raised moral problems, but "the acting makes laughter easy"; the *Observer* (Review of *An Ideal Husband*) was content to note that the play had been "sumptuously (by wartime standards) revived at the Westminster."

The Importance of Being Earnest. 1895. Opened 14 February during a raging snowstorm, at the St. James's Theatre, London, with George Alexander as John

Worthing, Rose Leclerq as Lady Bracknell, and Irene Vanbrugh as Gwendolen; produced by George Alexander, who had requested that the play be reduced from four acts to three, in which version it has most frequently been performed. Ran for 86 performances: Wilde's name was removed from the playbills and programs on 6 April, and the play was withdrawn, on Wilde's conviction, on 8 May. After Wilde's death the play was revived at the Coronet Theatre, Notting Hill Gate, London, on 2 December 1901; then at the St. James's Theatre in 1902, 1909, 1911, and 1913 (the second of these productions ran from 30 December 1909 to 23 September 1910). Since then the play has been performed in London, the English provinces, and elsewhere so many times that the word "revival" seems absurd. Particularly noteworthy productions have been Tyrone Guthrie's at the Old Vic (5 February–3 March 1934), with Roger Livesey as John Worthing, Athene Seyler as Lady Bracknell, Flora Robson as Gwendolen, Ursula Jeans as Cecily, Charles Laughton as Canon Chasuble, and Elsa Lanchester as Miss Prism; John Gielgud's at the Globe Theatre in 1939 and at the Phoenix Theatre from 14 October 1942, with Gielgud as John Worthing, Edith Evans as Lady Bracknell, and Peggy Ashcroft as Gwendolen; Michael Benthall's at the Old Vic (from 13 October 1959), with John Justin as John Worthing, Alec McCowen as Algernon, Fay Compton as Lady Bracknell, Barbara Jefford as Gwendolen, Judi Dench as Cecily, and Miles Malleson as Canon Chasuble. The play was also given a single matinée performance, produced by John Gielgud, at the Haymarket Theatre, London, 11 April 1946 as part of Theatre Festival week in aid of King George's Pension Fund for actors and actresses; it was attended by King George VI and Queen Elizabeth, and the cast included John Gielgud as John Worthing, Edith Evans as Lady Bracknell, Margaret Rawlings as Gwendolen, and Margaret Rutherford as Miss Prism.

"The author was called and applauded," said Nisbet. Not all reviews, however, were ungrudging in their praise. Whereas H. G. Wells [2] greatly enjoyed—after *An Ideal Husband*—Wilde's "delightful renewal of theatrical satire" mixed with "very good nonsense, excellent fooling," George Bernard Shaw [2] found the play amusing, but not touching, and therefore "heartless." Wilde's shift from social seriocomedy into a new register was implicitly grasped by William Archer [3], who found, though with great pleasure, that the play vanished like a mirage when closely approached; *Black and White* (Review of *The Importance of Being Earnest*) was similarly delighted, rather than chilled or irritated, by a play in which "all that happens is extravagant, ridiculous, futile and inconceivably amusing." Walkley [1] put his finger most accurately on the pulse of the play: "Better nonsense," he said, "our stage has not seen"; that nonsense resulted, in the best farce, from "the abandonment of realism for fantasy," but Wilde's play involved a further element—action that excited "the simultaneous recognition of the absurd and the natural in the thing laughed at," so that the playgoer remembered the endlessly teasing mixture of "something like real life in detail, yet, in sum, absolutely unlike it." This quality of inspired absurdity has continued to be commented on and perhaps accounts, more than anything else, for the continued special popularity of *The Importance of Being Earnest*. Its 1959 revival at the Old Vic produced in the *Times* (Review of *The Importance of Being Earnest*) these comments, which incidentally differentiate the play from others by Wilde: "*The Importance of Being Earnest* is one of the few plays of its period that it is possible to revive without the faintest hint of condescension. . . . Wilde's triviality, which is completely consistent with itself, is impervious to progress of any sort. . . . [The play excites] no outmoded sentiment or sympathy."

Salomé. 1896. First performed (in Wilde's original French) 11 February 1896 at the Théâtre de l'Oeuvre, Paris, with Aurelien-Marie Lugné-Poe as Herod and Lina Munte as Salomé; produced by Lugné-Poe. The production was favorably reviewed by Henri Bauer in *Echo de Paris* (Hart-Davis [1]). Also performed 15 November 1902 at the Kleines Theater, Berlin, directed by Max Reinhardt. The play was first performed in England on 10 and 13 May 1905 by the New Stage Club at the Bijou Theatre, Westbourne Grove, London, with Millicent Murby as Salomé and Robert Farquharson as Herod; directed by Florence Farr. As the play was still banned by the censor, the performances were private, with none but subscribers admitted, though "subscriptions" conveniently equated to the price of a single seat sold in advance. The play was also performed from 13–16 November 1905 at the Berkeley Lyceum in New York, by the Progressive Stage Society. A performance with design by Charles Ricketts was given on 10 June 1906 at King's Hall, Covent Garden, London; more performances of the play were given in New York in 1906 at the Astor Theatre, 15 November and London in 1911 and 1918, both at the Court Theatre. A real breakthrough was made when the play was performed as part of a triple bill at the Duke of York's Theatre, London, on 21 October 1931: the performance, directed by Nancy Price, was public, since Esmé Percy, Lady Asquith, George Bernard Shaw, and the play's translator, Lord Alfred Douglas, had combined to persuade the lord chamberlain to lift his ban. In this performance Nancy Price, who was honorary director of the People's National Theatre, played Herodias, Robert Farquharson again (as in 1905) played Herod, and Salomé was acted by Joan Maude, splendidly pictured on the program with upstanding "electric" hair and wide eyes, holding the head of Jokanaan. Earlier the same year (27 May 1931), the play had been presented at the Gate Theatre studio, London, with a very impressive cast: Robert Speaight as Herod, Flora Robson as Herodias, John Clements as Jokanaan, and Margaret Rawlings as Salomé (pictured in the *Sketch* of 3 June 1931 stripped down to a sort of decorated bikini); the music for the performance was by Constant Lambert, and the choreography was by Ninette de Valois. The most responded-to revival of *Salomé*, with little doubt, was its production, from 20 July 1954, at the St. Martin's Theatre, London (on a double bill with Jean-Paul Sartre's *La Putain Respectueuse*, mistranslated as *The Respectable Prostitute*); Salomé was played by Agnes Bernelle, Herod by the 6' 5" Australian actor, Frank Thring.

The *Daily Telegraph* (Review of *Salomé*) was carried away alike by the "fine drama, brilliant settings and sensitive imaginative production" of the 1931 revival. In the 1954 revival Frank Thring clearly stole the show with "a splendidly full-blooded, full-throated, full-hearted and full-bodied performance" (Review of *Salomé, Sunday Times*). Reviewers were less uniformly impressed by the play itself. Darlington found its language became "first cloying and then soporific" but conceded that "its exaggerated manner aside," *Salomé* was "far from being a negligible play," though likely to benefit from cutting; for the *Times* (Review of *Salomé*), "a thin line separates Wilde's notorious study in decadence from the ludicrous," and this production just managed to stay on the right side of it: Shulman [2], however, thought that *Salomé* managed "the not inconsiderable feat of being both repulsive and boring in about equal measure."

ASSESSMENT OF WILDE'S CAREER

It would be interesting, though profitless, to speculate on the kind of dramatist Wilde might have turned into had *Vera: or, The Nihilists* not been deprived, perhaps by political pressure, of its intended London production in 1881. Could it have achieved a longer run there than its mere week in New York in 1883 and established Wilde as an artist of high seriousness, passionately romantic yet socially "committed"? A sympathetic recent critic of Wilde's plays, Katharine Worth, has suggested that though *Vera*'s "melodrama might well defeat modern actors, . . . if performers with the right skills could be found, the play might well emerge as an interesting stage piece." But, in effect, Wilde's first play, set not in contemporary England but contemporary Russia, was stillborn, and Worth was unable to extend a would-be resurrecting hand to its successor, the quasi-Jacobean *Duchess of Padua*, whose only performance in England seems to have been its single one in 1907, put on to establish copyright. Either of these plays and *Salomé*, too, if performed in England during Wilde's lifetime and if successful, might have encouraged him to pursue a very different type of drama from that by which he became known in the 1890s. The enormous success of *Salomé* as turned into an opera by Richard Strauss in 1905 and its refusal to die as a stage play (the London Theatre Museum records list three performances in the 1950s and three more in the 1970s; in the 1980s it was performed professionally in St. John's, Newfoundland) suggest that Wilde's return, after release from prison in 1897, to possible biblical subjects for his plays was rather more than the counsel of despair of a writer who had lost his audience and no doubt felt some revulsion from the English high society he had used and amused.

Nevertheless, while it is worth remembering that Wilde tried to begin, and might have finished, his dramatic career with exotic settings, high-flown sentiments, poetry, and passion, it was as a commentator, cool and concerned by turns, on the morals and manners of his English contemporaries that Wilde found public success, the attainment of which was his strongest motive for writing plays. Americans might see, and some admire, Wilde the social libertarian,

Wilde the would-be Shakespeare; members of the French artistic community could in 1896 express their solidarity with an Irish tragedian who wrote in French and had been imprisoned by English philistines. But what English play-goers saw in Wilde's lifetime was Wilde the provider of social comedy, and him alone, though "social comedy" is a rough-and-ready term for plays that, between 1892 and 1895, ranged from melodrama, through problem play, to protoabsurdist farce. Wilde's career as a successful playwright was a very short one, as things turned out, but it seems the more brilliant for that brevity, each of the first three plays being sufficiently well constructed, of sufficient human interest, and amusing enough to overcome by a handsome margin its occasional clichés of plot and sentiment, and the last one, *The Importance of Being Earnest*, rising quite beyond earnestness and social observation into a self-sufficient realm of existential wit that A. B. Walkley was perhaps the only critic in 1895 to categorize but that has continued to give delight ever since the play was first performed.

If, since then, *The Importance of Being Earnest* has been the most often performed of Wilde's four social comedies, the phenomenon is easy to under-stand; but there have also been, most recently in the early 1990s, London pro-ductions of the other three, which have suggested that not only Wilde's paradoxical wit but his concern for tolerance and fair treatment strike a sym-pathetic chord with modern audiences. While continuing to value highly Wilde's verbal wit and sense of the absurd, that critical study of him that has been revived over the past twenty-five years could fruitfully expand, now, to consider the qualities of those plays scanted in his lifetime and virtually extinct since. Wilde wrote none of his plays as closet dramas; all of them were for the stage. A critical atmosphere needs to be created in which, while the social comedies continue to flourish, more theaters will risk putting on *Salomé* and even, with perhaps descending likelihood of luck, *Vera* and *The Duchess of Padua*. Only then will Wilde's drama be seen, if not admired, whole.

ARCHIVAL SOURCES

The significant holdings of Wilde's play manuscripts are in the British Li-brary, The Clark Library, the Pierpont Morgan Library, the New York Public Library, and the Harry Ransom Humanities Research Center at the University of Texas, Austin. The Bodmer Library in Geneva holds the earliest text of *Salomé*.

PRIMARY BIBLIOGRAPHY

Plays

An Ideal Husband. London: Leonard Smithers, 1899.
The Importance of Being Earnest. London: Leonard Smithers, 1899. Original four-act
    version (ed. Vyvyan Holland), London: Methuen, 1957.

Lady Windermere's Fan. London: Elkin Mathews and John Lane, 1893.

Salomé. Paris: Librairie de l'Art Independante; London: Elkin Mathews and John Lane, 1893 (in French). Translation published, London: Elkin Mathews and John Lane; Boston: Copeland and Day, 1894.

Vera: or, The Nihilists. London: Rankin, 1880; New York: privately printed, 1882 (see Stuart Mason, *Bibliography*, p. 253).

A Woman of No Importance. London: John Lane, 1894.

Anthologies

The First Collected Edition of Wilde's works (London: Methuen, 1908, thirteen volumes) prints Wilde's plays as follows:

Vol. I: *The Duchess of Padua*
Vol. II: *Salomé; A Florentine Tragedy; Vera*
Vol. III: *Lady Windermere's Fan*
Vol. IV: *A Woman of No Importance*
Vol. V: *An Ideal Husband*
Vol. VI: *The Importance of Being Earnest*

The Complete Works of Oscar Wilde. London: Collins, 1948, one volume.

SECONDARY BIBLIOGRAPHY

Agate, James. "Wilde and the Theatre." *Masque*. London: Curtain Press, 1947, 5–23.

Archer, William. [1]. [Review of *The Duchess of Padua*.] *Daily Chronicle* (21 Nov. 1904).

———. [2]. [Review of *An Ideal Husband*.] *World* (9 Jan. 1895).

———. [3]. [Review of *The Importance of Being Earnest*.] *World* (20 Feb. 1895).

———. [4]. [Review of *A Woman of No Importance*.] *World* (26 Apr. 1892).

———. [5]. *The Theatrical "World" for 1893–97*. London: Walter Scott, 1894–1898.

Beckson, Karl, ed. *Oscar Wilde: The Critical Heritage*. London: Routledge and Kegan Paul, 1970.

Bentley, Eric. *The Playwright as Thinker*. New York: Reynal and Hitchcock, 1946.

Bird, Alan. *The Plays of Oscar Wilde*. London: Vision Press, 1977.

Burgess, Gilbert. [Interview with Wilde.] *Sketch* (9 Jan. 1895).

Cookman, Anthony. [Review of *Lady Windermere's Fan*.] *Tatler and Bystander* (29 Aug. 1945).

Darlington, W. A. [Review of *Salomé*.] *Daily Telegraph* (21 July 1954).

Donohue, Joseph W., Jr. "The First Production of *The Importance of Being Earnest*." In *Essays in Nineteenth-Century British Theatre*. Ed. Kenneth Richards and Peter Thomson. London: Methuen, 1971, 125–43.

Duguid, Lindsay. [Review of *A Woman of No Importance*.] *Times Literary Supplement* (11 Oct. 1991).

Duncan, B. *The St. James's Theatre*. London: Barrie and Rockliff, 1964.

Ellmann, Richard. [1]. *Oscar Wilde*. London: Hamish Hamilton, 1987.

———, ed. [2]. *Oscar Wilde, A Collection of Critical Essays*. Englewood Cliffs, N.J.: Prentice-Hall, 1969.

Erikson, Donald. *Oscar Wilde*. Boston: Twayne, 1977.

Fido, Martin. *Oscar Wilde*. London: Hamlyn, 1973.

Gagnier, Regenia. [1]. *Idylls of the Market Place: Oscar Wilde and the Victorian Public*. Stanford, Calif.: Stanford University Press, 1986.

————, ed. [2]. *Critical Essays on Oscar Wilde*. New York: G. K. Hall, 1991.

Ganz, Arthur. [1]. "The Divided Self in the Social Comedies of Oscar Wilde." *Modern Drama* 3.1 (May 1960): 16–23.

————. [2]. "The Meaning of *The Importance of Being Earnest. Modern Drama* 6.1 (May 1963): 42–52.

Gielgud, John. *Stage Directions*. London: Heinemann, 1963.

Goodman, Jonathan. *Oscar Wilde File*. London: W. H. Allen, 1988.

Gregor, Ian. "Comedy and Oscar Wilde." *Sewanee Review* 74 (1966): 501–21.

Gross, John. [Review of *A Woman of No Importance.*] *Sunday Telegraph* (6 Oct. 1991).

Hart-Davis, Rupert, ed. [1]. *The Letters of Oscar Wilde*. London: Rupert Hart-Davis, 1962.

————. [2]. *More Letters of Oscar Wilde*. London: John Murray, 1985.

Holland, Vyvyan. *Oscar Wilde and His World*. London: Thames and Hudson, 1978.

Review of *An Ideal Husband. Black and White* (12 Jan. 1895): 39–40.

Review of *An Ideal Husband. Daily Telegraph* (4 Jan. 1895).

Review of *An Ideal Husband. Sketch* (9 Jan. 1895).

Review of *An Ideal Husband. Theatre* (1 Feb. 1895): 104–5.

Review of *An Ideal Husband. Times* (17 Nov. 1943).

Review of *An Ideal Husband. Observer* (21 Nov. 1943).

Review of *The Importance of Being Earnest. Black and White* (16 Feb. 1895).

Review of *The Importance of Being Earnest. Graphic* (23 Feb. 1895).

Review of *The Importance of Being Earnest. Theatre* (1 Mar. 1895).

Review of *The Importance of Being Earnest. Times* (4 Oct. 1959).

Review of *Lady Windermere's Fan. Black and White* (27 Feb. 1892): 246.

Review of *Lady Windermere's Fan. Times* (22 Aug. 1945).

Mason, A. E. *Sir George Alexander and the St. James's Theatre*. London: Macmillan, 1990.

Morgan, Margery. *File on Wilde*. London: Weidenfeld and Nicholson, 1976.

Morley, Sheridan. *Oscar Wilde*. London: Weidenfeld and Nicholson, 1976.

Nightingale, Benedict. [Review of *A Woman of No Importance.*] *Times* (3 Oct. 1991).

Nisbet, James. [Review of *The Importance of Being Earnest.*] *Times* (15 Feb. 1895).

Pearson, Hesketh. *The Life of Oscar Wilde*. London: Methuen, 1946.

Powell, Kerry. *Oscar Wilde and the Theatre of the 1890s*. Cambridge: Cambridge University Press, 1990.

Ransome, Arthur. *Oscar Wilde: A Critical Study*. London: Macmillan, 1911.

Reed, Francis Miriam, ed. *Oscar Wilde's Vera: or, The Nihilists*. Lewiston: Edwin Mellon Press, 1989.

Rutherford, Malcolm. [Review of *A Woman of No Importance.*] *Financial Times* (3 Oct. 1991).

Review of *Salomé, Daily Telegraph* (28 May 1931).

Review of *Salomé, Sunday Times* (25 July 1954).

Review of *Salomé, Times* (21 July 1954).

Scott, Clement. [1]. [Review of *Lady Windermere's Fan.*] *Illustrated London News* (27 Feb. 1892).

————. [2]. *The Theatre of Yesterday and Today.* 2 vols. London: Macmillan, 1899.

Shaw, George Bernard. [1]. [Review of *An Ideal Husband.*] *Saturday Review* (London) (12 Jan. 1895).

————. [2]. [Review of *The Importance of Being Earnest.*] *Saturday Review* (London) (27 Feb. 1895).

————. [3]. *Our Theatres in the Nineties.* 2 vols. London: Constable, 1932.

Shewan, Rodney. "*A Wife's Tragedy*: An Unpublished Sketch for a Play by Oscar Wilde." *Theatre Research International* 7 (1982): 75–131.

Shulman, Milton. [1]. [Review of *The Importance of Being Earnest.*] *Evening Standard* (14 Oct. 1959).

————. [2]. [Review of *Salomé.*] *Evening Standard* (21 July 1954).

Thomas, W. Moy. [Review of *Lady Windermere's Fan.*] *Graphic* (27 Feb. 1892).

Toepfer, Karl. *The Voice of Rapture: A Symbolist System of Ecstatic Speech in Oscar Wilde's "Salomé."* New York: Peter Lang, 1991.

Tydeman, William, ed. *Wilde: Comedies.* London: Macmillan, 1982.

Walkley, A. B. [1]. [Review of *The Importance of Being Earnest.*] *Speaker* (23 Feb. 1895): 212–13.

————. [2]. [Review of *Lady Windermere's Fan.*] *Speaker* (23 Feb. 1892): 257–58.

Wearing, J. P. [1]. *American and British Theatrical Biography: A Directory.* Metuchen, N.J.: Scarecrow Press, 1979.

————. [2]. *The London Stage, 1890–1899: A Calendar of Plays and Players.* Metuchen, N.J.: Scarecrow Press, 1976.

Wells, H. G. [1]. [Review of *An Ideal Husband.*] *Pall Mall Gazette* (4 Jan. 1895).

————. [2]. [Review of *The Importance of Being Earnest.*] *Pall Mall Gazette* (15 Feb. 1895).

Wilson, A. E. [Review of *Salomé.*] *Star* (21 July 1954).

Wilson, Cecil. [Review of *Salomé.*] *Daily Mail* (21 July 1954).

Review of *A Woman of No Importance. Sketch* (26 Apr. 1893).

Review of *A Woman of No Importance. Illustrated London News* (29 Mar. 1893).

Review of *A Woman of No Importance. Illustrated Sporting and Dramatic* (6 May 1893).

Review of *A Woman of No Importance. The Theatre* (1 June 1893): 332–33.

Woodfield, James. *English Theatre in Transition 1881–1914.* London: Croom Helm, 1984.

Woodward, A. G. "Oscar Wilde." *English Studies in Africa* 2 (1959): 218–31.

Worth, Katharine. *Oscar Wilde.* London: Macmillan, 1983.

BIBLIOGRAPHIES

Mason, Stuart (Christopher Millard). *Bibliography of Oscar Wilde.* 1914. New Edition. London: Bertram Rota, 1967.

Mikhail, E. H. *Oscar Wilde: An Annotated Bibliography of Criticism.* London: Macmillan, 1978.

Mikolyzk, Thomas A. *Oscar Wilde: An Annotated Bibliography.* Westport, Conn.: Greenwood, 1993.

Jack B. Yeats
(1871–1957)

GRACE BAILEY BURNEKO

In the stage talk before the 1949 production of *In Sand*, Jack B. Yeats jested that he hoped his play had succeeded in "putting a little salt on the tail of the Peacock" (MacGowran 5). The Peacock was then, and is now, the experimental wing of the Abbey Theatre, and two of Yeats' plays, using techniques and conventions a decade or more before they became synonymous with the theater of the absurd and antitheater, had innovative performances and full-length runs there. Only *La La Noo* (1949) played in the mother establishment around the corner, and that for one performance only. Though Yeats considered his plays entertainment for general audiences, only three of his eight major plays have been produced. Not surprisingly, then, Yeats, considered Ireland's finest modern painter and an imaginative writer, is little known as a dramatist.

Yeats' aesthetic influences, according to his friend Ernest Marriott, were sweeping: "Nothing [was] to be despised. Everything in his net [was] counted as fish" (11). He was born 29 August 1871, in London to Susan Pollexfen Yeats and John Butler Yeats, and Jack B. Yeats always thought of himself as "the son of a painter" (quoted in Pyle [1], 3). Yeats spent much of his youth in Sligo with his maternal grandparents, as his "prodigal" father sought to make an artist's living in London and Dublin. Thus, Jack B. Yeats began what he called the artist's work of "assembling memories" in the West of Ireland, digging in the good turf of Irish self-sufficiency, rambunctious storytelling, and his mother's supernatural beliefs. Private school in Sligo and a few art classes at the Westminster School of Art in London represented Yeats' formal education, but his father asserted that Jack's was "the education of a man of genius," having "the habits of a man who knows his own mind" (quoted in Pyle [1], 21); like Jack's friend York Powell, Oxford history professor, Jack's thinking was free, tumultuous, charitable, and all-embracing (Pyle [1], 28).

With this extrovert's education, Yeats began earning a living in London illustrating for a number of journals and drawing cartoons for *Punch* under the pseudonym "William Byrd." His drawings, characterized by human action and the uninhibited worlds of the sea, circus, boxing ring, racecourse, country dances, and the marketplace, transformed into his early dramatic enterprise— plays for a miniature stage. As Yeats explains in "My Miniature Theatre," he and his beloved wife, Mary Cottenham White Yeats, whom he married in 1895, entertained the neighborhood children of Surrey "with swashbuckling tales of pirates and extravagant circus events, all on a stage with a proscenium opening three foot nine inches wide and one foot ten inches high" (*Collected Plays* 17). When Elkin Mathews began advertising the publication of these miniature, hand-painted theater sets, he called them "sensations of theatrical management" (Marriott 29); and indeed, Yeats' father would call *James Flaunty: The Terror of the Western Seas*, published in 1901, a most "poetical play" (quoted in Pyle [1], 64), while W. B. Yeats and Gordon Craig adapted Jack's miniature theater for their collaboration on set designs. Yeats' miniature plays *The Scourge of the Gulph, The Treasure of the Garden, The Bosun and the Bob-Tailed Comet*, published in 1903 and 1904, kept his dramatic hand active while he continued his drawings for his brother's *Broadsides* or illustrated poems and experimented with painting mediums. When Jack and Cottie visited New York in 1904 and saw the commedia dell'arte puppet theaters of the boroughs, Yeats reflected upon the universality of the exuberant life, though he would leave off writing for his miniature theater in 1907.

In June and July 1905, Yeats traveled through Ireland with John Millington Synge, illustrating Synge's articles for the *Manchester Guardian*. Yeats and Synge both admired the Irish peasant, "delighted in crude power" (Saddlemyer 29), and indulged this sympathetic humanity in their theatrical art. According to Saddlemyer and biographer Pyle, Jack B. Yeats acquainted Synge with the Queen's Theatre melodramas, which link the "grotesque and violent" in the same euphoric way as Synge's *The Playboy of the Western World* and Jack Yeats' pirate stage adventures (Saddlemyer 29; Pyle [1], 93). While critics compare Yeats' late paintings to Synge's lyric dramas, *Deirdre of the Sorrows* and *Riders to the Sea*, they might also note the dramatists' similar handling of what Jack Yeats called the individual's short-lived "splendour" and "memory" of splendor within the continuum of life and death (quoted in Reid 4). As Yeats joyously wrote in his novel *Sligo*, "With laughter we come, with laughter we go" (11).

By the time Yeats met Samuel Beckett in late 1930, he and Cottie had been settled in Dublin since 1917, and he had written his first play for the larger theater, *Deathly Terrace* (1929), a drama analyzing the actor's relationship to audience. Since 1910, when he began painting consistently in oil, Yeats' artistic focus was painting, but in 1929 his pen became prolific, too, producing six novels and nine plays within a fourteen-year period, from 1929 to 1944. In his lifetime, he saw four of his plays for the larger theater published—*Apparitions, The Old Sea Road*, and *Rattle* in 1933 and *La La Noo* in 1943.

Despite vigorous campaigns to see his plays staged, Yeats saw performances only of *Harlequin's Positions* (1939), *La La Noo* (1942), and *In Sand* (1949). When the Lyric Players in Belfast revived *La La Noo* alongside W. B. Yeats' *The King's Threshold* in 1956, Yeats was too ill to attend, but he conveyed his pleasure at the family success. Yeats continued to assert the importance of his dramatic art, despite an ever-increasing reputation as a painter: by his death on 28 March 1957, Yeats had seen his drawings and paintings exhibited in the prestigious National Gallery of London, the Tate, the Victor Waddington Galleries, the National College of Art in Dublin, and a retrospective exhibition in the United States; he had received honorary degrees from Trinity College and the National University of Ireland; and he had been invested as an officer of the Legion of Honor and received an Italian diploma. In contrast, Yeats knew only a limited, chiefly lackluster appreciation for his theatrical art. Even the centenary-year celebrations at the Peacock produced but a brief reading from *La La Noo* and *James Flaunty*. Despite the publication of *The Collected Plays of Jack B. Yeats* in 1971, two recent book-length studies on his literary work, and another on Samuel Beckett's indebtedness to the Yeats brothers, that "theatre was a lifelong addiction" of Jack B. Yeats' finds only sporadic acknowledgment and the rare, experimental staging (James White 29).

Selected Biographical Sources: Brian P. Kennedy; Pyle [1]; Rose [3]; James White.

MAJOR PLAYS, PREMIERES, AND SIGNIFICANT REVIVALS: THEATRICAL RECEPTION

Harlequin's Positions. 1939. Opened 5 June at the Peacock Theatre, Dublin, and closed 17 June, twelve performances in all by the Abbey Experimental Theatre. Produced by Ria Mooney and Cecil Ford. Settings designed and painted by Anne Yeats and constructed by Gearóid Ó h-Íceadha.

Though there was report of Dublin theatergoers' positive response to the artist's unusual play, critical notices had been fairly negative: the *Irish Times* (Review of *Harlequin's Positions*, 6 June 1939) labeled *Harlequin's Positions* "a strange piece of material," with Clive labeling it a "rejected" Abbey play, an "interesting" experiment. While *Harlequin's Positions* portrayed Ireland in the late 1930s, life under Dr. Eamon de Valera's 1937 Constitution promoting a haven of self-sufficiency and what Yeats termed "war's alarums," critics failed to see its immediacy.

La La Noo. 1942. Special performance on Sunday, 3 May, by the National Theatre Society at the Abbey Theatre (double-billed with Lord Dunsany's *A Night at an Inn*). Produced by Ria Mooney. Settings and costumes created by Michael Clarke. Revival: Lyric Players, Belfast, 9–12 March 1956 (double-billed with W. B. Yeats' *The King's Threshold*). Revivial produced by Mary O'Malley. Centenary-year revivial: the Peacock Theatre, Dublin, on 22 November 1971. Scenes from *La La Noo* and other writings of Jack B. Yeats were read, entitled "The Gift of the Gab"; Hilary Pyle, Jack B. Yeats first biographer, compiled the writings, and Edward Golden directed. Recent revival: Toronto Irish Players, Tarragon Theatre, Toronto, 24–28 August 1994. Produced by Jude Hession. Directed by Lucy Brennan. Stage designed by Brendan Lynsky.

La La Noo, Jack B. Yeats' only play to reach the Abbey stage, had two double-billed productions, first with Lord Dunsany's thriller and next with his brother's play about a poet's hunger strike.

The *Dublin Evening Mail* (Review of *La La Noo*) thought Dunsany's action piece a perfect contrast to Yeats' "lovely talk, simple, grand, inconsequent talk"; furthermore, this Yeatsian talk fitted "the tradition of noble speech" inspired by the Abbey Theatre. This Abbey production, according to the *Irish Times*, achieved "a mood of wonder." Though "not hoisted as a comedy," as Yeats noted in a 1948 BBC interview with Thomas MacGreevy, *La La Noo*'s comedy turns into tragedy. Critics also noted the audience's approval of antimodernist speeches, and the producer Ria Mooney emphasized this theme. Mary O'Malley recalls how the play's talk of war and death seemed to result in a production fiasco: first, a cast member resigned after losing her brother on the heels of her father's unexpected death; second, the new cast member, who was pregnant, lost the baby in a bicycling accident; and, third, the final replacement completed the play's four-day run and the next day lost her brother to an unusual boarding school accident (86).

In the 1994 Toronto Irish Players' production of *La La Noo*, the jinx phenomenon continued: Brennan recalls that her "Publican" broke a rib just prior to opening night. While Yeats' directions call for the Publican to carry the dead body of the Stranger back on stage, Brennan improvised a shutter-gurney so the Publican could be assisted by one of the play's seven women characters.

In Sand. 1949. Opened 19 April at the Peacock Theatre, Dublin, for 12 performances by the Abbey Experimental Theatre. (The actors did not perform the play's prologue, *The Green Wave*.) Produced by Séan Mac Shamhráin. Directed by Jack MacGowran. Settings designed by Gene Martin and assistant Leslie Scott. Costumes designed by Gene Martin and executed by Eileen Tobin. Gunther Stumpf composed the incidental music. Revival: Lantern Theatre, Dublin, 29 September 1964, played with *The Green Wave* prologue for a two-week run. Patrick Funge produced the revival; Liam Miller and Noel Keating designed and painted the settings. Radio revivals: BBC Third Program broadcasts by producer Frederick Bradnum: 19 February 1956; 14 February 1956; and 7 May 1965.

Like *Harlequin's Positions* and *La La Noo*, *In Sand* helped secure the careers of actors in the Abbey Experimental Theatre. Brennan noted "some of the best acting that has come from the Abbey in a very long time,'' and J. J. Hayes praised ''a convincing'' cast whose performance was ''as taut as a violin string,'' with ''tonal verities [being] clear as crystal.'' Brian O'Higgins received the *Dublin Evening Mail*'s (''Jack Yeats' Play at Peacock'') praise for his delightful performance of the old sailor, Yeats' garrulous philosopher, played with ''a mixture of impudence, laziness, philosophy and wisdom.'' When director Jack MacGowran said *In Sand* ''was acclaimed a major success by critics and public alike,'' he was reaching only a little. The *Dublin Evening Mail* (''Jack Yeats' Play at Peacock'') noted these merits: ''fun,'' ''satire,'' ''humour,'' and ''the author's shrewd observation of life,'' stemming from a play about time and memory. The *Dublin Evening Herald* (Review of *In Sand*) called *In Sand* ''an evocative work of superlative beauty . . . making for a rare evening.'' The *Irish Times* (Review of *In Sand*) noted a ''Shavianism enriched with mellow humanity,'' producing a ''melancholy allegory, with Death the only real character.'' To derive ''keen enjoyment,'' according to the *Dublin Evening Mail* (''Jack Yeats' Play at Peacock''), audiences should ''surrender themselves to the mood of the piece'' and play by Jack Yeats' rules. Curiously, critics missed the charged political content of the play, what Rose [2] calls Jack B. Yeats' ''essential radicalism'' (95). His references to the pro-Unionist Primrose League, Nelson's Pillar, and the Four Courts present familiar Dublin symbols of British rule; yet not one critic noted the appropriateness of the play's opening one week prior to the Abbey's advertised Easter Rising tributes: Lady Gregory's *Dervorgilla* and *Rising of the Moon* and Roibeárd Ó Faracháin's *Lost Night*. As surprising is the absence of critical note on the songs woven into the dialogue and extended soliloquies, songs Yeats viewed as essential to the play's meaning: they lament emigration and recruitment of Irishmen for European wars and wars in foreign Catholic countries. Over at the Queen's Theatre, *The Flame* played as a salute to the New Republic, but no one noted the serendipity of the Peacock's production of *In Sand* or its extended run into the Easter Week festivities.

The Lantern Theatre revival fifteen years later produced *The Green Wave*, a humorous prologue about a painter and an unenlightened art collector. Though defined as ''A Compact Evening's Theatre,'' the revival lacked the 1949 ''magic,'' according to the *Irish Times* (''Revival of *In Sand*''), and Patrick Funge failed ''to impose an adequate unity of style on amateur actors of varying abilities, and pedestrian realism kept breaking in.'' The broadcasts of *In Sand* for the BBC Third Program produced a ''heavily cut'' version of the play. Yeats' comment to his friend Victor Waddington, ''They're trotting this out . . . I wish they'd forget this stuff'' (quoted in Rose [6], 38), more likely results from his distrust of cut versions of his work than from a rejection of his drama's merits.

PLAYS FOR THE MINIATURE THEATRE AND OTHER PRODUCTIONS

As an annual Christmas entertainment, Jack Yeats and his wife, Cottie, produced his miniature drama for the valley children near their early home, Snail's Castle (Cashlauna Shelmiddy) at Strete, near Dartmouth in Devon: *Timothy Coombewest or Esmeralda Grande* in 1900, *Onct More's Great Circus* in 1901 and 1902, *The Treasure of the Garden* in 1902, *James Dance or the Unfortunate Ship's Boy* (a pantomime) in 1903 and 1904, *The Mysterious Traveller or the Gamesome Princes and the Pursuing Policeman* in 1903 and 1904, and the "Galanty Show" in 1905 and 1906. *Esmeralda Grande* and *Onct More's Great Circus* entertained family and friends during the summers of 1900 and 1901, respectively. The children's reactions to his melodramas must have been mixed: in 1904, Yeats wrote his friend T. A. Harvey of his delight in their amusement, but in a 1906 letter to John Quinn, Yeats said he looked forward to playing his miniature theater before the more responsive Irish children (Pyle [1], 63). Written reviews of the "toy theater," in contrast, were never mixed. Carric called Yeats' miniature theater "the most natural Europe possesses" (47), while the 1904 *Manchester Guardian* suggested, "If Mr. Andrew Lang ever finds the 'Odyssey' losing its power to affect the mind like ocean thundering on a Western beach, he should try 'The Scourge of the Gulph' " (quoted in Marriott 28).

"Gift of the Gab," a reading of Yeats' works at the Peacock on 22 November 1971, was directed by Edward Golden. The centenary-celebration reading, as compiled by Hilary Pyle, included extracts from *James Flaunty, La La Noo*, and several novels. Readers were Michael Hennessy, Eamon Kelly, Peadar Lamb, Joan O'Hara, Pat Layde, Gerry Walsh, and Catherine O'Rourke. Kelly praised the presentation—deserving "more than a one-night stand"—and suggested a revival of Yeats' plays.

ASSESSMENT OF YEATS' CAREER

Early in Jack B. Yeats' career as a painter, his father acknowledged him to be "an initiator" (Murphy [2], 209). In a 1925 letter to his brother, Jack Yeats boasted "the immodesty of a spear head" (quoted in Pyle [1], 124). Divergent critical appraisals of his visual and literary art intersect on this point: Jack B. Yeats is peerless, original, no school's disciple; "[he] belongs to nobody but himself," notes the reviewer of the 1921 Dublin Painters' autumn exhibition (quoted in S. B. Kennedy 28). Even the severest critic of his dramatic work concedes its "inimitable" nature (Hogan and O'Neill 1037). But whereas this forerunner stance has led to international recognition of Yeats—chiefly posthumously—as a "solitary titan" in the history of Irish art (Rosenthal 1), his reputation for dramatic and verbal gamesmanship has suffered from his inventive plethora.

Jack Yeats' novel *Sligo*, published in 1930, is a case in point. "His high jinks are like nobody else's," notes Robin Skelton, though *Sligo* anticipates Flann O'Brien and T. H. White, recalls *Finnegans Wake*, and rivals Sterne's humor and Swift's satire (*Selected Writings* 9). But *Sligo*'s uncanny style, favoring a plurality of meanings, baffled most of its few early readers, as yet unaccustomed to the postmodern subversiveness to Western narratives of power. Reading *Sligo* or the six other major narratives, the reader is asked to explore the vagaries of Yeats' mind, what he referred to as his "jettison[ed] memories" (*Sligo* 28), and to question the very effectiveness of language to communicate personal truths. As McHugh explains, "Reading *Sligo* or *Ah Well* or *And to You Also* is like listening to a rambling talker who doesn't give a rambling damn whether you listen or not" (18). While McGuinness' study of his "literary universe" explores the integrity of Jack Yeats' nonlinear narratives, many admirers of his visual art have dismissed the literary works due to their innovations, assuming them to result from a painter's dilettantism (Mays 35).

The Collected Plays of Jack B. Yeats roundly affirms him as an initiator and experimenter in theatrical art. There are seven melodramas and a pantomime for the miniature theater; a trilogy—consisting of a comedy, tragedy, and romantic tragedy—systematically linked by music; a tableau piece of five acts linked with five harlequin poses; a tragicomedy; a one-act conversation piece; a romantic comedy; a supernatural comedy; and a metatheatrical comedy, a film within a play. There are plays observing all the unities, some breaking all the unities. Some plays require a proscenium; others, a theater-in-the-round. Some plays are politically charged; others, purely philosophical. Action propels some plays, whereas talk is the action in others.

Not surprisingly, Jack Yeats' theatrical art has proved impossible to label. Though his *La La Noo* had a one-night Abbey performance, Yeats cannot be identified with the Irish National Theatre movement. Indeed, he wrote Lady Gregory, one of the founders, that he was sorry the Mechanics Theatre, "where they played the most beautiful plays," would be superseded by the national dramas of the Abbey (7 August 1904). Though Lennox Robinson, as an Abbey director, praised *La La Noo* for its "pure Synge" and Fitzmaurice qualities (350), and critics have noted its faithfulness to local color (Rose [3], 39), Yeats was too idiosyncratic in his tastes to fit the Abbey mold. Yeats' droll solution to the *Playboy* riots, for instance, included "the old Music Hall style [of welting] the drums every time the language gets too high for the stomachs of the audience" (quoted in Pyle, [1], 93). As well, Yeats preferred "crook-drama" to "Thinking Drama," disparaging authors who think too hard and require actors to think doubly hard to enliven the drama (*Sligo* 42). Though critics have noted the "Shavian length" (Hogan and O'Neill 1038) of his characters' monologues, Yeats disliked established dramatists like Shaw, the "Woodbine Willie of Literature," as he called him (Letter to Joseph Hone, quoted in Rose, [3], 22). *Harlequin's Positions*, Yeats' projection of native independence, may be a riposte to Shaw's *John Bull's Other Island*. Finally, Yeats' Republicanism—

though he was opposed to violence—may have put him at odds with the Abbey's literary nationalism.

For lack of a category, O'Faoláin called the trilogy—*Apparitions*—"odd plays" (35). Indeed, Jack Yeats' plays do not fit a particular theatrical and literary rubric despite some felicitous correlations. There is much of the theatre of the absurd in Yeats' plays, and Samuel Beckett's well-known admiration for Jack Yeats' art has, no doubt, influenced scholars to look for parallels. *Harlequin's Positions* presents the *Waiting for Godot* paradigm, a benighted, middle-class people readied for adventure until war rumors leave them stranded at the train station. Theirs is the "paralysis of Ireland" (McGuinness 215). Like the circuses Yeats loved, notes Joseph Connelly, "each action [of the play] turns in a circle upon itself" (139). Its acts stylized on a harlequin's poses, this play "represents the farthest Jack Yeats went towards antidrama and the nearest he got to anticipating the methods of such later playwrights as Pinter and Mortimer," according to Skelton (see *Selected Writings* 22). Yet another scholar sees *Harlequin's Positions* as a Chekhovian drama, stiffened against change (Armstrong, [1], 210).

As in the theatre of the absurd, Yeats' characters generally are not individualized enough to appear like real people, unlike Shaw's or O'Neill's (Rose [1], 101). Anne Yeats, the artist's niece, notes this to be particularly true of his female figures or characters, as if at some point he failed to see changes in fashion or women's lives. Some critics note the "marionette-like" characterizations resembling those in the symbolist dramas of Maurice Maeterlinck. Yeats also follows the symbolists in portraying clairvoyance through his *petit peuple* (Rose, [3], 39); they are types more than individuals. Again, in the absurdist vein, characters are vehicles for talk. The characters' talking is a way to focus "on the momentary" (Connelly 153), "to freeze an experience by reformulating it as anecdote or cliché" (Rose [5], 78). As in Ionesco's or Pinter's absurdist plays, we witness talk preventing communication (R. Patrick Murphy 121). Beckett's *Happy Days*, in fact, contains no more "talking" than Yeats' *La La Noo*, deemed "a vaudeville of frustration" anticipating Flann O'Brien's novel *At Swim-Two-Birds* (Starkie 99).

In Sand stresses the ephemeral quality of personality, "the gesture" of life (O'Doherty, "Promise and Regret" 90), and all of Yeats' plays enact the *danse macabre* theme; *Rattle* plays on the death groan from its outset. Comedies, no less than tragedies, "contain a trap-door to disaster" despite the playful, local talk (McHugh 16). Death is often the practical joker, as in *The Deathly Terrace* when the filming of a scene produces a "real suicide, not a reel suicide" (Armstrong [1], 189). Similarly, a suicide and murder conclude *The Old Sea Road*, a drama that may well be a link between Synge and Beckett.

While the pell-mell plots, static scenes, and garrulous characters—including the familiar odd couple—help critics define the dramas as precursors of the absurd theater or antidrama (Rose, "Mixed Metaphors" 93; McHugh 18), ultimately Yeats is not an absurdist dramatist, remaining an individualist with no school. He distrusted what he called Beckett's "amoral" structure of life (quoted in Pyle, [1], 146); without didacticism, Yeats creates a moral framework for his art, and the greatest sins appear to be an unforgiving heart, a pleasureless life, and the posture of hypocrisy. Yeats is particularly hard on postmen and police-man, as "Wordsworth was on gypsies," according to Mays (39). They are "people doing things they don't get anything out of, drawing the breath of Life for a starter" (*The Old Sea Road* 154). "To know all is to forgive all" is the philosophy dramatized in *Rattle* (204). Just how far this forgiveness extends is revealed when Michael of the Song in *The Old Sea Road* asks the joker who has poisoned him, "Would it be any offence if I said a prayer for you?" (158).

Linked to this pervasive generosity of heart is Yeats' anything-but-absurdist theme, what McGuinness frames as "the need to immerse oneself in the rhythms of the universe" (186). This "current of life" (Skelton, *Collected Plays* 7) or "continuum of process" (Armstrong [1], 218) is taken to its extreme in *Silencer* and *Apparitions*, dramatizations of the supernatural. The séance in *Apparitions*, moreover, is a lighthearted jest at his brother's séance involvement and presents a competing, comical view to that of W. B. Yeats' séance drama, *The Words upon the Window-Pane*. When the garrulous Irishman in *Silencer* haunts his English murderer by speaking incessantly through a Dictaphone, the continuum of life is given not only comic expression but also communication through mechanical media—the recorded or cinematic voice—reminding us as well of Beckett's *Krapp's Last Tape*. Perhaps, as Mary O'Malley conjectures, Jack Yeats was competing with W. B. Yeats for dramatic prowess. Both dramatists, nonetheless, found themselves at odds with the realist, naturalist dramas of their time; Jack Yeats' few produced plays found only "experimental" stages, and in 1917, conceding the unpopularity of his dramatic vision, W. B. Yeats turned to Noh-styled dramas that could be played in drawing rooms. Both dramatists would have to wait for more hospitable audiences.

Just as Jack Yeats admitted that his visual art did not always "attract the human herd" (Letter to Lady Gregory, 17 June 1901), he was quick to acknowl-edge the difficulty of staging his experimental "odd" dramas. In a 1938 inter-view with Oshima, he spoke of his play *Apparitions* as "not fit for the stage in Ireland, to say nothing of England" (55). An innovator, Yeats sought to chal-lenge the theatergoer's perspective, having experimented with the confrontation between performer and public since his early creation of a miniature theater. The exchange between supernatural and natural phenomena, the influence of the cinema on the theatrical view, the influence of memory—these Jack Yeats sought to dramatize without benefit of technological advances that could now, for example, create the necessary illusion of hair turning white in *Apparitions*. Recent scholarly interest in Jack Yeats' dramatic works may indicate an aus-picious time and an audience amenable to his universe, having "the good thought" (*In Sand*, passim) for Jack B. Yeats and his one-of-a-kind dramatic world.

ARCHIVAL SOURCES

Private papers—including playbills, clippings, photographs, and several typescripts—are in the personal collection of Anne Yeats in Dalkey, Ireland. Other manuscript sources are housed in the National Library of Ireland; University College, Dublin, Library; Trinity College, Dublin, Library; National Gallery of Ireland Library; University of Reading Library; Bodleian Library, Oxford; University of London Library; University of Kansas, Kenneth Spencer Research Library; New York Public Library, Berg Collection; University of Victoria, MacPherson Library; University at Carbondale Library, University of Delaware Library; Southern Illinois, Morris Library; and the BBC Script Library, Drama Library and Sound Archives. The Dublin Public Library houses many first editions of his plays. Jack B. Yeats' letters to Mary O'Malley are in her personal papers in Dublin.

PRIMARY BIBLIOGRAPHY

Plays

Apparitions: Three Plays. London: Jonathan Cape, 1933; Secker and Warburg, 1971.
The Bosun and the Bob-tailed Comet: A Play for the Miniature Stage. London: Elkin Mathews, 1904.
The Deathly Terrace. London: Secker and Warburg, 1971.
Harlequin's Positions. London: Secker and Warburg, 1971.
In Sand. A Play, with The Green Wave, a One-Act Conversation Piece. Edited with a Preface by Jack MacGowran. Dublin: Dolmen 1964; London: Secker and Warburg, 1971.
James Flaunty or The Terror of the Western Seas: A Play for the Miniature Stage. London: Elkin Mathews, 1901; Secker and Warburg, 1971.
La La Noo. Dublin: Cuala Press, 1943; London: Secker and Warburg, 1971.
A Little Fleet: A Play for the Miniature Stage. London: Elkin Mathews, 1909.
The Old Sea Road. London: Secker and Warburg, 1971.
Onct More's First Circus. London: Secker and Warburg, 1971.
Onct More's Great Circus. London: Secker and Warburg, 1971.
Rattle. London: Secker and Warburg, 1971.
The Scourge of the Gulph: A Play for the Miniature Stage. London: Elkin Mathews, 1903; New York: Viking, 1929; London: Secker and Warburg, 1971; also published in Paul McPharlin, *A Repertory of Marionette Plays.* New York: Viking, 1929. 12–28.
The Silencer. London: Secker and Warburg, 1971.
Timothy Coombewest or Esmeralda Grande. London: Secker and Warburg, 1971.
The Treasure of the Garden: A Play in the Old Manner. London: Elkin Mathews, 1903; Secker and Warburg, 1971.
The Wonderful Travellers or The Gamesome Princes and The Pursuing Policeman. London: Secker and Warburg, 1971.

Anthologies

The Collected Plays of Jack B. Yeats. Ed. Robin Skelton. London: Secker and Warburg, 1971; Indianapolis: Bobbs-Merrill, 1971.

La La Noo. The Genius of the Irish Theatre. Ed. Sylvan Barnet, Morton Berman, and William Burto. New York: New American Library, 1960, 212–44.

The Scourge of the Gulph. A Repertory of Marionette Plays. Ed. Paul McPharlin. New York: Viking, 1929, 12–28.

The Selected Writings of Jack B. Yeats. Ed. Robin Skelton. London: André Deutsch, 1991.

Essays, Articles, and Letters on Drama and Theater

"How Jack B. Yeats Produced His Plays for the Miniature Stage." *Mask* 5.1 (1912): 49–54. Rpt. in *The Collected Plays of Jack B. Yeats.* Ed. Robin Skelton. Indianapolis: Bobbs-Merrill, 1971. 380–82.

"Jack B. Yeats." *Eason's Bulletin* 4.5 (1948): 3.

Letters to John Quinn. Manuscript Collection. New York Public Library.

Letters to Lady Gregory. Berg Collection. New York Public Library.

Letters to Ria Mooney. Berg Collection. New York Public Library.

"Life in Manchester: The Melodrama Audience." *Manchester Guardian* (9 Dec. 1905): 7.

"My Miniature Theatre." In *The Collected Plays of Jack B. Yeats.* Ed. Robin Skelton. Indianapolis: Bobbs-Merrill, 1971. 17–19.

"A Theatre for Every Man." *Music Review* 1.3 (1912): 83–85.

Novels with Significant References to Drama

The Careless Flower. London: Pilot Press, 1947.

Sligo. London: Wishart, 1932.

SECONDARY BIBLIOGRAPHY

Review of *Apparitions. Irish Book Lover* 21.6 (1933): 139.

Armstrong, Gordon S. [1]. *Samuel Beckett, W. B. Yeats, and Jack Yeats: Images and Words.* Lewisburg, Pa.: Bucknell University Press, 1990.

———. [2]. "Symbols, Signs, and Language: The Brothers Yeats and Samuel Beckett's Art of the Theatre." *Comparative Drama* 20 (1986): 38–53.

Arnold, Bruce. "Noble Deeds: Jack B. Yeats." *Éire-Ireland* 6.2 (1971): 48–57.

Beckett, Samuel. [1]. "Hommage à Jack B. Yeats." *Les Lettres Nouvelles* (April 1954). Rpt. in *Jack B. Yeats: A Centenary Gathering.* Trans. Ruby Cohn. Ed. Roger McHugh. Dublin: Dolmen, 1971. 75–76.

———. [2]. "MacGreevy on Yeats." *Irish Times* (4 Aug. 1945): n.p. Rpt. in *Jack B. Yeats: A Centenary Gathering.* Ed. Roger McHugh. Dublin: Dolmen, 1971. 71–74.

Bell, Sam Hanna. *The Theatre in Ulster: A Survey of the Dramatic Movement in Ulster from 1902 until the Present Day.* Dublin: Gill and Macmillan, 1972.

Booth, Mark Haworth. "Jack B. Yeats until Now." *Jack B. Yeats: The Late Paintings.* Bristol: Arnolfini, 1991.

Brennan, Lucy. "Jack Butler Yeats as Playwright." Unpublished paper, American Conference for Irish Studies and the Canadian Association for Irish Studies Conference, Belfast, 1995.

Carric, Allen. "Captain Jack B. Yeats: A Pirate of the Old School." *Mask* 5.1 (1912): 42–47.

Clive, Kitty. "Echoes of the Town." *Irish Times* (9 June 1939): 4.

"A Compact Evening's Theatre." *Irish Times* (30 Sept. 1964): 6.

Connelly, Joseph F. "Jack Yeats: Entertaining the Common Man." *Éire-Ireland* 17.4 (1982): 152–58.

Corkery, Daniel. "Jack B. Yeats Once More." *Irish Monthly* 73 (Sept. 1945): 363–67.

Curran, Constantine P. "Jack B. Yeats, RHA." *Studies: An Irish Quarterly Review* 30 (Mar. 1941): 75–89.

"Curtain's Up." *Social and Personal* (Dublin) (May 1949).

"The Gift of the Gab." *Irish Times* (22 Nov. 1971): 10.

Gorman, Michael. "The Yeats Play." *Leader* (Dublin) (4 June 1949).

Review of *Harlequin's Positions. Irish Times* (6 June 1939): 6.

Review of *Harlequin's Positions. Irish Times* (9 June 1939): 4.

Review of *Harlequin's Positions. Irish Independent* (9 June 1939): 10.

Hayes, J. J. "A New Drama by Jack Yeats." *Christian Science Monitor* (7 May 1949): 12.

Hogan, Robert, and Michael J. O'Neill, eds. *Joseph Holloway's Irish Theatre.* Vol. 3. Dixon, Calif.: Proscenium, 1970.

Hone, Joseph, ed. *J. B. Yeats: Letters to His Son W. B. Yeats and Others, 1869–1922.* London: Secker and Warburg, 1983.

Hutchins, Patricia. "Jack Yeats and His Publisher." *Yeats Studies* 2 (1972): 121–27.

Hyman, Timothy. "Jack B. Yeats's Self-Created Pageantry." *Times Literary Supplement* (19 Apr. 1991): 18.

Review of *In Sand. Irish Times* (14 Apr. 1949).

Review of *In Sand. Dublin Evening Herald* (20 Apr. 1949): 5.

Review of *In Sand. Irish Press* (20 Apr. 1949).

Review of *In Sand. Irish Press* (25 Apr. 1949).

"An Irishman's Diary" by Quidnunc. *Irish Times* (30 March 1957): 8.

Jack B. Yeats and His Family. Exhibition Catalog. Sligo County Museum and Library, 1971.

"Jack B. Yeats's *In Sand.*" *Irish Times* (20 Apr. 1949): 3.

"Jack Yeats' Play at Peacock." *Dublin Evening Mail* (20 Apr. 1949): 5.

Kelly, Seamus. "Reading of Yeats' Work at Peacock." *Irish Times* (23 Nov. 1971): 10.

Kennedy, Brian P. *Jack B. Yeats.* Dublin: National Gallery of Ireland, 1991.

Kennedy, S. B. *Irish Art and Modernism: 1880–1950.* Belfast: Queen's University, 1991.

Kennelly, Brendan. [1]. "*In Sand* by Jack Yeats." *Dubliner* 3.3 (1964): 71.

———. [2]. "Yeatsian Symbolism in New Play." *Irish Independent* (20 Apr. 1949).

Review of *La La Noo. Irish Times* (4 May 1942): 2.

Review of *La La Noo. Irish Independent* (4 May 1942): 3.

Review of *La La Noo. Dublin Evening Mail* (4 May 1942): 3.

Review of *La La Noo. The New Alliance* (April–May 1943): 12.

Review of *La La Noo*. "Play without Drama: Scene in an Irish Public House." *Times Literary Supplement* (3 Apr. 1943): 166.

Le Brocquy, Louis. "The Ballad World of Jack B. Yeats." Le Brocquy typescript, 24,268, in the National Library of Ireland.

Lyric Players: 1951–59. Belfast: Doric, 1960.

"Lyric Players Succeed in Two Short Plays." *Northern Whig* (12 Mar. 1956): 6.

MacGowran, Jack. Preface. *In Sand*. By Jack B. Yeats. Ed. Jack MacGowran. Dublin: Dolmen, 1964. 5–7.

MacGreevy, Thomas. *Jack B. Yeats: An Appreciation and an Interpretation*. Dublin: Victor Waddington, 1945.

Marriott, Ernest. "Jack B. Yeats Pictorial and Dramatic Artist." London: Elkin Mathews, 1911.

Masefield, John. "Mr. Jack B. Yeats." *Dublin Magazine* 1.1 (1923): 3–4.

Mays, James. "Jack B. Yeats: Some Comments on His Books." *Irish University Review* 2.1 (1972): 34–54.

McGuinness, Nora A. *The Literary Universe of Jack B. Yeats*. Washington, D.C.: Catholic University of America Press, 1992.

McHugh, Roger. "Jack B. Yeats: 1871–1957." *Jack B. Yeats: A Centenary Gathering*. Ed. Roger McHugh. Dublin: Dolmen, 1971. 7–21.

Molloy, Tony. "Review of *In Sand*." *Irish Press* (24 Apr. 1949).

Murphy, R. Patrick. "Nudity and Nakedness: Jack B. Yeats and Robert Graves." *Éire-Ireland* 10.2 (1975): 119–23.

Murphy, William M. [1]. *Family Secrets: William Butler Yeats and His Relatives*. Syracuse, N.Y.: Syracuse University Press, 1995.

———. [2]. *Prodigal Father*. Ithaca, N.Y.: Cornell University Press, 1978.

O'Doherty, Brian. [1]. "Jack B. Yeats: Promise and Regret." *Jack B. Yeats: A Centenary Gathering*. Ed. Roger McHugh. Dublin: Dolmen, 1971. 77–91.

———. [2]. "Obituary—Jack Butler Yeats, 1871–1957." *Dublin Magazine* 33.3 (1957): 55–57.

O'Faoláin, Sean. "Jack B. Yeats." *Bell* 1.4 (1941): 33–36.

O'Malley, Conor. *A Poet's Theatre*. Dublin: Elo, 1988.

O'Malley, Mary. *Never Shake Hands with the Devil*. Dublin: Elo, 1990.

Oshima, Shotaro. "An Interview with Jack Butler Yeats." *Jack B. Yeats: A Centenary Gathering*. Ed. Roger McHugh. Dublin: Dolmen, 1971. 51–56.

"The Peacock Theatre: New Play by Jack B. Yeats." *Irish Times* (6 June 1939): 6.

"Puzzling Play by J. B. Yeats." *Irish Press* (6 June 1939): 7.

Pyle, Hilary. [1]. *Jack B. Yeats: A Biography*. London: Routledge and Kegan Paul, 1970.

———. [2]. " 'Men of Destiny'—Jack B. and W. B. Yeats: The Background and the Symbols." *Studies* (Summer/Autumn 1977): 188–213.

Reid, B. L. *The Man from New York: John Quinn and His Friends*. London: Oxford University Press, 1968.

"Revival of *In Sand*." *Irish Times* (30 Sept. 1964): 6

Robinson, Lennox. [1]. *Ireland's Abbey Theatre: A History 1899–1951*. Port Washington, N.Y.: Kennikat, 1968.

———. [2]. "A Review of *La La Noo*." *Bell* 6.4 (1943): 348–51.

Rose, Marilyn Gaddis. [1]. "Mixed Metaphors: Jack B. Yeats's Writings." *Jack B. Yeats: A Centenary Gathering*. Ed. Roger McHugh. Dublin: Dolmen, 1971. 92–106.

————. [2]. "Jack B. Yeats: Irish Rebel in Modern Art." *Éire-Ireland* 7.2 (1972): 95–105.

————. [3]. *Jack B. Yeats: Painter and Poet.* Frankfurt: Herbert Lang Berne, 1972.

————. [4]. "Kindred Vistas of W. B. and Jack B. Yeats." *Éire-Ireland* 5.1 (1970): 67–79.

————. [5]. "Solitary Companions in Beckett and Jack B. Yeats." *Éire-Ireland* 4.2 (1969): 66–80.

————. [6]. "Sub Rosa: The Writings of Jack B. Yeats." *Éire-Ireland* 3.2 (1968): 37–47.

Rosenthal, T. G. *The Art of Jack B. Yeats.* London: Andre Deutsch, 1993.

Rynne, Stephen. "Tea with Jack B. Yeats—1940." *Éire-Ireland* 7.2 (1972): 106–9.

Saddlemyer, Ann. "Synge and Some Companions, with a Note concerning a Walk through Connemara with Jack Yeats." *Yeats Studies* 2 (1972): 18–34.

Sheehy, Edward. "Jack B. Yeats." *Dublin Magazine* 20.3 (1945): 38–41.

Shields, (Daniel). "Jack B. Yeats." *Irish Monthly* 77 (December 1949): 549–51.

Skelton, Robin. [1]. "Themes and Attitudes in the Later Drama of Jack B. Yeats." *Yeats Studies* 2 (1972): 100–120.

————. [2]. "Unarrangeable Reality: The Paintings and Writings of Jack B. Yeats." *The World of W. B. Yeats.* Ed. Ann Saddlemyer and Robin Skelton. Seattle: University of Washington Press, 1967. 262–63.

Starkie, Walter. "Memories of John Synge and Jack Yeats." *Yeats Studies* 2 (1972): 91–99.

"Three Yeats' Plays." *Irish Press* (18 July 1933): 8.

White, James. *Jack B. Yeats: Drawings and Paintings.* London: Secker and Warburg, 1971.

White, Terence de Vere. "The Personality of Jack B. Yeats." *Jack B. Yeats: A Centenary Gathering.* Ed. Roger McHugh. Dublin: Dolmen, 1971. 22–50.

Yeats, Anne. "Jack Yeats." *Yeats Studies* 2 (1972): 1–5.

William Butler Yeats
(1865–1939)

JAMES FISHER

William Butler Yeats was born near Dublin on 13 June 1865, son of the painter
John Butler Yeats and Susan Pollexfen. A sickly and shy child, Yeats was
particularly fond of the Irish countryside of County Sligo, where both of his
parents had been born. In 1874, Yeats and his family (including his siblings)
moved to London, where they remained for six years. Yeats was unhappy out
of Ireland, and he did poorly at the Godolphin School in Hammersmith, which
he attended before the family returned to Dublin.

Following the completion of his secondary education, Yeats began to write
poetry before enrolling in the Metropolitan Art School in 1883, which he attended for three years with the intention of following in his father's footsteps.
During these years, he was drawn to mysticism and the occult (partly as a
response to his own confused religious upbringing and partly as a result of his
first participation in a séance in 1886), and he also became passionately interested in Irish politics through his acquaintanceship with John O'Leary, leader
of the Fenian movement. In 1887, Yeats' family returned to London, where he
involved himself in a number of intellectual societies, as well as the burgeoning
literary community, befriending such artists as Oscar Wilde, Aubrey Beardsley,
and William Morris. He was most drawn to the French symbolist writers, and,
during the late 1880s, he began publishing his own poetry. When he met actress
Maud Gonne in 1888, he fell in love with her, and although she refused his
repeated proposals of marriage, she was a significant force in his evolving interest in the theater.

Although his enduring fame during his own life and since has been for his
poetry, Yeats' plays and his theatrical work are significant. He wrote his first
play, *The Countess Cathleen*, around 1889, but his first major step was its subsequent production as the inaugural presentation of the Irish Literary Theatre,

which Yeats cofounded in 1899 with Lady Augusta Gregory, George Moore, and Edward Martyn. This group evolved into the Irish National Theatre in 1902 and finally settled into a permanent home as the Abbey Theatre in 1904. While continuing to write poetry and other literary works, Yeats remained active as a playwright and theater manager until his death.

In 1915, Yeats refused a knighthood, and the following year he again proposed marriage to Maud Gonne and was refused. Yeats finally married Georgina Hyde-Lees, twenty-six years his junior, in 1917, and they subsequently had two children. Following the Irish civil war, Yeats accepted an appointment to the Senate of the Irish Free State. In 1923, he received the Nobel Prize in literature, but chronic ill health slowed his pace during the last two decades of his life, despite the fact that he produced many of what are now acknowledged as his finest works during this era. He made numerous tours of the United States and Europe before his death on 28 January 1939 in the South of France. Yeats was subsequently buried in Drumcliff, near his beloved Sligo.

Selected Biographical Sources: Armstrong; Bloom; Clarke [3]; Donoghue [3]; Ellmann [4].

MAJOR PLAYS, PREMIERES, AND SIGNIFICANT REVIVALS: THEATRICAL RECEPTION

The Countess Cathleen. Written ca. 1889, published 1892. Produced at the Ancient Concert Rooms (Dublin), 8 May 1899.

This earliest of Yeats' plays is set during the Irish Famine. The good Countess Cathleen sells off her castles and property in order to feed the hungry, but demons roam the land disguised as merchants attempting to buy souls to send to perdition. Many of the poor sell their souls for food, but Cathleen offers herself in place of those who have gone before. She dies of grief for her own lost soul, but because her motives were pure, she is permitted to enter heaven. Yeats himself described this early work as "ill-constructed, the dialogue turning aside at the lure of word or metaphor" (Jeffares and Knowland [1]), and Nathan has written that Yeats seemed "willing to compromise the supernatural reality that he took seriously in theory. Perhaps he feared the consequences of an unqualified challenge to orthodoxy." However, noting that the themes of the play are "extremely difficult to unravel," Flannery [2] has explained that it vividly "represents the perennial Yeatsian conflict of dreams versus human responsibility" that would be explored in greater depth in Yeats' later dramatic works.

The Land of Heart's Desire. Written 1894, published 1894. Produced at the Avenue Theatre, London, 29 March 1894; Abbey Theatre, Dublin, 16 February 1911.

This one-act verse play involves a newly wed peasant woman, Mary Bruin, who longs to escape the mundane reality of everyday life by reading Celtic mythology. She is enchanted by the legends of the Sidhe ("Faery Folk"), who suggest a land of wild imagination and freedom she seeks; she begins to think of their world as "the land of heart's desire." Increasingly dissatisfied with reality, Mary calls to the faeries to save her. A Faery Child appears, beckoning to her, and despite the protests of her parents and husband, Mary goes to her demise, hoping to be liberated by death. The play was first presented in London on a bill with George Bernard Shaw's *Arms and the Man*. Although Yeats was ultimately embarrassed by this early play's sentimentality, *The Land of Heart's Desire* became one of his most consistently produced works throughout the first half of the twentieth century, for the "characteristic and dramatically unassimilated lyricism dominates the tone of the play" (Nathan), and Flannery [2] believes that in this work, and Yeats' other plays of this period, he deliberately "intended to manifest the influence of the invisible upon the visible world and thus reawaken Ireland's sense of her ancient holiness."

Cathleen Ni Houlihan. (with Lady Augusta Gregory). Written 1901, published 1902. Produced at St. Teresa's Hall, Dublin, 2 April 1902.

A verse drama and easily the most nationalistic of all of Yeats' plays, *Cathleen Ni Houlihan* tells the tale of an elderly woman representing the eternal spirit of Ireland. She arrives at the house of a peasant family in the midst of hectic preparations for the marriage of their eldest son, Michael. Cathleen bemoans the loss of her lush lands and properties and protests the fact that mysterious strangers have arrived to occupy her house. After she departs, neighbors appear with the news that the French have entered the town's harbor and are enlisting young men to assist them in fighting the English. The words of old Cathleen come again to Michael, who abandons his fiancée and rushes off to join up. Nathan has written that *Cathleen Ni Houlihan* "exhibits a clarity of motive that strengthens the conflict and makes the play effective, if not profound, drama," while Flannery [2] has emphasized its relation to contemporary Irish politics, noting that the play "became one of the sacred works of the Sinn Fein and Republican movements."

The Hour-Glass. (with Lady Augusta Gregory). First version in prose written 1902, published 1914. Produced at the Molesworth Hall, Dublin, 14 March 1903. Second version in verse written 1903, published 1913. Produced at the Abbey Theatre, Dublin, 1912.

Based on an Irish folktale that subsequently became Lady Wilde's story "The Priest's Soul," *The Hour-Glass* tells of a clever priest who denies the existence of the soul, heaven, purgatory, and hell. After the visit of an angel who offers him a choice of a joyful one hundred-year life to be followed by eternity in hell or twenty-four hours of agonizing life after which he will be cast into purgatory, the priest discovers belief and faith with the help of a mysterious child who convinces him of the life of the soul. The priest recants his blasphemy and asks the child to kill him before his pupils so that they may watch his soul escape. Yeats worked on, and changed, this play periodically from 1902 to 1922, and Flannery [2] has explained that "the poetic version of *The Hour-Glass* is far more actable than the previous prose versions. This is accomplished by means of a number of precise and imaginative histrionic actions that enrich the characterizations and lend a much deeper theatrical verisimilitude to the whole play.''

On Baile's Strand. Written 1903, published 1905. Produced at the Abbey Theatre, Dublin, 27 December 1904.

In this first of Yeats' tragedies involving the Irish hero Cuchulain, *On Baile's Strand* owes much to the traditions of classical tragedy. It concerns an anonymous young man from the lands belonging to Aoife (a warrior queen loved and subsequently rejected by Cuchulain long before), who challenges Cuchulain to a fight. Cuchulain refuses and offers instead to befriend the young man, who seems familiar to him. King Conchubar orders the two to fight, and Cuchulain kills the young man. When he discovers to his horror that the young man was his own son by Aiofe, Cuchulain rushes into the sea to drown himself. This central plot is set in counterpoint to the relationship of a Fool and a Blind Man, which, according to John Rees Moore [2], ''mirrors in a distorting glass the bonds linking Conchubar and Cuchulain. The two worlds intersect and the Fool and the Blind Man enter directly into the action.'' Nathan has written that with this play, Yeats came to ''realize in his experience with stage production that the dramatic form depended for life on vital action and vivid characterization.''

Deirdre. (with Lady Augusta Gregory). Written 1904–1907, published 1907. Produced at the Abbey Theatre, Dublin, 24 November 1906.

This one-act verse tragedy concerns the last day in the life of Deirdre, a well-known character from Celtic myth similar to Helen of Troy. A chorus of two musicians relates several years of events leading up to the return of Deirdre and her lover, Naoise, to the court of King Conchubar, who has apparently forgiven Deirdre, his onetime intended bride, for leaving his court with Naoise. Before long, the lovers discover that they have been betrayed by Conchubar, and they play a game of chess, waiting for him to wreak his revenge. Conchubar, who wants Deirdre to return to him, catches Naoise in a net and kills him. But Conchubar is foiled when Deirdre serenely stabs herself to death as the citizenry proclaims the impending demise of Conchubar's kingdom. John Rees Moore [2] has written that Yeats attempted ''to lift out of its place in legend a heroic climax, give it a Yeatsian gloss, and return it brighter and more beautiful than it was before.''

At the Hawk's Well. Written 1916, published 1917. Produced at Lady Gregory's drawing room, London, 2 April 1916.

In his youth, Cuchulain journeys to a well that is reputed to offer eternal life, but he learns from an old man, who has come on a similar journey, that the dry well will fill with the life-giving water only when the hawk-woman guarding it dances. However, if one looks upon her as she dances, the gazer will be rendered helpless. The hawk-woman dances her enchanting dance, and Cuchulain looks and falls under her spell. When the spell wears off, he discovers that the well is dry again. Undaunted, Cuchulain departs to face life's challenges, with his spear slung over his shoulder. The influence of Yeats' interest in the Japanese Noh theater is vividly evident in this play, which, as Taylor [1] has noted, employed "the strangeness of the costumed characters and ritualistic action" typical of the Noh style, creating a play that is "amazingly forceful and effective" and, as Nathan has stated, revealing "a fairly wide range of human feeling."

The Only Jealousy of Emer. Written 1916, published 1919. Produced in Amsterdam, 1922.

In this Cuchulain play, Yeats depicts the hero on his deathbed, where he is tended by his wife, Emer. She summons Cuchulain's mistress, Eithne Inguba, in hopes that a kiss from her will rouse him. Instead, the kiss brings forth the god of discord inhabiting Cuchulain's body. The god offers to return Cuchulain to life if Emer will abandon her hope of regaining Cuchulain's love. She refuses, and the god offers a vision of Cuchulain's spirit being tempted by inhuman love. Emer finally renounces her hopes, and Cuchulain springs back to life, calling for Eithne Inguba. John Rees Moore [2] has argued that in this play Yeats continued to pursue a dominant theme from his earlier plays, such as *The Countess Cathleen* and *The Land of Heart's Desire*: "Man would like to seize the moment of most perfect beauty, pleasure, peace and forget his heartache, but he is bound to the wheel of life and cannot stop its turning," and Flannery [2] has found it "one of Yeats's most deeply moving plays."

Calvary. Written ca. 1920, published 1921.

Yeats' vision of the events involving Christ on Good Friday include Lazarus protesting Christ's intervention, which has robbed him of death's sleep, and Judas bragging that he has slain Omnipotence in an exercise of his free will. As Christ goes to the Cross, his guards throw dice in hopes of winning his robe. In despair, Christ calls to God, wondering, "Why has Thou forsaken me?" By showing a Christ "riven with terror and spiritual loneliness at the thought that His sacrifice for mankind was meaningless" (Flannery [2]), *Calvary* reflects the increasingly bleak resonances of Yeats' later plays.

The King of the Great Clock Tower. First version in prose written 1933, published 1934. Produced at the Abbey Theatre, Dublin, 30 July 1934. Second version in verse written 1934, published 1935.

A wandering poet arrives at the King's court and claims that the gods have proclaimed that the King's bride, whose background is veiled in mystery and whom the poet has praised in his poetry, must dance for him and that he is to sing while she dances. In a furiously jealous response, the King has the poet decapitated. However, the poet's severed head sings to the Queen's dance, and the King falls to his knees in awe. In this play, as in *A Full Moon in March*, Yeats is experimenting, as John Rees Moore [2] has written, with "a kind of drama that 'purifies' character into symbol, transforms scene into emblem, and condenses action into epiphany.'' Flannery [2] states that as ''Yeats's own life continued to unfold, his expression of tragic ecstasy became increasingly harsh, astringent, and violent,'' beginning with *The King of the Great Clock Tower.*

A Full Moon in March. Written 1934, published 1935.

This one-act verse play, one of Yeats' ''Plays for Dancers,'' is based on a Celtic legend involving an Irish queen and her beheaded peasant lover. It is clearly inspired by Yeats' interest in Japanese Noh theater and the story of Salomé. The Noh influence is seen particularly in the play's ritualistic style and symbolic use of gesture and dance. Wooed by a Swineherd poet, the Queen is insulted and orders the would-be suitor beheaded. Before the execution, the Swineherd tells the Queen that a drop of his blood will enter her womb and impregnate her with his child. Following the beheading, the Queen dances in adoration of the severed head and kisses it, and beneath a unifying full moon, the Queen and the Swineherd are symbolically reunited in a vision of sacred and profane love. In this play, as John Rees Moore [2] has explained, everything is ''fable and song; the irrelevant humors of the outside world are strictly excluded. Everything is mythical; nothing historical or 'real.' ''

Purgatory. Written 1938, published 1939. Produced at the Abbey Theatre, Dublin, 10 August 1938.

This highly symbolic one-act verse play involves an old man and his son. They come upon the ruins of a mansion where, years before, as the old man explains, his upper-class mother lived with her drunkard husband, a stable hand, until she suffered and died while giving him birth. The husband then squandered her fortune, abused his son, and, in a drunken fit, burned the mansion to the ground. While the house burned, the son murdered his father and fled. The tragedy is relived by the spirits of the old man's parents, and, as the story ends, the old man kills his son to prevent him from repeating the sins of his wastrel grandfather. However, he realizes that his act has failed to end his mother's eternal suffering. John Rees Moore [2] felt that in this play Yeats went further ''in the direction of unredeemed and apparently unredeemable blackness'' than in any of his other works.

ADDITIONAL PLAYS, ADAPTATIONS, AND PRODUCTIONS

With Lady Augusta Gregory, Yeats also wrote *Where There Is Nothing* (also with Douglas Hyde; 1902), *The Pot of Broth* (1902), *The King's Threshold* (1903), *King Oedipus* (an adaptation of Sophocles' *Oedipus the King,* 1905), and *The Unicorn from the Stars* (1907). Another adaptation from Sophocles, *Oedipus at Colonus* (1927), furthered Yeats' interest in classical tragedy, and he adapted his own prose drama, *The Golden Helmet* (1907), under the title *The Green Helmet* (1909). His remaining plays include *The Shadowy Water* (1894– 1906), *The Player Queen* (ca. 1908), *The Dreaming of the Bones* (1917), *The*

Cat and the Moon (ca. 1917), *The Resurrection* (1927), *Fighting the Waves* (1927), *The Words upon the Window-Pane* (1930), *The Herne's Egg* (1937), and *The Death of Cuchulain* (1938).

ASSESSMENT OF YEATS' CAREER

Although it is possible to believe that Yeats' theatrical work, at least in its earliest phases, was inspired mostly by his fervor to awaken Irish pride in their literary and theatrical heritage, it is also possible to view him as a true theatrical reformer promoting poetic drama and symbolic staging techniques. His dramatic output was only a part of his vast achievement as a writer, but the power and influence of his plays have been profound. Written in the 1890s, Yeats' earliest plays, *The Countess Cathleen* (1889), *The Land of Heart's Desire* (1894), and *Cathleen Ni Houlihan* (1901), were particularly nationalistic, but after the establishment of the Abbey Theatre, he wrote *The King's Threshold* (1903), a highly personal drama concerning a poet who gives his life to secure a higher place for poets in society. Seeking a style that would illuminate the emotions and yearnings of the soul instead of merely offering a naturalistic portrait of real life, Yeats looked for inspiration toward the work of some contemporary theatrical innovators. In 1902, Yeats saw one of Edward Gordon Craig's early productions in London. He recognized that within Craig's simple, highly evocative, nonrealistic stage settings, lighting techniques, and staging touches existed the visual manifestations of what he himself was attempting to do with the drama. He became a champion of Craig's work and other forms of theater and drama, particularly classical tragedy and other ritualized forms featuring symbolic elements and poetic language. Ultimately, Yeats was most significantly influenced by the traditions of the Japanese Noh theater, which he first discovered through translations by Ernest Fenollosa and Ezra Pound in 1916. His appreciation of the systemized gestures and symbolic techniques of Noh had profound impact on his post–World War I plays, which he labeled "plays for dancers." Utilizing masks, choruses, and dancers accompanied by music produced by string and percussion instruments, Yeats' later plays, *The Dreaming of the Bones* (1917), *The Cat and the Moon* (ca. 1917), *Calvary* (ca. 1920), *The Resurrection* (1927), *The King of the Great Clock Tower* (1933), and *A Full Moon in March* (1934), often focused on supernatural and religious themes and were intended for small audiences in intimate settings. Also among his most important dramatic achievements was a cycle of five plays, *On Baile's Strand* (1903), *The Golden Helmet* (1908; revised as *The Green Helmet* in 1910), *At the Hawk's Well* (1917), *The Only Jealousy of Emer* (1919), and *The Death of Cuchulain* (1939), all concerning the life of the legendary Irish folk hero Cuchulain.

ARCHIVAL SOURCES

Bibliothèque Nationale; National Library of Ireland; Trinity College; the Yeats family.

PRIMARY BIBLIOGRAPHY

Plays

(There are many reprintings of Yeats' plays; only the first-known editions are listed.)

Cathleen Ni Houlihan. London: A. H. Bullen, 1902.

The Countess Cathleen. London: T. Fisher Unwin, 1892.

The Death of Cuchalain. Dublin: Cuala Press, 1938.

Deirdre. London: A. H. Bullen, 1907.

A Full Moon in March. London: Macmillan, 1935.

The Green Helmet. Churchtown, Dundrum: Cuala Press, 1910.

The Herne's Egg. London: Macmillan, 1938.

The Hour-Glass. London: Heineman, 1903.

The King of the Great Clock Tower. Dublin: Cuala Press, 1934.

The King's Threshold. New York: "Printed for Private Circulation," 1904.

The Land of Heart's Desire. London: T. Fisher Unwin, 1894.

On Baile's Strand. Dublin: Maunsel, 1905.

The Player Queen. London: Macmillan, 1922.

The Pot of Broth. London: A. H. Bullen, 1905.

Purgatory. Dublin: Cuala Press, 1938.

The Shadowy Waters. London: Hodder and Stoughton, 1900.

Sophocles's King Oedipus. London: Macmillan, 1928.

Where There Is Nothing. The United Irishman (1 November 1902).

The Words upon the Window Pane. Dublin: Cuala Press, 1934.

Anthologies

(There are many reprintings of Yeats' plays in anthologies; only the first-known editions are listed.)

The Cat and the Moon and Certain Poems. Dublin: Cuala Press, 1924.

The Collected Plays of W. B. Yeats. London: Macmillan, 1934.

The Collected Plays of W. B. Yeats: New Edition with Five Additional Plays. London: Macmillan, 1952.

The Collected Works in Verse and Prose of William Butler Yeats. Stratford-on-Avon: A. H. Bullen, 1908.

Four Plays for Dancers. London and New York: Macmillan, 1921.

The Green Helmet and Other Poems. Churchtown, Dundrum: Cuala Press, 1910.

The Herne's Egg and Other Plays. New York: Macmillan, 1938.

The Hour-Glass and Other Plays. New York and London: Macmillan, 1904.

The King's Threshold and On Baile's Strand. London: A. H. Bullen, 1904.

Last Poems and Two Plays. Dublin: Cuala Press, 1939.

Later Poems. London: Macmillan, 1922.

Nine One-Act Plays. London: Macmillan, 1937.

Plays and Controversies. London:Macmillan, 1923.

Plays for an Irish Theatre. London: A. H. Bullen, 1904.

Plays in Prose and Verse. London: Macmillan, 1922.

The Poetical Works of William B. Yeats. New York and London: Macmillan, 1912.

Responsibilities and Other Poems. London: Macmillan, 1916.

Responsibilities: Poems and a Play. Churchtown, Dundrum: Cuala Press, 1914.
Seven Poems and a Fragment. Churchtown, Dundrum: Cuala Press, 1922.
Two Plays for Dancers. Churchtown, Dundrum: Cuala Press, 1919.
The Unicorn from the Stars and Other Plays by William B. Yeats and Lady Gregory.
    New York: Macmillan, 1908.
The Variorum Edition of the Plays of W. B. Yeats. Ed. Russell K. and Catherine C.
    Alspach. New York: Macmillan, 1957.

SECONDARY BIBLIOGRAPHY

Anon. [1]. "Memorable First Night." [Review of the Abbey Theatre productions of *The
    Resurrection* and *The King of the Great Clock Tower*]. *Sunday Times* (5 Aug.
    1934): 5.
————. [2]. "Mr. Yeats at the Abbey Theatre." *Irish Times* (9 September 1911): 8.
Archibald, Douglas. *Yeats*. Syracuse, N.Y.: Syracuse University Press, 1983.
Armstrong, Gordon. *Samuel Beckett, W. B. Yeats, and Jack Yeats. Images and Words*.
    Cranbury, N.J.: Bucknell University Press, 1990.
Barnes, T. R. "Yeats, Synge, Ibsen and Strindberg." *Scrutiny* 5 (Dec. 1936): 257–62.
Becker, William. "The Mask Mocked: Or, Farce and the Dialectic of Self (Notes on
    Yeats's *The Player Queen*." *Sewanee Review* 59 (1953): 82–108.
Beerbohm, Max. "Some Irish Plays and Players." *Saturday Review* 97 (9 Apr., 1904):
    455–57.
Bentley, Eric [1]. "On Staging Yeats's Plays." *New Republic* 120.8 (15 June, 1953):
    17–18.
————. [2]. "Yeats as a Playwright." *Kenyon Review* 10.2 (Spring 1948): 196–208.
Bertha, Csilla. *A Drámairo Yeats*. Budapest: Akadémiai kiadó, 1988.
Bjersby, Birgit. *The Interpretation of the Cuchulain Legend in the Works of W. B. Yeats*.
    Uppsala: Lundequistska Bokhandeln; Copenhagen: Monksgaard; Dublin: Hodges,
    Figgis, 1950.
Block, Haskell M. "Yeats's *The King's Threshold*: The Poet and Society." *Philological
    Quarterly* 34 (1955): 206–18.
Bloom, Harold. *Yeats*. New York: Oxford University Press, 1970.
Bottomley, G. "His Legacy to the Theatre." *Arrow* (Summer 1939): 11–14.
Boyd, Ernest A. [1]. *Contemporary Drama of Ireland*. Dublin: Talbot Press, 1915; Bos-
    ton: Little, Brown, 1917.
————. [2]. *Ireland's Literary Renaissance*. New York: Alfred A. Knopf, 1922.
Bradford, Curtis B. *Yeats at Work*. Carbondale and Edwardsville: Southern Illinois Uni-
    versity Press, 1965.
Bushrui, Suheil. *Yeats's Verse Plays: The Revisions 1900–10*. New York: Oxford Uni-
    versity Press, 1965.
Bushrui, Suheil B., and D. E. S. Maxwell, eds. *W. B. Yeats: Centenary Papers on the
    Art of W. B. Yeats*. Ibadan, Nigeria: Ibadan University Press and London: Nelson,
    1965.
Byrne, Dawson. *The Story of Ireland's National Theatre*. Dublin: Talbot Press, 1929.
C. P. C. "Dramatic Notes: Oedipus at the Abbey." *Irish Statesman* (11 Dec., 1926): 326.
Cardullo, Bert. "Notes toward a Production of W. B. Yeats's 'The Countess Cathleen.' "
    CJIS 11.2 (1985): 49–67.

Carpenter, Andrew. *The Dramatic Imagination of W. B. Yeats*. Dublin: Gill and Macmillan, 1978.

Clarke, David R. [1]. "*Nishikigi* and Yeats's *The Dreaming of the Bones*." *Modern Drama* 7 (May 1964): 111–25.

Clarke, David R., and George P. Mayhew. [2]. *A Tower of Polished Black Stones: Early Version of "The Shadowy Waters."* Dublin: Dolmen Press, 1971.

———. [3]. *W. B. Yeats and the Theatre of Desolate Reality*. Dublin: Dolmen Press, 1965.

———. [4]. "Yeats and the Modern Theatre." *Threshold* 4 (Autumn–Winter 1960): 35–56.

Colbert, Judith A. "Masks of Ben Jonson in W. B. Yeats's 'The Green Helmet' and 'Responsibilities.' " *CJIS* 7.1 (1981): 32–48.

Colum, Padraic. "Poet's Progress: W. B. Yeats in the Theatre." *Theatre Arts Monthly* 19 (Dec. 1935): 936–43.

Courtney, Marie-Thérèse. *Edward Martyn and the Irish Theatre*. New York: Vantage Press, 1957.

Craig, Gordon. "Is Poetic Drama Born Again?" *Mask* 5 (1912–1913): 291.

Domville, Eric, ed. *A Concordance to the Plays of W. B. Yeats*. Ithaca, N.Y.: Cornell University Press, 1973.

Donoghue, Dennis, and J. R. Mulryne, eds. [1]. *An Honoured Guest: New Essays on W. B. Yeats*. London: Edward Arnold, 1965.

———. [2]. *The Integrity of Yeats*. Cork: Mercier Press, 1964.

———. [3]. *William Butler Yeats*. New York: Viking Press, 1971.

———. [4]. "Yeats and the Clean Outline." *Sewanee Review* 65 (Spring 1957): 202–25.

Dorn, Karen. *Players and Painted Stage. The Theatre of W. B. Yeats*. Totowa, N.J.: Barnes and Noble, 1984.

Ellis-Fermor, Una Mary. *The Irish Dramatic Movement*. London: Methuen, 1939, 1954.

Ellmann, Richard. [1]. *Eminent Domain: Yeats among Wilde, Joyce, Pound, Eliot, and Auden*. New York: Oxford University Press, 1967.

———. [2]. *Golden Codgers: Biographical Speculations*. New York: Oxford University Press, 1973.

———. [3]. *The Identity of Yeats*. London: Macmillan, 1954; New York: Oxford University Press, 1964.

———. [4]. *Yeats: The Man and the Masks*. New York: Macmillan, 1948; W. W. Norton, 1979.

Engelberg, Edward [1]. "Picture and Gesture in the Yeatsian Aesthetic." *Criticism* 3 (Spring 1961): 101–20.

———. [2]. *The Vast Design: Patterns in W. B. Yeats's Aesthetics*. Toronto: University of Toronto Press, 1964.

Fay, Gerard. *The Abbey Theatre: Cradle of Genius*. New York: Macmillan, 1958.

Flannery, James W. [1]. *Annie F. Horniman and the Abbey Theatre*. Dublin: Dolmen Press, 1970.

———. [2]. *W. B. Yeats and the Idea of a Theatre: The Early Abbey Theatre in Theory and Practice*. New Haven, Conn.: Yale University Press, 1976.

Frazier, Adrian. *Behind the Scenes. Yeats, Horniman, and the Struggle for the Abbey Theatre*. Berkeley: University of California Press, 1990.

Friedman, Barton R. *Adventures in the Deeps of the Mind: The Cuchulain Cycle of W. B. Yeats*. Princeton, N.J.: Princeton University Press, 1977.

Good, Maeve. *W. B. Yeats and the Creation of a Tragic Universe*. Totowa, N.J.: Barnes and Noble, 1987.

Gose, Elliott B., Jr. "The Lyric and the Philosophic in Yeats's *Calvary*." *Modern Drama* 2 (February 1960): 370–76.

Gould, Warwick. "W. B. Yeats's Dramatic Imagination." *Themes in Drama* 3 (1981): 203–21.

Gray, Terence. *Dance Drama: Experiments in the Art of the Theatre*. Cambridge: Cambridge University Press, 1926.

Gregory, Lady. *Our Irish Theatre*. New York: G. P. Putnam's Sons, 1914.

Gwynn, Denis. *Edward Martyn and the Irish Revival*. London: Cape, 1930.

Gwynn, Stephen. [1]. *Irish Literature and Drama in the English Language*. London: Nelson, 1936.

———. [2]. "Poetry and the Stage." *Fortnightly Review* 85. 506 (Feb. 1909): 337–51.

———, ed. [3]. *Scattering Branches: Tributes to the Memory of W. B. Yeats*. New York: Macmillan, 1940.

Harper, George. *Yeats's Golden Dawn*. London: Macmillan, 1974.

Hayes, J. J. "The Irish Scene." *Theatre Arts Monthly* (Nov. 1932): 922–26.

Henn, T. R. "Yeats and the Theatre." *Studies in the Arts*. Ed. Francis Warner. Oxford: Basil Blackwell 1968. 62–81.

Hoare, Dorothy M. *The Works of Morris and of Yeats in Relation to Early Saga Literature*. Cambridge: Cambridge University Press, 1937.

Hone, Joseph M., ed. [1] *J. B. Yeats' Letters to His Son*. London: Faber and Faber, 1944.

———. [2]. *The Life of W. B. Yeats, 1865–1939*. New York: Macmillan, 1943.

———. [3]. *W. B. Yeats, 1865–1939*. London: Macmillan, 1967.

Hunt, Hugh. *The Abbey: Ireland's National Theatre, 1904–1978*. New York: Columbia University Press, 1979.

Ishibashi, Hiro. *Yeats and the Noh: Types of Japanese Beauty and Their Reflection in Yeats's Plays*. Ed. Anthony Kerrigan. Sligo: Dolmen Press, 1966.

Jeffares, A. Norman, and A. S. Knowland. [1]. *A Commentary on the Collected Plays of W. B. Yeats*. Stanford, Calif.: Stanford University Press, 1975.

———. [2]. *In Excited Reverie; A Centenary Tribute to William Butler Yeats*. New York: Macmillan, 1965.

———. [3]. *A Poet and a Theatre*. Groningen: Wolters, 1946.

———. [4]. *W. B. Yeats*. New York: Humanities Press, 1949.

———. [5]. *W. B. Yeats. A New Biography*. New York: Farrar, Straus & Giroux, 1988.

———. [6]. *W. B. Yeats: The Critical Heritage*. London: Routledge and Kegan Paul, 1977.

———. [7]. *Yeats, Sligo and Ireland*. Totowa, N.J.: Barnes and Noble, 1976, 1980.

Kavanaugh, Peter. *The Story of the Abbey Theatre, from Its Origins in 1899 to the Present*. New York: Devin-Adair, 1950.

Kermode, John Frank. *The Romantic Image*. London: Routledge and Kegan Paul, 1957.

Knapp, Bettina. "A Jungian Reading of William Butler Yeats's 'At the Hawk's Well'— An Integrated Anima Shapes a Hero's Destiny." *Etudes Irlandaises* 8 (1983): 121–38.

Knowland, A. S. *W. B. Yeats, Dramatist of Vision*. Gerrards Cross, Buckinghamshire: Colin Smythe; Totowa, N.J.: Barnes and Noble, 1986.

Koritz, Amy. "Women Dancing: The Structure of Gender in Yeats's Early Plays for Dancers." *Modern Drama* 32.3 (September 1989): 387–401.

Lapisardi, Fred. "The Redemption of W. B. Yeats." *American Theatre* 9.4 (July–Aug. 1992): 52–55.

Levine, Herbert J. "The Inner Drama of Yeats's 'Four Plays for Dancers.' " *Comparative Literature Quarterly* 16 (1980): 5–18.

Lucas, F. L. *The Drama of Chekhov, Synge, Yeats, and Pirandello*. London: Cassell, 1963.

Mac Liammóir, Micheál. *The Theatre in Ireland*. Dublin: Cultural Relations Committee of Ireland, 1964.

MacNamara, B. *Abbey Plays: 1899–1948*. Dublin: At the Sign of the Three Candles, 1949.

MacNeice, Louis. "Yeats's Epitaph." *New Republic* 102. 26 (24 June 1940): 862–63.

Malone, A. E. *The Irish Drama, 1896–1928*. London: Constable, 1929.

Marcus, Phillip L. *Yeats and the Beginning of the Irish Renaissance*. Ithaca, N.Y.: Cornell University Press, 1970.

Martin, Heather. [1]. "Of Blood and Fire: A Study of 'The Player Queen.' " *CJIS* 7.1 (1981): 49–60.

———. [2]. *W. B. Yeats: Metaphysician as Dramatist*. Waterloo, Ontario, Canada: Wilfrid Laurier University Press, 1986.

McCann, Sean, ed. *The Story of the Abbey Theatre*. London: Four Square Books, 1967.

McCully, Karin. "Reinventing Yeats." *Theater* 23. 1 (Winter 1992): 46–49.

McGreevy, Thomas H. "Mr. W. B. Yeats as a Dramatist." *Revue Anglo-Américaine* 7 (1929–1930): 19–36.

McHugh, Roger, ed. *Ah, Sweet Dancer*. New York: Macmillan, 1970.

Miller, Liam, ed. [1]. *The Dolmen Press Yeats Centenary Papers 1965*. Dublin: Dolmen Press, 1968.

———. [2]. *The Noble Drama of W. B. Yeats*. Dublin: Dolmen Press, 1977.

———. [3]. "W. B. Yeats and Stage Design at the Abbey Theatre." *Malahat Review* 16 (1970): 50–64.

Mills, John G. "W. B. Yeats and Noh." *Japan Quarterly* 2 (1955): 496–500.

Miner, Earl. "A Poem by Swift and W. B. Yeats's *Words upon the Window-Pane*." *Modern Language Notes* 72 (Apr. 1957): 273–75.

Moore, George. *Hail and Farewell*. Vol. 1. London: William Heineman, 1911.

Moore, Gerald. "The 'No' and the Dance Plays of W. B. Yeats." *Japan Quarterly* 7 (Apr.–June 1960): 177–87.

Moore, John Rees. [1]. "Cuchulain, Christ, and the Queen of Love: Aspects of Yeatsian Drama." *Tulane Drama Review* 6 (Mar. 1962): 150–59.

———. [2]. *Masks of Love and Death*. Ithaca, N.Y.: Cornell University Press, 1971.

Myles, Ashley E. *Theatre of Aristocracy: A Study of W. B. Yeats as a Dramatist*. Salzburg: Institut für Anglistik und Amerikanistik, Salzburg University, 1981.

Nathan, Leonard. *The Tragic Drama of William Butler Yeats: Figures in a Dance*. New York: Columbia University Press, 1965.

Nelick, Frank C. "Yeats, Bullen, and the Irish Drama." *Modern Drama* 1 (Dec. 1958): 196–202.

Newton, Norman. "Yeats as Dramatist: *The Player Queen*." *Essays in Criticism* 8 (July 1958): 269–84.

"O'Connor, Frank" (Michael O'Donovan). "A Lyric Voice in the Irish Theatre." *New York Times Book Review* (31 May 1953): 1, 16.

O'Driscoll, Robert, and Lorna Reynolds, eds. *Yeats and the Theatre*. Niagara Falls, New York: Maclean-Hunter Press, 1975.

Oppel, Frances Nesbitt. *Mask and Tragedy: Yeats and Nietzsche, 1902–1910*. Charlottesville, Va.: University Press of Virginia, 1987.

Orel, Harold. "Dramatic Values, Yeats, and *The Countess Cathleen*." *Papers of the Bibliographical Society of America* 56 (First Quarter, 1962): 79–103.

Oshima, Shotaro. [1]. "Yeats and Michio Ito." *Annual Report of the Yeats Society of Japan* 6 (1971): 15–20.

———. [2]. *W. B. Yeats and Japan*. Tokyo: Hokuseido Press; London: Luzac, 1965.

Parkin, Andrew [1]. *The Dramatic Imagination of W. B. Yeats*. Dublin: Gill and Macmillan; New York: Barnes and Noble, 1978.

———. [2]. "Women in the Plays of W. B. Yeats." *CJIS*, 8.2 (1983): 38–57.

Parkinson, Thomas. [1]. "W. B. Yeats: A Poet's Stagecraft, 1899–1911. *ELH* 17 (1950): 136–61.

———. [2]. *W. B. Yeats: Self-Critic*. Berkeley and Los Angeles: University of California Press, 1951.

Patterson, Gertrude. "W. B. Yeats in the Theatre: The Challenge of the Poetic Play." *Threshold* 31 (1980): 17–30.

Peacock, Ronald. *The Poet in the Theatre*. New York: Harcourt Brace, 1946; Hill and Wang, 1960.

Pearce, Donald R. [1]. "Philosophy and Phantasy: Notes on the Growth of Yeats's 'System.' " *University of Kansas Review* 18 (Spring 1952): 169–80.

———. [2]. "Yeats' Last Plays: An Interpretation." *ELH* 18 (Mar. 1951): 67–76.

Pitkin, William. "Stage Designs, Masks and Costumes for Plays of W. B. Yeats." *Bard Review* (Apr. 1949): 93–110.

Popkin, Henry. "Yeats as Dramatist." *Tulane Drama Review* 3 (Mar. 1959): 73–82.

Pritchard, William H., ed. *W. B. Yeats: A Critical Anthology*. Middlesex: Penguin, 1972.

Qamber, Akhtar. *Yeats and the Noh, with Two Plays for Dancers by Yeats and Two Noh Plays*. New York: Weatherhill, 1974.

Raine, Kathleen Jessie. [1]. "Death-in-Life and Life-in-Death: 'Cuchulain Comforted' and 'News for the Delphic Oracle.' " *New Yeats Papers VIII*. Dublin: Dolmen Press, 1974.

———. [2]. *Yeats, the Tarot, and the Golden Dawn*. Dublin: Dolmen Press, 1972.

Rajan, Balachandra. *W. B. Yeats, A Critical Introduction*. London: Hutchinson University Library, 1965.

Reid, Benjamin Lawrence. *William Butler Yeats, the Lyric of Tragedy*. Norman: University of Oklahoma Press, 1961.

Reid, Forrest. *W. B. Yeats: A Critical Study*. London: M. Secker, 1915.

Reinert, Otto. "Yeats's *The Hour-Glass*." *Explicator* 15 (1956): Item 19.

Rexroth, Kenneth. "The Plays of Yeats." *Bird in the Bush*. New York: New Directions, 1959.

Roberts, R. E. "W. B. Yeats, Dramatist." *New Statesman and Nation* 10 (2 Nov. 1935): 636–37.

Robinson, Lennox. [1]. *Ireland's Abbey Theatre: A History, 1899–1951*. London: Sidgwick and Jackson, 1951.

———, ed. [2]. *The Irish Theatre*. London: Macmillan, 1939.

————. [3]. *Lady Gregory's Journal, 1916–1930.* New York: Macmillan, 1947.

Ryan, M. Rosalie. *Symbolic Elements in the Plays of William Butler Yeats, 1892–1921.* Washington, D.C.: Catholic University of America Press, 1952.

Saddlemyer, Ann, ed. *Theatre Business: The Correspondence of the First Abbey Theatre Directors: William Butler Yeats, Lady Gregory, and J. M. Synge.* Gerrards Cross, Buckinghamshire: Colin Smythe; University Park, Pa.: Penn State University Press, 1982.

Sandberg, Anna. "The Anti-Theater of W. B. Yeats." *Modern Drama* 4 (Sept. 1961): 131–37.

Saul, George Brandon. [1]. *Prolegomena to the Study of Yeats's Plays.* Philadelphia: University of Pennsylvania Press, 1958.

————. [2]. *The Shadow of the Three Queens.* Harrisburg, Pa.: Stackpole, 1953.

Seiden, Morton Irving [1]. "W. B. Yeats as a Playwright." *Western Humanities Review* 13 (Winter 1959): 83–98.

————. [2]. *William Butler Yeats—The Poet as a Mythmaker.* East Lansing: Michigan State University Press, 1962.

Sharp, William L. "W. B. Yeats: A Poet Not in the Theatre." *Tulane Drama Review* 4 (Winter 1959): 67–82.

Sidnell, Michael J., George P. Mayhew, and David R. Clark. [1]. *Druid Craft: The Writing of "The Shadowy Waters."* Amherst: University of Massachusetts Press, 1971.

————. [2]. "Manuscript Versions of Yeats' *The Countess Cathleen.*" *Papers of the Bibliographical Society of America* 56 (First Quarter, 1962): 79–103.

Skelton, Robin, and Anne Saddlemyer. *The World of W. B. Yeats.* Dublin: Dolmen Press, 1965. Rev. ed., Seattle:University of Washington Press, 1967.

Skene, Reg. *The Cuchulain Plays of W. B. Yeats: A Study.* New York: Columbia University Press, 1974.

Smith, Peter Alderson. " 'The Countess Cathleen' and the Otherworld." *Éire-Ireland* 17 (Summer 1982): 141–46.

Starkie, Walter. "W. B. Yeats and the Abbey Theatre." *Southern Review,* new series 5.2 (1969): 886–921.

Staub, August W. "The 'Unpopular Theatre' of W. B. Yeats." *Quarterly Journal of Speech* 47 (Dec. 1961): 363–71.

Stucki, Yasuko. "Yeats's Drama and the Noh: A Comparative Study in Dramatic Theories." *Modern Drama* 60 (May 1966): 101–22.

Suss, Irving D. "Yeatsian Drama and the Dying Hero." *Southern Atlantic Quarterly* 54 (July 1955): 369–80.

Taylor, Richard. [1]. *The Drama of W. B. Yeats. Irish Myth and the Japanese Noh.* New Haven, Conn., and London: Yale University Press, 1976.

————. [2]. *A Reader's Guide to the Plays of W. B. Yeats.* London: Macmillan; New York: St. Martin's Press, 1984.

Thilliez, Christiane. "From One Theatrical Reformer to Another: W. B. Yeats's Unpublished Letters to Gordon Craig." *Aspects of the Irish Theatre.* Ed. Patrick Rafroidi, Raymonde Popot, and William Parker. Paris: Editions Universitaires.

Thwaite, Anthony. "Yeats and the Noh." *Twentieth Century* 162 (1959): 235–42.

Tindall, William York. *W. B. Yeats.* New York: Columbia University Press, 1966.

Torchiana, Donald T. *W. B. Yeats and Georgian Ireland.* Evanston, Ill.: Northwestern University Press, 1966.

Tsukimura, Reiko. "A Comparison of Yeats's *At the Hawk's Well* and Its Noh Version, *Take no izumi*." *Literature East and West* 11.4 (1967): 385–97.

Tuohy, Frank. *Yeats*. New York: Macmillan, 1976.

Unterecker, John. [1]. *A Reader's Guide to W. B. Yeats*. London: Thames and Hudson, 1973.

———, ed. [2]. *Yeats: A Collection of Critical Essays*. New York: Prentice-Hall, 1963.

Ure, Peter [1]. "The Evolution of Yeats's 'The Countess Cathleen.' " *Modern Language Review* 57 (Jan. 1962): 12–24.

———. [2]. *Towards a Mythology: Studies in the Poetry of W. B. Yeats*. London: Hodder and Stoughton, 1946.

———. [3]. *Yeats*. Edinburgh: Oliver and Boyd, 1963.

———. [4]. *Yeats the Playwright: A Commentary on Character and Design in the Major Plays*. New York: Barnes and Noble, 1963.

———. [5]. "Yeats's Christian Mystery Plays." *Review of English Studies*, new series, 11 (May 1960): 171–82.

———. [6]. "Yeats's 'Deirdre.' " *English Studies* 42 (Aug. 1961): 218–30.

———. [7]. "Yeats's Hero-Fool in *The Herne's Egg*." *Huntington Library Quarterly* 24 (Feb. 1961): 125–36.

Vendler, Helen Hennessey. *Yeats' Vision and the Later Plays*. Cambridge: Harvard University Press, 1963.

Weygandt, Cornelius. *Irish Plays and Playwrights*. London: Constable; Boston: Houghton Mifflin, 1913. Reprint, Port Washington, N.Y.: Kennikat Press, 1966.

Wilson, F. A. C. [1]. "Patterns in Yeats's Imagery: *The Herne's Egg*." *Modern Philology* 55 (Aug. 1957): 46–52.

———. [2]. *W. B. Yeats and Tradition*. London: Gollancz, 1958.

———. [3]. *Yeats's Iconography*. New York: Macmillan, 1960.

Wilson, Raymond J. "Delmore Schwartz and Purgatory." *Partisan Review* 57. 3 (Summer 1990): 363–71.

Worth, Katharine. *The Irish Drama of Europe from Yeats to Beckett*. Atlantic Highlands, N.J.: Humanities Press, 1978.

Yeats, Joseph Butler. *J. B. Yeats: Letters to His Son W. B. Yeats and Others, 1869–1922*. Ed. Joseph Hone. 1944. Reprint, London: Seckler and Warburg, 1983.

Zwerdling, Alan. *Yeats and the Heroic Ideal*. New York: New York University Press, 1965.

BIBLIOGRAPHIES

Cross, K. G. W., and R. T. Dunlop. *A Bibliography of Yeats Criticism, 1887–1965*. London: Macmillan, 1971.

Dougan, R. D. *Yeats: Manuscripts and Printed Books Exhibited in the Library of Trinity College Dublin*. Dublin: Printed for the Friends of the Library by C. OLochlainn, At the Sign of the Three Candles, 1956.

Gerstenberger, Donna. "Yeats and the Theatre: A Selected Bibliography." *Modern Drama* 6 (1963): 64–71.

O'Hegarty, P. "Notes on the Bibliography of Yeats." *Dublin Magazine* (Oct.–Dec. 1939, Jan.–Mar. 1940).

Roth, W. *Catalogue of English and American First Editions of Yeats*. New Haven, Conn.: Yale University Press 1939.

Symons, A.J.A. *A Bibliography of the First Editions of Books by Yeats*. London: First Edition Club, 1924.

Wade, Allan. *A Bibliography of the Writings of W. B. Yeats*. London: Rupert Hart-Davis, 1951.

Selected Bibliography

ED BALSAM

Bell, Sam Hanna. *The Theatre in Ulster: A Survey of the Dramatic Movement in Ulster from 1902 to the Present Day*. Dublin: Gill and Macmillan, 1972.

Bentley, Eric. *The Life of the Drama*. New York: Atheneum, 1967.

Bickley, Francis. *J. M. Synge and the Irish Dramatic Movement*. London: Constable, 1912.

Black, Hester M. *The Theatre in Ireland: An Introductory Essay*. Dublin: Trinity College, 1957.

Blythe, Ernest. *The Abbey Theatre*. Dublin: National Theatre Society, 1965.

Bourgeois, Maurice. *J. M. Synge and the Irish Theatre*. London: Constable, 1912.

Boyd, Ernest Augustus. *Appreciations and Depreciations: Irish Literary Studies*. Dublin: Talbot Press, 1918.

———. *The Contemporary Drama of Ireland*. Dublin: Talbot Press, 1918.

———. *Ireland's Literary Renaissance*. Dublin: Maunsel, 1916; Dublin: Allen Figgis, 1969.

Brustein, Robert. *The Theatre of Revolt*. London: Methuen, 1965.

———. *The Third Theatre*. London: Jonathan Cape, 1970.

Burton, E. J. *The Student's Guide to British Theatre and Drama*. London: Herbert Jenkins, 1963.

Byrne, Dawson. *The Story of Ireland's National Theatre: The Abbey Theatre, Dublin*. Dublin: Talbot Press, 1929.

Cahalan, James M. *Modern Irish Literature and Culture: Chronology*. New York: G. K. Hall, 1993.

———. *Plays of the Irish Renaissance*. New York: Macmillan, 1929.

Clarke, B. K., and Harold Ferrar. *The Dublin Drama League 1919–1941*. Dublin: Dolmen; New York: Humanities Press, 1979.

Colum, Padraic. *My Irish Year*. London: Mills and Boon, 1912.

Corkery, Daniel. *Synge and Anglo-Irish Literature: A Study*. Dublin and Cork: Cork University Press, 1931.

Courtney, Marie-Therese. *Edward Martyn and the Irish Theatre*. New York: Vantage Press, 1956.

Deane, Seumas. *Celtic Revivals: Essays in Modern Irish Literature 1880–1980*. London: Faber and Faber, 1985.

———. *A Short History of Irish Literature*. London: Hutchinson, 1986.

Donoghue, Denis. *The Third Voice: Modern British and American Verse Drama*. London: Oxford University Press, 1959.

Duggan, George Chester. *The Stage Irishman: A History of the Irish Play and Stage Characters from Earliest Times*. New York: B. Bloom, 1937.

Edwards, Philip. *Threshold of a Nation: A Study in English and Irish Drama*. Cambridge: Cambridge University Press, 1979.

Ellis-Fermor, Una. *The Irish Dramatic Movement*. London: Methuen, 1939; rev., 1954.

Esslin, Martin. *The Theatre of the Absurd*. London: Eyre and Spottiswoode, 1962; rev. ed., Woodstock, N.Y.: Overlook Press, 1973.

———. *Reflections: Essays on Modern Theatre*. New York: Doubleday, 1969.

Etherton, Michael. *Contemporary Irish Dramatists*. Houndmills, Basingstoke: Macmillan, 1989.

Fallis, Richard. *The Irish Renaissance*. Syracuse, N.Y.: Syracuse University Press, 1977.

Fallon, Gabriel, ed. *Abbey Theatre 1904–1966*. Dublin: National Theatre Society, 1966.

Fay, Frank. *Towards a National Theatre: Dramatic Criticism*. Ed. Robert Hogan. Dublin: Dolmen Press, 1970.

Fay, Gerard. *The Abbey Theatre: Cradle of Genius*. London: Hollis and Carter, 1958.

Field Day Theatre Company. *Ireland's Field Day*. London: Hutchinson, 1985.

Finneran, Richard, ed. *Anglo-Irish Literature: A Review of Research*. New York: Modern Language Association of America, 1976; *Supplement*, 1982.

———. *Recent Research on Anglo-Irish Writers*. New York: Modern Language Association of America, 1983.

Fitz-Simon, Christopher. *The Irish Theatre*. New York: Thames and Hudson, 1983.

Flannery, James. *Miss Annie F. Horniman and the Abbey Theatre*. Dublin: Dolmen Press, 1970.

Foster, John Wilson. *Colonial Consequences: Essays in Irish Literature and Culture*. Dublin: Lilliput Press, 1991.

Gregory, Lady Augusta. *Our Irish Theatre*. Gerrards Cross, Buckinghamshire: Colin Smythe, 1973.

Gwynne, Stephen. *Irish Literature and Drama*. New York: Nelson, 1936.

Harmon, Maurice. *Modern Irish Literature: 1800–1967; A Reader's Guide*. Dublin: Dolmen Press, 1967.

———. *Select Bibliography for the Study of Anglo-Irish Literature and Its Background*. Port Credit: P. D. Meany, 1977.

Harrison, Alan. *The Irish Trickster*. Sheffield: Sheffield Academic Press, 1989.

Henderson, W. A. *1909: The Irish National Theatre Movement*. Dublin: Privately printed, 1909.

Hobson, Bulmer. *The Gate Theatre, Dublin*. Dublin: Gate Theatre, 1934.

Hogan, Robert Goode, ed. *After the Irish Renaissance: A Critical History of the Irish Drama since* The Plough and the Stars. London: Macmillan, 1968.

———. *The Modern Irish Drama*. 4 vols. I: *The Irish Literary Theatre, 1899–1901*. With James Kilroy. Dublin: Dolmen Press, 1975; II: *Laying the Foundation, 1903–4*. Dublin: Dolmen Press, 1976; III: *The Abbey Theatre: The Years of Synge,*

1905–9. With Richard Burnham and Daniel Poteet. Dublin: Dolmen Press, 1978. IV: *The Rise of the Realists, 1910–15.* Dublin: Dolmen Press, 1979.

Hogan, Robert, and Richard Burnham. *The Years of O'Casey, 1921–1926: A Documentary History.* Newark: University of Delaware Press, 1992.

Hogan, Robert, and Michael J. O'Neill, eds. *Joseph Holloway's Abbey Theatre: A Selection from His Unpublished Journal, "Impressions of a Dublin Playgoer."* Carbondale: Southern Illinois University Press, 1967.

Hunt, Hugh. *The Abbey, Ireland's National Theatre, 1904–1979.* Dublin: Gill and Macmillan, 1979.

Irish University Review (*Silver Jubilee Issue: Teresa Deevy and Irish Women Playwrights,* ed. Christopher Murray.) 25.1 (1995).

Jeffares, A. Norman. *Anglo-Irish Literature.* New York: Schocken Books, 1982.

Kain, Richard Morgan. *Dublin in the Age of W. B. Yeats and James Joyce.* Norman: University of Oklahoma Press, 1962.

Kavanagh, Peter. *The Irish Theatre: Being A History of the Drama in Ireland from the Earliest Period up to the Present Day.* Tralee, Ireland: Kerryman, 1946.

———. *The Story of the Abbey Theatre.* New York: Devin-Adair, 1950.

Kersnowski, Frank L. *A Bibliography of Modern Irish and Anglo-Irish Literature.* San Antonio, Tex.: Trinity University Press, 1976.

Kilroy, James. *The "Playboy" Riots.* Dublin: Dolmen Press, 1971.

King, Kimball. *Ten Modern Irish Playwrights: A Bibliography.* New York: Garland, 1979.

Knight, G. Wilson. *The Golden Labyrinth: A Study of British Drama.* London: Phoenix House, 1962.

Kosok, Heinz, ed. *Studies in Anglo-Irish Literature.* Bonn: Bouvier Verlag, Herbert Grundmann, 1982.

Krans, H. S. *W. B. Yeats and the Irish Literary Revival.* New York: McClure, Phillips, 1904.

Krutch, J. W. *Modernism in Modern Drama.* Ithaca, N.Y.: Cornell University Press, 1953.

Law, Hugh Alexander. *Anglo-Irish Literature.* London: Longmans Green, 1926.

Lewis, Allan. *The Contemporary Theatre: The Significant Playwrights of Our Time.* New York: Crown, 1962.

Lynd, Robert. *Lyric Theatre 1951–1968.* Belfast: Lyric Theatre, 1968.

MacDonald, Thomas. *Literature in Ireland: Studies Irish and Anglo-Irish.* Dublin: Talbot Press, 1916.

Mac Liammóir, Micheál. *All for Hecuba.* London: Methuen, 1946.

———. *Theatre in Ireland.* Dublin: Cultural Relations Committee, 1964.

MacNamara, Brinsley, ed. *Abbey Plays 1899–1948.* Dublin: At the Sign of the Three Candles, 1949.

Magee, William Kirkpatrick. *Anglo-Irish Essays.* Dublin: Talbot Press, 1917.

———. *Bards and Saints.* Folcroft: Folcroft Library Editions, 1976.

Malone, Andrew E. *The Irish Drama: 1896–1928.* New York: B. Bloom, 1965.

Marcus, Philip. *Yeats and the Beginnings of the Irish Renaissance.* Ithaca, N.Y.: Cornell University Press, 1971.

Martin, Augustine. *Anglo-Irish Literature.* Dublin: Government of Ireland, Dept. of Foreign Affairs, 1980.

Maxwell, D. E. S. *A Critical History of Modern Irish Drama: 1891–1980.* Cambridge: Cambridge University Press, 1984.

McCann, Sean, ed. *The Story of the Abbey.* London: New English Library, 1967.

McCormack, W. J. *From Burke to Beckett: Ascendency, Tradition and Betrayal in Literary History.* Cork: Cork University Press, 1994.

McHenry, Margaret. *The Ulster Theatre in Ireland.* Philadelphia: University of Pennsylvania Press, 1931.

McMinn, Joseph, ed. *The Internationalism of Irish Literature and Drama.* Gerrards Cross, Buckinghamshire: Colin Smythe, 1992.

Mikhail, E. H., ed. *The Abbey Theatre: Interviews and Recollections.* Houndmills: Macmillan, 1988.

———. *An Annotated Bibliography of Modern Anglo-Irish Drama.* Troy, N.Y.: Whitston, 1981.

———. *A Bibliography of Modern Irish Drama 1899–1970.* London: Macmillan, 1972.

———. *Contemporary British Drama 1950–76: A Bibliography.* London: Macmillan, 1976.

———. *Dissertations on Anglo-Irish Drama: A Bibliography of Studies: 1870–1970.* Totowa, N.J.: Rowman and Littlefield, 1973.

———. *A Research Guide to Modern Irish Dramatists.* Troy, N.Y.: Whitston, 1979.

Monahan, Michael. *Nova Hibernia: Irish Poets and Dramatists of Today and Yesterday.* New York: M. Kennerley, 1914.

Moore, Alfred S. *The Little Theatre.* Belfast: Ulster and Dramatic Art, n.d.

Nic Shiubhlaigh, Maire, and Edward Kenny. *The Splendid Years.* Dublin: Duffy, 1955.

O'Connor, Frank. *The Backward Look: A Survey of Irish Literature.* London: Macmillan, 1967.

O'Donnel, Frank Hugh. *The Stage Irishmen of the Pseudo-Celtic Drama.* London: John Long, 1904.

O'Driscoll, Robert, ed. *Theatre and Nationalism in Twentieth-Century Ireland.* Toronto: University of Toronto Press, 1971.

Ó hAodha, Micheál. *The Abbey—Then and Now.* Dublin: Abbey Theatre, 1969.

———. *Theatre in Ireland.* Oxford: Basil Blackwell, 1974.

O'Mahony, Mathew. *Guide to Anglo-Irish Plays.* Dublin: Progress House, 1960.

O'Malley, William T. *Anglo-Irish Literature: A Bibliography of Dissertations: 1873–1989.* New York: Greenwood Press, 1990.

O'Neill, James. *A Bibliographical Account of Irish Theatrical Literature.* Bibliographical Society of Ireland Publications. Vol. 1, no. 6. Dublin: John Falconer, 1920.

———. *Irish Theatrical History: A Biographical Essay.* Dublin: Browne and Nolan, 1910.

Peacock, Ronald. *The Poet in the Theatre.* London: Routledge, 1946.

Pogson, Rex. *Miss Horniman and the Gaiety Theatre, Manchester.* London: Rockliff, 1952.

Power, Patrick C. *A Literary History of Ireland.* Cork: Mercier Press, 1969.

Price, Alan. *Synge and Anglo-Irish Drama.* London: Methuen, 1961.

Rafroidi, Patrick, Raymonde Popot, and William Parker, eds. *Aspects of the Irish Theatre.* Lille: Universite de Lille, 1972.

Robinson, Lennox. *Ireland's Abbey Theatre: A History 1899–1951.* London: Sidgwick and Jackson, 1951.

————, ed. *The Irish Theatre: Lectures Delivered during the Abbey Theatre Festival Held in Dublin in August 1938*. London: Macmillan, 1939.

Roche, Anthony. *Contemporary Irish Drama, from Beckett to McGuinness*. Dublin: Gill and Macmillan, 1994.

Ronsley, J., ed. *Myth and Reality in Irish Literature*. Waterloo: Wilfrid Laurier Press, 1977.

Ryan, Frank, ed. *Irish Literary Criticism: 1900–1970*. Lexington, Mass.: Ginn Press, 1985.

Saddlemyer, Ann. *Theatre Business, Management of Men, the Letters of the First Abbey Theatre Directors*. New York: New York Public Library, 1971.

Sahal, N. *Sixty Years of Realistic Irish Drama: 1900–1960*. Bombay: Macmillan, 1971.

Salem, James M. *A Guide to Critical Reviews, Part III: British and Continental Drama from Ibsen to Pinter*. Metuchen, N.J.: Scarecrow Press, 1968.

Setterquist, Jan. *Ibsen and the Beginnings of Anglo-Irish Drama*. Dublin: Hodges, Figgis, 1952.

Shaw, G. B. *Our Theatre in the Nineties*. 3 vols. London: Constable, 1932.

Simpson, Alan. *Beckett and Behan and a Theatre in Dublin*. London: Routledge and Kegan Paul, 1962.

Skelton, Robin, and David R. Clark, eds. *Irish Renaissance*. Dublin: Dolmen Press, 1959.

Stalder, Hans Georg. *Anglo-Irish Peasant Drama: The Motifs of Land and Emigration*. Bern: P. Lang, 1978.

Styan, J. L. *The Dark Comedy; The Development of Modern Comic Tragedy*. Cambridge: Cambridge University Press, 1968.

Taylor, Estella Ruth. *The Modern Irish Writers; Cross Currents of Criticism*. Lawrence: University of Kansas Press, 1954.

Todd, Loreto. *The Language of Irish Literature*. Houndmills: Macmillan, 1989.

Vance, Norman. *Irish Literature: A Social History, Tradition, Identity, and Difference*. Oxford: B. Blackwell, 1990.

Warner, Alan. *A Guide to Anglo-Irish Literature*. Dublin: Gill and Macmillan, 1981.

Waters, Maureen. *The Comic Irishman*. Albany: State University of New York Press, 1984.

Watson, George J. *Irish Identity and the Literary Revival: Synge, Yeats, Joyce and O'Casey*. London: Croom Helm, 1979.

Watt, Stephen. *Joyce, O'Casey, and the Irish Popular Theater*. Syracuse, N.Y.: Syracuse University Press, 1991.

Wauchope, A. G. *The New Irish Drama*. Columbia: University of South Carolina Press, 1919.

Welch, Robert. *Changing States: Transformation in Modern Irish Writing*. London: Routledge, 1992.

Weygandt, Cornelius. *Irish Plays and Playwrights*. London: Constable, 1913.

Witoszek, Nina. *The Theatre of Recollection: A Cultural Study of the Modern Dramatic Tradition in Ireland and Poland*. Stockholm: University of Stockholm, 1989.

Worth, Katharine. *The Irish Drama of Europe from Yeats to Beckett*. Atlantic Highlands, N.J.: Humanities Press, 1978.

Yeats, W. B., ed. *Beltaine; The Organ of the Irish Literary Theatre*. London: Frank Cass, 1970.

————. *The Irish National Theatre*. Rome: Reale Accademia d'Italia, 1935.

————. *Plays and Controversies*. London: Macmillan, 1923.

Index of Names

Page numbers in **bold-face type** indicate location of main entries.

Index of Titles

About the Editors and Contributors

LISA M. ANDERSON is an assistant professor of Theatre and African American Studies at Purdue University, where she teaches courses in Dramatic Literature, Critical Theory, and Black Theatre History and Literature.

ED BALSAM is a doctoral student in English at Memorial University in St. John's, Newfoundland. He is currently working on his thesis in the area of contemporary Atlantic Canadian fiction.

PATRICK BURKE is a Lecturer in the department of English at St. Patrick's College, Dublin City University. He has published extensively on Irish drama and theater in such volumes as *Perspectives of Irish Drama and Theatre* (1991) and *A Small Nation's Contribution to the World* (1993) and such journals as *Irish Literary Review, Graph, ATE*, and *Moderna Sprak* (Sweden), focusing on the work of Brian Friel, J. M. Synge, T. C. Murray, and Field Day. As actor, director, and adjudicator, he is also well known in Ireland as a theater practitioner. Notable productions by him in recent years include *The Winter's Tale* (1989), *Faith Healer* (1987), *Living Quarters* (1992), and *The Merchant of Venice* (1993), at the Shakespeare Studio and Andrew's Lane Theatre.

GRACE BAILEY BURNEKO is an associate professor of English at Augusta College, Augusta, Georgia. In addition to teaching English, humanities, and modern literature, she offers courses in Irish studies and directs the Freshman English Program. She has published in the *Yeats Annual of Critical and Textual Studies* and in *The Southern Quarterly*.

R. J. CLOUGHERTY, JR. is an assistant professor of English at Tennessee Technological University, specializing in contemporary British and Irish literature. He has published critical articles in journals in the United States, Ireland, and France, on authors including Patrick Kavanagh, Richard Murphy, W. B. Yeats, and others. His current reserach is on Nobel Prize winners. In the Spring of 1997 he will be a Fulbright lecturer at the University of Uppsala, Sweden.

KATHLEEN DANAHER was formerly assistant professor of English at Rosemont College, Rosemont, Pennsylvania, and editor of *The Journal of Irish Literature*. Danaher continues as an editor of Proscenium Press and is working on a biography of the actor and writer Robert Shaw. A longer version of her entry in this book, along with a brief history of the Ulster Literary Theatre, has been published in *The Journal of Irish Literature* 17. 2–3 (May–Sept. 1989).

WILLIAM W. DEMASTES is professor of English at Louisiana State University, Baton Rouge. He is series editor for Greenwood's *Research and Production Sourcebooks* and is author of that series' *Clifford Odets* (1991), editor of *American Playwrights, 1880–1945* (1995) and *British Playwrights, 1956–1995* (1996), and coeditor, with Katherine E. Kelly, of *British Playwrights, 1880–1956* (1996). In addition to writing numerous articles on theater and drama, he has also authored *Beyond Naturalism: A New Realism in American Theatre* (1988) and *Theatre of Chaos* (forthcoming) and edited *Realism and the American Dramatic Tradition* (1996).

KAY S. DIVINEY teaches English and coordinates teaching enhancement activities at the University of Prince Edward Island, Charlottetown. She has taught at the University of Alberta and at Hubei University in Wuhan, China.

DAWN DUNCAN is assistant professor of English at Concordia College, Moorhead, Minnesota. She is author of "Entertainment at Home and Abroad," *1941: Texas Goes to War!* (1991), and the radio farce *Sam Steerman: San Antonio's Super Sleuth* (KNTU broadcast, 1991). She also edited a recent special edition of Working Papers in Irish Studies devoted to *Studies in the Plays of Brian Friel*, to which she contributed "Pushing the Post-Colonial Boundaries: Freeing the Irish Voice in Brian Friel's *Translations*" (vol. 3: 1994). Duncan has forthcoming essays on Irish drama, melodrama, and George Bernard Shaw in *Reader's Guide to Literature in English*.

KURT EISEN is assistant professor of English at Tennessee Technological University, Cookeville. He is author of *The Inner Strength of Opposites: O'Neill's Novelistic Drama and the Melodramatic Imagination* (1994), as well as articles in *Comparative Drama, Essays in Literature, Modern Drama*, and *Studies in the American Renaissance*.

DANINE FARQUHARSON is completing a Ph.D. in contemporary Irish fiction at Memorial University of Newfoundland. She has published in the areas of cultural studies, critical theory, and Canadian fiction, and is currently the assistant editor of *The Canadian Journal of Irish Studies.*

WILLIAM J. FEENEY is professor emeritus of English at De Paul University, Chicago. He is author of *Drama in Hardwicke Street, A History of the Irish Theatre Company* (1984) and editor of the Irish Drama Series and of an anthology of plays performed at the Irish Theatre. Among the journals to which he has contributed are *Éire-Ireland, The Journal of Irish Literature,* and No. 6 of *The Yeats Annual.*

JAMES FISHER is professor and chair of Theatre at Wabash College, Crawfordsville, Indiana. He is author of *The Theatre of Yesterday and Tomorrow: Commedia dell'arte on the Modern Stage* (1992), *Al Jolson: A Bio-Bibliography* (Greenwood 1994), *Spencer Tracy: A Bio-Bibliography* (Greenwood 1994), and the forthcoming *Beyond the Theory: The Early Productions of Edward Gordon Craig (1900–1906).* He serves as book review editor of the *Journal of Dramatic Theory and Criticism* and has contributed articles for numerous journals, including *Theatre Journal, Films in Review, Modern Drama, The Drama Review, Theater, The Annual of Bernard Shaw Studies, Studies in American Drama, Theatre Research International, The Mississippi Quarterly, Comparative Drama, New Theatre Quarterly, Theatre Symposium, Soviet and East European Performance,* and *The New England Theatre Journal.*

AVERIL GARDNER is professor of English at Memorial University of Newfoundland, Canada. She has published articles on Oscar Wilde in *Dalhousie Review* and *English Studies in Canada.* She is author of *Angus Wilson* (1985) and *George Orwell* (1987), and coauthor of *The God Approached: A Commentary on the Poems of William Empson* (1978), together with various articles on twentieth-century British literature. She is a member of International P.E.N. (English center).

CLAUDIA W. HARRIS is associate professor and Drama Specialist in the English Department of Brigham Young University, Provo, Utah. She is a member of the Executive Committee of the American Theatre Critics Association. Her essays about Irish theater appear in several collections; she has also published articles and theater reviews in the *Colby Quarterly, Fortnight, Graph, Theatre Forum, Theatre Ireland,* and *Theatre Journal,* as well as various newspapers. She is the author of *Inventing Women's Work: The Legacy of Charabanc Theatre Company* (forthcoming).

MAUREEN S. G. HAWKINS is assistant professor of English at the University of Lethbridge, Alberta, Canada. She has coedited *Global Perspectives on Teaching Literature: Shared Visions and Distinctive Visions* (1993) and has published articles on intertextuality and cultural identity, the development of Anglo-Irish historical drama, and dramatic works by Dion Boucicault, Lady Gregory, Louis MacNeice, W. B. Yeats and LeRoi Jones, Brendan Behan and Neil Jordan, and Brendan Behan and Wole Soyinka.

RICHARD JONES has taught theater and related courses at Union College in Barbourville, Kentucky and, more recently, at Cornell College in Mt. Vernon, Iowa. He has published in *Classical World, New England Theatre Journal, Theatre Journal*, and *Theatre Survey*.

SISTER MARIE HUBERT KEALY is professor of English and chair of the English Department at Immaculata College, Pennsylvania, where she also directs the dramatic activities. Her previous publications include *Kerry Playwright: Sense of Place in the Plays of John B. Keane* (1993). She is an active member of the American Conference for Irish Studies and regularly writes and lectures on Irish theater.

EILEEN KEARNEY specializes in Irish and women's studies.

JOSÉ LANTERS is assistant professor of classics and letters at the University of Oklahoma. She is the author of *Missed Understandings: A Study of Stage Adaptations of the Works of James Joyce* (1988). Her articles on Irish fiction and drama have appeared in *Dutch Quarterly Review, Etudes Irlandaises, Éire-Ireland, Irish University Review, The Journal of Irish Literature*, and *Modern Drama*.

HELEN LOJEK is professor of English at Boise State University, Idaho. She has written articles for *Éire-Ireland, Canadian Journal of Irish Studies, Western American Literature, Contemporary Literature, New England Quarterly*, and *Southern Literary Journal*.

JAMES McALEAVEY is a doctoral student at the Institute of Irish Studies, Queen's University, Belfast. His thesis is on the Gaelic sources in the poetry of Edmund Spenser.

CARLA J. McDONOUGH is associate professor of English at Eastern Illinois University Charleston. Specializing in modern drama, she has published essays in *Theatre Journal* and *The Journal of Dramatic Theory and Criticism*. Her book, *Staging Masculinity: Male Identity in Contemporary American Drama*, is forthcoming.

BERNARD McKENNA teaches in the English Department of Wesley College, Dover, Delaware. He is the associate editor for *The Dictionary of Irish Literature* and has published numerous articles on Irish theater and literature, including studies in *Éire-Ireland* and *Nineteenth Century Prose*. In addition, he publishes a regular column on the history of Northern theater for the *Belfast News Letter.*

BRENDAN O'GRADY is professor of English at the University of Prince Edward Island. He has presented papers in Ireland and the United States on the writings of Seumas O'Kelly. His articles and reviews have been published in *The Canadian Journal of Irish Studies, The Clogher Record* (Ireland), and *The Abegweit Review* (Prince Edward Island). His essays have appeared in *The Untold Story: The Irish in Canada* (1988), *James Joyce and His Contemporaries* (1989), and *Celtic Languages and Celtic Peoples* (1992). He recently completed a study of the Irish settlers of Prince Edward Island.

NOEL PEACOCK is assistant professor of English at the University of Western Ontario, where he teaches courses in twentieth-century British and Postcolonial literature. He has previously published on Joseph Conrad, Les Murray, and John Le Carré.

SANDRA MANOOGIAN PEARCE is associate professor of English at Moorhead State University, Moorhead, Minnesota. She has written articles on James Joyce and Edna O'Brien and is currently working on a book on O'Brien, tentatively titled, *Redemption through Reconciliation: Edna O'Brien's Isolated Women.*

KATHLEEN A. QUINN is coeditor of *Silent Voices: An Anthology of Plays by Irish Women* (forthcoming). She has written articles for a number of journals, including *The Canadian Journal of Irish Studies* and *Theatre Ireland.*

BERNICE SCHRANK is professor of English at Memorial University of Newfoundland, Canada. She is the author of numerous articles on O'Casey and the editor of the *Canadian Journal of Irish Studies.* Her book, *Sean O'Casey: A Research and Production Sourcebook,* was published in 1996 (Greenwood Press).

DAVID J. SORRELLS is instructor of English at Lamar University–Port Arthur, Port Arthur, Texas. His publications include critical articles on *The Scarlet Letter,* Texas authors, and technical writing pedagogy.

TRAMBLE T. TURNER is assistant professor of English at Penn State University, Abington-Ogontz Campus. The 1992–1994 Mid-Atlantic representative for the American Conference for Irish Studies, he has written articles on Shaw for *Éire-Ireland* and delivered a talk on John Arden and Margaretta D'Arcy's Connelly cycle of plays at the 1992 MLA Conference. He wrote a chapter in a study of John Arden and Margaretta D'Arcy published in 1995, and his article on William Kennedy appeared in the Spring 1993 issue of *MELUS.*

TJEBBE WESTENDORP teaches at the University of Leiden, The Netherlands. He is the author of *Robert Penn Warren and the Modernist Temper* (1987), and editor, with Valeria G. Lerda, of *The United States South: Regionalism and Identity* (1992), and *Politics and the Rhetoric of Poetry* (with Jane Mallinson) (1995). His articles deal with the American South (the Nashville Agrarians), T. S. Eliot, W. H. Auden, the literature of war, Irish poetry, and Samuel Beckett.

GORDON M. WICKSTROM is professor emeritus of drama and chair at Franklin and Marshall College in Lancaster, Pennsylvania. He has specialized in the Irish dramatic movement and will take credit for rediscovering MacDonagh.

ISBN 0-313-28805-4

EAN

9 780313 288050

HARDCOVER BAR CODE